HISTORY OF THE UNITED STATES ARMY
Russell F. Weigley
Temple University

Volumes in preparation

THE COLONIAL WARS
Douglas E. Leach
Vanderbilt University

THE AMERICAN REVOLUTION
Don Higginbotham
Louisiana State University

THE WAR OF 1812
R. A. Preston
Royal Military College of Canada
S. F. Wise
Queens University (Canada)

THE INDIAN WARS, 1700–1848
Francis Paul Prucha, S.J.
Marquette University

FRONTIERSMEN IN BLUE, 1848–1865
Robert M. Utley
National Park Service

FRONTIERSMEN IN BLUE, 1865–1898
Robert M. Utley
National Park Service

THE MEXICAN WAR
Richard W. Van Alstyne
Henry E. Huntington Library and Art Gallery

THE CIVIL WAR
Jay Luvaas
Allegheny College

WORLD WAR I
Harvey DeWeerd
The Rand Corporation

THE MEXICAN INTERVENTION
Clarence C. Clendenin
Hoover Institution on War, Revolution, and Peace

WORLD WAR II (Pacific)
Louis Morton
Dartmouth College

HISTORY OF AMERICAN MILITARY DOCTRINE
Fred Greene
Williams College

HISTORY OF THE UNITED STATES AIR FORCE
James C. Olson
University of Nebraska

History of the United States Army

THE WARS OF THE UNITED STATES

General Editor

Louis Morton
Dartmouth College

HISTORY
OF THE
UNITED STATES
ARMY

☆ ☆ ☆ ☆ ☆ ☆ ☆ ☆ ☆ ☆ ☆ ☆ ☆ ☆

by Russell F. Weigley

The Macmillan Company, New York

Collier-Macmillan Ltd., London

Library of Congress Catalog Card Number: 67-16051

FIRST PRINTING

The Macmillan Company, New York
Collier-Macmillan Canada, Ltd. Toronto, Ontario

Printed in the United States of America

For Emma

☆ CONTENTS ☆

PART FOUR: SINCE 1945

Preface

THIS IS A history not of battles and campaigns but of the Army as an institution maintained by the nation to fight its battles and campaigns, or to deter a need to fight them.

A history of the United States Army must be, however, a history of two armies. Inheritance from England, geography, and democratic ideology have given the country two: a Regular Army of professional soldiers and a citizen army of various components variously known as militia, National Guards, Organized Reserves, selectees.

A history of the United States Army ought of course to attempt to weigh the merits of both armies fairly. Not all histories have done so. No history of the United States Army existed until Secretary of War Elihu Root saw to the publication of Brevet Major General Emory Upton's *Military Policy of the United States* in 1904. Upton was a Regular Army professional bitterly contemptuous of citizen soldiers. Though he was contemptuous also of many of the values of American society in general, his pioneer work so long stood alone and had such great influence that his interpretations have colored almost everything written about American military history. Other professional soldiers essaying history tended to find his opinions congenial. Civilian historians, for many reasons slow to explore Army history, found no guidebook comparable to Upton's and accepted his interpretations all too readily. More balanced assessments than his of the citizen army, perhaps most notably those of Brigadier General John McAuley Palmer, have been slow to gain currency. Recent civilian historians have still written disparagingly of "the myth of the militia,"[1] borrowing their terms from Emory Upton. This book will attempt to avoid the partisanship of professional versus citizen soldiers that has been so prominent in the writing of military history under Upton's example.

Upton and the champions of the Regular Army have held that only a military policy entrusting war primarily to professionals can give the United States true military security. The partisans of the citizen army have argued that only a military policy built mainly upon a citizen soldiery can assure democracy against the possibility of subversion by the very military forces that are supposed to protect that democracy. They argue that a citizen army can be an adequately strong army, but their primary interest is in assuring the compatibility of American military policy with a democratic society. During the early years of the Republic, the internal military threat against which a citizen army was supposed to stand guard was a military coup against constitutional government. American history has long since made such a threat seem altogether remote. The modern threat of the military to a democratic state lies in the danger that continuous international peril will make military considerations appear paramount over all others in the construction of national policy. Champions of the citizen army continue to assert its usefulness against more subtle dangers: an army tied closely to the whole body of the nation is most likely to respect nonmilitary national aims, while a citizenry accustomed to military service is best prepared to pass judgment on military issues.

Though the historian of the Army may try to shun Uptonian partisanship, the historic tension between the two American armies, professional and citizen, must remain his major theme. The effort to balance and harmonize their rival claims, in order best to assure both military security and a democratic polity, has dominated the history of American military institutions, apart from the Navy. The claims of the superiority of one over another kind of soldiery have caused the history of American military policy to focus disproportionately upon issues of manpower, often to the neglect of problems in strategy, weaponry, and logistics. They have also caused partisans of one or the other kind of army often to lose sight of the possible advantages to the United States of being able to call forth either type of army or both.

Next to the historic tension between the two American armies, a history of the United States Army must find a principal theme in the persistent question of how the armies shall be commanded. The citizen army is defended as essential to ensuring an appropriate subordination of military to civil policy; that subordination must also and more directly be sought through arrangements for military responsibility to civil authority. Here again a harmony between military aims and civil democratic ones has not been easy to assure. Emory Upton's disdain for civil interference in the conduct of military policy and war, though lightly veiled, or at least underplayed, by some of his disciples, ran as deep as his contempt for citizen soldiers, and has also profoundly influenced the writing of American military history. Out of a Regular Army accustomed to Uptonian views came General of the Army Douglas MacArthur's opinions on civil and military authority, to which few soldiers expressed cogent dissent even if they believed President Truman was right to dismiss MacArthur in the circumstances of 1952. MacArthur said to the Congressional committee investigating his dismissal:

The general definition which for many decades has been accepted was that war was the ultimate process of politics; that when all other political means failed, you then go to force; and that when you do that, the balance of control . . . is the control of the military. A theater commander . . . is not merely limited to a handling of his troops; he commands that whole area politically, economically, and militarily. You have got to trust at the stage of the game when politics fail, and the military take over, you must trust the military. . . .[2]

Genuinely pertinent and cogent challenges to such a view of military prerogatives have come with notable rarity from civilian as well as military commentators. Throughout our history, civilian Americans have tended to ignore military questions altogether whenever they could do so. Their usual avoidance of military knowledge and thought has contributed to an ambivalent attitude when they have had to cope with things military. Frequently they have stood in excessive awe of the mysteries attendant upon the conduct of war, too ready to abdicate national policy to the judgments of military professionals when a military emergency is at hand. Unhappy to have to make such concessions, civilians have reverted when the occasion permits to reciprocating the military's Uptonian attitudes with their own disdain for the military: what better way to rationalize an ignorance of military policy and military history than through persuading oneself that military questions after all appeal only to a low order of intelligence, the "regimented military mind?" But neither awe of the military nor contempt for the military can offer a satisfactory foundation for a democracy's military policy.

At a time when the nature of war and of armies is thoroughly in flux, it is difficult to be confident about the value of a history of the American Army. Nevertheless, a measure of acquaintance with the past may help to dissipate both the awe and the contempt that alternately have hobbled American deliberation upon military issues.

In writing this book I have incurred innumerable debts of gratitude. I should mention especially my thanks to Temple University, whose administration allowed me reduced teaching schedules and awarded me a summer research grant; to Professor Louis Morton of Dartmouth College, the general editor of this series, who gave of his time, his military knowledge, and his critical acumen beyond the call of duty; and to Peter V. Ritner and his staff of The Macmillan Company, who have been most tolerant and patient with a very long manuscript.

October, 1966

RUSSELL F. WEIGLEY
Temple University
Philadelphia

The well-being of the people equally with the well-being of the Army requires a common sympathy and a common interest between them.

—MAJOR GENERAL JOHN POPE,
to the veterans
of the Army of the Tennessee

☆ PART ONE ☆

The Foundations: 1607-1794

Article I, Section 8. The Congress shall have power . . . :

To declare war, grant letters of marque and reprisal, and make rules concerning captures on land and water:

To raise and support armies, but no appropriation of money to that use shall be for a longer term than two years:

To provide and maintain a navy:

To make rules for the government and regulation of the land and naval forces:

To provide for calling forth the militia to execute the laws of the union, suppress insurrections and repel invasions:

To provide for organizing, arming and disciplining the militia, and for governing such part of them as may be employed in the service of the United States, reserving to the states respectively, the appointment of the officers, and the authority of training the militia according to the discipline prescribed by Congress. . . .

Article II, Section 2. The president shall be commander in chief of the army and navy of the United States, and of the militia of the several states, when called into the actual service of the United States. . . .

—The principal military clauses
of the Constitution

ONE

The Colonial Militias: 1607-1754

Moreover, let each and every [freeman] . . . swear that . . . he will possess these arms and will bear allegiance to the lord king Henry . . . and that he will bear these arms in his service according to his order and in allegiance to the lord king and his realm. And let none of those who hold these arms sell them or pledge them or offer them, or in any other way alienate them; neither let a lord in any way deprive his men of them either by forfeiture or gift, or as surety or in any other manner.

—The Assize of Arms (1181)[1]

THE ROOTS of the American military tradition reach back to King Henry II's Assize of Arms, transplanted to America and nourished here after it became moribund in England itself.

Every English freeman had once been a part-time soldier in the Anglo-Saxon fyrd. William the Conqueror and the Norman kings gradually tamed this popular militia and then revitalized it to turn it to their own purposes. The Assize of Arms required every freeman to provide himself with arms, to train periodically under the local militia officer, and to be ready for the King's call to service. The Statute of Winchester of 1285 and the Instructions for General Muster of 1572 elaborated upon these requirements and reinforced them, and the popular militia became conspicuous in England's preparations for defense against Spain during the Elizabethan wars. The militia of the Elizabethan age was among the English institutions carried to the new colonies in America just after the Queen's death.

In the course of the seventeenth century, however, the English popular militia fell into eclipse, as similar militias had already done in Europe. The existence of the militia helped cause the travail of the English Civil War, and to restore stability Oliver Cromwell relied increasingly upon standing professional regiments of soldiers. Charles II had good reason to depend upon professional soldiers almost exclusively, and the history of the English regular army is usually dated from his reign. When England joined in the wars against Louis XIV at the end of the century, the predominance of professional armies on the continent confirmed her own new reliance upon professionals. The English militia fell into desuetude, not to be revived until well into the nineteenth century, and the professional army became the almost exclusive land force of the state.[2]

But while the history of seventeenth-century England shriveled the popular militia, the different history of England's American colonies nourished that militia into a vitality that has survived much adversity to persist into the twentieth century.

The American colonies in the seventeenth century were much too poor to permit a class of able-bodied men to devote themselves solely to war and preparation for war. Every colonist had to contribute all the energy he could to the economic survival of his colony, and no colony could afford to maintain professional soldiers. Yet through most of the century every part of the colonies remained subject to military danger, potentially from Spain and France and actually from the Indians. Therefore every colony needed military protection, and every colony save the Quaker settlements sought to obtain it by invoking the historic English principle of a universal obligation to military service, in order to create a military force of armed civilians.

The English promoters of the first colonies knew something of the hazards of America, and from the beginning the colonial charters authorized defensive armaments. The first ships to America carried military stores in their cargoes, and the first settlers brought with them men experienced in war, such as Captain John Smith of Virginia and Captain Myles Standish of Plymouth, to train and lead them in the bearing of arms. When the Jamestown settlers landed in 1607, they heeded the instructions of their English sponsors to form themselves immediately into three groups: one to erect fortifications for defense, one to serve as a guard and to plant a crop, the third to explore. Within the first month of the settlement the Indians launched a severe attack, and it was fortunate that the ships from England still rode at anchor to help overawe the aborigines with their cannons. About the end of the first month a fort was completed, a triangular structure with a "Bulwarke" mounting four or five artillery pieces at each corner. For the next few years the first permanent settlement in English America was practically coterminous with the fort.[3]

Governor Sir Thomas Dale arrived at Jamestown in 1612 when the colony was close to extinction from starvation. A soldier by profession, Dale reacted to the crisis by imposing military discipline upon every colonist, based on "the laws governing the Armye in the Low Countryes." He so strengthened the military force of the colony and thereby so impressed the Indians that

a peace was concluded [wrote John Rolfe] which still continues so firme, that our people yearly plant and reape quietly, and travell in the woods a fowling and a hunting as freely and securely from danger or treacherie as in England.[4]

This happy result of a muster of military force, combined with Dale's restoration of the economy, permitted a gradual relaxation of universal military discipline. Nevertheless, with the introduction of representative government through the assembly of 1619, Virginia civil law continued to declare a general military obligation. After the colony had barely managed to put down Opechancanough's rising of 1622, the assembly in 1623 imposed a statutory requirement that all citizens hold arms. In accordance with instructions from the Crown, which had newly assumed direct control of the colony from the Virginia Company, Governor Sir George Yeardley three years later defined the military obligation as extending to all males between seventeen years and sixty. The next year one Richard Bickley declined to take up arms after being ordered to do so by an Ensign John Utie; thereupon Bickley was arrested and, having been convicted by the General Court, sentenced to be "laid neck and heels for the space of twelve hours" and to pay a fine of one hundred pounds of tobacco. In 1639 the assembly reinforced the governor's instructions by providing that every male of legal age, unless a Negro slave, should be compelled to furnish his military services whenever the occasion for it arose. The next year it declared that every master of a family should be held responsible for the performance of military duties by each member capable of bearing arms.

As the settlement of Virginia crept up the rivers westward and northward from Jamestown, the governor came to exercise his functions as commander of the military forces by appointing subordinate commanders over militia districts. The district commanders then chose their own juniors, though all commissions came from the governor, and through them saw to it that the freemen supplied themselves with proper arms and equipment. The officers drilled their companies, supervised construction of defenses, and kept custody of the public gunpowder supply. The district militia commander took on certain civil duties as well, such as compelling church attendance, and became sufficiently busy that lieutenant commanders eventually were commissioned to give assistance.[5]

In similar circumstances the later colonies soon established similar systems of universal military obligation. Plymouth did so early, and a Massachusetts Bay law of 1631 decreed that all males between sixteen and sixty must provide themselves with weapons and form units for training. In Maryland and New York, the governors, working under instructions from the proprietors, had militia organizations well established before the legislatures got around to passing military laws, but generally the obligation to military service came to rest upon legislative enactment. In Massachusetts Bay, until the Dominion of New England was established, the assembly delegated command of the militia to an elected official known as the sergeant major–general. Elsewhere the legislatures entrusted command to the governors but with the assemblies retaining surveillance and ultimate control: they voted the necessary funds, oversaw their expenditure, and investigated the conduct of operations. Thus the colonial assemblies, their educated members mindful of classical examples of caesarism and praetorianism, and with the spectacle of Cromwell's military dictatorship arising before them, established in America and guarded jealously the principle of civilian control of the military.[6]

New England preceded Virginia in prescribing regular training periods for the militia. The General Court of Plymouth initially stipulated that drills be held six times a year. The Massachusetts law of 1631, passed when the colony was so new that it was extremely insecure, called for weekly drills, to be held every Saturday. Later it seemed safe enough to drill less often, and in 1637, training days were set at eight a year. When danger reappeared, training again intensified proportionately; there were twice-weekly drills during King Philip's War in 1675–76. On the training days, a town's militia company generally assembled on public grounds, held roll call and prayer, practiced the manual of arms and close order drill, and passed under review and inspection by the militia officers and other public officials. There might also be target practice and sham battles, followed in the afternoon—when times were not too perilous —by refreshments, games, and socializing. A system of fines enforced attendance and helped finance the system.

New England militiamen elected their company officers: in Massachusetts Bay, a captain, a lieutenant, an ensign, sergeants, and corporals. Companies numbered from sixty-five to two hundred men, two-thirds musketeers and one-third pikemen. When a town harbored more than two hundred able-bodied males of military age, several companies were formed there; towns of fewer than sixty-five banded together to establish companies. As early as 1636 the General Court of Massachusetts Bay organized the companies into regiments, the North, East, and Boston Regiments; the former two still exist as units, the 182nd Infantry Regiment (5th Massachusetts) and 101st Engineer Battalion respectively, and are the oldest units in the United States Army. Eventually each Massachusetts county came to have a regiment, so that regimental strengths varied greatly. A sergeant major commanded the regiment, assisted by a muster master. Supervising the whole was the sergeant major–general of the colony, who mobilized units and procured supplies. Military policy was defined by a council of war established by the assembly, and ultimately by the assembly itself.[7]

Pennsylvania, the Quaker colony, was an exception to the rule of compulsory military obligation. William Penn himself was a sufficiently worldly Quaker to make it his practice (he made only one exception) to appoint a non-Quaker as his lieutenant governor, so that in case of war someone could take command of the province untroubled by scruples concerning the use of force. The conversion of the proprietary family to Anglicanism after the founder's death assured the continuance of this policy. But Quakers long remained in control of the assembly, manipulating the distribution of seats to maintain their ascendancy long after their share of the population ceased to warrant it, and as long as they did so, they obstructed measures of self-defense. Eventually the non-Quaker inhabitants felt obliged to form an extralegal voluntary militia. In July, 1747, during King George's War, French and Spanish privateers sailed up Delaware Bay, put landing parties ashore to plunder two plantations just below New Castle, Delaware, and captured a ship coming in from Antigua. The printer and civic leader Benjamin Franklin then published a pamphlet pointing out that there were sixty thousand Pennsylvanians of military age who were not Quakers and calling on them to organize their own defense. Characteristically, he followed up by arranging a mass meeting, out of which came a volunteer association that soon grew to ten thousand men, who furnished themselves with arms, formed companies and regiments, and met to drill. Franklin organized a lottery to finance a fort and artillery and talked the governor of New York into sharing his cannons with Philadelphia. Later, when the Indians were raiding the western frontier of the province at the crisis of the French and

Indian War, the Pennsylvanians pressed the Quakers into yielding control of the assembly and created an official military force, though still without compulsory service.[8]

Thereafter the Pennsylvania military system was not much different in practice, as distinguished from principle, from the systems of the other colonies. For in those colonies which did fix the principle of universal military service, there grew up a distinction between the "common militia" and the "volunteer militia." Few occasions arose requiring the whole able-bodied manpower of a colony or a district, the compulsory-service militia companies and regiments in their entirety. Even when some planned military expedition might have made complete mobilization desirable from the military viewpoint alone, other considerations such as home defense and the need to tend to crops generally forbade it. Therefore the compulsory-service companies and regiments rarely took the field in all their strength; rather they served as training commands and replacement pools from which troops were drawn in emergencies to form the units that actually conducted operations. When troops were needed for a campaign, the legislatures assigned quotas to the local militia districts. The local officials then called for volunteers and could impress or draft men when sufficient numbers did not come forward. Usually, compulsory service was limited to expeditions within the colony, but militia laws often empowered the governor to employ troops outside the colony's boundaries for stipulated periods in special circumstances.

Out of these methods there naturally grew more or less permanent formations of those persons willing to volunteer for active duty. The "common militia" were the militia based on the principle of compulsory service; the "volunteer militia" were the formations whose recruits chose membership in them, generally with the understanding that they would respond first to calls for active service. Such a distinction had existed in England. The volunteer militia often took on a kind of elite status. As early as 1643, in a reorganization following the Pequot War, Massachusetts Bay provided that thirty soldiers in each militia company were to be ready for service at a half-hour's warning. Volunteers were sought for this role, out of which the minutemen of 1775 were to grow. Such cavalry and artillery formations as the militia managed to muster tended to be elite volunteer units, since cavalry and artillery entailed high expenses. Eliteness often became social as well as military, with the volunteer militia sometimes choosing their recruits on some basis of exclusiveness. The Ancient and Honorable Artillery Company of Boston, organized in 1636, is an example of a very early volunteer militia unit with overtones of eliteness. It was modeled on the

Honourable Artillery Company of London, and it still exists, although it has never been a part of the United States Army.[9]

No reasonable man would expect farmers and tradesmen who receive military training in their spare time to be instantly ready to take the field against armies of well trained military professionals. Programs for training citizen soldiers are based not on that expectation but rather on the assumption that some military training and organization is better than none, so that citizens' military training will offer a useful foundation upon which to build something more in a military emergency. Furthermore, the militia organizations of the English colonies in America had little expectation of having to fight large armies of professional soldiers, and until the War of the Revolution rarely did so, even during the French war of 1754–63. Their function was mainly to fight Indians, or occasionally white troops of their own character, such as the French-Canadian militia. Nevertheless, the colonies wanted to extract as much military value as possible from limited periods of training. To design a training program to achieve this goal posed difficult problems, as it always must.

As long as a colonial community remained a frontier community, the part-time soldiers of its militia company were likely to be fairly competent Indian fighters no matter what occurred on training days. When allowance is made for the romanticism that tends to infect even the best histories of the American frontier, it still seems true that frontier life in the forests of eastern North America demanded skill in the use of firearms from early boyhood, since hunting brought in much of the family's food supply. Forest-dwelling white men became skillful enough woodsmen to emulate the Indians in tactical use of the woods.

In the eighteenth century, moreover, Swiss and German craftsmen on the Pennsylvania frontier developed the Pennsylvania rifle, a far more accurate firearm than any musket and a lighter and less cumbersome weapon than the rifles that the Englishmen had known in their homeland. Hitherto the Indians had possessed in the bow and arrow a weapon which in good hands was superior to the matchlock and flintlock muskets of the whites: more accurate, more reliable, and with a more rapid rate of fire. Though even the best rifles of the eighteenth century posed troublesome difficulties of loading and firing, the Pennsylvania rifle did much to cancel out the Indians' previous advantages in weaponry. Its use spread so rapidly over the frontier that it is better known as the Kentucky rifle. Its users earned so impressive a reputation for marksmanship that during the Revolution, George Washington urged American soldiers to clothe themselves in the buckskin costume of the frontiersman, to play upon the British soldiers' supposed fear that all Americans were sharpshooting riflemen. The smoothbore musket, then still used along with the rifle and more numerous than the rifle, became more effective as it evolved during the colonial period from primitive matchlock to snaphance to flintlock.[10]

Unfortunately for the prowess of the colonial militia, however, as the frontier receded, the inhabitants of older communities gradually lost their skills in shooting, forest lore, and Indian fighting. More and more the militia of long-settled communities had to rely not on frontier experience but on European military manuals to guide them in their training. Those manuals taught not Indian warfare but the increasingly formalized type of war being developed by European professional soldiers, with tactical systems designed for the open plains that Europeans favored as battlegrounds. The Indians, in contrast, fought a stealthy forest warfare of cunning, ambuscades, and hit-and-run raids. By the time of King Philip's War, consequently, the colonial militia were already finding themselves repeatedly frustrated because their tactics had become too formal and European for Indian warfare.

Throughout King Philip's War, the Indians were able to strike the colonials at unexpected places, because colonial scouting was not up to tracking the Indians through the forest. Exploiting the inability of colonial reconnaissance and security measures to cope with them in their own habitat, the Indians repeatedly executed murderous ambushes upon colonial marching columns. In August, 1675, Captain Edward Hutchinson's column was ambushed and badly mauled while marching to a supposed parley with the Nipmucks near Brookfield, Massachusetts, the lucky ones escaping only because they had horses and the Nipmucks did not. In September, Captain Richard Beers with a company of thirty-six was marching to Squakeag in the upper Connecticut Valley to help evacuate the town. He fell into an ambush and more than half his force was slain, including Beers himself. In the same month another company under Captain Thomas Lathrop met an almost identical fate while assisting in the evacuation of Deerfield. The following March, Captain Michael Pierce and a company of sixty-five Plymouth Colony militia, with several Indian auxiliaries, were bushwhacked by Narragansetts along the Pawtucket River, and the whole force was destroyed.

So inferior were the militia to their Indian enemies in tracking and fighting in the woods, that in the closing phases of King Philip's War the New Englanders increasingly relied on friendly Indians to do their scouting and even much of their fighting. It became axiomatic that the only way to march safely into the enemy's lair was with friendly Indian guides. Benjamin Church's company, which finally captured and killed King Philip himself, was a mixed contingent of Indians and whites.[11]

Through the following century the divorcement of more and more Americans from frontier experience further widened the gap between white men and red in the skills of forest war. By the time of the French and Indian War, Colonel George Washington of the Virginia militia felt obliged to write that "without Indians, we shall never be able to cope with those cruel foes to our country." "Indians are the only match for Indians; and without these we shall ever fight upon unequal Terms."[12]

Despite this acknowledgment of a need for Indian assistance, Colonel Washington himself studied war from Humphrey Bland's *Treatise on Military Discipline*, first published in 1727 and the leading English tactical manual of the day. He recommended it to other militia officers, that they might better mold their part-time soldiers into approximations of the men-at-arms of Europe. Evidently it was widely used throughout the colonies.[13] Although the American militia made certain concessions to Indian-style warfare, as illustrated most famously when the Virginia militia took to the woods during Braddock's battle on the Monongahela in 1755, the militia was less a distinctively American than a European institution. Though its English prototypes were in decline, it stood squarely upon English precedent and continued to draw its discipline and tactics from the Old World. It represents not a Turnerian triumph of the New World environment but the colonials' persistent Europeanness.

Notwithstanding their frequent lack of their enemies' forest skill, the colonial militias served reasonably well to guard the westward-moving edge of settlement against Indian counterattacks. The advance of settlement was accomplished less through militia action than through the simple appropriation—or dubious purchase—of lands by white men supported by numbers too great for the Indians to offer effective resistance. When the Indians retaliated for the loss of their lands with terrorizing raids against the fringes of settlement, the whites took arms and assembled in their militia companies to defend themselves. The militia thus gathered to drive off raiders in hundreds of skirmishes, and more or less in this manner they won the Pequot War in New England in 1637, King Philip's War, and the Yemassee War in South Carolina in 1715.

The militia proved less useful when they were not fighting directly and obviously in defense of their own homes. The New England expeditions that took Port Royal in Acadia in 1690 and

1710—facing weak opposition—and the famous expedition that seized the fortress of Louisbourg in 1745—despite much stronger opposition—were exceptions. In general the colonial militias were not a reliable instrument of offensive war distant from their own firesides.

The reasons are evident. Few men came to America to be soldiers. More likely, they came in part to escape soldiering. They would fight when they had to, to preserve the homes and farms and way of life they had crossed the ocean to find. But they did not wish to abandon homes and farms for months or a season, to go off soldiering in pursuit of objects only remotely connected with their own aspirations or security. Militia training did not prepare them for extended campaigns, nor did militia organization befit the maintenance of long expeditions. A long campaign to distant fields that also involved meeting Indian tactics of stealth and ambuscade was a campaign for which colonial militia, except units recruited from frontiersmen, were especially unsuited. When the French and Indian War demanded such campaigns, the militia system did not suffice. Therefore regiments of the British regular army appeared in America, to fight the French and their Indian allies and to add their contribution to the influences that were to shape the United States Army.

☆ TWO ☆

The Arrival of Regulars:
1754-75

I am still of Opinion with[ou]t Force from Home, we shall hardly be able to drive the French from the Ohio; we want Military Men, and particularly Ingineers.

—Governor Robert Dinwiddie[1]

"THE Great War for Empire," Professor Lawrence Henry Gipson's title for the Franco-British struggle of 1754–63, is an apt designation in many ways. Among others, it connotes, as the old "French and Indian War" does not, the aggressive character of the struggle waged by Great Britain and her colonies against the French. Only most indirectly did the colonies wage a war of self-defense; if France had secured the title to the Ohio Valley asserted by the leaden plates she planted there, one day in the future she might have squeezed the British out of North America altogether. Much more immediately, the British fought an aggressive war of their own to win new lands and carry destruction to the French. Virginia precipitated the struggle when she aggressively sent militia detachments into the Ohio country to assert the expansionist claims of the Ohio Company investors against the rival, and of course similarly expansionist, French claims. Only after the war had well begun as a clash of aggressive empires did it become partly a war of self-preservation against French and Indian raids in parts, and then limited parts, of the colonies. Mainly it was a war of military offensives reaching far beyond the existing limits of British settlement. The militia system was not designed for such a war, and authorities in both Great Britain and America soon decided they had to call upon professional soldiers to fight it.

For such a war, remote from the interests of most inhabitants of the colonies, insufficient numbers of colonists volunteered for active duty, and the assemblies proved unwilling to impose a sufficiently rigorous draft on the militia, to permit colonial forces alone to fight effectively. Virginia discovered this fact before the war had officially begun. After the French overran the colony's outpost at the Forks of the Ohio in 1754 and rebuffed Washington's reconnaissance in force at Fort Necessity, Governor Robert Dinwiddie secured supplementary appropriations for defense from his assembly and proposed to raise a regiment of 2,000 volunteers. A few weeks of recruiting efforts served to lower his sights to 1,000 men and then soon to 800. Those coming forward failed to approach even the last figure, and Dinwiddie had to suggest that one in ten of the militia be drafted. The assembly did not comply.[2]

By the time Braddock's expedition gathered the next year, Virginia did manage to contribute nine companies, although of distinctly less than their authorized strength of 100 men each. Braddock's defeat presently wrecked this force; in September, of the nine Virginia companies plus one company each from North Carolina and Maryland that had marched with Braddock, only 198 soldiers and a dozen officers remained fit for action at Fort Cumberland. Virginia had to begin again. In August, 1755, the assembly granted immunity from civil process for debt as an inducement to recruits. Foreseeing that this would prove too small an inducement to the risking of lives, the law also provided for a draft of unmarried men if an adequate force were not recruited within three months. Or rather it seemed to provide a draft; it stipulated that any man drafted might offer a substitute. If he neither appeared in person nor presented a substitute, he nevertheless could not be jailed and could not be fined more than £10.

By December, 1755, Virginia had restored its military force only to about 500. At the beginning of April of the next year, Washington, at Winchester on the frontier, could count no more than forty armed men taking his orders. He appealed to Lord Fairfax, the county lieutenant, and the senior militia officers of Frederick County to muster their companies, but the officers replied that their men would not obey orders to assemble. The officers did offer to call for a voluntary meeting and then deliver an appeal. Washington agreed and set April 15 as the assembly date, but the effort produced only fifteen recruits.

In May the legislature agreed to a goal of 1,500 men as the colony's military force for the year, and again it formally decreed a draft of militia. But many militia officers studiously delayed the drawing of names for the draft, and nothing effective was attempted to hasten them. By June 25 Washington had seen his force at Winchester grow to no more than 264. The next spring, the general assembly reduced its goal to 1,272 men. It authorized a variety of expedients to assist recruiting: first, all vagrants were to be drafted; then one in forty of the able-bodied militia were to follow, not including "free-holders or house-keepers qualified to vote at an election of Burgesses"; then if the double draft did not suffice, a bounty of £5 was to be offered to any man who volunteered. Improvement was slight. Washington, still fretting at Winchester, sought a draft in Culpeper County. Of the hundred chosen by lot, fewer than eighty put in an appearance with Washington in the Shenandoah Valley, and only twenty-five of them were well armed.

When militiamen reported for duty, there was no assurance of their remaining to face danger. Washington dispatched 121 Prince William County men to an outpost on Patterson's Creek in the upper Potomac country in 1756, and a sergeant and fourteen privates deserted during the first night. On May 13 an express galloped into Winchester shouting that he brought news of a strong Indian foray in the area of Patterson's Creek and the South Branch of the Potomac. Forthwith much of Washington's militia strength evaporated. The Louisa County detachment numbered about seventy at dusk on May 13; by morning only six remained. The Stafford County contingent shrank from fifty-eight to eight, the Caroline County detachment from about one hundred to forty, the Spotsylvania County men from about seventy-one to thirty-two.[3]

The experiences of other colonies in attempting to raise and hold militia armies for the French war were similar. After Fort Necessity fell, Maryland was able to do no better than to muster a company of 100 men to take station at Wills Creek, the later Fort Cumberland, though that place was within her own borders. The New England colonies may have done somewhat better, possibly because they were closer to the centers of French power and considered the French a more direct menace. But in August, 1756, with plans afoot for an advance toward Canada on the Hudson River–Lake George–Lake Champlain route, and with the campaigning season already far advanced, the colonial army of Massachusetts, Connecticut, New Hampshire, Rhode Island, and New York troops on the northern frontier stood at less than two-thirds its authorized strength of 8,700.[4]

The militia system had done better in earlier wars when its members had responded to attacks on their own homes. But in the Great War for Empire, part-time soldiers demonstrated that they felt no inclination to take the field for extended campaigns that did not involve their own interests and aspirations in any direct ways that they could understand. The militia system had shown it could be useful when the citizenry felt involved in a military crisis. It was not a fit instrument for prolonged warfare on distant frontiers.

Colonel George Washington, the plantation aristocrat whose attitudes toward ordinary men bore a touch of the patronizing at best, did feel his interests involved in the French War and was also uncommonly self-disciplined. When the militia failed to meet his own standards of behavior, he drew generalized conclusions about their uselessness which, because of his later eminence, were to have a far-reaching influence upon later American military thought. He wrote:

Militia, you will find, Sir, will never answer your expectations, no dependence is to be placed upon them; They are obstinate and perverse, they are often egged on by the Officers, who lead them to acts of disobedience, and when they are ordered to certain posts for the security of stores, or the protection of the Inhabitants, will, on a sudden, resolve to leave *them*, and the united vigilance of their officers can not prevent them.[5]

By the time Washington was setting down these lugubrious conclusions, the ministry in London had long since been developing the thought that to carry the War for Empire to the enemy in the remote American forests, and in Canada itself, was a task for regular regiments, adapted to long offensive campaigns as the militia could not be. The ministry had also concluded that a unified British command must be imposed upon the American war, for not the least of the defects of the existing militia system was the separateness of each colony's armed force from the others, while colonial governors and assemblies were remarkably jealous of each other and slow to cooperate.[6]

Already in the seventeenth century, London had essayed to force cooperation on the colonies in such matters as warfare; indeed, Sir Edmund Andros's Dominion of New England would simply have consolidated the colonies from New Jersey and New York northward. That attempt had stirred up so wild a hornet's nest of colonial opposition, however, that the ministry believed it must now proceed toward colonial military unity by more subtle methods and by degrees. After the French seizure of the Forks of the Ohio seemed to put the enemy in a fair way to establishing his supremacy in North America, the ministry decided to appoint a British general as commander in chief of all military forces raised or to be raised on the North American continent. If the colonies would not submit to a

Dominion of New England, they ought at least to accept British military command, since in theory they were already doing so: the royal governors were the commanders of the armed forces of royal colonies, and charter limitations required British command of the troops of proprietary and corporate colonies in war emergencies. The commander in chief in North America would simply arrogate to himself the military authority to which officers of the Crown were already entitled. To fill this post, the ministry chose a veteran career officer, Major General Edward Braddock.[7]

Braddock's authority should permit him to deploy colonial troops as he wished, although he would remain dependent upon the American assemblies to raise and support them. But colonial troops would now pass into an auxiliary role, for with Braddock two regular regiments would be dispatched to America. To avoid undue expense, they would be regiments of the Irish establishment which were on a peace footing and therefore overofficered and undermanned, numbering a mere 310 men each. The regiments would be brought toward full war strength by recruiting Americans; but to escape intercolonial jealousies and to assure European military proficiency the British military themselves would do the recruiting and the training. In addition, two new regular regiments would be raised entirely in America, but again with British officers and under British auspices rather than the auspices of any individual colonies. Four regiments of regulars in America should reduce dependence on colonial troops to a minimum.[8]

This British plan met the expectations of its authors reasonably well. For a few years from 1755 onward, even the recruiting of British regiments in America yielded harvests beyond anything that the Americans' own recruiting efforts had given cause to anticipate. The two regiments of the Irish establishment that came to America with Braddock were the 44th and 48th of Foot. Together, having been augmented somewhat before sailing, they numbered a thousand men when they landed in America. By the time they set out from Wills Creek for Fort Duquesne, recruiting in America had lifted them to a total of 1,454. They lost 372 in Braddock's march to the Monongahela and back, but by June of the following year, 1756, they were up to 1,700 men. A report of August, 1756, credited them with having enlisted 1,562 men in America. The two new regiments raised in America, the 50th and 51st, had a total of 1,300 men by the fall of 1755. A severe winter reduced them by half, but by June, 1756, they were up to 1,260 again. Three British regiments already in Nova Scotia (the 40th, 45th, and 47th) enjoyed similar recruiting success in the New World. These encouraging experiences helped lead the ministry to decide in 1756 to recruit in America still another four battalions of a thousand men each, to form an oversize new regiment, the Royal Americans (at first the 62nd, later the 60th).[9]

These encouraging experiences might also seem to refute what has been said about the unwillingness of the colonists to leave their firesides for extended war. In part the British enlistment campaign surely does show that the colonies themselves might have raised larger volunteer forces if their efforts had been less halfhearted, since not every American had prospered in building a home and a farm or a trade, and the American population must have included persons for whom soldiering could promise escape from an unhappy civil career. But the initial success of British recruiting seems to have owed more to the not too scrupulous activities of British sergeants among indentured servants. To these men the army offered relative freedom, and many of them were therefore willing to break their indentures by enlisting. The historian of Lord Loudoun, Braddock's successor in the American command, estimates that from one-seventh to one-fifth of all American recruits in 1755 and 1756 were indentured servants from Pennsylvania alone.[10] Enlisting these men was legal, provided the government compensated their masters. But the government and the masters were likely to differ over what was a proper recompense, and often no compensation could be adequate for the loss of an experienced workman. Therefore colonial protests grew loud enough to persuade the British government to abandon its recruiting of indentured servants.[11]

Early British recruiting efforts were also ruthless. There are many evidences of fraud and trickery and the employment of drunkenness to net American recruits. When Loudoun became commander in chief in 1757, he apparently believed that American recruiting would benefit if it was given a firm legal basis. Therefore he saw to it that the terms of the Mutiny Act that regulated recruiting in England and Scotland were extended to America.[12] But the practical effect of this step turned out to be the curbing of abuses and thus a curtailment of the recruiting squads' success. Furthermore, British army regulations made recruiting a heavy expense for the regiments engaged in it, and the British recruiters had to compete against bounties and higher pay offered by the American provincial forces. From 1757 onward, consequently, recruiting in America did not garner enough men to keep the regiments stationed there up to strength.[13]

The ministry decided that the only recourse was to dispatch full-strength regiments from Great Britain. As early as 1756 the government in London, having agreed to send the 35th and 42nd Regiments of Foot to America, changed its original plan of filling their ranks in the New World and decided to fill them at home before shipping them overseas. In 1757 the new policy went into full effect; only 1,200 men for the regular regiments were enlisted in the colonies that year, while 11,000 were sent out from the British Isles. Regular regiments of the British army, composed mainly of men from the home islands, came to carry the brunt of the Great War for Empire and permanently to influence American ideas about the nature of armies and war.[14]

Many of the British regulars were excellent practitioners of the then current European methods of war. The Great War for Empire was, of course, the global extension of the Seven Years' War in Europe. In that European conflict, the generalship of Frederick the Great of Prussia was carrying the formal, classical age of war to its apogee. It was an age when peculiar political, economic, and technological circumstances made European war a ritualistic institution.[15]

Modern nationalism not yet having appeared, and the emotions of Europe's religious wars having burned themselves out, the European populations at large were divorced from interest in the political goals of their monarchs. The monarchs entertained rival territorial ambitions and also tried to enhance their own power and weaken opponents by juggling dynasties, especially those of the lesser states. But usually they did not seek to overthrow each other altogether, for to do that might have unleashed uncontrollable forces that would endanger all monarchs. Therefore they warred against each other for limited aims and thus were content to employ limited means: small professional armies. To have enlisted huge numbers of men into their armies would have been difficult, since most of their subjects were indifferent to the purposes of their wars. The only means of recruiting soldiers was to enlist not their emotional loyalties but their financial interests, and a really large army would have been prohibitively expensive. Under the creaky financial institutions of the old regime, excessive expense was to be avoided studiously.

Common soldiers were in fact the dregs of European society, vagabonds, ne'er-do-well's, and criminals, the only sorts of men who were willing to risk their lives for the little pay bestowed upon them. Indeed, even the dregs of society usually preferred to avoid the risks and discipline of army life, and recruits largely had to be impressed into service by one forcible means or another. Recruiting armies from the most shiftless and criminal of men necessitated in turn an extremely stiff discipline, which, in a vicious circle, made army life still more unattractive and required still more impressment of undesirables.

On the other hand, once a soldier was disciplined and trained in warfare, he represented a considerable financial investment, and therefore his government did not desire to see him killed. Accordingly, commanders planned campaigns and battles in such a way that loss of life would be minimized. As Daniel Defoe put it:

The present maxims of war are—
 Never fight without a manifest advantage.
 And always encamp so as not to be forced to it.
 And if two opposite generals nicely observe both these rules, it is impossible that they should ever come to fight.[16]

If eighteenth-century European armies fought a very limited kind of war, however, they sometimes fought it with a fine skill. If casualties were to be limited, maneuver had to be conducted with finesse. There must be no clumsy marching into unwanted combat, and officers and men must so comport themselves as to seize every possible tactical advantage on the battlefield. For these reasons an army had to be an instrument delicately responsive to its commander's wishes, able to throw itself from marching column into line of battle promptly and to take up designated positions on the battlefield precisely. Here was another reason for extremely intensive training: the men had to be drilled and drilled again to transform a collection of doltish recruits into a sensitive military mechanism.

Although armies thus resembled precision instruments, no military profession in the modern sense existed at all. That is, modern officers are required to develop sufficient expertise and a sufficient corporate sense of responsibility to be professional men much in the manner of physicians and lawyers, but in the eighteenth century no sufficient theory or philosophy of war, no specialization of the function of military leadership as compared with other activities, had yet developed to make such professionalism possible. Partly as an inheritance from medieval notions of war as an honorable activity suitable only to noblemen, partly as a means by which monarchs controlled the nobility and made them useful, commissioned ranks were generally regarded as the appropriate preserve of titled gentlemen, except possibly in the technical branches, artillery and engineering. In the British army, wealth united with birth as a criterion for officership, since for two hundred years after the Restoration a British commission generally had to be "purchased" for a substantial sum of money; the idea was to guard against a second Cromwell by insuring that officers would be persons with a stake in the existing social order.[17] Here was a further curb on the violence of war, since officers of all armies felt a mutual bond through the international qualities of nobility.

Despite the forces that limited eighteenth-century war, once battle began the casualties tended to be high in proportion to the numbers engaged. This fact offered still another reason for rigorous training and discipline. By the eighteenth century the matchlock musket with its clumsy prop, which was used by John Smith's first Virginia soldiers, had given way to the lighter and more serviceable flintlock. But eighteenth-century muskets were still crude weapons. The "Brown Bess," the .75-caliber smoothbore used by the British army from Marlborough's time onward through the century, had a maximum effective range between eighty and one hundred yards. Without a rear sight, and in the hands of soldiers whose training did not include marksmanship, it had a practical range of even less. Under these conditions the only useful kind of firing was volley firing. A primary object in battle had to be to fire by volley against the enemy, and so again the necessity was to train solders to maneuver precisely in careful alignment. It was the exchange of volleys at close range by battalions formed in lines three men deep that inflicted the proportionately high battlefield casualties of the eighteenth century, and only thoroughly disciplined troops would stand up under such a fire.

After a volley had been expended, the process of reloading muskets was so slow that the decisive combat was likely to be the closing of rival lines who had fired their muskets, to fight it out with the bayonet. The army likely to break the enemy was the one better trained to maintain its solid line of bayonets in this climactic clash. Once again, complete discipline was the prerequisite of battlefield success.

European war with its exchanges of volleys by disciplined, tightly drawn battle lines could be fought only in open and level country. Armies fought in lines of battalions or brigades; smaller units did not maneuver independently. Battlefields were chosen for their resemblance to gladitorial arenas or modern football fields, for only there could the armies maintain their alignments and avoid being broken up into fragments. Furthermore, campaigning had to be restricted to good weather, because flintlocks were useless in rain or snow.

These latter facts obviously raised questions after all about the wisdom of choosing British regulars to fight the Indian allies of the

French in the American wilderness. American Indians fought their own very informal style of war, and in forest campaigns the French often adapted themselves to Indian methods. The Indians did not do battle in open arenas; they used the ample cover of their wooded homelands. They were not about to give British regulars battle in the open field if they could avoid it, for they were skillful in the ambush and the hit-and-run raid in the forest and were hardly sufficiently foolish to abandon their resulting advantages for a mode of combat in which they would not have had a chance. The international brotherhood aspects of the European officer corps encouraged Europeans to fight under generally accepted rules of war, codified by Grotius and Vattel; but the Indians did not know the rules and would not have abided by them if they had. The Indians saw nothing wrong in employing stealth, trickery, and ruthlessness. Quite contrary to European practice, they made a special point of picking off officers. They did not always wait for good fighting weather, for although they grew increasingly dependent upon firearms, they still possessed bows that could fling arrows in any weather. The Indians fought not a polite, limited war, but a cruel war which included noncombatants among its victims. Indian warriors did not fight for merely limited objectives; they represented their nations in arms, resisting the advance of British settlement for the sake of their very existence.

The North American war would have to be fought on the Indians' own ground. There would be many forests but few open arenas for European-style battles. In the forests the tight formations of British infantry might well be fragmented. While British infantrymen were dull men dulled still further by the kind of discipline they endured and therefore not well prepared to fight in small groups or individually, the Indians excelled in individualized warfare. They encouraged the development of individual prowess, of the individual warrior's making the most of his knowledge of the ground to conceal himself and to strike quickly and destructively from cover.[18]

One of the principal problems of British campaigning in America was bound to be the fundamental one of provisioning the armies. European forces were accustomed to elaborate bases of supply, established at fairly regular intervals as the army advanced at a leisurely pace. Supplying campaigns in the North American wilderness, with inadequate base facilities, and with limited transport moving over bad or nonexistent roads, was bound to create problems of great severity.

It appeared then that British regulars might face in aggravated form the handicaps that European tactics imposed upon American militia in Indian warfare, and that their virtues in European war might be their undoing in America. The sequel proved otherwise. British regulars proved so formidable even in a kind of war that was new to them that they made an unforgettable impression on certain Americans, who later were to form an American regular army essentially in the image of the British regulars. Their rigorous discipline gave the regulars a tough competence that could carry them through trials and dangers whether foreseen or unforeseen by British tactical precepts. They might sometimes flinch before Indian ambuscades, but often their superior discipline and self-control enabled them to transform a battle from one fought on the Indians' terms to one fought on their own. Though the Indians had real skills in what later generations would call guerrilla war, they had no Mao Tse-tung to give them a doctrine of war that might have saved them from lapses that permitted the regulars to force them into open battle. Most of all, Indians simply could not match the steady persistence of the disciplined British.

Even the unhappy Braddock expedition demonstrated many of the assets of the British military system. Braddock attempted to march more than a thousand men across 110 miles of rough, wooded country between Wills Creek and Fort Duquesne in one leap, without establishing intermediate bases, and in that purpose he succeeded. He had to clear his own road most of the way across the Appalachians, and anyone familiar even with the automobile roads (other than the Pennsylvania Turnpike) across Allegheny Mountain, Laurel Hill, and Chestnut Ridge will attest that any military march across them would be a considerable feat—especially when the ridges were still covered with virgin forest so thick that a man might go "Twenty Miles without seeing before him ten yards."[19] Braddock crossed the mountains carrying with him twelve-pounder guns from the upper battery of H.M.S. *Norwich* and even larger eight-inch siege howitzers—although the Virginians in 1754 had abandoned as futile an effort to get four-pounders over the mountains. The French at Fort Duquesne did their best to harry or turn back the march with raiding parties, but their commander had to testify that the British "troops remain so constantly on guard, always marching in battle formation, that all the efforts our detachments put forth against them are useless."[20] Despite the obstacles of nature and man, Braddock was only eight miles from the Forks of the Ohio on July 8, early in the campaigning season.

The battle of the Monongahela itself was not so disgraceful an episode for British arms as many thought it then and many historians have made it seem. It was not an ambush but a meeting engagement, and if Lieutenant Colonel Thomas Gage, in command of Braddock's vanguard, had pushed energetically to gain a hill that commanded the route of march from the right, or to open ground suited to the British type of warfare and lying just ahead of the point of encounter, the superior numbers and discipline of the British would probably have effected the rout of the enemy. Instead, Gage fell back and created a traffic jam on Braddock's narrow twelve-foot road, exposing a dense mass of men to the French and Indian fire from wooded ravines to the left and right. Lieutenant Colonel Ralph Burton tried to do the tactically sound thing by pushing on to take the commanding hill, but the press of men on the road prevented him. Braddock made his way to the head of the column too late to retrieve the situation and then fell mortally wounded.

Almost certainly, adopting the methods of the colonial auxiliaries who accompanied him would not have saved Braddock. Many of the Virginians with him moved into the woods to seek cover and fight Indian style. But it was too late for that; fighting against an enemy already well placed and concealed, they suffered exceptionally heavy losses and fought to little effect. For the British soldiers generally to scatter into the woods would have been simply further playing of the Indians' game.

Braddock has been criticized for his long uninterrupted march from Wills Creek, despite its character as a notable achievement, since if he had managed to take Fort Duquesne he might have found it hard to stay there, more than a hundred miles from the nearest supporting base. When Brigadier John Forbes led a similar but successful expedition to the Forks of the Ohio in 1758, he met the supply problem in more conventional fashion by pausing to establish fortified depots along the way. He so slowed his march that he nearly failed to reach the Ohio before winter set in, but he ensured his ability to stay once he got there. Forbes showed that the roads and depots of European military supply could be scratched out of the American wilderness by a commander who had the will to do it, and regulars could be thus supported. But the poor roads and vast distances of America posed problems that were not altogether soluble and would continue to plague armies until the coming of the railroads.[21]

Colonel Henry Bouquet, Swiss mercenary turned British officer, showed how regulars might triumph in a battle much like Braddock's. Bouquet led still another expedition to the Forks of the Ohio during Pontiac's Rebellion in 1763 and, like Braddock, he collided with Indians who halted his advance along a narrow road and then worked their way around his flanks. But Bouquet had introduced

one tactical innovation of great importance to the Scots Highlanders under his command: he had had them trained to maneuver
by companies rather than only by battalions. Because of constricting woods, Bouquet could not have formed a battalion line, but this
fact did not reduce him immediately to fighting a battle of individuals such as the Indians fought. Retaining the advantages of his
regulars' discipline, he maneuvered his companies to lure the Indians out from cover, whereupon he overcame them with a European-style bayonet charge.[22]

The skill and discipline of British regulars were as valuable, then,
in America as in Europe, but they could best be employed when
coupled with adjustments to American conditions in the manner that
Bouquet demonstrated. Another useful adjustment was the improvement of reconnaissance and march and camp security in the face of
the Indians' fondness for concealment and surprise. To that end the
colonials had learned to employ Indian scouts, and similarly Major
General William Shirley, commander in chief in North America
from Braddock's death until the arrival of Lord Loudoun, enlisted a
company of Stockbridge Indians to serve the British forces. He considered the formation of an Indian regiment.[23]

Shirley's idea of an Indian regiment collapsed for want of enlistments, but both Shirley and Loudoun then turned to recruiting white
frontiersmen proficient in the ways of the forest. One such man was
Robert Rogers of New Hampshire. Rogers reconnoitered French and
Indian positions on Lake Champlain as captain of a company in the
New England provincial forces in 1755. He proved so capable that
the next year Shirley commissioned him to raise an independent
company of "rangers," and before 1756 was out Shirley called for
three similar companies, to be recruited to sixty men each and to be
financed out of Shirley's contingency fund and thus from the British
treasury. The ranger companies in effect were independent companies of the British army, and their mission was to act as scouts and to
guard the lines of march and supply of the army by beating the
Indians at Indian-style warfare. Loudoun reorganized them as companies of a hundred men.[24]

The latter-day fame of Robert Rogers notwithstanding, the ranger
companies were sometimes a disappointment. With the characteristic
individualism of the frontier, their soldiers were less than models of
obedience to orders and discipline, from Rogers himself on down.
Rogers took his company out without orders; the rangers stole provisions and rioted to free comrades imprisoned by their own officers.
Lord Loudoun prepared to break the rules of formal warfare himself
by mounting a winter expedition against Ticonderoga in 1757–58,

but Rogers helped ruin the plan by failing to carry out his assigned task of making snowshoes for the march. His fight and escape at Rogers's Rock in January, 1758, is one of the principal incidents in his fame, but Rogers had to flee a tight spot partly because he had plunged toward Ticonderoga without the support he might have had if other troops could have followed in the snowshoes he was supposed to have made.

Nevertheless, many of Rogers's exploits were both real and astonishing. Repeatedly he ventured into the enemy's country to bring back information which no one else was willing to try to get. He harassed the periphery of French operations in the Lake George–Lake Champlain–Richelieu River campaigns as annoyingly as France's Indian allies had earlier harassed the British. His raid against the Indian town of St. Francis avenged decades of bloodshed and pillage on the New England frontier. Few soldiers have been fortunate enough to have their adventures chronicled with the talent for dramatic narrative that Francis Parkman and Kenneth Roberts exercised upon Rogers's Rangers, but few have so well deserved that happy fate. When the United States Army in 1942 decided to call its raiding specialists the Rangers after Rogers's men—reprinting Rogers's rules of 1757 as a training aid—it chose a worthy designation.[25]

Meanwhile Lord Loudoun decided that a few companies of ranger auxiliaries were not enough and that larger parts of the British army must learn something about the special techniques of American forest warfare. With his encouragement some fifty-five British volunteers served with Rogers to absorb the Rangers' skills. Twenty-three of these men later received commissions in various regiments where they might share their knowledge, five of them in a new regiment of light infantry formed under the colonelcy of Thomas Gage in 1758. This regiment, eventually designated the 80th, was proposed by Gage himself, but it fitted well into Loudoun's purpose. It consisted as far as possible of men experienced in the forest, officered largely by men schooled under Rogers, and equipped with short, light muskets for forest service. Loudoun hoped that it might combine the unorthodox techniques of Indian and ranger warfare with the discipline of regulars. Unfortunately, Gage was no Rogers, and partly for that reason the regiment proved a disappointment. For example, it failed to provide the reconnaissance and security expected from it when it led the march on Ticonderoga in the summer of 1758.[26]

Other regular regiments tried to adapt to forest warfare through less drastic innovations. The four battalions of Royal Americans were trained and equipped for forest warfare from the beginning. To that end, they were the first British regiment to remove the lace from

their uniforms and to shorten their coats. Loudoun instructed that
they be trained

to fire at Marks, and in order to qualify them for the Service of the
Woods, they are to be taught to load and fire, lyeing on the Ground and
kneeling. They are to be taught to march in Order, slow and fast in all
sortes of Ground. They are frequently to pitch and fold up their Tentes,
and to be accustomed to pack up and carry their necessaries in the most
commodious manner.[27]

The idea of firing from a prone position and loading while kneeling
was an innovation comparable to maneuvering by companies. Henry
Bouquet, whose troops so maneuvered in 1763, was commissioned
in the Royal Americans, and his interest in adapting to forest warfare began with them.[28]

Increasingly, all British regiments in America received some such
training. British soldiers learned to march through woods single file
and to fend for themselves at the command "Tree all," each man
finding the cover of a tree and fighting his own fight—although this
tactic, an expedient for desperate moments, threw away too many
advantages to be used often. John Forbes resolved as he set out for
Fort Duquesne in 1758

upon getting some of the best people in every Corps to go out a Scouting in that [Indian] stile. . . . And I must confess in this country, wee
must comply and learn the Art of Warr from Ennemy Indians or anything else who have seen the Country and Warr carried on in itt.[29]

By 1770 every regiment of foot in America incorporated a light
infantry company, composed of lithe, agile men chosen for their
aptitude in relatively informal tactics and capable of maneuvering as
a company. Presently such companies began to appear in the regiments stationed in the home islands as well. In 1774 Sir William
Howe undertook to standardize their training.[30]

All such responses to the American environment, however, were
adaptations in detail. Essentially the British regular army transplanted European methods of war to America, and did so successfully. When British regulars faced European rivals on American soil,
as at the Plains of Abraham in 1759, they fought in the European
manner almost without modification. Quebec was a volley-fire and
bayonet battle of the classic type. American experience had only the
most limited influence on contests of Europeans versus Europeans.[31] Even against the Indians, European discipline and tactics
prevailed, modified mainly by improved reconnaissance and march
security, aimed firing, and maneuvering by companies. Called to

America when the Great War for Empire demanded a long-service soldiery in greater numbers than the local militia system could supply, British regular regiments took on the brunt of the fighting, won the war, and set a standard of expert soldiering for Americans to emulate. After George Washington had seen British regulars in action, his fondest hope for his Virginia provincial troops was that they might pattern themselves on the regulars.

Discipline [he wrote] is the soul of an army. It makes small numbers formidable; procures success to the weak, and esteem to all; and may, in a peculiar manner to us, who are in the way to be joined to Regulars in a very short time, . . . [be the means of distinguishing us] from other Provincials.[32]

THREE

The Creation of an American Army:
1775-82

Let us have a respectable Army, and such as will be competent to every contingency.

—George Washington[1]

ANY OF FOUR days in June, 1775, or perhaps the fourth of July of the same year, might be considered the birthday of the army that became that of the United States. The date generally accepted is June 14, when the Continental Congress first authorized the muster of troops under its own sponsorship. To assist the New England provincial forces then laying siege to Boston, it called for the raising of ten companies of expert riflemen, six from Pennsylvania, two from Maryland, and two from Virginia. Congress specified the manner of enlistment and the tables of organization; each company was to consist of a captain, three lieutenants, four sergeants, four corporals, a drummer or trumpeter, and sixty-eight privates. Together, these companies subsequently became the 1st Continental Regiment.[2]

On June 15 Congress voted the appointment of one of its own members, Colonel Washington of the Virginia militia, "to command all the Continental forces." On the sixteenth, Washington accepted the command, Congress appointed a committee to prepare his commission and instructions, and the delegates went on to adopt a plan of organization for the line command and the staff departments of an army, providing for two major generals and eight brigadiers subordinate to Washington, an Adjutant General's Department, and offices of a commissary general, quartermaster general, and paymaster general.[3]

On June 30 Congress authorized the first increment of national troops and adopted a modification of the British Articles of War for the governance of the new army.[4] General Washington meanwhile journeyed from Philadelphia to Cambridge, where he announced in general orders on July 4 that the "Troops of the UNITED PROVINCES of North America" were henceforth under the authority of Congress.[5]

From its first measures establishing a Continental Army, Congress was acutely mindful that the similar Parliamentary army of England little more than a hundred years before had turned upon its legislative creator and erected the military dictatorship of Oliver Cromwell. As men whose education was heavily classical, the members were thoroughly aware of the military autocracies of the ancient world. The dangers of a standing army as a threat to liberty were close to everyone's thoughts, since the attempt to station British regiments permanently in America despite the elimination of New France had been among the leading causes of the imperial crisis; many Americans had objected not only to taxation of the colonies for the support of British forces in the New World, but also to the very presence of those forces as, in the absence of external enemies, a bludgeon with which Great Britain might pommel American liberty. Therefore, from its first military resolutions onward, Congress looked to the assurance of its ascendancy over the Army. Washington's instructions emphasized his subordination to Congress and his duty to report regularly. Congress, not Washington, chose the principal line and staff officers. To limit the possibility that Washington might become a Cromwell, his instructions enjoined him on "any occasions that may happen, to use your best circumspection and (advising with your council of war) to order and dispose of the said Army as may be most advantageous." Washington consequently felt obliged to secure the approval of his generals for every major decision; Congress had bound him to a council of war.[6]

When Washington arrived at Cambridge to take command, the troops of the United Provinces consisted mainly of New England men besieging Boston, and New England and New York men, under the immediate command of Major General Philip Schuyler in the "Northern Department," guarding the lakes-and-river route from Canada. The Continental Army was destined to remain largely a New England army for a year to come. As the colonial quarrel with Great Britain had intensified after 1773, the New England colonies had undertaken increasing military preparations. On October 26, 1774, the Provincial Congress of Massachusetts Bay had created a committee of safety with power to collect military stores and to call out the militia. Reviving a seventeenth-century procedure, the Provincial Congress had instructed the field officers of militia to attempt to organize a quarter of their men into companies of fifty that would be ready for immediate service on call: the minutemen. After the Massachusetts forces thus instituted clashed with the British garrison of Boston at Lexington and Concord, on April 19, 1775, the committee of safety issued a circular letter on April 20 calling for the enlistment of an army, and the next day the strength of the army was set at 8,000 men.[7]

Especially after Lexington and Concord, large numbers of New Englanders evidently viewed the redcoats in Boston as a menace to their safety and their future about as direct as the redskins of King Philip had been. From the volunteer militia companies and the mass of the common militia they came forward for military duty, and their militia officers and legislative representatives spurred them on, as they had never done for the more remote issues of the Great War for Empire, and as they had not done since the Indian wars of the previous century. On April 23 the Provincial Congress of Massachusetts Bay raised its sights to call for 13,600 men and to appeal to New Hampshire, Rhode Island, and Connecticut for troops in the same proportion to their populations, for an army of 30,000 altogether. Individual volunteers and volunteer companies such as the Kentish Guards of Rhode Island—Nathanael Greene among its privates— streamed to Boston. By late May the New England colonies believed they had gathered 24,500 men.

They organized their companies on the British pattern into regiments of ten companies each (except the Rhode Island regiments, which consisted of eight companies). This New England Army fought the battle of Bunker Hill in late June, and for the time being its adoption by Congress, the presence of a Virginian commander in chief, and the approach of the Middle Colonies' riflemen gave the Yankee Army only the merest semblance of a continental force.[8]

The war enthusiasm that followed Lexington and Concord could hardly have failed to abate in some measure as siege operations dragged into the summer, and among an unmilitary people enthusiasm alone could not prevent a host of unaccustomed problems. Among Washington's first acts after he reached Cambridge in July was an effort to determine the strength of his Army precisely. He was told at first that 18,000 to 20,000 were currently around Boston, but his insistence on greater precision revealed that in fact he had only some 16,600 privates and n.c.o.'s, with only 13,743 foot and 585 artillerymen present for duty, fit. These returns were a disappointment, and the very manner in which Washington received them gave him another disappointment, which revealed much about the amateur quality of the Army he commanded:

Could I have conceived [he wrote], that what ought, and, in a regular army, would have been done in an hour, would employ eight days, I should have sent an express [to the Continental Congress] on the second morning after I arrived, with a general account of things; but expecting in the morning to receive the returns in the evening, and in the evening surely to find them in the morning, and at last getting them full of imperfections, I have been drilled on from day to day, till I am ashamed to look back at the time which has elapsed since my arrival here.[9]

From the beginning Washington encountered what was going to be a perennial plague, short supply. His troops did have plenty to eat; in the first enthusiasm New England offered provisions so abundant that the Yankee soldier's diet was held before the British as an incitement to desertion. If only a handful of men, mostly Rhode Islanders, wore anything resembling uniforms, nevertheless the Army was also tolerably well clothed. But there was an acute shortage of powder. The powder used at Bunker Hill had been seized by New Hampshire militia from Fort William and Mary in Portsmouth harbor, and its virtual exhaustion had ended the battle. Few American powder mills existed. Washington called on the colonies to send him every grain, and he inspired efforts to import powder from France, the West Indies, and Spain. But through 1775 he had to fear that if the British sortied from Boston, he would not be able to fire enough rounds to halt them. At the end of July, for example, at a time when the British were making motions suggesting an advance, Washington was told that there was scarcely enough powder to issue nine cartridges to each man.[10]

An inspection of the small arms in the hands of the troops late in the year showed many of them grossly defective. There was not much artillery, until the winter made it possible to haul to Boston on sledges the guns captured when Ethan Allen and Benedict Arnold seized Fort Ticonderoga.[11]

For all that, thanks in no small part to the mechanisms of the militia system, Washington did command a kind of army. The British respected it enough after Bunker Hill that despite their occasional alarming movements they did not venture another attack. Washington himself came to feel sufficient confidence to detach about 1,000 men in September for an attempt at the conquest of Canada in conjunction with General Schuyler's force.

But at the end of 1775 Washington's Army was due to evaporate. Almost everyone, apparently including Washington, had expected that the armed rising of the colonies would oblige Great Britain to hasten negotiations for the settlement of grievances, and in an amenable mood. Few Americans thought that there would be more than one campaign. The Army was enlisted only until the end of the year. As pronouncements emerged from London during the closing months of 1775, however, they evidenced not a softening but a hardening of British policy; the King stigmatized the Americans as rebels and Parliament agreed to enlarge military forces. Autumn brought a certainty that the need for an American army would extend into 1776, though the enlistments of the existing Army did not. In the autumn of 1775 even the powder shortage paled before the impending dissolution of the Army and the larger problem implicit in Britain's decision to strengthen her army to resist the American rebellion: could the colonies raise a military force capable of resisting British regular soldiers in formidable numbers?[12]

Washington believed that the only way to do that was to create an American approximation of the British regular army. Parliament had voted an army of 55,000 men. British recruiting parties immediately met trouble in trying to raise the regiments to that total, since the usual recruiting difficulties were aggravated by the considerable unpopularity of a war against the colonies. In any event, the whole of the British army could not be thrown against Washington. Late in 1775 Washington therefore believed that his goal for 1776 should be 20,000 men enlisted in the Continental Army, that is, enlisted in formations authorized by and responsible to the Continental Congress. Since the hope would be that, as in 1775, the Continental Army could be recruited largely from volunteer militia units already possessing some military organization and discipline, much of the Continental Army would be roughly comparable to modern National Guard units in federal service. They would be sufficiently "Congressional" or "Continental," however, that the regiments of the 1776 Army were to be designated not by their numbers in their respective provincial military forces but by a Continental nomenclature. It was with the organization of the 1776 Army, for example, that the Pennsylvania, Maryland, and Virginia rifle companies authorized in June, 1775, became the 1st Continental Regiment. Washington evidently intended that the Continental Army should rise as much as possible above its origins in part-time soldiering to become an army disciplined and skilled in the British pattern. A Continental Army of 20,000 men would obviously be none too large, but an army of this size was one that Congress might realistically hope to recruit and maintain. Washington would count on support and reinforcement when needed from the various provincial militias, from which units could be formed for short terms of active duty in the established manner. The provinces would also have their traditional militia systems to which to turn for home defense.[13]

In the fall of 1775, however, a Continental Army of 20,000 men for the next campaign was only a hope, and the first task of Washington and Congress was to persuade the men of the 1775 Army to sign on again. This effort proved discouraging. The Connecticut men were due to depart at the beginning of December, the rest of the New Englanders at the beginning of January. These men had neglected their fields and crafts for most of a year and had left their homes expecting a reasonably prompt return. They now believed they had done their share for the American cause. They had opened the contest; let those who had enjoyed comfort and safety meanwhile now take their places.

A survey in October revealed that probably no more than one-half, at most two-thirds, of even the company officers would stay to fight in 1776. In mid-November eleven regiments reported a total of only 966 willing to remain. Appeals to the Connecticut men to stand by the colors at least another month fell mostly on deaf ears.

Therefore Washington had to disband one army and create another in the presence of the enemy. He determined to interpret the Connecticut regiments' obligation to service as dating from the time not of their call to arms but of their actual mustering in, which meant he would compel them to stay at least until December 6 or December 10. He used the bayonets of other troops to enforce this decision. The respite thus secured permitted Massachusetts and New Hampshire to call out militia and send it to Washington's camps before the Connecticut troops disappeared.

The men of other states booed and hissed the Connecticut men when they left as soon as Washington permitted, but this display did not deter the jeerers themselves from leaving when their time arrived. Those companies that remained did so upon generous promises of furloughs, which cut still further into Washington's strength. New recruits were slow to come forward.[14]

We are now left [Washington wrote at the beginning of the New Year] with a good deal less than half-raised Regiments, and about five thousand militia, who only stand ingaged to the middle of this month; when, according to custom, they will depart, let the necessity of their stay be never so urgent.[15]

Fortunately, the British did not sortie from Boston, although other American commanders were less fortunate than Washington: the disintegration of the American army in Canada ruined the effort to take Quebec.

When Washington received his first strength returns for the new Army on January 9, he learned that enlistments totaled only 8,212, and that the number of men present for duty, fit, was only 5,582. He felt obliged to issue another call for New England militia, thirteen regiments to serve through February and March. By the beginning of March, Continental strength was up to 9,170, with 4,970 militia also on hand. With this force, and with the cannons from Ticonderoga, Washington undertook the advances that forced the British from Boston. But his Army had survived merely the first of many threats of dissolution, Continental strength in 1776 never approached 20,-000, and again even the disappointing numbers that came in did so pledged to only one year's service.[16]

Though the British ministry was experiencing its own difficulties in trying to increase its army to 55,000 men, it decided to supplement the redcoats by renting soldiers in the Germanies. It eventually managed to hire 29,875 of them. In the summer of 1776 Major General Sir William Howe led the strengthened British forces in a renewed effort to suppress the American rebellion, landing 32,000 British and German troops on Staten Island in July and August to begin with the conquest of New York. His men were well armed, well trained, and well equipped, carried to America aboard hundreds of transports and supported by more than ample sea power in the form of ten ships of the line and twenty frigates. Meanwhile the British were also setting in motion an advance from Canada down the river-and-lakes route, hoping to link up with Howe and thus to sever the rebellious colonies.

Washington believed that few if any of even his best Continentals were ready to meet European professionals on equal terms, and he decided that to oppose the formidable combinations gathering against him he ought to have a two-to-one superiority in numbers. He was able to lead to the defense of New York a mere 9,000 Continentals. So he turned again to militia. As early as June 3, Congress called on Pennsylvania, Maryland, and Delaware for 10,000 militia, to assemble in New Jersey and serve Washington as a reserve force to be known as the "Flying Camp."[17] Presently, Congress called Massachusetts, New York, New Jersey, and Pennsylvania to muster 15,000 more militia. All these troops were to serve until December 1, 1776.

The summer of 1776 was the summer of the Declaration of Independence, and that event seems to have inspired renewed zeal for the American cause. The militia came forward promptly and in numbers not too far short of the Congressional quotas. By the time General

Howe, habitually a leisurely officer, got around to moving troops from Staten Island to Long Island, Washington was able to oppose him with about 23,000 men. This figure fell short of the British strength, much less a two-to-one superiority, but Washington would be standing on the defensive on ground his Army knew better than the British, and for a brief moment as the campaign opened he felt sanguine.

He should not have. The campaign for New York turned into a disaster. It is difficult to assess what it revealed about the quality of the new American Army. Time and again American formations, Continentals and militia both, failed to stand up against the disciplined British and Hessians, but time and again bad leadership, from Washington on down, put them into situations where hard fighting might have been worse than useless, leading only to entrapment. Washington, somewhat more tolerant of weaker men than he had been as a young colonel, but still inclined toward impatience, frequently railed against inept and frightened soldiers. He called the flight of Connecticut militia before the British landings at Kip's Bay, Manhattan, "disgraceful and dastardly," and he indulged in similar epithets throughout the campaign. Yet American detachments can be credited with fighting very well on some occasions, especially in view of the fact that the battles were fought in the enemy's accustomed style, with geography permitting Howe to employ the formal tactics of Europe, and Washington making no effort to fight in any other manner. William Smallwood's Maryland Continentals and John Haslet's Delawares at the battle of Long Island laid the foundation of their coming fame as the crack troops of the Continental Army, some of Smallwood's men returning to the attack six times before retreating in the face of British reinforcements. John Glover's Marblehead men not only saved the Long Island forces with a skillful evacuation, but along with other Massachusetts troops they fought a brave holding action at Pell's Point. At Harlem Heights, Thomas Knowlton's Connecticut Rangers and three companies of Virginia Continentals lost their commanding officers in the course of a flanking march against the Black Watch; nevertheless they pushed on to enjoy the unaccustomed spectacle of the backs of the fleeing 42nd Highlanders.

The fairest verdict on these first open-field battles of the new American Army seems to be that the unevenness of American conduct demonstrated a general and predictable inferiority of American troops to European professionals in European-style combat, although those units whose officers had taken pains to train them diligently and well were ready to give a good account of themselves. If American soldiers were not all that might have been desired, the deficiencies of their leaders were greater. A handful of exceptionally good company and regimental leaders accounted for the best American performances, but most American leadership was indifferent or worse, from the company and regimental levels to such generals as John Sullivan, Israel Putnam, and Washington himself. Officership was not yet a profession, but nevertheless it was harder to develop good officers than good soldiers—while good officers could make good soldiers.

Anyway, the good performances by American troops were too few to offset the bad ones and bad generalship, and New York City was lost, along with numerous casualties and 2,837 officers and men, 146 cannons, 12,000 shot and shell, 2,800 muskets, and 400,-000 musket cartridges in the fall of Forts Washington and Lee alone. The Americans had no substantial tradition of military victory to sustain their self-confidence before such losses, and it is not surprising that in the sequel to defeat, "the contagion of desertion . . . raged after the manner of a plague."[18] The militia shrank to a shadow of their summer's strength long before December 1, and one month after that date whatever Continentals were left were due to go home again. Having been pressed to desperation even when he had troops on hand, Washington again faced the predicament of losing one army and building another in the midst of war.

Writers of the Emory Upton persuasion have spared no scorn in castigating Congress for the one-year enlistments which for the second successive winter imposed a crisis upon the Revolutionary cause. But the Congress were not such fools as to be blind to the dangers of their system. They knew that short enlistments created risks; if they had not known it, Washington's letters had certainly informed them. But they acted upon what seemed good reasons. When the 1776 Army had been enlisted, the Revolutionary cause was a plant of very uncertain vigor. The discovery that the war would be a long one, after most men had hoped for a negotiated peace in 1775, might have damaged it badly. Should Congress at this delicate moment have experimented with the forced-feeding of the cause through the harsh medicine of long-term enlistments? Did not wisdom counsel a gentle nurturing of the cause, avoiding the shock to morale implicit in the suggestion of a war that might go on not only for more than one or two campaigns but indefinitely? Might not an effort to enlist men for long terms play into the hands of Loyalists and their propaganda?

In any case, would enough men have enlisted for substantially more than a year? The soldiers of 1775 were mostly unwilling to remain in service after enduring less than a year. As events demonstrated, insufficient numbers enlisted in 1776 even for a one-year term. Washington himself seems to have been unready to urge long-term enlistments for the 1776 Army. When he did conclude that a long-term army was essential, he urged a draft as the only means of getting it; but Congress did not dare invoke that instrument in any year of the war. The one-year enlistments of 1776 were a grave handicap to the Revolutionary War, but the basic cause of that policy was not Congressional folly but the caution necessary in creating a professional army among a people who had fled Europe partly to escape such armies.

Nevertheless, the events of 1776 dictated a harsher military policy despite the obstacles. By the late months of the independence year, the presence of Howe's formidable army in New York, combined with the impending dissolution of Washington's forces, so much imperiled the whole American cause that any risk seemed secondary to the need for a reliable army. If a new army could not be raised, all other dangers would be irrelevant because the Revolution would be lost. And the crisis of 1776 was so severe that, could it be overcome, almost any risk seemed preferable to its repetition. Therefore Congress voted on September 16 to raise eighty-eight battalions—battalion being then a term equivalent to regiment—by quotas from the several states, "to serve during the present war." Additional emergency measures projected an army of 76,000 men, aggregating 104 battalions. To appeal to local pride, Congress dropped the Continental numbering system of 1776 and restored the state designations of the regiments.[19]

Unhappily, at this juncture Congress did display folly. Washington naturally hoped to reenlist as many as possible of the 1776 troops, both to benefit from their experience and to minimize the dangers of transition from the old Army to the new. But Congress provided that the states were to send committees to the Army to investigate the conduct of officers and men and then to appoint the officers of the new regiments. This was a well-intended plan to eliminate unfit officers and appoint only good ones, but the principal result was to impede reenlistment. For only officers of the new regiments could recruit those regiments, and until the state committees made their decisions, no one knew who would be the officers and there could be no recruiting among the 1776 troops. And the states proved extremely dilatory in sending their committees. By November 4, not a single officer had been chosen for the new Army and empowered to recruit.

Congress on that date changed course and empowered Washington to designate officers to begin recruiting. But Washington had to tread warily among jealousies military and political to exercise this power, and meanwhile Massachusetts, Connecticut, and Maryland had thrown a new impediment in his path by offering recruiting bounties in excess of those voted by Congress, thus hampering enlistments in the regiments of other states.[20]

These various difficulties obliged Washington to call upon several states for militia again to fill his ranks until new Continentals arrived. But by the time he did so he was fleeing through Brunswick and Princeton with Lord Cornwallis in pursuit, with the British apparently about to cross the Delaware River, descend upon Congress at Philadelphia, and add Pennsylvania to their conquests in New York and the Jerseys. Militiamen were not eager to board an evidently sinking ship, and few of them appeared. On November 30, Washington's immediate command was down to 5,410 men, with more than 2,000 of them entitled to start home the next day.[21]

Washington hastily put the Delaware between himself and the British and ordered the destruction of all boats on the east bank, to halt Cornwallis there as long as possible. But to do these things and nothing more was practically to abandon the cause. " . . . *if every nerve is not strain'd* to recruit the New Army with all possible expedition, *I think the game is pretty near up*," Washington wrote;[22] yet men were unwilling to enlist in an army whose record for nearly a year was one of utter defeat. And one day the British would collect boats to cross the Delaware.

Washington decided that he must recross the river first, to strike some blow at the enemy before they could strike at him. Only by this desperate measure could he hope to restore American morale and make possible the recruitment of the new Army to continue the war. After midnight on December 31 he would have only 1,400 to 1,500 men, together with whatever militiamen might join him. Before that hour arrived, though the old Army had but a week to live, he must use that Army to fight.[23]

So he crossed the Delaware on Christmas Day and surprised the celebrating Hessian outpost at Trenton, gobbling it up. His desperate stroke brought happy results, perhaps beyond expectation. The Germans withdrew from all their posts on the Delaware. Cornwallis lost a furlough to England and had to return to New Jersey to try to chastise Washington. The American cause returned from the edge of the grave. Two-months militia hurried to Washington's camps to await the mustering of the new Army. Congress voted the commander in chief "full, ample, and complete" powers to raise sixteen battalions of infantry beyond those previously voted, 3,000 light horse, three regiments of artillery, and a corps of engineers. In these units Washington himself might appoint and dismiss all officers under the rank of brigadier general. Throughout the Army he and his council might establish whatever system of promotion they thought likely to produce the widest satisfaction. He was

to take, wherever he may be, whatever he may want for the use of the army, if the inhabitants will not sell it, allowing reasonable price for the same; to arrest and confine persons who refuse to take the continental currency, or are otherwise disaffected to the American cause. . . .

He was

to use every endeavour, by giving bounties and otherwise, to prevail upon the troops, whose term of inlistment shall expire at the end of this month, to stay with the army so long after that period, as its situation shall render their stay necessary.[24]

Having thus boldly reversed the momentum of the war, Washington had determined upon the latter step even before Congress authorized it, so that he might strike the enemy again before he recovered his balance. One by one he assembled and addressed the Continental regiments due to be discharged on the thirty-first, reviewing the success of Trenton, urging that Trenton had created opportunities that must not be wasted but could be seized if the veterans remained six weeks more, offering a reenlistment bounty, and pleading with the veterans to stay. Half or perhaps slightly more consented, enough to encourage another foray across the Delaware.[25]

This second recrossing brought victory over a detachment of Cornwallis's troops at Princeton and reinforcement of the verdict of Trenton. The British withdrew eastward across the Jerseys, the Americans reoccupied most of the province, and Washington's Army took position on the heights of Morristown to command the route of any new British march toward the Delaware.

Trenton and Princeton stimulated enough enlistments and reenlistments to save the Army, but they did not end Washington's struggle to create and maintain the Continental Army. That struggle had to be fought as long as the war was fought. Despite Trenton and Princeton, the new Continentals of 1777 remained agonizingly slow in joining. As late as April 3 Washington wrote that "except for a few hundred men from Jersey, Pennsylvania, and Virginia, I have not yet received a Man of the new Continental Levies." Congress offered a bounty of $20 plus one hundred acres to anyone who enlisted for the war, or $10 to a three-year enlistee. But more men preferred to settle for $10 than to risk the longer term, and still more preferred state bounties for enlisting in state companies of volunteer militia, to serve mainly as home guards; the Massachusetts bounty of 86 2/3 dollars was one example of the reason why.[26]

In consequence, Washington himself had to continue calling for successive short-term levies of militia. Their shifting arrivals and departures left him never sure how many he had in camp. But he called for them when Howe renewed the war by shifting from New York to Head of Elk in Maryland and thence toward Philadelphia, and he had to repeat the process in every major campaign of the war.

The commander in chief believed that the states should have it impressed upon them that theirs was much of the responsibility for recruiting the Continental forces and apprehending deserters therefrom. Only the states possessed administrative machinery at all adequate to the task. But the states varied in enthusiasm for the war, and they often thought parochial problems more important than continental ones. Some states forbade recruiting for the Continentals until they were satisfied with their local defenses. Congress sometimes perversely encouraged the states to put obstacles in the way of recruiting. A Congressional resolution of April 14, 1777, suggested to the states that they exempt from militia duty any two men who together would supply an able-bodied Continental recruit for three years or the duration of the war. Despite the apparent possible advantage, the effect was to encourage a traffic in substitutes, with well-to-do men buying their way out of service while dubiously qualified recruits came to the camps. The old problem of the enlistment of indentured servants reappeared.[27]

All such experience strengthened Washington's growing belief that only compulsion could fill the Continental battalions.

Voluntary enlistments seem to be entirely out of the question [he wrote as early as 1778], all the allurements of the most exorbitant bounties and every other inducement that could be thought of, have been tried in vain, and seem to have had little other effect than to increase the rapacity and raise the demands of those to whom they were held out. We may fairly infer, that the country has been already pretty well drained of that class of Men whose tempers, attachments and circumstances disposed them to enter permanently, or for a length of time, into the army. . . .[28]

But Washington also had to recognize that compulsory service for the length of the war imposed upon an unlucky portion of the national manpower was a policy the country was not likely to accept. He eventually recommended annual drafts of quotas from the state militias, for twelve months' service to begin each January 1. Then as many as possible of the drafted men should be persuaded through bounties and otherwise to remain beyond a year.[29]

Congress did fix manpower quotas for the states, but the states responded variously through recruiting efforts and militia drafts, and as often as not they responded indifferently. The strength of the Continental Army remained subject to violent fluctuations. In the summer of 1778 it reached its maximum: Washington had 16,782 rank and file fit for duty. But by the summer of 1781 the Continental force he could spare from New York to seize the opportunity of Cornwallis's retreat to Yorktown was a deplorably small one: two New Jersey regiments, two New York regiments, the Rhode Island regiment, Hazen's "Canadian Regiment," light infantry detachments, Colonel John Lamb's artillery regiment, and a small "corps" of engineers, sappers, and miners—altogether about 2,000 men. The total force around New York had been about 3,500. It is true that many of the Continentals from Pennsylvania and the southern states were already campaigning in the South, but Washington's capacity to exploit a remarkable opportunity was pitifully small nonetheless, and the outcome hinged excessively upon good fortune.[30]

The Continentals were always too few.

I most firmly believe [wrote Washington in October, 1780] that the Independence of the United States never will be established till there is an Army on foot for the War; that if we are to rely on occasional or annual Levies we must sink under the expence; and ruin must follow.[31]

But the fact was that the American cause did have to rely upon occasional or annual levies to rescue it in every emergency.

The subsequent history of the American Army suggests a speculation about Washington's prolonged struggle to raise and maintain an adequate force of Continentals. Perhaps his troops were too few because he always asked for too few. The later United States was repeatedly to find it in many ways easier to call for a general rising of its military manpower than to separate only a limited portion of that manpower from their homes while many of their brothers remained in safety and comfort. Almost the whole potential military population served in World War II practically without complaint; but even the conscription machinery of the modern state found it harder to maintain an adequate Army for the Korean War or for Vietnam, when only a segment of the military manpower was needed, because few were eager to be part of that segment when many others remained civilians. To curb discontent among those called, a rotation system was introduced into the Korean War, with effects not unlike those of the short-term enlistments of Washington's day. Perhaps one reason that few joined the Continental Army was that Washington, seeking to build a relatively small regular army on the

British model, never sought more than a relative few. Perhaps his manpower problems would have been smaller if he and Congress had called for a general levy, for a rising of the nation in arms. Though a revolution, the American War of Independence was fought to a remarkable extent as an eighteenth-century limited war; the history of the Korean War and the Vietnamese War has given us a new awareness of the difficulties awaiting leaders in a popular government who must cultivate public support not for a crusade but for a war employing limited means.

Suggesting that Washington and Congress might have invoked a general levy raises unanswerable questions about whether the American governments were strong enough to make such a call and whether enthusiasm for the war was great enough to sustain it. Whether a general levy could have been equipped and supplied is also questionable. Still, the ability of Revolutionary France to do something of the sort a few years later suggests that a general levy might not have been altogether a chimerical idea but a real alternative to Washington's method of building a relatively small regular army as much as possible of the European type.

George Washington, however, was not given to speculative and thoroughly revolutionary methods. He could be bold on the battlefield, but his general military policy bespoke the caution of a man who could all too easily lose the war should he turn reckless. Building the kind of army he knew from his service with the British, he finally raised a large enough Continental Army and maintained it long enough to win the war—with French help.

FOUR

The Continental Army: 1775-82

We want nothing but good officers to constitute as good an army as ever marched into the field. Our men are better than the officers.

—Nathanael Greene[1]

To FIND MEN for the Continental Army was a labor of continual frustration, which frequently came close enough to failure to threaten the American cause. To find or fashion good officers was a task marked by fewer dramatic crises but finally even more difficult. One way or another, men were enlisted, never really enough but in numbers sufficient to keep the Army and the cause alive. But the Continental Army remained always an uncertain weapon, because to create an army to match the British regulars required officers capable of some tactical skill in battlefield leadership and, perhaps even more important, officers and sergeants who could train the men in the school of the soldier. Here the best of will and intelligence could not match in a few seasons the tactical skill and assurance that the British army drew from more than a century of existence and experience.

Officers were needed to administer and supply the Army, and the difficulties of finding good ones for those purposes sometimes drove Congress and Washington close to despair; but the skills required were related to various civilian skills, and more or less adequate persons could be found. Technical specialists in engineering and artillery were needed, but the numbers required were not great and could be met partly by employing European specialists, and in the artillery mainly through the remarkable self-taught abilities of Henry Knox. The nearly insoluble problem was that of leadership for campaign and battlefield and still more for training.

In these circumstances Washington not only had to carry the usual duties of a commanding general, but he often had to serve as his own military staff and in battle to do the job of a brigade or battalion commander. His own military preparation was deficient in the technical aspects of the profession; his service with regulars had been short, and his role with them that of an aide or a leader of auxiliaries. But the Continental Army depended upon him as no other army in American history was to depend upon a single leader.

Congress regularly appointed supervisory boards over the Army and sent investigating committees, in part as an expression of its perennial fear of a military bid for ascendancy. Washington meanwhile was so self-effacing that he deferred to Congress beyond the call of constitutional duty. But Congress was usually distant and always preoccupied, and it was inherently unsuited to exercise military command. Such a staff as the commander in chief possessed consisted mostly of young aides diligent as letter writers and couriers but unable to do much more. It was fortunate that Washington was physically robust, for a less hardy man would have collapsed under the mere physical and nervous strain of his labors.

The extent to which Washington participated in the Congressional choice of his principal subordinates tended to fluctuate with the fortunes of war. In general, when the Revolution was in no immediate mortal danger, Congress was inclined to go its own way in commissioning subordinate general officers; when affairs were in crisis, it turned to Washington for advice. Thus in June, 1780, Congress named Horatio Gates to head the Southern Department of the Army without so much as asking Washington's opinion; many knew that if Washington had expressed an opinion candidly it would have been unfavorable. But after Gates's defeat at Camden had brought the war in the South to the brink of collapse, Congress followed Washington's recommendation of Nathanael Greene to succeed Gates.

The effort of Congress to ensure the subordination of the Army spawned a growing Congressional administrative machinery. Early in the war there were merely a series of *ad hoc* committees on military matters, a new one being formed for each problem that arose. One such was a committee on organization and regulations for the Army on which Washington himself served while he was preparing to leave Philadelphia to assume his duties as commander in chief in 1775. The more important of the occasional committees had thirteen members, representing all the colonies in revolt. Between 1775 and

1780 six additional special committees were dispatched to visit the armies in the field.[2]

To increase the permanency of military administration, Congress established early in 1776 a committee of seven to consider the creation of a war office and the powers that should be granted to it. But the long colonial quarrel with the royal governors had given Congress an acute fear of "executism," and not until Washington sent an urgent appeal did it act on June 12 to create the Board of War and Ordnance. John Adams was chairman, Roger Sherman, Benjamin Harrison, James Wilson, and Edward Rutledge, all congressmen, were members, and Richard Peters was secretary. The board was to be responsible for "the raising, fitting out, and dispatching [of] all such land forces as may be ordered for the service of the United Colonies." It was to maintain an accurate roster of those forces and of the various provincial forces and exact accounts of arms, ammunition, and military stores. These tasks proved impossible. More important, the board was to conduct all Congressional correspondence dealing directly with the war. In practice it concerned itself mainly with preparing estimates of needed supplies, keeping account of supplies on hand, and arranging for the establishment of arms manufactories. It took on enough detailed work that John Adams found himself in "continual employment, not to say drudgery," day and night.[3]

The Board of War gave a new continuity to Congressional administration of the Army, but the demands it placed on its members left them little time for other duties. Therefore in late 1776 Congress reluctantly formed a committee to consider the delegation of military and other executive business to "boards composed of persons, not members of Congress." The resulting deliberations brought about the creation of a reformed Board of War, on July 18, 1777, to consist of three men not congressmen. But the new board never got off the ground.[4]

Thomas Mifflin, quartermaster general of the Army, received an appointment to the board, agreed to serve, and entered readily upon a career of offering advice, which he found far more congenial than his rather thankless duties as quartermaster general. But Timothy Pickering was slow to join Mifflin on the board because Washington could not find a suitable replacement for him as adjutant general, and Colonel R. H. Harrison of Washington's staff declined to serve. Thus only one member was ready to do anything. Congress responded by increasing the membership to five, adding to Mifflin and Pickering a former commissary general, Joseph Trumbull; the secretary to the former Board of War, Richard Peters; and as chairman, the military lion of the hour, the victor of Saratoga, Horatio Gates.

Nevertheless, the change produced only two men available for duty, Mifflin and Peters. In these circumstances Congress vacillated between resolutions that such new members as were present should sit with the old Board of War, or that the old board should continue until there was a quorum of the new.

Eventually Gates arrived at the seat of Congress (in exile from Philadelphia at York), and by early 1778 the new board organized itself. With Congressional sanction it ventured into strategic planning, canvassing the idea of a new invasion of Canada and thus contemplating a major extension of its activity. But Mifflin soon left York in a huff resulting from a growing estrangement between him and Washington, and Gates's activities were shadowed by his involvement in the mysterious "Conway Cabal" or whatever approximation of such a thing actually existed. Meanwhile closer acquaintance with such men as Gates and Mifflin, and others who like them had been free with criticism of Washington, renewed Congressional respect for Washington himself and dissuaded many members that there should be closer supervision of him. The Board of War, barely assembled, fell apart again. In April, Congress sent Gates back to his former field command in the Northern Department. Joseph Trumbull resigned because of ill health, and Timothy Pickering, now at last arrived, and Richard Peters were left as the only members of the board. Hence the board abandoned policy planning and reverted to the detailed labors over accounts and correspondence that had occupied John Adams's original board. These functions did not demand much military expertise, and Congress voted in October, 1778, that two congressmen should rejoin the board.[5]

The Congressional fear of "executism" was strongest among the most radical of the American revolutionaries, the men who hoped most fervently to utilize independence to achieve a new democracy and who tended to glide readily from suspicion of the British government into suspicion of any government. By 1780, however, the political weight of this group was diminishing. In certain states, notably Pennsylvania, they had carried their revulsion against government so far that they weakened state government badly enough to stir up a reaction against themselves. Paradoxically, their reluctance to create through Congress a central office to manage the war encouraged military autonomy—breeding the very sort of dangers they feared—and could with some reason be blamed for making it more difficult to hold an army together and prolonging the war. More conservative men, who supported or were reconciled to independence but who believed nevertheless in a government strong enough to function effectively, began to enjoy a resurgence of influence. A growing conviction that the war effort of the states must be better concerted spurred the ratification of the Articles of Confederation. Meanwhile, as ratification proceeded, the strong government men turned to establish executive departments for foreign affairs, finance, and war.

On February 7, 1781, Congress voted the creation of a War Department. The department was to have a single chief, with the British title of Secretary at War that dated back to Charles II. The Secretary would of course be responsible to Congress. He and his department were to assume the records keeping and liaison functions of the Board of War, they were to investigate the "present state" of the Army, and they were to transmit and execute the military orders of Congress.[6]

Though the new department was intended to hasten victory, the fortunate opportunity of Yorktown brought most operations to an end before it began to function. Having created the department, Congress consumed most of the year in choosing the Secretary, with the initially strong candidacy of Major General John Sullivan becoming hopelessly entangled in political rivalries. At length, on October 30, Congress named Major General Benjamin Lincoln, probably in part because he was a fat, gouty, and somewhat lethargic individual who therefore displayed no dangerous ambitions. His military record was scarred by his surrender of Charleston, but he had been a reasonably capable officer and he possessed administrative ability. It may be noted that Congressional fears of the military did not preclude choosing a general officer as the first head of the War Office.[7]

Congress did not trouble itself to define clearly the respective functions of the Secretary and the commander in chief, but Lincoln and Washington were able to work out a satisfactory arrangement. On matters of reorganization and demobilization of the Army they conferred together, both in writing and through visits. Though the Secretary theoretically headed the military establishment, he left actual control of the armies in the field to Washington and, in the South, Nathanael Greene. At the same time, he relieved Washington of various routine administrative duties that had thitherto burdened him, such as matters involving prisoners of war, courts-martial, and the issuing of discharge papers. Future secretaries and commanding generals were to quarrel bitterly about the division of authority between them, but apparently only once did a suggestion of those later troubles arise between Washington and Lincoln. When Washington learned that inspectors were reporting directly to the Secretary at War, he enjoined them to report to the commander in chief; otherwise it would "in affect render the heads thereof [of the various staff departments] independent" of the commander in chief.[8]

Congress provided Lincoln with an Assistant Secretary, a secretary to serve as chief clerk, and two additional clerks. With this staff the Secretary undertook, in addition to liaison between Congress and the Army, activities in supply, pay, personnel, intelligence, and recruiting. Although Superintendent of Finance Robert Morris contracted for supplies, Secretary Lincoln stored and distributed them, assisted by Quartermaster General Timothy Pickering and Commissary of Military Stores Samuel Hodgdon. Lincoln also arranged for paying the troops, although throughout his tenure there was little money for this purpose. He compiled rosters of the Army. He wrestled with the delicate question of which officers to retain after the war. Attempting to make his office a clearing house for military information, he prepared intelligence estimates for Washington. Through recruiting agents appointed by the states, he directed efforts to maintain the strength of the Army as long as formal hostilities lasted.

All these activities developed, however, only as the war was guttering out. Benjamin Lincoln presided merely over the dissolution of the war effort and the Army, never over any military crisis. The Revolutionary War had passed in experiments with the central administration of military affairs under the eye of Congress, and the launching of a respectable war office occurred only when the war no longer posed much need for one.

Any reduction of his burdens, however belated, was welcome to the overworked Washington. Until Lincoln became Secretary at War, the commander in chief himself had reported to Congress every event and problem of moment, in detail and by letter or interview. When security considerations prevented his sharing thoughts and information publicly with Congress, he told them as much as he could through private letters to individual members. Lincoln eased this responsiblity.[9]

Washington's staff often was barely adequate to conduct his voluminous correspondence, let alone to fulfill the other functions of a military staff. Early in the war the commander in chief found great value in the services of Horatio Gates as adjutant general, for Gates was an officer of long experience in the British army, bad blood had not yet developed between him and Washington, and he brought to his key administrative post a knowledge of European military procedure that Washington lacked. But Gates's experience seemed to be needed even more in a line command, and he was transferred to the Northern Department in June, 1776. Fortunately, he had had enough time to get much of the headquarters routine established. His successor, Joseph Reed, was a young Philadelphia lawyer of more than ordinary ability who had been Washington's first secretary from the beginning of the war. He could not begin to match Gates's military knowledge, but he was so diligent and trustworthy and so sound in his judgments that Washington came to regard him as invaluable, and a bond of affection developed between the young man and the general.

Then Reed resigned in January, 1777, to return to politics and private business in Pennsylvania. Washington went five months without finding another man he believed fit for the post. Arthur St. Clair, George Weedon, and Morgan Connor each filled in briefly as adjutant general until Colonel Timothy Pickering took over. Pickering proved competent enough without either Gates's knowledge or Reed's flair, though he was one of those persons who found it easy to condescend to the apparently slow-thinking commander in chief. After Pickering went to the Board of War, Alexander Scammel and Edward Hand each served for an interval; both performed much as Pickering had, though with more pleasant personal relationships with Washington.

Except for Gates, these adjutants general were hardly of more value than the military secretaries, a succession of young volunteers of whom the most notable were Reed, Tench Tilghman, John Laurens, and Alexander Hamilton. To these men Washington's senior aide, Colonel Robert Hanson Harrison, was "the old colonel" because he was in his early thirties. They performed all manner of clerical duties for the general, and it was they especially who wrote dispatches and remarks for public occasions; when he himself took pen in hand, Washington found that his mind did move slowly.[10]

A staff post that produced great trials and then remarkable success was that of inspector general. Washington and his lieutenants recognized that the difficulties of training the new Army were so great and the results so vital that someone ought to devote himself to training and virtually nothing else. They recommended that Congress create an inspector general's office, to be filled by an experienced soldier who would prepare and supervise a training program. Unfortunately, during the period of Gates's popularity and Washington's relative eclipse following Saratoga, Congress chose for the post an ambitious and intriguing partisan of Gates, Thomas Conway. Conway was an Irish soldier of fortune with considerable experience in the French army but little else to commend him. He provoked Washington to one of his rare displays of personal animosity and soon disillusioned Congress by showing far more interest in intraservice politics than in training the soldiers. Finally, when he sought to further his vendetta against Washington by offering his resignation, Congress surprised him by accepting it. His departure opened the way for Friedrich Wilhelm von Steuben to take the post, with the results that Washington had hoped for, and more.[11]

Distinguished and able though some of its members were, Washington's staff remained inadequate both in size and experience. Partly the fault was Washington's own: he disliked to increase the public expense for his own convenience, and he was addicted to doing his own paperwork. He tried to administer the Continental Army almost alone, but the job was too great, and the Army in consequence was not well administered.

The heads of the supply departments were formally members of the commander in chief's staff, but their association with Washington was looser than that of the adjutants general, Inspector General von Steuben, and the military secretaries. When Congress adopted a plan for the organization of the Army on June 16, 1775, it included provision for a quartermaster general and his deputy and for a commissary general of stores and purchases. Duties and regulations for these offices were not stated but remained to be worked out in practice and then gradually written into law.[12]

On July 19 Congress appointed Joseph Trumbull, commissary of the Connecticut troops, commissary general of the Army. The same day it authorized Washington to make his own choice of a quartermaster general, and in August the commander in chief named Major Thomas Mifflin of Pennsylvania, until then one of his aides. Both Trumbull and Mifflin entered into their duties with an energy and success that failed to portend the misfortunes to follow. Each organized his department into units corresponding to the divisions into which Washington organized the line of the Army, then three in number. Each supply division was to issue materials to the line division to which it was attached, with various deputy officers responsible for purchases and for depots in the rear, and with Trumbull and Mifflin supervising activities and accounts from their posts near Washington's headquarters at Cambridge.[13]

Mifflin laid plans to replace the motley clothing of the troops around Boston with some kind of uniform, and Washington recommended the hunting shirt and long breeches or overalls, both made of tow cloth, as the most practical garb. Congress failed to act on this suggestion, so no standard was agreed upon. Mifflin canvassed the states for clothing, Congress purchased imports and the loot of privateers, and, from the beginning, French assistance included tentage and clothing. Congress followed British practice by stipulating that each soldier was to pay for his own clothing, at the rate of one and two-thirds dollars a month deducted from his wages. With no agreement on a uniform, American military dress ran to browns and greens, especially the former, for which dyestuffs were easily made. Through 1775 and into the New York campaign of 1776 the troops were tolerably well clad.[14]

Tentage was not so easily come by as some kind of clothing. Congress directed that all likely expedients be tried, to the point of stripping the yards of sailing vessels. But tents nevertheless were in short supply as the weather turned cold in 1775, and the men around Boston began constructing shelters of their own planning:

> Some are made of boards, some of sailcloth, and some partly of one and partly of the other. Others are made of stone and turf, and others again of Birch and other brush. Some are thrown up in a hurry and look as if they could not help it—mere necessity—others are curiously wrought with doors and windows done with wreaths and withes in the manner of a basket.[15]

The quartermaster general also assumed responsibility for transportation, seeking the best means of acquiring and organizing wagons, and concerning himself also with hiring, building, and maintaining boats for the Army's amphibious operations around New York. Procuring forage for the animals, building permanent and semipermanent quarters, and supplying knapsacks and canteens also became quartermaster functions and were destined to remain so for generations to come.[16]

Meanwhile Commissary General Trumbull had been dispatching agents and creating a network of channels for the purchase and supply of food from throughout New England and New York. Congress established a uniform ration for the Continental Army on November 4, 1775, which is worth quoting since it too was to have a long history, remaining in its essentials the United States Army ration for more than a century, until the advent of modern nutritional science:

> RESOLVED, That a ration should consist of the following kind and quantity of provisions: 1 lb. beef, or ¾ lb. pork or 1 lb. salt fish per day; 1 lb. bread or flour, per day; 3 pints of peas or beans per week, or vegetables equivalent, at one dollar per bushel for peas or beans; 1 pint of milk, per man per day, or at the rate of 1-72 of a dollar; 1 half pint of rice, or one pint of Indian meal, per man per week; 1 quart of spruce beer or cider per man per day, or nine gallons of molasses, per company of 100 men per week; 3 lbs. candles to 100 men per week, for guards; 24 lbs. soft, or 8 lbs. hard soap, for 100 men per week.[17]

This ration was generous for the time, and Trumbull was actually able to exceed it during the first months of the war. It was thus that the Continental Army could appeal to British soldiers in Boston to desert by offering the lure of more and better food.

Thomas Mifflin, an ambitious man, persuaded Congress to commission him brigadier general in May, 1776. Thereupon he resigned as quartermaster general to take a line command. Washington selected Stephen Moylan, another of the commander in chief's aides, to follow Mifflin. But Moylan was neither happy nor especially successful in the post. His department incurred Washington's blame for failing to provide enough boats for the evacuation of Long Island and Manhattan, which Washington believed would have permitted withdrawal without loss. Congress too was displeased, and a Congressional committee persuaded Moylan to resign after less than four months in office. Mifflin agreed to return to his old post in Moylan's stead, but the time of troubles of the Revolutionary supply system was beginning.[18]

The rapid movements of the Army during the New York campaign and then the retreat across the Jerseys naturally created supply problems far beyond those of the previous prolonged encampments or relatively unhurried movements. Constant marching wore out uniforms and especially shoes. By now Congress had attempted to relieve the quartermaster general of excessive responsibility by creating an office of clothier general; but the occupant of the post, a Philadelphia merchant named James Mease, proved careless and lazy. Textiles had become scarce, furthermore, and had to be purchased abroad. Mease took insufficient precautions against their disappearance on the long trip from seaports to camps. False economy led him to issue uniforms that were generally too small, a condition that hastened their wearing out. He was supposed to procure shoes by exchanging the hides of animals slaughtered by the Army for finished shoes. But the supply of shoes was always small compared with what the hides seemingly should have brought in, and by the summer of 1776 Washington was complaining that the Army received shoes "almost entirely incapable of doing duty."[19]

Joseph Trumbull had made a good start in the commissary department, but his health was uncertain and he was hypersensitive to criticism. These factors seem to have contributed to his departure from Washington's headquarters just when subsistence problems became severe, as the Army began its retreat across New Jersey. Trumbull returned to his home state of Connecticut, on the plea that he was needed there to organize New England storehouses and to examine accounts. He left his deputy, Carpenter Wharton, with Washington, and Wharton proved both incompetent and corrupt. Meanwhile, retreat compelled the abandonment or movement of subsistence stores, with constant losses en route; and the Army's marches disrupted the usual late fall and early winter activity of slaughtering animals and curing meat for the late winter and spring. Not surprisingly, this combination of difficulties broke down the infant commissary system, and by May Washington was writing that unless food came into his Morristown camps quickly, the Army would have to disperse to look for it.

By that time the impatience of both Washington and Congress had caused the dismissal of Carpenter Wharton and an investigation of his affairs. Trumbull was summoned to the scene of war in the Middle States, but once he was in Philadelphia Washington found it almost as difficult to budge him from the capital as it had been to pry him out of New England. Meanwhile, the Army had to think about getting enough food for the immediate present without regard to the next winter, a method that promised greater difficulties to come.[20]

Through 1777, matters went from bad to worse. Congress tried to reform the commissary department, and it accepted a recommendation from Trumbull to divide the purchasing and distributing functions into two separate departments, leaving Trumbull simply as commissary general of purchases. This step accorded with Washington's belief that Trumbull's responsibilities had been beyond the capacities of any individual. At the same time, however, Congress angered both Trumbull and his deputies by changing their compensation from a commission system to a straight salary. Only with great difficulty could Trumbull be persuaded to remain in the service, and a number of deputies resigned.

Trumbull's health was also growing worse, and in late 1777 he seems to have been preoccupied with health and anger. All the less therefore did he plan for winter. Resignations and new appointments disrupted his department, and the British capture of Philadelphia left both principal Atlantic seaports closed to the coastwise shipping of foodstuffs as well as to imports. When Washington's Army encamped at Valley Forge for the winter of 1777–78, the British held the leading beef-producing sections of the Middle States, and shipment of foodstuffs from the South was hampered by British control of the mouth of Chesapeake Bay. The immediate vicinity of Washington's encampment was depleted by previous demands—meat prices had risen rapidly in the preceding months, and the butchers of Philadelphia had outbid the Army. Even such food as was available was often kept from camp by a shortage of wagons or taken by its producers to the British in Philadephia for higher prices.[21]

There followed the starving time of Valley Forge. As early as December, Washington feared mutiny provoked by hunger. James Varnum's division went two days without meat and three days without bread. Washington had to inform Congress that he had "not a single hoof of any kind to Slaughter, and not more than 25. Barls. of Flour!" The general sent out parties of soldiers to thrash wheat and collect all available wagons to haul provisions, and for a time the shortage was eased. But by early in the New Year the commissary was once again bare, absolutely bare, and the Army fasted.[22]

Thereafter small quantities of food came in to be consumed on a hand-to-mouth basis, the Army never feeling sure it would eat on the morrow. The second week of February brought a bitter storm, which closed the roads and compelled another period of fasting. The staple food of the encampment came to be "fire cakes," thin cakes concocted by baking a flour-and-water paste. Dr. Albigence Waldo's journal records the soldiers' sentiments about them:

Fire-cake and water for breakfast! Fire-cake and water for dinner! Fire-cake and water for supper! The Lord send that our Commissary for Purchases may have to live on fire-cake and water![23]

At Valley Forge the Army was naked as well as starving. The marching and countermarching in New Jersey and Pennsylvania that occupied 1777 had been highly destructive of clothing and shoes; Clothier General Mease was as indolent as ever; the vagaries of a transportation system dependent upon the hiring of private wagons and wagonmasters were a hindrance here as in the subsistence department; the Army was usually distant from American-controlled seaports; and Quartermaster General Mifflin busied himself late in 1777 in recruiting activities and in conferences with Congress. He did so partly at Washington's urging and partly because of his own inclinations, but meanwhile he neglected his quartermaster duties.[24]

In February, Washington was walking through a company street when he saw a soldier emerge from one hut and dash to another. The man was wrapped in a blanket, but beneath that Washington could see his bare body and legs. At the time, some 4,000 men were reported to be lacking in the simplest apparel. Much of the Army could attend to few duties because the men could not leave their quarters.[25]

Both Mifflin and Trumbull resigned their offices before the end of 1777, out of both discouragement and resentment of criticism. Congress attempted to stimulate the supply system, and it prevailed upon a capable man, Jeremiah Wadsworth, to become commissary general of purchases and the still more capable Nathanael Greene to be quartermaster general. Greene observed unhappily that "No body ever heard of a quarter Master, in History," but his conscience and

Washington persuaded him to take the job. In the commissariat, a commission system of paying the agents was restored, after its abolition had helped wreck the department.[26]

But the supply problems of the Continental Army ran deeper than the ability of any individuals to remedy them. Once supply had collapsed, little was possible thereafter but to go on living from hand to mouth. The disastrous inflation of Continental currency compounded the woes of purchasing agents. Any crisis of nature or campaign was likely to provoke a new crisis of supply. The winter of 1779–80 turned out to be worse than the Valley Forge winter, with the worst storms in memory isolating the Morristown encampments and obliging Washington to write in December that the Army had been

five or six weeks past on half allowance and we have not more than three days bread at a third allowance on hand, nor any within reach. When this is exhausted, we must depend on the precarious gleanings of the neighbouring country. Our magazines are absolutely empty everywhere, and our commissaries entirely destitute of money or credit to replenish them. We have never experienced a like extremity in any period of the war.[27]

"Those who have only been in Valley Forge or Middlebrook during the last two winters, but have not tasted the cruelties of this one," Baron Johann de Kalb wrote of the same season, "know not what it is to suffer."[28] The men starved again, again their clothing was little better than rags, and an extreme cold persisted all winter, packing the snow hard and deep and torturing the men. As soon as the roads cleared sufficiently to make it possible, Washington resorted to the stern expedient of fixing quotas of grain upon the various districts of New Jersey and sending out armed parties to get it. But once real thaws set in, the roads became quagmires, and in mid-March the Army was still without more than five days' supply of bread on hand.[29]

Despite the Morristown winter, it is possible to say that Greene, Wadsworth, and eventually James Wilkinson as clothier general worked a certain improvement in supply. Especially did Greene improve the transportation system, upon which all else depended. Mifflin had announced a wagon department but had done little to create it; Greene energetically procured wagons for the department, repaired old ones, and enlisted wagoners. He lobbied with some success to remove restrictions that the states had imposed on hiring and impressing private wagons. By the spring of 1778, Washington was able to praise Greene for making possible an expeditious movement such as could not have been accomplished before: from Valley

Forge to Monmouth and thence to the Highlands of the Hudson.[30]

Improving the clothing supply was harder, because the Army was dependent upon imports from France. Nevertheless, Washington felt sufficiently encouraged in 1779 to get around to prescribing uniform colors for the Continental Army: blue faced with white for the New England Lines; blue and buff for New York and New Jersey; blue and red for Pennsylvania, Delaware, Maryland, and Virginia; and blue and lighter blue for the Carolinas and Georgia. The appearance of the Army never gave much evidence of the existence of these regulations, and they remained in effect only until 1782; but until the twentieth century, blue was to remain the basic uniform color of the American Army.[31]

By 1780 the collapse of the currency was so complete that Congress reorganized the food and forage procurement system on a kind of barter basis. Henceforth each of the states would be assigned a quota of commissary and quartermaster supplies, its shipment of which would be credited to its quota of money to be raised for Congress. Here were possibilities for complexity thrice compounded, and the worst possibilities were usually realized. The arrival of supplies in the Continental camps became more erratic than before, if that could be. In May, 1780—spring, not winter—Lafayette found Washington's Army "reduced to the very verge of starvation." The merchants of Philadelphia rose to this occasion by immediately dispatching five hundred barrels of flour. But sometimes state legislatures adjourned without meeting their quotas, while others sat but procrastinated; and starvation and nakedness would threaten again.[32]

Nathanael Greene was never happy as quartermaster general, and in July, 1780, he lost patience and resigned. He had grown disgusted in the conviction that Congress was far more zealous to investigate and to regulate than to assist his department. The last straw was a Congressional reorganization plan of 1780 which—seeking to find economies in the new system of the states' furnishing specific supplies —eliminated his two most trusted deputies, left him with a staff he considered too small, and kept pay at a level he thought excessively low. Rightly or wrongly, Greene had also concluded that personal enemies in Congress were deliberately contriving his ruination, and so he accompanied his resignation with a verbal blast at the legislature that nearly caused his dismissal from the Army. Washington could ill afford to lose him as quartermaster general; to have lost him altogether would have been a catastrophe, and Washington mustered all his influence to avert it.[33]

The commander in chief had feared mutiny early in the Valley Forge winter, and the famine of May, 1780, precipitated open rebelliousness in two Connecticut regiments. A veteran Pennsylvania brigade had to be called on to break the mutiny and arrest the ring-leaders. Then, on New Year's Day, 1781, hunger, nakedness in the cold, and general neglect from the civil powers, together with too little pay, provoked another of the crises that endangered the very existence of the Army: the mutiny of the six regiments of the Pennsylvania Line.

The Pennsylvanians had been reliable enough to suppress the Connecticut mutiny as recently as the previous May. They were among the most experienced soldiers of the Army and may have been the best of the state lines. But like the rest of the Army they had gone into the winter on half rations and in rags, and unlike some of the Army they had not been paid for a year. Other states were offering high reenlistment bounties; Pennsylvania was pinching pennies. But while she offered reenlisting veterans little, Pennsylvania did offer generous bounties to raw recruits, including those who signed up from the Philadelphia jails. Much of the Pennsylvania Line had enlisted at the beginning of 1777 for three years or the war; the state and Congress now interpreted their obligation as the war, whether or not three years had elapsed. Any soldier who protested that his circumstances were exceptional and his enlistment therefore expired was likely to receive at most the reply that nothing could be checked because records were not available at Morristown.

A round of rum in honor of the New Year helped inspire open expression of these grievances on January 1, 1781. The Pennsylvania Line paraded that night without orders, seized several field pieces, and dealt roughly with officers who tried to restrain them, killing a captain. About eleven P.M. they marched off toward Philadelphia, announcing that they had business with Congress. Their commanding officer, Brigadier General Anthony Wayne, intercepted the march and tried to halt them, going so far as to open his coat to challenge them to shoot him. They would not shoot him, declaring that they had no wish to harm their officers, but neither would they halt.

When the news reached Washington, his inclination was to deal sternly with the mutineers. To do otherwise would encourage further defections, and already he feared that the British would march from New York to take advantage of the affair. New England troops seemed reliable enough to be used against the Pennsylvanians; some of the Connecticut men had good reason to want to be used. But Wayne, the Pennsylvania authorities, and Congress preferred to negotiate lest an attempted showdown tear the Army apart; and Washington deferred to them, though he dispatched New Englanders to bar the crossings of the Delaware should negotiations fail.

Washington's former aide Joseph Reed was now president of the Supreme Executive Council of Pennsylvania. He journeyed to Princeton to confer in Nassau Hall with a committee of sergeants representing the mutineers. The British were also attempting to communicate with them; two British agents sent to them were seized by the mutineers and turned over to Reed as an earnest of loyalty. Then, disturbingly, the sergeants changed their minds and announced that they had better retain custody of the agents until agreement on a settlement.

The sergeants drove a hard bargain, and Reed and Wayne believed they had no choice but to meet most of their terms. The mutineers received assurance of additional clothing and part of their back pay. Men who had enlisted for three years or the war and who had served three years were to be discharged. If a soldier claimed to have served three years and his papers were not available to verify the claim, he was to be discharged upon his oath. Since the Pennsylvania records were extremely fragmentary, this last provision especially favored the mutineers.

To have followed Washington's inclinations and attempted the suppression of the mutiny would have been risky, and Reed's conciliatory policy was probably wise. But Washington feared the terms would mean the dissolution of the Pennsylvania Line, and he was not far from wrong. About half the line went home.[34]

And the infection did spread. On January 20 the New Jersey Line at Pompton mutinied. Fortunately, the New Jersey Line of three regiments was much smaller than the Pennsylvania, and on this occasion Washington could not be dissuaded from forceful suppression. Major General Robert Howe surrounded the New Jersey camps with loyal New England troops during the night of January 26–27 and trained cannons on them. He then ordered the New Jersey men to parade without arms in five minutes. He would offer no talk of conditions; instead he called on the senior New Jersey officers to name the ringleaders. He placed the three most prominent mutineers on the parade ground before the troops, then formed a firing squad of the twelve next most prominent offenders, and compelled them to execute their comrades.[35]

This action ended the Jersey mutiny, and the example allayed restlessness for the time being. Happily, the great victory of Yorktown intervened before winter returned to the Army again.

The mutinies were in part testimony that the new quartermaster general, Colonel Timothy Pickering, was having no more success than his predecessors. The same was true of the new commissary general of purchases, Ephraim Blaine. Pickering was diligent, but all the familiar plagues persisted, and he was both limited by and to some degree a partner in the Congressional passion for economy that had provoked Greene's resignation.[36]

In February, 1781, Congress elected Robert Morris to the newly created office of Superintendent of Finance. Morris included among his conditions for acceptance the proviso that he control the financial affairs of the quartermaster, commissary, and medical departments of the Army. He replaced the system of requisitions upon the states with the European practice of supply through private contractors. This method clearly opened new opportunities for speculation and profiteering, and Washington was soon to denounce the chief contractor as a practitioner of "*low dirty* tricks." In fact, that personage had to be dismissed and a new contractor found.[37] But aided by the close of active hostilities, Morris's system worked some improvement. When the approach of the Comte de Grasse's fleet to the Chesapeake presented the supreme military opportunity of the war, the commander in chief himself assumed careful supervision of the immediate arrangements for moving his Army to Virginia, and for once both wagon and water transport were adequate to all demands. By the spring of 1783 Washington found his troops "better covered, better clothed, and better fed than they have ever been in any former winter quarters." Of course, by that time a system could be far from good and still seem better than what had gone before.[38]

The Army could survive all these trials in part because the circumstances of time and place were such that, though other supplies might sometimes disappear, at least it had enough of the weapons of war. The frontier was still sufficiently close to have placed a considerable quantity of firearms in American hands and to have created a small gun-making industry. Also, American militiamen had habitually carried their weapons home with them after service in the French wars, so that numerous British Brown Besses were scattered through the country. Even before the contracting of the French alliance, French sympathy for the enemies of Great Britain made possible the procurement of French Charleville muskets. There were a few occasions when American troops found themselves in some danger through shortages of small arms, notably on the eve of the New York campaign of 1776; but generally, enough arms were available for the limited numbers in the American ranks if the armies were willing to make do with greatly assorted types.[39]

With powder and lead it was much the same. There occurred the initial dangerous shortage of powder; and as late as February, 1776, when Washington was planning his final effort against Boston, he calculated that if he issued twenty-four rounds to each man the

Army's store would be reduced to about one hundred barrels, a mere five tons. In March, the American force in Canada had only sixty rounds per man—if it allotted nothing to its artillery. But again the development of existing small mills, an inheritance of the frontier, and a more efficient mobilization of their output sufficed to give Washington's Army enough powder for the New York campaign of the summer, and thereafter shipments from France helped. The Americans never grew sufficiently desperate to conserve powder by adopting Benjamin Franklin's suggestion that they resort to the bow and arrow.[40]

The New England army of 1775 began the siege of Boston with one cannon. Boston patriots soon managed to slip out of town three brass 3-pounders cast in England which the Massachusetts assembly had imported for the volunteer militia. Additional cannons came from various stocks left over from the French wars and from armed ships, some of them taken from British vessels by American privateers. In the early winter of 1775–76, the Army around Boston had fifty-one guns: five 24-pounders, six 18-pounders, twenty-five lighter cannons, seven mortars, and eight howitzers. These guns included a great brass mortar of thirteen inches' bore and 2,700 pounds' weight, which had been seized from an enemy brig in November and in a jubilant ceremony christened "Congress" with a bottle of rum. Henry Knox, a Boston bookstore operator who had been among the militia proprietors of the brass 3-pounders smuggled from the city and was an amateur student of guns, soon replaced Colonel Richard Gridley as chief of artillery. In January, Knox arrived at the artillery park at Framingham with the guns captured at Ticonderoga. He had dragged them across wilderness, rivers, and mountains with remarkable speed, using sleds to cross snow and ice. It is not certain how many he brought; Knox himself reported fifty-nine usable pieces, and the number may have been as high as sixty-six. Thereafter, lesser acquisitions alternated with misfortunes such as the loss of 114 cannons at Fort Washington in 1776, and for a time in 1777 the artillery allotment had to be restricted to two guns per brigade. But American forges and foundries for the first time undertook the manufacture of cannons, and Henry Knox chose Springfield, Massachusetts, as the site of a Continental cannon foundry, the beginning of the Springfield Arsenal. Though the inception of artillery foundries posed technical problems that Americans did not altogether solve in the course of the war, the Army was able to go through the war without suffering any critical shortage of guns.[41]

In supply, combat equipment could be had while supporting materials were scarce. In the search for officers for the Army, a kind of reverse of that situation persisted: officers could be found, such as Greene, Jeremiah Wadsworth, and Pickering, to administer the supporting agencies of the Army about as well as conditions permitted; but officers qualified to train the troops for combat and lead them in it sometimes seemed as scarce as regulation uniforms.

In consequence Washington never believed he had enough formations comparable in training and tactical leadership to the British to permit him to challenge the main body of a British army to battle with Americans alone unless he stood in a prepared defensive position. He took the offensive at Germantown, but only a portion of Howe's army was within supporting distance of the battlefield. At Monmouth it was the British rear guard that Washington struck. He never felt he had enough long-service troops, but still more he lacked officers and drill sergeants.

The Continental Army of 1775 comprised thirty-eight regiments of greatly varying size. The Massachusetts, New Hampshire, and Rhode Island regiments stood on a basis of 590 enlisted men, while Connecticut regimental tables of organization sometimes called for 1,000 enlisted men, sometimes for 600. Washington organized these regiments into six brigades generally of six regiments each, and into three divisions of two brigades each. The brigades and divisions were primarily administrative headquarters. The key tactical unit was the battalion, which was usually the same body of men as a regiment, "regiment" being another term denoting an administrative unit, while "battalion" was the tactical term. The possibilities of employing as tactical entities units larger than battalions but smaller than an army were only beginning to be realized in Europe. The advent of the division as a tactical formation mainly awaited the Wars of the French Revolution. Since Washington and his lieutenants patterned the tactics of the American Army on what they knew of European armies, the Army tended to fight not by divisions or brigades but as a tactical whole, its constituent units of maneuver being the battalions.[42]

When the Army had to be made over for 1776, Congress prescribed the regimental tables of organization, calling for twenty-eight regiments of 728 officers and men. This plan made for a more compact and, it was hoped, a more efficient Army, but it also discouraged recruiting, since the elimination of some regiments and the rearrangement of companies would exclude and therefore embitter numerous officers. The regiments were to be formed into eight companies, each listing one captain, two lieutenants, one ensign, four sergeants, four corporals, two "drums and fifes," and seventy-six privates. Though Continental designations were planned for the regiments of 1776, they would mainly be organized through the efforts of the states, and their officers would be chosen by the states.

The emergency legislation of the fall of 1776 provided for an Army of eighty-eight regiments, but nothing near this number materialized. Gradually in subsequent years the paper establishment shrank closer to reality: eighty regiments in 1779, fifty-eight (forty-nine of infantry, four of cavalry, four of artillery, one of artillery artificers) in 1781. Even if fifty-eight regiments had been filled, there would have been less than 43,000 men enrolled, a number which the Army did not approach even in the fortunate summer of 1780.[43]

Washington tried to facilitate molding these formations into an army by means of harsh discipline and punishments not unlike those of the British army. For misconduct of almost any kind, infractions of camp sanitation or absence without leave, Washington's sovereign remedy was the lash. The first articles of war adopted by Congress prescribed the New Testament maximum of thirty-nine strokes. With Washington's encouragement, a revision of the articles on September 20, 1776, permitted 100 strokes. In 1781 the commander in chief recommended 500. Congress was unwilling to go so far, but the Continental Army appears often to have wrung the maximum pain from the permissible 100 by inflicting half of them and then waiting a while before lashing an inflamed back fifty times again. Washington sometimes approved also the unauthorized punishment of running the gauntlet. Whether these methods were appropriate to the Army of a popular revolution may be dubious, but they were consistent with Washington's general purpose to build the Continental Army into an approximation of its adversary.[44]

It is difficult to estimate just how much Steuben accomplished when he joined in the effort to give the Army tactical training comparable to European standards. Friedrich Wilhelm, Baron von Steuben took over the duties of inspector general in the spring of 1778, while the Army was at Valley Forge. He owed the aristocratic "von" in his name to his middle-class father's bland appropriation of it, and he had never been the lieutenant general in the army of Prussia or of some other German state that he variously claimed to be. But he had been a staff officer in the army of Frederick the Great during the Seven Years' War, and thus he had learned the conventional warfare of the day from the master who practiced it most expertly.

Perhaps Steuben was more sensitive than Washington to the propriety of adjusting European discipline and training to American conditions. When the baron took over the training of the Continental Army, he made no effort to translate Prussian discipline and tactics literally. He tried to incorporate American experience into his tactical system. He decided that it would never do simply to order the

American soldier to carry his musket in a certain way or to march in a certain manner; the American must be told why he was to do a thing. Steuben believed that once the American understood the reason for something, he did what he was supposed to do very well. Steuben was sufficiently unassuming that he took a drill sergeant's work upon himself. He introduced his system of minor tactics to a model company of officers by drilling them personally, then dispatched the company to transmit his lessons through widening circles of the Army. With assistance from Hamilton and Tilghman, he committed his precepts to paper, *Steuben's Regulations for the Order and Discipline of the Troops of the United States* (1779); this *Blue Book* remained the official American military manual for thirty-three years, prescribing drill regulations, tactics, and general military routine.

Not the least of Steuben's services was the organizational one of consolidating the Continental formations. He found the regiments so skeletonized by the time he undertook their training that they could not function effectively in maneuver. Therefore he amalgamated them into training battalions of a standard 200 men each. These training battalions could coalesce on the battlefield as well as on the parade ground. The regiments, the administrative units, ceased to be identical with the tactical battalions. Now the Continental Army could maneuver in battle in Steuben's battalions, of calculable size and therefore able to work relatively calculable results.

One mark of deficient training before Steuben was that American units had difficulty moving from column of march into line of battle. Steuben's drilling emphasized the proper way to do so, and he greatly increased the speed with which the Army could deploy. Before Steuben, also, the Army had often marched in Indian file; Steuben insisted on columns of fours and thus speeded the rate of march.[45]

So there is little doubt that Steuben improved the Army. Nevertheless, Washington continued to avoid open confrontations with the British, because he believed that the Continental Army continued to fall short of European proficiency. Partly the trouble may have been that Steuben, however energetic he was, could not be everywhere at once to ensure that every regiment trained as carefully as he had drilled his model company. As before Steuben's coming, so afterward, the best American units were those whose own officers were most diligent and conscientious, notably the Maryland and Delaware Continentals; and most officers were content with lower standards of training and discipline.

More than that, if Steuben accomplished reasonably good training, the problem of combat leadership remained. Washington continued to lack officers sufficiently versed in combat tactics and experienced in the stress of combat to make the right decisions consistently and promptly, or even to understand and carry out orders reliably. The reader of histories of Revolutionary battles finds plausible plans going awry time and again because officers failed to lead their troops into doing what was expected of them. Failures occurred on every level of leadership. Since the Continental officers had not climbed gradually up the commissioned grades, there had been no means of weeding them out before the war. Some who had seemed able enough in small roles in the French war proved inadequate under larger responsibilities, notably the New England hero Israel Putnam. Service in the British or some foreign army was no guarantee of capacity for high place in the American Army, as Charles Lee demonstrated, and as Washington tried to persuade Congress at a time when it seemed to be dispensing commissions wholesale to foreign adventurers.

Through all the Revolutionary War, only a handful of Washington's generals fully measured up to their trusts. Nathanael Greene was not only a good supply officer but more than adequate as a combat officer, all the way to an army command. Henry Knox became an admirable chief of artillery despite the technical handicaps of a book-taught soldier. Steuben, Lafayette, and on a lower level Anthony Wayne performed superbly on occasion, but all three were erratic. Benedict Arnold may have been the most brilliant soldier of the Continental Army, but grave faults of character and temperament were evident even before his treason. The list could not be much longer. A review of the battles suggests that faulty leadership lost more of them than any other single cause, and the weaknesses of leadership must surely have been a primary reason for Washington's reluctance to challenge the British to more decisive contests that might have shortened the war.

Since his Army suffered from defects that might have made decisive contests fatal ones, Washington chose the methods of warfare that gave him his reputation as the American Fabius. He could not conduct frontal assaults. He could rarely outflank the enemy once he confronted him on the battlefield, since his Army was a clumsy instrument for that delicate undertaking. Unless he enjoyed unusual advantages of position, he believed he must evade direct tests of battle. But he had to try to wear down the enemy. So he resorted to swift raids against the enemy's detachments and periphery, with Trenton and Princeton the outstanding examples. "General Washington," Nathanael Greene wrote in 1776, "as every defender ought, has . . . [been] endeavoring to skirmish with the enemy at all times and avoid a general engagement."[46]

To carry out his forays successfully, Washington counted on surprise. "Secrecy until the moment of execution," he said, "is the life of enterprise."[47]

Surprise required not only secrecy to shroud Washington's own movements but a knowledge of what the enemy was doing. Therefore Washington devoted special attention to his intelligence services. He employed spies as numerous as his resources would permit. He was careful to give close personal attention to what his agents reported. The weakness of his staff compelled him to be his own chief intelligence officer, but at least in this situation he avoided that gap between intelligence analysis and responsible decision that has so often plagued modern intelligence services.

To learn where the enemy was and what he was doing and then to strike a surprise blow demanded also swift movement. It was proverbial that Washington always tried to get his Army off to an early start.[48]

The deficiencies of his Army in the conventional style of war familiar to his adversaries might have persuaded Washington to experiment with tactical innovations, but he preferred caution here as in his avoidance of direct confrontations and his very methods of recruiting the Army. His nearest approach to innovation in tactics was his interest in developing light infantry, bodies of picked men who would be distinguished by their special skills in the swift movements and sharp striking power on which he relied.

The ten companies of riflemen voted by the Continental Congress in June, 1775, had much in common with the rangers of the French wars. They were frontiersmen adept in marksmanship, and they should have been especially valuable for scouting and harassing missions. But they displayed the same serious shortcoming that had weakened Rogers's Rangers: they were so undisciplined that Washington wondered whether they were more of a plague than an asset.

The British had tried to retain the advantages of rangers and to escape their defects by training selected regular infantrymen in an approximation of ranger tactics in addition to their ordinary training in linear tactics. The resulting "light infantry" appeared as an elite company within each conventional regiment, sometimes formed specialized regiments such as the 80th, and sometimes campaigned in task forces (to use a modern expression) formed by detaching the elite companies from several regiments. The British column that marched to Lexington and Concord in April, 1775, was such a task force, composed of the light infantry companies and the grenadier companies—the latter made up of unusually tall and strong men—from the regiments in Boston.

Similarly, Washington encouraged the formation of light infantry companies, and then he adopted the habit of detaching them to form an elite command. He emphasized that he wanted a special class of men to be chosen for the light infantry:

The General [he wrote] is persuaded that the Officers commanding Regiments will be very careful in the choice of Men for these Companies as the good of the service and the honor of their Regiments will be materially concerned in it; The Men should be mostly of a middle size, Active, robust and Trusty, and the first Twenty [chosen for each light company] must be all old Soldiers the remainder will have a proportion of Levies. . . .[49]

The light infantry, which came to carry a special weapon, the fusee, a firearm lighter than the musket, first appeared as a separate command in 1777, when the riflemen had gone north to join Gates's army and Washington drafted 100 picked men from each brigade to form the "light brigade" under Brigadier General William Maxwell. By July, 1779, the light infantry command, now under Anthony Wayne, had grown to 1,312, a substantial number as compared with 9,755 conventional infantry of the line. Their most famous exploit occurred that month when Wayne led them to the storming of Stony Point, a model of the kind of operation on which Washington had to depend and for which light infantry were an appropriate instrument.[50]

Washington's light infantry experiments were hardly of surprising boldness, however, since they followed upon earlier British experiments which the British were continuing simultaneously. Much less did Washington essay any tactical innovations so unconventional as to approach what later generations would call guerrilla war. Major General Charles Lee, an interesting military thinker whatever his shortcomings as a leader or patriot, flirted with the notion of irregular, partisan warfare as an appropriate method for a people's uprising weak in conventional military power. He viewed irregular war as making possible effective employment of militia, which would all the more draw war making and the people together as befitted a popular revolutionary cause. In the southern theater of war, far from the direct influence of Washington's conservatism, citizen soldiers spontaneously demonstrated that Lee's ideas were not wholly chimerical.

In the South, Indian warfare was still closer than it was in most of the North, and a higher proportion of the inhabitants retained competence in Indian fighting. The Carolina hill country was still subject to Cherokee and Catawba raids, and the colonists had launched major retaliatory campaigns in 1775 and 1776. As late as 1752 a trader had been scalped just outside Charleston itself. So the citizen soldiers of the southern militia establishments clung to fighting skills of a kind that most of their northern counterparts had lost. Many southern militiamen were crack marksmen, and although most probably did not carry rifles, many were adept at jamming wadding tightly into the barrels to enhance the accuracy of smoothbore muskets. They knew something, too, about effecting surprise in hit-and-run raids.

Southern partisan leaders emerged to put these abilities to good use. After Cornwallis occupied Charlotte in 1780, Brigadier General William Lee Davidson's North Carolina militia so tormented foraging parties and messengers that they did much to persuade the British to abandon the settlement. William R. Davie took time off from his duties as a Continental commissary officer to lead successful partisan raids to gobble up British detachments. Francis Marion raided British supply convoys passing through the Carolina swamps. Daniel Morgan, already famous as the outstanding figure of the rifle companies of 1775, went farthest toward elevating partisan tactics to a consistent system of war. Cornwallis was probably the best British general in America, and the British southern army was no ordinary British force but one organized throughout as light infantry for quick movement and open-order fighting. But the stings inflicted by the American partisans, combined with Nathanael Greene's excellent handling of the American southern army, made every British victory a Pyrrhic one. Cornwallis finally marched out of the Carolinas happy to reach the Virginia tidewater, where he expected the Royal Navy to succor him.[51]

Perhaps Washington would have done well to share more than he did in Greene's policy of encouraging and cooperating with irregular warriors. But he did not, and he could have cited good reasons for his own caution. If the partisans contributed much to winning the war in the South, his own and Greene's conventional armies were essential; partisan warfare alone was not decisive, while conventional warfare at Yorktown won the victory that ended the war. Furthermore, partisan warfare appropriate to the unpopulated swamps and hill country of the South might have brought only excessive destruction and bitterness to the more densely populated areas from Virginia northward. Related to such dangers, furthermore, could have been considerations of the dignity of the American cause and of methods of war both appropriate to that dignity and conducive to harmony at home and lasting peace with the Mother Country once the present conflict came to an end.

Washington's experiences and predilections made him not only a conservative general but primarily an infantry general. The development of American artillery, engineering, and cavalry depended especially upon the quality of assistance he could secure from other officers. In this situation, circumstance and historical accident combined to give him a good artillery, an adequate military engineering force, and a generally weak cavalry.

The historical accident of the presence of Henry Knox largely accounted for a good artillery, although the availability of cannons from the colonial wars and of an American iron industry of respectable dimensions were also essential. Perhaps already the American soldier, product of a society that nurtured self-reliance and versatility, had acquired something of the mechanical aptitudes that were to help distinguish American artillery in later wars. Knox could train his junior officers with some thoroughness because of their relatively small numbers as compared with the infantry officers, and he utilized foreign artillerists such as his adjutant, the Chevalier du Plessis. Though he always had to work with a conglomeration of guns and missiles, he turned the artillery into what Lafayette called "one of the wonders of the Revolution."

By the time of Brandywine, Washington felt able to report that his artillery fired more accurately than the British. Knox was not merely an unusually competent book-taught soldier; he could be an innovator as well. He broke from the conventional emphasis on artillery as mainly a siege weapon and tried to improve gun carriages for greater mobility to keep the cannons moving with the troops (although light guns were still hauled into action by men, not horses). Partly as a consequence Washington took eighteen guns across the Delaware with him for his Christmas attack on Trenton, an unusually high number to accompany 2,400 men, especially in an expedition requiring rapid movement. The guns then played a decisive part in trapping the Hessians in the streets of Trenton. An uncommonly high quota of field pieces was present again for the second foray to Trenton and the battle of Princeton, and on both occasions they gave the Army an invaluable shield.

Unlike the infantry in their "lines" representing the states, the artillery, as well as the engineers, served "under immediate Continental inspection." Originally the artillery formed a "corps" of independent companies, as late as the summer of 1776 numbering only 585 men. Late in 1776 there was a reorganization into four regiments. In 1778 these formations were established on a basis of twelve companies each, except for the 4th Regiment of only eight companies. In 1780 they were reorganized into ten companies each. By that year authorized artillery strength was 2,646 men; 1,607 were actually present in 1779.

Exceptionally mobile for its day, Knox's artillery could also serve well in traditional siege operations. It did so at Yorktown and proved itself capable by now of serving without embarrassment beside the French. Few branches of the American Army have been so fortunate in their founders as the artillery with Henry Knox, and Knox set what was destined to be a lasting tradition of excellence: in almost every American war through World War II and Korea, the artillery was the arm most frequently regarded as outstanding.[52]

Washington's military engineering was adequate because he was able to find sufficient qualified foreigners to undertake this most technical of eighteenth-century military specialties. The French engineer Louis Lebègue Duportail became Washington's chief engineer in time to plan the defenses of Valley Forge, and he distinguished himself especially in his contributions to the fortifications at West Point and the siege lines at Yorktown. The Pole Tadeusz Kościuszko, trained at the French artillery and engineering school at Mézières, contributed notably to defensive works at Saratoga and West Point. By 1782, Duportail's principal assistants were fourteen other French engineers. When the Revolution ended, native American military engineering remained in embryo.[53]

Washington's whole service in the French wars had been with infantry; while he was with that arm he had been able to observe the utility of cannons and military engineering. He entered the Revolution with virtually no acquaintance with cavalry. This fact helps account for his failure to do anything about organizing an American cavalry until July, 1776. Connecticut then sent the Army at New York a regiment of about 400 "light horse," composed of picked men "of reputation and property." Washington responded by sending the troopers home almost immediately. The Connecticut light horse had enlisted on the understanding that they would be exempt from guard duty and unpleasant fatigue details so they could use the time caring for their horses. Washington decided that such an exception was bad for morale and that he had little use for cavalry anyway. On the first point, there was something to be said for his view; on the second he was almost surely wrong.

Even a small cavalry patrol of the roads leading to the rear of the Continental position at the battle of Long Island might have prevented the disastrous outflanking that occurred there. The absence of cavalry in the Revolutionary Army is sometimes explained by reference to the lack of suitable country for its operations. But Long Island was relatively open countryside, and so was the greater part of southern New York, New Jersey, and southeastern Pennsylvania, the theater of war in the Middle States. On the Brandywine in 1777 a small force of cavalry might have served the same purpose as on Long Island in 1776. In the Monmouth campaign of 1778, cavalry might have harassed the British retreat across the Jerseys badly, since

Sir Henry Clinton's column was encumbered by a cart train a dozen miles long. Good cavalry reconnaissance might also have helped turn the battle of Monmouth into the decisive engagement Washington hoped it would be. The geography of the Middle States does not explain Washington's failure to develop a cavalry there; the geography of his early experiences in war, the Appalachian wilderness and mountains, more likely does.

In the Trenton-Princeton campaign, the Pennsylvania militia that turned out included the First Troop, Philadelphia City Cavalry, founded in 1774 and today the oldest cavalry organization in the country. But the First City Troop was misused by breaking it into driblets of individual scouts or very small details or simply headquarters guards and couriers. In 1777 Congress, perhaps prompted by observation of the Philadelphia cavalry, authorized four regiments of dragoons. But these organizations failed to acquire sufficient horses and equipment, and to the extent that they came into being at all they were wasted much as the First City Troop had been. Congress had commissioned Count Casimir Pulaski the first commander of cavalry, but Pulaski's blend of vanity with ignorance of both the English language and the American countryside did nothing to help make his arm effective, and he soon resigned. Stephen Moylan replaced him, a more suitable officer but by no means an outstanding one. His appointment attested to continued indifference in higher places, and the cavalry still failed to prosper. As late as 1780 Moylan reported that the 2nd Dragoons had only seven men fit for duty, equipped, and this regiment was not untypical.[54]

Neglect of cavalry is the more remarkable because the proper kind of mounted arm could have served so well in the cautious, mobile sort of warfare Washington had to wage. In the southern theater, where central command on both sides was loose and events occurred more spontaneously, mounted troops, like partisans, made themselves count in the outcome.

Among the sparse settlements of the South, men were accustomed to covering the great distances between homes and towns on horseback. When partisan bands sprang up, they naturally rode to their objectives, dismounted to fight, then rode away again. Since marksmanship was important to them, the partisans were not prepared to do their actual fighting on horseback, and their mounts were neither heavy nor swift enough for combat anyway. But they introduced a new mobility into the war.

Meanwhile the British reacted to the distances of the South and the scattered nature of American resistance there by dispatching to the area the two cavalry regiments they had in America, the 16th and 17th Dragoons. Both were understrength, and under the command of Colonel Banastre Tarleton they were combined as the Queen's Dragoons. Along with mounted Loyalists, and occasional mounted companies from infantry regiments, they raided American outposts and supply lines in an irregular war similar to the Americans' own. They also engaged in mounted battlefield action, as at the Cowpens, where almost fifty per cent of Tarleton's force were dragoons.

These methods led the Americans to counter with horsemen of their own who could fight mounted as well as ride to the scene of action. They found effective commanders in "Light Horse Harry" Lee and in William Washington, the latter a sort of cavalry counterpart of Henry Knox in his combination of obesity and energy. At the Cowpens the American mounted force of about eighty Continental dragoons and Georgia militia delayed the British advance and then helped drive home Daniel Morgan's counterattack. At Guilford Courthouse, William Washington's cavalry joined the 1st Maryland Continentals to break the charge of the 2nd Guards Battalion. Still, Lee's and William Washington's mounted forces were always tiny.[55]

In the main, then, the Continental Army was an infantry army modeled on the conventional European infantry of its day. Its greatest weakness was probably the inexperience of its officers in every grade. The shortages of good junior officers and sergeants to train the men and of reliable combat leaders were probably the chief causes of that erratic battlefield performance which led Washington to avoid direct confrontations with the main body of the British. If the tactics of the Continental Army were somewhat more ragged than those of established European armies, they remained essentially the same tactics. If the weapons were more varied in manufacture and model, they were the same types of weapons. Like European infantry, the Continentals carried chiefly smoothbore muskets, and they relied on volleys of musket fire followed by closing with the enemy to fight with bayonet and clubbed musket. Though their lines were more ragged, their volleys may have been somewhat more accurate than European volleys, since the Continentals put greater stress on aimed firing. The greater looseness of their battlefield tactics was partly deliberate; the British too were opening their ranks somewhat and placing increased emphasis on skirmishing as a means of feeling out and softening the enemy and on marksmanship. British battalions abandoned a battlefield formation of three linear ranks for two, with wider intervals between the men. They departed enough from the rigidity of European battle formations that by 1785 Cornwallis was commenting scornfully on maneuvers of Frederick the Great's army:

Their manoeuvres were such as the worst General in England would be hooted at for practising; two lines coming up within six yards of one another, and firing in one another's faces till they had no ammunition left; nothing could be more ridiculous.[56]

But the innovations of both British and Americans were variations on a theme, and the theme consisted of the standard modes of war of the classical age. Washington fought the British as he had seen the British fight the French: using American citizen soldiers as auxiliaries, but with his principal reliance upon European-style regulars, in his American approximation of them, the Continental Army.

FIVE

Arms and the Constitution: 1778-94

A standing force . . . is a dangerous, at the same time that it may be a necessary provision.

—James Madison in *The Federalist*[1]

GEORGE WASHINGTON believed that the military experience of the Revolution proved America's need for a professional army of the European type.

Regular Troops [he said] alone are equal to the exigencies of modern war, as well for defence as for offence. . . . *No Militia* will ever acquire the habits necessary to resist a regular force. . . . The firmness requisite for the real business of fighting is only to be attained by a constant course of discipline and service. I have never yet been witness to a single instance that would justify a different opinion. . . .[2]

The Jealousies of a standing Army, and the Evils to be apprehended from one, are remote; and in my judgment, situated and circumstanced as we are, not at all to be dreaded; but the consequence of wanting one, according to my Ideas, . . . is certain, and inevitable Ruin.[3]

But Washington himself could not base his prescriptions for the future military policy of the United States solely upon the combat experience of the Revolution. The nature of a permanent American Army was a political issue, the decision of which could influence the whole larger question of the nature of the United States. A society of free men had grown up in America partly because at the beginning the citizenry had relied on themselves for their own defense. To establish a standing army would be to accept a European import that had been designed in the first place to buttress monarchy. Even if American circumstances minimized any likelihood that an American standing army would promote a despotism, the creation of such an army might nevertheless contribute to a more centralized and more powerful government than many leaders of the Revolution thought wise. As Samuel Adams put it, a

standing army, however necessary it may be at sometimes, is always dangerous to the liberties of the people. Soldiers are apt to consider themselves as a body distinct from the rest of the citizens. They have their arms always in their hands. Their rules and their discipline is severe. They soon become attached to their officers and disposed to yield implicit obedience to their commands. Such a power should be watched with a jealous eye.[4]

Disbanding the Army that had fought the Revolutionary War posed ample difficulties to reinforce such fears. An alarming train of events issued from questions of pay for officers and men at the close of the war and for a time seemed to threaten civil government.

The Continental officers, mindful of British and European practice, had begun early in the war to agitate for half pay for life after its close. To many congressmen this proposal for a special concession to officers suggested the class consciousness of European officer corps and the very sort of Old World military custom that America should avoid. Congress resisted the officers' plea. In contrast, to many officers their appeal suggested nothing more than a just recompense for the financial sacrifices the war demanded of them. They argued that their military pay did not permit them to maintain the style that their status required, especially with the depreciation of Continental currency.

At first Washington sympathized with Congress and opposed his officers on this issue, but eventually he told Congress that unless it complied the officers might go home and leave the Revolution in the lurch. He recommended a compromise, half pay for seven years to those officers who agreed to serve for the duration, with a gratuity of eighty dollars to enlisted men who did likewise, to dilute the class aspect of the plan. In 1778 Congress yielded to the compromise, but still there persisted both agitation for half pay for life and a disturbingly large stream of officer resignations. So the next year Congress recommended that the states grant half pay for life to duration officers, a bounty to enlisted men, and pensions to widows of officers and men killed in service. The trouble with this action, of course, was the usual tepid response of the states. Thus, though the summer of 1780 saw the Army at peak strength, by fall the Army seemed closer to dissolution than it had been at any time since the retreat across New Jersey in 1776, and this time for lack of pay.

Aided by an increment of members favoring a stronger government, Congress, on October 21, 1780, responded by voting at last for half pay for life. But this issue was now less pressing than that of arrears in current pay. Also, the decision would depend again on the states' cooperation to supply the funds, and the states remained unenthusiastic.

In late 1782 a committee of Massachusetts officers appealed to the General Court of their state for financial relief both immediate and prospective. The General Court referred them to Congress. Thereupon the Massachusetts officers urged that Continental officers as a body take action for redress. Certain leading malcontents proposed that the whole officer corps resign. Washington managed to bury that scheme, but he did suggest that regiments draw up lists of grievances. The outcome was the appearance of an officers' memorial, to be delivered to Congress by a committee of three men headed by Major General Alexander McDougall. The memorial recited grievances regarding food and clothing as well as pay, it asked that enlisted men be assured payment of the eighty-dollar bonus promised them, and it offered to settle for a flat sum in place of half pay for life.

In Philadelphia, General McDougall's committee found Congress debating not only how to pay off the Army but also how to make terms with its whole numerous array of creditors. The strong-government men were urging that the only solution was to establish a national source of revenue without recourse to the states. These congressmen persuaded the officers' representatives that their principal hope lay in combining the Army's influence with that of the strong-government cause generally. ". . . What if it should be proposed," McDougall asked Henry Knox, "to unite the influence of Congress with that of the army and the public creditors to obtain permanent funds for the United States which will promise most ultimate security for the army?" The plan made enough headway that strong-government congressmen began using the threat of a mutinous Army to strengthen their hand.[5]

Thus certain congressmen, such as Gouverneur and Robert Morris and Alexander Hamilton, were not above using the Army as a tool for political purposes. But the Army, as Washington was soon to warn, "is a dangerous instrument to play with,"[6] and some of the officers in turn were not above trying to exploit the situation for the purposes of a political army. Despite its link with some politicians of influence, the McDougall committee had to return to camp with the disappointing news that Congress had turned down a proposal to commute half pay for life to six years' full pay. Thereupon the Newburgh Addresses began to circulate in the camps. Issued anonymously but probably the work of Major John Armstrong, Jr., aide-de-camp to General Gates, these addresses threatened that the Army would take matters into its own hands if its grievances were not remedied. They suggested that the Army might become unwilling to disband. If Congress should show "the slightest mark of indignity . . . the army has its alternative." If peaceful requests should fail, the Army could march west and defy Congress to destroy it.[7]

Washington acted promptly to squelch such notions. He called a meeting of the officers for March 15, 1783, to hear the report of the McDougall committee. Then he made a dramatic personal appearance before the meeting. Finding words difficult as usual, he drew from his coat a prepared statement, began reading it, faltered, and put on his eyeglasses, saying, "Gentlemen, you will permit me to put on my spectacles, for I have not only grown gray, but almost blind, in the service of my country." An appeal from the old commander so presented could hardly be resisted. Washington deplored the addresses as unmilitary and unreasonable, expressed confidence in the justice of Congress, and offered to use all his influence to achieve just redress. The officers voted to commit their case to his hands.

The day Washington's report of these events arrived, Congress further eased the situation by voting the officers full pay for five years; the question of how to raise the money was postponed by stipulating that payment would be either in cash or in securities at six per cent. The enlisted men were to get full pay for four months. The Army accepted this arrangement, and the danger of an officers' mutiny passed. But behind the incident lingered doubts over the Army's course if a different man had held command.[8]

Furthermore, despite demonstration of the risks involved, some political figures persisted in hoping to use the Army as a political instrument to strengthen the central government. Hamilton openly suggested, even while ostensibly deploring, the possibility of the Army's intervention in government, causing Washington to warn him that he regarded such ideas "with astonishment and horror."[9] To add to fears of the military's pretensions, Henry Knox and a circle of friends chose this unfortunate juncture to organize the Society of the Cincinnati, on May 13, 1783, at Steuben's headquarters. This association was to band together the Revolutionary officer corps in a permanent union, with their sons inheriting their membership. Probably the founders were sincere in claiming that their purposes were mainly social and charitable; Washington's acceptance of the presidency fits only that interpretation. But a public now hypersensitive to threats of military or aristocratic counterrevolution saw the society as a step toward hereditary nobility and an engine for pursuing the theme of the Newburgh Addresses. Numerous legislators denounced it, Washington became embarrassed, and the political views of Henry Knox were such that there was probably an element of truth in the fears.[10]

The news of preliminary terms of peace brought another threat of mutiny, this time from the enlisted men. The men wanted to go home immediately, but Congress hesitated to discharge them before peace terms became final. The men also wanted payment before they departed, because otherwise they would have to go home, in Washington's phrase, as a "Sett of Beggars." The commander in chief recommended that they receive three months' pay. By the end of April, 1783, he was reporting that the soldiers were rioting and insulting their officers:

I believe it is not in the power of Congress or their officers, to hold them much, if any, longer; for we are obliged at this moment to increase our guards to prevent rioting, and the insults which the officers meet with in attempting to hold them to their duty. The proportion of these men amount to seven-elevenths of the army. . . .[11]

Congress proposed merely to furlough the troops with assurance of a discharge upon the signing of a peace treaty and promise of a financial settlement later. But again a group of officers petitioned for financial relief before being sent home, and a committee of sergeants in Philadelphia, making a plea for payment, phrased it as a sharp demand. On June 17 eighty mutinous recent recruits marched from Lancaster to Philadelphia, aroused the several hundred Pennsylvania soldiers—also mostly new men—quartered in the city, and barricaded Congress and the Executive Council of Pennsylvania in the State House while demanding immediate redress of grievances. Fortunately, a twenty-minute time limit set by the soldiers passed without violence, and when Congress took up courage to walk out of the State House it met nothing worse than insults, despite the fact that the rioters had now been drinking freely. The whole affair fizzled, but Congress saw fit to transfer its sessions from Philadelphia to Princeton.[12]

Meanwhile, Washington had announced the Congressional plan to furlough the troops, and the desire to go home proved stronger than the desire to have money in the pocket while going. By June 13 most of the soldiers and many of the officers had begun their journey from the camps. Except for about 700 men retained for garrison duty, the

Continental Army disbanded, unhappily, in an atmosphere of disgruntlement and of threats of mutinies and coups.[13]

Even when the Continental Army had comported itself with greater subordination than during its final unfortunate months, by its very existence it had been a political force, and it had not always been a passive one. The Army and especially the officer corps had been by no means the least potent agency in the movement for independence. Once men accepted commissions in the Army, they found the logic of their situation pointing them toward independence, and under Washington's leadership they had acted accordingly in hastening the great Declaration.[14] Similarly, officers such as Knox who favored strong government had capitalized upon their military positions to push the creation of the executive departments.[15] The memory of the political potency of the Army was fresh in mind when Congress faced the question of a permanent military establishment and regarded it as a political issue.

Naturally, the congressmen most eager to create a permanent establishment of respectable proportions were the proponents of a stronger central government. In 1783 they secured a Congressional committee to study the military question. Hamilton became chairman, and James Madison, James Wilson, Samuel Osgood, and Oliver Ellsworth would serve with him. This membership was sure to be generally friendly to military strength. They sought mainly the advice of Washington and Steuben, two generals whose advocacy of a reasonably strong permanent military system was well known. Stephen Higginson, a congressman of contrary views, wrote that

there are those also among us who wish to keep up a large force, to have large garrisons, to increase the navy, to have a large diplomatic corps, to give large salaries to all our servants. Their professed view is to strengthen the hands of government, to make us respectable in Europe. . . .[16]

In fact, the financial weakness of the new nation and the prevailing political climate ensured that the military recommendations even of those most friendly to military strength had to be modest ones. Suggestions for a standing army had to be played down. Experience with the redcoats both before and during the Revolution, closely followed by the problems of disbanding the Continental Army, had multiplied all the traditional fears of a standing army, and Congress would surely not substitute an American army of any considerable size for the departing British army.

Therefore Washington and Steuben in their recommendations to the committee and Hamilton in his report proposed merely a small standing army, albeit about as large a one as there was any hope of getting in the face of much opposition to any at all, with ultimate reliance upon improved versions of the historic citizens' militia. Washington proposed a permanent force of four regiments of infantry and one of artillery and artificers, aggregating 2,631 officers and men, whose major duties would be to see to Indian defense and to patrol the national frontiers. He also proposed a respectable navy to guard the coasts against invasion. Behind these forces would stand a militia system enrolling all male citizens between eighteen and fifty and holding them liable for service to the nation in emergencies. Apart from the general enrollment, able-bodied young men between eighteen and twenty-five who had a "fondness for military Parade (which passion is almost ever prevalent at that period of life)" should be recruited into a special force, to be trained in encampments twelve to twenty-five days a year, brigaded in readiness for call, and commanded by officers commissioned not by states but by the United States. Washington's three types of forces clearly had their roots in the British and Continental Armies, the common militia, and the volunteer militia, respectively, with the latter now to be subject to United States rather than merely state control.

Steuben's proposals were similar, with a somewhat more thorough training suggested for the new version of the volunteer militia: Steuben would have had young men volunteer for three years to train for thirty days a year under regional defense commands. In this respect Washington stated that he preferred Steuben's recommendation to his own. He confessed that in preparing his plan, he "glided almost insensibly into what I thought *would*, rather than what I conceived *ought* to be a proper Peace Establishment for the country."[17]

Despite such caution, Washington's "Sentiments on a Peace Establishment" far exceeded what Congress was willing to provide. Hamilton of course was receptive, and he incorporated features of the Washington and Steuben plans into his own more ambitious recommendations, which would have had all single men enrolled in the militia assemble into companies once a month, and into regiments every three months.[18] But when final peace terms at last were ratified and Washington resigned as commander in chief, Congress refused to heed even Washington's short-term recommendation that 500 infantrymen and 100 artillerists be retained from the Continental Army. Instead it turned to the states and their militias for its immediate as well as permanent military needs.

On June 2, 1784, Congress directed Henry Knox, the senior officer remaining, to discharge all but fifty-five men at West Point and twenty-five at Fort Pitt. These eighty men, with a proper complement of officers, would guard the military stores at those places.[19]

Benjamin Lincoln had already resigned as Secretary at War. His Assistant Secretary and two clerks had preceded him, and Congress did not fill the vacancies. The Department of War now consisted only of the secretary in the War Office, that is, the chief clerk, Joseph Carleton. Timothy Pickering stayed on as quartermaster general and Samuel Hodgdon as commissary of military stores, but much of their business consisted of finding buyers for the supplies remaining from the war.[20]

In discharging the Continental Army, Congress destroyed the possibility that regiments of a future United States Army might draw directly upon the traditions of the Continental regiments. The eighty-six or so regiments and independent battalions of the Continental service now disappeared entirely; no modern regiment descends directly from any of them. The only, and minor, exception is Battery D, 5th Field Artillery Battalion. Through Captain John Doughty's garrison at West Point this unit claims a somewhat tenuous connection with Alexander Hamilton's Provincial Company of Artillery of the Colony of New York, organized in 1776, and therefore ranks as the oldest organization in the Regular Army.[21]

The well-known picture of the era of the Articles of Confederation as the critical period of American history may be overdrawn. But the Articles were not designed for the vigorous development of military power. The war powers of Congress under the Articles were much the same as those the Continental Congress had exercised, and the Revolutionary War had not been conducted with efficiency, economy, or vigor. Under the Articles, Congress could declare war, but it had to requisition the states for both militia and money. It could enlist volunteers, but if dread of a standing army could be overcome and men persuaded to sally forth, Congress remained dependent on the states for the means to equip and supply them. It would be difficult to raise and maintain a Confederation force of any dimensions.

Nevertheless, the Confederation did need a larger force than the eighty men of June 2, 1784. The states had ceded the Northwest to Congress, and the cession gave Congress a problem of Indian defense over a vast area. To aggravate the problem, popular land hunger demanded that the Confederation try to capitalize upon the military successes of the Revolution to overawe the Indians into extensive land sales. In the Northwest also were the forts that the British continued to garrison in defiance of the Treaty of Paris. And although the states of Georgia, South Carolina, and North Carolina still held jurisdiction over the Southwest, they were sure to appeal to Congress if their Indians got out of hand. Georgia especially was feeble compared with the Creeks and the Cherokees, and perhaps only the unwillingness of Spain to encourage the Indians to a show-down at this time spared the Confederation from insoluble difficulties.

By 1784 the pendulum of political power had swung away from the strong-government men and back toward the states' righters, but Congress could hardly deny that the Indians and the British garrisons demanded some semblance of a national army. Therefore, having eliminated all political danger from the Continental Army by reducing it to eighty men, Congress the next day called on Pennsylvania, New Jersey, New York, and Connecticut to furnish 700 men from their militias. The filling of this call would afford one regiment, at the table-of-organization strength of 612 privates and corporals that had prevailed at the end of the war. Pennsylvania was assigned a quota of 260 men, New Jersey 110, New York 165, and Connecticut 165. The term of national service was to be one year.[22]

Only Pennsylvania, which felt the Indian menace directly, met its quota. A Pennsylvanian, Lieutenant Colonel Josiah Harmar, received command of the troops. Soon Knox retired, and Harmar became the ranking officer of the Army. The first activity that Congress had in mind was to try to take over the British-held forts, but since the turnout was disappointing, nothing was attempted. Nevertheless, Harmar began the organization of the 1st American Regiment, opening the history of what remains the oldest regiment in the Regular Army, the present 3rd Infantry.[23]

The next spring, 1785, Congress decided upon another effort to provide defense against the Indians and discouragement for the British garrisons. This time, hoping that the matter might be pursued more energetically, the delegates began by filling the vacant post of Secretary at War with the ample person of Henry Knox. Knox remained a partisan of a stronger government than the Articles provided, but he would do what he could to improve one department from within. Congress then called on the same four states as the previous year to fill the regiment of 700 men, to be enlisted now for three years' service.

Once again, Pennsylvania surpassed the effort of her sister states. When it appeared that few of the 1784 troops would reenlist, the state went so far as to arrange the transfer of as many as possible to the remoter frontier posts, to make it difficult for them to get home and thus to provide further persuasion. Meanwhile Knox pressed the other states, and by June, 1786, he was able to report that all but 60 of the 700 had been recruited. Thereupon he began requesting more.[24]

The Secretary realized that recruiting 640 men was a small achievement though a difficult one, and that the possible Indian troubles in the West remained disproportionate to his regiment's strength. Congress placed the two Superintendents of Indian Affairs, for the Northern and Southern Departments, under his authority, and he tried to follow a conciliatory policy, discouraging pressure for land cessions lest the Indians be provoked into an uprising. Much of the activity of the troops came to be the eviction of squatters from Indian lands, although there was no catching up with all of the perhaps 50,000 who entered the Indian country by the end of the decade.[25]

The 1st American Regiment consisted of ten companies, eight of infantry and two of artillery. The stations from which it tried to impress the Indians and restrain squatters were a series of stockades in the Ohio River country, from Fort Franklin on the upper Allegheny River downstream to Fort Steuben near Louisville and Fort Knox at Vincennes. Usually it was scattered among the outposts by companies or even smaller detachments. Its weapons came from Revolutionary stocks that were more than ample for its needs. Five supporting agencies had survived from the war until 1785—quartermaster, commissary, hospital, marine, and clothier departments. In March, 1785, Congress abolished these agencies, turning over their functions in June to two commissioners responsible to Knox. Timothy Pickering had been eager to resign as quartermaster general anyway, having been disappointed at not becoming Secretary at War. Knox himself largely took over the quartermaster duties. He modified Samuel Hodgdon's role, making him commissioner of military stores, while one of his own formal duties was to visit the depositories of those stores twice annually. By 1787 Knox's own office consisted merely of three clerks and a messenger. Despite its miniature size, the military establishment was one of the most costly departments of the Confederation. The total expenditures of the government from 1784 to 1787 averaged something over $500,000 a year. In 1784 military expenditures amounted to $297,323.75; in 1787 the military appropriation was $176,757.17.[26]

Unfortunately, the commissioner of military stores proved inefficient, and the private contractors on whom the Army was still relying to furnish supplies were often both inefficient and corrupt. Comfort Sands, the man whom Washington had described as a practitioner of "*low dirty* tricks" when he was a wartime contractor, turned up as a contractor again. Turnbull, Marmie, and Company, the subsistence contractors in 1786, did their job so badly that Colonel Harmar had to reach into his own pockets to keep his men from starving. Clothing was chronically scarce; veteran soldiers did not get new clothing in 1788 because what was available had to be issued to the recruits. Pay always came late, if at all.[27]

The Springfield Arsenal was especially close to Henry Knox's heart. He had suggested the site, and he gave it special attention on his tours of military installations. Its facilities now included a foundry for casting brass cannons as well as a brick magazine and the stores of weapons. Knox was a conservative man who would have been alarmed and angered by Shays's Rebellion of 1786 in any case; its threat to the Springfield Arsenal multiplied his anger.[28]

For to Knox's disgust, the Confederation proved unable to protect its own arsenal. In the face of Shays's Rebellion, Congress voted to increase the Army to 2,040. Ostensibly the purpose still was to deal with the Indians; but the Army would now have had the equivalent of two full regiments of infantry plus supporting troops, organized in a "legionary corps" of mixed arms, and much of this strength would not have been needed immediately on the frontier. Of the new men, however, only two companies of artillery could be assembled. Massachusetts itself obstructed the effort to send Massachusetts recruits to Springfield lest the state's own efforts to suppress the Shaysites be diverted. Knox finally dispatched 125 Connecticut men to the arsenal, but only after Massachusetts militia had already secured the place. To complete the humiliation, even the Massachusetts militia defied the authority of the Confederation. Major General William Shepherd of the militia asked Knox's permission to use the Confederation arms at Springfield against the Shaysites. Knox, jealous to protect national prerogatives, refused until Congress should consent. Shepherd, growing desperate, used the arms anyway.[29]

Shays's Rebellion galvanized the movement to replace the Articles of Confederation with a stronger frame of government. To conservative men and to those generally who hoped to see the United States a respectable power, the Shaysites' humiliation of both national and state governments seemed an insult that must not be borne again. No man was more strongly affected than Henry Knox. The official most directly concerned with the military strength of the United States, he regarded Shays's Rebellion as final evidence that the Confederation not only condemned the United States to weakness against foreign foes but also deprived the nation of power to keep order within.

Among men of all parties the future of the Army was a central issue in the movement leading to the Constitutional Convention of

1787 and in the ratification struggle that followed. Hope for a government that could support a more powerful army was high among the causes animating the strong-government men. Fear of a military engine that might threaten American liberties was high among reasons for opposition to the new Constitution.

In Pennsylvania at least, the surviving officers of the Continental Army whose political opinions are still known were unanimously partisans of the new Constitution, forty-four out of forty-four. Surviving militia officers who had served in the Revolution were divided, but here too a significant fact appeared: those officers who had done active militia duty without leaving Pennsylvania were almost all opposed to the new Constitution, but those militia officers who had served outside the state almost all favored it. Firsthand knowledge of the military limitations of the Continental Congress and the Confederation seems therefore to have been a critical factor in determining attitudes toward the Constitution of 1787. And former officers of the Revolutionary Army were often potent figures in the ratifying conventions of their states.[30]

In contrast, traditional fears of a standing army continued to excite the opponents of a stronger government. Patrick Henry warned the Virginia ratifying convention that under the new Constitution:

Congress by the power of taxation, by that of raising an army, and by their control over the militia, have the sword in one hand and the purse in the other. Shall we be safe without either? Congress have an unlimited power over both; they are entirely given up by us. Let him candidly tell me where and when did a freedom exist when the sword and the purse were given up from the people? Unless a miracle in human affairs interposed, no nation ever retained its liberty after the loss of the sword and the purse.[31]

And for what need, the opponents of the Constitution asked, was the central government to receive powers which would permit the erection of a standing army?

Had we a standing army when the British invaded our peaceful shores? Was it a standing army that gained the battles of Lexington and Bunker Hill, and took the ill-fated Burgoyne? Is not a well regulated militia sufficient for every purpose of internal defense? And which of you, my fellow citizens, is afraid of any invasion from foreign powers that our brave militia would not be able immediately to repel?[32]

Elbridge Gerry tried to have written into the Constitution a specific limitation of the national army to 2,000 or at most 3,000 men. On this occasion, Washington is said to have departed from the impartiality of his chairmanship of the Constitutional Convention to offer a stage-whispered amendment making it unconstitutional for any enemy to attack with a larger force.[33] But if Washington could afford a small sarcasm, the strong-government men generally seem to have felt apologetic about the Constitution's possibilities for a strong permanent army. Certainly James Wilson phrased the goal mildly to the Pennsylvania ratifying convention:

When we consider the situation of the United States, we must be satisfied that it will be necessary to keep up some troops for the protection of the western frontiers and to secure our interest in the internal navigation of that country.[34]

Madison went so far as to tell the Virginia convention that "with respect to a standing army, I believe there was not a member in the Federal Convention who did not feel indignation at such an institution."[35]

In truth, the military clauses of the Constitution follow a cautious compromise course between the hopes of those who favored greater military strength and the fears of those who anticipated a military despotism. The new national government received sufficient authority to raise and maintain about as powerful an army as the resources and public sentiment of the country would permit. Congress received categorically the powers "To declare war" and "To raise and support armies." It might call the state militias into federal service "to execute the laws of the union, suppress insurrections and repel invasions." It might "provide for organizing, arming and disciplining the militia, and for governing such part of them as may be employed in the service of the United States." Unlike the Continental and Confederation Congresses, furthermore, and as Patrick Henry emphasized in his warning to the Virginia convention, the new Congress would also command the power of the purse, with taxing authority adequate to give practical effect to its authority "To raise and support armies." There are few limitations here upon Congress's ability to mobilize national resources for military purposes.

At the same time, however, the Constitution erected a series of hedges against the possibility that military power might become military despotism. While Congress might create armies, appropriate money for their support, and make rules for their discipline, military command was vested not in Congress but in another branch of government, the executive, with the President as Commander in Chief of the Army and Navy of the United States and of the militia when in federal service. The President commissioned the officers, with the advice and consent of the Senate. But while the President and his officers commanded the Army, lest they pursue purposes of their own choosing they remained dependent upon Congressional appropriations. The Constitution did not prescribe the British practice whereby the legislature authorized military discipline only for periods of one year, so that armies would disintegrate if something like the Mutiny Act were not renewed annually; but it did prescribe that no appropriation of money for the Army's use should be for a longer term than two years. Thus the Constitution drew from British experience to guard against military despotism either from an executive army, like the Royal army under Charles I, or a legislative army, like the Parliamentary army under Cromwell; it made the Army responsible to and dependent upon both Congress and the President.

While thus dividing military authority within the new federal government, the Constitution also divided military power between the federal government and the states. The states retained their historic militias, with authority to appoint their officers and to conduct their training (although Congress might prescribe the system under which training was to be conducted, and although no state might keep up troops without the consent of Congress). The militias might be called into federal service only for limited purposes, "to execute the laws of the union, suppress insurrections and repel invasions." The Second Amendment further guaranteed the status of the militias by declaring: "A well-regulated militia being necessary to the security of a free state, the right of the people to keep and bear arms shall not be infringed." It was possible to regard the state militias as a check against a federal standing army, since they had just accomplished a very similar purpose: they had given birth to the Continental Army to check the threat of a military despotism from the British army.

The strong-government men had desired sufficient authority to create a strong national army, and the Constitution fulfilled their wish. But in the Constitution they retained the dual military system bequeathed to the United States by its history: a citizen soldiery enrolled in the state militias, plus a professional army of the type represented by the British army or, more roughly, the Continental Army.

In this vein *The Federalist Papers* urged the ratification of the Constitution on grounds of the flexibility it would give to American military power. John Jay wrote in *The Federalist*, Number 4:

Our Government can collect and avail itself of the talents and experience of the ablest men, in whatever part of the Union they may be found. It can move on uniform principles of policy— It can harmonize, assimilate, and protect the several parts and members, and extend the benefit of its foresight and precautions to each. . . . It can apply the resources and power of the whole to the defence of any particular part, and that more easily and expeditiously than State Governments, or separate confederacies can possibly do, for want of concert and unity of system. It can place the militia under one plan of discipline, and by putting their officers in a proper line of subordination to the Chief Magistrate, will as it were consolidate them into one corps, and thereby render them more efficient than if divided into thirteen or into three or four distinct independent bodies.[36]

An improved military system was one of the main issues to the three writers of *The Federalist*. Eight of the papers especially concern the military establishment: Number 4, by Jay; Numbers 23, 24, 25, 26, 28, and 29, by Hamilton; and Number 41, by Madison. While Hamilton wrote too of the advantages of coordinating the militias, not surprisingly he was most outspoken on the merits of a standing army and the deficiencies of a citizens' militia:

Here I expect we shall be told, that the Militia of the country is its natural bulwark, and would be at all times equal to the national defence. This doctrine in substance had like to have lost us our independence. . . . The steady operations of war against a regular and disciplined army, can only be successfully conducted by a force of the same kind. Considerations of œconomy, not less than of stability and vigor, confirm this position. The American Militia, in the course of the late war, have by their valour on numerous occasions, erected eternal monuments to their fame; but the bravest of them feel and know, that the liberty of their country could not have been established by their efforts alone, however great and valuable they were. War, like most other things, is a science to be acquired and perfected by diligence, by perseverance, by time, and by practice.[37]

Despite what he said on the subject to the Virginia convention, Madison wrote in Number 41 of *The Federalist* that though it is dangerous, a standing army may also be a necessary provision.[38]

In military affairs as elsewhere, the Constitution laid foundations upon which a stronger national power might be built in the future. Its ratification did not immediately revolutionize America's military posture. Like the other executive departments of the Confederation, the War Department and the Army simply continued to function under the new government until appropriate successors could be established by statute of the new Congress. When that body did legislate for a Department of War on August 7, 1789, it mainly extended the status quo. The title of the head of the department was changed from Secretary *at* War to Secretary *of* War, but Henry Knox continued in office. More fundamentally, the Secretary would be directly responsible now not to Congress but to the President; how important a change this was, however, was not immediately apparent, since the Secretary still participated in occasional sessions of Congress to lay War Department business before it. In 1790, one new clerk was added to Knox's staff; by 1792 the number grew to ten. The superintendencies of Indian affairs were combined with the offices of governor in the Northwest and South Territories, but the Secretary of War remained the agent of the government to supervise Indian policy. On September 29, 1789, Congress legalized the Army inherited from the Confederation, confirming a law of 1787 which had raised the authorized strength to 840 men, in one infantry regiment of eight companies plus four independent companies of artillery. Only some 672 of these men were actually in service. At the same time, the President was authorized to call out militia when necessary to provide additional protection against Indians.[39]

Congress expected Knox to be ready with recommendations for a permanent military system when the second session of the First Congress convened in 1790. Knox complied. He proposed a moderate strengthening of the standing force to 2,033 officers and men, which would have filled out the "legionary corps" contemplated at the time of Shays's Rebellion but never completed. To improve the militia, he reiterated a plan he had earlier offered soon after becoming Secretary at War and which resembled the Washington and Steuben proposals of 1783. All able-bodied men between eighteen and sixty would be enrolled in the militia, with mariners designated as a naval militia. The general body of militia manpower, however, would be divided into three categories: an Advanced Corps of men from eighteen to twenty, a Main Corps of men from twenty-one to forty-six, and a Reserved Corps of older men. Eighteen- and nineteen-year-old's should be required to drill thirty consecutive days a year, twenty-year-old's ten days. Passing into the Main Corps, men should be required to continue drilling four days a year. Like the standing army, the active parts of the militia would be organized into legions, miniature armies incorporating all arms. Each militia legion should assemble every three years, and each constituent regiment of the legions annually. The whole should be subject to a relatively strict federal supervision.[40]

This plan was too ambitious and required too much of the citizens' militia to meet a friendly reception in Congress. Senator William Maclay of Pennsylvania grumbled that "The first error seems to have been the appointing of a Secretary of War when we were at peace, and now we must find troops lest his office should run out of employment." Maclay was exceptionally testy and considered himself exceptionally democratic, but on this issue most members shared his views.

With no immediate threat of foreign or, except on the frontiers, Indian invasion, most citizens were prepared to give only limited obeisance to the theory of universal military obligation. Having escaped British taxation through the war, most citizens were prepared to accept only limited taxation from an American government, as several political crises of the 1790's were to demonstrate. Congress did nothing about Knox's militia plan in 1790, and the next year when the Secretary offered a diluted version that Washington had helped prepare and endorsed, Congress still did nothing.

The standing force fared slightly better. With Indian relations in the Northwest worsening, Congress voted an increase to 1,216 enlisted men on April 30, 1790. This increment permitted the reorganization of the infantry regiment into three battalions of four companies each. The company would consist of one captain, one lieutenant, one ensign, four sergeants, four corporals, two musicians, and sixty-one privates. A major, an adjutant, a quartermaster, and a surgeon or surgeon's mate would round out each battalion. The artillery would form a separate battalion. While calling for more men, Congress simultaneously served economy by cutting the private's pay from four dollars to three dollars a month.[41]

Henry Knox's Indian policy, now supported by President Washington, remained one of restraining the rush of squatters into the territories and of seeking conciliation with the red men. In the South Territory, the former western lands of Georgia and South Carolina, Knox was able to arrange the satisfactory Treaty of New York to keep peace with the Creeks and their allies. In the Northwest and in Kentucky, however, the flow of settlers was too heavy to permit conciliation of the Miami, Shawnee, Kickapoo, and such. Far from being reconciled to continual white advances, they insisted, with the encouragement of the British in their remaining garrisons south of the Great Lakes, that the white frontier must fall back to the Ohio. Even peace negotiations in the Northwest became a kind of war, with the Indians taking advantage of parleys to steal from the whites and cut off Army patrols. Therefore when Congress voted the increase of the 1st Regiment to three battalions, Governor Arthur St. Clair of the Northwest Territory and Josiah Harmar, now a brigadier, decided to stage a show of force.

The first major military expedition of the standing Army of the United States, it ended in disaster. By authority of the President, Harmar reinforced the Army by calling out 1,000 militia from the District of Kentucky and 500 from Pennsylvania. But he mistakenly divided his force and sent it into the Indian country in two columns, both of which were mismanaged. Major John F. Hamtramck, commanding one of them, lacked resolution and turned back from his march without accomplishing anything. Harmar showed resolution but little skill and divided his column still again, whereupon the Indians mauled his detachments in detail. The troops from the 1st Regiment evidently fought more firmly than the recently assembled militia, but the whole affair was so badly conducted that this hardly surprising fact has even less significance than it would otherwise. The result of the expedition was not to overawe the Indians but to embolden them.[42]

Since the Indian harassment of the frontier increased, Congress voted in the spring of 1791 to create a second infantry regiment, organized much like the first although smaller by fifty men. The same law authorized a major general, brigadier general, brigade major, quartermaster, and chaplain for the Army. It also authorized the President to call into service two regiments of six months' levies— that is, temporary federal troops—or whatever militia might be needed for six months. Washington named Governor St. Clair to command a new expedition.

But although the President had urged the new legislation as early as December 8, 1790, Congress had not passed it until March 3, 1791. A Congressional committee later remarked that this slow response left time "hardly sufficient to complete and discipline an army for such an expedition during the summer months of the same year."[43] The War Department then dawdled further. Knox appointed Samuel Hodgdon to the revived office of quartermaster general, though by now he had ample reason to distrust Hodgdon's competence. William Duer received the contract for supplying the troops beyond Fort Pitt, though Knox also had ample reason to know that Duer's main interest was filling his pockets through speculation; indeed, Knox was Duer's partner in some such activities. When Hodgdon and Duer displayed the lassitude that should have been anticipated from them, Knox failed to goad them; fatter even than in his Revolutionary years, he seems to have become also much less zealous and much too fond of comfortable living. While the gathering of supplies lagged, so did enlistments. For three dollars a month, minus one dollar for clothing and medical expenses, not much came in except men "purchased from prisons, wheelbarrows and brothels." When something of an army finally assembled, St. Clair neither moved it rapidly nor utilized his time to train it.[44]

Not until September 17 did St. Clair leave Ludlow's Station near Cincinnati. Then his drums seldom beat the march before nine in the morning, and in a typical three-day period the Army covered only nineteen miles. The general himself was ill. His troops knew little of arms. The 1st American Regiment was detached from the main body. On November 4 St. Clair blundered into an Indian attack. His militia fled in panic, his "regulars" of the 2nd Regiment could do little better, the wounded were left to the scalping knife, and 632 men, about half the column, perished. Like the Continental Army in 1783, the surviving levies were sent home without pay, save for three dollars and a note specifying that "some" advances had been paid on account.[45]

So the whole job of raising the standing Army to what seemed adequate strength and trying to pacify the Indians had to begin again, for a third time. On March 5, 1792, Congress authorized the recruiting of the two infantry regiments and the artillery battalion to full strength; established three additional infantry regiments to be enlisted for three years, plus four troops of light dragoons, the type of horsemen, armed primarily with firearms, not sabers, who had proved most useful in the Revolution; ended the deductions from soldiers' pay for uniforms and medical supplies; and offered an eight-dollar enlistment bounty. The Treasury Department, upon the plea of its energetic Secretary Alexander Hamilton, was to replace the War Department as purchaser of Army supplies.[46]

On December 27 Congress agreed to the reorganization of the new Army as the Legion of the United States. Knox had been proposing a legionary organization since the 1780's. The term legion had come into renewed military use during the eighteenth century, especially in eastern Europe, to denote small mixed bodies of cavalry and infantry. As such it appeared in the American Revolution on both sides, as in Tarleton's Legion or Pulaski's Legion. Now the United States applied it to a much larger force, but still denoting a mixture of the military arms. The Legion of the United States was to consist of four sublegions of 1,280 men each, commanded by brigadier generals. Each sublegion would include two battalions of infantry, one battalion of riflemen, one company of dragoons, and one company of artillery. With the disappearance of regiments, the rank of colonel also disappeared, the battalions being commanded by majors. The military purpose of the legionary organization was to enhance tactical flexibility by creating four miniature armies in the four sublegions. Here, for the same reason that the French army was concurrently developing the modern division, was a departure from the eighteenth-century tendency to regard a whole army as a single tactical unit. A more sentimental purpose of the legionary organization resided in the young American Republic's delight in drawing parallels between itself and the ancient Roman Republic.[47]

With some misgivings about the impetuosity that had won Anthony Wayne the nickname Mad Anthony, Washington named him as major general commanding the Legion. The misgivings proved needless. Far from proceeding impetuously, Wayne took full advan-

tage of long delays occasioned by new negotiations with the Indians
to ensure that before the Legion fought it should become an army.
Through two years he drilled the Legion. Unwilling to have his men
distracted by the fleshpots of frontier Pittsburgh, he early moved
them from that first assembly point to a clearing in the wilderness
down the Ohio. He placed Steuben's *Blue Book* in the hands of every
company officer and saw that they used it, until the Legion could
impress the Indians with close-order drill on the parade ground or,
hopefully, hold its lines firmly on the battlefield. He also taught the
art of field fortification, so that when the Legion moved into the
country of the Miami and the Shawnee, it could throw up redoubts
and abatis to protect its encampments. In line with American experience, he taught individual marksmanship. To stimulate an *esprit de
corps*, he gave each sublegion its distinctive color for cap ornaments
and uniform facings: white for the First Sublegion, red for the Second, yellow for the Third, green for the Fourth. The sublegionary
colors appeared also in the banners of the dragoon troop, artillery
battery, and infantry battalions of each sublegion.

By the time peace talks had broken down and the Army had to
invade the Indian country again, in the summer of 1794, Anthony
Wayne had created a good, reliable army. Reinforced by 1,600
mounted Kentucky militia, who also fought well, he won the battle
of Fallen Timbers on August 20. Thereby he broke the power of the
Indians in the eastern region of the Northwest and gave a decisive
push toward British evacuation of the garrisons below the Lakes. He
also erased much of the stigma of the Harmar and St. Clair expeditions and gave the infant standing Army of the United States its first
model of excellence. With good reason he could be called the Father
of the Regular Army.[48]

Meanwhile, the same flurry of military interest that led to the
authorization of Wayne's Army had inspired Congress at last to
place the historic citizens' militia upon a legal footing under the
Constitution. The Militia Act of May 8, 1792, fell far short of
Knox's plans for a well trained militia under careful federal supervision, but it did fix the principle of a universal military obligation in
the statutory law of the new government. It required the enrollment
of every free, white, able-bodied male citizen between eighteen and
forty-five in the militia of his state. Company commanders were to be
responsible for such enrollment in their districts. Each citizen was to
equip himself, within six months

with a good musket or firelock, a sufficient bayonet and belt, two spare
flints, and a knapsack, a pouch, with a box therein to contain not less

than twenty-four cartridges, suited to the bore of his musket or firelock, each cartridge to contain a proper quantity of powder and ball; or, with a good rifle, knapsack, shot pouch and powder horn, twenty balls, suited to the bore of his rifle, and a quarter of a pound of powder; and shall appear, so armed, accoutered, and provided, when called out to exercise, or into service. . . .

The law similarly prescribed the equipment of officers. It prescribed an organization of the whole force into divisions and brigades made up of lower units corresponding to the regiments and companies of the standing force (the legionary pattern not yet having been adopted when the Militia Act was passed). The President might call militiamen into national service, for the constitutionally prescribed purposes, for no more than three months in any one year, "nor more than in due rotation with every other able-bodied man of the same rank."[49]

Because providing arms was left to individual militiamen and enforcement was left to the states, with no federal standards of training and competence, and because the terms of possible federal service were so drastically limited, the Militia Act has received a good deal of contempt from historians of the Emory Upton school. Judged by standards of military efficiency, the act indeed lacked much; judged in terms of Congress's larger need to consider how best to apportion the energies and resources of a young and still poor nation, it is not so certain that military purposes should have been served more generously. The Militia Act of 1792 was not useless; it preserved if it did not improve the inherited tradition of a citizen soldiery, and that tradition was to assist the nation often in future years. To have expected more of the law was probably to expect unrealistically much of the new constitutional government and the scattered, undisciplined, agrarian society it represented.

Henceforth the American Army would continue to be built upon two foundations, represented now by the Militia Act of 1792 and by the Regulars disciplined under Anthony Wayne.

☆ PART TWO ☆

The Formative Century:
1794-1898

Of all the civilized states of Christendom, we are perhaps the least military, though not behind the foremost as a warlike one.
— Dennis Hart Mahan[1]

SIX

Arms and the Young Republic: 1794-1812

. . . a well-disciplined militia, our best reliance in peace, and for the first moments of war, till regulars may relieve them . . .

—Thomas Jefferson[1]

THOUGH PROVOKED partly by the Indian troubles of the Northwest, the Militia Act of 1792 was an effort to fix military policy for a prolonged era of peace. Instead, its passage coincided with the opening of a long era of threats of war, culminating in the actuality of war. The year of the Militia Act was the year of the beginning of the wars of the French Revolution. By 1794 the victory of Fallen Timbers was important not only for the safety of the Northwest frontier but also as a makeweight against the danger of war with England. Out of the new era of danger was to come an unexpectedly prompt testing both of the constitutional system of control of military institutions and of the military qualities and respective roles of the new federal standing Army and federal militia system.

By 1794 the efforts of Revolutionary France to enlist the cooperation of the United States in war against England, the willingness of one of the American political parties to respond, and England's customary wartime highhandedness on the oceans were carrying the United States swiftly toward a new conflict with the Mother Country. President Washington believed the new Republic was yet too feeble to risk such a conflict, and he bent all the diplomatic energies of his administration to avert it. At some sacrifice of American concepts of neutral maritime rights, his envoy extraordinary to London, John Jay, succeeded in doing so through Jay's Treaty.

In the meantime the new national government had to give its first thought to the historic twin of the Indian problem in American military history, the question of coastal defense. On March 27, 1794, Congress passed the Naval Act, ostensibly to deal with the Algerine pirates, but with the British threat obviously in mind. A navy was to be built, and the Navy would be one of the responsibilities of the Secretary of War. Furthermore, Congress voted to erect coastal fortifications and four arsenals for storing munitions. The War Department acquired sites for the forts through purchase or cession by the states, citizens of seaports contributed part of the necessary material and labor, and an act of May 9, 1794, added 764 rank and file to the corps of artillerists to man the forts. The total authorized artillery strength now stood at 56 officers and 992 men. Outright invasion by sea was unlikely, but a war against England, or against France, might bring raiding expeditions into American harbors. By the time of the War of 1812, twenty-four forts had been built along the Atlantic coast. They consisted mainly of earthwork and masonry redoubts in the star patterns associated with the name of Vauban and familiar to visitors to Fort McHenry, which was one of them. Altogether they mounted 750 guns in thirty-two batteries, but at least until the war there were never half enough artillerists to serve them.[2]

The easing of American relations with Great Britain, at least for the time being, through Jay's Treaty, did not please the French. Already they were annoyed by the Washington administration's rebuffs of such of their schemes for enlisting American help against England as those advanced by Citizen Edmond Gênet. Their imagination colored by the genuine Anglophilia of some Federalists, they now thought they saw in Jay's Treaty more than was really there: a secret agreement of partnership between England and her former colonies. Thus Jay's Treaty patched up relations with Great Britain at the expense of friendship with France, and the United States and France now drifted into increasing hostility, the arrogant mood of Revolutionary France encouraging the process. The French became the most notorious violators of American commercial rights, and some American crews landed in harsh French prisons. Three months after John Adams became President in 1797, he felt obliged to send Congress a grim message recommending another increase in coastal defenses, enlargement of the artillery and cavalry, and a new start toward creating a navy.

In 1795 Congress had voted to recruit the Legion of the United States to full strength, despite Wayne's success against the Indians and the consequent easing of western military problems. In response to Adams's message, on June 23, 1797, Congress appropriated an additional $115,000 for harbor fortifications, asking also that the states supplement this amount with moneys they owed the federal government. Meanwhile Adams had sent a special mission to France to try to clear the air as Jay had done in England, but the mission sailed into the notorious XYZ Affair. Having received from the French not negotiations but intolerable hauteur, Adams asked his cabinet their opinion on additional military proposals. His Secretary of War, James McHenry, was an amiable nonentity inherited from the last and less happy years of the Washington administration. Mc-Henry had nothing to suggest, as was his custom; but as was also his custom, he consulted Alexander Hamilton, and after receiving Hamilton's advice relayed it to the President as his own. Hamilton recommended a regular army of 20,000 men, supported by a provisional army of 30,000.[3]

Adams preferred to rely on the Navy, backed up by a moderate increase in the coastal defenses; he regarded Hamilton's army plan as utterly disproportionate to the problem. But Hamilton, not Adams, happened to be the real leader of much of the Federalist party, and Congress deliberated upon the Hamilton plan. It did not swallow the plan whole, but it appropriated $250,000 more for fortifications and $800,000 for arms; voted a three-year provisional army of 10,000 men whenever the President might choose to raise it; voted an increase in the strength of the existing four infantry regiments (the legionary organization having been abandoned for more conventional forms in 1796); authorized twelve new infantry regiments and six troops of dragoons for the emergency; and early in 1799 empowered the President to recruit still another 30,000 men if war should occur or invasion be threatened.[4]

Anthony Wayne was dead at fifty-one on the shores of Lake Erie, worn out by fevers, gout, and a restless military life. In the hours of patriotic enthusiasm that followed publication of the XYZ dispatches, everyone expected Washington to emerge from Mount Vernon to command the Army again. Adams did not disappoint the expectation; he commissioned Washington a lieutenant general. But Adams did not intend to cooperate also with the Federalist intention that Hamilton should be second in command, to lead the Army whenever the elderly Washington was absent. The President instead proposed that the major generals should be, in order of rank, Knox, Charles Cotesworth Pinckney, and Hamilton. The Hamiltonian faction then enlisted Washington's help, persuading him to threaten to decline his own services unless Hamilton became inspector general and his immediate subordinate. Adams had to acquiesce.[5]

The President had good reason to distrust Hamilton. Adams still believed that the Navy was the appropriate military instrument for the hour, and he concentrated on building it while doing almost nothing to fill up the Army. Inspector General Hamilton did all he could to override the President, attempting to recruit the new regiments and commissioning more than enough officers for the additional army of 30,000. This activity created so much bad feeling that John Quincy Adams later wrote: "The army was the first decisive symptom of a schism in the Federal Party itself, which accomplished its overthrow and that of the administration."[6]

Even if the Franco-American crisis had erupted in a formal declaration of war, a French invasion of North America was wholly unlikely. The French army was busy with European antagonists. Washington believed a French invasion beyond the realm of possibility. President Adams said: "At present there is no more prospect of seeing a French army here than there is in Heaven."[7] Why then did Hamilton pursue the inflation of the Army, so destructive to his and the President's party?

Hamilton hardly had in mind the invasion of Canada, for reasons apart from the impracticality of the idea. Invasion of Spanish America was a more real possibility—in fact Hamilton's bold imagination entertained the thought—but it was certainly a remote one. The most likely employment of a large army was neither defensive nor aggressive war but the cowing of the Republican party opposition. This idea has often been scoffed at, no doubt partly because political employment of the Army has come to seem so alien to American experience. But in 1798 American experience was new—and what other use for Hamilton's Army existed?

Hamilton was the most influential figure in the new Army, and it was no secret that the notion of political uses for the Army had long intrigued him. The Army—or rather, and more ironically, the militia —had already served such a purpose on a limited scale in suppressing the Whiskey Insurrection in 1794.

In western Pennsylvania, persistent opposition to the whiskey excises of 1791 and 1792 had culminated during the summer of 1794 in calls for armed resistance to the tax and the riotous burning of the house of John Neville, the district inspector of revenue. President Washington soon concluded that the western counties of Pennsylvania were in "open rebellion," and commissioners dispatched to the scene reported "that we have still much reason to apprehend, that the authority of the laws will not be *universally* and perfectly restored, without military coercion." A necessary preliminary to the use of federalized militia in this sort of contingency was notification by a federal judge of obstruction of the law. Such notification reached Washington on August 4. With the Legion of the United States occupied in Indian war to the westward, the President then called on the governors of Pennsylvania, New Jersey, Maryland, and Virginia for 12,950 militia.

The citizens' militia felt little eagerness to march against fellow citizens. Especially did Pennsylvanians feel reluctant, and in that state Governor Thomas Mifflin's halfhearted calls for volunteers bore so little effect that there had to be a militia draft. In the western counties the draft itself was ineffective, for there the militia were much involved in the insurrection. Furthermore, despite the provisions of the Militia Act of 1792, the Pennsylvania militia proved badly deficient in both arms and supplies. Nevertheless, the requisite Pennsylvania and New Jersey troops rendezvoused at Carlisle, and the Virginians and Marylanders assembled at Cumberland under "Light Horse Harry" Lee, now governor of Virginia. The President rode to Carlisle to take personal command, accompanied by Alexander Hamilton. Washington's column then followed Forbes's old route across the mountains; Lee's followed Braddock's. The mountains and the weather resisted the march, but nothing else did. Before the "Army of the Constitution," the Whiskey Insurrection evaporated.

The newly formed Jeffersonian Republican party felt inclined to denounce the use of the militia as the kind of armed tyranny they had feared from the Federalists. Historians since have bestowed considerable sympathy upon the whiskey rebels, on the grounds that the excise bore disproportionately upon western Pennsylvania and that military enforcement of civil law is distasteful and dangerous. Much of the sympathy for the whiskey rebels seems to be sympathy misplaced. The real root of their grievance was apparently a desire to pay no taxes at all, and in fact to respect no government. (Since the argument that they shipped much whiskey to distant markets appears specious, the tax could have borne disproportionately upon them only if they drank more than other sections.) And if the use of the military arm to enforce civil law is distasteful and dangerous, it is nevertheless preferable to lawlessness and anarchy. Twentieth-century Presidents of both parties have recognized that fact and have followed in George Washington's footsteps to federalize the militia when doing so was necessary to uphold the law.[8]

On the other hand, Hamilton's military activities during the later French crisis, as well as Madison's acquaintance with Hamilton, give reason to ponder Madison's reflections on the Whiskey Insurrection despite their partisan source:

If the insurrection had not been crushed in the [swift and easy] manner it was [Madison said], I have no doubt that a formidable attempt would have been made to establish the principle that a standing army was necessary for enforcing the laws.[9]

If Madison was unduly suspicious, Hamilton's friend Gouverneur Morris nonetheless wrote after Hamilton's death:

Our poor friend Hamilton bestrode his hobby to the great annoyance of his friends, and not without injury to himself. . . . He well knew that his favorite form [of government] was inadmissible, unless as the result of civil war; and I suspect that his belief in that which he called "an approaching crisis" arose from a conviction that the kind of government most suitable in his opinion, to this extensive country, could be established in no other way.[10]

Madison's notes indicate that in the Constitutional Convention Hamilton argued that force, "a coercion of laws or coercion of arms," is among "the great and essential principles necessary for the support of government." "A large portion of military force is absolutely necessary in large communities." In 1799 Hamilton told Jonathan Dayton that the government ought to be strengthened by a permanent army regardless of the course of foreign affairs and that to increase the central power the larger states ought to be reduced in size, a project that could scarcely have been accomplished except by force.[11]

Suspicion of the purposes of the Army of 1798 must be all the greater because of the partisan fashion in which its officers were chosen. No other American army has ever been so political in composition. Hamilton saw to it that Republicans were systematically excluded from commissions, especially from the higher ranks; often they were excluded from the Army altogether. President Adams would have liked to use some commissions as plums for tempting Republicans into a transfer of allegiance, but at the outset he agreed to defer to the lieutenant general in all military matters, and Washington left much to Hamilton. Secretary of War McHenry wrote:

In the present crisis of our affairs, and state of party in the country, it was, and is deemed important not to accept companies composed of disaffected persons who may for improper motives, be desirous to intrude themselves into the army, under the pretense of patriotic associations; and to guard against it, certificates have been, and are required, from prominent and known characters, or those whose virtues, talents, and usefulness have given them a weight and respectability in the community, setting forth the principles of the associates, those of the officers elect, especially, and that the company have complied with the conditions prescribed by law.[12]

Washington himself was in a partisan mood; a list of forty-nine appointees he suggested for important military posts included not a single Republican.[13]

President Adams feared that these activities would backfire:

Regiments are costly articles everywhere [he said], and more so in this country than any other under the sun. If this nation sees a great army to maintain without an enemy to fight, there may arise an enthusiasm that seems to be little foreseen.[14]

He meant, of course, an enthusiasm to remove the Federalists from office and bring the Republicans in. In one area of the country, albeit small, the Army and the taxes to support it did provoke an outbreak similar to the Whiskey Insurrection. John Fries led a rebellion against the window tax in eastern Pennsylvania, tax collections broke down, and Adams had to call again upon a portion of the Pennsylvania militia and to send 500 Regulars into the disaffected area as well. He then stood off Hamiltonian attempts to have a monitory example made of the Fries rebels through stern punishment, and he eventually pardoned Fries and all his associates.[15]

Just as firmly, Adams set his face against any larger political employment of the Army, and he also reopened negotiations with France as soon as it seemed honorably possible, in order to eliminate the pretext for the Hamiltonian military activities that he believed were harming rather than helping Federalism. The French were sufficiently preoccupied elsewhere that they dropped most of their arrogance toward the United States. Thus Adams was able to avert war, over the opposition of much of his party, and to put an end to the military buildup. The Hamiltonians cried that in doing so he had ruined Federalist chances for the election of 1800, but there seems good reason to believe that, in the face of the unpopularity of Hamilton's Army, he instead had done all that was possible to restore them.

But it was too late. In the election the Republicans carried Thomas Jefferson into the Presidency, playing upon fears of the Army as well as of the Alien and Sedition Acts. Actually, Adams's caution plus a quick collapse of popular fervor after the initial XYZ crisis had kept the Army of 1798 a shadow rather than a substance. None of the provisional regiments had been recruited, except for the officers, and little of the temporary Regular regiments.

It may be that by backfiring against their authors, the Federalist efforts to forge the Army into a political weapon assured the continuance in America of the post-Restoration English tradition of the nonpolitical army. At the same time the decline of the Federalist party opened an era of political consensus, limiting the opportunities for political maneuver by the Army. With the temporary forces discharged after May, 1800, by December 19, 1801, in the early Jeffersonian era, the Regular Army numbered 248 officers, 9 cadets, and 3,794 men, in four regiments of infantry, two regiments of artillerists and engineers, and two companies of light dragoons.[16]

The standing Army was not to be an instrument of politics; the approach of Thomas Jefferson to the Presidency suggested some doubt whether it would be retained as any kind of instrument at all. Jefferson had announced his hostility to standing armies on many occasions. When the Army had been increased for the Indian campaigns of the early 1790's, he had deplored the possibility that

every rag of an Indian depredation will . . . serve as a ground to raise troops with those who think a standing army and a public debt necessary for the happiness of the United States and we shall never be permitted to get rid of either.[17]

Of the distinction between the civil and the military, he said that it was "for the happiness of both to obliterate [it]." In his inaugural address he listed among the "principles [that] formed the bright constellation which has gone before us, and guided our steps through an age of revolution and reformation, . . . a well-disciplined militia, our best reliance in peace, and for the first moments of war, till regulars may relieve them . . ."[18]

As these statements suggested, Jefferson's military program was to rely almost wholly on the citizens' militia and by this means to abolish the distinction between the civil and the military. "None but an armed nation can dispense with a standing army," he said; "to keep ours armed and disciplined is, therefore, at all times important. . . ." But as this statement suggested in turn, Jefferson believed that the indispensable condition for abolishing the standing Army was to have the citizenry trained and organized in arms. The universal military obligation should be transformed from theory into practice, and with the citizens armed the natural aristocracy of talent and virtue would serve as their officers, for appropriate military training would become part of all collegiate education.[19]

This program, however, was one that Jefferson never discovered how to realize in practice, for the same reasons that Congress had been unwilling to write meaningful enforcement provisions into the Militia Act of 1792. And when Jefferson failed to realize any of his utopias, he habitually made a flexible adjustment to the world as he found it. Though he felt an optimistic confidence in the essential goodness and rationality of man, unlike some later Jeffersonians he did not anticipate an imminent disappearance of violence from human affairs. He believed the country needed an army. Lacking an armed and disciplined citizenry, it would have to settle for a standing army. So when Jefferson came into office, he reduced the standing Army, but he did not eliminate it; and when foreign affairs became more turbulent again, he did not hesitate to increase it. Under his chosen successor, James Madison, and through the actions of a Jeffersonian Congress, the Regular Army was destined to reach its highest authorized strength before the Spanish War of 1898.

If a standing army must be tolerated, however, Jefferson believed it should be as useful as possible, and not merely in military ways. If the Army was to be useful, it ought to have intelligent and educated officers. Therefore Jefferson not only retained the standing Army but added to it the institution that was to give it intellectual direction and doctrine, the United States Military Academy at West Point, founded under Jefferson's aegis by act of Congress of March 16, 1802.

Washington and Hamilton had long advocated a school for the education of officers, such as the schools beginning to appear in rudimentary form among the European military powers. Hamilton in fact had envisioned a hierarchy of military schools ascending from those concerned with technical and tactical studies to those dealing with the higher theory and philosophy of war; no such system was to exist anywhere until the Prussian *Kriegsakademie* was founded in 1810, and then it was to be decades until most other European nations established similar systems and nearly a century until the United States did so. Meanwhile Washington did establish at West Point in 1794 a school for the regiment of artillerists and engineers. He hoped to escape that dependence on foreigners for the technical skills of those branches that had characterized the Revolution and was still evident in the leadership of the West Point school by such officers of French origin as Stephen Rochefontaine and Louis de Tousard. President Adams sought the services of no less a figure than Benjamin Thompson, Count Rumford of Bavaria, to head and improve the school, and Secretary of War McHenry tried to persuade Congress to grant it formal authorization and financial support.[20]

Jefferson succeeded where McHenry had failed, although in keeping with the straitened circumstances of the Army and the federal budget, the Military Academy was made identical with the Corps of Engineers. The law of March 16, 1802, said of that corps:

> . . . the said corps . . . shall be stationed at West Point, in the state of New York, and shall constitute a military academy. . . .

. . . the principal engineer, and in his absence the next in rank, shall have the superintendence of the said military academy. . . .[21]

More than immediate financial economy was involved in these stipulations, however. The association with the Corps of Engineers comported with Jefferson's concept of an academy of more than military utility. If Jefferson had hoped that the citizen would become a soldier, he hoped also that the soldier would serve the nation as a citizen in peaceful pursuits. He appointed as superintendent Jonathan Williams, merchant, jurist, and most importantly a scientist, but not a professional soldier; Williams could best develop not the military but the scientific aspects of the West Point program. Under such auspices West Point was soon to develop as the preeminent seat of engineering and scientific education in America, the first American engineering school; but it was slow to develop as a school of the art of war.[22]

Under such auspices, too, it is not surprising that the principal distinctions of the Army in general during Jefferson's Presidency should have been earned in works of peace, not war. Jefferson set the soldiers to roadbuilding, on the Natchez Trace to the Southwest, and the officers to renewed treaty making with the Indians. Most important, he set the Army to exploring. Before the Louisiana Purchase, he persuaded Congress to underwrite an exploration up the Missouri River and to the Pacific. After the purchase, Captain Meriwether Lewis accepted the transfer of upper Louisiana for the United States at St. Louis and then marched out with Lieutenant William Clark, four sergeants, twenty-three privates, and Indian interpreters for the journey to the western ocean. The military discipline of the Lewis and Clark expedition played no small part in carrying it through thousands of hostile miles with only one casualty, and permitting it to become the climactic act in man's delineation of the face of North America. Meanwhile, Lieutenant Zebulon Montgomery Pike, searching with a lieutenant, a sergeant, two corporals, and sixteen privates for the headwaters of the Arkansas, ended by linking his name permanently with the Front Range of the Rocky Mountains and pointed the nation toward the next step of Manifest Destiny down the road to Santa Fe.[23]

But if Jefferson was indifferent neither to the issues of national defense nor to extending the usefulness of the Army, he was an indifferent administrator for whom the Army stood on the periphery of his concerns. The Regular Army did suffer decay during the Jefferson years, not from Presidential malice but from slipshod leadership. The Secretary of War was Henry Dearborn. Dearborn had left the practice of medicine to serve as a Revolutionary officer, and he had served with bravery, notably in Benedict Arnold's march up the Kennebec into Canada and as commander of the 1st New Hampshire at Freeman's Farm. But the former gallant young officer was now fifty and a plodding Republican politician, his most salient characteristic a devotion to governmental thrift surpassing Jefferson's and approaching niggardliness. He did nothing to compensate for Jefferson's preoccupation elsewhere.[24]

The ranking officer was Brigadier General James Wilkinson, whose name has become synonymous with deviousness and who defies biographical rehabilitation. Since the early 1790's Wilkinson had been regularly in the pay of Spain, earning his pensions with advice on how the Spanish might subvert the American West. By 1801 there was no longer much chance of achieving that object, and Wilkinson saw to it that his advice was misleading anyway; but his Spanish pensions and the oath of allegiance he had sworn to Spain hardly qualified him to exercise conscientious command in the American Army. When he tired of duping merely Spain and the United States, he went on to play games of deception with his fellow Kentuckians and with British officials in Canada as well. Eventually he consorted with Aaron Burr during the latter's mysterious visits to the West, until he decided that greater advantage lay in betraying Burr. Even on the staider level of land purchases and Mississippi River commercial investments, Wilkinson gave his energies mainly to his own pocketbook, only secondly to the Army.[25]

Winfield Scott, soon to become an officer of the Army, described his fellow officers as "swaggerers, dependents, decayed gentlemen and others fit for nothing else . . . totally unfit for any military purpose whatever." Too many of them were veterans of the Revolution grown far too elderly for their grades. The War Department had to concern itself with such problems as their tendency to turn the garden patches they cultivated adjacent to the forts into their principal source of livelihood and interest. The intellectual tone of the officer corps appears to be well illustrated by the case of Colonel Thomas Butler, a veteran of the Independence War who decided to make a major issue of Wilkinson's order, following the new fashions of the French Revolution, that hair must be cut short and especially that queues be removed. Bulter defied the order, stood trial before two courts-martial, and thirteen days before the order of the second court was to become effective, died with queue still conspicuous, reportedly being buried with the appendage protruding from the coffin. Such an officer corps devoted itself little to improving the soldierliness of the men, who continued to be recruited from unpromising ranks of society.[26]

West Point itself remained "a puny, rickety child," always on the verge of death. Williams resigned the superintendency in disgust in 1803, only to have Jefferson persuade him to return in 1805, for another frustrating tour of duty that ended with another disgusted resignation in 1812. Cadets varied in age too widely to permit consistent instructional policies—one of the first was only twelve—and the extent of their academic preparation varied even more. Quarters and buildings were inappropriate for a school; for a time the cadets shared the barracks of the enlisted men of an artillery company. Teaching equipment was scarce and good faculty members scarcer. One instructor was dismissed after fighting with a cadet. Besides the superintendent, the only faculty formally provided by Congress were a professor of mathematics and a professor of drawing and French. ". . . the military academy as it now stands," said Williams, "is a foundling, barely existing among the mountains, and nurtured at a distance out of sight, and almost unknown to its legitimate parents. . . ."[27]

Since the close of the quasi-war with France and the decline of Hamilton's influence, a greater share of the responsibility for Army supply had returned to the War Department from the Treasury. Purchases of all supplies except subsistence, however, remained with a purveyor of public supplies in the latter department. He contracted for all clothing, shoes, military stores and equipage, and medicine and hospital stores, and then turned them over to a superintendent of military stores in the War Department, who held them until issue. Usually both these officers centralized their purchasing and storage activities in Philadelphia. For some articles there was competitive bidding, while for others the purveyor preferred to rely on known contractors; in either case inspection for quality appears to have been consistently lax. Uniforms were fashioned by Philadelphia tailors to whom the purveyor distributed cloth for the purpose. Barracks and quarters for the Army were constructed by a Quartermaster's Department. Subsistence was still procured by Robert Morris's contract system, with responsibility for feeding the troops in a given area assigned to the lowest bidder. Sometimes the bids were so low that they obviously would not permit both adequate subsistence and a return for the contractor, so just as obviously the contractors skimped and the soldiers suffered. Anthony Wayne had insisted upon "the absolute necessity of some [more] effectual & certain mode of supplying the Army than that of private Contract," but the system persisted. With the impediments to transportation among scattered outposts in a large, road-poor country added to a weak supply organization, the Army endured continual shortages of food, clothing, and shelter, and sometimes the officers described the living conditions of the men as "inhuman."[28]

The initial Jeffersonian reductions in the Regular Army fell disproportionately upon the officer corps. For a time the enlisted strength rose slightly, to 3,794 in December, 1801, before declining by June, 1802, to 3,040. In the same period the number of officers fell from 248 to 172. This reduction was caused mainly by reorganization under the law of March 16, 1802, which reduced the number of infantry regiments from four to two, reduced the artillery to one regiment, and eliminated cavalry altogether. The infantry regiments had been organized as single battalions for tactical purposes since the disbanding of the Legion; they would now consist of ten companies of four officers and seventy-six men each. The artillery regiment would be a large formation of four battalions, each of five companies of five officers and seventy-six men.[29]

However distasteful it was to him, Jefferson had to take increased interest in the Army after the intensification of England's war with France, the latter now led by Napoleon, once more stepped up the interference of both powers with American shipping. The President was able to avert war over the nasty *Chesapeake-Leopard* incident in 1807, but the incident led directly to his embargo policy. By now it was evident that the militia could contribute little in a sudden emergency. The states had neglected to train and make ready the battalions and divisions enrolled under the act of 1792, and a Congressional enactment of 1803 requiring them to make periodic reports on the condition of their militias failed to prod them enough. So Jefferson recommended, and on April 12, 1808, Congress authorized, a virtual tripling of the Regular establishment, to nearly 10,000 men. There were to be five new infantry regiments, one of riflemen, one of light—that is, unusually mobile—artillery, and one of light dragoons. New funds were also voted to hasten the coastal fortifications. To prod again and this time to assist the states with their militias, an annual appropriation of $200,000 was authorized for the purchase of arms and equipment, to be distributed among the states and within each state expended as the legislature might provide.[30]

Somewhat embarrassingly, the embargo policy, through which Jefferson hoped to assert American interests and yet avoid having to send the Army to fight, now drove the administration into repeating the sort of domestic employment of armed force that the Jeffersonians had condemned when the Federalists practiced it during the Fries and Whiskey Insurrections. Jefferson had held in 1794 that grand juries and not armed force were the proper means for dealing with the whiskey rebels. But the embargo provoked resistance beyond the ready capacity of civil officers and courts to overcome, and with characteristic pragmatism Jefferson called out the militia. He employed it with less restraint than Washington.

Resistance to the embargo was especially strong in the Lake Champlain area, and on April 19, 1808, Jefferson proclaimed the area in a condition of insurrection and implored all civil and military authorities to quell disturbances. The local authorities were unwilling to respond, and the proclamation became an awkward nullity. Thereupon, in August, the President attempted to induce the governor of New York to do the job of mustering the militia to police the area, upon assurance that the federal government would reimburse the state. With some reluctance the governor complied. To ensure against further difficulties, however, Jefferson sought a new enforcement act which would "invest the Executive with the most arbitrary powers and sufficient force to carry the embargo into effect." Congress produced a law permitting calls upon the militia with little formality. Secretary of the Treasury Albert Gallatin believed that the militia could now be turned out on the mere call of federal district revenue commissioners. Jefferson at first held that the calls should at least be made through the governors, but at the first crisis he shifted to Gallatin's view, and invoked it. Even when he did attempt to continue working through the governors, he so enmeshed them in federal law enforcement that the Massachusetts legislature rebuked the governor of that state for cooperating on Jefferson's terms. Occasionally, Jefferson also used Regulars in a police capacity to enforce the embargo. As usual, he valued the achievement of practical ends more than theoretical consistency.[31]

During this period of renewed military interests there were two notable innovations in the Regular Army, of which perversely the less fortunate was destined for a long life and the more promising was soon canceled. In 1806 the Army began awarding brevet rank. Borrowed from the British service, brevet rank was honorary rank awarded to an officer for meritorious conduct. But the practical significance of brevet rank was not clear and never became so. The articles of war now prescribed that brevet rank had no practical effect in its holder's own organization, but that brevet rank might be recognized as real rank when the officer was assigned to provisional formations made up of several regiments, or to detachments composed of various corps (that is, arms of the service), or in courts-martial, or "on other occasions." The consequent confusion increased with the growth of the Army. It got utterly out of hand when the Civil War caused a promiscuous scattering of brevets, and captains who were brevet generals turned up commanding majors and colonels. In the early 1870's, brevets were at last put on the way to extinction by permitting only actual rank to be referred to in orders and prohibiting the wearing of brevet uniforms. Thereafter, brevets ceased to be awarded and medals gradually replaced them as means of conferring honor. But for more than half a century the Army had to live with the perplexing brevet system.[32]

The happier experiment opened in 1808. Napoleon then commanded the attention of the whole European military world. Napoleon was first of all an artillerist, and much of the power of his armies came from his employment and extension of certain artillery reforms first introduced in the French army during the eighteenth century by Jean Baptiste Vaquette de Gribeauval. Gribeauval had lightened the pieces and standardized a relatively small number of calibers, mounted the cannoneers on horses or the gun carriages, and replaced with soldiers the civilians who had hitherto driven animal teams drawing guns. Compared with the artillery of the past, slow-moving and on the battlefield wrestled into position by hand, Gribeauval's artillery was so rapid in motion and maneuverable as to be almost revolutionary. Napoleon's horse-drawn guns habitually raced to the front of his battle lines, standing just out of effective range of the enemy's musketry to work him over and soften him, often fatally, for the French assault to follow.

American artillery officers became aware of the Napoleonic system and urged its introduction into their service. The act of April 12, 1808, included a regiment of light artillery in its increases of the Army. Captain George Peter's company of the new regiment was issued sufficient horses to mount itself and thus to become the first American battery of light artillery in the new Napoleonic style. On July 4, 1808, Peter's company staged an impressive demonstration for Congress, and it soon conducted a route march from Baltimore to Washington at the then remarkable speed of six miles an hour. Unfortunately, the experiment proved abortive. After Jefferson left office, President Madison's Secretary of War decided the horses were a waste of money and sold them. No other company of the Regiment of Light Artillery was mounted before the War of 1812; during the war a few were, but only briefly.[33]

The fate of Peter's company was typical of the Madison administration during the years before the war. James Madison was a man less capable of decisive action than Jefferson and perhaps more wedded to theory. By the time Madison assumed the Presidency in 1809, it was apparent that domestic opposition and little evident effect abroad would compel the repeal of the embargo. Though the Republican party still had a few additional economic weapons in its arsenal, the likelihood of having to use the Army to defend American interests against Great Britain became greater than before. But one senses in the Madison administration a stronger nostalgia for the old Jeffersonian dream of eliminating the distinction between civil and military than in the practical President Jefferson himself, and the early military policy of Madison therefore proved more ambivalent than Jefferson's. On the one hand, after the collapse of the Erskine Agreement and a hardening of British policy early in 1810, Madison recommended filling the Regular regiments, recruiting 20,000 volunteers, and extending an earlier law to require the states to arm and equip 100,000 militia. On the other hand, Madison allowed Gallatin to precede these requests with a budget in which the federal deficit was to be eliminated by cutting military and naval expenditures in half, with estimates based on an average of the six *lowest* years of military expenditures under Jefferson. Not surprisingly, Madison's and Gallatin's recommendations canceled each other out, so that Congress simply drifted. By 1812 the Army stood not near its authorized 10,000 but at 6,744 men.[34]

Administration of the military establishment remained as indifferent as under Jefferson, or worse. The new Secretary of War, William Eustis, like Dearborn a former physician, was a less capable man than Dearborn and perhaps even more singlemindedly devoted to thrift. In 1808 and 1809 Wade Hampton of South Carolina and Peter Gansevoort of New York joined James Wilkinson as brigadier generals; their honesty was greater than Wilkinson's but their ability and energy less.[35]

On the eve of war the administration and Congress cooperated to restore some of the staff offices which had had only occasional existence since the Revolution, especially those of quartermaster general and commissary general of purchases. But the law that did so also assured continued difficulties in the management of supply by creating a nearly complete conflict of jurisdictions. The quartermaster general was "to purchase military stores, camp equipage and other articles requisite for the troops." At the same time the commissary general of purchases was "to conduct the procuring and providing of all arms, military stores, clothing, and generally all articles of supply requisite for the military service of the United States." To compound the confusion, there was also established an Ordnance Department, with a commissary general of ordnance. The peacetime duty of this department involved supervising the construction of ordnance carriages and apparatus, inspection of ordnance, and keeping records of ordnance on hand. These duties did not impinge upon those of the other supply officers, but in wartime the Ordnance Department was able to move into the purchasing of ordnance and ammunition, thus encroaching upon the territory of both the quartermaster general and the commissary general of purchases. Meanwhile Congress failed to approve administration requests for increases in the clerical assistance of the War Office itself.[36]

Slothful and negligent management under Madison permitted one of the Army's worst peacetime disasters of any era, the Terre aux Boeufs tragedy of 1809–10. Early in 1809 the increasing peril of war led the Jefferson administration to decide to strengthen the defenses of New Orleans. Wilkinson was sent to command there, with about 2,000 troops. As early as mid-April, soon after the change of administration in Washington, over 500 of Wilkinson's men were on sick call, evidently the result of lax camp sanitation in a semitropical climate plus the effects of the well-known vices of the Creole City. The new Secretary of War was sufficiently troubled by the first reports he read from New Orleans that he encouraged Wilkinson to move his force outside the city, preferably to the higher, healthier ground upriver at Fort Adams or Natchez. Wilkinson, however, was reluctant to leave, since he had business interests in the city and a full social life that included a growing interest in one of New Orleans's Creole belles. When after much delay he agreed to move the troops at all, they marched not upriver but downriver to a place called Terre aux Boeufs. Here the Army was to pay $630.34 rent for its campground for three months, a high amount considering that the camp had to be redeemed from jungle and swamp.

The Army arrived on June 9 to spend the hot months. When rains came, the river rose, drainage ditches overflowed, and the area became a mass of mud. Filth could not be disposed of properly, and it littered the camp. The available tents leaked. Mosquitoes swarmed. Food turned bad, and the men ate sour bread alive with worms and bugs, rancid pork, and noisome beef, all washed down with muddy river water or cheap whiskey. Wilkinson was in collusion with the contractor, who could therefore complacently order his agents to disguise the condition of flour when it became unfit for use by mixing it with a bit of sweet flour. The sick list grew more rapidly than in New Orleans. Medicines were insufficient, especially since Dearborn had ordered the military agent at New Orleans to allow no expenditure greater than fifty dollars unless it had been previously authorized by Washington, and Eustis took a conservative view of admissible charges. Especially the new Secretary frowned on such extravagances as fresh fruit for the sick. But Eustis did feel troubled, and on June 22 he gave an outright order to move to higher ground. Still, Wilkinson remained busy in the city and then became sick himself, and the move did not begin until September 10. By then it was an army of invalids that dragged itself upriver, with boats only for the most desperately sick. Between February, 1809, and January, 1810, a force of 2,036 enlisted men suffered over 1,000 losses, including 166 desertions and the rest deaths. Some 40 officers resigned or died.[37]

Even short of a Terre aux Boeufs, the available information on the Army at the end of the century's first decade suggests an unhappy Army, continually on the verge of demoralization. It is significant that even so promising a young officer as Winfield Scott—who had joined during the excitement after the *Chesapeake-Leopard* affair—withheld pay from his men, at least carelessly if not from worse motives, and also got himself in trouble by intemperately damning his commanding officer, Wilkinson, as a traitor, liar, and scoundrel. Scott's epithets may have been accurate, but it was still destructive of discipline for him to mouth them indiscriminately. He faced a court-martial for both his offenses and was found guilty of both, being sentenced to loss of all rank, pay, and emoluments for a year.[38]

Partly the troubles of the Army were no doubt the natural and virtually inevitable trials of a military organization in a nation whose general aspect was one of individualism and social incoherence so great—an invertebrate society, in Allan Nevins's phrase—as to have been almost incompatible with an efficient war office. Partly the Army's troubles were not inevitable but the results of mere lack of interest on the part of the Republican administrations; despite the handicaps of an invertebrate society the Treasury Department was well managed by Gallatin during most of the time when the War Department was poorly managed by Dearborn and Eustis. It may be argued—as the government's military policy argued by implication —that there existed far more important calls upon the national energies and resources than those of the Army, and that the War Department deserved a peripheral place. But as long as the Napoleonic wars lasted, this argument was vitiated by the inescapable tug toward war with England, such a war being sure to involve land combat on the Canadian border. Furthermore, during the Madison administration, military policy became increasingly inconsistent with foreign policy. Though it neglected the Army, the Madison administration, whether of its own volition or pushed by the Congressional War Hawks or both, hardened its policy toward Great Britain and added momentum to the already existing drift toward war. The United States in 1811 was hardly a military nation, but in foreign policy it was nevertheless a warlike one.

Whatever their causes, the Army's deficiencies were too great to be corrected hastily when war became imminent and President and Congress abruptly thought to restore harmony between military and foreign policy. It was late 1811 when Madison felt obliged to discard his antimilitary sentiments and to ask again for enlargement of the Army. He asked that the existing regiments be filled, that 10,000 men be enlisted in new regiments, and that the Regulars be reinforced by 50,000 federal volunteers. Congress voted 30,000 volunteers and authorized raising the Regular Army to 25,000, including thirteen new regiments of all arms. Presumably the volunteers were to be secured largely by enlisting existing volunteer militia organizations into federal service, much as the Continental Army had been raised, since the states were to choose the officers of the volunteer regiments. Oddly, in view of growing infatuation with the thought of invading Canada, the volunteers were to have the status of militia as far as foreign service was concerned, and thus presumably were to be in-eligible for invasion duty. To finance the volunteer regiments, Con-gress appropriated not the $3,000,000 that Madison wanted but $1,000,000. The whole Congressional package suggested a continu-ing casualness of approach to military questions.[39]

Such words as casual and indifferent sum up the military policy of the Republican party under Jefferson and Madison. The Federalists had conducted military matters more purposefully, but their interest in the Army was tainted by the inclination of some of them to use it as a bludgeon against domestic political rivals. Once the Republicans had squelched that menace, they substituted no consistent military policy of their own. Jefferson proposed a nation in arms, but his own Congress showed no interest in providing the "well-disciplined mili-tia" that he thought indispensable if professional soldiers were to be dispensed with. Thereupon Jefferson had to reconcile himself to maintaining the Regular Army he had inherited from the Federalists. But he gave the Army none of his enthusiasm, and his lieutenants and his successor were less interested in improving it—or more dogmatically hostile to it—than he.

So in 1812 the nation faced a new war with a central government of more ample powers than in the Revolution but with little more existing military strength or military administrative machinery than in 1775. The Regular Army of something under 7,000 was not only small but dispersed in scattered garrisons. Its senior officers were men of little talent. The older regiments were still commanded by aging Revolutionary veterans; the regiments raised since 1808 were officered largely by well-connected men drawn from civil life. Only seventy-one West Point graduates were available. The officers seem to have been lax in training their men, and the dispersion of units was such that few battalion exercises could have been possible. Sup-ply departments and staff were scarcely adequate for peacetime needs. Moreover, any advantage this Regular Army represented in the military situation of 1812 over 1775 was largely canceled out by the tendency if not necessity to continue scattering it across the long Canadian border and Indian frontier and along a coastline that now reached to the mouth of the Mississippi. A sustained war effort would again have to be built, as in the Revolution, upon volunteer militia companies and the amorphous common militia behind them.

SEVEN

War, Nationalism, and the Army:
1812-21

The battle of Chippawa was the only occasion during the war when equal bodies of regular troops met face to face, in extended lines on an open plain in broad daylight, without advantage of position; and never again after that combat was an army of American regulars beaten by British troops. Small as the affair was, and unimportant in military results, it gave to the United States army a character and pride it had never before possessed.

—Henry Adams[1]

THE INFORMAL and unsystematic qualities of Republican military policy persisted even into war itself. The "invertebrate society" fought from 1812 to 1815 an inchoate, almost planless kind of war. This manner of war making carried the nation to a series of humiliating defeats, including the loss and destruction by fire of the Capitol itself. Amidst the reverses and chaos, however, the training program of a few exceptional Regular Army officers, combined with the fortunes of war and the valor of a small body of American infantrymen, permitted a few Regular Army regiments to win uncommon distinction for themselves and to bestow upon the whole Regular Army an unaccustomed luster. These events, the war's dramatization of military deficiencies, contrasted to the exceptional discipline and bravery of part of the Regular Army, were to combine after the war with an awakened American nationalism, galvanized by hardship and battle, to open a new era in the history of the Army. It became possible for Secretary of War John C. Calhoun to offer in 1820 proposals at which no prewar Secretary could have hinted: that the citizens' militia should be relegated to the background and to peripheral military roles and that American military policy should stand foremost and unquestionably upon the Regular Army.

When Congress voted for war with Great Britain on June 18, 1812, the authorized strength of the Regular Army consisted of seventeen regiments of infantry, four of artillery, two of dragoons, one of riflemen, and a Corps of Engineers of 24 officers, 250 cadets, and 94 enlisted men in a company of bombardiers, sappers, and miners. Except for seven infantry regiments, two of artillery, one of dragoons, and part of the Corps of Engineers, these formations had been authorized too recently to have achieved much substance. Their tables of organization were extraordinarily diverse, infantry regiments ranging from ten to eighteen companies. Only after war began, on June 23, 1812, did Congress standardize the organizations, fixing the infantry regiments at ten companies of ninety privates each, and in the process of shrinking some of them raising the total number of infantry regiments to twenty-five.[2]

The aggregate strength of the Regulars authorized at the time the war began was 35,603. In addition Congress had voted the 30,000 federal volunteers, and on April 10 it had asked the governors to have 80,000 militia ready to respond to a federal call. The government might well have regarded such numbers as ample, at least for the first campaigns, whatever their various conditions of preparation, since there were fewer than 5,000 British troops in Canada, most of the British army was needed against Napoleon, and the Canadian militia was at least as uncertain a quantity as the American citizen soldiery —some Americans hoped they would prove disloyal to the Crown— and much smaller in numbers.

Unhappily, the authorized strengths could not be attained. Governors responded erratically to calls for militia. Perhaps the most fruitful plan of recruitment would have been to concentrate on seeking organized companies of volunteer militia to come forward as federal volunteers. This method had initially built the Continental Army, and it would have drawn on partially ready formations of men with some taste for arms. In the course of the year 30,000 volunteer militia may actually have entered federal service, but this program was treated rather offhandedly. The War Department emphasized filling the Regular Army. Such an approach was paradoxical in a Republican administration, but the Republicans were dedicated to strict construction of the Constitution, and the law stipulating that federal volunteers retained the status of militia pointed to the constitutional questionability of militia service outside the United States. So Congress approved enlistment bounties totaling forty dollars for

Regular recruits, plus three months' pay in advance and 160 acres of land. Despite these inducements the Regular Army grew only to about 15,000 by the end of 1812.[3]

Good leadership might still have accomplished something substantial in the first military project of the war, the invasion of Canada. But good leadership did not appear. James Madison had little taste or ability for the role of wartime Commander in Chief. Secretary Eustis failed also to provide effective direction. It was typical of his performance that on the day war was declared, he ordered Brigadier General William Hull to hurry from Dayton to take command at Detroit but neglected to inform him that war had begun. Hull's consequent carelessness allowed the British to take the first trick on the Northwest frontier, the capture of a hospital schooner with the roster of Hull's forces. Similarly, for weeks Eustis allowed Major General Henry Dearborn to command on the northern frontier without correcting Dearborn's misapprehension that his sector extended westward no farther than the Niagara and that Hull at Detroit was independent of him.

To fill the highest professional ranks, Madison had to choose between young men of little or no experience or proven military skill and aged Revolutionary veterans. He chose the latter. Henry Dearborn, the former Secretary of War, and Thomas Pinckney of South Carolina, a veteran of the southern campaigns of the Revolution, received the two major generalships authorized by Congress on the eve of war, and the roster of newly authorized brigadiers was completed with men who brought the average age of all general officers to sixty years. None of the generals served as professional commander of the whole Army. Instead, Secretary Eustis sought to coordinate nine military districts with a general officer over each.[4]

Supply was as badly managed as the conflicts of authority recently decreed by Congress had made likely. The quartermaster general at the beginning of the war was Brigadier General Morgan Lewis, another veteran of the Revolution, who would have preferred a line command and did not strenuously exert himself. He was unwilling to take responsibility, and he burdened the Secretary of War with requests for instructions on matters he should have decided for himself. His subordinates in turn complained of lack of instructions from him. The district commanders habitually complained of shortages of everything, including horses and wagons with which to transport anything else they might need, and of bad quality when materials did arrive. In the month of October, Regulars on the Canadian border had not yet received winter clothing and were standing sentry in growing storms and cold still clad in linen. Throughout the war subsistence was still to come from private contractors, with all the evils attendant upon that method. The diet was an unvarying one, featuring fried meats with little to balance them.[5]

Despite the handicaps of the district system, Dearborn might have coordinated movements on the Canadian border if he had bothered to inquire into the extent of his authority, if Eustis had informed him of it promptly, or if he had shown a reasonable amount of energy. None of these things happened, and so there occurred three uncoordinated attempts at invasion, all of which failed. Hull ventured into Canada from Detroit but soon lost his nerve, retreated, and ended up besieged in Detroit and finally surrendering that place. Brigadier Generals Stephen Van Rensselaer and Alexander Smythe launched inept punches across the Niagara River. Late in the year Dearborn himself finally began moving down Lake Champlain toward Montreal, where a concentrated effort might have broken enemy communications with everything in Canada farther west. But he fell back when militia in his mixed command refused to cross the international border. Such refusals had also marked the Niagara campaign, and so the misgivings that probably accounted for the stress on Regular Army recruiting were realized.[6]

The historic evolution of the citizens' militia, after all, was as a home defense force, and the Constitution had heeded that fact by stipulating that Congress might "provide for calling forth the militia to execute the laws of the union, suppress insurrections and repel invasions." The Constitution provided no clear sanction for militia to become invaders themselves. By the next foreign war, the government would skirt part of the problem by regarding organized militia companies that had volunteered themselves for federal service not as militia but as forces raised under the more general authority to raise and support armies. But for the present the constitutional scruples of the administration were too great and its public support too uncertain to force into Canada those citizen soldiers who chose to balk. And though part of the problem could be skirted, the question whether men called into federal service under the militia clause could somehow be dispatched outside the country was to cloud the status of the militia for more than a century.

The failures of 1812 seemed to demand a new recruiting effort, and in January, 1813, Congress voted to increase the total of infantry regiments to forty-four. To tap the best source of recruits and arrange a limited escape from the constitutional problem, it invited members of volunteer militia organizations to join the Regular Army for one year. The authorized strength of the Regular Army was now 57,351, but again the actual turnout was disappointing. It is doubtful that more than 20,000 Regulars were on the muster rolls by the end of 1813.[7]

That year brought no spectacular achievements in the field, but the naval victory of Lake Erie did secure the Northwest against British counterinvasion and made possible the success of a new major general, William Henry Harrison, in a limited probe into Canada from recaptured Detroit to the Thames River. The approach of the next campaigning season, however, carried ominous possibilities. Napoleon's fortunes declined rapidly after his defeat at Leipzig in October, 1813, and his fall from power seemed imminent for some months before he abdicated in April, 1814. The British would now be able to spare for the war in America veterans of the Duke of Wellington's campaigns. In fact the British government planned to invade the United States from three points, Niagara, Lake Champlain, and New Orleans, while extending and tightening the naval blockade and raiding along the Atlantic coast.

So many unfilled regiments existed in the American Army that there was little to be gained by authorizing still more. Congress contented itself with voting for a regiment of "sea fencibles" for coastal defense in July, 1813, and for three additional regiments of riflemen in February, 1814. The aggregate Regular Army authorization then stood at 62,274, the highest point it was to reach until 1898. But the problem was still recruitment. In this regard, the increase in British resources proved a partial blessing. Until now recruitment had suffered not only from all the customary impediments to men's leaving their homes for war and danger, but also from a decidedly mixed popular support for an aggressive war of invasion against Canada. But men who would not take arms to invade Canada would do so when British redcoats appeared again as invaders in their own country, and by September the Regular Army climbed to about 35,000. About an equal number of men took the field in volunteer militia organizations on extended duty, so that late in the year the federal government and the states together could muster nearly 70,000 men in active service. This number was exclusive of those men from the volunteer and common militias who served for short periods against British raids and invasions in their own districts and who may have numbered in the hundreds of thousands.[8]

By 1814 the war effort was receiving somewhat better leadership, and the improvements in both leadership and recruitment, though modest, proved sufficient to turn back British invasion and to end the war, not with tangible gains for the United States, but with enough of a show of military prowess to earn American nationhood a new respect in both foreign and American eyes.

Secretary of War Eustis resigned under well-deserved Congressional fire in December, 1812. Madison's selection to replace him was John Armstrong, an eccentric choice but one that brought some benefits. Armstrong's principal fame, although he had served gallantly at Trenton and Princeton in the Revolution, was as Horatio Gates's aide who reputedly wrote the Newburgh Addresses. After the Revolution he studied law and followed an erratic political course as a Federalist, a protégé of the Livingston family of New York by virtue of marriage to the sister of Robert R. and Edward Livingston, a George Clinton Republican, a DeWitt Clinton Republican, an unexpected supporter of Madison in the election of 1812, and then a harsh critic of the administration's war effort. Madison tried to silence the critic with a grant of responsibility. Much of Armstrong's energy as War Secretary proved to be expended in intrigues to replace the Virginia Dynasty with a Pennsylvania–New York dynasty headed by himself.

To further his ambitions he also succumbed to the temptation posed by the lack of a professional commander of the Army and took the field himself. In 1813 he accompanied James Wilkinson and Wade Hampton in a march on Canada from Lake Ontario down the St. Lawrence. His presence not only signaled his inability to perceive the proper functions of his office but also worked harm in Canada. He confused the lines of command, and when he recognized that Wilkinson and Hampton were about to botch the campaign—with his help—he withdrew into the background to escape blame for failure.

Armstrong took the field still again when a British force landed from the Chesapeake and approached Washington in August, 1814. The Secretary had persistently scoffed at the possibility that the enemy might try to seize the capital and had failed to do much to forestall such a move. A wholly inadequate army of seamen, marines, and both organized and common militia had to be patched together for the occasion, and Armstrong was present when this command stood across the path of the British advance at Bladensburg. Also present were President Madison and Secretary of State James Monroe, Madison merely observing, Monroe disposing troops without authority and contributing to a situation in which three American battle lines were so deployed as to be incapable of supporting each other. The Americans were mainly citizens enrolled in common militia units that had not trained regularly since the passing of the need for Indian defense. Naturally, the British walked over them and on into the capital. Armstrong with partial justice became the scapegoat, and Madison replaced him with the busy Mr. Monroe.[9]

Meanwhile the good that had come of Armstrong's tenure had been in the form of institutional improvements in the War Department and the Secretary's nominations for new generalships. Armstrong did much to secure from Congress a law of March 3, 1813, which gave the Secretary of War the assistance of a General Staff. That term now appeared for the first time in American legislation, and the General Staff was established substantially as it was to remain for nearly a century. It was not a general staff in the present sense. Rather, Congress established the War Department administrative offices which in modern terminology would become the special staff. But the improvement over a condition in which the Secretary of War's principal assistance came from a few clerks was crucial. The Secretary could henceforth call upon an adjutant and inspector general with two assistants, the inspector general and the assistant adjutant general; a quartermaster general; a commissary general of ordnance together with two deputies and an assistant; a paymaster; and an assistant topographical engineer. These officials, unlike previous holders of some of the same titles, were expected to settle in Washington and act as the permanent management staff of the War Department.[10]

Also commendable was Armstrong's 1813 list of promotions. Armstrong began the task of weeding out elderly misfits and replacing them with younger officers proven during the first campaigns. The 1813 list still included three old men of doubtful quality among the four new major generals, but their influence made them difficult to escape: James Wilkinson, William Henry Harrison, Wade Hampton, and Morgan Lewis. The seven new brigadiers were mainly youthful. They included the explorer Zebulon Pike, who was showing himself adept as a warrior but whose career was about to end with tragic abruptness in the explosion of a powder magazine when an American force entered the Canadian capital of York. Armstrong's 1814 list was better still. It brought the average age of general officers down to thirty-six, twenty-four years lower than it had been when the war began. George Izard, thirty-nine, became the senior major general in active service; he was a promising officer who had studied in British, French, and German military schools. Somehow Izard never quite fulfilled his promise, but the major generals of 1814 also included Jacob Brown and Andrew Jackson. Among the new brigadiers was Winfield Scott. These three would have been useful leaders in any army, and they gave the American Army in the closing campaigns of the war far better direction than prewar neglect made it reasonable to anticipate. Significantly, only one of them was a product of the prewar officer corps, and in its atmosphere he had drifted to court-martial and the verge of ruin. Brown and Jackson both came from the volunteer militia.[11]

Improvements in supply in 1813 and 1814 did not equal those in leadership. For the enlarged and newly defined post of quartermaster general in March, 1813, Armstrong replaced Morgan Lewis with Brigadier General Robert Swartwout, formerly a colonel of New York militia. Swartwout was probably an abler man than Lewis, but the preparations for the year's campaign were well advanced, or should have been, before he could take charge effectively. Through the rest of the war, furthermore, he was hampered by the increasing financial embarrassment of the Treasury. Many of the supply problems were insoluble. The arena of war was vast, from New Orleans to Plattsburg, and communications were still primitive. Like the Regular Army generally, Swartwout concentrated on the Canadian border and neglected the Southern Department. The American clothing industry was still an infant despite forced-draft growth under embargoes and war, and the quality of uniforms—or more accurately, whatever was supplied in lieu of uniforms—remained low. Shoes were described as made of leather "as porous as Sponge." Jacob Brown said that the reason why five men died of disease for each one who fell in battle was a policy that assumed the soldier "could bear all the vicissitudes of climate and weather without requiring either quarters or covering."[12]

Since the Revolution the federal government had nurtured an arms industry. It manufactured small arms, ammunition, and gun carriages in its own arsenals and foundries while acquiring supplementary materials by contract, the most notable contractor having been Eli Whitney. The federally supported arms industry did much to advance the precision manufacture of interchangeable parts, so immensely important for the American future. Cannons were contracted for from private manufacturers, who were assured of continued government support in return for satisfactory work. By these means sufficient stocks had been accumulated before the war and sufficient production was possible to prevent any severe shortages of weapons from hampering the fighting. Quality of weapons, however, did not match quantity. The guns varied greatly. A captain inspecting the 12th Infantry in the autumn of 1812 said that the muskets were good, though some were out of repair and neither gun slings nor enough tools to keep them in repair had been supplied. But another inspector during the same season found arms in "infamously bad order." Some bad powder was supplied, and sometimes troops had to be detailed to make their own cartridges.[13]

The adversities of 1814 lessened but did not destroy the popular indifference which hampered raising and supporting troops in many areas, and still less did they destroy the outright hostility of much of

New England. New England's opposition to Mr. Madison's war approached treason in several ways, and especially it denied the mobilization of most of New England's militia through most of the war. On June 12, 1812, Madison requested the New England governors to order into federal service as many men as General Dearborn of the Northern Department deemed necessary for the defense of the coast. Governor Caleb Strong of Massachusetts responded with silence and inaction. Governor Roger Griswold of Connecticut at first offered compliance, then took to a sickbed, then refused troops by citing the constitutional argument on which New England thereafter came to rely.

The relevant passage of the Constitution was again the one granting Congress power "To provide for calling forth the militia to execute the laws of the union, suppress insurrections and repel invasions." The Militia Act of 1792 as amended in 1795 sought to give effect to this provision by authorizing the President to make calls in "imminent danger of invasion." Connecticut now asserted that militia could not lawfully be offered since the state officials knew of no declaration by the President that an invasion had taken place. Secretary Eustis replied that the President declared that an imminent danger of invasion existed. Governor Griswold in turn argued that war was not invasion and that the presence of a hostile fleet off the coast represented only "a slight danger of invasion, which the Constitution could not contemplate."

Rhode Island, New Hampshire, and Vermont followed Connecticut's line. The political leaders of New England also discouraged recruiting and enlistments for the Regular Army, lest their state policies be undermined by patriotic individuals. When Madison managed to prod Governor Strong at least into making a statement, Strong sought the opinion of the Massachusetts Supreme Court and secured from its three Federalist judges the observation that "no power is given to the President, or to the Congress" to determine that either invasion or insurrection exists; "the decision must be that of the commander in chief of state militia." The federal government was still too weak to find an adequate response to this phalanx of resistance.[14]

In time Massachusetts did suffer invasion, when the British decided to detach the eastern part of the District of Maine and in 1814 descended upon Eastport and Castine, announcing the annexation of the Passamaquoddy and Penobscot Bay areas to the British Crown. Some towns on Cape Cod fell under contribution to British ships. Governor Strong now wanted to use the state's armed force, and the legislature authorized him to recruit 10,000 volunteers and arrange a loan of $1,000,000. The governor also besought the War Department to defray the costs of the troops. But because Massachusetts still had no intention of committing its troops to federal command, the War Department refused. A joint committee of the legislature thereupon adopted a report asserting that the federal government was not protecting the state and implying that the state might accordingly employ for its own purposes the money it was now paying in federal taxes. With such notions in mind, some of the Federalist leaders began arranging for the Hartford Convention.[15]

The administration's own Republican states'-rights inheritance made dealing with New England's recalcitrance all the more awkward. But the conduct of New England, combined with the general disappointments of recruiting everywhere, drove Madison and his lieutenants to the thought of conscription. Secretary Armstrong said in late 1813 that conscription was the only means of raising an adequate force for the dangers of the coming year. At that time, Madison and Secretary Monroe reacted with horror, saying that the idea was politically impossible and manna for the Federalists. After they witnessed the battle of Bladensburg and the fall of Washington, however, the President and Monroe reconsidered. When he became Secretary of War, Monroe urged that the means of bringing the Regular Army to its authorized strength was to classify the militia— that is, the whole able-bodied citizenry—according to age and similar criteria and to impose a draft upon it. To make soldiers of them, drafted men should serve a term of two years.

The same events that had spurred the administration aroused the Senate sufficiently to push through a bill stronger even than Monroe's proposals, providing for a draft of 80,000 militia for two years. But the bill did not reach a conference committee of the two houses until the late days of 1814, when much of the urgency of the late summer and fall was gone, and there it died when the war soon ended. The topic of conscription disappeared with it, for half a century.[16]

The new officers of 1813 and 1814 proved able to mold the growing numbers of recruits into an army good enough to fend off a need for conscription, despite New England's attitudes and every other handicap. Winfield Scott especially created regiments that were to influence decisively not only the course of the war but also the whole future relationship between Regulars and citizen soldiers.

After the court-martial which had sentenced him to a year's suspension from rank and pay beginning in January, 1810, Scott returned to his native Petersburg district in Virginia to console himself in the social rounds of the gentry, among whom he had once practiced law. He was fortunate to have among his friends there a young lawyer and legislator named Benjamin Watkins Leigh, who suggested that Scott improve his idleness by studying the literature of the military art, and who offered his own excellent library on the subject. Scott agreed, and a year with his friend's books gave him a good grounding in the theory and history of war.

Returned to duty, Scott was both gallant and conspicuous at the battle of Queenston in the first campaign on the Niagara frontier, but he became a prisoner of war when that battle turned into a fiasco. He was exchanged in time to join Dearborn's northern army in the spring of 1813, and there his textbook knowledge and confident manner sufficiently impressed the old commander to win Scott appointment as Dearborn's adjutant general. Characteristically, Scott produced a French staff manual from among his baggage and used it to reorganize Dearborn's staff in the Napoleonic manner. He drew up the orders that brought about the capture of Fort George on May 27, 1813, and according to Morgan Lewis's report to Secretary Armstrong, Scott "fought nine-tenths of the battle." To Scott's disgust, Dearborn failed to follow up the victory.[17]

Now colonel of the 2nd Artillery, Scott participated in Wilkinson's campaign on the St. Lawrence in the late fall of 1813. That bungled affair gave no one much opportunity to win credit, but Scott garnered some by swiftly marching his regiment (serving as infantry) from Fort George to join the campaign and then energetically leading the advance as long as Wilkinson kept an advance going. With competent officers scarce, these accomplishments gained Scott his commission as a brigadier general.

On March 24, 1814, Scott arrived at Buffalo to command a small force of Regulars assembled there, intended to be the nucleus of an army to reopen the Niagara campaign when warm weather returned. Scott had been disturbed to observe how little the movements of any American troops resembled the evolutions described in the books of Benjamin Leigh's library, prescribed by William Duane's *Hand Book for Infantry* (1812), which was the latest American tactical manual, and sometimes actually performed before Scott's eyes by the enemy. Like the Revolutionary army, the American Army still lacked officers and sergeants capable themselves of imparting tactical knowledge. Scott determined to remedy the situation in the force under his command. With the prospect of several weeks before campaigning resumed, he took in hand a textbook again and set out to use it to train soldiers.

In the armies of continental Europe, the French Revolution had considerably modified the tactics of the eighteenth century. French conscription laws had gone far toward realizing Jefferson's idea of the nation in arms, and the early armies of the French Revolution had overwhelmed their adversaries partly through weight of numbers alone. The other continental powers had to respond by invoking the levy en masse themselves. The enlarged armies were managed by the more systematic use of divisions as tactical formations, abandoning the effort to conduct a whole army as a single tactical unit. Several divisions would form a *corps d'armée*, and several corps might unite in a single field army. The new levies would enter battle much less thoroughly trained than the long-term soldiers of Frederick the Great, but in the French armies especially, the rising emotional force of nationalism provided an *élan* to compensate in part for inferior discipline and inferior tactical skill. The loosening of battlefield tactics already in process naturally developed still further in enlarged armies of lightly trained men. Not thin lines but clouds of skirmishers preceded the French armies in the attack, and the armies themselves attacked not in lines but in columns. The column was more easily controlled than a line, French numbers gave it weight, and good soldiers at the head of a column might be hoped to carry the more faint-hearted along with them. In addition, the new mobile artillery softened the way for French attacks, and it might be argued that the success of the armies of Revolutionary France and Napoleon derived from good artillery and good leadership covering the deficiencies of the infantry.

These changes had influenced the British army far less than the continental armies. Since their main military reliance continued to be upon sea power, the British did not need an army so large as those of the continental powers. Principally, the British army remained the volunteer army of the eighteenth century. It was supported in home defense by an active militia on full-time duty, formed by imposing district quotas that were filled in part by volunteering and completed through conscription. The old citizens' militia became merely a third line of defense. Since pay and allowances were higher in the Regular regiments than in the active militia, men drafted into the latter were likely to make the best of bad circumstances by moving eventually into the Regulars. This indirect form of compulsion sufficiently enlarged the Regular army to make possible the expeditionary forces that England sent to the continent.

As British recruitment had changed relatively little, so had British tactics. Partly because they had to serve at the end of long lines of sea communications, British expeditionary forces had proportionately less artillery than the French. Unable to depend upon artillery as the French did, but still commanding relatively small numbers of long-service men who could be trained thoroughly, the British continued to rely on discipline and skill in the eighteenth-century fashion. They fought in lines—not in the old-fashioned three ranks in which the third rank could make itself felt very little, but in the two ranks they had employed since their American wars—and they emphasized a musketry training that enabled them to get off volleys with deadly effect. Before Wellington went to the continent, he believed that the French tactical system was "a false one against steady troops," and indeed his steady red lines did turn back the French. The French had gained a moral ascendancy over earlier enemies; but now a French officer had to write ruefully that when they witnessed the unwavering, disciplined lines of the British, "An indefinable sensation nailed to the spot many of our men."[18]

The prospect for 1814 was that the American Army would have to face growing numbers of such British forces fresh from their victories over the French. The Americans were not likely to be able to bring against them numbers comparable to the French even should conscription be imposed; the government was too weak and public sentiment on the war too divided for that. Winfield Scott believed therefore that the only remedy was better training.

Jacob Brown, now the major general commanding the district, authorized Scott to establish a camp of instruction. Between March and June, Scott had in it from time to time somewhat over 3,000 men in understrength Regular regiments, the 9th, 11th, 21st, 22nd, 23rd, and 25th Infantry, plus two companies of the 2nd Artillery. These formations all were new units raised on the eve of war or since war began, so that not much was "Regular" about them except their names. Scott put the men in tents, and remembering Terre aux Boeufs, he imposed strict rules of sanitation. He began as Steuben had begun at Valley Forge, acting as his own drill sergeant and instructing first the officers, including those of field grade, in tactics he drew from his books. He was influenced by some French texts, but mainly his system was one of linear tactics similar to the British and in general conformity with Duane's *Hand Book for Infantry*. He taught the use of the musket and the bayonet and moved systematically from the school of the soldier to the school of the squad, company, and battalion. In keeping with his own precautions he included camp and field police and sanitation in his course. From his personal instruction, the officers in turn went on to teach the men to march, wheel, deploy, fire, and attack and defend with the bayonet. Ten hours of drill per day became the usual regimen. When a run of desertions threatened, Scott executed four offenders before the whole camp drawn up in a hollow square. While some tried to escape and many grumbled, the general was pleased with his men: "If, of such materials, I do not make the best army now in service by the 1st of June, I will agree to be dismissed [from] the service."[19]

It was not long since Jacob Brown had been a York State farmer, and he had little of Scott's knowledge of the refinements of the military art. But he was extremely aggressive. On July 3 he led across the Niagara the army Scott had trained. The troops were organized now into two Regular brigades, under Scott and Brigadier General Eleazar Wheelock Ripley, and a militia brigade, under the former War Hawk Congressman Peter B. Porter, went along. They first captured Fort Erie, across from Buffalo. On July 5 somewhat careless tactical arrangements on Scott's part brought first his brigade and then the bulk of the army into unexpected conflict with three partial regiments of British infantry regulars, supported by artillery and dragoons plus Canadian militia and Indians. This engagement was the battle of Chippewa, fought in open fields along Chippewa Creek with the Niagara River to the Americans' right, within sound of the Falls. In it Scott's training had its reward. For the first time in the war American soldiers stood up to approximately equal numbers of British regulars in the most brutal kind of sparring without entrenchments. In fact the British engaged were somewhat superior in numbers. But the Americans drove them from the field and exacted more casualties than they suffered.

Chippewa was a prelude to the similar but larger and longer battle of Lundy's Lane, fought just west of Niagara Falls on July 25. The British had brought reinforcements to the Niagara frontier under Lieutenant General George Gordon Drummond, and Drummond had crossed to New York and captured Fort Niagara at the mouth of the river. Brown characteristically tried to force him back into Canada by mounting an offensive of his own on the Canadian shore. Scott stormed a hill bisected by Lundy's Lane and took it after a series of attacks climaxed by murderous exchanges of musketry at virtually point-blank range. Then, the effort having brought Drummond to the scene, the British regulars threw three attacks against Scott. When night fell Scott held the hill, but his brigade hardly counted the strength of a battalion. Brown and Scott were both among the wounded, and the Americans pulled away during the night. They left the hill and Lundy's Lane to the British, but they had proved again they could hold their own against British regiments that carried on their muster rolls veterans of the long wars against Napoleon.[20]

In the summer of 1814, few phases of the war were going well for the United States. The British were about to occupy Washington. Amidst the surrounding gloom, the success of the Regulars at Chippewa and Lundy's Lane seemed all the more impressive. Furthermore, the remaining months of the war, though they saw the British repulsed at Baltimore and on Lake Champlain, brought no comparable American achievement on land except the battle of New Orleans, and there the Americans stood up to Wellington's veterans from behind cotton bales rather than in the open field. Chippewa and Lundy's Lane remained unique, the only extended open-field actions of the war in which the Americans fought at least as well as British veterans. And the Americans at Chippewa and Lundy's Lane were principally Regulars. From that time forward, advocates of the Regular Army as the only reliable instrument of war were to contrast Chippewa and Lundy's Lane with the less happy battles of the War of 1812 as a primary argument for their case. Largely because of Chippewa and Lundy's Lane, Secretary Calhoun could argue soon after the war that the nation's future reliance must be on Regulars, with Regular formations so numerous that at the outset of war "there should be nothing either to new model or to create." To this day, recruiting posters of the United States Army depict the battle of Chippewa and recall proudly the British commander's supposed exclamation of dismayed surprise at the Americans' steadiness: "Those are regulars, by God!"

Few incidents contributed so much to the prestige of the Regular Army and its acceptance as the necessary axis of American defense as Chippewa and Lundy's Lane. But to rely on those actions to demonstrate the superiority of Regulars to citizen soldiers is surely dubious. Scott had demonstrated again the importance of good officers acquainted with the art of war. When he opened his camp of instruction his Regulars were hardly distinguishable from any volunteer companies possessing a modicum of military skill but not yet real soldiers. Though he was assisted by his ability to impose the sanctions of Regular Army discipline, Scott probably could have accomplished essentially what he did with any similar body of American citizens recently placed in uniform. The truly notable aspect of his accomplishment was the brevity of the time in which he created an army able to stand up to British veterans. The extent of his accomplishment of a few months should have thrown doubt on all assertions that making a good soldier is a labor of years; instead the emphasis of champions of the Regular Army and of Uptonian historians on the point that Chippewa and Lundy's Lane were fought mainly by the Regular Army was to make the Niagara campaign of 1814 serve an almost diametrically opposite conclusion.

The War of 1812 demonstrated no clear superiority of Regular Army formations over those based upon volunteer militia (which included some of the Regulars). In the early years of the war, the defeats of the Regulars compared all too closely with those of citizen soldiers in frequency and humiliation. On the other hand, if volunteers bore the brunt of no battle of the prolonged intensity of Lundy's Lane, on several occasions they fought admirably. Kentucky volunteer militia were prominent in William Henry Harrison's advance to the Thames in 1813. Before its supports melted away, compelling retreat, the 5th Regiment of the Maryland militia, a volunteer militia regiment, charged the British at Bladensburg in fine parade-ground style, holding its alignment across open fields against fire from a sheltering grove of trees, forcing some of the British into a momentary withdrawal, and pulling away only when ordered. The regiment later faced its adversaries again on North Point in defense of Baltimore, and two of its privates took much of the energy out of the British march on that city by firing the shots that killed Major General Robert Ross. On the Niagara frontier, after Jacob Brown recovered from his Lundy's Lane wound, he led a sortie against General Drummond's British regulars who were besieging Fort Erie; Brown's men this time were volunteers, but they broke the advanced positions of some Scots Highlanders and captured two batteries. If the main battle of New Orleans was no fair test of prowess, Jackson's volunteers, drawn largely from volunteer militia organizations, fought a tough action with bayonets, knives, and clubbed muskets on the night of December 23 at the Villeré plantation; they scored as much of a win as Jackson expected of them, imposing heavier losses than they took and causing the enemy to hesitate in his advance.[21]

The crucial issue was again one of leadership, of finding officers who could train their men and handle them properly. When Regulars were led by "the old officers," as Winfield Scott described them, "[who] had, very generally, sunk into either sloth, ignorance or habit of intemperate drinking," and who neither drilled their troops nor led them with skill or bravery on the battlefield, American Regulars were no match for British regulars. When volunteer companies were led by a William Henry Harrison or an Andrew Jackson, who used them with regard to their limitations but who both disciplined and inspired them, meeting the British was not likely to end in rout and might even lead to victory. Nathanael Greene's observation of the Revolution was still true and pertinent: "We want nothing but good officers to constitute as good an army as ever marched into the field."

Mixed though the military record of the War of 1812 was, and inconclusive the terms of peace, the war greatly awakened American nationalism. Samuel Flagg Bemis has suggested that the nation experienced the same surge of renewed self-respect that an individual feels when, having been tormented intolerably by a bully, he forgets any odds against him and turns to fight. In such a circumstance it is the resolve to fight that counts most, not winning or losing. Whatever the reasons for this effect of the war, Albert Gallatin testified to its presence:

The War has renewed and reinstated the national feelings which the Revolution had given and were daily lessened. The people have now more general objects of attachment with which their pride and political opinions are connected. They are more American; they feel and act more like a nation; and I hope that the permanency of the Union is thereby better secured.[22]

Even more cogently than Gallatin's words, the policies of the federal government and of the Republican party which controlled it after the war testified to the same galvanizing effect. The postwar period brought nationalist legislation in the Tariff of 1816, the establishment of the Second Bank of the United States, and federal road construction bills, and nationalist jurisprudence in a series of decisions written by Chief Justice John Marshall that were more in harmony with general opinion than any Marshall had written before or after a few years would write again. The War Department too reflected the nationalist mood, and the Army was to profit from it. Into the War Office went the nationalistic young South Carolina War Hawk John C. Calhoun. Encouraged by the nationalist fervor of the day, by both public shame at the setbacks of the war and desire to avoid their repetition and by the credit the Regular Army had won, Calhoun proposed a new military policy that would make the Regular Army the cornerstone of national defense. He did not accomplish all he wanted, but he did both enhance the place of the Regular Army in national policy and work far-reaching practical improvements in the Army and the War Department.

James Monroe was briefly Secretary of War as well as Secretary of State during the closing months of the war, from September, 1814, after Armstrong's fall from grace accompanying the loss of Washington, to March, 1815. Too busy trying to be general factotum of the Madison administration in practically all departments, with the pursuit of the Presidency in mind, he did not especially distinguish himself. At that late stage of the war, in fact, he did not have much chance to do either great harm or great good. When his official duties were confined again to the State Department, and he then succeeded in moving to the Presidency, William H. Crawford became Secretary of War. Crawford too was preoccupied with Presidential ambitions.

As President, Monroe gave Crawford the Treasury. Seven months of Monroe's Presidency passed before he turned up a permanent occupant for the War Department. He offered the Secretaryship to Governor Isaac Shelby of Kentucky and Congressman William Lowndes of South Carolina and was rejected. He probably considered William R. Drayton, Andrew Jackson, William Henry Harrison, and David R. Williams. Only on October 10, 1817, did he approach Calhoun.[23]

At thirty-five Calhoun was self-confident and even brash, already experienced and powerful as a legislator and determined to prove his executive capacity. The shortcomings of the Army and the War Department thus far owed much to the fact that there had never been an Alexander Hamilton of the War Office to give to the military service the traditions of energy, efficiency, and foresighted purpose that Hamilton had bestowed upon the Treasury. Calhoun essayed the role, and comparisons with Hamilton soon were heard.

The new Secretary came into a department whose unsettled accounts amounted to $45,000,000, and he reduced them to $3,000-000. His strict control over departmental finance cut defalcations from three per cent of the amount disbursed annually to two-tenths of one per cent. He seized upon the organizational reforms of the war, such as the General Staff and an improved supply service, broadened them, and made them permanent foundations of a better Army. He secured an adequate staff of responsible assistants and advisers for the Secretary of War and with their help asserted the Secretary's control over the whole Army, to transform what had been a miscellaneous collection of companies and regiments into a semblance of a unified organism. He brought line command to a focus by fostering the office of commanding general. He presented to Congress and the nation a series of comprehensive reports which were reminiscent of Hamilton's great documents and in which Calhoun explored the problems and necessities both of Army organization and of military policy on the highest level, the role of the Army in peace and war.[24]

The completion of the General Staff, so that the Secretary would not have to do too much alone, was the first task Calhoun set for himself.

In fact [he said], no part of our military organization requires more attention in peace than the general staff. It is in every service invariably the last in attaining perfection; and, if neglected in peace, when there is leisure, it will be impossible, in the midst of the hurry and bustle of war, to bring it to perfection.[25]

On Crawford's recommendation, Congress had already acted to perpetuate the General Staff centralized in Washington which had appeared during the war. To this permanent management group Calhoun secured the addition of a commissary general of subsistence, heading a Subsistence Department, and a commissioned surgeon general, as head of a Medical Department. The Subsistence Department at last ended the evils of farming out to private contractors the job of feeding the Army; instead the commissary general contracted for regional and individual items of subsistence but supervised the whole process. In 1821 Calhoun added also an inspector general's office separate from the adjutant general. He brought the chief of engineers from West Point to Washington, saying he "should be stationed at the seat of Government, to superintend, under its immediate control, the great and important duties assigned to the corps."

Calhoun's choice as first surgeon general was Joseph Lovell, a Harvard Medical School graduate with a good war record as surgeon of the 9th Infantry. Lovell quickly demonstrated his aptitude for military medicine and administration in his first report, an analysis of the relationship between the Army diet and the soldier's health. Similarly characteristic of Calhoun's staff appointments was Thomas S. Jesup as quartermaster general. As a major, Jesup had commanded the 25th Infantry at Chippewa and Lundy's Lane, winning his brevet as lieutenant colonel in the first battle and as colonel in the second. Only thirty years old at the time of his staff appointment, he gave the Quartermaster's Department essentially the organization it would retain into the twentieth century and earned the accolade of the modern historian of the Quartermaster Corps as "Father of the Corps." Calhoun carefully selected his staff officers, cultivated their loyalty, and held them. The head of every staff department served from the time Calhoun came into office or the time of his own appointment through Calhoun's eight years in the War Department. To support his own reports the Secretary drew from the heads of the staff departments a series of unprecedentedly comprehensive studies of the condition of every branch of the Army.[26]

Calhoun believed that his staff department system gave him ample technical advice to inform him of the issues of Army management and that through his agents, the staff heads, he could exert the unified control of the military which was his responsibility as civilian chief. But the bureau system also meant dividing the management of the Army into specialized segments, with the General Staff not so much a coherent entity as a collection of varied experts. It also left unclear the relationship between the staff headquarters in Washington and the line officers who commanded the military districts into which the country was divided. Time was to reveal and to aggravate difficulties in the system, but it survived until the Army had to bear the responsibilities of twentieth-century world power.

Questions about the chain of command from the staff department headquarters into the military districts were arising before Calhoun took office. His predecessor, Secretary Crawford, ordered Major Stephen Long, a topographical engineer assigned to Major General Andrew Jackson's Southern Division, to report to Washington. Jackson received no copy of the order, and he asked for an explanation. Acting Secretary of War George Graham brusquely replied that "this department at all times exercises the right of assigning officers to the performance of special duties, at its discretion." Offended, Jackson took the case to the newly installed President Monroe, protesting the War Department's assumption that it could move staff officers around the country without even the knowledge of the geographical division or district commander. So far Jackson was on firm ground; but when Monroe did not reply promptly enough to please him, he indulged his usual lack of patience by ordering officers within his division to obey no War Department order unless it came through him.

This order provoked a reply from Monroe, but not the one Jackson had been awaiting. Instead the President rebuked him for his action, saying, "The principle is clear, that every order from the dept. of war, to whomever directed, must be obeyed." Characteristically, Jackson filed the rebuke with a note: "This is to be filed, and the further explanation waited for. . . ." He told Monroe:

I will continue to support the Government in all respects when the orders of the War Dept. do not, in my opinion, go to infringe all law and strike at the very root of subordination and the discipline of the Army.

Jackson having overreached himself, Monroe now insisted that the issue had become "the naked principle, of the power of the Executive, over the officers of the army, . . . for the department of war cannot be separated from the President." The orders of the War Department, Monroe said, are the orders of the President.

The commander of a district, is, it is true, charg'd with its defense . . . but still he is no further responsible, than for the faithful application of the means committed to him for the purpose, by the Executive. The whole means provided by law . . . are committed to the Executive. . . . He must therefore be the judge how those means are to be applied, and have full power to apply them . . . as he may find expedient. . . .[27]

Jackson's impetuosity had obscured the original and practical issue of the nature of the chain of command by opening a debate on the Presidential power as Commander in Chief, from which the division commander eventually had to back down. When Calhoun took office, he attempted both to resolve the immediate issue and to reassert the prerogatives of the President in general orders. Ordinarily, he said, orders to all officers would be issued through division commanders, and always those commanders would receive copies of orders issued by the War Department to officers attached to them. On the other hand, when necessary the War Department would dispatch orders directly to any officers. But were officers of staff departments who were serving in districts to look first to the division or district commanders, or to consider themselves mere transients in any district and responsible mainly to Washington? That point was still unclear.

The reorganization act of April, 1818, seemed to make deputy commissaries responsible directly to the commissary general, whatever their station. A deputy commissary in Jackson's division thereupon disregarded an order from Jackson that he considered at variance with his instructions from commissary headquarters. Jackson returned to the charge, court-martialing the deputy commissary. Calhoun then canceled the court-martial.

Similarly, the surgeon general ordered assistant surgeons general and post surgeons to forward their reports directly to Washington. For some time those in Jackson's command failed to comply; evidently Jackson had insisted that all post surgeons in his division report to Washington only by way of the assistant surgeon general at his headquarters. Calhoun wrote Jackson that he must change his policy. He said that for reports to go through division headquarters caused excessive delay and that the division commander could be kept informed by means of duplicate reports. Meanwhile, he hoped he would be relieved

from the necessity of determining whether I shall permit the orders of the Government to be habitually neglected, or resort to the proper means of enforcing them. Should the alternative be presented I will not hesitate to do my duty.[28]

The Secretary's stand was firm enough to bring acquiescence from Jackson for the brief remainder of his military career. There matters rested for the time being. But if Jackson was unduly rash, nevertheless he had raised real problems. The distribution of authority between staff and line remained unsettled, and under the staff department system it was to continue so for nearly a hundred years.

For all Calhoun's achievements with the General Staff, one senses an uneasiness in his approach to the principal line commanders. These were powerful figures in their control of thousands of armed men, and among them Jackson at least was headstrong and independent-minded as well as powerful. On one occasion more momentous than any of the staff squabbles, Jackson succeeded in having his way contrary to his orders from the War Department and the inclinations of Calhoun. The event was his seizure of the Spanish outpost Fort Barrancas at Pensacola in 1818. His orders permitted him to pursue marauding Seminoles into Spanish Florida but not to take action against Spanish authority without first consulting the War Department. Calhoun would have reprimanded him, but the larger diplomatic interests of the United States—Secretary of State John Quincy Adams's determination to bludgeon Spain into the cession of Florida—prevented another confrontation between the Secretary and the general.[29]

Perhaps Calhoun's interest in strengthening the staff departments was partly a quest for a counterpoise to the line commanders over whom the Secretary's control was unsure. Despite his eagerness to centralize staff operations in Washington, Calhoun significantly allowed the line command to remain divided through about half his term. One of the command improvements of the war had been to create two division headquarters, a Northern and a Southern, over the various districts. Calhoun delayed the next logical step of consolidating the divisions or creating a headquarters superior to them. Instead, Major General Jacob Brown continued in command of the Northern Division, comprising the First through Fifth Districts or Departments, while Jackson commanded the Southern Division, the Sixth, Seventh, and Eighth Districts.

The success of Secretary Adams's and General Jackson's pressure against Spanish Florida brought about Jackson's retirement from the service to become governor of Florida in 1821. With Jackson out of the way, Calhoun felt able to give the Army at last a single commanding general. He summoned Jacob Brown to Washington for that purpose. But the Secretary's relationship with the line command remained uneasy. Upon the creation of the office of commanding general, who really commanded the Army, the Secretary or the commanding general? The Secretary as the President's deputy was constitutionally responsible, but if he commanded, then the senior professional office became a post of empty honor. The commanding general possessed, presumably, professional expertise that the Secretary lacked, but his constitutional position was uncertain, and no statutory authority defined his role clearly either upon the establishment of his office or throughout the subsequent long history of the office. Closely related to the problems between line commanders and officers of the staff departments in the field, the relationship between the Secretary of War and the newly created post of commanding general was another problem that was to continue unsettled and thorny for almost a century.[30]

Fortunately, Jacob Brown, unlike Jackson, reserved his aggressiveness for the enemy in war and did not vent it upon his civilian superiors, and he and Calhoun managed to drift along in an ambiguous relationship without crisis. If the strength of the line commanders disturbed Calhoun, as a nationalist he nevertheless hoped to foster the strength of the Army itself. In Jacob Brown he had a cooperative partner who would quietly assist in that effort.

When Calhoun entered the War Office the Army was completing a reorganization decreed by act of Congress of March 3, 1815. Congress had moved hastily to reduce the wartime Army, for on March 3, 1815, the United States and England had not yet exchanged their ratifications of the Treaty of Ghent; but its provision for the peace establishment was nevertheless generous by prewar standards, a maximum of 10,000 enlisted Regulars exclusive of the Corps of Engineers. The force was to include eight regiments of infantry (ten companies each, with one captain, one first lieutenant, one second lieutenant, four sergeants, four corporals, two musicians, and sixtyeight privates to a company, for an infantry total of 5,440 privates), a Rifle Regiment (ten companies, 660 privates), one regiment of light artillery (again ten companies, 660 privates), and a Corps of Artillery for the permanent fortifications (eight battalions of four companies, 100 privates per company). The regiment of dragoons disappeared; cavalry was expensive and of limited usefulness in forest warfare against the Indians. Commissioned officers wishing to be retained must have served in the war, with preference given to Military Academy graduates. Vacancies in the officer corps were filled from the list of disbanded officers until May, 1816.[31]

To reduce the war to the peace establishment, the War Department had devised a plan that dealt cavalierly with all regimental traditions that had grown up since the first muster of Josiah Harmar's 1st American Regiment, but which produced the numbering system for infantry regiments that has survived ever since. Four or five of the wartime infantry regiments were assigned to each of the eight military districts. There they were consolidated into a single regiment. The consolidated regiments received new numbers, bearing no relation to their previous designations but based on the order of seniority of the new regimental commanders. The 2nd Infantry, the old 2nd American Regiment raised for St. Clair's campaign in 1791, became part of the new 1st Infantry. The old 1st became part of the 3rd Infantry, establishing the claim of that regiment to be the oldest in the service. Winfield Scott's wartime 9th, 11th, 21st, 22nd, 23rd, and 25th Regiments became variously parts of the 2nd, 5th, and 6th Regiments, and later regiments bearing their old numbers have no connection with them.

The postwar Rifle Regiment represented a consolidation of the four wartime regiments of riflemen. Several infantry regiments and the dragoons were amalgamated into the artillery. Each military district received one of the eight battalions of fortress artillery, the battalion to carry the number of the district.[32]

Congress's relatively generous regular establishment of 1815 can be attributed both to the nationalism of the hour and to the failures of improvised regiments during the war. But by late 1818 a contrary trend was developing in the legislature, a movement to reduce the Army more nearly to Old Republican dimensions. Displeasure among some congressmen over Andrew Jackson's reckless incursions into Spanish Florida had something to do with the movement, and so did a desire to depreciate the Presidential stock of both General Jackson and War Secretary Calhoun, and to advance that of such nonmilitary figures as William H. Crawford and Henry Clay. Calhoun resisted the trend, arguing that in proportion to responsibilities that had enlarged with the growth of national population, wealth, and territory, the Army was no more excessive now than the Jeffersonian 3,000 or so of 1802 had been.[33]

Nevertheless, on May 11, 1820, the House of Representatives directed Calhoun to prepare, by the beginning of its next session, a plan for reducing the Regular Army to 6,000 enlisted men. Calhoun responded on December 12 with the most important of his War Department messages. In it he argued that if the Regular Army must be reduced, the reduction must be on such a plan that the Army would remain ready to expand instantly in war; for experience had now proven, he argued, that only the Regular Army and not the citizens' militia was a fit instrument for all the major operations of war:

I am aware that the militia is considered, and in many respects justly, as the great national force; but, to render them effective, every experienced officer must acknowledge, that they require the aid of regular troops. Supported by a suitable corps of trained artillerists, and by a small but well-disciplined body of infantry, they may be safely relied on to garrison our forts, and to act in the field as light troops. . . . To rely on them beyond this, to suppose our militia capable of meeting in the open field the regular troops of Europe, would be to resist the most obvious truth, and the whole of our experience as a nation. War is an art, to attain perfection in which, much time and experience, particularly for the officers, are necessary.[34]

Therefore the military policy of the United States ought to focus upon the Regular Army and so to organize the Regular Army as to permit it to carry the principal burden of war:

The great and leading objects, then, of a military establishment in peace, ought to be to create and perpetuate military skill and experience; . . . and the organization of the army ought to be such as to enable the Government, at the commencement of hostilities, to obtain a regular force, adequate to the emergencies of the country, properly organized and prepared for actual service.[35]

To reconcile such purposes with the Congressional instructions to plan a reduction to 6,000 men was a task that Calhoun thought difficult but possible. He would create a full skeleton of a wartime Regular Army in time of peace, in which all wartime formations would already exist, and such that wartime recruits would be absorbed directly into them. In such an Army wartime recruits would quickly take on the tone and even the skill of Regulars, and Regulars would always stand at the recruits' side.

It was especially important that the staff of the war Army should be ready in peace, "every branch of it . . . completely formed."

With a complete organization, and experienced officers, trained in peace to an exact and punctual discharge of their duty, the saving in war (not to insist on an increased energy and success in our military movements) would be of incalculable advantage to the country.[36]

Similarly, Calhoun would retain in the reduced Army the two major generals and four brigadiers retained in 1815, for the same reasons that demanded a full staff and to offer sufficient high ranks to keep talented and ambitious men in the officer corps. Throughout the line of the Army he would retain a disproportionately high number of officers, for "The qualifications of the officers are essentially superior to those of the soldiers, and are more difficult to be acquired."[37]

Finally, Calhoun would keep up the organization of every company that the wartime Army would require. He proposed to reduce the peace strength of artillery and infantry companies to sixty-four and thirty-seven enlisted men respectively. Retaining the existing companies would then yield an aggregate enlisted strength of 6,316, approximating the figure that Congress desired. Then, without adding a single officer but simply bringing the enlisted men to a reasonable war strength, the Army could be expanded to an enlisted strength of 11,558. Calhoun believed that by adding 288 officers but again without increasing the number of companies, the Army could absorb enough additional privates and n.c.o.'s to raise the total to 19,035 officers and men.

The war organization, thus raised on the basis of the peace establishment, will bring into effective operation the whole of the experience and skill of the latter, which, with attention, would, in a short period, be communicated to the new recruits, and the officers recently appointed, so as to constitute a well-disciplined force.[38]

The leading principle in the formation of the Regular Army ought to be, said Calhoun:

that at the commencement of hostilities, there should be nothing either to new model or to create. The only difference, consequently, between the peace and the war formation of the army, ought to be in the increased magnitude of the latter; and the only change in passing from the former to the latter, should consist in giving to it the augmentation which will then be necessary.[39]

Here was the fruit of Chippewa and Lundy's Lane and the new awakening of nationalism: from a Secretary of War of Jefferson's party came proposals that stood Jefferson's military policy on its head, not eliminating but emphasizing the distinction between citizen and soldier, consigning the citizens' militia to auxiliary roles, and seeking means "at the commencement of hostilities, to obtain a regular force, adequate to the emergencies of the country."

It was too strong a brew for Congress even in the nationalistic "Era of Good Feelings." The military legislation of 1821 cut the Regular Army to about 6,000 enlisted men without including Calhoun's plan for an expansible army; instead it consolidated the 6th Infantry and the Rifle Regiment, eliminated the 8th Infantry, and consolidated the Corps of Artillery, the Light Artillery Regiment, and the Ordnance Department in four regiments of artillery.[40] But Calhoun's plan could not have been announced at all by any earlier Secretary of War, and as memories of the war and the mood of war-born nationalism faded, it became impossible for the War Department to advance that plan officially for many years again. The plan of an expansible Regular Army as the central military reliance of the country was a direct legacy of the War of 1812. Despite its initial setback, it was to prove a permanent legacy.

The idea of expansible companies as a means of making an enlarged Regular Army the principal instrument for war was to be nourished by the Regular Army itself, to reappear in the late nineteenth century as the chief proposal of Emory Upton and the military reformers and historians who followed him, and to persist into the twentieth century as a favorite idea of those who believed that the Regular Army and not citizen-soldier formations must be the focus of war planning. For the first time a responsible statesman had urged repudiation of the militia tradition, at least for primary military purposes, and a stress upon the professional establishment as the only part of the country's military inheritance to possess unimpeachable military value. This event was one result of the War of 1812 that would reverberate through the next century of American military history.

Its persistence would owe much to a part of Calhoun's work which he could carry forward with less dependence upon Congress. Calhoun sponsored a revival of the Military Academy at West Point from the verge of extinction and its growth into something new: the incubator of an American military profession in the full modern sense of that noun. The appearance of a Regular Army that was professional in an unprecedented way would both enhance the persuasiveness of the expansible army idea and provide corporate guardianship for the idea. Calhoun could say: "War is an art." The next stage in the history of the Army would permit his followers to say, more persuasively: "War is a profession."

EIGHT

The Professionalization
of the Regular Army:
1821-46

War is not, as some seem to suppose, a mere game of chance. Its principles constitute one of the most intricate of modern sciences. . . .
—Henry W. Halleck[1]

THE CADETS AT West Point first received gray uniforms in 1815 or 1816. A familiar tradition has it that the purpose of the new uniforms was to honor the Regulars who fought at Chippewa and Lundy's Lane. In 1814 the habitual shortcomings of supply had deprived Winfield Scott's soldiers of regulation blue jackets, and they had gone into battle wearing rough gray kersey. Their feats of arms then demanded some memorial, and West Point has memorialized them ever since. If the tradition is true, its significance is more than superficial. Before the achievements of the Regulars of the War of 1812, the fate of the Military Academy was highly uncertain. With those achievements, it was possible immediately after the war to lay the foundations of the modern Academy, and with them the foundations of the true professionalization of American arms.[2]

Already the war had carried the Academy beyond its original design as an adjunct of the Corps of Engineers. In 1808, with the expansion of the Army after the *Chesapeake* affair, two cadets were attached to each company of infantry, riflemen, and artillery and detailed to West Point, creating an authorized cadet body grown to

150. When Congress expanded the Army for war on April 29, 1812, the authorization grew to 250, and the cadets were no longer to be attached to particular companies of the staff or line. At the same time, three professors were added, one of natural and experimental philosophy, one of mathematics, and one of engineering both civil and military, and each professor was to have an assistant. The training was henceforth to include all duties of a private and a noncommissioned and commissioned officer.[3]

Calhoun counted the Academy high among his means of improving the Army, and he proposed to build still further: to detach the Academy altogether from the Corps of Engineers by separating the superintendency from command of the Corps; to add a professor of chemistry and one of artillery; to increase faculty pay in order to attract thoroughly competent men; to raise the minimum age of admission from fourteen to sixteen; and to clarify the uncertainty of whether the Articles of War applied to the cadets by establishing a special disciplinary code appropriate to them. As part of his expansible army plan, he proposed a second academy to help develop the surplus of officers required by the plan.[4]

Encouragement from the War Department was badly needed, since although the legislation of 1808 and 1812 had opened important possibilities for growth and improvement, the actual condition of the Academy at the close of the war was one close to foundering. The war had drained off cadets as soon as they acquired a modicum of military knowledge. The first of the Academy's graduates and one of the most able of the early cadets, Joseph G. Swift, had become superintendent during the war, but his duties as chief of engineers had mostly carried him elsewhere. Captain Alden Partridge followed him, a talented teacher but a poor administrator, a nepotist, and a personality incapable of moving without generating controversy and bad feelings. Partridge interpreted rules to his own tastes and feuded with both teaching staff and cadets, keeping the Academy in a continual uproar which threatened to be the death of it, until in June, 1817, President Monroe visited West Point in person and decided to court-martial Partridge and replace him with Captain (Brevet Major) Sylvanus Thayer.[5]

Thayer was fitting himself into his new post when Calhoun entered the War Department. Calhoun gave him the support he needed to restore and transform West Point and win his place in history as the father of the Academy. He was a product of Dartmouth College as well as of the Academy itself (class of 1808), and he respected education in general as well as military training. He was also a man of great intellectual curiosity who had proposed to go abroad after the war to study the military schools of Europe and who had so impressed Secretary of War Monroe that he went with an official commission for the task. He found West Point hardly serving its original purpose as a training school for Army engineers; he left it after a sixteen-year superintendency as a college educating men for the profession of officership.[6]

The law of 1812 provided that the cadets were to "receive a regular degree from an academical staff." To give substance to this provision and make West Point genuinely a seat of higher academic education, Thayer created the Academic Board, in which the permanent professors, in effect the department chairmen, would meet with the superintendent to determine academic policy. The Academic Board still serves this purpose. It developed a standard four-year curriculum and set the requirements of proficiency the cadets would have to meet. Under Thayer's leadership it extended the curriculum beyond courses directly associated with engineering to include chemistry, general history, moral philosophy, geography, law, and ethics. To encourage study, Thayer instituted weekly class reports of cadets' standing and merit rolls on which the cadets were ranked in order of general proficiency, the weight of each branch of study in the total ranking being regulated by multiplying the cadet's grade in that branch with a number corresponding to its importance. The first five cadets in each class were to have their names published in the annual Army Register.

Thayer's means of academic instruction was the small class in which each student might recite daily, an innovation which came to be almost sacred at West Point and still prevails in many disciplines there. Sections of about twelve men were set up in each subject by dividing the cadets according to their proficiency in the subject. The professor would conduct the first section, his assistants the other sections, with the professor periodically visiting all sections. To a degree, instruction and assignments were adjusted to the abilities of the sections.

To escape parochialism, and also as a means of disseminating interest in West Point, Thayer welcomed and encouraged the annual Board of Visitors, made up of distinguished officers, educators, and government leaders from around the country. Instituted in 1815, the Board of Visitors became an annual fixture after 1819, preparing a report embodying recommendations to the Academy and to Congress.

As he developed the academic aspect of the Academy beyond engineering subjects, so Thayer also developed the military aspects of the Academy beyond training in military engineering. He took seriously the legislative injunction of 1812 that the course was to include all duties of a private, a noncommissioned officer, and an officer. He created the office of commandant of cadets, to conduct the military training and discipline of the cadets. He organized the corps of cadets into tactical units under cadet officers. The cadets participated in three two-months' summer encampments, for military exercises in the field. In their final encampment they both studied the current tactical manuals for infantry and artillery and practiced their precepts. A cadet's standing on the roll of merit was based in part upon his military proficiency and his adherence to a stern disciplinary code of conduct.[7]

The European military schools which gave Thayer his models and standards of excellence were principally those of France, especially the École Polytechnique for the training of military and civil engineers and the School of Application for Engineers and Artillery at Metz. This influence reflected both the association with the French army during the War for Independence and the magnetism of Napoleon, as well as the geographical proximity of France among the European military powers. Under the French influence, however, American officers were long to remain almost unaware of a military school system that had advanced well beyond that of France, the schools of Prussia. Thus Thayer's reforms, admirable as they were, proved in time to have severe limitations in preparing the United States Army for adjustment to military events in Europe later in the century. French military schools continued to stress military engineering, fortification, and tactics. Prussian schools emphasized strategy, military policy in its highest aspects, and a regard for arms as a true profession, not a mere craft but a discipline based upon broad historical knowledge and thought. One day the differences between their military schools would contribute to a reversal of the power balance between Prussia and France, and then the United States Army, like many other armies, would have to hasten to reassess French examples it had long revered.

Not all that the Prussians did in the meantime to make military officership a true profession was lost upon America; some of it filtered through France. Nor did Prussia initiate all the steps in that direction. The emergence of a genuine military profession was a by-product of the changes in warfare accompanying the French Revolution. War in the age of Frederick the Great had become so stylized and routinized that it demanded little save polished craftsmanship from even the most successful commanders. Frederick the Great himself attained first rank among the captains of his day mainly by training his army with such painstaking thoroughness that it could carry out the standard battlefield tactics of the day better than its opponents. His principal innovation was to employ again in attack the oblique order of battle made famous by Epaminondas of Thebes in the battle of Leuctra in 371 B.C. But the developments of the French Revolutionary era vastly increased the complexity of war: mass armies drawn from the conscripted "nation in arms" in place of small long-service armies; relatively untrained but often zealous soldiers; management and administrative problems much increased by mass armies; the new tactics with their use of growing numbers of skirmishers, the column of attack rather than the line, and mobile light artillery. To understand the new developments, to know how best to employ the citizen soldiers of the Revolutionary era to compensate for their inexperience but exploit their enthusiasm, to know how to manage and support mass armies, demanded study and thought and a military literature that could offer guidance.

Napoleon's special mastery of the Revolutionary style of war naturally inspired a search for the principles that he followed and that presumably explained his success. Antoine Henri de Jomini presently offered the most persuasive exposition of Napoleonic war. A Swiss bank clerk fascinated by war, he enlisted for a time in the French army, then returned to clerking while he wrote his *Traité des grandes opérations militaires*. He sent a copy to Marshal Ney, and Ney was sufficiently impressed to grant him a staff appointment. Then Jomini saw to it that a copy of the book went with a set of dispatches from Ney to the Emperor. Napoleon was also impressed, and Jomini graduated to the Emperor's own staff and won his growing approbation in the Jena and Austerlitz campaigns. But Jomini's rapid ascent, combined with a swollen self-esteem, pricked the jealousy of the chief of staff, Marshal Berthier, and Jomini quarreled with him and then left in a huff to join the Russians. After the war he alternated between the service of the French Bourbons and the Russians again, meanwhile writing his magnum opus, the *Précis de l'art de la guerre*. This book became not only the principal French interpretation of Napoleonic warfare but also the model which was to inspire a new American military literature.[8]

Such a volume as Steuben's *Blue Book* had been typical of earlier military publications. The *Blue Book* was a manual of tactics and of military practice, but it also approached being a complete guide to the art of war as understood in Steuben's day. In 1807–9 Colonel William L. Duane had published his two-volume *Military Library* with the purpose of offering Americans a survey of all military knowledge; but the book was not much different from a tactical manual. A few European writers of the eighteenth century, notably Marshal de Saxe, had begun to go beyond this kind of thing toward a theory of war. But like the division, the creation of a theory of war was an eighteenth-century innovation that awaited the Revo-

lutionary era for its fruition. The advent of a theoretical and historical approach in such works as Jomini's then became an important
event in transforming officership into a profession.[9]

Meanwhile Napoleon's crushing defeat of Prussia in 1806–7, in
which Jomini assisted, had provided motives for the first officer corps
that was to become genuinely professional. The battle of Jena and
the peace of Tilsit humiliated Prussia when the time of her Frederi-
cian military glory seemed but yesterday. The leaders of this state, so
identified with its army, determined that Prussian arms must be glorious again. The Treaty of Tilsit limited the Prussian army to 42,000
men, but the Prussians evaded its intent by passing large numbers of
conscripts through the ranks to be trained by a relatively small permanent cadre. They thus inaugurated a military training system
which would bear fruitful further development. Meanwhile, possessing able military leadership in Graf Gerhard von Scharnhorst and his
coterie, but no genius of the order of Frederick the Great to compete
with Napoleon, they turned to the expedient of refining and pooling
such leadership talent as they had. They established a military educational system superior to anything that had gone before. Where previously the Prussian officer corps perhaps more notoriously than
most had been a refuge for arrogant but ignorant noblemen, Scharnhorst required officer candidates to have a liberal education. He then
established division schools to train the officers in the elements of the
military art, and above the division schools he created the *Kriegsakademie*, the first true approach to a modern professional school.
Out of the schools, especially the *Kriegsakademie*, there came the
first collective studies of the principles and theory of war. In addition, Scharnhorst established the rudiments of the first general staff
in the modern sense of that term, a body of officers selected for their
outstanding professional competence and assigned to advance their
professional development by constant study and to serve also, through
shared knowledge of the principles of war, as a collective brain for
the army.[10]

After the defeat of Napoleon these Prussian innovations suffered a
certain decay, as the conservative *Junkers* sought to reassert their old
perquisites in the army. Enough of the general staff survived, however, to nourish a later renewed growth of the institution, and the
studies at the *Kriegsakademie* culminated in the posthumous publication of its director's masterwork, Karl von Clausewitz's *Vom Krieg*,
in 1831. Furthermore, the Prussian example compelled the other
powers to cultivate at least in some measure a germ of genuine
professionalism in their own officer corps.

It was French efforts in that direction that inspired the next advances toward professionalism at West Point and in the American Army. Thayer knew no better way to continue the improvement of the Military Academy than to continue sending officers to study in France, and in 1826 he chose for that purpose Dennis Hart Mahan. Mahan was an Academy graduate of the class of 1824, a diffident youth too frail to suggest a soldier. He had come to West Point hoping to learn something of the fine arts through the drawing classes but had found himself fascinated by engineering and war. Mahan had caught Thayer's eye before his first cadet year was out, and the superintendent had made him acting assistant professor of mathematics, that is, student instructor in some of the mathematics sections. He remained with the faculty after graduation, but his uncertain health soon seemed to require a respite. Still believing him a promising prospect for the faculty, Thayer decided to offer him both opportunity and release from routine by sending him to France.

There Mahan enrolled in the School of Application for Engineers and Artillery. He also toured the French border fortresses. When he returned to West Point in 1830, he became acting professor of engineering, and two years later Professor of Civil and Military Engineering. As such he taught the capstone course of Thayer's curriculum, the first classmen's course in civil and military engineering, including civil and military architecture, field fortification, permanent fortification, and the science of artillery. Since suitable textbooks in English were lacking, he provided his own, based on the notes he had gathered in Europe. He produced the texts upon which subsequent American engineering education was founded. But significantly, he insisted that there be added to the title of his professorship the phrase, "and of the Art of War." For he also initiated the American branch of the new military theory.

Here too he felt obliged to provide his own texts. Using a lithograph press he had brought back from France, he prepared lithographed notes. Out of the notes there developed eventually the pioneer American study of the art of war, first published in 1847 and running through several editions, cumbersomely but deceptively titled and soon called by the cadets simply *Out-Post*.[11]

The basic assumption of Mahan's military teaching was that an officer could become accomplished only if he acquired a broad historical knowledge of war. Only from such knowledge could he draw the essential principles of military strategy and the nature of war which remain valid in all ages, and only from knowledge of its historical evolution could he comprehend the art of war of his own day and project its coming development. But to say that officership must be based upon a broad historical knowledge was to say that officership must become a profession.

No one can be said to have thoroughly mastered his art, who has neglected to make himself conversant with its early history; nor, indeed, can any tolerably clear elementary notions, even, be formed of an art, beyond those furnished by the mere technical language, without some historical knowledge of its rise and progress; for this alone can give to the mind those means of comparison, without which everything has to be painfully created anew, to reach perfection only after many cycles of misdirected mental toil.

It is in military history that we are to look for the source of all military science. In it we shall find those exemplifications of failure and success by which alone the truth and value of the rules of strategy can be tested.[12]

Mahan recognized that the historical approach to war suggested a risk that officers would become bound to past and bookish solutions of problems. He himself emphasized that while principles of strategy remain constant, the methods of applying them must change. But he argued that even in this light, history is invaluable, for history is the only substitute for experience in acquainting the fledgling officer with the variety of possible approaches to war. The professionally trained soldier is the one most likely to perceive all the possiblities in a situation and thus to choose the best response; "no soldier, who has made himself conversant with the resources of his art, will allow himself to be trammelled by any exclusive system."[13]

Mahan had been urging his students to a historical and theoretical approach to war for nearly two decades before he published the first edition of *Out-Post*. By that time, one of his pupils had preceded him with the first published American study of the new military theory. In 1846 Lieutenant Henry Wager Halleck, class of 1839, published *Elements of Military Art and Science*. Already in the previous year Halleck had submitted to Congress a perceptive report on the problems of national defense. His *Elements* was a much more systematic and coherent statement of military theory than Mahan's *Out-Post*, which too often reverted to the style of a handbook of military maxims. Some critics have dismissed Halleck's *Elements* as a paraphrase of Jomini, and in fact Jomini was the most important single influence upon it. But it was more than that: it was a review of the history and theory of war from an American perspective, designed to draw from that review a military policy for the United States. It argued that the principles of military art and science constitute a body of knowledge to be understood and mastered only through a professional education and that accordingly the duties of a modern officer can no more be entrusted to an unschooled civilian than a carpenter can do the work of a physician.[14]

Significantly, the military policy that Halleck recommended

closely paralleled that of Calhoun: the defense of the United States ought to be entrusted to a cadre of experienced soldiers under professional officers, so organized as to permit the rapid expansion of the cadre in wartime. In war, "*science* must determine the contest."

No people in the world ever exhibited a more general and enthusiastic patriotism than the Americans during the war of our own Revolution. And yet our army received, even at that time, but little support from irregular and militia forces in the open field.

The great difficulties encountered by Washington in instructing his inexperienced forces in the more difficult branches of the art, made him the more earnest, in after years, to impress upon us how important it was for us *In peace to prepare for war*. The preparation here meant is not the keeping up, in time of peace, of a large standing army ever ready to take the field; but rather the formation of a small body, educated and practised in all the scientific and difficult parts of the profession; a body which shall serve as the *cadre* or framework of a large army, capable of imparting to the new and inexperienced soldiers of the republic that skill and efficiency which has been acquired by practice.[15]

The professional approach to war exemplified by Mahan and Halleck and nurtured by Thayer's West Point now expressed itself also in the appearance of the first American military periodicals which, in at least part of their content, approximated professional journals. These periodicals included the *Military and Naval Magazine*, 1833–36; the *Army and Navy Chronicle*, 1835–44; and the *Military Magazine*, 1839–42. Worth mentioning also is the *Southern Literary Messenger*, which reflected the characteristic southern interest in things military by publishing several of the best articles on military affairs to appear anywhere, notably the series by "A Subaltern" in 1845.[16]

Out of West Point came an American military literature of a high quality disproportionate to the constricted circumstances of the American Army, and out of West Point there grew also professional attitudes in the American officer corps remarkable in a group so small and so isolated from the military institutions of Europe. But West Point was not a developed military school system like the Prussian. At best, it offered only an undergraduate education (albeit medical and law schools of the day offered little more), and so it could afford only an incomplete professional curriculum. The resources and public support available to the Army in Calhoun's and Thayer's day permitted the development of little in the way of higher military schools.

It is a tribute to Calhoun's perceptions, however, that he recognized something of the need for such schools, and made a beginning toward establishing them.

. . . whatever degree of perfection may be given to the Military Academy at West Point, as an elementary school [he said], yet our military education, in the higher branches of the art of war, must remain imperfect, without a school of application and practice. The education at the Military Academy will be full and complete for officers of infantry; but those who may be promoted into the artillery and the corps of engineers, ought to have the means, in a school of application and practice, to complete their theoretical knowledge in the higher branches of the science connected with their profession, and to apply the knowledge acquired to practice.[17]

In April, 1824, Calhoun ordered the establishment of the Army's first postgraduate school, the Artillery School of Practice at Fortress Monroe. Ten companies of artillery were to be drawn from the four regiments and assembled there as an "Artillery Corps for Instruction." The faculty was detailed from the artillery at large, including departments of mathematics, engineering, chemistry, and drawing. After graduating from the Military Academy, each lieutenant assigned to the artillery was to receive a year's additional training at Fortress Monroe. Through a plan of rotation, all artillery companies would eventually pass through the school.[18]

In 1827 Calhoun's successor established a more rudimentary and informal Infantry School of Practice at Jefferson Barracks, Missouri, but for the present the school system developed no further.[19] Instead, during the age of egalitarianism which was shortly ushered in with the Presidency of Andrew Jackson, military education barely held its own. The egalitarianism of the 1830's and 1840's was a different phenomenon from Jeffersonianism, and its nationalist aspects did not include a high regard for the Regular Army in the manner of Calhoun. Jefferson had believed in equality of opportunity out of which would arise a natural aristocracy of virtue and talent. He believed strongly in the value of learning, and he believed that the natural aristocracy should receive ample education. If the distinction between civil and military were to be erased, for example, all colleges throughout the country should offer instruction in the art of war. The new egalitarianism inclined toward another view. It was impatient of any aristocracy, even a natural one of virtue, talent, and learning. Its idea of equality implied that education should command no special privileges or consideration and that offices of public trust should be open to all, without regard to special qualifications of schooling but on a basis of natural abilities which overrode educational distinctions. In any area, civil or military, the new egalitarianism distrusted the kind of professionalism that Thayer and Mahan were introducing in the Army. In war as in other fields, it so disliked any suggestion of special privilege that it tended toward outright deprecation of learning while exalting native unschooled genius.

In military affairs, not Chippewa and Lundy's Lane but Andrew Jackson's victory at New Orleans came to symbolize the new egalitarian attitudes. New Orleans was interpreted as a triumph of the natural American—strong precisely because he was unschooled and therefore natural—over the trained and disciplined but therefore artificial and even effete European. "Their system, it is true," said one congressman of the heroes of New Orleans, "is not to be found in Vauban's, Steuben's or Scott's military tactics, but it nevertheless proved to be quite effective." Jackson himself viewed his victory in a similar light:

Reasoning always from false principles, [the British] expected little opposition from men whose officers even were not in uniform, who were ignorant of the rules of dress, and who had never been caned into discipline. Fatal mistake! a fire incessantly kept up, directed with calmness and unerring aim, strewed the field with the brave officers and men of the column, which slowly advanced, according to the most approved rules of European tactics, and was cut down by the untutored courage of the American militia.[20]

Such views called into question the value of any Regular establishment, not simply military schools. After the reductions of 1821, however, the Regular Army could barely fulfill its peacetime duties and hold the Indians in check; so it suffered no further reductions and in fact grew slightly in response to Indian alarums. But the center of professionalism, West Point, underwent a drumfire of criticism.

In 1831 the legislature of Jackson's native state, Tennessee, resolved that the Military Academy was inconsistent with republican institutions and dangerous to the principles of free government, and requested the state's congressmen to seek its extinction. The Ohio legislature followed with similar resolutions the next year. The federal House of Representatives established a select committee to investigate the Academy, and in 1837 the committee reported that West Point violated "constitutional principles, principles of sound policy, and principles of fiscal economy." To permit West Point graduates to monopolize the commissioned ranks of the Army was denounced by the committee as an especially gross violation of democratic principle. The committee was all the more shocked because the cadets undemocratically favored by such a system all too often spent their years of publicly financed education in insubordination and misconduct. In 1831, it pointed out, 150 cadets had earned up to 50 demerits; 88 had earned up to 100; 34 had earned up to 150; 16 had earned even more. The committee believed that no other institution suffered "annual delinquencies and mal-conduct" to compare with West Point. "It is seen that scarcely one in twenty escapes the contamination of the evil associations engendered there."[21]

Sylvanus Thayer became a special target of the Jacksonian branch of the egalitarian movement. He was vulnerable as the very father of American military professionalism, but this fact may have been no more important in provoking the Jacksonians' wrath than certain differences of opinion that had developed between Thayer and Andrew Jackson Donelson when the latter was a cadet. Donelson had then identified himself with several classmates who collided with Thayer's stern discipline; as Andrew Jackson's nephew, he went on to become private secretary to the President. Whatever Donelson's influence on Jackson, it became a feature of Jackson's Presidency that cadets who ran afoul of the disciplinary code could count on sympathy from the White House and often on Presidential reinstatement. It also became apparent that Jackson did not like Thayer and had no use for his opinions. Thayer grew more exasperated as Jackson seemed to be jeopardizing the whole structure of Academy discipline, overruling the verdicts of both the Academic Board and courts-martial. In 1833 Thayer resigned.[22]

He had built too solidly for his resignation alone to undermine the Academy. His successor, Major René de Russy (class of 1807), competently followed the course Thayer had charted until 1838, when Major Richard Delafield (class of 1814) took over to pursue an administration of distinction until 1845. But a zeal for progress passed from the Academy with Thayer, and no one has ever quite recaptured it.

How seriously the egalitarianism of Jackson's times threatened the very existence of the Military Academy is questionable. The annual Board of Visitors could be relied on to defend the Academy all through the era; even the appearance of a hostile minority report composed by southern and western members in 1840 was unusual. The unfriendly House of Representatives committee report of 1837 did not challenge the basic worth of military education; on the contrary, it reverted to the somewhat Jeffersonian suggestion that private colleges should take over the work of the Military Academy, with West Point to become an advanced school for officers already commissioned. But a rumble of opposition did persist in Congress, the legislatures, and many newspapers throughout the era, and the articulated opposition reflected an underlying disharmony between military professionalism and the ethos of the egalitarian age.[23]

It was not professionalism alone that was suspect. America in Andrew Jackson's day was an utterly unmilitary society, the martial attributes of the national hero notwithstanding. Public disfavor therefore fell upon the militia system as well as West Point and the Regular Army, and the militia was less able to withstand it. With the Indian menace vanished as far as most of the population was concerned, and danger of foreign attack gone since Napoleon's downfall and the Treaty of Ghent had removed the threat of involvement in Europe's wars, most Americans saw no reason to train the nation in arms. Militia duty came to seem pointless to all but a minority of military enthusiasts. At the same time, the militia system came to appear not an asset of democracy but an instrument of inequality. When citizens could recognize no immediate reason why they should attend annual militia musters, compulsion as a means of getting them there had to become more prominent than before. The customary means of compelling fulfillment of militia obligations was a schedule of fines. The effect, egalitarians argued, was to relieve the well-to-do of any militia obligation, since they could readily pay the fines and buy their way out; while the citizen who could not so readily pay the fines was subjected to inconvenience, if not worse, at least annually. Therefore state officials often neglected to impose penalties and militia obligations upon anyone, claiming democratic principle by way of justification, and the militia system fell into further decay.[24]

Decay set in despite the militia's continued rhetorical role, in the words of Jackson's first inaugural address, as "the bulwark of our defense . . . which in the present state of our intelligence and population must render us invincible."[25] Joel Poinsett of South Carolina, Secretary of War to Martin Van Buren, did take such rhetoric more seriously than most and proposed a reform of the militia. Perhaps that was because he was a southerner, for the plantation society persisted in attaching peculiar value to military virtues, and being fearful too of slave uprisings, it neglected the citizen soldiery less than the rest of the country. Poinsett would have recruited 100,000 men, by volunteering if possible and by draft if necessary, for a special "active" militia, reminiscent of George Washington's and Henry Knox's plans. But Congress rejected the scheme, and a much later Congressional committee concluded that "This appears to have been the last decided attempt to save the decaying system from dissolution. . . . The militia system by this time was virtually dead."[26]

More accurately, it was the common militia based upon a universal military obligation that was close to death. The minority of men who felt inclined toward arms added up to a fairly large group throughout the country, especially in the South, and they managed to preserve the volunteer militia companies in considerable vigor. The growing affluence of the country encouraged more and more elaborate uniforms and elegant social occasions, which encouraged recruiting even if not for the best of reasons. The New England Guards of Boston, the 7th Regiment of New York "National Guards," the First Troop of the Philadelphia City Cavalry, the Light Infantry Blues of Richmond, the Washington Artillery of New Orleans, and some scores of similar if less famous units thus became fixtures of the American scene and favorite subjects of folk artists and popular lithographers. They paraded on battalion days (that is, the annual militia muster days), escorted distinguished visitors, celebrated patriotic holidays with banquets and balls amidst the silver trophies that ornamented their headquarters, assisted in local emergencies of fire and flood, and somehow, as subsequent campaigns were to demonstrate, cultivated a surprising amount of genuine military skill.[27]

Nevertheless, the volunteer companies were at least as much a social as a military phenomenon, and they barely detract from the generalization that egalitarian America in the time of Andrew Jackson was an unmilitary country, indifferent to its military institutions at best and inclined toward downright hostility to military professionalism.

In the Regular Army and at West Point the development of the new professionalism continued all the same. To a degree the indifference and hostility of civilian society may even have encouraged professionalism; officers convinced of the value of what they were doing could be stimulated by the pride of doing it in the face of obstacles. For the future, however, the most important result of the divergence between civilian egalitarianism and military professionalism was an increased isolation of the Army from the rest of American life. As much as the eighteenth-century founding fathers had been suspicious of standing military establishments, civil-military relations of the eighteenth century had been smoothed by the lack of clear distinctions between civil and military careers. George Washington and his officers felt handicaps because they had not devoted their whole lives to war, but once a profession of arms had developed, what seemed striking in retrospect was not the difficulty but the ease with which Washington had shifted between civil and military occupations. Such shifts would be harder in the future. Never again would a man so new to armies as Washington, or Andrew Jackson, or Jacob Brown, lead the United States Army in war. And since the growth of military professionalism occurred at the very period in American history when the nation was least sympathetic to any kind of elite, a gulf far wider than anything the eighteenth century had known came to separate the Army from the rest of America in attitudes, values, and beliefs. However valuable to the Army was the growth of a military profession, the consequent isolation of the Army was scarcely an unalloyed blessing.

Henceforth except in occasional war, and until the responsibilities of world power in the twentieth century brought a new rapport between the Army and people, the Regular Army was sufficiently isolated to resemble sometimes a monastic order, isolated often physically as it patrolled the distant Indian frontiers, and isolated still more in mind and spirit as it cultivated specialized skills within a sprawling nation of jacks-of-all-trades.

When Calhoun entered the War Department in 1817, the Army's westernmost outposts were Fort Howard at Green Bay and Fort Crawford at Prairie du Chien in the Wisconsin country, Fort Armstrong at Rock Island in Illinois Territory, Chickasaw Bluffs (Memphis) in Tennessee, and Natchitoches, Louisiana. Already the postwar rush of settlement had crossed the Mississippi in certain areas, to reach longitudes beyond these forts. Calhoun therefore proposed to leapfrog the Army beyond the line of settlement to form a shield across the whole foreseeable westward advance. He proposed to push the garrisons eighteen hundred miles up the Missouri River to the mouth of the Yellowstone, with intermediate stations at the Mandan Village (near present Bismarck), where the Missouri swung closest to the Hudson's Bay Company outpost on the Red River of the North; at the Big Bend of the Missouri; and at the Council Bluffs. He was concerned more about the northwestern than the southwestern frontier for the reason suggested by his selection of the Mandan Village site: his desire to eliminate British influence from among the Indians of the United States. The northwestern tribes seemed considerably more hostile then the southwestern, and he believed the British influence explained why.

Congress authorized Calhoun's posts all the way to the Yellowstone, then retreated to a less ambitious plan for reasons of economy. But Calhoun did succeed in pushing the military frontier across what would become the first tier of states beyond the Mississippi. At the junction of the Minnesota River with the Mississippi, the Army built Fort St. Anthony, which Calhoun soon renamed Fort Snelling for its first commandant. Thence the new posts reached southward to Council Bluffs, where the Platte enters the Missouri; Fort Gibson, on the Arkansas River beyond the present eastern boundary of Oklahoma; Fort Towson, due south from Gibson and on the Red River; and Fort Jesup in western Louisiana. Here and at posts intermediate between them and the settlements, most of the Army spent most of the postwar years, passing most of its days in a routine of discipline, training, and housekeeping, punctuated by occasional arduous marches and more occasional skirmishes and battles. Early in Jefferson's Presidency the Army had garrisoned twenty-seven posts, the most remote of them Mackinac Island in the north and Fort Stoddert on the Mobile River to the south; by 1818, Calhoun pointed out in one of his efforts to dissuade Congress from reducing the Army, the posts had multiplied to seventy-three.[28]

The advance from the forests of the East into the prairies and plains westward from Illinois brought the Army to its first combat with mounted Indians. Red horsemen began to sneer contemptuously at infantry as "walk-a-heaps." In consequence, mounted units reappeared in the Regular Army, to carry in time the brunt of the later Indian Wars. The Sac and Fox tribes led against the whites by Black Hawk in 1832 were still forest Indians and not mounted, but the distances of the campaign made horsemen useful, and mounted militia were called out from Illinois and Michigan. They served well enough, and their commanding officer, Colonel Henry Dodge of Michigan, proved skillful enough, that Congress authorized a six-company battalion of mounted rangers for the Regular Army, with Dodge receiving a United States commission as major to lead them. Before the mounted ranger battalion could complete its organization, a law of March 2, 1833, raised the authorization to a full regiment. This was the 1st Dragoons, to comprise ten oversize companies and a total of 1,832 men. Dodge would command, with Stephen Watts Kearny, a Regular veteran of much campaigning and exploring on the plains, as lieutenant colonel in charge of both recruiting and training and tactics. As the name "dragoons" implied, like virtually all previous American horse soldiers the new regiment was expected to ride to its objectives but to fight mainly on foot, as geography and the nature of the enemy might decree.[29]

The 1st Dragoons got off to an unhappy start, which reflected all too well the character of military service on the new trans-Mississippi frontier. The officers, transferred from the infantry, and the recruits began to assemble at Jefferson Barracks in the summer of 1833. There they found little equipment ready for them and no horses. Not until October did enough horses arrive to mount three companies. Then, in early November, the Western Division of the Army made the ill-considered decision to send such of the regiment as was sufficiently organized on an immediate march to Fort Gibson, the stockade far up the Arkansas River in present-day Oklahoma. The three mounted companies, hardly practiced cavalrymen, and two others had to attempt a 500-mile winter march through almost uninhabited territory. In the face of storms typical of the Great Plains, most of the men made it; the recruits did so by transforming themselves almost into veterans on a single march.

The remaining five companies moved upriver in better weather the next spring. As soon as all the companies, now mounted, were at Gibson, Brigadier General Henry Leavenworth led them off to a new trial, a march to Pawnee and Comanche villages 250 miles farther upstream, to reconnoiter the country and make treaties with the Indians. The weather now turned intensely hot, as high as 114 degrees in the shade, and bad water induced "a slow and distressing bilious fever." At the junction of the Canadian and Little Rivers, Colonel Kearny had to be left behind with an encampment of sick men and horses. At the False Washita River, only half of the original force was still on its feet, and Leavenworth himself turned back, instructing Dodge to press on with about 200 men. Dodge managed to reach the Pawnee and Comanche and to arrange for the desired treaties. By the time the 1st Dragoons reassembled, the regiment was little more than a band of invalids.[30]

A march in distant Florida the following year came to a still less happy end and plunged the Army into one of the bitterest and most difficult of its Indian wars. On December 28, 1835, Captain Francis L. Dade was leading a company of the 4th Infantry, a company each from the 2nd and 3rd Artillery, a six-pounder gun, and a ration train from Tampa Bay to Fort King, 130 miles northeast. His guide had assured him the journey was almost finished, and he relaxed his march discipline. But his guide had also told hostile Seminoles of his approach, and Dade marched into an ambush, which wiped out his whole command, 107 officers and men. The Dade Massacre opened the Seminole War.

The professionalization of the American officer corps was preparing the Army to fight with new skill in any campaigns of the kind conventional in the European world. It did not serve so well as preparation for unconventional, irregular war. The United States Regular Army was patterned sufficiently on British and European models, in fact, that in 1835 it was not much better prepared for guerrilla warfare against the Seminoles in Florida than Napoleon's soldiers had been for the guerrillas of Spain. This was true despite experience in fighting forest Indians and the irregular campaigns that Americans themselves had sometimes waged during the Revolution.

A historical pattern was beginning to work itself out: occasionally the American Army has had to wage a guerrilla war, but guerrilla warfare is so incongruous to the natural methods and habits of a stable and well-to-do society that the American Army has tended to regard it as abnormal and to forget about it whenever possible. Each new experience with irregular warfare has required, then, that appropriate techniques be learned all over again. So it was in the Seminole War, for even more than forest Indians farther north, the Seminoles refused to stake their future upon showdown battles but preferred instead to wear out their adversaries by means of raids and terror, and by turning their forbidding homeland itself into a weapon against their foes.

The Seminole War was to last six years by official reckoning, and in ugly incidents still longer. After the Dade Massacre, a succession of commanding officers, including some of the best in the Army, led a succession of futile expeditions designed to pacify the Seminoles by the conventional means of bringing their warriors to battle and defeating them. Brevet Brigadier General Duncan L. Clinch tried in 1836. So in the same year did both Brigadier General (Brevet Major General) Edmund P. Gaines, commandant of the Western Department in a new division of the country into two geographical divisions, and Brigadier General Winfield Scott, commandant of the Eastern Department. Neither earned any laurels, and a long-standing personal feud contributed to that result. In unauthorized operations Gaines used up supplies that Scott was counting on; Scott got his movements started too late in the year; and communications between the two generals became so hostile that the War Department reprimanded both of them.

Quartermaster General Thomas Jesup next received temporary field command for a try at the Seminoles, and he managed to win enough pitched battles to feel hopeful of complete success. When the Seminole chieftain Osceola kept fighting when by conventional standards he should have acknowledged defeat, Jesup persuaded him to attend a council under a flag of truce and then made a prisoner of him. This expedient reflected a certain understanding of the nature of the war, but its violation of customary standards of honor outraged public opinion and Congress, and the effect on the Seminoles seems to have been mainly to infuriate them and stimulate their resistance.[31]

Meanwhile the war was draining away the strength of the tiny Regular Army and causing garrisons to be weakened all through the rest of the country. The actual strength of the Army was down to about 4,000 men when the war began. During most of the war at least 1,000 Regulars were kept in Florida. On May 23, 1836, Congress therefore voted an additional regiment of dragoons and authorized enlistment of 10,000 emergency troops for six or twelve months. General Scott gathered some 4,000 militia from neighboring states under the provisions of the militia acts. But many of the militia reported without arms, illustrating the lack of enforcement powers in the Act of 1792; they insisted that their service be limited to three months; and their performance was as uneven as might have been expected when men essentially civilians were thrown into war against a practiced adversary.[32]

In 1838 Congress added sixteen privates to the authorized strength of every artillery company and thirty-eight to every infantry company. It added an eleventh company to each regiment of artillery, and created the 8th Infantry Regiment. The staff departments were allowed proportionate increases. The total authorized strength of the Regular Army grew to 12,539 officers and men.[33]

By now the field commander was Colonel Zachary Taylor, a one-time Kentucky farmer who like Winfield Scott had entered the Army in the expansion of 1808. He was best known as a hero of the Black Hawk War. On Christmas Day, 1837, he brought the Seminoles to the biggest pitched battle of the war, on the shore of Lake Okeechobee, and won his brevet as brigadier general by giving them a resounding defeat. When the Indians predictably faded into the swamps to revert to guerrilla tactics, Taylor made the most appropriate response yet. His policy would require great patience but should work: he divided the entire disaffected region into districts twenty miles square, proposed to establish a stockade and a garrison in each district, and commissioned each district commandant to comb his district on alternate days.[34]

Washington lacked the requisite patience. The War Department optimistically ordered Taylor to suspend hostilities, and when the Indians then renewed their raids, Taylor asked to be relieved of his command.

Colonel William J. Worth succeeded him. Worth also adjusted his thinking to the nature of the campaign, offering a plan that might be swifter than Taylor's though also crueler. Rather than indulge in wild goose chases after the elusive enemy, Worth would hunt down the enemy's crops and dwellings and destroy his means of subsistence. To do so he would campaign straight through the hot months of 1841, which was the only way to keep the Seminoles from raising and harvesting their crops. The cost to Worth's own men in fever and dysentery was high, but the method succeeded. The Indians were broken into small bands that barely subsisted, and concerted resistance to United States authority came to an end.[35]

So complete was Worth's pacification of the Seminole that on August 23, 1842, Congress reduced the Regular Army to 8,613 officers and men. The reduction differed from earlier ones, however, by following to a degree Calhoun's old prescription of 1820. No regiments were disbanded and no commissioned officers released. Instead, only the enlisted strength of each company was reduced, along with a few cuts in the staff departments. The 2nd Dragoons became a rifle regiment, but that change was reversed within less than a year.[36]

The Regular Army of the 1820's and 1830's was most conspicuously an Indian-fighting army, but as always since the days of the 1st American Regiment much of its energy was expended also in shielding the Indians, in the territories assigned to them, from the restless pressures of the whites. When the government could or would not restrain those pressures, the Army sometimes received other unpleasant duties besides outright war. In 1838 and 1839, for example, it forced the Cherokee out of its southeastern homeland—obeying Presidential orders that rested on the most dubious of legal grounds —and escorted them on the tragic march to Oklahoma which took the lives of one-fourth of their nation on the way. In frontier areas, furthermore, the Army not only enforced federal authority upon and regarding the Indians; it often served as the principal instrument of United States marshals for the enforcement of law and order generally.[37]

A small part of the Army, artillerymen and engineers mostly, found themselves spared the physical isolation of most of their comrades through assignments to build and man the coastal and border fortifications guarding the cities of the East. The War of 1812 had renewed interest in such defenses: a principal reason why Baltimore held out against British attack while Washington did not was the presence of Fort McHenry where the Patapsco River approached the former city. Most of the principal harbors had defenses of some kind dating back to colonial times, and the coastal fortifications had been strengthened by the Federalists during the foreign troubles of the 1790's. But Jeffersonian economy had caused neglect, and the Royal Navy had been able to enter and command American bays and harbors all too freely. So Congress took up the subject of coastal defense immediately after the war.

In 1816 it appropriated $838,000 to initiate a systematic program of fortification that might forestall repetition of the cruises of Sir George Cockburn. To survey the coast and select sites, the War Department nominated a Board of Engineers, consisting of Simon Bernard, formerly an engineer officer of Napoleon's armies, Joseph G. Swift, the initial West Point graduate now chief of engineers, and a Navy captain. The Board had detailed suggestions ready for Secretary Calhoun to present to Congress in 1818. Calhoun proposed a series of fortresses to be erected under the supervision of the Corps of Engineers; private contractors would perform the actual construction, but the Corps of Engineers would be accountable for expenditures and responsible for the final product. Congress voted sufficient funds to begin construction as soon as final surveys of selected sites were complete. From January 1, 1817, to September 30, 1824, the Corps of Engineers expended over $3,000,000 in launching the program, seventy per cent as much as all previous expenditures for coastal fortification.[38]

As the War of 1812 receded, however, Congress grew neglectful again, and after 1824 the fortress walls rose slowly. Furthermore, as Andrew Jackson pointed out during his Presidency, appropriations for ordnance lagged far behind those for the fortresses themselves, and completed casemates often stood empty of guns. The reminder did little good. Much of the history of the Corps of Engineers from the War of 1812 to the Civil War concerns the slow erection of the red-brick-faced masonry battlements, many of which were to become famous during the 1860's: Fortress Monroe at Old Point Comfort, Fort Sumter on an artificial island in the jaw of Charleston harbor, Fort Pulaski on Cockspur Island off the mouth of the Savannah River, and the rest of them. Despite more than a generation of labor, however, Fort Sumter was still incomplete when Confederate cannon shot arched toward it at dawn on April 12, 1861, and so were most of its sisters. And by that time masonry walls proved to be obsolete against rifled guns.[39]

The officers of the Corps of Engineers were by far the least isolated of Regular Army men. Not only did their military engineering carry them into the coastal and Canadian border cities, but since West Point was the only engineering school in the country until Rensselaer Polytechnic Institute was founded in 1824 (not producing its first graduates until 1835), West Point graduates were far too valuable to be utilized on military works alone. One of the problems of Army manpower was the ability of West Point engineers to find better paying jobs in civil life, and those who remained in the Army were sent to civil works as well. The career of Montgomery Cunningham Meigs, future quartermaster general of the Army, was exceptionally successful but not untypical of that of the engineer officer. Brevetted a second lieutenant in the Corps of Engineers as the fifth-ranking graduate of the West Point class of 1836, Meigs first assisted in the building of Fort Mifflin, on the Delaware below Philadelphia. Next he collaborated with Lieutenant Robert Edward Lee in planning the improvement of Mississippi River navigation near St.

Louis. After returning to Philadelphia, he worked on both Fort Delaware in the river and the Delaware Breakwater, which was being built south from Cape May to aid navigators entering the Delaware. After a tour of duty at Washington with the Board of Engineers for Atlantic Coast Defenses, he became superintendent of construction at Fort Wayne on the Detroit River. Thence he went back to corps headquarters in Washington as assistant to the chief of engineers, thence to Fort Montgomery at Rouses Point, New York, then back to the Philadelphia projects, and finally to Washington again to build the Washington Aqueduct and the wings and dome of the Capitol of the United States. The last assignment, along with a captain's commission, came in 1853; Meigs remained with it until the eve of the Civil War.[40]

Active as the engineers were in civil works, the civil works program never achieved all that Calhoun had envisioned for it as a means of tying the Army more closely to the country and easing communications and commerce throughout the country, to the advancement of that national sentiment which seemed so important to the South Carolinian when he was Secretary of War. Calhoun believed that Congress should finance and the Army build an intracoastal waterway from Boston to Savannah, a road paralleling the coast and the waterway and reaching to New Orleans, and a complex of canals and roads to link the East with the trans-Appalachian West and to bind together the parts of the West. Such a system would exceed the financial capacities of the states, and it should be national too because every section of the country had a stake in communication with every other section. The extent of the country demanded roads and canals over which the Army could be shifted for defense, but:

The road or canal can scarcely be designated, which is highly useful for military operations, that is not equally required for the industry or political prosperity of the community.

The beneficial effects which would flow from such a system of improvement would extend directly and immediately to every State in the Union; and the expenditure that would be required for its completion would bear a fair proportion to the wealth and population of the several sections of the country.[41]

This ambitious plan ran aground on constitutional scruples, the governmental retrenchment following the Panic of 1819, the Presidential politics of 1824, and the post-War of 1812 decline of both interest in military affairs and nationalist enthusiasms. Nevertheless, Calhoun set the Army to limited road building, the soldiers themselves carrying out much of the labor, to ease travel between various military posts: from Plattsburg to Sacketts Harbor in the strategic Canadian border area; from Detroit to Fort Meigs near modern Toledo, another area that had figured prominently in the War of 1812; and from the northern border of Tennessee toward the Mississippi River and Madisonville, Louisiana, the Jackson Military Road. Congress subsequently approved similar projects though not a national road system: the Chicago Road, for example, from Detroit to Fort Dearborn (the site of Chicago), built in 1825, and the Fort Howard–Fort Crawford Road, from Green Bay to Prairie du Chien on the Mississippi, authorized in 1832. As Calhoun had said they would, they served far more than military purposes, the latter two doing much to open Michigan and Wisconsin, respectively. As the railroad revolution got under way, the Corps of Engineers had a hand in it as well; President John Quincy Adams lent Army engineers for the construction of the Baltimore and Ohio, for example.[42]

Civil works such as Meigs's on the Delaware Breakwater and the Mississippi channel resulted from the Rivers and Harbors Act of 1824, which gave the Corps of Engineers charge of improving seaports and inland waterways. From that act dates the special relationship between the Corps of Engineers and Congress, whereby the corps has enjoyed the special favor of Congress as the instrument of local and regional improvements dear to many Congressional hearts, while the corps in turn has used its resulting influence to become a conspicuous part of the rivers and harbors lobby, seeking expanded improvements and the assurance of its own role in developing them. During most of the nineteenth century, waterways improvements were especially conspicuous as one of the few overt projections of federal activity into economic affairs; in the twentieth century this aspect of federal economic activity has declined in relative importance, but the Corps of Engineers has retained its status as a sort of army within the Army as far as Congressional relationships are concerned. Sometimes involvement in civil works and thus in Congressional appropriations battles has drawn the engineers and individual members of the corps into notably unmilitary postures. To cite the career of M. C. Meigs again, during the James Buchanan administration that officer sought to keep his place on the public works in Washington despite a hostile Secretary of War by lobbying—successfully, as it turned out—to have Congress appropriate funds with the express proviso that he be in charge of expending them.[43]

The civil activities of Army engineers included also continued exploration of the national domain in the tradition of Lewis and Clark and Zebulon Pike. In 1816 Congress provided that the General Staff should include three topographical engineers, and in 1831 the Secretary of War established the Topographical Bureau as a separate staff department. Congress approved this step the following year, and the Topographical Engineers continued to exist separate from the rest of the Corps of Engineers until 1863. The most famous Army explorers of the middle years of the century included Major Stephen Long, who explored the Platte, the Arkansas, and the Canadian Rivers between 1817 and 1820; Captain Benjamin L. E. Bonneville of the 7th Infantry, who with 107 volunteers from his regiment and on leave of absence undertook a semiofficial exploration to the Rocky Mountains and beyond between 1832 and 1835, seeking a fortune in the fur trade for himself and information about the northwestern Indians for the War Department, and succeeding in the latter while failing in the former purpose; and Lieutenant John Charles Frémont of the Topographical Engineers, who began the map making that was to win him his sobriquet, "The Pathfinder," with a journey up the Oregon Trail in 1845. In 1837 the Topographical Engineers made their services available for commercial purposes, announcing they would undertake

surveys of a national or highly interesting commercial character applied for by states or incorporated companies. In those cases, such officers as can be spared (with their instruments) are allowed to be assigned. All other expenses . . . are supplied by the parties interested in the survey.[44]

Explorations, if arduous and often dangerous, at least were clearly purposeful, and so were the civil works of the Corps of Engineers, which held the additional advantage of bringing contacts, often pleasant, with civil life. But the post-War of 1812 years brought little activity so immediately purposeful to most of the Army, and most of the Army had to live largely isolated from civil life and influences, except for contact with sparse settlements in the West. Accounts of Army life in the 1820's and especially in the 1830's and 1840's often give impressions of restless unease and discontent, in an Army that led a hard life but felt itself little appreciated, and too often could not itself discern immediate and tangible usefulness in its activities.

The routines of frontier posts were harsh and uninspiring, interrupted mainly by occasional danger. The private's pay began at five dollars a month and rose to six dollars by 1833 and eight by the Mexican War. His release from routines, danger, and boredom had to be found in such dives as frontier villages on the edge of Army posts offered, if his neighborhood happened to afford that much. Until 1830 the Army also attempted to cheer him with a whiskey ration, amounting to 72,537 gallons at a cost of $22,132 during the year 1830; but some officers' complaints of drunkenness, together with the rising temperance movement, put a stop to that amenity.

Especially under such circumstances the quality of the men who would sign up with the Army, in a country of expanding economic opportunities, was scarcely what the War Department desired. Hard times such as those of the Panic of 1837 spurred recruiting and brought something of an improvement in the character of the recruits. But officers and visitors to Army posts spoke mostly of the men's low intelligence, loose morals, and especially their habitual drunkenness. Despite various restrictions upon the enlistment of aliens, the Army had to rely on them in considerable numbers; in the 1840's some forty-seven per cent of recruits were immigrants, about half of them Irish, many of the rest German. Withal, however, the evidence of the Indian wars and of constructive peaceful labors—including the building of posts mainly by the enlisted men themselves—indicated that a considerable capacity for both bravery and hard work could be found in the ranks.[45]

Still again, the number of men who would see a three-year enlistment through was smaller than the quantity who would sign up at all. Desertion was a persistent plague. In 1823 the adjutant general reported that desertions totaled about one-fourth of the enlistments for the year, and in 1826, an unusually bad year, the number was more than half. In 1853 Secretary of War Jefferson Davis calculated that the usual total of desertions, added to discharges and deaths, compelled the replacement of one-third of the Army annually. No one knew what to do about it. In 1830 Congress abolished the death penalty for desertion in peacetime, since so rarely did military courts feel willing to invoke it that it was a nullity anyway. But no substitute punishment worked. To be confined to the guard house of a frontier post was not much worse than simply serving at the post like any loyal soldier who had not tried to desert. Major General Alexander Macomb proposed to enlist boys of twelve for twelve-year terms, thinking thus to bend them to discipline at a malleable age. After several Secretaries of War had recommended it, Congress voted in 1838 to withhold two dollars of the soldier's monthly pay until the expiration of his enlistment, to persuade him to stay on. It was at the same time that coffee and sugar replaced the whiskey ration, in the fond hope that sobriety would breed faithfulness. Restrictions on the number of chaplains who could be recruited were also relaxed, to permit every post commandant to employ one, for similar reasons. Not even the first of these expedients seems to have had much effect; the Army could be unpleasant enough to make even the loss of withheld pay appear a small price for escaping it.[46]

The life of the officers was little more appealing than that of the enlisted men. One result of the developments at West Point was a tendency for travelers visiting Army posts to comment with remarkable frequency upon the high attainments of the officers in character and knowledge. But an intelligent, cultivated officer was all the more likely to think a hot, dusty, and remote outpost on the Plains a poor place even after the Spartan regimen of the Academy. For an officer without a family, the usual frontier post was dishearteningly lonely; for an officer with a family, it was generally no fit place for his family to be. In 1842 a second lieutenant's pay was twenty-five dollars a month and four rations. Prospects for promotion were dismal, since the Army was barely growing. There was no retirement system, and promotion was by seniority within each regiment or staff department.

Often the vacancies in the rank of second lieutenant were too few to absorb the West Point graduates, few though they were (about forty-five a year), and cadets had to be merely brevetted and assigned to special duties. A distasteful fate for a newly graduated cadet was to be set to some clerical task such as that of acting quartermaster, acting paymaster, or disbursing agent for the Indian Bureau. Such work was dull and routine, nothing of the sort the West Point aspirant had bargained for, and there was a risk of auditors' disallowances and consequent personal expenses. To discourage career officers further, when the 8th Infantry was raised in 1838, its officers were chosen from civilian life, and the next year Secretary Poinsett instituted an annual board to examine civilian candidates for commissions. These steps were responses to the popular and political sentiment for democratizing the Army, but they still further constricted opportunities for advancement. As one means of dealing with desertion the War Department in 1837 began an experiment in improving enlisted men's morale by offering a few promotions to commissioned grades from the ranks, but again the effect was to hurt the morale of the officers even while presumably advancing both democracy and the morale of the n.c.o.'s.

Therefore, while enlisted men deserted, the officers resigned. Their doing so was facilitated by the fact that until 1838 the Military Academy graduate was committed to only one year of active service. After 1838 the obligation was extended to four years. By 1847, of 1,330 West Point graduates, only 597 were in the Regular Army. Perhaps the wonder is that so many stayed, and that of those who did, so many remained good officers in the face of many temptations to go to seed.[47]

The disappointments and frustrations so pervasive in the officer's life, as well as the existence of an officer corps so small that almost everyone knew everyone else, do much to account for the extraordinary quarrelsomeness of the officers. A biographical study of almost any officer is virtually certain to be filled with persistent arguments, recriminations, and feuds. These unpleasantries reached to the very top, producing a notably contentious high command, which in turn could hardly have improved morale down through the ranks.

Eastern and Western area commands replaced the Northern and Southern Departments during Jacob Brown's tenure as commanding general. In the new department headquarters the two brigadier generals then in the Army were to alternate in two-year tours of duty, shuttling back and forth between the two commands. Unfortunately, the two brigadiers, Scott and Gaines, would cooperate with each other only under the severest pressure, for they feuded interminably over a question of rank which was to persist as long as both were in the Army. Each claimed seniority over the other; their brigadiers' commissions bore the same date, but Gaines's name preceded Scott's on the list; on the other hand, Scott possessed a brevet as brigadier antedating Gaines's.

When Brown died in 1828, the War Department decided that to put either Gaines or Scott in his place would be to drive the other out of the service; so Alexander Macomb, who had commanded bravely on the Plattsburg front in 1814, was advanced to major general instead. Scott responded characteristically by resigning rather than serve under Macomb. The department was able to smooth his feathers sufficiently to produce a retraction, but for a time he refused to have anything to do with Macomb beyond the strictest demands of duty. The original feud had thus spawned a second one; and meanwhile Scott did not confine his quarrels to his superiors, but indulged in disputation whenever anyone of any rank gave him the merest pretext. He had written the section of the Army regulations which forbade dueling, but no officer was freer with challenges to the field of honor. When Macomb died in 1841 there seemed nothing to do but choose between Scott and Gaines to succeed him after all; and Scott, able soldier but difficult if not juvenile personality, became commanding general. Gaines disappointed some expectations by not resigning but choosing to stay in the Army, where his and Scott's mutual dislike could continue to stir up trouble.[48]

Winfield Scott was something of a mirror of the Army itself. His flaws were great, but he had large virtues as well. Like the Army itself, he was in transition from military amateurism to professionalism. Commissioned from the legal profession and no West Pointer, he nevertheless encouraged the Academy and its new professionalism as much as he could, and studied to enhance his own expertise. The outstanding drillmaster of the War of 1812, after the war he was the most influential member of a board of officers which revised William Duane's *Hand Book for Infantry* to present the first infantry tactical manual drawn up under official auspices. Reflecting in part European as well as American experience, the new manual included among its innovations a more rapid march cadence (ninety rather than seventy-five steps per minute), an explicit emphasis on target practice, and the adoption at last of two rather than three ranks as the normal formation of American infantry in order to increase the rate of fire. In 1822 Lieutenant Colonel Pierce Darrow published a *Cavalry Tactics* which conformed to Scott's infantry system, and in 1826 Scott himself assisted in preparing both cavalry and artillery manuals to supplement his infantry tactics. Three years later Scott was the principal author of a still more complete statement of infantry tactical regulations, organizing the drill regulations under three headings, the school of the soldier, of the company, and of the battalion.[49]

Perhaps the most important of the Army's efforts to apply its increasing study of European military methods to practice concerned the artillery. The War of the Revolution and the War of 1812 had been mainly infantry wars. The contribution of Knox's artillery had been mainly to the winning of sieges. Despite Knox's efforts to make his guns more useful in open combat, the cannons of the Revolution could not dominate a battle of maneuver; they were either too small and light to do much damage or too heavy and clumsy to be manhandled into position rapidly enough. Napoleon's development of Gribeauval's artillery improvements transformed the guns into a decisive weapon of mobile war, with the use of better light guns drawn into position by horses, the cannoneers themselves either riding the limbers into action or, in horse artillery, going in mounted; but the new system made little impression upon the War of 1812. The British lagged in applying it and brought few guns to America, and the American experiment with Peter's battery had been abortive. Following the Napoleonic wars, however, the British turned their attention to their artillery to catch up with and improve upon the French. They improved the design of both field guns and carriages, and the French in turn copied the British improvements. Presently Lieutenant Daniel Tyler of the 1st Artillery returned to the United States from Europe with copies of the latest artillery regulations, information on the new guns, and advice that the United States adopt them.[50]

The Army reorganization act of 1821 had provided that one company in each of the four artillery regiments be a battery of light artillery. For seventeen years this provision of the act was a dead letter. The artillery served mainly as foot soldiers, stationed in coastal and frontier forts but largely doing the work of infantry, for which the Indian frontier seemed to present a far greater need. Then

Joel Poinsett, altogether the most vigorous and foresighted War Secretary since Calhoun, decided in 1838 to begin mounting four light batteries as the law provided. Captain (Brevet Major) Samuel Ringgold's Battery C, 3rd Artillery, became the first to receive six new field guns and the appropriate complement of horses. The next year Poinsett held a summer "camp of instruction" near Trenton, where Ringgold's battery maneuvered in company with infantry and dragoons, before an audience of invited and influential guests. Major Ringgold was a dashing young cavalier, and he put on an excellent dramatic performance which facilitated Congressional appropriations for mounting the remaining three light batteries.[51]

A few other technical improvements occurred about the same time. The fulminate of mercury percussion cap was adopted for the infantry musket, the flintlock could thus be replaced, and muskets could be serviceable in rain and snow. The United States arsenals ceased production of flintlocks in 1842, and the Model 1841 Springfield caplock officially became the standard shoulder arm. Actually, General Scott distrusted the percussion cap as too complicated, and because of his influence the guns in service were still mostly flintlocks when the Mexican War began. In Europe, meanwhile, experiments with rifled shoulder arms were going far toward solving the problems of fitting a bullet into the rifling of a muzzle loader. It was not until about the time of the Mexican War, however, that the French Colonel Minié presented his workable solution to those problems, and meanwhile the United States wisely retained smoothbore weapons.[52]

This chapter has been mainly an optimistic one. With an increasingly professional officer corps, interested in technical and tactical improvements, and leading eight seasoned regiments of infantry, two of dragoons, and four of artillery, all with a reasonably efficient special staff, the Army entered the Mexican War in 1846 immensely better prepared than it had been for the War of 1812. So far the new professionalism seemed to have brought pure gain toward a more effective Army. Even the isolation of the Army from much of American life, physical and otherwise, encouraged its efficiency in an untidy age. Isolation and professionalism had not yet proceeded far enough to suggest many misgivings that the divorcement of the Army from the mainstream of American society might somehow also weaken the Army by impairing its access to the sources of national vitality and strength. Jacksonian suspicions of professionalism took more superficial form and barely touched that idea. For the moment, the new professional Army was highly confident of itself, and—the Mexican War would seem to show—with good cause.

☆ NINE ☆

Regulars and Volunteers:
1846-61

[The citizen soldiers] were associated with so many disciplined men and professionally educated officers, that when they went into engagements it was with a confidence they would not have felt otherwise. They became soldiers themselves almost at once.

—Ulysses S. Grant[1]

ON February 4, 1846, Colonel (Brevet Brigadier General) Zachary Taylor was stationed at Corpus Christi in the newly annexed state of Texas with as large a force as the Regular Army could well assemble: five of the infantry regiments, one of dragoons, and sixteen companies of artillery, altogether not quite 4,000 men. That day he received orders from Washington to advance into the disputed ground between the Nueces River and the Rio Grande. Taylor's force was as large as it was because Mexico had threatened war if the United States so much as attempted to annex Texas. Conciliatory overtures from the United States now having failed, Taylor's new orders sent him into an area claimed by Texas but never recognized by Mexico as part of that state. The effect was to provoke a Mexican attack upon Taylor that opened the Mexican War.[2]

Second Lieutenant Ulysses S. Grant, 4th Infantry (USMA 1843) was to reflect, after he had seen much larger armies fight a much greater war, that the United States had been fortunate to begin the Mexican War with the Regular Army fashioned in the years since the War of 1812. Himself a member of Taylor's force in 1846, he wrote later that "A better army, man for man, probably never faced an enemy than the one commanded by General Taylor in the earliest two engagements of the Mexican War." Its troops, he said, were "under the best of drill and discipline," and "Every officer, from the highest to the lowest, was educated in his profession, not at West Point necessarily, but in the camp, in garrison, and many of them in Indian wars."[3]

More than a generation had passed when Grant wrote these impressions of the war, and no doubt time had obscured his recollection of certain less pleasant features of the Army's condition. Sylvanus Thayer's West Pointers filled many of the captaincies and lieutenancies in 1846, but the older officers still were older indeed, retaining their ranks in the absence of a retired list and perpetuating many of the Army's weaknesses of their own youth, when a lack of systematic military education and training had persisted all the way from the close of the Revolution to the War of 1812. Grant himself told how the colonel of his regiment, a "most estimable . . . old gentleman," decided that with war imminent he should conduct battalion drill, which he had not done in years; after two or three evolutions he fell dead. Colonel Ethan Allen Hitchcock, (USMA 1817) believed that General Taylor, no West Pointer, could not choose gun positions properly and failed to pay due regard to his supply lines, and that neither Taylor nor the other senior officers of the army that crossed the Nueces could form a brigade into line in proper fashion. "As for maneuvering, not one of them can move a step in it. Egotism or no egotism, I am the only field officer on the ground who can change a single position of the troops according to any but a militia code."[4]

Yet there was much to be said for Grant's later assessment. A generation of campaigning in the West and the Seminole country had made the Regulars extremely tough and able fighting men. They proved capable of passing on much of their knowledge to recruits very quickly. If the officers sometimes found it difficult to maneuver battalions and brigades by the rule book, many of them were so thoroughly experienced as commanders of smaller bodies and so fully accustomed to responsibility that they could pick up sufficient knowledge of tactical niceties as rapidly as they had to. Such a regiment as the 1st Dragoons had patrolled up and down the Indian frontier for so many seasons that mere marching could never again inflict on them the losses of their first year. In 1845 Colonel Stephen W. Kearny had led five companies of the regiment from Fort Leavenworth up the Oregon Trail to Fort Laramie and the Continental Divide at South Pass, thence back to Leavenworth by way of the foot of Pike's Peak, Bent's Fort, and the Arkansas River—2,200 miles in ninety-nine days, with every man well on the return.[5]

At the highest levels of command, the relationship between the Secretary of War and the commanding general remained an unsettled problem, especially as regarded the position of the staff department chiefs. Nevertheless, Calhoun's staff reforms had given the War Department ample ability to administer a war at least of the dimensions of one with Mexico, notwithstanding that the Army would have to exert its power much farther from the national heartland than ever before, and for the first time—to reach Mexico City—conduct what amounted to a campaign overseas.

The Mexican War President, James Knox Polk, rarely receives the highest marks for his performance as Commander in Chief. But the country could have been far less fortunate. Especially for the balance of military and civil power, it was well that a man of Polk's strong character should have occupied the White House. The only previous wartime Commander in Chief under the Constitution had practically abdicated the part, so it was Polk who first outlined the boundaries of powers later to be explored by Abraham Lincoln, Woodrow Wilson, Franklin D. Roosevelt, and Harry S Truman. Civil control of the military had survived the Revolution largely because the military commander, George Washington, was so circumspectly dedicated to it; otherwise the weakness of Congress might have undone it. In the War of 1812 neither the President nor his Secretaries of War were strong enough to lend the principle much meaning, but civilian weakness was offset by the corresponding weakness and ineptitude of most of the military chiefs. Polk first demonstrated how a strong executive, untroubled by the diffusion of power that had hampered the Continental Congress, could reconcile civil supremacy and the effective conduct of war, to the enhancement of both.

He accomplished it almost in spite of himself. He had no military knowledge or experience, and he lacked Abraham Lincoln's intuitive flair for military combinations. He was so zealously partisan a Democrat that he could hardly abide the Whiggery of his two principal generals, Scott and Taylor. He seriously proposed to Congress the revival of the rank of lieutenant general, so that he could give it to Senator Thomas Hart Benton, as little a soldier as himself but a Democrat. Frustrated in that design, he did impose upon the Army a dubious set of political commanders of brigades and divisions, with his own law partner, Gideon J. Pillow, the worst of them. He helped perpetrate a needless repetition of the short-term enlistment difficulties of the Revolution, which was to leave Scott sitting dangerously weak at Puebla on the road from Vera Cruz to Mexico, while seven of his regiments went home and he waited for new men to join.

But Polk had enough energy and enough common sense to compensate for a variety of shortcomings, and enough intelligence whatever his deficiencies that control of the war was probably better in his hands than in those of anybody else available. And he did control the war. Once fighting began, he kept himself in constant contact with the War Department and applied himself constantly to military plans, down to such details as the sailing date of ships. He selected the commanders of all expeditions, and he himself prepared their basic instructions. He had the Secretary of War bring dispatches from the field promptly to the White House. He chose the objectives of the campaigns, pushing Taylor southward across the Rio Grande to commence pressure upon Mexico as soon as war was declared, assuring the conquest of New Mexico and California through the march of Stephen Kearny's Army of the West, and finally deciding that the enemy would make peace only upon the fulfillment of Scott's proposal for a march from the Gulf to Mexico City. Polk consistently urged the war forward when the generals preferred to move more cautiously, as when he disallowed the eight-week truce negotiated by Taylor at Monterrey and ordered the resumption of that officer's southward march. The pervasiveness of his influence in the Army is illustrated by the reply of the Secretary of War to a congressman trying to get a commission: ". . . it is proper to say what I presume you are not ignorant of, that the selections are not made by the War Department, but by the President himself."[6]

Always Polk overshadowed Secretary of War William L. Marcy. When the summer came and Marcy fled Washington, Polk remained to take on all of Marcy's duties as well as his own. When Marcy was present but nevertheless inadequate, Polk remedied his deficiencies. In making the bureau chiefs strong, Calhoun had neglected the possiblility that under lesser leadership than his own they might become stronger than the Secretary of War. There was plenty of opportunity for them to do so: they were career professionals who stayed in their offices for decades while Secretaries came and went. Marcy could not control them. When Polk wanted to reward the heroism of some noncommissioned officers by promoting them to vacant second lieutenancies, for example, the adjutant general tried to sabotage the plan by withholding the list of vacancies. Marcy could not extract it from him. Polk had to restore the bureau chief to his proper status. He summoned the adjutant general, immediately refused to engage in debate, and offered an emphatic reminder "that he must regard what I said as a military order & that I would expect it to be promptly obeyed."[7]

Partly because of President Washington's deference to Alexander Hamilton, the custom had developed and prevailed since Washington's day that the Secretary of the Treasury collected the estimates of expenditures of the executive departments and sent them directly to Congress. In accordance with his determination to control his own administration and especially its war effort, Polk insisted upon inserting his own review between the Treasury Department and Congress, most especially in regard to War Department estimates. In 1846 he instructed Marcy to submit those estimates to him before sending them further. When the following year his new procedure convinced him that the estimates were excessive, he personally huddled with the General Staff, and the final estimates were very directly his own. This immediate supervision of the bureau chiefs and their finances was still another expression of Polk's high sense of executive responsibility, but it lapsed again under succeeding Presidents.[8]

Everywhere Polk sought to lead and control the military establishment in a manner commensurate with his constitutional responsibilities, and he left for his successors what was in many ways a model performance. The whole effort was complicated, however, not only by his own candid partisanship but also by a new kind of military politics: active aspiration for the Presidency by successful generals. This development was inconsistent with the new professionalism of the officer corps, but it was probably inevitable in a war which, unlike the nation's previous conflicts, brought an unbroken train of victories. Furthermore, the generals to whom the White House beckoned were transitional figures and not yet as fully professional soldiers as many of the graduates of Thayer's West Point. For Zachary Taylor and Winfield Scott, the Mexican War made the Presidency too immediate a possibility for either to ignore or reject it readily. Their military and political campaigning became intermingled. To make matters worse, since both of them were Whigs, their ambitions stimulated the Democrat Polk's own natural tendency to mix politics with war making.

Whigs who recognized his potential as an ornament to their party cultivated Taylor's ambitions almost from the time he crossed the Nueces, and "Old Rough and Ready"—a wonderful appellation for political purposes—became so enchanted that he began seeing in every disagreement with the War Department evidence of a Democratic plot to bar the White House doors. He became so quick to take offense that the administration began to distrust him in turn and to seek in fact the ruin of his political prospects. When Taylor's army went from victory to victory despite Polk's loss of enthusiasm for his campaign, the President decided that someone else must by all means lead the final thrust to the Mexican capital.

Since General Scott's politics were as unpalatable as Taylor's, Polk tried as long as he could to escape the obvious alternative to

Taylor as chief of the climactic expedition. It was at this juncture that he contemplated tailoring a lieutenant general's uniform to Thomas Hart Benton's measurements. By the time he concluded that he had to use Scott, the latter had joined Taylor in believing himself the target of an administration conspiracy. Scott now read ulterior motives into Polk's actions even where they did not exist, as when Polk attempted to hurry his army into the field before Scott considered the preparations complete.

I smelt the rat [the general said], and immediately told the Secretary that I saw the double trick, first, to supersede me, and, at the end of the war, say in six or eight or twelve months, disband every general who would not place Democracy above God's country.

So Scott went to Mexico believing himself endangered by "*a fire upon my rear, from Washington, and the fire, in front, from the Mexicans.*"⁹

Friction between Scott's headquarters and the President was bound to follow, especially once thousands of miles lay between them. Since Scott's officer corps included many of Polk's partisans, misunderstandings between the general and the President generated a host of quarrels within Scott's army itself. It is hard to estimate who behaved worst, Polk, Taylor, or Scott, in infecting the war effort with party and personal politics. Fortunately, both subsequent Presidents and subsequent generals seem to have profited from the example. Hereafter the rise of the West Pointers helped the Army cultivate in its officers a political style less that of Winfield Scott than of Dennis Mahan, who believed any hint of political activity inconsistent with his obligation of service to the nation; even the most politically ambitious generals felt increasingly obliged by custom and tradition to curb the open expression of their ambitions. The inhibiting of military partisanship in turn assisted Presidents to spare themselves some of Polk's worst troubles by inhibiting their own partisanship when they acted as Commander in Chief. And after all, even the intensely Democratic Polk finally allowed Taylor and Scott to lead on to victory, whatever his distaste for them and their politics.

Politics aside, the functioning of the professional headquarters of the Army was among the less successful features of the Mexican War. Calhoun's War Department bureaus did reasonably well in carrying out their assigned specialized tasks, but the war demonstrated that there was no adequate machinery for professional direction of strategy and operations. As commanding general, Scott had to perform the functions of a modern general staff almost single-handed: to devise a variety of possible war plans and inform the President of their merits, to estimate their requirements in men and supplies, to work out the details of plans agreed upon, to keep in touch with and supervise their execution. He had to do so without adequate intelligence of Mexican capacities or even geography and climate. Maps were so lacking that the campaign against Vera Cruz had to be planned from sketches made by a former United States consul at the city. Scott looked up two gentlemen who had traveled in Mexico to ask them about climate and especially about campaigning during the rainy season. When he tried from Washington to coordinate the assembly and movement of troops to the seat of war and Taylor's first advances into Mexico, he was balked by inadequate communications. The Army had no courier system; the mails were slow and uncertain, and in them many dispatches were lost; there were no codes or ciphers to conceal dispatches from prying readers. Once preparations were reasonably complete for the invasion at Vera Cruz, Scott had to abandon his Washington office for the field, leaving only the President, the Secretary of War, and some of the bureau chiefs to act as headquarters of the Army. With his departure a one-man general staff gave way to none at all.[10]

The work of the supply departments, the chief test of the War Department bureau system, was fairly good though capable of improvement. When the outbreak of war caused a hasty effort to raise volunteers and enlarge the Regular Army, and supplies and equipment had to be found for forces eventually growing to about 50,000, much had to be done in a hurry, and advance planning for such an emergency turned out not to have been one of the virtues of the staff departments. There followed much misdirected effort, waste of time and money, and profiteering by ambitious suppliers and agents who chose to exploit loose and improvised supply activities. On one occasion Quartermaster General Jesup allowed himself to be persuaded to requisition $2,000,000 of quartermaster funds for transfer to New Orleans, although there was no pressing need for the money in that city at the time. The Washington banking firm of Corcoran and Riggs did the persuading and acted as agent for the transfer. They promptly paid $400,000 to the proper agent at New Orleans, but they used the rest of the money for a time in stock speculation. Experiences of this kind helped lead Polk to devote more of his energies to supervising supply arrangements than to any other military activity.

The President felt continually upset over what he encountered here, especially since by his lights the supply departments made habits of both procrastination and extravagance. Ships rarely sailed promptly enough to satisfy him, goods rarely reached their destination soon enough, and everything seemed to cost too much. But there was also merit in Jesup's naturally more favorable view, that

with our depots farther from the sources of supply than Algiers is from Toulon or Marseilles, we accomplished more in the first six months of our operations in Mexico, than France, the first military power in Europe, has accomplished in Africa in seventeen years.[11]

Arms, equipment, and uniforms were procured in quantities that proved sufficient, and they were kept flowing to the troops at the front, by sea and across long stretches of hostile territory.

For the first time the Quartermaster's Department alone was responsible for clothing the Army in war; the offices of the commissary general of purchases, which had purchased clothing and much equipment, and the Clothing Bureau, which had estimated clothing requirements, had been consolidated into the Quartermaster's Department in 1841. Uniforms were provided by purchasing cloth from manufacturers, cutting it into garments at the Schuylkill Arsenal in Philadelphia and at another depot in New York City, and sending it out to seamstresses and tailors for finishing. Though Congress at first required that the volunteers requisitioned from the states furnish their own clothing (or more realistically, be supplied by their states), the Quartermaster's Department ended up supplying many of them as well as the Regulars. Troops and supplies for Scott's Army of Invasion traveled by steamers and sailing ships chartered by the Quartermaster's Department and on that department's own fleet of thirty-five steamers and thirty-five sailing ships purchased or constructed during the war.

In Mexico the armies largely had to subsist themselves, because of the great distances involved and especially after Scott virtually cut loose from his base on the Gulf. Foodstuffs were either purchased or requisitioned by commissary officers accompanying the armies, or gathered up more informally by the men. In the desert campaigns, the soldiers often dined abstemiously, but along the route of Scott's march Army hard-water crackers and salt pork could be supplemented with a variety of vegetables, fruits, breads, chickens, and eggs. The Army had permitted civilian sutlers to accompany the troops since Washington's day, and they went along to Mexico, vending delicacies, tobacco, and alcohol. In the latter line they faced competition from enterprising soldiers who bought up from the Mexicans and retailed aguardiente, muscal, and other local potations.[12]

The major deficiencies in supply resulted at least as much from mistakes of the field commanders as from failures of the supply bu-

reaus at Washington or the supply base at New Orleans. Zachary
Taylor's forte was battlefield command, not administration or staff
work. Scott tried to minimize Old Zach's shortcomings by providing
him with an excellent assistant adjutant general, Captain William
Bliss; but "Perfect Bliss" could not assume the whole administration
of Taylor's army or make important decisions. So Taylor chose as his
base for preparing the invasion of Mexico the town of Camargo, a
hundred miles from the Gulf of Mexico by air line and much farther
up the snaking Rio Grande, too far for boats to supply it well. Furthermore, it was an unhealthy place, where fetid air stagnated between limestone rocks. Taylor's sanitary precautions were slack, and
while his army spent most of August, 1846, there, 1,500 died and
almost every volunteer regiment had a third to a half of its men on
sick list by the time Taylor was ready to march away.

Incredibly, Taylor had not in the meantime arranged with the
Quartermaster's Department for transport once he began to move
southward. Hearing nothing from him, the Quartermaster's Department was trying to purchase sufficient wagons for his army. When
Polk learned of the wagons, he suggested characteristically that it
would be cheaper and just as satisfactory to use mules for transportation in Mexico. Jesup said he agreed, and he proved unable to
explain clearly why in that case the wagons were being purchased.
By fall and into the winter, furthermore, the need for transport became so urgent that quartermasters bought expensive horses and
mules in the United States for shipment to Mexico, a country famous
for its pack animals.[13]

Taylor's haphazard supply arrangements were symptomatic of
other deficiencies in the higher ranks of the Army. West Point professionalism had not yet reached those ranks, and without systematic
education in the administration and command of large bodies of
troops, the ranking officers still had much of the amateur about
them, and their qualities were uneven. Through native ability, experience, and military self-education, Winfield Scott had become a
consummate soldier, an able strategist, tactician, and logistician who
triumphed in the end over both the enemy and the pettinesses of his
own character. But most of the other generals could hardly have
measured up to the demands of a bigger war and barely qualified for
the relatively small one at hand. Zachary Taylor was a brave, inspir-
ing, and determined leader on the battlefield, but only a fair tactician
and a worse administrator. Stephen Watts Kearny led the small
Army of the West ably on its long march from Fort Leavenworth to
the conquest of California, and he was one officer who might have
done well with larger forces in a larger war.

The troops in Mexico were the first American soldiers to be organized systematically into divisions, the somewhat autonomous armies in miniature that had appeared with the growth of armies during the French Revolution. But it was almost as difficult to find officers capable of handling a division well as to find army commanders. Among the division commanders, William J. Worth had qualities of brilliance but was erratic and self-centered, and his quarrels with Taylor and Scott limited his usefulness to both of them. David E. Twiggs was blunt and unimaginative, devoted to the frontal assault because everything else was too sophisticated for his taste. John E. Wool may have been the best of the division commanders because he was the steadiest, but he demonstrated no capacities that were strikingly large.[14]

The great strengths of the United States Army were in its junior officers, especially the West Pointers, and its enlisted men. They not only made the Regular Army which opened the war a formidable force for its size; they also demonstrated again what Scott had shown when he fashioned the force that won at Chippewa and Lundy's Lane, that the leadership and example of a relatively small number of officers and n.c.o.'s who knew the business of soldiering could make good soldiers out of willing citizens in a remarkably short time.

When the Mexican War began in May, 1846, the Regular Army numbered 734 officers and 7,885 enlisted men, in eight regiments of infantry, two of dragoons, and four of artillery, in addition to the staff corps and departments. In the War of 1812 the government had authorized rapid multiplication of the Regular formations, giving the Regular Army a paper strength far beyond anything it could hope to achieve in practice. Rather than repeat this delusory method of enlarging the national military strength for war, Congress now voted only moderate increases in the Regular Army, such as it might reasonably hope to achieve, and otherwise relied on the volunteer militia companies, which in part were already recruited and in which additional men were more willing to enlist than in the Regulars.

In May, 1846, Congress raised the Regular Army infantry companies from an authorized sixty-four privates to a war strength of a hundred privates. It also voted a 100-man company of sappers, miners, and pontoniers, and a ten-company regiment of mounted riflemen. The Regular Army enlistment term continued at five years. In February, 1847, the legislature voted an additional nine regiments of Regular infantry and one of dragoons, with more attractive enlistment terms; men might sign up for the duration of the war only, and upon honorable discharge they might receive a land bonus. The next month each artillery regiment was increased by an additional two companies, with two companies of each regiment rather than only one to be organized as light batteries. Altogether, 30,476 men served in the Regular Army during the Mexican War.[15]

At the same time that Congress enlarged the companies of the Regular Army, in May, 1846, it authorized 50,000 volunteers, to serve for twelve months or for the war at the discretion of the President. In addition, the President was authorized to call militia into federal service for six months rather than the three months provided by the peacetime laws. Since the Mexican War was fought entirely on foreign soil, the common militia, in essence a home-defense force, was not suitable, and the latter provision was never invoked. Congress understood that the 50,000 volunteers would be sought largely by enlisting companies and larger tactical formations of volunteer organized militia into federal service, and the War Department proceeded in that manner. Congress authorized the President to apportion field, staff, and general officers of volunteers among the states according to the quantities of troops they offered. The volunteer units were to be organized according to the militia laws of the various states.

One of Polk's mistakes was to delegate to the states or the volunteer units the option of enlisting for twelve months or the war. The consequence was Scott's embarrassment at Puebla on the way to Mexico City. After February, 1847, however, no enlistment was permitted for less than the duration of the war.[16]

A total of 73,532 men served in units other than the Regular Army during the war. Both this figure and the Regular Army aggregate are misleading. Some of the men included were called up for three months under the old militia laws before wartime legislation got under way. Zachary Taylor called on Texas for militia when war was impending, and he received 1,390 men. His immediate superior, General Gaines, commanding at New Orleans, made an unauthorized call for militia from the southwestern states, for which he was reprimanded and relieved from command; but meanwhile 11,211 men presented themselves under his call. Some of these same men surely enlisted again and were counted again under the later calls for volunteers, and some men were counted twice because they volunteered first for twelve months and then for the duration. The total number in service at a given time was probably never much more than 50,000. Significantly, also, some 15,000 of the Regulars were enlisted in Mexico, which means that those 15,000 largely passed into the Regular Army from the volunteers, with whom they had reached the enemy's country.[17]

The numbers engaged in any one battle were always relatively small. At Monterrey, Taylor commanded about 6,000 men; at

Buena Vista not quite 5,000. Scott landed about 10,000 to take Vera Cruz, and he led only about 700 more than that out of Puebla in August, 1847, for the final advance into the Valley of Mexico. The small numbers engaged were largely Regular Army in enough of these battles to permit the growth of a legend that the Mexican War was won by the Regular Army almost alone, and of the consequent argument that the brief duration of the war and the uniform success of American arms demonstrated a requirement that the Regulars be strengthened to carry the main share of the burden in other wars.

The performance of the Regular rank and file and of the junior officers was indeed encouraging. This was especially true of that technical arm, the artillery, and of the new mobile batteries. On the eve of the war, in 1845, Scott wrote into still another of his tactical manuals the experience of the first such batteries in adapting the English and French systems. The available weaponry was still appropriate to Napoleonic artillery tactics, in which the gunners would pound the enemy's guns and infantry from relatively short range. The war's first combat of consequence, Palo Alto, was mainly an artillery victory. Maneuvering with almost the flexibility of cavalry, standing beside or sometimes in front of the infantry, Ringgold's and Captain James Duncan's batteries, assisted by two heavy eighteen-pounders, got off some 3,000 rounds to 750 for the rival Mexican guns and broke up every Mexican advance before it could become a serious threat. "The gallant Major Ringgold" died while proving his guns; but General Taylor, hitherto a skeptic, was moved to report that it was to the artillery that "our success [is] mainly due."[18]

The small forces engaged in the battles of the war permitted the handful of light batteries, mostly Regular Army, to go on fighting with almost equally conspicuous value. In his last battle, Taylor had cause for special gratitude to the guns again. Outnumbered more than four to one at Buena Vista, and with all but four light batteries and two companies of dragoons of the Regular Army departed to serve with Scott, Taylor won the battle although in General Wool's words, "Without our artillery we could not have maintained our position a single hour." "Our artillery did more than wonders," was Taylor's comment this time.[19]

If the combat experience of the Regular Army was mainly in small unit actions, the terrain of the Mexican War often broke up larger battles into multiple fragmentary actions to which this experience was highly relevant. At Resaca de la Palma, the second important engagement, a heavy cover of chaparral atomized the fight into contests of squads and even individuals. Elsewhere mountainous terrain had a similar effect. So did the street fighting at Monterrey and the advance along the Belén and Verónica causeways into the City of Mexico.

For the first time in an American war, the skill of the junior officers was commensurate with the bravery of the soldiers. Though Sylvanus Thayer's and Dennis Mahan's curriculum was better calculated to produce good engineers than skillful battlefield leaders of platoons and companies, the tactical training of West Point proved sufficient, augmented by experience, to turn out such leaders. The biography of almost every officer destined for high command in the Civil War is ornamented with feats of skill and valor in the Mexican War. Winfield Scott's encomium to his young West Pointers is famous but evidently well deserved:

I give it as my fixed opinion [he said] that but for our graduated cadets the war between the United States and Mexico might, and probably would, have lasted some four or five years, with, in its first half, more defeats than victories falling to our share, whereas in two campaigns we conquered a great country and a peace without the loss of a single battle or skirmish.[20]

The graduated cadets were as useful as they should have been in military engineering as well as in combat. They demonstrated their skills in the selection and field fortification of positions, in the reduction of enemy fortresses at Monterrey and Vera Cruz, and especially in their reconnaissance of lines of march from Vera Cruz to Mexico and of the approaches to the enemy's position before almost every battle. Scott never sent troops to the attack without a full report on the approaches from the engineers. Captain R. E. Lee of the Corps of Engineers discovered the invaluable flanking route around Cerro Gordo; Lieutenant P. G. T. Beauregard supplied the survey and situation estimate that led Scott to choose the route to Mexico City by way of the citadel of Chapultepec. It was in the Mexican War that American artillery and engineering, hitherto entrusted so often to foreign officers, at last came of age.[21]

The West Point graduates also permitted Scott to assemble for his Army of Invasion the first American field army staff to approach adequacy. Lee was a staff engineer, along with Major (Brevet Colonel) John Lind Smith, the chief engineer. The perceptive and literate Colonel (Brevet Major General for gallant conduct at Molino del Rey) Ethan Allen Hitchcock was inspector general, and Captain (Brevet Lieutenant Colonel) Henry Lee Scott assistant adjutant general. Scott called these West Pointers his "little cabinet." One of their most notable services was Hitchcock's in organizing a company of spies from among the Mexican population and deserters, which together with a network of agents in Mexico City gave Scott easily the best American intelligence system since George Washington's.[22]

At least as important as the quality of the Regular Army rank and file and junior officers, however, was the performance of the Mexican War volunteers. For the existence of a professional leadership for the Regular Army, and especially of good junior officers, permitted the citizen recruits to secure training far more adequate than anything generally available in any previous war. If nothing else, the officers and n.c.o.'s of the volunteer regiments had Scott's various tactical manuals at hand. In 1821 the War Department had begun to publish *The General Regulations for the Army of the United States*, and it had appeared in revised editions at frequent intervals since then, with another new edition arriving in 1847; this work provided volunteer officers with a guide to procedure, administration, and organization that they had not possessed in previous wars. Once in Mexico, the volunteer regiments could drill side by side with Regulars. Taylor compelled "the volunteers with him to receive six hours drilling per day and relieves them of all other duties, to make soldiers of them." Scott was at least as thorough. The results were summarized by Lieutenant Ulysses Grant in the quotation appearing at the head of this chapter; the volunteers

were associated with so many disciplined men and professionally educated officers, that when they went into engagements it was with a confidence they would not have felt otherwise. They became soldiers themselves almost at once.[23]

Professional officers accustomed to European ways of military thought still insisted that the making of a soldier required years, and they were to continue to insist so into the twentieth century. Yet the United States Army was to discover that it could produce acceptable soldiers for the much more complex warfare of World War II with a basic training program of about thirteen weeks, and accordingly it should hardly come as a surprise that acceptable soldiers for the simpler war of 1846–47 could be trained at least as quickly. Until now, American citizens had rarely become soldiers (except for Scott's small regiments of Chippewa and Lundy's Lane) because not enough soldiers, and especially officers, who were already trained could be found to teach them. Now that the teachers were available, Nathanael Greene's rueful dictum of the Revolution, that the soldiers were better than the officers, gave way to Grant's, that men exposed to disciplined fellow soldiers and professionally educated officers become "soldiers themselves almost at once." After all, about half of the Mexican War Regulars, some 15,000 out of 30,000, themselves began as volunteers and became Regulars merely by virtue of a new oath administered in Mexico.

Some volunteer regiments occasionally fought less than well in Mexico, such as the unhappy 2nd Indiana at Buena Vista, to provide grist for the mills of the Uptonian historians who were to be determined to find little that was good to say about them. But in this war another kind of example was easier to find. If Taylor could not have won Buena Vista without his Regular artillery, neither could he have won it without his volunteers, such as the 3rd Indiana, who redeemed the honor of the Hoosier State, the 2nd Kentucky, the 1st and 2nd Illinois, and Colonel Jefferson Davis's Mississippi Rifles. The latter may have been the best of all the volunteer regiments; significantly, its colonel was a West Pointer. If Buena Vista was a defensive battle, albeit an uncommonly fluid one, the volunteers and the new Regulars mainly carried Scott's army to its offensive successes at Churubusco and Chapultepec.

Among the volunteer regiments also was citizen-soldier (erstwhile lawyer) Alexander William Doniphan's 1st Missouri Regiment, "unwashed and unshaven, . . . ragged and dirty, without uniforms, and dressed as, and how, they pleased." Starting from Santa Fe in November, 1846, 856 strong, they marched down the Rio Grande; across the dread desert called the Jornado del Muerto to Brazito near El Paso, where they routed 1,200 Mexican soldiers; southward to Chihuahua, subsisting on the country and on the way routing 2,700 enemy soldiers and 1,000 armed rancheros at the battle of the Arroyo Seco; thence to Saltillo and to Monterrey, to join Taylor's army. Altogether their anabasis covered 6,000 miles, during which they received neither supplies nor pay nor instructions. They were of course somewhat uncommon citizen soldiers, "ring-tailed roarers" of the frontier; but as they could do so much, many other citizen soldiers proved in the Mexican War that they could do a great deal.[24]

Its first conquest of foreign territory gave the Army its first, brief experience in military government of alien soil. Its record ranged from excessive brutality to excessive generosity in the treatment of the inhabitants. Taylor always guided his men with a loose rein, and sometimes he allowed them to get out of hand at the expense of the invaded population. The Regular officers charged that it was especially the volunteers who ran riot; Scott, writing to the Secretary of War after visiting Taylor's army, said:

But, my dear Sir, our militia & volunteers, if a tenth of what is said to be true, have committed atrocities—horrors—in Mexico, sufficient to

make Heaven weep, & every American, of Christian morals, *blush* for
his country. Murder, robbery & rape of mothers & daughters, in the
presence of the tied up males of the families, have been common all
along the Rio Grande. . . . Truly it would seem unchristian & cruel to let
loose upon any people—even savages—such unbridled persons—free-
booters, &c., &c. . . .[25]

When Scott took his own army into the enemy's country, he tried
to suppress firmly such crimes against persons or major crimes
against property. In fact, his restraint of his men and his effort to
maintain the normal forms of civil order as far as possible may have
helped lead his division commander William J. Worth into one exceptional display of generosity. Worth accepted the capitulation of
the city of Puebla on terms that not only maintained much of the
local administration but also gave the native courts the right to try
Mexicans who attacked and even murdered American soldiers. Such
defendants could therefore anticipate unusual tolerance.

One of the difficulties of the time was the absence of generally
accepted international law on the subject of military occupations.
Scott largely had to devise his policy for himself. He proclaimed a
code of "martial law" for occupied areas, and he appointed military
governors to enforce it. Both civilian and military offenders were to
be tried by military commissions. At the same time he stressed the
idea that the American quarrel was with the Mexican government
and not with the Mexican people, insisted that the Mexicans must be
treated in accord with general American standards of justice and
fairness, and tried to use his military government policies to drive a
wedge between the Mexican people and those of their authorities
who were waging war against the United States. This policy did not
preclude Scott's governing through the native municipal officials,
and he did so as much as possible. He promised the Mexicans protection against all wanton impositions upon either persons or property,
and he ordered that cash be paid for all Army purchases and requisitions. In Mexico City he organized 400 picked soldiers as a police
force to supplement the native establishment. He respected the local
customs and religion, although not so much that he failed to essay
characteristic Anglo-Saxon improvements. For example, he tried
diligently to improve the public sanitation of Mexican cities; one
object of his cleansing campaign was the loathsome prison of Ulúa in
Vera Cruz, which a later American observer with the occupation
forces of 1914 believed was not cleaned again until the Americans
returned.

Scott's efficient and honest regime, operating in an age when nationalist sensibilities were not yet so acute as in the twentieth century, seems to have won a surprising amount of admiration and

friendship from Mexican officials. Adjutant General Hitchcock was astonished by the warmth and lavishness of the entertainment that the Mexico City *ayuntamiento* eventually offered in tribute to Scott. When Scott departed for a court of inquiry called to examine his customary quarrels with his fellow officers, Major General William O. Butler succeeded him and maintained his policies until Mexico was evacuated.[26]

Partly because the Army had fought so well in Mexico, partly because any changes in military policy might have affected the sectional balance, few innovations marked the history of the Army from the Mexican War to 1861. As the sectional crisis mounted during those years, both sides preferred to exempt the Regular Army from involvement in it, lest either secure a potential military advantage over the other. The sectional crisis now joined other considerations in dictating that the Regular Army remain small; the South would not have awarded the central government a powerful weapon of suppression. Since 1843 Congress had tried to assure against sectional imbalance in the officer corps itself, by formally legislating a policy that had developed since Jackson's day, whereby cadets of the Military Academy were appointed from Congressional districts.[27]

The Army preferred its political neutrality. Even Taylor and Scott sought to divorce their military from their political roles to the extent of never voting while they remained in uniform, a practice in which they concurred with the example set by Dennis Mahan.[28]

As the Mexican War ended, the volunteers were discharged and most of the new Regular formations created during the war disbanded. The Regiment of Mounted Rifles was an exception, remaining in service, along with the two companies added to each artillery regiment. The company tables of organization reverted to peace strength: forty-two privates in each infantry and artillery company, fifty in a dragoon company, sixty-four in a company of mounted rifles. To encourage the officers, they were allowed to retain whatever rank they had achieved in the war, being carried as additional numbers in their grades but returning to their old units. Brigades and divisions disappeared, and the regiment became again the largest tactical unit. For administration of the Army the old Eastern and Western Divisions had been replaced since 1842 by some nine smaller geographical departments.[29]

During the Presidency of Franklin Pierce, the Army benefited from the leadership of one of the most energetic of Secretaries of War, Jefferson Davis. Already the colonel of the Mississippi Rifles was assuming the mantle of southern political leadership passed on by the recently deceased Calhoun, yet the sectional quarrel had not advanced so far as to make it inappropriate for Calhoun's heir to follow him in the national War Department. A reforming Secretary on the model of Calhoun, Davis persuaded Congress that the new territorial accessions required more military patrols, and in 1855 the 9th and 10th Infantry Regiments and the 1st and 2nd Cavalry were added to the Army, raising its authorized strength to 17,867 officers and men. The prospective employment of the new mounted regiments against the light horse of the Plains Indians probably influenced their designation as cavalry, but in fact they became primarily dragoons on the established American pattern, rather than saber-wielding cavalry of the European type.[30]

Like Calhoun before him, Davis was also highly interested in the peaceful services of the Army. He took an especially close interest in Captain Meigs's work on the wings and dome of the Capitol and toward a pure water supply for the capital city through the Washington Aqueduct. He helped make the decade of the fifties the high point in the history of the Corps of Topographical Engineers and of military surveys of the trans-Mississippi West. Army engineers did much of the mapping both of the new border with Mexico and of the vast territories newly acquired. Davis became one of those Americans almost obsessed with the vision of a transcontinental railroad to the Pacific shore and of the possibilities that would flow from it, and despite his attachment to a southern route, he sponsored the Army's exploration of four trails that the road might follow (giving the fullest supplies to the northernmost party, to emphasize his fairness). The routes thus surveyed became in time the approximate paths of the Northern Pacific, the Denver and Rio Grande, the Santa Fe, and the Southern Pacific.[31]

Davis also sponsored the last important advance in military technology before the Civil War, the adoption of a rifled infantry musket. By now, Captain Minié in France had made the rifle practical as a mass weapon by inventing a shell with a hollow base so designed that the gases of the gun's firing would expand the shell to fit the rifling snugly—the "minnie ball" of the Civil War. The United States now adapted the Model 1855 Springfield rifle, to take Minié ammunition of .58 caliber. The acceptance of the rifle demanded a new system of tactics, and under Davis's leadership the Army adopted *Hardee's Rifle and Light Infantry Tactics* in 1855. For the present the principal changes over previous tactical manuals consisted of the instructions for handling the new weapon and appeared in the "school of the soldier." The effects upon battlefield tactics were destined to be immense but could not altogether be foreseen and remained to be digested by later tactical writers.[32]

Related changes in artillery were waiting in the wings. European armies were experimenting with both rifled and breech-loading cannons, Italian and German inventors having produced such guns independently in 1846. The American Ordnance Department, though inclined toward conservatism, had some justification for awaiting further developments before settling upon a fixed design. So the South Boston Iron Foundry and the West Point Foundry manufactured a few rifled cannons before the end of the decade, but the first extensive introduction of them did not occur until the Army ordered 300 three-inch rifles at the beginning of the Civil War. American acceptance of breechloaders came still later.[33]

Davis wanted to increase the Army's awareness of such European developments, and he was principally responsible for sending an American military commission to observe the Crimean War and the armies of Europe generally. The visit was an outstanding success. The three commissioners were intelligent, perceptive, and thoroughly imbued with the new professional outlook; and each of them, Major Richard Delafield (USMA, 1818), Major Alfred Mordecai (USMA, 1819), and Captain George B. McClellan (USMA, 1846), presented a report that ranks as a landmark in the new American military literature. All three reports reflected the West Point emphasis upon military engineering in perhaps excessive degree, but each writer had something important to say about his specialty as well: Delafield, fortification; Mordecai, artillery; and Mc-Clellan, cavalry.[34]

Davis's additional reforms were as varied as a pay increase for officers and men (to eleven dollars a month for the private) and the famous introduction of thirty-three camels into the American West for military freight-carrying. The camel experiment was not so ludicrous as it has often been made to seem; Davis was pleased with the results, and his successor proposed to purchase 1,000 more of the beasts. But the Civil War intervened, and soon afterward the railroads made camels unnecessary.[35]

The Secretary could not succeed in everything he attempted. He tried but failed to discover a remedy for the plague of desertion. He wanted to encourage the better officers and to advance them rapidly; but by now the Army had become accustomed to a system of promotion by seniority, and by seniority in regiment or staff corps at that; and the charms of a system without delicate puzzles were too great for the service to be willing to weigh nice alternatives in order to stimulate and reward merit. Davis believed strongly that the United States should manufacture its own arms in government factories, but he failed to secure an additional armory on the Pacific

Coast. Most important, he failed to remedy the most conspicuous weakness revealed by the Mexican War, that of the command system.[36]

Davis gave special attention to the vexed questions concerning the relationship among President, Secretary of War, and commanding general. During the war, a strong President had maintained his constitutional ascendancy, but at the expense of constant quarrels with his principal professional soldiers, unpleasantly overt assertions of his will over the bureau chiefs, and a considerable limitation of his ability to receive candid professional advice and guidance. He had controlled over-all strategy most thoroughly when Scott vacated the office of commanding general to lead a single field army, but that departure had also left the Army without a professional head and Polk without access to a suitable military counselor. How could the responsibilities of President, Secretary of War, and commanding general be defined to assure the constitutional ascendancy of the civil authorities and yet bring into full play the professional expertise of the senior general? This question and its many corollaries were to plague the Army for two generations more; Davis's effort to solve it merely aggravated the difficulties.

Davis was inclined, not unnaturally, to elevate the role of the Secretary of War in the command of the Army, and his inclination found a certain sanction in the law and the Constitution. If civil control of the military was to be fortified with institutional safeguards, the Secretary would have to become the focus of civil control. Polk had maintained civil ascendancy through an uncommonly vigorous assertion of Presidential power, but Presidents have many duties, and future Presidents could not be counted on to supervise the Army as diligently and minutely as Polk had done; often they simply would not have time for it. The Secretary of War, however, was the President's deputy for military matters and could apply himself wholly to the Army. Until now most Secretaries had lacked effective control of the Army, and the strongest of them, Knox and Calhoun, had not held the office in wartime. But the regulations of the Army, based upon statute law, did state that the Secretary of War as the President's deputy was to exercise direct control of the military arm. In contrast, no statute defined the duties of the commanding general. To have defined those duties would have required facing up to the anomalous nature of the office; for if the general in chief commanded the Army, he usurped the legal and constitutional place of the Secretary of War. The only means of guarding the law and the Constitution and yet retaining suitable professional expertise in the command of the Army was to make the general in chief a deputy and adviser to the Secretary. Davis evidently aimed at such a solution.

Unfortunately, he pursued it with a roughshod arrogance that ensured his failure, especially since he had to deal with Winfield Scott.[37]

Scott not only took his rank as commanding general seriously but interpreted it literally. That is, he took so dim a view of civilian authority over his right to command as to approach setting himself up as an independent potentate. After the Mexican War he did not fully resume the office of commanding general until Zachary Taylor became President, because even Scott recognized the inexpedience of issuing orders to an officer who was about to inhabit the White House. Therefore Scott confined himself for a time to a restored Eastern Division, while Taylor commanded the Western Division. Once Taylor did become Commander in Chief, however, Scott's jealousy of him asserted itself, and the commanding general insisted on commanding the Army from New York, not Washington, so that the President and the War Department could less well influence his conduct and policies. In this condition the War Department and the commanding general abandoned all but the most minimal intercommunication. When Taylor died and Millard Fillmore succeeded him, Scott consented to return to Washington; but as soon as Franklin Pierce, victor over Scott in the election of 1852, installed himself in the Presidency, the commanding general forthwith returned to New York.

Jefferson Davis resolved to eliminate the division of authority between Washington and New York. But his personality was little better suited to harmonizing differences than Scott's. He was coldly vain where Scott was emotionally and impulsively vain. He had a confidence in his own military knowledge which assisted him in his lesser military reforms but was sure simply to offend Scott. He had no tact and easily grew angry. Given the personalities involved, Davis's effort to resolve the command problem promptly degenerated into a mere contest for supremacy.

Scott had been long in the habit of making short trips on Army business on his own authority and charging mileage compensation for them. The regulations sanctioned compensation only for those officers who traveled "under written and special orders from their proper superiors," but Scott assumed that as commanding general he had no such superior. Davis was sure that he did—the Secretary of War. Therefore, about two months after Davis took office, a War Department auditor found grounds for exception in one of Scott's mileage vouchers. Scott protested that there was no "proper superior" to the commanding general other than the President, and that he need not consult the President every time he traveled. Davis stiffly upheld the auditor.

Must Scott regard the Secretary as speaking for the President and thus be subordinate to him, or was the commanding general his own master except when the President in person intervened in military matters? Scott came to assert that no order of the Secretary bound him unless it expressly stipulated "by order of the President." Scott's interpretation of his status, then, would largely have divorced the Army from the civil authority, since the President cannot maintain constant contact with the activities of the Army and its commander. Once the issue was drawn, Scott and Davis fought over it through the rest of Davis's term. Scott's intransigence grew, if that were possible, when Congress voted him the brevet rank of lieutenant general, the first lieutenant generalcy since George Washington. Then the quarrel extended itself to the nature of Scott's emoluments in his new rank. The general and the Secretary fought too over Scott's reimbursement for expenditures he had made in Mexico for "secret service" activities, the nature of which he said he could not reveal without betraying confidences. Davis questioned Scott's right to grant Colonel and Brevet Brigadier General Ethan Allen Hitchcock leave of absence when his regiment was under orders for an Indian campaign, and Hitchcock finally suspended that phase of the quarrel by resigning his commission.

At length Davis brought in the Attorney General, who issued an opinion that the Secretary of War could legally command the ranking general without specifying that he spoke "by order of the President"; the orders of the Secretary must be assumed to be those of the President. But the practical questions remained unsolved. Scott continued to sulk in New York, more and more aloof from Washington except when he chose to hurl one of his periodic diatribes at Davis, whom he described as the "scribbler . . . at his dirty work again." In practice his absence left control of the Army to Davis, who exploited his position at the center of power in Washington to conduct most of his reforms without reference to Scott. But even with the Attorney General's opinion, nothing was really solved; granting that opinion, the question remained: what were the duties and responsibilities of the commanding general?[38]

When Davis turned the War Department over to President James Buchanan's Secretary, John B. Floyd, friction between the department and Scott eased, if only because Floyd was an ineffectual bumbler who therefore posed no personal threat to Scott's preeminence. But the general was so soured (and accustomed to the amenities of New York) that he remained outside the capital—to return old and fat and feeble only when the southern states seceded and duty called him again to defend the flag he had served since Jefferson's time.

Notwithstanding the feud with Scott, Jefferson Davis's tenure in the War Department was mainly a success. John B. Floyd's was unhappy in almost every way. Though personally honest, Floyd weakly allowed himself and the department to become enmeshed in scandal when he propped up the finances of the Army's freighting contractor on the Plains with unauthorized borrowing from the Indian Bureau funds. A similar easygoing tolerance for the vagaries of politically influential contractors on the public works at Washington led Floyd into a hassle with the superintendent of construction, Captain Meigs, who was both unbendingly honest and irritatingly self-righteous. This unpleasantness climaxed in Floyd's exiling Meigs to duty at Fort Jefferson on the Dry Tortugas amidst a welter of legal and constitutional problems, since Meigs had persuaded his friends in Congress, led by Jefferson Davis, to appropriate funds for the public works only on condition that Meigs be entrusted with their expenditure.[39]

Twice during Buchanan's term, moreover, the Army faced the unwelcome task of curbing domestic turmoil, standing between free-soilers and slave-staters in Kansas, and marching against the Mormons in Utah after they had practically forced federal officials out of the territory. The "Mormon War" of 1857–58 nearly became a war in fact, since the Mormons captured and burned supply trains serving the Army and prepared their militia for resistance. Only skillful diplomacy by a Presidential emissary sympathetic to the Mormons' legitimate grievances enabled the Army to march into Salt Lake City unopposed in the spring of 1858.[40]

The implications of Kansas were much more frightening than those of Utah. During the Buchanan years, there developed a growing insistence among the southern states that the War Department ship them the full quotas of arms due their militia under the law of 1808. Secretary Floyd complied with the law. Since he happened to be a Virginian, some northern men began to find grounds beyond his careless finances on which to question his fitness for his post.[41]

If one of the principal military features of the Mexican War had been its demonstration of the ability of citizen soldiers to fight notably well once they received a modicum of training, Regular officers had sometimes shown an equally notable reluctance to acknowledge the fact. The citizen soldiers' display of their fighting qualities in the armies of Taylor and Scott had been accompanied by an inordinate amount of grumbling and magnifying of their faults on the part of professional officers, especially such young West Point graduates as George G. Meade and John F. Reynolds. Evidently the professionalization of the officer corps was encouraging, along with its beneficial results, the not uncommon self-protective tendency of skilled men to regard their skills as so arcane that nobody could or should share in their work at all except at the most menial levels. But professionals' skepticism about them had not deterred the citizen volunteers of 1846–47 from fighting, and their performance then should have suggested that the southern militia arming themselves in the 1850's, and the northern companies beginning to arm in response, might be capable of staging a considerable war.

TEN

The Grand Army: 1861-65

Practically considered, then, the nation has no army in time of peace, though, when the clarion voice of war resounds through the land, the country throughout its vast extent becomes, if necessary, one bristling camp of armed men. . . . It is a circumstance quite unique in character. . . . It is so new that it has no precise parallel in all history: it belongs to the genius of the American Republic. . . .

—John A. Logan[1]

THE WARS OF the French Revolution had first demonstrated the immense military powers that might be unleashed when the popular passions of nationalism enlisted themselves for war. Those passions produced the nation in arms, with mass armies irresistible except by other mass armies formed out of similar national emotions. Before the armed nationhood of Revolutionary and Napoleonic France the regular armies of the eighteenth century, overwhelmingly dwarfed, could not stand, not even the army of Frederick the Great's Prussia.

The United States had been spared participation in the mass warfare of the beginning of the nineteenth century. The War of 1812 still resembled more closely Europe's eighteenth-century wars, as the American War for Independence had been fought conservatively enough that it only hinted at the possibilities of the nation in arms. But although in 1861 the United States had never yet participated in a mass warfare of hordes of armed citizens, the patriotic enthusiasms that swept North and South after Fort Sumter were such as to nourish an almost instinctive realization that such a war was at hand. Though many expected the war to be brief, all expected it to be an epic struggle. The South believed it must fight to defend its very way of life, all the values of home, family, and civilization. The North fought for the Federal Union, which a generation of schoolboys reciting Webster's reply to Hayne had come to regard as carrying the democratic hopes not only of Americans but of mankind. Both sides set out immediately to muster mass armies many times larger than any hitherto mobilized in the Western Hemisphere.

Two days after the inauguration of Abraham Lincoln, the Congress of the Confederate States of America voted an army of 100,-000 volunteers to be enlisted for one year, and within about a month one-third of them were under arms. Soon the Confederates began to enlist men for the duration of the war. After Bull Run their Congress voted 400,000 men for three years. In December, 1861, they voted various bounties and privileges to induce one-year men to reenlist for two years more. When it became evident in early 1862 that these inducements were insufficient, the Confederates turned to the drastic expedient of conscription, to force the one-year men to stay and to ensure the filling of the depleted regiments.[2]

The Confederacy stood in the extreme situation of fighting for its very national life, and with inferior numbers and resources. The Union, with superior numbers and resources and facing less direct peril, felt slightly less desperate and moved slightly more slowly into extreme measures to recruit and maintain mass armies. But only slightly more slowly. On the day after the evacuation of Fort Sumter, April 15, 1861, President Lincoln issued his proclamation calling on the states for 75,000 militia for three months' federal service, to put down rebellious combinations in seven southern states. He also announced an extra session of Congress to meet July 4. The militia call was based on the Militia Act of 1792. Under it the War Department assigned each state a quota of militia. Since the common militia consisted mainly of enrollment lists, the states sought to meet their quotas mainly by recruiting the organized companies and reinforcing them. Patriotic enthusiasm and popular pressure brought the organized volunteer companies and individual recruits forward in greater numbers than the governors of the states and the President were prepared to accept. Thanks to the existence of the organized volunteer companies, however, Lincoln could mobilize a fairly substantial army with some measure of equipment and training, quickly and without recourse to Congress.

Under the Militia Act as amended in 1795, he might retain this force "until the expiration of thirty days after the commencement of the then next session in Congress." By that time, the July 4 special session could have acted to provide a more permanent force. Meanwhile, the militia institutions permitted Lincoln to delay the convening of Congress long enough that he might give some thought to his military proposals and the means of implementing them rather than rush forward headlong. Merely by giving the Union a stopgap army and a breathing spell, the country's militia institutions amply justified themselves.[3]

The Union was fortunate to retain the enlisted strength of the Regular Army virtually intact. Lincoln was to use this fact as evidence "that the plain people understand, and appreciate" that the war was "essentially a People's contest." ". . . not one common soldier, or common sailor," he told Congress on July 4, "is known to have deserted the flag." Though defections among officers were contrastingly numerous, they were not so many as they might have been, considering that proportionately more southern than northern graduates of West Point had made the Army their career; of the 1,108 officers in the Army on December 31, 1860, 313 resigned. While retaining the Regular Army gave moral encouragement to the Union, however, its military weight in a mass war must be relatively small. At the beginning of 1861 it numbered only slightly more than 15,000 enlisted men. Merely to assemble them would consume time. One hundred eighty-three of the 198 companies were scattered along the western frontier in seventy-nine posts, and when Texas seceded, General Twiggs had surrendered to its authorities his whole Department of Texas, numbering about one-fourth of the Army. Hostilities not yet having begun, the troops were allowed to make their way north from Texas, but all the public property of the Department of Texas stayed behind.[4]

How much the small Regular Army might assist the Union would depend on the way it was used. When Lincoln took office, Winfield Scott was back in Washington to lend the government the wisdom and prestige of "the first soldier of the age." Scott rejected proposals to scatter Regular officers and soldiers among the new formations in order to use them as teachers. He insisted that instead the Regular Army must be kept intact, as a solid if tiny nucleus for the war armies and a model rather than a swarm of instructors. Lincoln accepted this advice; the wisdom of it has been debated ever since. Much can be said for the opposite idea that regiments of citizen soldiers should have received as many experienced officers and n.c.o.'s as possible. In time the government did relax Scott's policy to a degree, and when state governors learned that professional officers could be useful and began to plead for them, some were released to the volunteers. Also, the states secured many of the West Point graduates who had entered civil life but now returned to the sword:

393 such men accepted state commissions, while 115 reentered the Regular Army. Meanwhile, under Scott's policy the solid discipline of a bloc of Regulars did prove invaluable and served as a useful example on many of the early battlefields. At First Bull Run, the Regulars were conspicuous even though they consisted only of one battalion, along with a battalion of marines. The retention of separate Regular Army formations proved itself sufficiently that such formations again retained their identity in the twentieth-century world wars. But less even than during the Mexican War did the government repeat the War of 1812's disappointing effort to build a large Regular Army while volunteer units were also recruiting; Congress was to increase the authorized Regular establishment merely by nine regiments of infantry, one of cavalry, and one of artillery.[5]

Under Lincoln's call for three-months' militia, the government actually accepted 91,816 men. They served the country well; they rescued the city of Washington when it was in grave danger of falling to a secessionist coup, and it was their commanders' fault more than their own that they did not win the First Battle of Bull Run. With additional men still clamoring to enlist in federal service, Lincoln decided to anticipate Congress and to create new formations without authorization of law. Thus he called on May 3 for 42,034 volunteers to serve for three years, unless sooner discharged, and increased the strength of the Regular Army and the Navy by 22,714 and 18,000 men respectively. Indeed, he accepted troops in excess of all of his calls. By July 1, Secretary of War Simon Cameron reported to him that 310,000 troops were under arms, of whom about 80,000 would soon be discharged as three-month men. The call of May 3 had been for 40 regiments of three-year volunteers, but by July 1, 208 such regiments had been accepted, of which 153 were in active service and 55 almost ready.[6]

As Lincoln had expected, Congress was prompt to sanction his emergency measures. In his message of July 4, he requested authorization for 400,000 three-year volunteers. Congress quickly voted 500,000. On the day after Bull Run a bill for still more troops was introduced into the Senate; as finally passed it authorized 500,000 volunteers "for the war." Thus Congress voted a volunteer army of a million men. Eventually some 700,000 were enlisted under the two acts and officially credited to the call of May 3, although none were enlisted "for the war" despite the terms of the second act. By August 3 the War Department reported 485,640 three-year volunteers already in service, organized in 418 regiments of infantry, 31 regiments of cavalry, and 10 regiments of artillery.[7]

So American nationalism turned its mighty energies to war, and in a few weeks it produced mass armies such as the world had seen only once before since the half (or more than half) legendary armies of the ancients. Not only the armies but the speed with which they assembled reflected the tremendous urgency of patriotic fervor and the readiness with which the government responded to it. Kenneth P. Williams has pointed out that in the approximately four months from Fort Sumter's fall to the War Department report of August 3, the United States Army grew to twenty-seven times its original strength; and that in 1917, without the handicaps of a divided country, defecting officers, and an imperiled capital, in a similar period the Army grew less than threefold.[8]

While patriotic enthusiasm could bring forth hordes of soldiers, however, it alone could not arm, equip, and train them. It is hardly remarkable that while asking for an authorization of 400,000 men, Lincoln also told Congress on July 4: "One of the greatest perplexities of the government, is to avoid receiving troops faster than it can provide for them."[9] It is hardly remarkable that histories of the first months of the war generally emphasize accounts of confusion, fumbling, and ineptitude in organizing and supplying the troops, with not a few instances of corrupt men battening on the occasion, and with soldiers even in the national capital standing guard clad only in their drawers because uniforms were not numerous enough or good enough.

But these lugubrious tales can easily be overdone. In the matter of supply, the Civil War was not yet a gross-national-product war on the order of World War II, demanding the intensive mobilization of the whole national economy. It was still a war of rifled muskets, bayonets, and relatively primitive cannons, rather than of automatic weapons, self-propelled guns, tanks, airplanes, and radar. Its armies did require mass production of certain products; but they were comparatively simple ones, and by the time of the war the United States had taken off on its rise as a modern industrial power, enough so that the productive and technological capacity of the country could meet the war's demands. The really remarkable point about military needs in the Civil War is how well even the agricultural South was able to improvise sufficient war industry for the purpose, so that southern armies did not fail for lack of equipment and supplies until northern encroachments upon Confederate territory had deprived the South of necessary resources, such as the copper mines of Tennessee and the coal and iron fields of Alabama. Both sides now had railroads to move the large armies and the telegraph to coordinate their movements, granted the relative backwardness of the southern facilities. As far as organizing the hordes of recruits into armies was concerned, West Point, observation of Europe, and the experience of smaller wars provided sufficient knowledge of what to do, and the country had cultivated enough executive ability to do it.

When the war began, a fairly large supply of small arms was on hand, because stores of them had been accumulated not only for the Regular Army but also for the militia, under the Act of 1808. It is putting it mildly to say that not all of them were the most modern of weapons. Also, they varied so much that as late as Second Bull Run the ordnance officer of the Federal Army of Virginia asked on one requisition for eleven different kinds of ammunition for carbines, rifles, and muskets. Still, the weapons could serve for a time against an enemy similarly armed. Altogether, the North held in its arsenals at the beginning of the war 457,660 percussion muskets and rifles judged suitable for service, 35,335 of which were muskets altered to rifles or .58-caliber 1855 rifles. The South seized from United States arsenals some 120,000 muskets, 10,000 of which were rifles, in addition to some 300,000 weapons already in the hands of southern militia. The latter, however, often were especially outmoded—Virginia's were mainly flintlocks—and many of them had to be kept in the states for home defense against the persistent fear of slave insurrection.[10]

The South could arm its first recruits, then, but it faced real limitations in arming additional troops. Southern agents quickly tried to purchase weapons in Europe. But the North moved at least as quickly to forestall them, and northern purchasing agents had both more money and more reliable credit to offer. Northern agents bought up all sorts of European guns, even extremely ancient ones, to keep them from southern hands. Nevertheless, the Confederacy eventually purchased about 200,000 arms in Europe. In the course of the war its armies captured another 150,000. Meanwhile, at the beginning of the war the Confederates held Harpers Ferry with its United States arsenal, and before they evacuated the place they carried off the rifle-making machinery to Richmond and to Fayetteville, North Carolina. They used the machinery to build up their own arms manufactories with considerable success, producing about 40,000 weapons by the time of Gettysburg. Altogether, some 600,000 small arms were available to the Confederacy in the course of the war, enough to equip the men who were available for mobilization.[11]

On the eve of the war the productive capacity of the Springfield and Harpers Ferry arsenals was some 22,000 pieces annually. The North retained the larger of the two, Springfield, and immediately set out to increase its capacity. It is another evidence that Lincoln soon abandoned the delusion of a short war that he early pushed for the establishment of a new arsenal at Rock Island, Illinois. By November 21, 1862, the North had purchased 726,705 foreign muskets and rifles plus 30,788 rifles, 31,210 carbines, and 86,607 pistols from American manufacturers. By that time the Springfield Arsenal had manufactured 109,810 rifles, and its capacity had grown to 200,000 rifles a year. By the end of the war, the government arsenals produced nearly 1,700,000 pieces.[12]

At the beginning both North and South were less well off in artillery than in small arms. In the North, United States arsenals listed 4,167 guns on hand, but only 163 were serviceable field guns and howitzers. Therefore securing artillery for the new mass armies did demand immediate industrial activity, but this was one of the areas in which American industry proved sufficiently mature to meet the requirements of the war. Even in the South, by mid-June, 1861, Virginia with its Tredegar Iron Works at Richmond was able to supply from limited stocks on hand and from new manufactures 115 guns for twenty field batteries. By the time McClellan advanced on Richmond, he could approximate his desired artillery quota of 3 guns per thousand men, and the Confederates were not markedly inferior. In the Gettysburg campaign the Federal Army of the Potomac had 4 guns per thousand men, and the Confederate Army of Northern Virginia 3.4. (The Prussians in 1870 had 3.5 per thousand.) During the war, northern foundries cast 7,892 cannons.[13]

The equipment and supply of many of the early troops, North as well as South, was undertaken by the states, and even by cities, towns, and groups of individuals. Neither the government at Washington nor the government at Richmond as yet possessed administrative machinery sufficient to provide for the needs of so many men; the War Department at Washington consisted only of the Secretary himself, the bureau chiefs, and a handful of assistants and clerks. Already the states and the members themselves had equipped the organized militia companies which formed the nucleus of the first volunteer armies. Each state had its own small war department to administer militia affairs, and though none of them amounted to much, each was more adequate to the needs of the state's own troops than the federal War Department was to the needs of a mass army. So the states conducted the enlistment of the men, the state governors chose the regimental officers, and the states and their citizens largely saw to outfitting the recruits as soldiers. In Philadelphia, for example, a Committee of Public Safety voted to raise $250,000 to arm and equip ten regiments. This sort of activity brought on an unfortunate competition for the purchase of military supplies and thus drove up prices. It also made for a motley assortment of supplies. But by this means the first armies were equipped when no other means were available. As rapidly as it could, the federal government enlarged its administrative machinery to take over the responsibilities. Through citizens', state, and federal activity, and with the federal government by now carrying most of the burden, Brigadier General Irvin McDowell could comment in December, 1861, that he believed the Union forces were supplied more lavishly than any in the world: "I believe a French army of half the size of ours could be supplied with what we waste."[14]

The individual who signed up for the Army in 1861, out of patriotism, desire for a job, pressure of family or sweetheart, or some other cause, generally had some choice of officers and comrades with whom he would serve. Even in rural counties and small towns more than one company was likely to be recruiting, perhaps the established volunteer militia company filling its ranks, perhaps a company forming under the auspices of a private citizen who wanted a commission and had been authorized by the governor or the War Department to raise troops, perhaps a company enrolling under some representative of the governor. In large cities the choice of organizations was wide. At this juncture most companies still appealed to recruits by means of colorful titles, such as the Ringgold Light Artillery or the Washington Grays; these names would soon be swallowed up in relatively drab regimental designations. When a company or regiment reached the minimum strength prescribed by law, which for most volunteer organizations was sixty-four privates to a company, with ten companies forming a regiment, it would march off or entrain—often parading amidst grand civic demonstrations—to a designated mustering point. There a Regular Army officer inspected it before mustering it into federal service. At first the mustering officer was simply charged with determining that the enlistees were between eighteen and forty-five years of age and "in physical strength and vigor"; after August 3, 1861, a surgeon was to conduct thorough medical examinations of recruits, but most testimony suggests that the examinations were not all that they were supposed to be.

The mustering officer then administered the oath of allegiance, and the regiment or company passed into federal service. The federal government now attempted to remedy any deficiency in the equipment and uniforms supplied by the states. The officers had either been elected by the men or appointed by the governors in reward for recruiting or for political service—the two methods tending in practice to be identical, since political pressures figured in the elections. Crude though this system of officer selection was, there was no better method available to the citizen armies, and the federal government accepted the officers and commissioned them.[15]

"We thought the rebellion would be over before our chance would come," wrote a boy who passed through such a process to enter the 6th Wisconsin Regiment under Lincoln's call of April 15, 1861. That half-fear, half-hope underlay much of the frenzied activity of the first months and did much to make recruiting easier. When it developed that there was plenty of time to grapple with the rebellion, and that the dangers were many and the experience unpleasant, main- taining the mass armies proved a much more difficult task.[16]

After the first enthusiasm faded, casualties, desertions, and a con- stant tendency of the war to continue enlarging itself demanded a perpetual stream of recruits. Invariably since its birth in the French Revolution, modern mass warfare has imposed conscription upon the young manhood of warring nations, rationalized on the ground that the rights guaranteed to the individual by the new popular na- tional governments imply an obligation upon him to defend his rights by defending the government that assures them. To keep up their mass armies, both North and South had to turn to this principle.

The Confederacy resorted to conscription only a year after shoot- ing began. On April 16, 1862, the Confederate Congress imposed an obligation to military service upon white men between the ages of eighteen and thirty-five. Amendments in September, 1862, and Feb- ruary, 1864, extended the age limits to seventeen and fifty. Under a supplementary law of April 21, 1862, men in various occupations deemed essential or at least highly useful were exempted; after Feb- ruary, 1864, exemption was subjected to executive discretion, and drafted men could be detailed to war industries. More invidiously, the law also exempted one slave owner or overseer for every twenty slaves he owned or supervised, or after February, 1864, one for every fifteen, and thus provoked an outcry about class legislation. Until December, 1863, the law also permitted the hiring of a substi- tute, another dubious provision, though in the Confederacy rela- tively few substitutes were available for hire. By means of the draft law, the Confederacy was able to hold most of its one-year men of 1861 in service and to justify their retention to them by pointing to the general obligation. Eventually, the draft law seems to have pro- vided directly or indirectly some 300,000 soldiers, about a third of the Confederate total, and thus to have contributed to the Confederacy's remarkable harvest of military manpower from a white population of about five and a half million.[17]

Before 1862 was over, the North felt obliged to assert the prin- ciple of national conscription as well, if not yet to invoke it effec- tively. The universal obligation to military service had of course been implicit in the militia system since colonial days; the innovation of the Civil War was not only to enforce the obligation more consistently than before but also to make it an obligation to the national government rather than merely to the states. For this reason it is usually cited as noteworthy that the states'-rightist South imposed national conscription before the North.

On December 3, 1861, in War Department General Orders No. 105, Secretary of War Simon Cameron promulgated an intelligent plan for maintaining the strength of the new Army, which by that time numbered 660,971 men. He put an end to state and private recruiting by stipulating that once the units in process of organization were completed, additional troops would be recruited only by requisition of the War Department. He further provided for War Department general superintendents of recruiting, who would take charge of recruiting in each state at the beginning of the new year and who would supervise regimental recruiting parties in the states. The superintendents would assemble recruits at central depots, see to their equipment and instruction, and then forward them to established regiments. Thus the federal government would control the recruiting process, and the effect would be to keep up the strength of old regiments rather than continually to create new ones.[18]

Unfortunately, after Edwin M. Stanton became Secretary of War on January 15, 1862, he upset Cameron's plan. Stanton was intent on minimizing the extravagance and waste that supposedly infested Cameron's administration of the department, and believing that the existing Army was ample to crush the Confederacy, one of the methods he chose to save money was to close the recruiting service. The casualties of Shiloh and the Peninsular Campaign and the failure of those actions to defeat the enemy soon disabused Stanton and compelled him to reopen recruiting. On May 1 he instructed army commanders to requisition governors for replacements for casualties, and on June 6 he restored the federal recruiting service. But he did not restore Cameron's replacement plan. Instead, he decided that widening operations and growing lines of communications demanded new regiments, and he adopted a procedure which led to their creation wholesale and to the neglect of replacements for the existing regiments.

The War Department arranged that the governors should appeal to the President to accept 300,000 more volunteers, and the President responded with a proclamation of July 2, 1862, calling for them. This was the call that inspired the song *We Are Coming, Father Abraham*, but otherwise the response was less exuberant. After the initial calls of 1861, state quotas had become hopelessly confused and the quota system had been abandoned, but now each state was again assigned a share according to its population. Everyone could recognize that recruits were no longer likely to hasten to the

colors as rapidly as the year before, so the War Department authorized immediate payment of $25 to each recruit from a bounty of $100,
the remainder to be paid on discharge; and to enlist the efforts of
influential men who might assist in recruiting if they could become
officers, all the states except Wisconsin chose to raise completely new
regiments rather than fill the old ones, a course made possible by
Stanton's abandonment of Cameron's replacement plan.[19]

Eventually, in 1863, the War Department did revert to a program
of filling up the old regiments, not with complete consistency but
with some success. By then, however, there were so many regiments
that to have brought them toward full strength would have increased
the total manpower of the Army beyond what seemed expedient.
Consolidating regiments was a possible alternative, but to deprive
men of their accustomed officers, flags, and regimental traditions did
not appear wise. Meanwhile, as regiments and their officers grew
experienced, they also shrank in personnel, the numerical losses going
far to offset the gains in military skill. At the same time, new organizations joined the Army, strong in numbers but weak in experienced
officers and n.c.o.'s and therefore slow to make good soldiers of their
men except at the price of additional heavy losses. Because Wisconsin adhered to the different policy of filling up her old regiments,
William T. Sherman wrote in his memoirs:

. . . we estimate a Wisconsin regiment equal to an ordinary brigade. I
believe that five hundred new men added to an old and experienced
regiment were more valuable than a thousand men in the form of a new
regiment, for the former, by association with good experienced captains,
lieutenants, and non-commissioned officers, soon became veterans, whereas
the latter were generally unavailable for a year.[20]

Despite the inducement of the bounty and the encouragement of
recruiting by influential citizens, the response to the call of July 2,
1862, was disappointing. On July 17, however, the federal Congress,
by means of amending the militia laws, took a halting step toward
following the Confederate Congress into conscription. The Militia
Act of that date reiterated the militia obligation of all able-bodied
male citizens between eighteen and forty-five. It provided further that
when calling the militia into federal service the President might specify the period of such service, not to exceed nine months, and most
importantly, that for those states which did not have adequate laws
governing the militia he might make all necessary rules and regulations. On this basis the President instituted on August 4 a draft of
300,000 militia for nine months. He announced that any state which
had not met its quota of three-year volunteers by August 15 would

be subjected to the draft. Where no state system of conscription existed, the War Department called upon the governors to designate certain officials to carry out an enrollment, consider exemptions, and draft conscripts. The War Department would also appoint civilian provost marshals for the states, nominated by the governors, to enforce compliance upon individuals.[21]

This proclamation of a draft under the Militia Act of 1862 was the first assumption of the conscription power by the United States government. In practice, the draft of 1862 never went into effect. The governors protested their quotas and the shortness of the time allowed to meet them before invoking conscription, and the people protested by means of scattered riots and threats of riots. Thereupon Secretary Stanton permitted the governors to postpone the draft, first for a month and then indefinitely. But the threat of the draft probably helped bring forward the desired recruits. The government accepted either three-year volunteers or nine-month militia, under a curious accounting system whereby four of the latter would count as one of the former in meeting a state's quota. Eventually the War Department counted 431,958 volunteers and 87,558 militia under the calls of July 2 and August 4, 1862.[22]

In the months following those calls, however, casualties climbed far above those that had prompted the calls, and the war went badly. This was the unhappy time of Second Bull Run, Antietam, Perryville, Corinth, Fredericksburg, Stones River, and Chancellorsville. After Chancellorsville also the nine-month militiamen went home, their terms expired. In early 1863 the war seemed no closer to victory than a year before, and attrition was shrinking the armies. After the newspapers and picture weeklies had described the horrors of Antietam and Fredericksburg, new enlistments were few. Reluctantly, Congress turned to a more forthright draft, the Enrollment Act of March 3, 1863.

This act imposed a federal military liability upon all able-bodied male citizens and declarants between the ages of twenty and forty-five. Bypassing the militia clauses, it was based squarely on the constitutional power "to raise and support armies." Exemptions were granted only to the physically and mentally unfit, certain high federal officials and the state governors, only sons of dependent widows, and only sons of infirm parents. Enrollees were divided into two classes, Class I consisting of all persons between twenty and thirty-five and all unmarried persons between thirty-five and forty-five, Class II comprising all other enrollees. No men were to be drafted from Class II until the Class I pool was exhausted. For two years after enrollment, enrollees were subject to draft. Once drafted, they would remain in service for three years or the war, whichever ended first. The act provided for an enforcement machinery including enrollment officers organized by Congressional districts, enrollment boards, and military provost marshals in the states, with the newly established Office of the Provost Marshal General in Washington supervising the whole draft under the Secretary of War.

The assertion of the principle of national conscription in the act of March 3, 1863, was a bold one, but Congress much diluted the principle in practice. Instead of making it an obligation of the citizen to come forward to enroll, the act sent enrolling officers on house-to-house canvasses to seek out enrollees, which detracted from the dignity of the proceedings by making enrollment dependent on a kind of snooping and led in fact to occasional unpleasant altercations. Much worse, the act permitted substitution, whereby a drafted man could hire another person to perform military service for him, and commutation, whereby a drafted man could purchase outright relief for $300. Substitution and commutation were inheritances from the militia system of the past; if unjust they had at least been workable when militia drafts were for short service and there was no need to tap the whole reservoir of manpower. But in a long war where the whole manpower pool was potentially needed they were anomalies as well as injustices. Perhaps the best that can be said for them is that they defrayed the cost of administering the draft and the recruiting service.[23]

In time the anomalies were reduced. After February 24, 1864, the commutation fee bought exemption only from the specific call involved, not from later calls. After July 4, 1864, commutation was possible only for conscientious objectors. (The conscientious objector who refused to pay the commutation fee remained a problem, but in general, members of recognized pacifist sects were treated generously by administrative instructions, and Congress had provided on February 24, 1864, that religious objectors should be assigned to duty in hospitals, or to the care of freedmen, or were to pay the commutation fee for the benefit of sick and wounded soldiers.) Substitution remained, but substitutes had to be men not subject to the draft themselves (this provision was repealed March 3, 1865, but by then the war was almost over), and an enrollee's exemption lasted only as long as his substitute was in service.

Diluted though they gradually were, commutation and substitution remained impediments to the effective application of the draft law. Their persistence suggests not only a Congressional suscepti- bility to class interests but, more than that, a larger reluctance to apply conscription thoroughly. In part this reluctance mirrored the resistance to the law which erupted in the New York draft riots as well as in lesser demonstrations, but it was also something that ran deeper than mere timidity in the face of resistance.

The main practical use of the draft proved to be to stimulate volunteering. Districts could still avoid the draft by meeting their quotas through volunteering, and so the Enrollment Act stimulated recruiting campaigns and helped perpetuate the hope that the United States could still wage its wars mainly with volunteers. The nation evidently cherished that hope dearly and would cling to it as long as possible. Altogether, only six per cent of the 2,666,999 men who served in the Union Army during the Civil War were secured directly through conscription. Of 249,259 persons "held to service" under the Enrollment Act of 1863, 86,724 escaped by payment of commutation, leaving 168,649 "men raised." But of the latter, 116,188 were substitutes, and only 46,347 were "held to personal service."[24]

One of the worst crises in keeping up the Union armies came after the draft act, in 1864, when a repetition of George Washington's old problem of expiring enlistments threatened to destroy the Army. The enlistments of the three-year men of 1861 were due to expire largely in May, June, and July, 1864, just as Grant would be beginning his drives against the Confederacy on all fronts. During the early months of the year before the resumption of campaigning, the War Department staged an elaborate effort to persuade veterans to reenlist so that the armies would not lose their backbone on the eve of the climactic campaigns. Persuading them was not easy, since these men had seen a lot more of war than they had bargained for in 1861, and they could readily feel that it was time for someone else to take up the burden. But the government offered to each reenlisting veteran a bounty of $400 plus whatever his state or community might pay him, which could often add up to $700; a thirty-day furlough; the right to call himself a "veteran volunteer"; and an appropriate chevron for the sleeve. Since it was important to retain regiments, if three-fourths of the members of a regiment would reenlist, they could go home as a unit for their thirty-day furlough and return to keep their organization and their flag. These terms were offered to the men to the accompaniment of oratory, band music, and sometimes whiskey; and when three-fourths of a company or regiment signed up, there were likely to be further celebrations and parades to encourage the others. In the Army of the Potomac, 26,767 veterans reenlisted by the end of March, less than half the total but enough to hold the army together. Finally a total of 136,000 three-year veterans signed on again, all in all a respectable number. Together with the draft, they ensured the endurance of the Army to the end of the war.[25]

By the time the three-year veterans were being offered bounties as high as $700 to reenlist, the system of offering bounties for volunteers was clearly getting out of hand; but it seemed an inescapable expedient as long as the nation refused to face up to thoroughgoing application of the draft. In every war, bounties had proven a necessary sweetener in recruiting; the unprecedented manpower demands of the Civil War turned them into a national scandal. City and state authorities, following custom, had begun offering enlistment bounties from the start. The War Department soon followed suit, and Congress sanctioned the practice by authorizing a bounty of $100—initially to be paid when the soldier was mustered out—in the act of July 22, 1861. Thenceforth the federal bounties climbed to $300 for new recruits and $400 for veterans in 1864, and state and local bounties grew proportionately, or more so. The federal government eventually paid a total of $585,000,000 in bounties, and the states are believed to have paid at least $286,000,000. Bounties cost as much as the whole pay of the Army for the war, more than the quartermaster services, and five times the cost of ordnance. They threw communities into expensive competition with each other, and they led to the bounty-jumping racket, whereby professional bounty takers enlisted and deserted and reenlisted again as long and as often as they could get away with it.[26]

Still another expedient for evading a thorough application of conscription was to tap the pool of Negro manpower, despite the notions of Negro racial inferiority which pervaded the North as well as the South. The idea that the Negroes might assure their freedom by joining in the fight for it held a certain romantic appeal for antislavery idealists, and for most northerners it held a still larger appeal by promising to reduce the number of white men who would have to face inconvenience and danger. Recruiting of Negroes began under the local auspices of Major General David Hunter in the Department of the South as early as April 12, 1862. When Hunter was disappointed with the response, he resorted in fact to impressment, and Thomas Wentworth Higginson, the well-known abolitionist, said the Negroes were "driven like cattle" into the Army. Similar efforts continued sporadically on the initiative of various other commanders. Stanton gave his implied approval, while Lincoln stayed aloof and noncommittal. On July 17, 1862, Congress authorized recruiting of Negroes while passing the antislavery Second Confiscation Act. On August 25 the War Department first extended official sanction to such recruiting, but only to the limit of 5,000 men for guard and labor duties.

Then the Emancipation Proclamation put the matter in a new

light for the executive branch. In the proclamation Lincoln stated that former slaves "of suitable condition will be received into the armed service of the United States to garrison forts, positions, stations, and other places, and to man vessels of all sorts in said service." The Negro troops recruited by Hunter and later, more humanely, by Brigadier General Rufus Saxton meanwhile received regimental organization as the 1st South Carolina Volunteers, Thomas Wentworth Higginson becoming their colonel. Some northern states now thought of raising Negro regiments under their own recruiting quotas. Stanton gave Governor John A. Andrew of Massachusetts permission to attempt it. Andrew proceeded enthusiastically, but in Massachusetts he found insufficient Negro recruits. He then sent George L. Stearns, like Higginson a former sponsor of John Brown, to recruit in other northern states, and Stearns was able to create not only the 54th but also the 55th Massachusetts Regiments. However, his activities provoked complaints from other states that Negroes enlisted on their soil ought to count toward their quotas, not Massachusetts's. Some other states began Negro recruiting of their own, but Stanton now decided that the only way to avoid endless confusion and acrimony was for the War Department itself to take charge. On May 22, 1863, the department established a Bureau of Colored Troops to organize and supervise Negro units. Stearns became assistant adjutant general in charge of Negro recruiting for the federal government. Some recruiting by northern governors and crediting of Negroes to northern state quotas persisted, but mainly agents under Stearns enlisted the Negroes into regiments of United States Colored Volunteers, or later, more simply, United States Colored Troops.

The Negro regiments were officered almost entirely by white men, and the abolitionists had to wage a hard fight before relieving them of discrimination in pay just before the war ended. They finally aggregated 120 regiments of infantry, 12 of heavy artillery, 1 of light artillery, and 7 of cavalry, altogether 186,017 men, an impressive total. They fought well on several occasions which received much publicity, notably when the 54th Massachusetts stormed Fort Wagner near Charleston; but mainly they were used as laborers and garrison troops. They received little chance to prove their mettle as soldiers, but conversely the government withstood the temptation to use them as cannon fodder. Negroes had served in the Revolution, with Andrew Jackson at New Orleans, and in other early wars. But they had been barred from the Regular Army and, under the Militia Act of 1792, from the state militia, and the Civil War marks their official entrance into American military history. With many of their race still held as a species of property, the United States Colored Troops at last could sing

> We look like men a-marching on;
> We look like men o' war.[27]

The United States Colored Troops were also part of another innovation in American military history. When the Civil War began, the federal government did not repeat the experiment of the War of 1812, of attempting a large wartime expansion of the Regular Army. Instead it raised war formations through the states, which could build around the nucleus of the organized militia companies and exploit local patriotisms. Mustered into federal service, volunteer regiments still retained their state designations. Nevertheless, once the resources of state pride and the state militia organizations had built the initial war armies, the federal government, having exploited those resources, gradually took a more direct hand in recruiting, groping toward a bypassing of the states. Writers on civil as well as military affairs have emphasized the tendency of the war to aggrandize the federal government at the expense of the states. In military recruitment, the assertion of a universal obligation to military service to the federal government, not merely to the states, was an outstanding expression of that tendency. Another was a drift toward direct federal enlistment of volunteers as well as conscripts. The United States Colored Troops were one example of federal volunteer formations, without official ties to specific states. They were one of a growing number of such examples. In the distant past of 1775 the Continental Congress had attempted to erase state regimental designations from the Continental Army enlisted for 1776, but the experiment had failed; now a stronger national government cautiously moved again toward such a recognition of the war Army as a national Army.

The first United States volunteer regiments to be designated as such were only two in number and less an expression of a grand nationalizing tendency than of a specific military need. In the summer of 1861, selected companies from eight different states, from among those companies which were left over when the states formed their first three-year regiments, were collected into the 1st and 2nd Regiments of Sharpshooters, United States Volunteers. They served conspicuously with the Army of the Potomac and eventually had to be consolidated into a single regiment at the end of 1864.[28]

More important in the organizational history of the Army than the Sharpshooters were experiments to create a federal military reserve, perhaps to substitute for the state militias in backing up the active Army. On April 23, 1863, War Department general orders created the Invalid Corps, United States Volunteers, to be composed of officers and enlisted men no longer fit for front-line service but who enlisted for further duty. At one time or another 60,000 men served in this corps, in 24 regiments and 186 separate companies. In each of the full regiments, a first battalion of six companies comprised men capable of limited field duty who might act as guards and an emergency reserve, while a second battalion of four companies enlisted men able only to serve as clerks, cooks, hospital orderlies, and the like. In 1864 the organization's unfortunate title, a French derivation, gave way to the more acceptable Veteran Reserve Corps. But the corps remained an organization of United States, not state, regiments.[29]

Emergencies such as Lee's invasions of the North in 1862 and 1863 made it desirable to have a reserve army more imposing and numerous than the "invalids." A few states responded by revitalizing their militia institutions, despite the absence of their best young manhood with the active Army. Most conspicuously, New York maintained a National Guard—a name she had borrowed from her 7th Regiment to apply to her whole militia—in an advanced state of organization and readiness to move, if not in a condition of thorough training. When Lincoln and the War Department called for emergency troops to meet Lee's advance in June, 1863, Governor Horatio Seymour could quickly dispatch some eight to ten thousand New York troops to Harrisburg, where they were mustered into federal service for thirty days. Pennsylvania owed a debt of gratitude to her sister state, for her own organized militia had practically ceased to exist after it was drained for the war Army, and in the invasion emergency Pennsylvania officials had to scurry about trying to conjure up home guards out of little except amorphous manpower, and not much of that.

Meanwhile, Stanton had responded to Lee's invasion with a suggestion that would have created a long-term reserve, not just one for the present emergency, and under federal auspices. He proposed to establish in the border Military Departments of the Susquehanna and the Monongahela a corps of volunteers between the ages of eighteen and sixty who would agree to serve during the "pleasure of the President or the continuance of the war" but who would go on active duty only during emergencies. The inclusion of men both younger and older than draft age would have contributed to the permanence of the corps. The federal government was to train, equip, and command it. In its presence, the historic state militia would have fallen into its shadow. In the circumstances of threatened invasion, Pennsylvania officials proved amenable to the idea; but recruits proved less willing to respond, no doubt partly because indefinite terms of service frightened them. Through want of recruits Stanton had to abandon the scheme and settle for a hodgepodge of emergency men, some enlisted for the duration of the emergency, some for thirty days, some for six months, and some of them ninety-day state militia.[30]

Altogether, states such as New York managed to keep between 125,000 and 200,000 men in more or less organized state militia formations through the war. They were of value not only in crises of invasion but also in guarding certain prisoner of war camps and important industrial establishments and railroad lines and in relieving Regular garrisons on the Indian frontier.[31] The War Department responded to the requirements of the Indian frontier also by organizing still another kind of federal volunteer. The 1st through 6th Infantry Regiments, United States Volunteers, consisted of veterans of the Confederate States Army, enlisted out of the prisoner of war camps for duty against the Indians only.[32]

Though Stanton's idea of a federal military reserve had fallen flat, the War Department pursued the organization of United States Volunteers. The Colored Troops formed the largest increment in that category. President Lincoln's last two major calls for men differed from earlier ones in being directed not to the states or the governors but to the manpower of the Union. On July 18, 1864, Lincoln called for 500,000 to enlist for one, two, or three years, on the basis of a new law authorizing such options. Despite the form of the call, the states undertook to raise additional regiments, and almost all the men credited to the call were state, not United States, volunteers. The quotas actually assigned to the states totaled not 500,000 but 346,746; with the help of the draft, 384,882 men were recruited.

A more strenuous effort to enroll United States Volunteers followed Lincoln's final call, of December 18, for 300,000 men. By that time Major General Winfield Scott Hancock had been detached from the Army of the Potomac to take charge of recruiting experienced soldiers as United States Veteran Volunteers. Hancock had never recovered altogether from his Gettysburg wound, and as a field commander he was not the general he once had been. But he carried much prestige, and the hope was that he might assemble a reconstituted I Army Corps of Veteran Volunteers. Without the persuasive resources of state and local political leaders, however, his effort fizzled. Only the 1st through 9th Regiments of United States Veteran Volunteers ever assembled, none of them in time to see action. Of the 204,568 men eventually credited to the final call, most as usual were in regiments organized by the states. So the effort to organize a war Army directly under federal auspices was not much more successful than the Continental regiments of 1776 had been, but the very persistence of the War Department's effort was an expression of the rise of nationalism and a harbinger of the future.[33]

Of the 2,666,999 men enrolled in the United States Army during the Civil War, the total "present and absent" strength at any one time never reached much over one million, and the total present for duty never reached quite a million. Nevertheless, the mobilization of the war armies—the Grand Army of the Republic, in the Napoleonic phrase later perpetuated by the veterans' organization—was an impressive achievement, especially for a nation with so limited a permanent military force. In no small measure, the achievement derived from the historic citizens' militia, whose organized companies became the nucleus of the war armies. In no small measure too, however, the citizens' militia made possible the great war itself, by giving the states sufficient military strength, and thus a sufficient residue of sovereignty, to wage war against each other. Some perception of the relationship between the military institutions of the states and the very existence of the war probably underlay the War Department's eventual efforts toward direct federal recruiting. Initially nourished by the organized militia companies, the Civil War was also the great war of the volunteer armies, since at least ostensibly almost all the Union soldiers were volunteers. But it proved to be the last major war both of state-affiliated and of volunteer armies. After reviewing the problems and anomalies of the effort to maintain the volunteer armies of the 1860's, the United States would never again attempt to raise a mass wartime army by that method. Federal conscription would be the principal legacy of the Civil War experience to future American war armies.

To supply the Civil War armies was almost as impressive an achievement as to enlist them. The history of the supplying of the Union armies is a far cry from the history of supply in the Revolutionary War and demonstrates the advance of the United States in fourscore years toward both the affluent society and the military status of a great power.

No more does the mention of supplying the Army suggest soldiers naked and starving in the winter at Valley Forge. Instead it suggests the wartime photographers' pictures of the great Union depots such as City Point, Virginia, where more than a mile of wharves served forty steamers, seventy-five sailing vessels, and a hundred barges a day, and groaned under great piles of ammunition, guns, uniforms, equipage, and foodstuffs. Once the 1861 recruits were equipped, no Union army suffered from want of any essentials except the occasional army under siege. The main defects of the supply system were themselves those of a rich economy: not shortages, but plundering of the public treasury by unscrupulous contractors and supply officers who could not resist the temptation to cut themselves in when lavish sums flowed by. Once the initial frenzy passed, even that sort of activity was kept to a notable minimum through the efforts of such aggressively honest men as Secretary of War Stanton and Quartermaster General M. C. Meigs.

In the mobilization of 1861 much of the work of supply fell not only upon the states but also upon irregular, ad hoc committees and agents of the War Department. The justification for their appointment was that the permanent staffs of the War Department and its bureaus were hopelessly inadequate for the work of organizing and equipping armies rapidly growing to more than 500,000 men: the Quartermaster's Department began the war with only thirteen clerks in its Washington office, thirty-seven officers, including the quartermaster general, and seven storekeepers. But the special appointees of 1861 were inexperienced in military supply and often unqualified in every other way—many of them were merely political allies of Simon Cameron—and much of the worst extravagance, misdirected effort, and downright robbing of the public purse in collusion with contractors came from them. It is not certain that many of the irregular agents were really needed, since despite the smallness of the supply offices, those offices grew relatively little through the whole war and yet managed in time to get control of their duties. The roster of the Quartermaster's Department grew only from thirty-seven officers to sixty-four in the course of the war. Furthermore, if special appointees were needed in 1861, they should have been put under the supervision of experienced supply officers; there was no good reason to have Cameron's newspaperman friend Alexander Cummings buying independently in New York City, for example, when an experienced quartermaster officer was in the city and could have guided the purchases. There did exist a feeling in the civilian administration that Regular Army officers were too hidebound by small routines to conduct the huge task of mobilization; but the Regular supply officers should have been given more of a chance from the beginning to show just what their abilities were, since a Congressional committee later concluded that only the Regular Army supply officers almost uniformly did a good and honest job.[34]

After the summer of 1861, supply operations mainly returned to their usual places in the War Department. Three War Department bureaus were principally concerned with supply: the Ordnance Department, which manufactured or purchased and distributed arms and ammunition; the Subsistence Department, which purchased and distributed food supplies; and the Quartermaster's Department, which gathered in all supplies not secured by the other two departments—uniforms, equipment, tentage, barracks, horses, fodder—and transported supplies of every kind over rails, rivers, lakes, oceans, and wagon roads. With some but not excessive exaggeration, Quartermaster General Meigs said of his office:

It is . . . the second place not in military rank but in actual real influence over the war, in the army. A major general commands a corps d armee on a single line. The Lt General commands the whole army. The Q. M. Genl. supplies the means of moving that army, & his command extends from the Atlantic to the Pacific the Lakes to the Gulf.[35]

During the early years of the war, Meigs presided over a much decentralized quartermaster purchasing system. In addition to the main quartermaster depot at Philadelphia, he established new depots at Boston, New York, Cincinnati, Louisville, Indianapolis, St. Louis, Detroit, and Springfield, Illinois. The depot quartermasters purchased for the area and armies for which they were responsible, the bulk of supplies was collected at the depots, and thence the supplies were distributed to the armies in the field. In an emergency, when supplies could not be secured from a depot, the chief quartermaster of a field army or of a detachment might purchase supplies by order of his commanding officer. In Washington, Meigs sought to coordinate the various purchases, and his staff carefully audited the accounts of all quartermaster officers. Here his clerical assistance did grow to include 184 clerks and 29 women copyists by the end of 1864. Six department inspectors, holding after 1864 the rank of colonel, visited armies and depots to scrutinize their activities.

The supervisory business of the Washington office fell naturally into various categories, but before the war only one division within the Quartermaster's Department had existed for a specialized purpose, the Clothing Bureau, whose separate status owed something to its various predecessors that had been outside the Quartermaster's Department. In response to the complexities of the war, Meigs created an informal series of specialized subdepartments, and eventually he persuaded Congress to authorize nine divisions of the Quartermaster's Department, by statute of July 4, 1864. These were the First Division, providing animals for the armies; Second Division, clothing and equipage; Third Division, ocean and lake transportation; Fourth Division, rail and river transportation; Fifth Division, forage and fuel; Sixth Division, barracks and hospitals; Seventh Division, wagon transportation; Eighth Division, inspection; and Ninth Division, records and correspondence. With this reorganization, furthermore, a more centralized purchasing system was instituted, whereby all supplies, except in emergencies, were contracted for by the appropriate divisions of the Quartermaster's Department in Washington.[36]

Under long-established law, reiterated by Congress in 1861, all purchases and contracts were to be negotiated by advertising for proposals, receiving competitive bids, for which adequate time was allowed, and making the award to the lowest bidder. However, the law did permit direct purchase without competitive bidding in an emergency. During 1861 much purchasing took place without competitive bidding, partly because of the prevailing sense of urgency, partly out of carelessness, partly because supplies were needed in such quantities that all available sources had to be tapped. When reports of extravagance and corruption stirred up a Congressional investigation, however, and Congress found that often such reports were true, the law on contracting was stiffened. On June 2, 1862, Congress provided that all contracts must be in writing, that their terms must be sworn to in affidavits before magistrates, and that a copy of every contract, together with all bids, offers, and proposals and a copy of the advertisement published, must be filed in the Interior Department. General Meigs's honesty and concern for honest performance were beyond question, yet he commented sarcastically: "Let any member propose a new provision of law stated to be intended to restrain contractors or officers and it goes through with little examination." He considered the new law so stringent as to be unworkable, and Stanton agreed with him. Consequently, the War Department evaded its severities by means of Stanton's administrative ruling that it applied only to such contracts as had been required to be in writing at the time of its passage.[37]

In 1861 the Army purchased clothing from almost every available supplier and sometimes of inferior materials. Meigs commented:

. . . the troops were clothed and rescued from severe suffering, and those who saw sentinels walking post in the capital of the United States in freezing weather in their drawers, without trousers or overcoats, will not blame the department for its efforts to clothe them, even in materials not quite so durable as army blue kersey.[38]

Once sufficient stocks were on hand, however, the Quartermaster's Department procured uniforms mainly through its traditional method, that of manufacture under its own auspices. Some uniforms continued to be bought from private contractors, but mainly the department simply purchased uniform cloth, cut it to patterns at the expanded Schuylkill Arsenal in Philadelphia and at new establishments in New York, Cincinnati, and St. Louis, and issued the cut cloth to seamstresses and tailors, who returned hand-finished uniforms to the depots. The recently invented sewing machine was not utilized for standard Civil War uniforms; the Army considered hand-sewn garments more durable.

Blankets, tentage, and shoes were purchased from private suppliers. Until the Civil War, American Army tents had been either ordinary wedge tents, wall tents, or the cylindrical-conical Sibley tent. Without sufficient tentage material early in the war, the Quartermaster's Department introduced what the French army called the d'Abri tent, that is, the shelter tent so familiar ever since, of which each soldier carries one-half. In purchasing shoes the Quartermaster's Department lent more encouragement to the Industrial Revolution than in procuring uniforms, since it purchased machine-sewn shoes, manufactured with the machine for sewing the uppers to the soles which Lyman R. Blake had patented in 1858 and Gordon McKay promoted and improved. The demands of the Army and a shortage of skilled shoemakers led to the industry's rapid adoption of the Blake-McKay machine and the growth of the factory system in shoe manufacturing.

Volunteers seemed to be much more wasteful of clothing and such equipment as knapsacks than Regulars, and clothing and equipment allowances based on the experience of the Regular Army did not work well with the volunteers. Nevertheless, by the end of 1861 Meigs was already concerned lest an excessive surplus be accumulated in the depots, and for a time he suspended advertisements for new contracts. The President's calls for militia and volunteers in the summer of 1862 then exhausted the supply of uniforms and compelled Meigs to go into his reserves of cloth, and contracting was resumed. By 1863 ample stocks were on hand again, and Meigs was able to retain adequate reserves through the rest of the war. The Philadelphia and New York depots each always kept on hand uniforms and equipment for 100,000 men.[39]

The Civil War was still largely a war of animal power. Most of the functions now served by the internal combustion engine had to be carried on by horses and mules, including all transportation of supplies away from rail and water lines. So the Quartermaster's Department's task of finding animals ranked in magnitude with its procurement of uniforms and equipment. In 1864 a group of armies numbering 426,000 men had 221,000 animals with them, more than one for every two soldiers, including 113,864 serviceable horses, 87,791 serviceable mules, and some oxen plus some invalided horses and mules. Cavalry and artillery animals were used up with special rapidity and demanded continual replacement; during the first eight months of 1864 the cavalry of the Army of the Potomac was completely remounted twice, receiving nearly 40,000 horses.

Fortunately, if the Army used hundreds of thousands of horses and mules, so did civilian America, and the Quartermaster's Department could draw on the stock of a rich agricultural country. The census of 1860 gave the northern states a horse population of 4,688,-878. The main problem then was to secure honest purchasing agents who were also good judges of horseflesh and to organize their activities properly. There were some false starts, and a good many sickly nags seem to have found their way into the Army in the early part of the war. But a careful reading of the *Official Records* makes it difficult to give much credence to the claims of immense shortages made by such generals as McClellan after Antietam and William S. Rosecrans about the same time; the reports of their own quartermaster and cavalry officers refute them.[40]

The Army ration had not improved much nutritionally or in palatability since the War of the Revolution, but in the Civil War it usually reached the troops in ample quantities. General McDowell was thinking mainly of the ration when he remarked that a French army half the size of the Union Army could live on the latter's waste. Regulations called for:

12 ounces of pork or bacon, or 20 ounces of fresh or salt beef; 18 ounces of bread or flour, or 12 ounces of hard bread, or 20 ounces of cornmeal; and to every 100 rations 8 quarts of beans, or 10 pounds of rice, or twice a week 150 ounces of desiccated potatoes and 100 ounces of desiccated mixed vegetables; 10 pounds of coffee, or 1½ pounds of tea; 15 pounds of sugar; 4 quarts of vinegar; 1 pound of sperm candles, or 1¼ pounds of adamantine candles, or 1¼ pounds of tallow candles; 4 pounds of soap; and 2 quarts of salt.

This was the ration for the camp. On the march, the soldier was issued one pound of hard bread, three-fourths of a pound of salt pork or one and one-quarter pounds of fresh meat, plus sugar, coffee, and salt.[41]

Herds of beef cattle followed the armies to supply fresh meat. The hard bread was the familiar "hardtack," flour and water biscuits. Coffee was supplied in the whole bean to prevent adulteration and was ground by the men themselves, often using rifle butts on stone. The desiccated potatoes and vegetables were an experimental compound issued from time to time, inevitably known to the soldiers as "desecrated vegetables." One soldier described them as coming "in sheets like pressed hops."

. . . a cook would break off a piece as large as a boot top, put it in a kettle of water, and stir it with the handle of a hospital broom. When the stuff was fully dissolved, the water would remind one of a dirty brook with all the dead leaves floating around promiscuously.[42]

The purpose of this concoction was to remedy the most glaring deficiency of the ration, the lack of an antiscorbutic; but that deficiency was probably better remedied by the occasional issue of potatoes, onions, or the like, or more frequently, by the men's own foraging. General William T. Sherman said that in order to find an antiscorbutic, "I have known the skirmish-line, without orders, to fight a respectable battle for the possession of some old fields that were full of blackberries." The search for embellishments to the ration was a constant activity in the invaded South.[43]

On appropriate occasions, troops and supplies moved by ocean and river steamer and sailing vessel. The Quartermaster's Department purchased and built 183 ocean steamers, 43 sailing vessels, and 86 barges in the course of the war, and it chartered or hired another 753 ocean steamers, 1,080 sailing vessels, and 847 barges. These ocean vessels were in addition to 599 river boats owned by the department during the war, including 91 steamers, and 822 river boats chartered, hired, or pressed into service, including 633 steamers. McClellan's army was moved to and supplied on the Peninsula by water, waterborne supplies reached the Army of the Potomac at Aquia Creek when it was campaigning in the Fredericksburg region, and Grant's Petersburg lines were supplied mainly from the James River base at City Point. The western armies naturally utilized the western rivers. When Sherman reached Savannah after his march to the sea, Meigs had a full outfit of clothing and abundant other supplies awaiting him on a fleet of quartermaster vessels, and those vessels continued to put in at ports in North Carolina to keep Sherman supplied as he moved northward. Here their cargoes included locomotives, rolling stock, and related equipment for reopening the railroads.[44]

The Civil War was also the first great railroad war. The railroads brought an immense new mobility to armies, most dramatically illustrated in "the accomplishment par excellence of Civil War logistics,"[45] the transfer of almost 25,000 men, 10 batteries and their horses, and 100 cars of baggage of the XI and XII Corps from the Army of the Potomac in Virginia to Chattanooga. In eleven and a half days the two army corps traveled 1,200 miles, much of it over track frequently devastated and reconstructed. Behind the troops came another set of trains bearing more than a thousand horses and mules, spare artillery, field transport, and all the impedimenta of a field army.

Army railroad transport was ably managed by railroad experts employed from civil life. In one of the first expansions of the War Department, Secretary Cameron appointed Thomas A. Scott, an executive of the Pennsylvania Central Railroad, Assistant Secretary of War, and Scott did much to coordinate railroad operations during the initial gathering of the armies. The railroads served efficiently, but with Scott drawing up the rate schedules, they also served under lucrative tariffs. Congress soon decided the government was being bilked, and for this reason and to ensure continued adequate service it passed the Railroad Act of January 31, 1862. The act empowered the government to take possession of any railroad lines in the United States whenever the public service required it, and in general to control and supervise all railroad transportation of troops and military supplies. The threat of public seizure never had to be applied in the loyal states, for Secretary Stanton and General Meigs were now able to work out reasonable rates in consultation with the roads, and northern railroad operators continued to give faithful support to military requests.

In the South, however, the government did apply the Railroad Act to operate eventually more than 2,000 miles of railroads. These lines were administered by the United States Military Railroads, under a military director and superintendent, Colonel (later Major General) Daniel C. McCallum, formerly superintendent of the Erie Railroad. McCallum's office was formally a part of the Quartermaster's Department, but McCallum reported directly to Stanton, while procuring materials through General Meigs. Herman Haupt, perhaps the most famous of Civil War railroaders, acted for a time as superintendent of railroads in northeastern Virginia independent of both McCallum and Meigs. To keep the military railroads running despite destruction by retreating Confederate armies and Confederate raiders, a Railroad Construction Corps appeared within the Quartermaster's Department, eventually numbering nearly 10,000 men. This corps grew so efficient that it inspired the despairing remark of Confederates resisting Sherman's march to Atlanta that there was little use in destroying tunnels on the railroad because Sherman carried a spare tunnel with him. To assist the Construction Corps, the Quartermaster's Department completed a rolling mill in Chattanooga whose construction had begun before the Confederates evacuated the city. The mill did not get into operation before the war ended, but the Quartermaster's Department worked it from April to October, 1865, and with its output rebuilt the Chattanooga-Atlanta line which Sherman had ruined before leaving Atlanta to march to the coast.[46]

The new mobility which the railroads gave the armies suffered from a severe limitation: it was imperative not to stray too far from the railroad lines. Some campaigns, such as Sherman's for Atlanta and Grant's around Petersburg, became largely contests for possession of the precious yet thin and brittle railroads. Without the railroads, movement of supplies remained almost as primitive as in the Revolution. Away from the railroads, supplies still moved by horse-, mule-, or ox-drawn wagon, mostly mule-drawn. In most parts of the United States, especially in the South where the armies campaigned, roads were abominable, rutted when dry and quagmires in the rain. Fortunately the Army's wagons were durable, since a sturdy design had been evolved to serve the outposts in the West. But problems were large. In 1862 the Quartermaster's Department found that it had to move 600 tons of supplies daily from supply depots and railheads to the advanced positions of an army of 100,000. Napoleon had held that twelve wagons should be allotted for every thousand men, but General Meigs learned that to carry forward the lavish supplies of an American army required many more wagons than that—twenty-six per thousand men during McClellan's Peninsular campaign, thirty-three per thousand at the beginning of Grant's 1864 campaign in Virginia. Much of the South was so short of forage, and becoming more so, that the animals that drew the wagons had to carry in subsistence for themselves. It took 150 wagons to haul a day's food for McClellan's soldiers on the Peninsula and 300 wagons to haul a day's food for the animals. Too much of an Army wagon train served nothing but its own animals.[47]

This dependence on wagon trains to sustain the armies in the field badly cramped Civil War logistics. The vexed question whether to develop breech-loading shoulder arms, for example, hinged partly on the problem of getting enough ammunition to the front to keep up an increasing rate of fire. Skillful management was required to prevent supplies simply from jamming up at the railheads, perhaps idling railroad cars in the process. To be the quartermaster of a field army in these conditions called for high managerial abilities, and fortunately the Union armies were mostly well served, especially the Army of the Potomac with Brigadier General Rufus Ingalls.

Discussion of the services that sustained the armies must include some mention of the Medical Bureau. Until the Civil War, medical service in the United States Army as in all armies was haphazardly organized, and the wounded soldier had been fortunate who happened to fall into the hands of a reasonably competent though overburdened doctor who had a reasonably good place in which to work.

The scandal of atrocious medical service in the Crimean War, the natural outcome of traditional methods, helped stimulate nineteenth-century humanitarians to seek something better. Inspired in part by the story of Florence Nightingale, a civilian organization to improve medical care in the Army sprang up almost as soon as the war began, the United States Sanitary Commission. It could draw upon those middle-class sensibilities so characteristic of the age, which had made the prewar decades an era of reform. Its members were largely middle-class humanitarian women, awakening to the possible benevolent influence of their sex; its public spokesmen were largely well-to-do and influential philanthropists, many of them already prominent in the Republican party through association with antislaveryism. Such types by no means lacked self-righteousness, and there developed an unseemly controversy between them and Stanton, who apparently feared—with some reason—that they were trying to take control of the Medical Bureau of the War Department out of his hands. They did pressure the government into replacing the elderly C. A. Finley as surgeon general with William Hammond, whereupon Stanton inaugurated a running fight with Hammond that culminated in Hammond's trial for improper conduct in January, 1864, a dubious verdict against him, and his replacement in turn by Joseph K. Barnes.

Meanwhile the Sanitary Commission did much that was good. It raised funds to provide a wealth of medical supplies. Stanton and Barnes persisted in Hammond's organizational reforms which the commission had inspired, to overcome bureaucratic inertia in the Medical Bureau. From the beginning of the war, the commission circulated "Rules for Preserving the Health of the Soldier," an unprecedented guidebook for both officers and men. On June 9, 1861, the commission secured a general order of the War Department providing for women nurses in military hospitals, though not in camps or on the march; applicants for such service had to be at least thirty years old, to have "certificates from two Physicians, and two Clergymen of standing," and they served under the superintendence of formidable Miss Dorothea L. Dix. In time Clara Barton commenced her own field ambulance service independent of Miss Dix and the Sanitary Commission, but she did such good work that she received special permission to travel with the Army of the Potomac.

Not all the impetus for medical improvement came from the civilian humanitarians. In the Army of the Potomac, Surgeon Jonathan Letterman developed a workable hospital system wherein regiments maintained first-aid stations from which the wounded were carried by ambulance companies to tented field hospitals. Thence in turn they were transferred to a series of base hospitals outside the war zone. McClellan supported Letterman's hospital reforms, the western armies took them up, and on March 11, 1864, Congress gave official sanction to the system. By the standards of the day, the Union armies received good medical service as well as generous supplies, to be altogether the best cared for and provided armies ever to wage war.[48]

The building block into which the masses of manpower were poured and from which armies were formed continued to be the regiment. In an order of May 4, 1861, the War Department prescribed the shape of the regiments to be drawn from Lincoln's call of that date; the pattern then described persisted in its essentials for all the volunteer regiments raised under all the subsequent calls. In general, the organization paralleled that of the existing Regular Army regiments. Each infantry regiment consisted of ten companies, each company composed of a captain, a first lieutenant, a second lieutenant, a first sergeant, four sergeants, eight corporals, two musicians, one wagoner, and sixty-four to eighty-two privates. The regiment was to have a staff consisting of a colonel, a lieutenant colonel, a major, an adjutant, a quartermaster, a surgeon, two assistant surgeons, a chaplain, three sergeants (sergeant major, quartermaster sergeant, commissary sergeant), a hospital steward, two principal musicians, and a band of twenty-four members. In practice the band was rarely retained. The minimum strength of a regiment was to be 869 officers and men, the maximum strength 1,049; failure to recruit depleted regiments meant that most of them eventually fell far below the prescribed minimum, with a typical regiment numbering perhaps 530 men by the time of Chancellorsville, perhaps 375 at Gettysburg, and thereafter recovering strength slightly. Although the presence of a lieutenant colonel and a major made it possible to maneuver a regiment as two battalions, for tactical purposes it continued in fact to be handled as a single battalion, as had been almost uniformly true since the close of the Revolution. Cavalry regiments had a squadron organization, consisting of six such units, which were composed of two companies each.[49]

In European armies the organization of the regiment into several battalions was growing in favor in the middle nineteenth century, since it made for greater tactical flexibility and permitted the detachment of battalions for recruiting duty. The nine new Regular infantry regiments which were called for on May 4, 1861, reflected this tendency. They were to be composed of two or more battalions each, of eight companies to the battalion. Each of them was to have the three majors appropriate to three battalions. Also reflecting European practice, each of them was assigned to a geographical region from which it was to recruit. But these regiments, the 11th through the 19th, failed to reach full strength, because recruits preferred the looser discipline and higher bounties of the volunteers. At Gettysburg none of the Regular regiments represented had more than eight companies present. When the war ended, the new Regular regiments were reorganized to the conventional one-battalion pattern.[50]

In the course of the war the United States raised 1,696 regiments of infantry, 272 of cavalry, and 78 of artillery. These regiments came to be gathered into higher operational organizations including brigades, divisions, army corps, and field armies. The War Department originally ordered the formation of brigades of four regiments each and of divisions of from three to four brigades. In practice, however, none of the units higher than the regiment was a table of organization unit in the modern sense; all of them rather were task forces, composed of varying constituent elements as circumstances and accident decreed. Brigades usually consisted of anywhere from two to six regiments, sometimes even more; divisions of two or more brigades. Perhaps the most usual alignment was five regiments to a brigade, three brigades to a division. In addition to their infantry, divisions generally had organic artillery, that is, artillery permanently allotted to them; in the Army of the Potomac from the Gettysburg campaign onward, however, artillery was organic principally to an army corps, with about nine batteries to each corps. Early in the war some infantry divisions had attached cavalry. Later, cavalry was organized mainly into divisions of its own. By the middle of the war, an infantry division averaged about 6,200 men.

In the 1860's the approved basic larger unit was not so much the division as the army corps of two or more divisions. Through late 1861 and early 1862 Lincoln urged McClellan, first when he was commanding general of the Army and then as commander of the Army of the Potomac, to begin introducing a corps organization. Without corps the Army of the Potomac was an unwieldy organization of some 150,000 men in an agglomeration of about fifteen divisions. McClellan nevertheless demurred, on the ground that no officers had yet proven themselves capable of corps command—an argument that applied equally to the army commander himself. At length Lincoln lost patience and ordered the establishment of four corps in the Army of the Potomac. Two more corps had been formed in that army and others were forming in other armies when Congress decreed a corps organization for the Army generally on July 17, 1862. Thereafter the corps were numbered consecutively throughout the Army, with divisions numbered consecutively within each corps. A corps commonly embraced three divisions, aggregating about forty-five regiments of infantry and nine batteries of artillery.[51]

The first system of standard unit badges in the United States Army grew out of the corps organization. When Major General Joseph Hooker became commander of the Army of the Potomac in the spring of 1863, he ordered that each corps be identified with a distinctive badge, as Major General Philip Kearny had already identified the 3rd Division of the III Corps with a red diamond. The badges were cut from flannel and were generally blue, white, or red to designate the 1st, 2nd, or 3rd division of a corps, respectively. They were worn conspicuously on the soldier's cap. They stimulated unit pride, and they incidentally eased the job of identifying stragglers. The corps of the other field armies adopted their own badges about a year after Hooker prescribed them for the Army of the Potomac.[52]

A greatly varying number of corps made up an army. An army usually possessed, in addition to its infantry corps, a generous allotment of artillery beyond what was organic to divisions and corps, and usually an army force of cavalry. By late 1862 the Army of the Potomac had no less than eight infantry corps, so McClellan somewhat haphazardly and his successor, Major General Ambrose Burnside, more systematically formed several corps into still other intermediate organizations, which they called grand divisions. Hooker ended this perhaps useful experiment. Usually an army included most of the forces in a single theater of war, although toward the close of the war the Union made frequent use of what today would be called army groups. The Army of the Potomac and the Army of the James jointly laid siege to Petersburg and Richmond, and Sherman led the Armies of the Cumberland, the Tennessee, and the Ohio together against Atlanta. There were at least sixteen Union armies during the course of the war. They took their names usually from the geographical military departments in which they were first organized and which in turn were named generally for rivers.[53]

For administrative, as distinguished from tactical, purposes, the peacetime division of the country into territorial departments persisted through the war. Some fifty-three territorial departments are listed in the index to the *Official Records*, marking the shifting alignment of these units. Obviously, not all the territorial departments had whole armies attached to them, but conversely a field army command usually was attached to the administrative direction of a territorial department. While deep in Georgia with Sherman, for example, the commander of the Army of the Ohio still had to concern himself with the administration of military affairs, such as posts and the apprehension of deserters, in the territorial Department of the Ohio, far to the north along the river of that name. Late in the war several territorial departments were sometimes joined in larger geographical commands, such as the Military Division of the Mississippi, which under Grant and then Sherman after October, 1863, included the Departments of the Ohio, the Cumberland, the Tennessee, and Arkansas.[54]

In the Civil War as in every major war, the crux of the problem of expanding the Army to war strength was the question of finding adequate officers: efficient commanders of regiments, brigades, divisions, corps, and armies, and good junior officers who could both train the men and then lead them in battle. As always, the latter aspect of the question was the more difficult and the more critical. If few men possessed the talent to command an army, only a few dozen such men were needed; but thousands of colonels and tens of thousands of subalterns had to be found. And if the junior officers could not train citizens to be soldiers, no amount of skill on the part of the high command was likely to compensate for it.

By 1861 the graduates of West Point formed a far larger reservoir of military knowledge than the United States had possessed in any previous war. The instruction they gave and the examples they set surely do much to account for a much more rapid and efficient transformation of recruits into regiments and armies than in any earlier war, except perhaps the much smaller Mexican War. Yet the numbers of available West Pointers were dwarfed by the magnitude of mobilization. Some 440 West Point graduates remained in the Regular Army after the southerners resigned, 115 returned to the Regulars from civil life, and 393 entered volunteer regiments. But with about 2,000 regiments eventually forming, and many of the West Pointers moving into higher commands, most of the colonels, let alone the junior officers, had to be military amateurs.[55]

Had the government dispersed the Regular Army to provide officers for the volunteers, the supply would still have fallen short of the demand. Under the circumstances it may well have been as good a plan as was possible to have the men elect their lieutenants and captains and to have the latter officers elect the field grade officers; at least the elections could be presumed to bring forward men of some leadership qualities, and there were hardly any other criteria available. Even if officer training schools had been quickly erected, they could not have supplied the first regiments, and there were not enough men qualified to instruct in such schools anyway.

After the first rush, the government began to think about eliminating unfit officers. In accordance with a law of July 22, 1861, the War Department ordered on July 25 that all officers of volunteer regiments appear for examination before a board of three to five officers appointed by the department commander and the general in chief. These were the first efficiency boards in the United States Army.

Those officers declared unfit by the boards were to be replaced by men who could pass the examinations. What the boards could accomplish was still limited by the general dearth of military knowledge, but considerable numbers of officers resigned rather than face the boards at all. Meanwhile an act of August 3, 1861, gave the Army its first retirement program, by authorizing retirement, with adequate pay and allowances, for officers who suffered physical disability or who had served forty years. This measure made possible the weeding out of high-ranking but superannuated officers inherited from the peacetime Regular Army.[56]

Without enough trained officers, training the men was bound to be a puzzling task, but it did not help that the War Department never prescribed any consistent training program. How much training a Union regiment took into battle was a hit-or-miss matter depending not only on the experience and knowledge of its officers but very much on their conscientiousness as well. Those amateur officers who possessed a large measure of the latter quality spent hours pouring over the Army Regulations, the tactical manuals, and any other military works they could find, emerging from their tents to try to transfer paper precepts to the parade ground. A Congressional gesture toward the training program was to make two appropriations of $50,000 to purchase tactical manuals for the volunteers. The most popular works of that genre were General Scott's *Infantry Tactics;* William J. Hardee's *Rifle and Light Infantry Tactics*, adopted as official in 1855 and still used despite its author's defection to the Confederacy; and Silas Casey's *Infantry Tactics*, a loyal officer's work which officially superceded Hardee in 1862. The proportion of conscientious officers who studied these books diligently was evidently high, and their success in putting their studies to use was also often notable. With the manuals easily available, and with military school graduates and Regular Army men supervising, assisting, and setting examples, the amateur officers did a reasonably good job of turning themselves and their men into soldiers at the same time; there was just enough military knowledge in the country to assist them so that this task was not the nearly impossible one it had been in the Revolution.[57]

As commanding general at the beginning of the war, Winfield Scott tried to set up a more systematic training program. Training was one of his characteristic preoccupations, and he persuaded Secretary Cameron to ask the governors to provide camps of instruction at the rendezvous points of the first three-month men. But the need to assemble an army quickly at Washington, for defense of the capital, and then popular pressure to use the army offensively broke up Scott's system before it really got started.[58]

McClellan's long delay in opening an offensive after he took command of the Army of the Potomac is often justified on the ground that he needed the time to train his army. But while he encouraged training after a fashion, there is no evidence that he set up any systematic program for the whole army. Anyway, no one in the 1860's, not the most professional of soldiers, carried training much beyond the parade ground to anything resembling simulated combat, or even to realistically difficult marches. Target practice varied widely according to various commanders' whims and the background of various regiments. The essence of military training in the 1860's was drill—drill designed to permit officers to move their regiments quickly from column of march into line of battle, and to keep their battle lines under disciplined control in the close-order fighting still envisioned by the manuals. While close-order drill required a lot of practice, it is difficult to believe that McClellan put to good use eight months of this sort of thing, when the enemy against whom he was preparing was no more professional than his own troops. In World War II a more complex basic training consumed only about three months.

After campaigning had gone on for a while, the volunteers could supply their own reservoir of seasoned officers and could themselves take in hand the training of recruits. As the war went on, the most common method of securing officer replacements was promotion from the ranks. Good army and corps commanders ordered all regiments, including veteran ones, to devote their available time to instruction in arms and tactics. On April 19, 1864, Major General George G. Meade, then commanding the Army of the Potomac, at last authorized expenditure of ten rounds of small arms ammunition per man to teach the men to use their rifles, and he ordered corps commanders to see that such instruction occurred. Unfortunately, the practice of raising new regiments rather than filling old ones minimized the value of veteran experience. Late in the war, unlucky soldiers in new regiments continued to go into battle under new officers who had not yet learned their business.[59]

The volunteer regiments faced a variety of disciplinary problems related to those of training. Citizen soldiers as usual were loath to pay unquestioning obedience to officers who had recently been their neighbors and whose advantages in soldierly knowledge were at best something culled from a book. To accommodate and attract recruits, the volunteer regiments relaxed the harsh disciplinary punishments of the Regular Army. Flogging was abolished in 1861, much to the satisfaction of humanitarians who had long campaigned against it. Discipline remained easygoing throughout the war, by Regular Army standards and in the eyes of foreign military observers. As the officers grew more competent and therefore more confident of themselves, however, they reverted toward a more consistent enforcement of the letter and spirit of the regulations and harsher penalties for miscreants. Bounty jumpers and substitutes and other unpromising military material sometimes seemed to give them no choice. By 1864, bucking and gagging in the infantry and spread-eagling in the artillery were brutal penalties once again seen frequently.[60]

The shortcomings of training no doubt help explain high casualty rates in the early battles of the war. Soldiers who learned little but parade-ground drill knew few methods of protecting their own lives while endangering the enemy. But casualty rates continued to be extremely high as the war went on, when growing battle wisdom might have been expected to offset improved marksmanship of the enemy. In World War II, losses of ten per cent in an engagement seemed barely tolerable; in the Civil War, regiments frequently lost fifty per cent in one battle and occasionally more than eighty per cent. Obviously, then, more than defective training was at fault; the technology of war had made certain advances to which tactics were slow to adjust or could not adjust.

Even so formidable an array as the Grand Army therefore found it hard to press battles to victorious decisions. In the resultant frustration, its leaders sought new means to victory, with large consequences for the nature of war itself.

ELEVEN

The Perplexities of Civil War: 1861-77

. . . war is simply power unrestrained by constitution or compact. If they want eternal warfare, well and good; we will accept the issue and dispossess them, and put our friends in possession.

—William T. Sherman[1]

It is whipped rebellion not repentant rebellion. . . .

I have no faith in all that we hear of the loyalty &c of the South. They are beaten, they are cowed . . . [yet] they will revenge themselves for their defeat upon the North & upon the black in every mode which may be safe.

—M. C. Meigs[2]

IN THE Civil War and Reconstruction, the United States Army first experienced both the exhilarating potency and the frustrating limitations of modern military power.

As it was to do still more markedly in the twentieth century, a new technology at once enhanced and hampered military power. The Civil War witnessed the first large-scale military application of three technological advances, the railroad, the telegraph, and the rifle.

The rapid movement over great distances introduced by the railroad could not have been exploited without the telegraph. Major Richard Delafield of the American military mission to the Crimea had been impressed by the potential usefulness of this instrument when the British initiated telegraph links between their headquarters and subordinate commands, and indirectly between their headquarters at Sebastopol and their government at London. The American Army now applied the lesson on a still larger scale. All the Union forces from the Potomac to the Gulf could be joined in a telegraph network responsive to the War Department and the commanding general. Such a network was developed under Colonel Anson Stager, former general superintendent of the Western Union Telegraph Company. The operatives were also mainly experienced civilian telegraphers. Technically the system was part of the Quartermaster's Department, with its funds coming from that source and its officers ranking as assistant quartermasters. Significantly, Stanton insisted that the system nevertheless be responsible directly to him.[3]

But the telegraph was sufficiently cumbersome that it could have only limited battlefield usefulness. Communications on the battlefield itself remained primitive, and because officers found it difficult to maintain contact with each other and with their men in combat, the tendency was to retain close-order tactics even when the third technological innovation, the rifle, made them horrendously murderous.

Colonel (eventually Brevet Brigadier General) Albert J. Myer tried to do something about tactical communications, and he achieved a certain amount of progress and founded the Signal Corps. Myer was a military surgeon who became interested in communications through writing a thesis on sign language for deaf-mutes as a student at Buffalo Medical College. He developed a method of signaling with flags which was tested from 1858 onward in the Indian wars. On June 21, 1860, the War Department named him chief signal officer of the Army with the rank and pay of a major of cavalry, the first such post in any army. Myer spent much of the summer of 1861 trying to interest the department in sponsoring a portable telegraph apparatus which could keep an army commander in touch with detachments on the battlefield. He received encouragement from McDowell and McClellan but little help from the War Department; still, by November 30 he had adopted the Beardslee portable telegraph and developed a field train for it. It served on the Peninsula and enabled Burnside to maintain telegraphic communication across the Rappahannock at Fredericksburg. Meanwhile, Myer also continued work on the flag signal system, and the principal concern of the Signal Corps at its birth in 1863 was with that type of communication. Myer's advances in both areas were useful but in both the tactical applications remained limited. Neither flags nor the portable telegraph with its delicate and cumbersome wiring, short range, and slow transmission could do very much to extend control over combat itself beyond the physical presence of the officers. Largely because of these facts, close-order tactics persisted.[4]

Most of the shoulder arms in American arsenals at the outbreak of the war were smoothbore muskets. These weapons generally had an extreme range of about 250 yards. Their effective range was far less; a Wisconsin backwoodsman remarked that it took a pretty steady hand to hit a barn door at fifty paces. The Model 1855 United States rifle, firing the Minié bullet, had an extreme range of half a mile or more, and its effective range was 200 to 250 yards. The Model 1861 rifle was still more satisfactory because it had a more reliable firing device, an improved percussion cap dispensing with the so-called Maynard Tape primer, which was spoiled by moisture. Thus the rifle was thoroughly superior to the smoothbore musket, and the War Department tried to replace smoothbores as rapidly as possible. By the fall of 1862 most Union regiments carried Springfield or Enfield rifles or muskets converted to rifles. By capture, importation, or manufacture with the help of the Harpers Ferry machinery, the Confederates equipped their infantry with rifles almost as promptly. The Civil War became the first great war of the rifle, and the rifle dominated the battlefields.[5]

Though battle lines had been loosening and skirmish lines had been increasing in importance since before the War of the American Revolution, infantry tactics until the Civil War had not changed essentially from those of the eighteenth century. The main idea was still that the attacker should bring a well-aligned mass of men close to the enemy's position, punish him with a volley, and then close with the bayonet. Dense formations remained important both to fall upon the enemy with a heavy weight and to permit the officers to control what was happening.

But the rifle with its increased range and accuracy confronted the old tactics with a variety of difficulties. The short-ranged smoothbore muskets often could get off only one effective shot against an advancing enemy line; the long range of the rifles permitted them to be fired effectively many times against an enemy line marching across open ground. In fact, Civil War battles soon demonstrated that rifles tended to tear any frontal attack to shreds before it could close. If attackers paused on open ground to get off their own shots against covered defenders, they only increased the duration of their exposure. Surgeons soon noted that bayonet wounds rarely appeared any longer; it was unusual for the attacker to get close enough for a bayonet fight. Because of the destructive power of the rifle, soldiers increasingly looked for the shelter of stone walls or dug rifle pits or trenches as soon as they halted anywhere; this habit of digging in then rendered the task of the attacker still more difficult, since less and less could he make effective reply to the hail of bullets which tore his ranks.[6]

Napoleon had strengthened the attack by developing his extremely mobile artillery and then sending the guns forward with or ahead of the infantry charge, to batter the defenders with a storm of heavy lead.

But the infantry rifle quashed Napoleonic artillery tactics too. If artillery drew close enough to sheltered defenders to hope to fire with effect, the defender's rifles could pick off the artillerymen at their guns.

Artillery itself went increasingly to rifled weapons during the war. Only a few experimental rifled cannons were available at the beginning, but by 1863 about half the guns of a Union field army were likely to be 3-inch rifles. The 4.62-inch twelve-pound Napoleon smoothbore had an extreme range of 1,680 yards and an effective range of about 800 to 1,000 yards; the 3-inch rifle could fire as far as 4,000 yards and had an effective range of about 2,500 yards. While rifling thus enhanced the accurate range of artillery as well as of shoulder arms, it did not restore artillery to its Napoleonic prominence in the attack. At distances at which the gunners were safe, rifled artillery could do little damage to entrenched infantry. For that purpose it was necessary to have a shell that would explode above the trenches and spew forth a hail of deadly pellets. Such a device, the modern shrapnel shell, was not used until the Franco-Prussian War, and even its success proved limited against well-designed entrenchments.

Union artillery upheld the high tradition inherited from General Knox and Major Ringgold, but its value was mainly defensive. In the artillery there occurred less dilution of the Regular Army than in the more numerous infantry, and especially in the Army of the Potomac the Regular batteries were so distributed that one of an infantry division's four was likely to be Regular Army (itself generally a mounted battery only since the beginning of the war). The volunteer batteries served in close association with the Regulars and quickly learned from them. Union artillery earned the acknowledged respect of the enemy very early, at a time when the Confederates still professed to regard Union infantry and cavalry with contempt. The Army of the Potomac became famous for its excellent artillery, commanded with great skill from Antietam onward by Brigadier General (later Major General) Henry J. Hunt.

Though his guns could carry out effective counterbattery fire against Confederate artillery, Hunt rightly recognized that the principal value of his arm under the prevailing tactical conditions was to supplement the infantry rifle in repulsing enemy attacks. In fact, he believed that in suitable circumstances his guns might do more than supplement the rifles of the defending infantry: with their longer range they might break an attack before it became a real threat to the infantry. At Chancellorsville his guns massed on such eminences as Fairview and Hazel Grove were instrumental, perhaps decisive, in halting Stonewall Jackson's flank attack, often firing over the heads

of their own infantry. At Gettysburg, Hunt ordered the Union batteries to cease firing relatively early in the artillery duel that preceded Pickett's Charge, in order to conserve their ammunition for
the infantry attack that would follow. General Hancock counter-
manded this order for the artillery of his II Corps, as was his prerogative. Hunt later maintained that if he had not done so, the Union
line would not have been penetrated, and the guns alone—having
been allowed to cool, and with plenty of ammunition—would have
broken Pickett's Charge. He could point to the fact that to Hancock's
left, where the guns did conserve their ammunition for the infantry
attack, the enemy did not reach the Union line.[7]

In firing against an infantry attack such as Pickett's, the artillery
opened at long range with rifle shells, then had its smoothbores join
in with solid shot as the enemy approached closer, and finally at
about 200 yards' range switched to case shot. Because smoothbores
were most effective for close-in fighting, spewing forth grapeshot or
canister, a large quota of them remained with the armies, perhaps
actually growing in favor late in the war. The twelve-pound Napoleon remained the most frequently used gun of all.[8]

If artillery alone could break an infantry attack, as Hunt argued,
then frontal assaults had become doubly hopeless. In the face of
withering fire from both infantry rifles and artillery, attack formations tended to open up much more than ever before, and attacks
tended to become series of short dashes from cover to cover, infantrymen working their way forward from rock to tree to irregularity
of ground to whatever other shelter their approach afforded. By this
means they might gradually build up a line which could deliver a
respectable blow to the entrenched enemy. But officers had to resist
such tendencies and finally had to retain much of the old two-rank
attacking line. They had to insist on relatively compact formations if
they were to retain control by voice and visual communications. And
strong entrenched positions are not carried by men moving in driblets from one shelter to another; the end of an assault had to be some
semblance of the traditional massed charge. Unhappily, that charge
led almost invariably to huge casualties and repulse. A skillful commander might sometimes avoid a frontal assault by turning the
enemy's flank; but if the enemy then chose to stand and fight, he
would often make the initial success temporary by forming a new
line to face the flank attack.

In short, the rifled fire power of a defending army well entrenched
brought battle to an impasse. The single decisive battle of the Austerlitz and Jena variety became practically extinct. A determined
attacking army might impose heavy casualties on the defenders despite the advantages of the defense, but only by absorbing very heavy

casualties itself. Since the enemy could no longer be shattered utterly in a decisive battle, the only way remaining to beat him was to wear him down by prolonged attrition. With the Civil War, warfare entered that phase of costly, inconclusive battles of attrition that was to last until the coming of the tank and the airplane.

Before the tank and the airplane gave new hope to attacking armies, the defender's means of repulsing an infantry attack were to grow still more deadly. Considerable controversy has surrounded the question of whether the Union Army in the Civil War might have carried those means beyond the muzzle-loading rifle and muzzle-loading artillery. The chief of ordnance when the war began was Brigadier General James A. Ripley, a conservative gentleman loath to adopt new weapons. Ripley's successor, Brigadier General George D. Ramsay, chief of ordnance from September, 1863, to September, 1864, quickly incurred Stanton's ill will, and the spite of the cantankerous Secretary may have hamstrung any improvements that Ramsay might otherwise have effected. Only after the appointment of Brigadier General Alexander B. Dyer to succeed Ramsay did the Ordnance Department enjoy a chief who was both vigorous and influential. Furthermore, the Army lacked a program for developing and testing new weapons.

Nevertheless, charges of culpable resistance to change on the part of the Ordnance Department seem to have little weight. They center on the claim that Union soldiers should have been issued breech-loading rifles. But few breechloaders were available when the war began, and to convert muzzle-loaders to breechloaders thereafter would have been a difficult business; the Ordnance Department undertook it on a limited scale only after the war and its urgency were gone, and then with limited satisfaction. Generals had qualms about the liberal amounts of ammunition soldiers were likely to expend if they were given breechloaders, and the necessity for ammunition to reach the battlefield by wagon train gave point to such concern. With transportation to the battlefield so cumbersome, the soldier in combat was mainly dependent on the forty rounds he could carry in his cartridge box plus about twenty more rounds in his pockets. A good metallic cartridge that could be mass-produced was not yet available, and with paper cartridges, breechloaders allowed an escape of gas which reduced their range. With paper cartridges and black powder, the breech mechanism easily became fouled, and an infantry rifle should be as reliable as possible.[9]

Along with the breechloader controversy, there are some subsidiary charges against the Ordnance Department, notably that it should have offered more encouragement to the development of some such forerunner to the machine gun as the Gatling gun. The trouble here was that the Gatling gun and its contemporaries were unwieldy and ready targets for enemy artillery. Napoleon III had great faith in the mitrailleuse, a similar weapon, but the Franco-Prussian War proved his faith misplaced.[10]

The 272 regiments of cavalry mobilized by the Union Army represented many times more mounted troops than the United States had ever had before, but the infantryman's rifle also assured that there would be no reversal of cavalry's descent into an auxiliary role. European military observers grew fond of debating the merits of American cavalry, which, they emphasized, remained more nearly mounted infantry than traditional cavalry of the lance- and saber-wielding kind. They often attributed the absence of traditional cavalry to the Americans' inexperience and the wooded and broken character of American terrain. But their own subsequent wars were to confirm a more basic cause, the futility of old-style cavalry tactics, a futility considerably greater even than the growing futility of old-style infantry tactics. The massed horsemen of old-fashioned cavalry charges were merely gun fodder to well-placed infantry wielding rifles.

Though an auxiliary arm, however, Civil War cavalry could still be extremely valuable, since there was as yet no substitute for it as a reconnaissance and counterreconnaissance arm. Because Union cavalry in the early days of the war was notoriously inferior to Confederate, Union commanders were notoriously hard put to discern, until it was too late, the enemy's strength and what he was doing with it. Their ignorance does something to explain several of the grossest blunders of Union generalship early in the war, and conversely Lee's excellent cavalry service made possible some of his finest battles; the information gained by Jeb Stuart's Confederate cavalry during their ride around McClellan's army on the Peninsula was the foundation of Lee's plan for the Seven Days battles that saved Richmond.

One of Stuart's salient qualities was his superior ability to interpret what he saw on such a ride and provide his superiors with a perceptive intelligence summation. Lesser leaders, fascinated by the example of his dramatic thrusts into the enemy's country, tended to emulate his raids but to achieve little more than spectacular waste of horseflesh and energy. In this fashion Major General Joseph Hooker reformed the cavalry of the Army of the Potomac by consolidating it into a compact division and then tossed away his reform by allowing most of the division to ride off toward Richmond when he needed it on the flanks and in advance of his army. Eventually Stuart himself may have become infatuated with the theatrical side of his long rides at the expense of the reconnaissance function, though debate continues about the motives for his raid during the Gettysburg campaign.

Another direction of cavalry development is associated with the resurgence of Union cavalry later in the war under such leaders as John Buford and Philip Sheridan. Cavalry might be employed somewhat like modern airborne troops, exploiting superior mobility to seize a position in advance of the army, but then fighting as infantry to hold on until reinforced. Unfortunately, the light weapons of cavalry, attributes of mobility, made prolonged resistance to infantry difficult. Breech-loading carbines partially compensated for the advantages of the longer-ranged infantry rifle over the cavalry carbine. Cavalry could adopt breech-loading weapons earlier than infantry, because with light carbines range could not be so important a consideration anyway as with infantry rifles, and carbines in any case could not stand up under prolonged firing as could infantry rifles. But this is to say that the inherent inferiority of carbines to infantry shoulder arms remained. The best carbines could not enable cavalry to stand up to infantry on equal terms. The possibilities for cavalry to take and hold ground continued to be limited. However useful it was as an auxiliary arm, cavalry could not break the tactical impasse.[11]

With a decisive Austerlitz battle virtually precluded by rifled firearms, strategy in turn had to concentrate upon variations on the theme of attrition. This necessity in its own turn posed hard problems for generals whose West Point training stressed the tradition of Napoleonic battle, and helps to explain the difficulties of the Union Army's command.

". . . the rank and file of the Army of the Potomac had begun to consider themselves better soldiers than their commanders," wrote a veteran of the war, echoing Nathanael Greene's observation about the officers and soldiers of the Revolutionary Army.[12] The problem was not quite the same as in the War of the Revolution, however. Despite the high proportion of amateur officers in the Union Army, enough basic military knowledge was in circulation in the United States that the company and field grade officers did reasonably well with fair consistency. The worst difficulties of the Civil War officer corps were in the higher command.

In Richard S. Ewell's famous phrase, the officers of the prewar Army learned everything about commanding a company of fifty dragoons on the western plains and nothing about anything else. Notwithstanding the merits of the Military Academy, the United States Army had no facilities for instructing officers in the theory and doctrine, let alone the practice, of commanding large bodies of troops. When the Civil War began, only the division commanders of the Mexican War had experience in leading any really sizable body of troops, and now those men were generally too old or otherwise disqualified to be considered for field command. There was no staff school, no adequate theory of staff work, upon which to found adequate assistance to army, corps, and division commanders in the complex work of caring for and moving thousands of men.

Thus all the techniques of command at its highest level had to be learned pretty much by doing, and men capable of exercising high command had to be sought out by trial and error. Naturally blunders occurred, some of them in matters of command and staff work that would later seem elementary. Army commanders expended their time and energies on tasks they had no business touching: Irvin McDowell personally reconnoitered roads while his army marched to Bull Run, and George McClellan personally sighted artillery pieces as his army came up to the Antietam. So ill served was McClellan by those staff officers who should have done the work of modern operations and intelligence officers that he tried to shift his whole army from its base on the York River to the James by a single road, when two other reasonably good roads paralleled that one at a short distance; nobody at his headquarters knew of their existence although McClellan had contemplated the shift to the James for weeks. After Major General Erasmus D. Keyes's IV Corps had stumbled upon the two roads and used them, nobody else was told about them, and they again fell idle until Major General William B. Franklin's III Corps also chanced upon them.[13]

Intelligence was the part of staff work probably least well handled through much of the war. Not only was McClellan perpetually uninformed about key geographical features in his own vicinity, but he was also victimized by utterly erroneous notions of the numbers and disposition of the enemy. To remedy the deficiency he resorted to hiring the Pinkerton detective agency; but he would have done better to have no intelligence estimates at all than those supplied him by the Pinkertons, for they simply aggravated his own tendency to exaggerate the enemy's strength. The quality of intelligence work in the Army of the Potomac improved somewhat when General Hooker assigned a staff officer, Colonel George H. Sharpe, specifically to the duties that today would go under that heading. The improvement was possible partly because anyone with military knowledge could avoid many of the Pinkertons' errors simply by applying such knowledge to information readily at hand; while the private detectives were misleading McClellan, for example, Quartermaster General Meigs drew up an accurate order of battle for the enemy army and accurate estimates of its strength merely by digesting what he read in southern newspapers. After employing Sharpe, however, Hooker was slow to make good use of him; the army commander continued to rely too much on the estimates of his cavalry commander, Alfred Pleasonton, which were remarkably unreliable, and everybody from Pleasonton upward was remarkably slow to discover what Lee was up to when the Pennsylvania campaign of 1863 began.[14]

The recitation of such blunders could go on at length. For all that, where command and staff work involved sheer technique, rather than such qualities as judgment and wisdom, the striking fact is how rapidly leaders of the Union Army became tolerably good and then increasingly better. By the summer of 1862 the Army of the Potomac could carry out its difficult movement from the Peninsula to Aquia Creek practically without a hitch. There are many military writers who think that Lee should have brought the Army of the Potomac to disaster after he had repulsed it at Fredericksburg and it stood with its back to the Rappahannock; however much Lee's opportunities there may sometimes be exaggerated, it was certainly no mean feat for Ambrose Burnside's staff to arrange the transfer of the army back to the north bank of the river without loss. The evacuation of the south bank after Chancellorsville was an almost equally impressive achievement.

By late 1862 and 1863 the Army of the Potomac had in staff posts several unusually competent men who had learned their work very rapidly. Ingalls as chief quartermaster and Gouverneur K. Warren as chief engineer are especially worth noting. For the first time in American military history, such men held rank commensurate with their duties; the principal staff officers now wore a brigadier's star on their shoulders. Good staff specialists had also been found for Winfield Scott's army in Mexico; the Army of the Potomac had something more in that it also possessed, in Daniel Butterfield and Andrew A. Humphreys, chiefs of staff fully competent to act and decide in appropriate instances in the absence of the commanding general and able to bear a variety of detailed work. The western armies appear to have been slightly less well served by their staffs, but only slightly less so. In general, the quality of Civil War staff work was surprisingly high despite the Army's deficiency in staff training, and the war was the first in which the Army consistently possessed reasonably adequate staffs.[15]

The great and tragic shortcomings of Civil War leadership were at a higher level, beyond the realms of technique and expertise. They were in the faulty tactics and strategy which lost campaign after campaign despite every advantage of numbers and matériel, sacrificed thousands of lives in futile combat, and by prolonging the war ensured its transformation into a "remorseless revolutionary strug-gle."[16] They were in the generalship of McClellan, Pope, Buell, Burnside, Hooker, and other men who demonstrated appalling unfit-ness for the highest military responsibilities but whose failures the country had to endure with patience because for too long the Army seemed to offer no commanders who were better.

Perhaps much of the trouble at the level of theater and army command lay in the absence of an established body of military doc-trine which could have guided officers through difficult situations. Too much of the conduct of Civil War campaigns rested solely on the accidents of intelligence, boldness, and even the daily state of mind of individual officers. The Prussians were beginning to work out a system that would partially overcome the hazards of those accidents, through their higher military schools and their general staff, whereby the military schools would fashion a coherent doctrine of war, and each higher commander would have at his side a general staff officer trained in the application of the doctrine to specific situa-tions. West Point's limited training in the maxims of Jomini did not afford Union officers the guidance of a coherent body of doctrine, and however good their staffs became in a specialized way, Union commanders could not turn to those staffs for guidance comparable to that provided by officers of the Prussian general staff.[17]

Yet such germs of an accepted corpus of military doctrine as can be found in West Point teaching, official manuals, and the Army Regulations do not offer much reason to suppose that, had it tried, the prewar Army could have developed a doctrine appropriate to the Civil War situation. Such approaches to a doctrine as existed often proved inadequate in the testing. The outstanding peacetime repre-sentatives of the new professionalism of the officer corps often proved most unsatisfactory generals.

McClellan and Henry W. Halleck had been among the most bril-liant of Dennis Mahan's pupils, and both had contributed books of their own to the literary expression of the new military professional-ism. But although knowledge of military history and of the teachings of military philosophers can be of high value in preparing competent officers, they cannot alone make good generals. McClellan and Hal-leck had mastered military literature as thoroughly as any Ameri-cans, but both of them suffered from flaws of imagination and char-acter which frustrated their efforts to apply their knowledge. Know-ing the maxims of Jomini well, they held to them too literally in conditions to which they did not apply. McClellan moved too slowly in part because he tried to insist on an academic perfection of equip-ment and organization before he committed his troops to danger. He conducted textbookish siege operations at Yorktown when bold action could have swept away the defenders almost instantly. Halleck was so obsessed with the Jominian principle of the advantage of interior lines that he long refused to acknowledge that the Union might exploit its advantage in numbers to press the Confederacy all along the borders. The untrained Lincoln wrote that the Union must menace the enemy

with superior forces at *different* points, at the *same* time; so that we can safely attack, one, or both, if he makes no change; and if he *weakens* one to *strengthen* the other, forbear to attack the strengthened one, but seize, and hold the weakened one. . . .

But Halleck scorned such advice as violating the Jominian principle of concentration of force; it "is condemned," he said, "by every military authority I have ever read."[18]

The shortcomings of McClellan and Halleck certainly lay in their own minds and character as well as in devotion to any maxims they had learned at West Point. Dennis Mahan, after all, had emphasized that the very purpose of studying military science is to escape rigid rules; "no soldier," he said, "who has made himself conversant with the resources of his art, will allow himself to be trammeled by any exclusive system."[19] Yet somehow the conviction must persist that the kind of military professionalism that West Point and the Regular Army had developed before the war was linked to the all too universal failure of the men thrown up to leadership at the beginning of the war. The trouble ran deeper than literal adherence to Jominian maxims; it extended to basic attitudes.

Because they had become conscious of their professionalism, the professional officers too often felt a sort of disdain for the military amateurs who filled out their armies. They resumed the grumbling letter writing on the subject of volunteers that had marred the records of some of them in Mexico. Sometimes they understood sufficiently little about commanding citizen soldiers that they lost the respect of their men in turn, so that amateur officers who could gain rapport with their men sometimes did better with companies and even regiments than professionals who could not.[20]

Distrusting amateurs at war, the professional officers could easily extend their distrust from the citizen soldiers to the citizens in the government who tried to direct war making. When Lincoln attempted to inform himself of McClellan's strategic intentions the better to sustain his general, McClellan reacted with annoyance and discourtesy and prayed to be free of "browsing presidents." Writing to McClellan on his familiar theme of the obstacles implicit in the Union's exterior lines, Halleck also complained "that the want of success on our part is attributable to the politicians rather than to the generals." McClellan blamed his civilian superiors for all his troubles on the Peninsula.[21]

Believing political impingement upon military domains an unmixed handicap, generals of the McClellan stamp tried to close their ears to the politicians. In doing so, they also closed their senses to many useful insights into the changing nature of the war. The politicians, certainly President Lincoln, grew increasingly aware that the Civil War differed from any previous American war, and that the means of winning it were likely to have to be new and different strategies. The new rifled weapons made decisive victory on the battlefield almost impossible to attain. At the same time the South conceived itself to be defending with the Confederacy its very way of life, all that men hold valuable, and mere victory on battlefields might not overcome the mind and will of the South anyway. No limited war making could well force the South to yield, for its citizens believed that the stakes at issue were unlimited. The situation drove Lincoln's government toward unlimited war making, against the property and people as well as the armies of the South. The desperation of southern resistance caused Lincoln at last to declare the emancipation of the Confederacy's slaves, as one means of undermining the southern war effort. In doing so he knowingly converted the war into a social revolution, unavoidably enhancing southern desperation even while weakening the southern means to resist.

Distrusting civilians and politicians in war, and as much as possible turning a deaf ear to them, many of the professional officers closed their minds to the tendencies toward unlimited and revolutionary war. Far from leading the trend toward more terrible war, many professional soldiers, outstandingly McClellan himself, called for moderation and for conciliation of the South, even while waging war, and in the face of that growing futility of any conciliatory efforts which the politically acute could recognize. A noteworthy number of professional soldiers were among those who drove Lincoln to bemoan the many who would restrict him to wage war "with elder-stalk squirts, charged with rosewater."[22]

Lincoln believed, and rightly by all our evidence of the southern state of mind, that the South would respond to no conciliation short of southern independence, and that given the desperation of southern resistance, the only alternative was to wage war aimed at the South's total defeat: to wage unlimited war that would reach beyond armies to the southern people and undermine their will. Those officers whose military professionalism closed their sensitivity to civilian influences, and thus to the character of the war, therefore became dispensable. To lead the Union armies Lincoln had to find other commanders, less thoroughly professional perhaps but better attuned to the national spirit and to the tides of the war. He turned away from the model professionals, McClellan and Halleck, to much less orthodox officers, West Pointers but hardly embodiments of professionalism, mainly Grant and Sherman.

Or more accurately, until, in Grant and Sherman, he found officers who would wage the sort of war he believed he needed, Lincoln felt obliged to conduct the war himself.

The institutions of the high command remained as unsatisfactory in the Civil War as they had been before. President, Secretary of War, and commanding general continued to play badly defined and overlapping parts.

Lincoln possessed at least the vigor and strength of will of James K. Polk, which had assured civilian ascendancy over the military arm during the Mexican War, and from the beginning he intended no mere titular role for himself as Commander in Chief. From the beginning he kept in constant touch with the armies, eagerly utilizing the new telegraph; from the beginning he intervened in strategy when he thought it wise to do so. At the beginning, however, he felt constrained by an acute consciousness of his own want of military expertise.

When the armies were gathering in the summer of 1861, Secretary Cameron and General in Chief Scott suspended the old rivalry of their offices for the crisis and followed a division of labor suggested by the Regulations, Cameron mainly seeing to the organization and administration of the new armies, Scott mainly determining strategy. But this arrangement broke down after First Bull Run. Once McClellan arrived in Washington to retrieve the first defeat and organize an army in and around the capital, he seized effective control of the Washington army away from the aging Scott. He considered the hero of Lundy's Lane and Chapultepec senile, incompetent, and an obstacle to the proper conduct of the war, and he made his feelings more and more plain. Scott's military mind remained in fact a good one, but he was fat, gouty, weary, and disinclined to contend for long against the ambitions of the young Napoleon of the West. On November 1, 1861, McClellan saw him off to the railroad station and into retirement at West Point, and the new Napoleon became commanding general himself. From the complacent Cameron he now set out to assume many of the functions of the War Department as well.

McClellan's idea of the War Department seems to have been that it was the agency from which he drew men and supplies. In the military province, which he defined broadly, McClellan acknowledged no superior except the President, and he often gave Lincoln short shrift. He appropriated to the commanding general's office the War Department series of general orders, so that the department issued no such orders, and the President eventually felt obliged to begin a new series of Presidential War Orders to regain a measure of control over the Army. When Stanton replaced Cameron as Secretary of War, he invited McClellan to establish his headquarters in the War Department building adjacent to the White House, so that the department and the commanding general might cooperate better; but McClellan preferred to remain in his own headquarters in a mansion on Jackson Square, and he rarely visited the War Department.

Stanton, however, was not Cameron, and he determined to fulfill that provision of the Regulations which described the Secretary of War as exercising direct control of the Army as the President's deputy. Significantly, he early removed the military telegraph center from McClellan's headquarters and planted it in the War Department. McClellan resisted him, and an intimate friendship between the two of them soured into bitter animosity. But Stanton persisted, and by the spring of 1862 McClellan's position was weakening under his failure to demonstrate capacity as more than an organizer of troops. McClellan withheld pertinent information of his strategic intentions not only from the Secretary of War but from the President himself and from his generals; so much did he gather all the reins of the Army into his own hands then when he fell ill, Lincoln despaired that "the bottom is out of the tub." But McClellan justified secretiveness and insistence upon power with no military results, and while he held the President at arm's length, he did not discourage the tentative overtures of the Democratic party opposition whose war views he shared. It took no great persuasion on Stanton's part to bring Lincoln at length to issue one of his Presidential War Orders on March 11, 1862, relieving McClellan as commanding general and restricting his command to the Army of the Potomac.[23]

No suitable replacement was in sight. No officer in the United States, except the retired Scott, was better qualified by experience than McClellan, yet along with everything else McClellan's shortcomings obviously came in part from inexperience. By default, the President and the Secretary of War decided to shoulder the office of commanding general themselves.

Their decision to do so has occasioned much amusement as well as some contempt among military critics. Indeed, there was something pathetic about their efforts to catch up with the new job by reading books about strategy late into the night. Nevertheless, they performed better than McClellan and probably did as well as anybody in the country could have at the time. They attempted, as McClellan never had, to coordinate operations in various theaters, and they succeeded in getting the several armies west of the Appalachians to work in harness under Halleck, in an offensive which coincided with McClellan's long-delayed advance against Richmond. They had to react to Stonewall Jackson's thrust down the Shenandoah Valley at the end of May, 1862, and they did so swiftly and intelligently, by attempting to grasp the opportunity to cut off Jackson's detachment and destroy it. Their effort to bring converging columns together south of Jackson nearly succeeded and might have done so had it not been for Major General John C. Frémont's blundering choice of route and for heavy rainstorms. They were right to look to the safety of Washington when McClellan took the Army of the Potomac to the Peninsula, but they saw to it that McClellan had ample resources out of which a more resolute general would almost certainly have fashioned success. In precision and completeness their orders to the field commanders consistently would have done credit to trained officers.[24]

Lincoln and Stanton were not pretentious men. They recognized their military limitations and wanted all the reliable professional assistance they could get. They brought out of retirement Ethan Allen Hitchcock, one of the most diligent military students of the pre-Mexican War Army, and made him their principal adviser. Unfortunately, Hitchcock was not only old and in dubious health but increasingly interested in spiritualism rather than war. After McClellan's Peninsular Campaign failed, while the armies under Halleck in the West won a measure of success, they ordered Halleck east and gave to him the office of general in chief on July 23, 1862.[25]

Stanton was willing now to curtail his intervention in events in the field and to emphasize administration of the War Department and the Army. Lincoln continued in close consultation with the general in chief, and occasionally the President communicated directly with subordinate officers. But the Secretary and the President were willing to consign military command mainly to Halleck. As events turned out, however, Halleck was unwilling to take it. He would not make decisions if he could possibly avoid them; he would not even press to implement the decisions of others unless the Secretary and the President pressed him in turn.

If in such a difficulty as this you do not help [Lincoln wrote when Halleck evaded one delicate military decision], you fail me precisely in the point for which I sought your assistance. . . . Your military skill is useless if you will not do this.

But Halleck continued to disappoint the President, and Lincoln and Stanton themselves had to return to the active control of the armies.[26]

Halleck faded into being little more than an agent for the translation of the President's will into military terms and its transmission to field commanders. He also served as a gossipy gatherer and purveyor of miscellaneous military information and rumors. When the President did not project his will into military affairs, Halleck confined the central direction of the Army to the proffering of good advice, consistently couched in such terms as would avoid responsible involvement. His familiarity with military rules, customs, and practice made his presence near Lincoln a convenience, but he was not a real general in chief.

Lincoln bore this situation for over a year because he concluded again, and with good reason, that if he himself had to act as commanding general, he could do the job as well as anybody available. Then Ulysses Grant at Vicksburg and Chattanooga proved himself a consummate officer. Lincoln gladly gave way to him. Early in 1864 Congress revived the full rank of lieutenant general, vacant since George Washington held it during the quasi-war with France, and Lincoln bestowed it upon Grant and appointed him commanding general of the Army. Thence emerged the structurally awkward but —thanks to the personalities involved—practically workable command system that carried the Union to victory. Grant brought unprecedented vigor and decisiveness to his post, and he brought all the armies in all the theaters of war into a single strategic design as had never been done before. Confident of Grant's ability, Stanton concentrated upon administrative work and Lincoln maintained only a loose and general supervision over Grant, although not so loose as Grant was to claim in his memoirs. While he supervised all the armies, Grant paid special attention to the critical Eastern theater and took the field with the Army of the Potomac, while retaining Major General George G. Meade in tactical command of that army. To assist Grant in keeping touch with the other armies, Halleck stayed on in Washington as chief of staff of the Army. His principal duty was to convert the decisions of others into detailed orders, and for that work he was well qualified. The legal status of the commanding general remained obscure, but Lincoln, Stanton, and Grant could see to it that the fact was of no practical consequence as long as the war lasted.[27]

Stanton's particular province, then, came to be the business management and maintenance of the Army through the War Department staff and bureaus. By the end of the war, the bureaus through which he worked had grown to be eleven in number: those of the adjutant general, the quartermaster general, the surgeon general, the judge advocate general (whose office was established March 2, 1849, reviving one that had existed off and on from the Revolution until 1821, but under whom the Bureau of Military Justice was created only on June 20, 1864), the chief of ordnance, the commissary general, the paymaster general, the chief of engineers (the Corps of Topographical Engineers being consolidated with the Corps of Engineers on March 3, 1863), the chief signal officer (the post of signal officer being established June 21, 1860, with a Signal Corps following on March 3, 1863), and the provost marshal general (from March 3, 1863).[28]

When Grant took command of the field armies and assumed the principal strategic direction of the war, many in the professional officer corps seem still to have felt misgivings about him, Vicksburg and Chattanooga notwithstanding. Especially the officers of the Army of the Potomac, McClellan's own army, reflected that Grant had not yet proven himself against the likes of Lee and the Army of Northern Virginia. His Old Army past was against him: his West Point record was mediocre, he was by no means a student of war as McClellan and Halleck were, but worst, he had resigned his commission in 1854 a notorious drunkard. Tales of occasional benders still followed him. He dressed carelessly, generally gave the impression of an easygoing rustic, and did not look like much of a soldier.

In the end, such doubts about Grant came to suggest some of the limitations of pre-Civil War professionalism. Grant was rustic and earthy partly because he did not feel set apart from the mass of Americans by his West Point education; he did not share the common professional distrust of citizen soldiers, and he made vigorous and successful campaigns with them from the beginning of the war. He was no master of those tactical precepts of Jomini that read like something out of a geometry text; but while Halleck, a translator of Jomini, displayed a geometric obsession with places and lines on the war map (after Corinth he allowed the enemy to slip away unmolested, content to take a fortress and a railroad junction), Grant always struck to destroy the enemy's army and ultimately all his power to make war. Jomini had expressed a horror of the ruthless, destructive campaign to which the guerrillas had provoked Napoleon in Spain; those who adhered to his precepts believed war should be restrained and gentlemanly much in the eighteenth-century manner. Grant did not know him so well and very much made his own rules anyway. He early drew new conclusions from the war's combination of tactical indecisiveness and impassioned southern resistance; the essence of his conclusions was to strike beyond the Confederate armies against everything the enemy used to sustain war:

Up to the battle of Shiloh [he wrote] I, as well as thousands of other citizens, believed that the rebellion against the Government would collapse suddenly and soon, if a decisive victory could be gained over any of its armies. Donelson and Henry were such victories. An army of more than 21,000 men was captured or destroyed. Bowling Green, Columbus, and Hickman, Kentucky, fell in consequence, and Clarksville and Nashville, Tennessee, the last two with immense amounts of stores, fell into our hands. The Tennessee and Cumberland rivers, from their mouths to the head of navigation, were secured. But when Confederate armies were collected which not only attempted to hold a line farther south . . . but assumed the offensive and made such a gallant effort to regain what had been lost, then, indeed, I gave up all idea of saving the Union except by complete conquest. Up to that time it had been the policy of our army, certainly of that portion of it commanded by me, to protect the property of the citizens whose territory was invaded, without regard to their sentiments, whether Union or Secession. After this, however, I regarded it as humane to both sides to protect the persons of those found at their homes, but to consume everything that could be used to support or supply armies.[29]

Grant's aim was to be complete conquest. The tactical impasse imposed by rifled weaponry decreed that the strategies employed must be strategies of attrition. Grant pushed forward the Anaconda Policy that Winfield Scott had offered at the beginning of the war, strengthening the naval blockade by encouraging joint Army-Navy expeditions against the Confederacy's remaining seaports, such as Mobile and Wilmington. Like Lincoln and in refutation of Halleck, he recognized that coordinated pressure by the stronger Union forces against the inferior Confederate numbers all along the Confederate frontier must force the enemy to spread his armies too thin, so that somewhere his lines must break. So he opened the campaign of 1864 with concerted attacks in every theater, and he tried to keep pushing those attacks constantly. Confederate generalship was sufficiently skillful, however, and the tactical deadlock on the battlefields was sufficiently hard to break, that pressure all along the frontier gobbled up territory but did not lead to the immediate destruction of the enemy armies. Thus Grant had to employ still another device of attrition: he had to accept heavy casualties himself in order to impose heavy casualties upon the enemy, knowing that he could afford to play that game but the enemy could not.

The aim of "complete conquest" implied still another kind of strategy, however, that went beyond Grant's methods of attrition. Under Grant's aegis, and more directly under Sherman and Sheridan, the Union armies employed that other strategy: to carry the war to the enemy's whole people and thus destroy their will to resist. The

Civil War was no eighteenth-century dynastic contest but a war of peoples. "Complete conquest" had to be the Union aim because the southern people believed their very way of life was at stake, and they would submit to nothing less. Upon their determination to resist rested the power of the Confederate armies. But if destruction was carried to their very way of life by the war itself, then their determination would lose its object, and the respite of peace might seem worth purchasing. If the Confederate people lost their determination to resist, their armies would collapse from loss of support. If the enemy's armies alone were destroyed, a guerrilla war might follow the end of formal fighting. If the will to resist was destroyed, that danger too would pass.

Thus Sherman conceived his marches through the enemy's heartland:

I attach much importance [he said] to these deep incisions into the enemy's country . . . : we are not only fighting hostile armies, but a hostile people, and must make old and young, rich and poor, feel the hard hand of war, as well as the organized armies.

My aim, then, was to whip the rebels, to humble their pride, to follow them to their inmost recesses, and make them fear and dread us.[30]

Grant had pursued "complete conquest" from Shiloh onward, he authorized and encouraged Sherman's marches, and his friend and biographer Adam Badeau expressed his final concept of the war in similar terms:

. . . he understood that he was engaged in a people's war, and that the people as well as the armies of the South must be conquered, before the war could end. Slaves, supplies, crops, stock, as well as arms and ammunition—everything that was necessary in order to carry on the war, was a weapon in the hands of the enemy; and of every weapon the enemy must be deprived.

. . . It was not victory that either side was playing for, but for existence. If the rebels won, they destroyed a nation; if the government succeeded, it annihilated a rebellion. It was not enough at this emergency to fight as men fight when their object is merely to outwit or even outnumber the enemy. This enemy did not yield because he was outwitted or outnumbered. It was indispensable to annihilate armies and resources; to place every rebel force where it had no alternative but destruction or submission, and every store or supply of arms or munitions or food or clothes where it could be reached by no rebel army.[31]

Henceforth the Civil War afforded the American Army its conception of a major war. In American military thought and teaching, and certainly in American memories, it far overshadowed the wars of Napoleon, and subsequent foreign struggles such as the Franco-Prussian War could not approach its impact upon American thought. When the men who were to lead the American Army in World War I went to West Point, and most of the commanders of World War II as well, the model of a great war most conspicuous in their studies was the Civil War, a war of "power unrestrained" unleashed for "complete conquest."

Yet wars must end and power once again be restrained, and then the conquest of an enemy people is likely to prove less complete than it seemed. So the Army learned, as the sequel to war making became disheartening entanglement in the politics of Reconstruction. Invading the South, the Civil War Army was bound to participate in shaping policy for the seceded states. Waging the war, its officers and soldiers were sure to form conclusions about the kind of war they should wage, mild and conciliatory or harsh, and that was a partisan issue. Especially, since slaves flocked to the refuge they believed the Union Army offered them even before the Emancipation Proclamation, the Army could not help but influence government policy toward the Negroes.

On May 23, 1861, three slaves of a Virginia owner arrived at Fortress Monroe seeking their liberty. Their owner demanded they be returned to him under the Fugitive Slave Act. Major General Benjamin F. Butler commanded the district. Notoriously a political general, he had been the Vice-Presidential candidate on the Breckinridge Democratic ticket but was now sniffing a change in the political winds. He refused the slave owner's demand, on the ground that since Virginia had seceded, her citizens could not claim the protection of federal law. In his report of July 30 to the Secretary of War, he referred to the slaves he harbored as "contraband of war."[32]

Brigadier General Charles P. Stone, (USMA 1841), began the war most promisingly. When James Buchanan and Winfield Scott grew fearful that secessionists might try to prevent the inauguration of Buchanan's successor, Scott appointed Stone to take charge of the District of Columbia militia, drill them and ensure their loyalty, and look to the defense of the capital. Nothing untoward happened, and Lincoln too came to trust and value Stone. On April 18, 1861, he became inspector general of the District of Columbia and commander of the District Volunteers. Thereafter he rose from colonel to brigadier general and commander of a division of the Army of the Potomac by October. But on October 21, 1861, his troops suffered a costly reverse at the battle of Ball's Bluff. By that time also, talk was circulating in the capital about Stone's attitudes on the South and the war. Stationed on the upper Potomac, his division had become a magnet for runaway slaves, but Stone published an order denying the fugitives asylum in his lines and insisted on returning them to their owners. Massachusetts soldiers of antislavery leanings reported these events to their antislavery governor, John A. Andrew, along with word that Stone fraternized with Maryland slaveowners and forwarded Confederate mail. Andrew then denounced the participation of any Massachusetts man in slave catching, and Senator Charles Sumner aired Massachusetts's grievance against Stone on the floor of the Senate. The general foolishly replied to such political interference with his control over his own division by writing Sumner a letter calling abolitionists troublemakers and virtually inviting the Senator to challenge him to a duel.

In the heated atmosphere of rebellion, many Republicans suspected a connection between Stone's tolerance for slavery and his defeat at Ball's Bluff. The time was the same autumn of 1861 when McClellan was refusing to prosecute the war vigorously. Significantly, Stone was a member of the McClellan circle. Significantly too, it seemed to many, Stone and McClellan with their disinclination to treat southerners harshly were both West Pointers, who had consorted with southern cadets in that socially conservative institution, while Ben Butler, who regarded slaves as "contraband," had not attended the Military Academy.[33]

Such suspicions led to a call for Congressional investigation of Ball's Bluff, and to that end Congress in December created the Committee on the Conduct of the War. The committee was destined to endure throughout the conflict and to investigate much more than Ball's Bluff.

General Stone was its first major target. He turned out to suffer extraordinary penalties, but otherwise the committee's handling of him set a pattern. Through January, 1862, the antislavery Republicans who dominated the committee heard witnesses in secret session and gathered evidence which they presented at the end of the month to Secretary Stanton, saying it "seemed to impeach both the military capacity and the loyalty of General Stone." The committee eagerly included in its evidence the most nebulous camp gossip as long as it was detrimental to Stone. Stanton thereupon ordered Stone's arrest, on unspecified charges. McClellan tried to insist on a military trial for Stone, but all that Stanton would allow was a return appearance before the Committee on the Conduct of the War. There Stone pathetically attempted to prove his loyalty without being able to confront either his accusers or the specific accusations against him. He returned to prison, where he remained for 189 days before less hostile congressmen secured an act to free him. No other officer was imprisoned without charges, but thereafter the committee conducted a series of similar inquiries consistently based on the theory that a conciliatory attitude toward the South and a willingness to retain slavery were equivalent to incompetence for military leadership. These inquiries helped unseat various officers of conservative and Democratic political views, including McClellan himself and many of his circle. As in the Stone case, Stanton blandly exposed to the committee those officers who were reluctant to fight a harsh war, because he tended to believe there was merit in the committee's view—that an officer who was unwilling to invoke harsh measures did not understand the kind of war he was fighting and would fail to apply the means which in this war were essential to victory. Increasingly, to Stanton this meant that officers must be willing to join in undermining slavery; on the other hand, he sustained William T. Sherman until the close of the war and until an egregious blunder in Sherman's handling of the Confederate surrender. Stanton did so because though Sherman was distinctly cool toward the slaves, he won victories.[34]

Much could be said for the judgments of the committee on the nature of the war. Nevertheless, mere antipathy toward the South and slavery did not guarantee a general's military ability. The committee too often assumed that it did, displaying conspicuous approval for such inept officers as Ben Butler and John C. Frémont. Less can be said in favor of the committee's inquisitorial methods of procedure. Still, the group did ferret out a large body of pertinent military information. If Harry S Truman profited from its mistakes in handling his own Congressional investigating committee during World War II, as he says he did, he also worked upon a foundation of Congressional prerogatives which the Committee on the Conduct of the War helped erect.[35]

As the war went on, antislavery men could count upon growing support from the Army. As Lincoln initially omitted the extinction of slavery from the purposes of the war, so few soldiers enlisted in the Army out of antislavery zeal. When the President issued the Emancipation Proclamation, he still provoked considerable grumbling from the Army. But as the Army penetrated the South, soldiers recognized more clearly that slavery was among the principal props on which the Confederacy rested and that to weaken it would surely ease their own task and hasten the end of the war. In the South the northern soldier knew that virtually every southern white man was his enemy, but the Negro was his friend. So northern armies more and more welcomed the runaway slaves that flocked to them, the Negroes more and more found substance in their vision of Lincoln's Army as the herald of the Year of Jubilo, and the Emancipation

Proclamation itself drew substance from the advance of the armies.[36]

In the face of the advancing Union armies, Confederate civil government crumbled, and the Army found itself the sole source of law and order in occupied areas. Therefore the Army had to improvise a system of government, and the method that most naturally developed was to extend the functions of the provost marshals from policing the Army to policing the occupied districts and in effect governing them. The provost marshals decided which southern civilians should be taken into custody and which should remain free to pursue their usual tasks; they regulated traffic and travel; in scarcity they distributed food, clothing, and other goods. Significantly, the provost marshal system of government was adopted everywhere except in Sherman's military division; despite his harshness in war, Sherman showed considerable tolerance of the local civil officials once resistance ceased.[37]

Almost everywhere, the provost marshals developed a system of loyalty oaths as a means of testing the inclinations of southern citizens and determining how much freedom to allow them. In December, 1863, Lincoln took up this system of oaths, to construct upon it in the occupied areas new state governments which would rival the state governments of the Confederacy and perhaps help undermine them. He offered pardon, with certain exceptions, to any southern citizen who would take an oath to support the Constitution of the United States and the Union. Whenever in any state persons as numerous as one-tenth of those who voted in the election of 1860 had taken the oath, they might establish a state government, which Lincoln would recognize when it abolished slavery.[38]

To assist in creating the new state governments, Lincoln also appointed military governors in much of the reoccupied South. At the outset of the war, he had seen to the election of a new governor of Missouri under military auspices, to replace a governor of secessionist leanings. As early as 1862 he had appointed military governors in Tennessee, Louisiana, and North Carolina. These officials were civilians functioning with military support; although Stanton told the military governor of North Carolina that he was to "be Dictator" there, in fact the powers of the governors were subordinate to those of the military department commanders.[39]

As long as the war lasted and thus as long as he lived, Lincoln was careful to avoid committing himself to a single specific plan for restoring the South to the Union. The governments under his ten-percent plan would have collapsed without military support, which is one good reason for thinking of them more as a wartime measure to weaken Confederate authority than as a program for Reconstruc-

tion. When the Confederate armies surrendered, the only firm foundation upon which Reconstruction could be built was the United
States Army and its military government. So for a time after the war
ended, the military provost marshals continued to govern the former
Confederacy.

The provost marshals soon met challenges to their authority. Some
came from southern whites, who hoped to win as much recognition
as possible for their accustomed local officials. More surprisingly,
other challenges came from the Freedmen's Bureau, another agency
of the War Department but an autonomous one. After several years
of effort on the part of antislavery leaders and considerable disagreement over where in the government such an agency belonged, Congress had authorized the bureau on March 3, 1865, to give protection and support to the freedmen, and also to the Unionist southern
whites. Major General Oliver O. Howard, a professional officer
known for his deep religious convictions and his long-standing opposition to slavery, headed the bureau, and his principal lieutenants
were mainly officers with views similar to his own, together with
several civilian antislavery leaders. The Freedmen's Bureau fed,
clothed, tried to find work for, and otherwise assisted needy freedmen, took control of abandoned and confiscated southern lands hoping to transfer them to the Negroes, and set up special tribunals to
administer justice in cases involving the rights of the former slaves.[40]

Many staunch antislavery men favored extension of the authority
of the Freedmen's Bureau at the expense of the provost marshals.
Reports from the South indicated that many provosts were much less
zealous than bureau agents in protecting the freedmen. By late 1865
Stanton agreed that the powers of the bureau ought to be increased,
since another advantage of it was its central direction and responsiveness to him, whereas the provosts were loosely organized and
their policies differed from department to department. Furthermore,
the Secretary had been receiving disturbing evidence that some
provosts took advantage of loose supervision to make a racket out of
the issuance of trade and travel permits. With Grant's approval
Stanton transferred most of the governmental functions of the provost marshals to the Freedmen's Bureau.[41]

By that time, it was important that War Department Reconstruction policy be as coherent and effective as possible, for the Army in
the South was encountering growing difficulties. During 1865 President Andrew Johnson pursued his Reconstruction plan based on the
Presidential pardoning power, whereby he pardoned most former
Confederates when they took a loyalty oath, and allowed them to
reestablish civil government. Johnson's program was so lenient as to
encourage southerners to swiftly renewed self-confidence, and with it

to a return to political views hardly changed from those that had led to secession. This process included a burgeoning southern arrogance not only toward the freedmen but toward Union soldiers as well. Soldiers as well as Negroes increasingly found themselves subject to jeers and insults and, worse, to danger of physical attack when they went abroad alone or in small groups. The Black Codes of the restored state legislatures expressed and sanctioned a determination to restore the Negro to a thoroughly subservient status. Restored state courts began to contest the jurisdiction of both the Freedmen's Bureau tribunals and the provost marshals' courts. With Johnson's permission the restored state governments reorganized their state militias, their personnel drawn from the disbanded Confederate armies, uniforms commonly of Confederate gray, and disarming of Negroes a principal activity.[42]

Soldiers in the South did not have to be zealously antislavery to feel that the Army's whole mission was being threatened. In the revived state courts, southern citizens began instituting scores of suits against soldiers asking damages for actions taken under martial law during and after the war. The state courts were sure to hear these suits sympathetically, and officers reported to the War Department that they feared to exercise their functions of military government lest the suits succeed and they be subjected to financial ruin. Secretary of War Stanton himself became the target of a damage suit initiated in the New York courts by Joseph E. Maddox, who claimed that he had been arrested during the war on false charges of disloyalty. Powerful Democratic politicians stood behind Maddox, and if he won his suit against the Secretary, subordinate officers in the South were sure to feel still more insecure.

The Army's concern for its ability to complete the pacification of the South and even for the safety of its soldiers there eventually forced its officers into political partisanship unparalleled since the formative years of the Republic. President Johnson was well disposed toward the restored southern state governments which he himself had sponsored, and he felt little sympathy for the Negroes. By implication he felt little sympathy for the Army's position in the South. In the face of the damage suits, the Army could count on no assistance from the President. It felt obliged to turn to Congress. As the Republican leadership of Congress itself moved into increasingly open conflict with Johnson's Reconstruction policy, first individual officers and then the Army stood more and more openly with Congress against the President, if only for the self-protection of the officers and men assigned to the South.

Unable to secure Presidential assistance in protecting the Army against the damage suits, Stanton and Grant sought Congressional

action. In the meantime Grant issued general orders by which soldiers, civil officers, and Negroes who asserted that the civil courts
of the South did not offer them justice could have any suits against
them transferred to federal courts or to the Freedmen's Bureau
tribunals. On May 11 Congress authorized federal court jurisdiction
in suits against soldiers, as well as assistance from the government's
legal officers to current and former public officers involved in litiga-
tion over actions performed under orders during and since the war.
Meanwhile Grant managed to arrange a compromise that led to the
dropping of the Maddox case against Stanton.[43]

These safeguards for the Army were soon shadowed by new setbacks. In April the United States Supreme Court issued a preliminary judgment in the case Ex parte Milligan, involving the validity of
military tribunals where the civil courts were functioning, and it was
clear that the final decision of the Court was not likely to look kindly
upon such exercise of military law. In the same month the President
proclaimed the rebellion at an end and the southern states restored to
the Union, thus increasing the pertinence of the Milligan case and
jeopardizing all military actions based on wartime powers.[44]

On the other hand, by that time Congress had renewed the charter
of the Freedmen's Bureau over the President's veto, explicitly sanc-
tioning the bureau's tribunals. With this assurance of Congressional
support, Stanton and Grant issued a secret circular to military commanders in the South, instructing them to comply with the President's recent proclamation but also reminding them of the Freedmen's Bureau Act and Grant's general orders on the subject of civil
courts and authorizing them to go on employing military courts
where necessary. On July 6 Grant reinforced this circular with a
new general order empowering all Army commanders in the South,
down to the post or company level, to arrest civilians charged with
crimes against federal personnel or against Negroes when necessary
for the protection of justice.[45]

This latter order was a strange bedfellow to the President's peace
proclamation, but Stanton, Grant, and many officers in the South
more and more felt justified in moving contrary to the President's
policy, sure as they were of the support of Congress. In July the
governor of Virginia requested arms to reactivate his state militia;
the President supported the request, but Grant delayed compliance.
At the end of the month a riot in New Orleans precipitated by a
procession of Negroes led to a slaughter of Negroes by white police-
men and citizens, with about 40 persons killed and 160 wounded,
mostly Negroes. The local military commander would have intervened, but his troops were stationed outside the city at the time.
Major General John Pope soon made a public speech, the text ap-

proved by Stanton and Grant in advance, in which he warned that all the old southern political influences would reassert themselves if military power did not control the South.[46]

Grant was careful to avoid an open break with Johnson and maintained outward good relations with him. But the general risked his own political ambitions by resisting the Commander in Chief even cautiously, since his popularity was such that he had only to avoid rocking the boat to be pretty well ensured of the Presidency. Stanton might well have resigned if he had followed his personal inclinations. Thus both seemingly acted as they did, not out of ambition but to serve the Army and the country. Together they ensured that the Army mainly served Congressional Reconstruction policy, not Presidential. But Johnson eventually moved to shift them from his path. He tried to persuade Grant to accept a diplomatic mission to Mexico. Rumors spread that he would remove Stanton from the War Department. Congress thereupon acted to keep Grant and Stanton in their places, through the Command of the Army Act and the Tenure of Office Act of March, 1867.[47]

The former was a constitutionally dubious measure that made the commanding general rather than the President the effective head of the Army. It provided that all orders to the Army from the President or the Secretary of War must be issued through the commanding general, whose headquarters must be at Washington and who was not to be removed without the consent of the Senate. At the same time, the First Reconstruction Act enhanced the power of Grant's Army in the South by dividing the ten unreconstructed states into five military districts, whose commanders were authorized to oversee the processes of civil government, and were presently instructed to reorganize southern state governments on a basis of Negro suffrage and exclusion of Confederate leaders. In case Johnson should yet displace him or Stanton, Grant instructed the district commanders that their duties were outlined for them by Congress and that thus they must conduct themselves as responsible to Congress, not the President, in Reconstruction policy. When Johnson threatened to override this view of things, Congress incorporated it into the Third Reconstruction Act in July, making the forces in the South virtually a separate Army under Congressional control, as distinguished from the frontier border forces which remained an arm of the executive.[48]

Infuriated by the circumscription of his office and the frustration of his policies, Johnson suspended Stanton. Congress was not in session at the time to apply the Tenure of Office Act, but Johnson was prepared to defy that act should the legislators invoke it against him when they returned. Meanwhile he appointed Grant Secretary of War in Stanton's place, evidently with the idea that free from

Stanton's influence Grant would prove malleable. Grant's limited political sophistication encouraged the thought, but Johnson failed to count on Grant's thorough devotion to the Army, whose welfare and safety in the South seemed to depend on Congressional Reconstruction. With some reluctance Grant accepted the Secretaryship while retaining his place as commanding general; but he did so out of loyalty not to the President but to the Army, and he encouraged the district commanders to conform to the letter and spirit of Congressional policy as before.

When Congress returned, the Senate invoked the Tenure of Office Act and refused to approve Stanton's removal, whereupon Stanton reclaimed his office and Grant disappointed Johnson by yielding it to him. Johnson asserted the unconstitutionality of the Tenure of Office Act and refused to recognize Stanton, attempting to seat Adjutant General Lorenzo Thomas in the War Department. By now Congress was as furious with Johnson as he with them, and it retaliated by impeaching him. The articles of impeachment mainly cited his defiance of the Tenure of Office Act, but they also alleged a conspiracy to defy the Command of the Army Act. While the impeachment trial dragged on from March into May, 1868, the Presidential powers as Commander in Chief lapsed further still; Stanton and Grant now sent reports direct to the Congressional military committees. It was difficult, however, to prove that the charges against Johnson accorded with the constitutional grounds for impeachment, high crimes and misdemeanors. The Senate finally failed to convict Johnson and remove him from office.[49]

The failure was by only one vote, however, and Johnson acted considerably subdued through the brief remainder of his term. With the Senate vote of acquittal, Stanton relinquished the War Department, as personal and family concerns had long tempted him to do. The chastened Johnson, Grant, and the Republican leaders in Congress agreed upon Major General John M. Schofield as a compromise Secretary of War; Schofield was acceptable to Congress, he would guard the interests of the Army, but as a district commander in the South he had not identified himself with Congressional Reconstruction closely enough to become anathema to the President. Since Grant remained as commanding general and soon became due for elevation to the White House, he was by far the leading figure in the military situation, and he commanded the Army much as he chose. So weak was Schofield's position that in 1868 the bureau chiefs, traditionally subordinate to the Secretary of War if to anybody, published their reports without referring them to the Secretary. The Army in the South was now firmly established as an instrument of the Congressional Reconstruction program, delaying the readmission of the southern states while attempting to assure the full liberation of the Negroes. A final decision from the Supreme Court in the Milligan case and several related cases might have threatened this arrangement, but Congress responded by limiting the appellate jurisdiction of the Court, and the Court profited from Johnson's example by restraining itself from further challenges to Congress.

The Army became a primary instrument of Congressional Reconstruction, but some of the problems of Reconstruction lay in the limitations of armed force as a means of social transformation. To effect by force the Negro's rise to full citizenship and the acquiescence of his enemies, when the latter included most of the population, required large numbers of troops. The North was never sufficiently zealous for Negro rights, or even for the punishment of rebels, to provide numbers that matched the Army's responsibilities. The wartime volunteers wanted to go home, and their families wanted to have them at home. The names of 1,000,516 officers and men were on the rolls on May 1, 1865; by the end of the year this figure had shrunk to 199,553. After another year only 11,043 volunteers remained, about 10,000 of them United States Colored Troops. Grant asked for an increase of the Regular Army to 80,000 men, with an eye to Maximilian in Mexico as well as to the former Confederacy; but neither Stanton nor Congress was willing to go quite so far. On July 28, 1866, Congress reorganized the Army and authorized expansible companies that in the infantry and cavalry could vary from fifty to a hundred privates. The War Department then called for companies of sixty-four privates and a total of 54,302 rank and file. But authorization remained one thing and recruiting another. Fewer than 40,000 troops were at hand when Congress enacted its legislation. The peak strength to which the Army was recruited during Reconstruction was 56,815 officers and men in September, 1867, and the peak strength for policing the South was about 19,000.[50]

This force was sufficient to maintain a general armed supervision over southern government and elections but not to prevent an appalling incidence of terror and violence directed against the freedmen and their friends and allies. Furthermore, northern voters and therefore Congress did not desire to expend money and men in a perpetual large-scale Regular Army policing of the South. An indigenous military force would be preferable if a reliable one could be found, and little time elapsed before some Reconstruction leaders began to think about organizing the freedmen for the military defense of their own new status. All the arguments that had brought about the arming of Negroes in the war seemed to bear at least equal force now. Thousands of former United States Colored Troops were at loose ends. To extinguish the gray-clad southern militia of some of Johnson's Reconstruction governments, Congress suspended the militia power in the southern states in 1867. In 1869 and 1870, however, it restored that power to the southern state governments fashioned under military supervision, with the idea of transferring much of the military burden to southern militias loyal to the new governments and therefore largely Negro. At the same time the authorized strength of the Regular Army was reduced to 45,000 men, and it was cut again to 30,000 the next year.[51]

Most of the Republican Reconstruction governments of the southern states now set out to restore their states' military forces for their own purposes, resuming the organization of volunteer militia companies. Georgia and Virginia governors thought it best not to enlist Negro militiamen, and Alabama enrolled Negroes but did not arm them. The other states organized both Negro and white companies, with the former much outnumbering the latter under the circumstances. All of them except Florida then used their Negro militia for general police duty and especially to watch over electioneering and voting, to ensure that freedmen could and would vote and that ineligible ex-Confederates stayed away. Sometimes the militiamen interpreted these duties aggressively. For a time their utility at elections was great. They were less effective in the general suppression of white terrorism, partly because of the old problem of insufficient numbers. More than that, their existence provoked a retaliatory terrorism, both to counteract their effect on elections and because southern whites gagged at the mere sight of black men in uniform. The whites took arms to resist the Negro militia, sometimes fighting pitched battles as in Arkansas and New Orleans, more often with night riders attacking isolated militiamen and their families and harassing them constantly to make life unbearable. White violence was effective enough to cool Negroes' enthusiasm for militia service at an alarming rate. By the early 1870's the Negro militia was already disintegrating, and with it much of the remaining military support for Reconstruction.[52]

Military force as an instrument for the uplift of the freedmen suffered from limitations more deep-seated than the problem of numbers. Yet force was often the only instrument available; if it is not an ideal instrument of social change it is sometimes an effective one (as the Second Reconstruction in the twentieth century has sometimes had to demonstrate), and perhaps Reconstruction fell short of full liberation for the Negro not because it used force too much but because it did not rely on it thoroughly and long enough.

The Army served Congressional Reconstruction loyally as long as the government itself permitted. As long as Congress supported it and maintained reasonable troop strength in the South, the Army tried to protect the freedmen, to crush such counterreconstruction organizations as the Ku Klux Klan, and to force public officials and state governments into policies of respect for Negroes, Unionists, and the federal Union. In the course of the battle between Johnson and Congress, the Army had become an active force in politics, and through the rest of the Reconstruction era it clung to the alliance then formed with the Congressional Reconstruction leaders. It deviated both from its apolitical tradition and from the social conservatism habitual to its prewar leaders. Its motive was largely one of self-preservation: the safety of soldiers in the South depended upon the Congressional alliance. But more than self-preservation was involved. The Civil War with its aim of unlimited conquest and its ruthless methods had brought tough and somewhat unorthodox leaders to the fore; Sherman was conservative enough to be distrusted by the Radical Republicans, but after waging war as he had, he could hardly quail at social revolution as McClellan might have done. Of sheer vindictiveness the Army displayed little, much less than many Congressional leaders; it respected its former adversaries and saluted them when they surrendered. But there appears to have existed in the Army a strong feeling that to acquiesce in Johnson's Reconstruction program would have been to break trust with the comrades who had died in the war. "I have no faith in all that we hear of the loyalty &c of the South," wrote Quartermaster General Meigs.

God has punished us [Meigs said] for allow[in]g slavery & oppression in the South & has more severely punished the South for it[s] greater & more active guilt. He lifted his hand from them for a time & they are returning like dogs to their vomit. They can not enslave but they will outrage & oppress. Their hearts are not changed. We are guilty again. We permit this oppression they are guilty again they enact it. God will surely visit both sections of the Union until the foul spot is wiped off our escutcheon & it blazes with unsullied brilliance as altogether free.[53]

TWELVE

Twilight of the Old Army: 1865-98

We're marching off for Sitting Bull
And this is the way we go—
Forty miles a day, on beans and hay,
With the Regular Army, O!

—Old Army song

PERHAPS THE GLOW of romance has lighted it because, amidst revolutionary change brought by the Civil War and the new industrial, urban age, the old Regular Army seemed to have changed so little. In the postwar years it was one remnant at least of the lost and simpler American past. The lean cavalrymen in dusty blue rode out from their wooden stockades to fight the Indians, and once more the Army appeared a place where officers learned all about commanding fifty dragoons on the western plains but nothing about anything else. The storm of the Civil War was gone, the citizen armies dispersed, and with the Regular Army all was much as it had been before.

But the romantic glow was of twilight. These were the Army's last years as the constabulary for pacifying Indians which it had been since its birth in the days of Josiah Harmar and Anthony Wayne, the last years of physical isolation on the frontier and of a deeper isolation from the main currents of American life. A restlessness of coming change was already present. The Civil War gripped all memories, and the portents for future war in its huge citizen armies, its frustrating tactics, and its "power unrestrained" could provide much to think or talk about in long hours in garrison. Uncle Billy Sherman was commanding general for a time, himself restless and erratic and, in an undisciplined way, different from Halleck or McClellan yet something of a military intellectual. Sherman gave the necessary encouragement to set young Emory Upton on his career as the most influential student of military policy the Army has ever produced. He also helped to establish a system of postgraduate military schools, which in turn helped stimulate a new interchange of professional information and opinion in professional journals. The Franco-Prussian War stirred interest in the German military system. By the nineties, officers were discussing America as the coming world power and the place of the Army in such a future.

The Reconstruction statutes whereby Congress deprived the constitutional Commander in Chief of effective command over the army of occupation in the South might have been expected to have a lasting as well as revolutionary effect on the place of the Army in the American system of government. Even at the height of the Congressional assault upon Presidential prerogatives, however, the purpose of Congress was the immediately practical one of preventing Andrew Johnson from thwarting Congressional Reconstruction. Therefore Congress interfered little with Presidential powers as far as the Army on the Indian frontier was concerned. In effect there were two armies during the Reconstruction era: the Congressional army in the South, and the army that conducted the usual peacetime duties under the usual executive command. When changing political attitudes caused the withering and in 1877 the abandonment of Congressional Reconstruction, with the withdrawal of occupation troops from the South, the Congressional army melted again into the conventional Army, and the service emerged from Reconstruction with its constitutional relationship to President and Congress surprisingly little disturbed.

The Regular Army authorization in 1865 was the prewar Army plus the regiments authorized in 1861, a total of nineteen regiments of infantry, six of cavalry, and five of artillery. The disbanding of the volunteers would have reduced the Army to this force had not the act of July 28, 1866, intervened, to provide a more adequate force for Reconstruction and the patrol of the Mexican border as well as the usual frontier duties. Under that law, the three-battalion regiments reverted to the older single-battalion ten-company type, an economy measure which provided more regiments at relatively lower cost in manpower. There would be forty-five such infantry regiments, plus ten twelve-company cavalry regiments and the prewar five of artillery, each of the latter with two mounted batteries. Lieutenants were to be chosen from among the wartime volunteers. Higher grades were to be filled in equal numbers from among volunteers and Regulars, all officers to have had at least two years' service with good conduct during the war. Officers reverted to their permanent ranks, and some wartime generals found themselves once again captains.[1]

When the southern states were authorized to restore their militias and Congress hoped that local troops might assume much of the Army's burden in the South, the 1869 reductions cut the number of infantry regiments to twenty-five. Some 750 officers had to be given a year's pay and released. The regimental tables of organization were reduced in turn in 1876, to limit the total authorized force to 27,442 officers and men. This authorization remained virtually stationary until the Spanish-American War, and during the intervening years the actual strength of the Army generally hovered below 25,000. One result of the Civil War was the inclusion of Negro regiments, mostly officered by whites: the 38th, 39th, 40th, and 41st Infantry and 9th and 10th Cavalry in the 1866 reorganization, the 24th and 25th Infantry and 9th and 10th Cavalry after 1869. Congress also provided for 1,000 Indian scouts.[2]

In 1869 the Army was scattered among 255 military posts. As in the prewar Army, regiments rarely assembled. Administration continued to be carried on through territorial departments. By 1879 there were eight departments and eleven districts, under the headquarters of three major territorial divisions, those of the Atlantic, the Pacific, and the Missouri. The headquarters of the Division of the Missouri gave a modicum of coordination to the Indian campaigns. Here in the years immediately following the war Sherman was permitted to ensconce himself, remote from attempts to elevate the southern black man which he believed foolish and futile. Sure of the racial inferiority of both Indians and Negroes, Sherman much preferred to elevate neither but rather to spend his time pushing one of them aside in the name of white civilization. When Grant's assumption of the Presidency obliged Sherman to accede unhappily to the office of commanding general, Phil Sheridan, equally fond of Indian fighting, replaced him at division headquarters in St. Louis. Sherman himself continued wandering restlessly among the outposts on the Indian frontier whenever he got the chance.[3]

Here indeed the Army seemed never to have left the simpler past. Its adversaries now as before the war were the mounted tribes of the High Plains. To combat them again put a premium upon mounted troops and a discount upon slow-moving artillery, and even upon infantry; they remained an elusive enemy, and their territories were vast. Nine hundred forty-three engagements against the Indians were counted by the Army from 1865 to 1898. Only a few, such as the Gibbon-Terry-Custer-Crook expedition against the Sioux and Cheyenne in 1876 and the long campaign against Chief Joseph of the Nez Percé in 1877, called together masses of three or four thousand men. The Indians usually fought a guerrilla-style hit-and-run war in which heavy columns were too cumbersome to track them down anyway. The Army's dilemma was to balance adequate strength with adequate mobility. To do that, it broke up into several columns concentrations such as those of 1876 and 1877, but this method posed the danger of defeat in detail, as the battle of the Little Big Horn so horribly demonstrated.

In truth, the Civil War had made at least one important difference in the Army's handling of the Indian wars; it had accustomed leaders and soldiers to conventional war fought according to white men's rules, and readjustment to guerrilla-style war was not easy. The Army had to grapple again with the perennial problems of a force whose reliance has been upon weight of numbers and armament, confronted with an enemy whose specialties are mobility and deception. To offset its handicaps in this situation it needed a first-rate intelligence and reconnaissance service; once again, the only way to get anything at all adequate was to employ Indians against Indians. Scouts from the Pawnee and Crow and other tribes traditionally antagonistic to the principal Great Plains tribes, or from dissident Apache groups, became essential to every important movement. Often they fought bravely unto death at the white man's side.

Even when intelligence was otherwise adequate, distributing information was a frustrating process. The telegraph could not crisscross Indian country, and the enemy kept a careful watch against couriers. So converging columns therefore failed to converge because they could not stay in touch with each other, and other columns blundered into losing battles they could have avoided if they had known all that their comrades knew.

Often moving half blind, the Army needed all the firepower superiority it could get. Sometimes it had no such superiority at all. In 1866 the Ordnance Department began converting muzzle-loading to breech-loading rifles in quantity, and when reliable center-fire metallic cartridges became available after 1867, the United States Army became the first in the world to adopt this invaluable adjunct to the breechloader. The new standard infantry weapon was to be the .45-caliber model 1873 single-shot breech-loading Springfield rifle; the standard cavalry weapon was to be the same rifle cut down to carbine size. When private arms manufacturers utilized the copper cartridge to develop magazine rifles and some of these weapons fell into the hands of the Indians as trade goods, some officers and a few soldiers armed themselves similarly at their own expense. For even the best single-shot breechloader could not give the Army that assured margin of firepower superiority it desired to offset its handicaps in gathering intelligence, in communications, and in mobility. The Indian wars cried for magazine weapons. Sometimes detachments got them; in the Wagon-Box Fight of 1867 Captain James Powell with a force of some thirty-two men stood off hundreds of Indians by virtue of having Springfield-Allen magazine rifles. But not until 1892 did the Army find a magazine rifle it considered sufficiently troublefree to make it standard issue. The Indians had no answer to artillery, and occasionally field artillery was decisive. But artillery complicated the mobility problem.

Considering the Army's tactical problems and the vastness of the areas it had to patrol with a bare minimum of troops, its defeats were remarkably few. A better disciplined and better led adversary using the Indians' general style of war could have given it a very rough time. But while the Indians were cunning and crafty, their leaders usually gave little sustained thought to tactics and none to strategy. Chief Joseph of the Nez Percé was one exception, and the contrast made him seem almost a military genius simply because he planned ahead. Other Indians did not do so, and such leaders as the tribes did produce maintained only a tenuous control over their followers. Simple discipline and thoughtful leadership therefore proved to be the Army's overwhelming assets.

The Army enjoyed one other prime advantage over the Indians: it could fight in winter. During the cold months the Indians huddled in their camps against impossible exposure. If they tried to move, snow and short rations would deny them their customary swiftness, and in the bare countryside they might even starve. But the Army could take the field at any time. The building of the transcontinental railroads immensely eased the task of the Quartermaster's Department. Unlike the Missouri River and its tributaries, the rail lines did not freeze over. They brought warm winter clothing to the men and, with the wagon trains, a continuous flow of supplies the year round. Thus supported, the Army again and again won its most decisive victories in the winter. Then George Custer won the battle of the Washita; then George Crook and Nelson Miles crushed Sitting Bull and Crazy Horse; then Chief Joseph vowed to Howard and Miles to fight no more forever.[4]

Romantic though Indian fighting had come to seem, and much as a bellicose officer of the Phil Sheridan stamp might enjoy it, holding the Indian frontier was as harsh and brutish a task as ever. The amenities of frontier posts were few. Since 1863 each company was authorized to detail one or two men as cooks, and after 1894 the cook was given a sergeant's pay; so in garrison the soldier no longer had to enhance the edibility of the ration himself. It was not until 1895, however, that a Presidential order established the post exchange, a cooperative store to sell goods not issued to the troops by the government; meanwhile sutlers or post traders preyed upon men desiring more than the minimum sustenance the Army offered them. Detail to the Indian frontier still meant mostly garrison duty served out in flimsy shanties through the dusty summers and bitter winters of the Plains. When occasional campaigning broke otherwise endless monotony, it was against formidable warriors, the bravest and best in the whole long history of American Indian wars. So limited were the attractions of this kind of life that, in the approaching flood tide of immigration, names of many nationalities had to fill out the muster rolls, along with the Irish and Germans who had been a staple since the first flood tide in the 1840's. Enlistment was for five years until 1894, when it was reduced to three; pay was $13 a month, although it had been $16 at the close of the war. With these conditions, desertion again became the plague it had been before the war. In 1871 some 8,800 men, one-third of the Army, deserted. The number fell during the depression years of the seventies, to rise again to 3,721 in 1882.[5]

Major General John Pope, (USMA 1842), was an intelligent and perceptive officer notwithstanding his unfortunate encounter with Lee and Stonewall Jackson at Second Bull Run. He was a successful leader of Indian campaigns and a successful administrator, and in the postwar Regular Army he early began to worry about the consequences of the Army's return to isolation, so strongly contrasting with the close bond between Army and nation that had prevailed during the war. "The well-being of the people equally with the well-being of the Army," he believed, "requires a common sympathy and a common interest between them."

Shall we especially of the Regular Army [he asked] be willing to contemplate without sorrow the certainty that . . . the strong affection which unites us to so many comrades who have returned to civil life will also perish, and that the unhappy and well-nigh fatal divorce which for years had separated the Regular Army from the people and which required a great civil war to reconcile, shall again be pronounced upon our descendants?[6]

In civilian America, remoteness from the Indian-fighting Army did indeed nourish again doubts about the very need for the Regular Army. In 1887 John A. Logan, founder of the Grand Army of the Republic as a veterans' organization and former citizen-soldier major general of the XV Army Corps, published posthumously his *Volunteer Soldier of America*, a 700-page diatribe against the un-democratic exclusiveness of the Regular Army and its West Point-ers, calling for military reliance on a citizen army and the native military genius of American citizens in the tradition of Andrew Jackson. The Regular Army could be called again a traditional enemy of the Republic.[7]

But Jacksonians like Logan were somewhat anachronistic in the post-Civil War industrial and urban world. The Jacksonians might deprecate the Regular Army, but they tended nevertheless to roman-ticize war. More profound doubts about the need for an Army came from an increasing number of influential Americans who affirmed the obsolescence of war itself. To industrialists and financiers of the increasingly international late nineteenth-century business world, war might well seem an archaic irrationality that would interrupt industrial progress and profits. The intellectuals who supplied the business world with its rationale, men such as Herbert Spencer, Wil-liam Graham Sumner, and John Fiske, thus claimed to regard war as part of an era in evolution now passing; while applauding a Dar-winian competition in the economic world, which would lead to the survival of the fittest and the betterment of civilization, they deplored as outmoded an armed version of the struggle for existence. Andrew Carnegie appropriately devoted much of his philanthropy to the search for world peace. Other businessmen were less pacifist than Carnegie, but the business community in general held back when other Americans entered the jingoistic mood of the 1890's that was to lead to the war with Spain.[8]

And until that mood set in at the end of the century, Jacksonians, the business community, and all Americans relieved upon emerging from a long war could join in indifference or hostility to the Regular Army. The Custer Massacre might create a flurry of concern for the soldier's safety and well being, but the flurry quickly subsided. Congressional military appropriations declined through the early 1870's, and in 1877 there was no appropriation whatever for the support of the Army until November 30; for the better part of a year soldiers had to depend on loans from frequently usurious bankers (though the enlisted men did receive rations). The final spasms of Reconstruction had much to do with this nadir of the Army's career, since the financial straits of the Army helped assure southern con-gressmen of the final evacuation of their states. But Congress's ne-glect could hardly have occurred in any climate but the existing one of unconcern.[9]

General Pope meanwhile feared the effects of the Army's isolation upon the attitudes of the soldier himself:

So long as the soldier remains one of the people; so long as he shares their interests, takes part in their progress, and feels a common sympathy with them in their hopes and aspirations, so long will the Army be held in honorable esteem and regard. . . . When he ceases to do this; when officers and soldiers cease to be citizens in the highest and truest sense, the Army will deserve to lose, as it will surely lose, its place in the affections of the people, and properly and naturally become an object of suspicion and dislike.[10]

For officers as well as enlisted men, the isolation and monotony of the frontier Army posed perils of stultification and worse.

In 1871 Dennis Hart Mahan died in tragic circumstances. The Academic Board of the Military Academy decided he must retire on account of age, and after hearing the decision, he stepped—intentionally or accidentally—from a boat into the Hudson River. With him, the sequel proved, went much of the vitality of the Military Academy. It is true that there were improvements in the postwar years: in 1866 the Academy was removed from the control of the Corps of Engineers, and officers of all branches became eligible for the superintendency directly under the War Department. The technical engineering part of the curriculum was somewhat constricted, and the genuinely military was expanded to include about one-third of the curriculum by the turn of the century. But with these changes the Academy lost its eminence among American engineering schools without commensurate gain in the quality of its military instruction. Such instruction continued to be narrowly technical in its own way: it stressed weapons and tactics, not a historical approach to war, military policy, and strategy. Sylvanus Thayer's instructional system of small classes permitting daily recitation by each cadet could become a constricting fetish, when to staff the small classes instructors of dubious capacity as teachers had to be detailed from the service. The curriculum remained heavily mathematical, with little of the liberal arts to encourage a less technicist approach to war. The West Point of the 1870's and 1880's trained reasonably competent junior officers, but it hardly began to educate men for higher military responsibility. It had no Dennis Mahan to make it a center of constructive military thought, and out of it came no stimulants to the professional growth of the American officer corps comparable to Mahan's and Halleck's books of the prewar era.[11]

Surprisingly nevertheless, though West Point languished and the quality of life in frontier garrisons was discouraging, the professional progress of the Army's officer corps did not halt. It may be that again the Army's very necessity to turn inward upon itself gave some stimulus to the officers to seek their own professional improvement—for what other purpose could sustain them? Also, the officers remained sufficiently in touch, if not with the civilian world then with the wider military world, to know of the spectacular Prussian victories in the wars of 1864, 1866, and 1870–71 and of the military innovations that contributed to them. Breech-loading artillery as well as breech-loading infantry rifles received their first large-scale test, and much more importantly the Prussians introduced the huge cadre-conscript army thoroughly organized for war before war began, the prearranged employment of railroad nets for the rapid mobilization and initial deployment of the army, and their own kind of thoroughly educated general staff to assume the formidable task of directing and controlling a massive military machine. To fill in the intellectual background of these developments, Clausewitz was translated into English in 1873, and a general awareness at least of his main ideas spread among American officers soon thereafter.

Fortunately, from 1869 to 1883 the Army possessed in William Tecumseh Sherman one of the most cerebral and innovative of all its commanding generals. It was significant that he had been a college president on the eve of the Civil War. His memoirs of the war were almost unique among such literary efforts in their thoughtfulness about the future of war. If the traditional vagueness of the authority of his office helped frustrate any reforms he might have accomplished in the Military Academy, he found other ways to encourage the professional advancement of the officer corps. Most especially, he fathered a system of postgraduate schools beyond the Military Academy, conceiving of a pyramid of institutions through which the officer could learn the special skills of his own branch of service and then the attitudes and principles of higher command.[12]

The first beginning toward such a system had been Calhoun's Artillery School at Fortress Monroe. After expiring in 1860 on the eve of war, this school was revived in 1868, and Sherman's accession to the high command immediately afterward permitted him to sustain it during a period of tenuous existence. When West Point was separated from the Corps of Engineers in 1866, a group of engineer officers had founded the Essayons Club at Willett's Point, New York, to perpetuate the study of engineering in the Army, and Sherman helped nourish this institution into the Engineering School of Application, comparable to the Artillery School. In 1881 he founded a School of Application for Infantry and Cavalry at Fort Leavenworth, Kansas. To it one lieutenant from each infantry and cavalry regiment was to be assigned every two years, for the gradual dissemination of its precepts throughout the Army.

At the beginning the Fort Leavenworth school was a fairly elementary center of instruction in infantry and cavalry tactics. But from the beginning, Sherman had higher plans for it. He hoped that his schools would "qualify officers for any duty they may be called upon to perform, or for any position however high in rank that they may aspire to in service." The final field of study at Fort Leavenworth was to be "the science and practice of war." During its first two decades of existence, the Leavenworth school gradually evolved toward the fulfillment of Sherman's aims. The credit for its doing so must go in no small part to Arthur L. Wagner, (USMA 1875), who served as instructor there from 1888 to 1904. Wagner was an admirer of the "excellence of the military system of Prussia," and he regarded the Prussian school system culminating in the *Kriegsakademie* as a model for American military schools to emulate. He eventually helped transform the Leavenworth school into the General Service and Staff College, and he was to be a founder of the Army War College. Meanwhile he published several notable studies of his own: *The Campaign of Königgrätz* (1889), and two studies, *The Service of Security and Information* (1893) and *Organization and Tactics* (1895), which led at least one officer to call him "the first of our military men to write anything readable on tactics."[13]

Sherman gave his blessings and encouragement also to professional institutions that could supplement the school system, a professional association and professional military journals. Major General Winfield Scott Hancock initiated the former when, commanding the Department of the East in 1878, he founded the Military Service Institution of the United States, approved by the War Department and with headquarters on Governor's Island. It was patterned on the Royal United Service Institution of Great Britain, its membership was open to Regular and National Guard officers and interested civilians, while its purpose was to promote writing and discussion about military science and military history. It inaugurated a bimonthly *Journal*. In 1879 the similar *United Service* journal also began publication. Previously there had been only ephemeral, commercially sponsored military journals. Now those of general military interest were soon supplemented by the *Cavalry Journal* in 1888 and the *Journal of the United States Artillery* in 1892.[14]

The journals and the schools cross-fertilized each other, with the journals affording an outlet for ideas and studies nurtured at the schools. Arthur L. Wagner wrote for them, and so did the remarkable John Bigelow (USMA 1877). The scion of a New England literary family and a company officer in the 10th Cavalry, Bigelow published a textbook, *Principles of Strategy*, into which he incorporated precepts drawn from Sherman's warfare against civil populations. His shorter monographs, *Chancellorsville* and *Mars-la-Tour and Gravelotte*, remain today among the outstanding studies of those campaigns.[15]

By far the most important of Sherman's intellectual protégés was Emory Upton. Upton was a much wounded and much honored veteran of the Civil War, who had graduated from the Military Academy in June, 1861, participated in First Bull Run a month later, and emerged from the war a brevet major general. In the process he had displayed gallantry and dash worthy of a George Custer, but he had also shown an uncommon concern for the welfare of his men, a keen intelligence, and a flair for tactical innovation. His method of assaulting the Mule Shoe salient at Spotsylvania, employing four lines of three regiments each to advance in quick succession, fan out, and support each other inside the enemy's lines according to a meticulous plan, offered about as good a prospect as was possible of breaking the infantry deadlock to carry a fixed position. The multiple lines amounted to heavy columns falling upon the enemy, their rear ranks protected by the front ones as they advanced, and the whole carrying enough weight that it might overawe the enemy and thus crack both his nerve and his line. If Upton had received proper support at Spotsylvania, his plan might have produced an important success albeit with no escape from a heavy cost in blood.

After the war Upton set out on a systematic search for means to escape tactical impasse, and he worked out a new system of infantry tactics which the Army adopted in 1867. His tactics took into account both the destructive power of the rifle and the ease of firing of the breechloader, which he recognized must come into universal use. He abandoned the traditional two- or three-line battle formation, since with breechloaders, infantry standing in a single line could reload often enough to maintain a sufficient rate of fire. He based his tactics upon groups of four men, which by means of much simplified commands could be ordered forward, left, or right to form a line facing in any direction. In the attack, he would have skirmishers move forward to within 150 yards of the enemy's position to protect the remainder of the attacking battalion as it advanced in column. The skirmish line could be built up gradually by feeding "fours" into it. When the skirmishers had formed their shield, at 200 yards from the enemy the main attacking column would deploy quickly into line and charge. If it was repulsed, supporting troops would move up to strengthen it, and more would be fitted into it until the opposing position could be carried. The emphasis on skirmishers followed Civil War experience. The advance in column as long as possible minimized exposure to the enemy's fire, while the final attack in line brought maximum fire upon the enemy. Upton recognized that the line must be much less dense than the traditional one, and with this consideration and the need for active skirmishing, he stressed the need to instill intelligent initiative into the troops, to compensate for the loss of ready communication between the commanding officer and his men. The essentials of Upton's tactics, especially the use of fours, served into the twentieth-century world wars. If the system did not resolve the tactical impasse after all, it was because only a new order of weaponry could do that.[16]

An innovative intelligence like Upton's naturally attracted General Sherman. Upton soon became commandant of cadets and instructor in tactics at the Military Academy, and Sherman began to discuss with him the idea of visiting the armies of Asia to seek out military lessons for the United States. The commanding general, most interested now in the Indian campaigns, believed the Army might learn something from the similar campaigns of British India and from the army that fought them. Upton already had been involved in an abortive scheme to provide American military instruction for China and had retained an interest in that country. So Sherman named Upton to a three-man commission to visit the armies of Asia, and before departure it was decided that the commission might as well come home through Europe and report on the European armies too.

This afterthought was fateful, for Upton's observation of the German army of 1876, fresh from its triumphs over Austria and France, led to an infatuation with it and to a decision to advocate the adoption of a similar military system by the United States. Upton was temperamentally receptive to the German system: he was intense, humorless, singlemindedly devoted to the military profession and to efficiency in it, a sober, even brooding, man sustained by an old-fashioned Protestant piety—in short, a man not unlike several of the German military reformers themselves. The Asian armies fell into the background as from Berlin he wrote of new plans for his report:

I shall devote most of my attention to the subject of officers, and to showing our reckless extravagance in making war. When Germany fought France she put her army on a war-footing in eight days, and in eight days more she had four hundred thousand men on French territory. It took us from April, 1861, to March, 1862, to form an army of the same size at an expense of nearly eight hundred millions of dollars. We can not maintain a great army in peace, but we can provide a scheme for officering a large force in time of war, and such a scheme is deserving of study.[17]

So Upton turned from tactics to the much larger question of a military policy for the United States. He sought a means to mobilize quickly the mass armies that the Civil War and the Franco-Prussian War had required. But in taking the German army's mobilization in

1870 as a model for the United States, he began by concentrating on means without much consideration whether the means were relevant to any reasonable American ends. Was there any conceivable situation in which the United States would require a mobilization system approximating the German one?

Heedless of that question, Upton's report on *The Armies of Asia and Europe* included recommendations that the United States adopt a modified form of the German cadre army. The traditional American citizen soldiery should be made thoroughly subsidiary to the Regular Army. The Regular Army should become the axis of all military policy. The Regular Army should be reorganized into skeleton formations, and in war those formations should be filled with the citizen volunteers. Thus the war Army should consist entirely of Regular formations, and all volunteers should serve under Regular officers. In peace the Regular officers should prepare for war through a military school system on the German model. This plan for an expansible Regular Army borrowed something from John C. Calhoun's old plan of the war Army with "nothing either to new model or to create," and Upton pointed to Calhoun as a preceptor. But mainly Upton was pleading for abandonment of the traditional dual military institutions of the United States, to replace them with a thoroughgoing emphasis on professionalism in the manner of Germany.

In *The Armies of Asia and Europe* Upton's reform proposals had to be squeezed into a book mainly devoted to his assigned descriptive report on foreign armies. But with characteristic zeal, Upton now decided he must become the prophet of the new military order, and he set out to prepare a full length exposition of his views, his book *The Military Policy of the United States.*

Upton did not live to finish the book, for he suffered increasing torment from what was evidently a brain tumor. Headaches more and more deprived him of sleep and made any concentration on his writing an effort of immense difficulty. Periodic seizures also erased his awareness and reason. At length he decided that the attacks had become so frequent that he ought no longer to exercise command, so on March 15, 1884, he wrote his resignation. Thus cut off from his profession, he shot himself.[18]

The unfinished manuscript was not published until 1904, but it was put in order by Colonel Henry A. DuPont, a friend and helper; it circulated among officers of the Army; and it attained a remarkable influence long before it appeared in print. Another friend, Professor Peter Smith Michie of the Military Academy, published in 1885 a biography of Upton which gave knowledge of the manuscript and its main arguments to the world at large. In order to advance his tenets, Upton had composed a history of American military policy, which he had carried as far as 1862. He wrote clearly and persuasively; no comparable American military history existed or was to exist for decades, and as history his book contained a wealth of useful information. Thus for many years to come anyone interested in American military history consulted Upton's book as the standard work in the field. The arguments which colored the history therefore persuaded many who would not otherwise have been receptive, because they studied the American military past from no other angle of vision. To the professional officers who read Upton, however, few special circumstances were necessary to make his reform proposals persuasive, since they offered the military efficiency that every good officer desired, through a system modeled on the proven German system. Awkward questions about the relevance of Upton's prescriptions to the American situation could readily be ignored, because by the late years of the nineteenth century the officer corps had fallen into the very alienation from the country at large against which General Pope had warned.[19]

Upton argued that the military past of the United States was a record of repeated failure and immense waste of treasure and lives at the outset of almost every war, redeemed only by the country's immense wealth, the native bravery of its soldiers, and the weakness or folly of its adversaries. The Regular Army, he said, had always fought well from the start, but except perhaps in the Mexican War it had never been large enough in a crisis, not even for many of the Indian wars. The nation had attempted to compensate for the numerical weakness of the Regulars through a variety of expedients employing citizen soldiers, all of them wasteful. The traditional militia system ought to be discarded altogether, for "No matter how absolute the necessity for calling out undisciplined troops, history teaches that useless extravagance, often accompanied by inaction or disaster, will surely ensue." In discussing the militia, Upton made no distinction between the mass of enrolled manpower and the organized militia; he simply damned "the militia system." Not only were militiamen invariably untrained and undisciplined, according to him, but their traditional short term of service compounded their uselessness, and so did the dual system of federal and state control. Citizen volunteers could become good soldiers in time, but their training always took too long, and historically they also had been subjected to the vagaries of dual federal-state control.[20]

Much of Upton's indictment of the American military past was accurate, although he consistently minimized any shortcomings of Regulars and their officers or any evidence of possible military usefulness in the militia and related citizen-soldiery systems. Thus he reiterated his plea that all military preparations in the United States be consigned to the Regular Army, by making the Regular Army the sole cadre around which a wartime Army would form. On the German model, every Regular Army battalion should henceforth be assigned a territorial district, whence it would be recruited and where it would always maintain a depot. In peacetime, the battalion depots would conduct military training among young men of their districts. (By what means would the trainees be recruited? The answer consistent with Upton's argument was conscription, but Upton dared approach that topic only obliquely, by arguing that history proved the necessity for conscription in wartime.) When war broke out, the citizens of a district would report to the battalion with which they had already trained, the battalions would thus swell to war strength, and the Army would go to war in established formations in which every man knew his officers and assignment, and with Regular officers commanding the whole. Sustained during wartime by the "truly democratic doctrine" of conscription, this program would avoid the wastes and dangers of earlier wars and bring the people and the Army into the kind of healthy relationship that prevailed in Germany.[21]

Upton went further. He argued that all the defects of the American military system rested upon a fundamental, underlying flaw, excessive civilian control of the military. American military policy was formed first by Congress, usually "a body of citizens who, in their individual experience, were totally ignorant of military affairs."[22] Congress having established military policy, control of the Army was assigned to another generally inexperienced citizen, the President as Commander in Chief. Upton dwelt in especial detail upon Lincoln's performance in that office during the Civil War, and he concluded that the excessive duration and wastefulness of the war were caused by a "bad system," that "defect in our laws which . . . tempted the President to assume the character and responsibilities of a military commander." In contrast:

In foreign armies it is the duty of the General Staff to draw up the bills relating to military organization, which, after approval by the War Minister, are presented to the representatives of the people. The latter may refuse to incur the expenses of reforms, but do not question the wisdom of the details.[23]

And just as foreign countries did not permit their legislatures to meddle in the shaping of military policy in the manner of the American Congress, so they left command to the professionals, not a civil Commander in Chief:

In every country save our own, the inability of unprofessional men to command armies would be accepted as a self-evident proposition.

The disasters [of the Civil War] . . . must therefore be credited to the defective laws which allowed the President to dispense with an actual General in Chief and substitute in his stead a civil officer supported by military advisers, disqualified by their tenure of office and occupations from giving free and enlightened opinions.[24]

To improve the American command system, Upton recommended again the establishment of military schools comparable to those of Germany, and he proposed also a general staff corps on the German model, to serve, in the phrase with which he anticipated Spenser Wilkinson, as "the brain of the army."[25] But such improvements could not get to the root of the problem, and here was the rub. Upton's book ended a deeply pessimistic one, pessimistic in tone no doubt partly because of the background circumstances of Upton's temperament, the tragic death of his youthful wife which had shortly preceded the writing, and his own gathering illness, but pessimistic also because Upton could entertain little hope that his prescriptions would be accepted. Knowing that the nation was not about to adopt a large peacetime Regular Army, Upton professed to believe that a relatively small one of 1,000 men for each 1,000,000 of the population would form a sufficient cadre; but he must have recognized, as General Hancock pointed out, that the cadre would be too small and wartime volunteers or conscripts would swamp it.[26] The country would not accept a Regular Army large enough in fact to dominate a war Army as Upton said it should, and the country certainly would not abandon the principle of civil control of the military. Upton replied to the assertion that a plan such as his would endanger free institutions by arguing that there was no alternative:

The student of modern history cannot fail to discover that the principles of organization, like those of strategy, are of universal application, and that no nation has ever violated them, except at its peril.[27]

So he went on insisting that the national institutions must adjust to military expediency, while to his despair the nation went on retaining its inherited institutions.

Upton's pessimism does not appear to have diminished the appeal of his arguments as they circulated among the officer corps; perhaps rather his pessimism fitted the mood of an Army neglected by the nation in thought and in financial support. Long before the publication of *The Military Policy of the United States*, the new military journals published frequent articles by young officers suggesting military programs of an Uptonian kind, and after the book was in print the articles became more frequent still. And the pessimism became more explicit, culminating in such flat statements as:

It is a self-evident proposition that a democracy based on the will of millions of people, expressed through devious and changing channels, cannot be as skillful or efficient in the conduct of military affairs as a monarchy headed by a wise and powerful chief.[28]

National characteristics, which become governmental ones in a democracy like ours, make it impossible to organize and discipline an effective army from the point of view of military experts.[29]

No doubt the importance of such statements by junior officers can readily be exaggerated, since their mood ran counter to the national optimism and was easily swallowed up in the exuberance of the Spanish-American War. But Emory Upton did lasting harm in setting the main current of American military thought not to the task of shaping military institutions that would serve both military and national purposes, but to the futile task of demanding that the national institutions be adjusted to purely military expediency.

By proposing a military policy that the country could not accept, Emory Upton helped ensure that the country would continue to limp along with virtually no military policy at all. Through most of the late nineteenth century no likelihood of foreign war existed, and the lack of any preparation for war was if not altogether wise at least more appropriate to the situation than many of Upton's proposals. Even as the decade of the 1890's unveiled a new national interest in possible foreign adventures, however, and the Navy entered upon an era of expansion, the Army continued to languish in neglect.

Apart from the intellectual renaissance that Sherman encouraged, such stirrings of military activity as did appear in the late years of the century did not always bear much relevance to what proved to be the requirements of the Spanish-American War. The industrial growth of the post-Civil War years and its consequent social maladjustment involved the Army in the unpleasant task of policing strikes, which was not the least reason for the unpopularity of the service in certain civilian quarters. The outstanding instances of strike duty occurred in the great railroad strikes of 1877, during which President Rutherford B. Hayes used the Army reluctantly and with restraint and with the primary motive of restoring order, and of 1894, when President Grover Cleveland was persuaded to employ Regulars from Fort Sheridan in a role that amounted to strike breaking. Beyond these spectacular appearances, the Army was called upon in more than three hundred labor disputes during the period. Whatever the pur-

poses of its employment, the usual effect was such as to prompt
Samuel Gompers' remark: "Standing armies are always used to exercise tyranny over people, and are one of the prime causes of a rupture in a country."[30]

The organized militia formations marched to strike duty still more
frequently than the Regulars, since they were the natural first resort.
It has sometimes been argued that their utility in protecting order
and property and possibly discouraging labor organization prompted
a new effort to breathe life into the state militias. It is true that
because of their social nature, the volunteer companies sometimes
consisted of men especially unsympathetic to strikers, and a few
journalists did suggest that they should be made increasingly elite
organizations of propertied gentlemen, the more thoroughly to assure their reliability in defense of the social order.

But the evidence for an organized militia revival growing out of
strike duty is scant. Policing fellow citizens would not have been
likely to be especially popular with most members of organized militia companies regardless of their own social status, and the members
were only rarely and in certain companies gentlemen of very large
property. Before the excitement of the Spanish War, the organized
militia of the 1890's was much smaller in proportion to population
than it had been before the Civil War; in 1893 it aggregated 112,507
in all the states and territories. The main effect of industrialism
seems to have been to reduce inclination and time for amateur soldiering, and thus to weaken the militia institutions inherited from the
rural past. Such small progress as the organized militia enjoyed was
associated mainly with its creation of an instrument to represent its
interests before federal and state governments and the public, the
National Guard Association. A national meeting of officers of organized militia formed the association at Richmond in 1877; the name
chosen reflected the fact that most states by now had followed New
York in borrowing the term "National Guard" from the French to
designate their organized volunteer companies. The association undertook lobbying activities in the various capitals, but the most conspicuous success to which it could point was a small one: in 1887
Congress increased the allotment of $200,000 annually to the mili-
tia, which had been constant since 1808, to $400,000. The effect of
the increase was diluted by adding other equipment besides ordnance
to the federal contributions to the states under the allotment.[31]

Another military development of only limited usefulness for any
possible mobilization was the first growth of military training in the
civilian colleges and universities. This growth was prompted initially
by the famous Morrill Land Grant Act of 1862, which included
military tactics among the subjects to be taught in the land-grant

colleges. The act of July 28, 1866, which reorganized the Army for peace also empowered the President to detail twenty officers to schools having more than 150 male students, there to teach military science; curiously, the details were not restricted to the land-grant schools. In 1870 Congress authorized issuing surplus small arms and ammunition to the colleges for military training, and the number of officer-instructors was gradually increased, from thirty in 1876 to a hundred in 1893. In practice, it was mainly the land-grant schools that instituted military programs. The quality of the offerings depended mostly on the instructors and must have varied greatly. Some of the training was probably very good: at the University of Nebraska First Lieutenant John J. Pershing was an enthusiastic instructor from 1891 to 1895. But nothing ensured utilization of the graduates of the courses, since the Army did not even keep a record of who received the training. Perhaps the program helped provide officers for the Spanish War, but it is impossible to be sure.[32]

Occasionally the War Department and the military committees of Congress showed a spark of interest in the possibility of foreign war, perhaps impelled by a natural desire to justify their own existence. Partly because of the sensation attending the Custer Massacre and the Chief Joseph campaign, partly under the influence of the railroad strike of 1877, and partly with the simple hope of finding ways to save money, Congress in 1878 established a joint committee under the chairmanship of Ambrose Burnside to consider the reorganization of the Regular Army. The committee recommended reductions and consolidations, but it also took some interest in proposals for a better citizen reserve and encouraged the principal leaders of the Army to set forth their views on the question. Except from Hancock, the committee received Uptonian opinions, notably from Upton himself and from Sherman, about which it naturally did nothing.[33]

The Army did share slightly in the interest in sea power which attended the more adventurous foreign policy of the closing years of the century and which contributed to the rise of the Navy. For one thing, the effort to build a modern steel navy quickly collided with the fact that American industry could not produce either armor plate or armor-piercing guns comparable to those appearing in Europe after the Franco-Prussian War. Therefore in 1883 the Naval Appropriations Act set up a joint Army-Navy Gun-Foundry Board to consider the problem. The board toured the armaments factories of Europe and eventually recommended that the government offer generous contracts to stimulate American industry to develop appropriate steels and forgings, and that the government itself undertake to assemble these materials into modern guns at the Naval Gun Factory and the Army's arsenals. One consideration here was to avoid both Germany's complete dependence on private arms makers, the Krupps, and France's almost equal dependence on a hidebound military armaments board. The recommendations were followed.[34]

Meanwhile, national interest in the Navy also called attention to the condition of coastal defenses, which seemed in need of improvement if the new Navy was not to be immobilized in defense of the principal harbors. Little had been done to strengthen the coastal fortifications since the Civil War, and the vertical masonry forts erected between the War of 1812 and that conflict had proven obsolete against the rifled cannon of the 1860's. To be worth anything the coastal fortifications would have to be dug into the earth, and they would have to be armed with the new breech-loading heavy ordnance that was being developed under the recommendations of the Gun-Foundry Board. The ordnance in turn should be shielded by the new armor plate. In 1885 Congress voted another board, under the chairmanship of Secretary of War William C. Endicott, to plan the restoration of the coast defenses. The board produced somewhat extravagant proposals for the fortification of the twenty-seven (later twenty-eight) principal harbors of the country, plus the Canadian border, with earthworks and steel-plated masonry sheltering 677 high-powered guns and 824 mortars, the whole to be supplemented by mine-laying in the harbors. The estimated cost would be some $127 million, and the extravagance lay not simply in that large sum but to a greater extent in the Endicott Board's inability to point to a foe likely to challenge the coasts to the point of requiring such extensive protection. Not only the world diplomatic situation but the naval technology of the day rendered such a challenge doubtful.[35]

But the Endicott Board did not go altogether unheeded, for in 1888 Congress voted an initial appropriation to begin carrying out the proposals and established within the Army a Board of Ordnance and Fortification headed by Major General John M. Schofield, the commanding general, to review detailed plans to be worked out by the Corps of Engineers. The work went slowly and was destined never to be completed, but during the 1890's the old forts of the Civil War era were abandoned around the major harbors for earthworks, armor-plated concrete pits, and ten- and twelve-inch "disappearing" rifled guns. Furthermore, merely working on the Endicott program offered the feeling that the country now possessed a kind of military policy looking toward foreign war, and this feeling was so reassuring that in the War Department reports and the military publications of the 1890's interest in the coastal defenses became almost obsessive.[36]

One of the principal reasons why the United States had no more complete military policy was that the Army had perhaps less of a directing brain than at any other time in its history. The old problem of the relationship between the Secretary of War and the commanding general effected a continued deterioration of the commanding general's office to the verge of nullity, and during the whole era witnessed no Secretary of War remotely approximating the strength of John C. Calhoun, or of Edwin M. Stanton before the quarrel with Johnson began to erode his strength.

For Ulysses Grant, Congress in 1866 created the new rank of full general, and Sherman and for a brief time Sheridan held it after him. But the office of commanding general that accompanied that rank remained a place of frustration.

The Regulations now said of the commanding general:

The command exercised by the commanding general of the Army, not having been made the subject of statutory regulation, is determined by the order of assignment. It has been habitually composed of the aggregate of the several territorial commands that have been or may be erected by the President.

The military establishment is under the orders of the commanding general of the Army in that which pertains to its discipline and military control. The fiscal affairs of the Army are conducted by the Secretary of War through the several staff departments.[37]

Thus the staff departments continued to be excluded from the "habitual" command of the commanding general, and in consequence his control of the territorial departments was also limited, since the distribution and diversion of these departments' support clearly could influence the operations of the troops. Furthermore, there remained the question of the Secretary of War's power to intervene in the territorial departments themselves, as Jefferson Davis especially had done.

The confidence and understanding that developed between Secretary Stanton and General Grant during the Civil War did not prevent disagreement over the commanding general's office after the war. The larger crisis of Reconstruction swallowed up their quarrel before much could come of it, and in that larger crisis Stanton and Grant cooperated, though not without suspicion of each other's motives. During Grant's interim tenure as Secretary of War while he remained commanding general, he studiously attempted to safeguard the domain of both offices by issuing orders in his capacity as Secretary of War and then crossing Seventeenth Street from the War Department to Army Headquarters to countersign them in his capacity as commanding general.[38]

Grant's sympathies lay mainly with the claims of the commanding general, however, and when he succeeded to the Presidency and his friend Sherman stepped up to the chief professional post, he assured Sherman that he would be commanding general in fact as well as in name, standing not only between the Secretary and the field forces but also between the Secretary and the War Department bureaus. He had John M. Schofield, then serving as another interim Secretary of War, issue an order to that effect. But to Sherman's disgust, Grant quickly reneged. The new Secretary of War was to be another old friend, Grant's wartime chief of staff and *alter ego* John A. Rawlins. Rawlins soon convinced Grant that the statutes required the Secretary's direct control over the bureaus, and he rescinded Schofield's order. Sherman in his *Memoirs* depicted himself as swallowing Grant's change of mind only with icy formality, one of the few recorded instances of coolness between the two.[39]

Rawlins softened his victory by conceding to Sherman in practice and sending all his orders through the commanding general's office. But Rawlins was already badly consumptive when he took office and soon died, and Grant's next Secretary, W. W. Belknap, proved intent on developing the powers of his office to the fullest. Sherman's lukewarm attitude toward the still continuing military Reconstruction of the South may have influenced Belknap and Grant's support of him. Belknap ignored Sherman in directing the War Department bureaus, and he began interfering in Sherman's control of the Army itself. As Sherman put it:

Orders granting leaves of absence to officers, transfers, discharges of soldiers for favor, and all the old abuses, which had embittered the life of General Scott in the days of Secretaries of War Marcy and Davis, were renewed.[40]

Indeed, the dreary old script of the Scott-Davis quarrel was played out again almost to the letter. Belknap took to tormenting Sherman seemingly with no purpose but to make life miserable for him, allying himself with Sherman's chief Congressional critic John A. Logan, who harbored a grievance because Sherman had denied him command of the Army of the Tennessee during the war and who was suspicious of all professional soldiers. When Belknap removed a sutler at Fort Laramie and appointed a man distasteful to the garrison, Sherman asserted himself to reinstate the original sutler. Thereupon Belknap's association with Logan produced a statute removing the appointment of sutlers from the commanding general's hands altogether, and Belknap restored his own man. Just as Scott before him had departed angrily from Washington to New York, so Sherman now decamped to St. Louis. He cited the high expense of living in Washington, and no doubt that was one of his considerations. But in effect he reduced himself to his old command of the Division of the Missouri—and not even that, since Sheridan now officially held the post. Sherman could do little more than make inspection trips, while Belknap commanded both the War Department and the Army. The commanding general finally left on an extended tour of Europe, as he might as well have done.

Sherman savored the fine taste of revenge when evidence became public that Belknap was selling sutlerships—the very focus of the controversy with Sherman—for private gain. The Secretary resigned hastily to evade impeachment, and in the crisis at the War Department Secretary Alphonso Taft urged Sherman to come back to Washington. Taft, an unassertive man, was so eager for Sherman's support that he offered to concede part of Sherman's views on the office of commanding general, and Sherman at length restored his headquarters to Washington. The orders announcing the change also declared that the departments of the adjutant general and the inspector general should report to the commanding general, and they explicitly reserved to him the military control and discipline of the Army under the President.[41]

By now it was 1876 and Reconstruction was dying anyway, so Sherman's position on that issue no longer mattered much. Taft was true to his word and pretty much resigned to Sherman any prerogatives that the general chose to assert, confining himself largely to matters of law and finance. Before Grant's second term was over he appointed still one more Secretary of War, but Donald Cameron was mainly in training for his father Simon Cameron's Senate seat and the political boss-ship of Pennsylvania, and he bothered Sherman no more than had Taft. Rutherford B. Hayes's Secretary of War, George Washington McCrary, an Iowa lawyer and judge, was more conscientious than Cameron but little more inclined to challenge Sherman. Garfield's appointee Robert Lincoln was a man of stature even apart from his distinguished parentage, but he was not much interested in the War Department. It was during this interval when his title of commanding general was meaningful that Sherman established the School of Application for Infantry and Cavalry at Fort Leavenworth and generally made his contributions to the Army's intellectual renaissance.[42]

Though Sherman's final years as head of the Army were relatively happy ones, all the constitutional and statutory difficulties over the command of the Army were merely obscured, not solved. Sherman retired in Sheridan's favor in 1882. With characteristic impulsiveness, Sheridan promptly sought a showdown to resolve the whole ancient controversy to the benefit of the commanding general, including authority over the staff departments. He met a rebuff that left him frustrated and brooding, and the atmosphere poisoned anew.[43]

So the bureau chiefs continued to go their own ways. They and their subordinates were permanently detailed to their respective departments, and thus they were men long experienced in departmental procedures and routines and the better able to guide their own destinies. M. C. Meigs, for example, remained quartermaster general from 1861 until his retirement in 1882, and John K. Barnes was surgeon general from 1866 to 1882. The Secretaries of War meanwhile continued to be men chosen for the sake of political balance in the cabinet who did not have much military interest or experience beyond possible volunteer service in the Civil War. They had neither the inclination nor the knowledge to interfere much in the operation of the bureaus. Nor did they have adequate staffs of their own, for except during the brief interval 1882–84, and after 1890, there was no Assistant Secretary of War, and they had no one to rely on but a chief clerk and his deputies.

In these circumstances the staff bureaus which administered and supplied the Army and on which the field forces depended became almost independent sovereignties, each going its own way without much heed to the others, let alone to the Army as a whole. The bureaus were not only uncoordinated but also routinized and conservative. Quartermaster General Meigs was probably one of the most intelligent and progressive bureau chiefs, but even he announced that the methods which had won the Civil War represented a perfection that could not be improved upon, and this attitude seems generally to have prevailed and persisted. Of course, even the methods that had won the Civil War were gradually forgotten over the long years of a small peacetime Army. In the 1890's the somnolent staff departments were by no means prepared for even a small foreign war.[44]

This condition was all the more natural since their day-to-day work had almost nothing to do with war anyway. The Engineer Department was busy as usual with civil improvements to rivers and harbors, in comparison with which the erection of fortifications was an occasional thing. The Signal Corps was busy with the useful but only partially military work of spawning the United States Weather Bureau. The supply departments had the existing Army to think about, small but far-flung as it was. The ultimate weakness of the staff bureaus, their lack of forethought for war, was also a source of present strength: their concern was with the Army of *now*; the commanding general only *might* have a real command, if there was a war.

Some hope of an effective and constitutional solution to the command problem was offered by General Schofield, who succeeded Sheridan as commanding general and held the office from 1888 to 1895. Schofield had briefly been Secretary of War. That experience had caused him to give considerable thought to the Secretary's relationship with the commanding general long before he stepped into the latter post, and he entered his duties in 1888 convinced that the only way to function in his new office was to acknowledge that it was anomalous: "that under the government of the United States an actual military commander of the army is not possible." Constitutionally, command must reside with the President or his civilian deputy; therefore, Schofield believed, "the general-in-chief, or nominal commanding general, can be at most only a 'chief of staff'—that or nothing,—whatever may be the mere title under which he may be assigned to duty by the President."[45]

So Schofield abandoned the pretensions of Sherman and Sheridan, and frankly resigned to the three Secretaries of War whom he served the command of the Army, both line and staff. But by offering his military knowledge to the Secretaries, as *de facto* chief of staff to the Secretary of War, he assured professional expertise plus coordination in the direction of all the branches of the Army, line and staff. "It is only in this country," he remarked, "where the chief of state has generally no military training, and his war minister the same, that a chief of staff of the army is supposed to be unnecessary." Schofield would remedy the defect, drawing on European practice for an innovation that especially well fitted American constitutional requirements.

Not by any means the least benefit [Schofield further believed] would be the education thus given to officers of the army in respect to the relation in which they stand to the commander-in-chief, and in respect to the reasonable limits of military ambition in a republic where the President is and must be commander-in-chief.[46]

Unfortunately, the prevailing rigid application of seniority caused Schofield to be followed as commanding general by Major General Nelson A. Miles. Miles neither followed Schofield's recognition of the constitutional realities nor gave the Secretaries of War much other reason to have confidence in him. A man who had risen from the ranks of the Civil War volunteers, and an Indian fighter of some ability, he was nevertheless perhaps the least qualified man to serve as commanding general since the inception of the post. Traditionalist in almost all his views, haughty and cantankerous in personality, possessed of a fantastic but consuming desire to become President, he quarreled continually with Secretaries of War Daniel Lamont,

Russell Alger, and Elihu Root. In the Spanish-American War he conducted the Puerto Rican campaign and demonstrated an utter ineptitude in strategy, carrying out five weak landings too dispersed to support each other, and escaping disaster only through the demoralization and greater ineptitude of the enemy. Under him the progress achieved by Schofield went lost, and the Army again had no directing head. When at last Elihu Root sought to remedy the command defect permanently by institutionalizing Schofield's chief of staff idea among a complex of reforms, Miles predictably obstructed him.[47]

Withal, the line of the Regular Army was not so badly prepared for the Spanish War of 1898 as many journalistic accounts then and histories since have made it seem. As almost every writer stresses, the Indian campaigns had honed the fighting skills of individual companies to a high level of excellence. Those campaigns were ending now—the last Indian action of consequence was the battle of Wounded Knee in 1890—but in 1898 their influence upon the troops was still alive.

During the late 1880's and the 1890's, furthermore, respite from the Indian wars had encouraged a few preparations for possible foreign war. Some regiments were assembled to exercise as a body for the first time in years—the 12th Infantry in 1887 and the 21st Infantry in 1889, for example, both for the first time since 1869. In 1892 a school of instruction for drill and practice of cavalry and artillery was established at Fort Riley, Kansas. Through the later years of the century, the Army encouraged target practice and experimented with improved systems of instruction in it. In 1884 the infantry rifle was equipped for the first time with a rear sight which allowed for the drift of the bullet. In 1893 the Army adopted a good repeating shoulder arm to replace at last the single-shot model 1873 Springfield. The new weapon was the Danish .30-caliber Krag-Jorgensen rifle, with a box magazine of five-round capacity, and firing smokeless cartridges. When war broke out in 1898 there were 53,508 such rifles and 14,895 Krag-Jorgensen carbines on hand, more than enough for the existing regiments recruited to war strength. In 1898 those regiments were maintained at a peacetime level of eight companies, with each company at less than full strength, so the Regular Army could readily expand in reasonable if not Uptonian proportions by filling its companies and increasing their number per regiment. On April 1, 1898, the aggregate strength of the Regular Army was 2,143 officers and 26,040 enlisted men; this force could and did grow without undue difficulty into one of over 50,000.[48]

In the years since the Civil War, the officer corps had begun to benefit from slight but real improvements in the old system of promotion by seniority within regiments, with virtually no retirement for superannuation. In 1861 Congress had provided for compulsory retirement for incapacity, and in 1862 and 1870 it had voted that officers might retire voluntarily after thirty years of service or by compulsion at the President's discretion. In 1882 it enacted compulsory retirement at age sixty-four, which occasioned the already mentioned departures of Sherman, Meigs, and Surgeon General Barnes that year. In 1890 it opened up the promotion system by basing promotions on seniority within each arm, corps, or staff department rather than within the regiments. At the same time it provided for an examination for all promotions below the grade of major. During the 1890's the Army instituted systematic efficiency reports on all officers.[49]

Not that everything went well in these years. When the Spanish War came in 1898, the Krag-Jorgensens were not available in sufficient numbers to equip the citizen soldiers who would swell the war Army. Though the possibility of tropical campaigning had become increasingly apparent all through the 1890's, nothing had been done to prepare uniforms and equipment for tropical conditions. And American artillery fell much behind European artillery.

In Europe, artillery improvements of the late nineteenth century began to rescue the gun crews from the extreme vulnerability to which rifled small arms had exposed them in the Civil War. There was to be a resurgence of artillery in the wars of the early twentieth century, albeit not one sufficient to break the tactical stalemate. Breech-loading artillery became virtually universal among the European armies. Other improvements included smokeless propellants, which helped permit concealment of gun positions and gave range, precision, and penetration much superior to black powder; truly effective explosive shells, which burst into numerous high-velocity fragments; and recoil-absorbing devices, which eliminated the need to re-aim a gun after every shot and opened the way to much-improved sighting instruments and thence to indirect fire. The American Army was slow to adopt all these innovations, partly because of a lag in the application of American scientific and inventive skills to war. The Prussians produced a smokeless powder in 1865, and its general adoption in Europe followed French improvements in 1884; but American artillerists were still using black powder in the War with Spain. American artillerists of 1898 had nothing comparable to the French 75-mm. gun invented the year before. They had, however, begun to experiment with the new devices, including steel carriages, pneumatic or hydraulic recoil brakes, and elevating, traversing, and sighting mechanisms.[50]

The years following the Civil War have sometimes been called the Army's dark ages.[51] The Regular Army went into the Spanish War smaller in proportion to the national population than in any war since the formation of the United States. Often it could have used more men to fight the Indian wars that intervened, and it certainly could have used a repeating rifle at an earlier date, to meet Indians who carried repeaters. But the picture of darkness can be overdone. If the Indian-fighting soldiers often found themselves in small bands fending off several times their numbers, such combats were implicit in the extent of the territories they had to patrol and would have been likely to occur even had the Army mustered several times 25,-000 men. Despite disasters like Fetterman's Fight and the Little Big Horn, the Army proved large enough in the end to win over the Indians a victory more unlimited than that over the Confederacy. If isolation from the main currents of American life encouraged an unhealthy introspection in such a figure as Emory Upton, it also freed the Army from any temptation toward political activity and encouraged the healthy aspects of concentration upon things military. The rapid accomplishments of the early twentieth century in building a new Army suited to world power were built upon foundations laid in the twilight years of the old and isolated Army.

☆ PART THREE ☆

A Destiny of World Power:
1898-1945

In the last days of the war I stood on the levee of the Elbe looking across at the New Russia on the other bank not a hundred yards distant and mused on the mutations of time. Not since the medieval end of the Völkerwanderung had an outsider pitched his tents so deep in Europe, and I confess to feeling an involuntary resentment at the intrusion. I could not imagine what the outcome would be. . . .

Then a stranger thought struck me: namely, that it was I who stood on the German Elbe—not a neutral visitor from Mars, but a taxpaying citizen of the U.S.A., without a passport or visa, five thousand miles from home. With me on the levee were fifty more Americans, behind us ten thousand more, and linked to us across half the width of Europe a hundred divisions more.

—Howard K. Smith[1]

THIRTEEN

The Leap Overseas:
1898-99

Iv coorse, they'se dissinsions in th' cabinet; but they don't amount to nawthin'. . . . We're all wan people, an' we look to Gin'ral Miles to desthroy th' Spanish with wan blow. Whin it comes, trees will be lifted out be th' roots. Morro Castle'll cave in, an' th' air'll be full iv Spanish whiskers.

—Finley Peter Dunne's Mr. Dooley[1]

AFTER THE BATTLESHIP *Maine* exploded in Havana harbor, Congress added two regiments of artillery to the Regular Army, to bring the authorized strength to 28,747 officers and men. The Spanish had about 80,000 soldiers in Cuba. The saving features as war approached were the quality of the small Regular Army, in combat proficiency if not in organization, and, as always and despite both their own deficiencies and the Regulars' Uptonian suspicions of them, the citizens' militia companies. Around these two poles the national strength was to rally, to begin successfully the adventure of world power.[2]

It was April 19, 1898, when Congress opened the adventure by authorizing the President to employ the entire land and naval forces of the United States to secure the independence of Cuba. Restrained until now from substantial military increases by the last misgivings about war itself, Congress soon acted to enlarge the miliary forces for the purpose. The professional officers of the War Department had been urging an expansion of the Regular Army to 104,000 men by filling the existing companies and creating three-battalion infantry regiments of twelve companies each. They also urged a federally sponsored volunteer force thoroughly under the Regular Army's control, which would avoid all the old problems of dual federal-state auspices that Emory Upton had deplored so emphatically.

But it would have been folly for Congress to ignore the existing regiments and companies of organized militia, the National Guard, since they were citizen soldiers partially ready for mobilization and war whatever their limitations. Anyway, the National Guard and its National Guard Association were probably too potent politically to permit being ignored. On April 22 and 26 Congress adopted a compromise expansion plan. The Regular Army would be supplemented by means of a Presidential call for volunteers for federal service, but any militia organization which volunteered in a body would be accepted as a unit, and the states might even raise new organizations, with officers appointed by the governors, also to be accepted as units into the federal volunteer army. Not more than one Regular officer could be appointed to any volunteer regiment, and efficiency boards composed of volunteers, not Regulars, would review the capacity of the volunteer officers. In fact, this plan gave the professional officer corps merely the appearance of the federal volunteer army they had sought, while giving the state militia organizations the substance of an army built upon their established units. By an act of April 26, the authorized Regular Army itself was enlarged, but only to an authorized 64,719 officers and men. This act did concede a tactically meritorious argument of the Uptonians: it prescribed for all the infantry regiments the three-battalion, twelve-company organization for which Upton's tactics had originally been designed.[3]

Congress granted a few additional limited concessions to the concept of volunteers directly recruited and controlled by the federal government. Recalling such specialized federal volunteer units of the Civil War as the United States Colored Troops and the Veteran Volunteers, an act of April 22, 1898, authorized the Secretary of War to organize from the nation at large volunteer units "possessing special qualifications." They were to have federally appointed officers but were not to exceed a total of 3,000 men. The troops thus authorized turned out to be the 1st, 2nd, and 3rd Regiments of United States Volunteer Cavalry—the latter two almost forgotten, the 1st Colonel Leonard Wood's Rough Riders, with Theodore Roosevelt as lieutenant colonel. It is not at all clear that most congressmen had intended the regiments with "special qualifications" to be simply three more cavalry regiments. Perhaps to fulfill the original intention, a law of May 11 authorized a 3,500-man brigade of federal volunteer engineers. The same statute also provided for 10,000 enlisted volunteers who possessed immunity to tropical diseases. Ten infantry regiments resulted from the latter provision, six of white men and four colored, designated the 1st through 10th United States Volunteer Infantry but generally known as "the Immunes." How immune they really were is questionable, since physical examinations appear to have been lax, and when the 3rd Regiment, recruited mainly in Georgia, was due to go to the yellow-fever country of Cuba during the fever season, Senator A. O. Bacon of Georgia raised a cry against exposing them. A few other oddments of federal volunteers appeared eventually, but nothing like a sizable Uptonian federal force unconnected with the state militia.[4]

President William McKinley followed up Congressional authorization with a call for 125,000 volunteers under the April 22 law. The call was similar to those made by Lincoln, and like his it set quotas for the states in proportion to their population. Service was announced as for two years, unless sooner discharged. In accordance with the wishes of the National Guard but also intelligently using such preparations as were at hand, McKinley asked first for volunteers from the organized militia, stipulating that he would receive additional men only when organized units fell short of a state's quota. The National Guard had been badgering their state governors to call them up during the excited "Remember the *Maine*" days before the war, and now they sprang forward with alacrity. They reported to places designated by their governors, where after varying delays they were sworn into United States service by federal officers. Newspaper writers and the populace thought the process of assembling and mustering in was slow, but 124,804 officers and men were in the volunteer army by the end of May.

Since the volunteers were intended for overseas service, the National Guardsmen were sworn in as individuals, not militia units, thus obviating the old questions surrounding the constitutional provision that the militia might be called "to execute the laws of the union, suppress insurrections and repel invasions." There was some confusion occasioned by the requirement that National Guard regiments also transform themselves into twelve-company, three-battalion units along the lines of the Regular reorganization. There was also some confusion because the War Department seemed to indicate through the press that company strength would be 106 men, while in fact it was set at 81; in this mixup some men were sent home, only to return later under a second Presidential call. A bit of confusion for historians of regimental lineages also turned up, since some states called out historic regiments which retained their historic numbers in federal service (the 71st New York National Guard Regiment becoming the 71st New York Volunteers), while others preferred to start a new sequence of regimental numbers to reserve the old numbers for their Civil War regiments (the 1st Minnesota National Guard becoming the 4th Minnesota Volunteers).[5]

Commodore George Dewey's victory at the battle of Manila Bay increased manpower requirements somewhat unexpectedly, since troops would now be needed to harvest the fruits of the victory by occupying the Philippine archipelago. Partly for this reason, McKinley issued his second call for volunteers on May 25. He asked for 75,000 men, to be utilized first to fill existing organizations and only then to form new units—an evident attempt to profit from the experience of the Civil War. Again the response was rapid, and some 40,000 had been sworn in under the second call when the early signing of an armistice agreement suspended recruiting on August 12.[6]

In short, securing enough manpower to fight a colonial war with Spain proved to be no problem. So plentiful were recruits that the Regular Army indulged itself in rejecting more than three-quarters of its applicants for failing to meet its physical, mental, or moral standards. The Regulars could easily have attained their full authorized strength; they contented themselves with 58,688 officers and men. Keeping enough competent officers on hand did prove something of a problem: some went into the volunteer regiments, though the number who could do so was strictly limited; others went on recruiting details to fill the Regular regiments; and several hundred were diverted to staff and training assignments. But this problem was never serious, since there were many capable n.c.o.'s. Altogether, when the war ended in August, 1898, the Army, Regulars and volunteers, counted a total of 11,108 officers and 263,609 enlisted men on its rolls.[7]

If getting enough men was not difficult, taking care of them was. When it was apparent that the volunteer army would be constructed mainly from the organized militia, General Miles believed they ought to be trained as long as possible in state camps, since the United States now as in 1861 had no adequate installations or equipment for receiving them. But the War Department—meaning the staff bureaus and especially Adjutant General Henry C. Corbin, who emerged as a kind of chief of staff to the Secretary and strong man of the department—decided they had better concentrate both Regulars and National Guards in relatively few camps, mostly in the Department of the Gulf. Transportation of supplies would be easier for a few camps than for many; the militia ought to be exposed to the influence of the Regulars; and the militia ought to be divorced as soon as possible from the parochial influences of their homes. Some fifteen campsites were used eventually for the assembly and training of troops, with the most important of them at Chickamauga Park, Georgia, and Tampa, Florida.

Colonel William S. Patten of the Clothing and Equipage Division of the Quartermaster's Department soon described the situation of his division as "a mess." The description applies to most aspects of the first weeks of mobilization. Historians of the war have generally chided the War Department and the staff bureaus for having made practically no preparations to receive a rapidly expanded Army, but they do not make altogether clear what they think should have been done. There was no agency in the department responsible for mobilization planning, and plans alone could have been of only limited utility. Certainly the War Department and the bureaus were unimaginative and complacent, and they made a few egregious mistakes which will be mentioned presently; but they were hardly so obtuse as to have given no thought during early 1898 to the likelihood of war. Yet they could do little more than think about it. Until war was declared, expenditures were limited mainly to the existing appropriations, and no contracts exceeding the appropriations could be sealed. At best the War Department bureaus could contract for certain limited items beyond their appropriations to fill the estimated necessities of the current year, in terms of existing peacetime needs. Congress had created such restrictions, and it was not the manner of the American Congress to proceed differently until war was upon them.[8]

Though carried along by popular war fever, the McKinley administration was sufficiently sincere in its hopes of avoiding war as to discourage military preparations that might have suggested offensive designs before Congress voted war. Congress appropriated an extraordinary $50,000,000 for defensive preparations on March 9, a little over a month before war began; but the Army's $20,000,000 share went mainly into hurrying the Endicott program. When war came, a shortage of Krag-Jorgensen rifles compelled the volunteers to be armed with single-shot, black-powder Springfields; but the Ordnance Department could hardly have prevented it. The Quartermaster's Department, unable to stockpile beforehand, had at the declaration of war clothing and equipage for three months' supply for the peacetime Regular Army plus 10,000 additional troops. To handle any expansion, that department had only fifty-seven officers and eighty sergeants; the Commissary Department had twenty-two officers and ninety-six sergeants. The National Guard regiments of course brought some clothing and equipment to begin with, but of uneven quality and quantity, most of it quickly having to be replaced.[9]

Naturally the coming of war overwhelmed the supply departments and produced a mess. Unfortunately, too, the war came during the exuberant birth of the modern popular press, and it was overreported by correspondents seeking sensation. Hopefully anticipating uniform American success, the newspapers tended to put the worst face on anything short of it. Though the press conveyed an impression of thorough ineptitude in the supply departments, the procurement of supplies actually seems to have gone fairly well for the circumstances.

Quartermaster General Marshall Independence Ludington was an old man and tired, but he had the advantage of having served under M. C. Meigs in the Civil War—the last quartermaster general of whom that was true. He promptly asked Congress for a war organization of the department similar to that which Meigs had secured in 1864, and he got it and put it into effect promptly. Many inexperienced purchasing agents had to be sent scurrying across the country, but they brought in huge quantities of supplies without touching off scandals comparable to those attending the early supply activities of the Civil War. Of course there was waste and the government often had to pay inflated prices, but none of the vague charges of fraud and corruption bruited about in the press have ever been substantiated. The Quartermaster's Department also bought a good deal of material that did not measure up to specifications, but no shoddy like that of the Civil War. The troops had to go to the tropics in woolen flannels, or in canvas duck that was not much cooler; but the fault here lay not in unpreparedness for war but in a more general and inexplicable obtuseness whereby the War Department had never yielded to pleas for a lighter uniform after the Army had spent decades compaigning in the Southwest. At least the Army had a tropical uniform by the end of the war, at long last.

American industrialism had advanced immensely since the Civil War. Once orders were placed for clothing and other quartermaster's supplies, American industry could turn out materials for a quarter of a million men very rapidly, and the supply departments were soon shipping them in great bulk in the direction of the camps. The depot quartermaster at New York reported that his labor force manufactured blouses and trousers for 100,000 men in two weeks. As much as possible, the Army continued to manufacture uniforms in its own depots, but in the emergency it also contracted with private suppliers. The production of weapons was harder to speed up, but by August the volunteers were fast receiving Krag-Jorgensens.[10]

Transporting supplies to the troops, and moving the troops themselves, was done much less well. It was unfortunate that the concentration for the invasion of Cuba took place in the South, where the transportation net was still not so well developed as in the North, and especially in Florida, where the modern tourist industry with attendant transportation facilities was just beginning to rise from the sand and swamps. Only two railroads served the concentration area at Tampa, and only one connected Tampa with Port Tampa. In the absence of railroad regulatory legislation like that of the Civil War, the two lines entering Tampa cooperated with each other only sluggishly and reluctantly, to the detriment of the Army. But inadequate rail service does not excuse the huge congestion of loaded freight cars that built up around Tampa and other southern camps, filling sidings from Tampa all the way back to Columbia, South Carolina. The Quartermaster's Department failed to develop an adequate system for unloading the cars and was inexcusably slow even to begin marking the cars to indicate their cargoes or to put car numbers on bills of lading. Until a car was emptied, nobody at the camps knew what it contained, and badly needed items often lay undiscovered for weeks—such as a fast freight trainload of clothing that disappeared for ten days before it turned up on a siding eighteen miles from Tampa.

To make matters worse, once anything was removed from the trains it still had to be carried to its final destination by mule- or horse-drawn wagon; the internal combustion engine was still in its earliest infancy. In a fit of peacetime obtuseness worse than its neglect of summer uniforms, the Army had concluded in 1895 that with the end of the Indian wars it would not need its wagon trains, and it had sold them off. "Wagons that sold for two hundred dollars," one quartermaster mourned, "were sold to farmers for fifteen—and their stock were unable to pull them!" When the Army now turned to the Studebaker Company for hasty replacements, the company revealed it had sold much of the machinery for making them. Again the industrial capacity of the country was able to remedy the deficiency in a comparatively short time, but it was well into July—and the main campaigning was over—before the Quartermaster's Department could supply as many as four wagons to each regiment. Meanwhile, even when there were wagons to haul supplies from railroads to southern camps, the wagon roads were as execrable as during the Civil War.[11]

The greatest single transportation problem of the war was that of transferring the Cuban expeditionary force from Tampa to Santiago, and it produced some of the most noteworthy of the scenes that gave the war a comic-opera aspect. Tampa was selected first as a campsite for a small force and metamorphosed into the concentration point for the Cuban expeditionary force without anyone's giving much thought to it. The railroad which connected the camp at Tampa with

Port Tampa was a single track, and at Port Tampa there was only one long pier from which men and supplies could board ship. Ships had to enter a canal to get to it.

When it became apparent that Major General William R. Shafter's force of about 17,000 men would nevertheless have to embark from Port Tampa for Cuba, quartermaster Captain James B. Bellinger worked out a careful schedule for moving the men and their supplies over the railroad to Port Tampa and onto ships. But after weeks of wavering, the McKinley administration pushed Shafter to depart in a rush, Bellinger's schedule would cause too much delay, and Shafter resorted on the evening of June 7 to an order announcing his intention to sail at daybreak with such troops as were on board transports. Bellinger tried to preserve a semblance of order and arranged to have a railroad train for each regiment and a wagon train to get each to the tracks; but knowing the inadequacies of both railroad and wagons, the troops rushed wildly to seize any means of transportation they could find, overloaded wagons so that they sank into the sand, and scuffled with each other for possession of railroad cars. Chaos reigned all night. But the men got themselves to the port.[12]

There the scramble to board thirty-eight assembled ships matched the turmoil of the race to the port. Word had spread that the ships' capacities were inadequate for the full expeditionary force and its supplies, and so they were. When the Quartermaster's Department began looking for ocean transports early in the war, it discovered that the Navy had already preempted most of the best and fastest shipping before the war. For this purpose the Navy had had a larger share of the special defense appropriation of March 9, and the administration had given it greater leeway than the Army, reasoning that any naval increments could be used simply for the defense of the coasts and therefore did not contradict McKinley's peaceful professions. When the Quartermaster's Department did begin chartering vessels, someone made the extraordinary policy decision that owners should be called upon only to provide such tonnage as they could spare without interfering severely with their normal activities. Furthermore, since only ships of American registry were eligible for charter, and since Congress opposed granting American registry to foreign ships, the only vessels actually available tended to be those plying the coastal trade. These were mostly small and mostly freight carriers.[13] There developed the usual newspaper charges of extortionate prices and fraud in the chartering of vessels, with little evidence ever advanced to support them. But it is certainly true that the ships available for Shafter's force were too few, too small, and generally dirty and somewhat rundown. Nor does the Quartermaster's

Department seem to have done all that it might have to ready them for troop carrying.[14]

Shafter's men got aboard the transports—only to sit in them in Tampa Bay for a week, because of a false alarm about Spanish cruisers. Much equipment had to be left behind, including some medical supplies. Furthermore, when the supplies were unloaded in Cuba, they proved to have been packed as haphazardly as they had been loaded on the railroads, and much time was lost and a good deal of wastage occurred before they were sorted out. Shafter chose to land on the southern coast of Cuba east of Santiago to secure the seemingly most advantageous route for an advance against the city, but this decision placed him at unsheltered roadsteads with inadequate landing facilities. Without help from Admiral William T. Sampson's blockading squadron more generous than Shafter's own subsequent cooperation with the Navy, the expedition could not have gotten ashore. Once ashore, its supplies had to follow its advance along roads worse than those in the American South; the limited supply of wagons could not supplement pack mules until some men were detached from the line to make road repairs. With bad roads, not enough wagons, inadequate landing facilities, and insufficient transports behind them, the troops at the front suffered shortages of almost everything, while great quantities of stores still rested in the southern United States.[15]

Deficient transportation was the principal source of many food problems. The volunteers would surely have complained about their Army diet in the best of circumstances, because except for the addition of a pound of vegetables daily after 1890, and a few authorized substitutions, the ration had hardly changed in a hundred years. But circumstances were rarely at their best in the Spanish War. The country could supply great quantities of foods, and the Commissary Department purchased generously if unimaginatively. For the first time in an American war it was not necessary to drive herds of cattle along with the armies, since troops near rail lines could receive refrigerated meat. In the southern camps, volunteers groused about tastelessness and monotony in the diet but not about lack of quantity. The problem was to get foodstuffs to the troops in Cuba over the creaky route to the front at Santiago. Almost four million rations of vegetables were sent to Cuba during June and July, but hardly any of the stuff found its way to Shafter's trenches. Much of the food originally shipped with the expeditionary force was packed on the transports before anything else went aboard, perhaps with the idea that it was of primary importance; but consequently it was unloaded last, and by the time it emerged, it had often spoiled in the steaming holds.

Meanwhile the expeditionary force subsisted largely on the travel ration, which posed further difficulties. For reasons unexplained, the Commissary Department had bought little of the canned corned beef which was the normal staple of the Regular Army's travel ration in the absence of fresh meat. It had substituted a product known variously as canned fresh beef or canned roast beef. This stuff was in fact a canned boiled beef, and it had never been well accepted among the Regulars. It was stringy, tasteless, and disagreeable in appearance. Colonel John F. Weston, who had pioneered its use, was however the chief commissary officer for Shafter's expedition, and he believed that when cooked with vegetables and condiments it made a palatable stew. It was never intended to be eaten straight from the can, uncooked, and without seasoning, and certainly not over a prolonged period of time. Yet in that manner the troops had to eat it for nearly two weeks, in the fetid heat of their transports. Since refrigerated beef could not reach them in Cuba until they captured Santiago, in that fashion they also ate it all through the campaign for the city. Vegetables and condiments disappeared somewhere along the supply line. The heat of the transports and of Cuba did nothing to improve the canned beef. Before long the very sight of canned beef began to nauseate the men, and fewer and fewer of them could keep it down if they could manage to eat it at all. But many men continued to receive little else until Santiago fell. Before the war faded into memory, the hated canned beef would serve as raw material for a national scandal with immense repercussions.[16]

Deficient transportation also helped explain the shortcomings of the Medical Service. Facilities for the wounded were inadequate after the battles around Santiago, partly because medical supplies had never found their way up the mule paths to the front, or sometimes had not been loaded in Florida. But much more than transportation went awry in this department. Surgeon General George M. Sternberg was a research scientist of ability and eminence in bacteriology and epidemiology. His encouragement of Major Walter Reed was to be instrumental in bringing about the identification of the yellow fever carrier. But Sternberg was startingly indifferent to administrative details.

He had been an Army surgeon long enough to be aware of the carelessness with which soldiers are likely to treat sanitary precautions, but when the recruits and National Guards gathered in improvised camps in the South, he contented himself with sending a circular of hygienic instructions to the officers. Virtually nothing was done to impress its precepts upon the recipients or to assure that they observed it, and sickness in the camps, especially typhoid, took more lives than both the enemy and the tropical fevers of Cuba. The state

GEORGE WASHINGTON

By James Peale, 1795

The Brixey Portrait

James Peale painted the first Commander in Chief in military uniform, recalling Washington's accomplishments as founder of the United States Army. (*Historical Pictures Service–Chicago*)

AN AMERICAN REVOLUTIONARY SOLDIER
AS SEEN BY A BRITISH PRISONER OF WAR

A British Colonel Campbell depicted the cunning but loutish prototype of Brother Jonathan, his attempts at splendid military dress incongruous with his bearing, his weapons, and his homely nag. (*Historical Pictures Service–Chicago*)

THE BATTLE OF BRANDYWINE

By Frank C. Yohn

If there was a typical soldier of the Revolutionary Army, a true depiction of him probably would lie somewhere between Colonel Campbell's caricature and the sturdy fighters standing off a British charge in this illustration by a modern artist of the Howard Pyle school. But Continentals sometimes did fight as well as those imagined here. (*Historical Pictures Service–Chicago*)

WASHINGTON REVIEWING THE WESTERN ARMY
AT FORT CUMBERLAND, MARYLAND

Attributed to James Peale

The federal government's use of the militia army depicted here to suppress the Whiskey Insurrection in 1794 opened a new stage in the history of the citizen soldiery and set a precedent followed by President Eisenhower at Little Rock, Arkansas, in 1957 and President Kennedy at Oxford, Mississippi, in 1962. (*The Metropolitan Museum of Art, gift of Edgar William and Bernic Chrysler Garbisch, 1963*)

FOUNDERS OF THE UNITED STATES ARMY

Henry Knox was painted by Gilbert Stuart as a major general, not yet so fat as when he became the first Secretary of War; the engraving after Stuart is by E. Prudhomme. Henry Elouis portrayed Anthony Wayne as the proud disciplinarian who fashioned the Legion of the United States. John C. Calhoun in his War Department years was the young man of the engraving by T. B. Welch from a drawing by J. B. Longacre. Robert W. Weir, who taught art at West Point, portrayed a more vigorous Winfield Scott than the old man seen after photography appeared. (*Historical Pictures Service–Chicago: Knox and Calhoun; Brown Brothers: Wayne; West Point Museum Collections: Scott*)

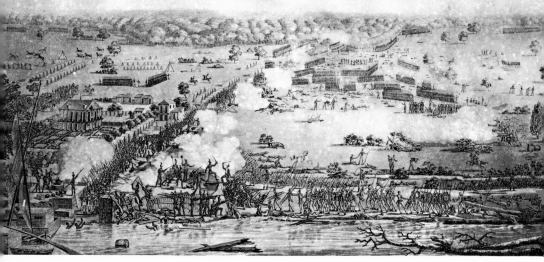

THE BATTLE OF NEW ORLEANS

Aquatint by Louis Philibert Debucourt after Hyacinthe Laclotte

Laclotte was an engineer in Andrew Jackson's army. He depicted the landmarks of the battlefield meticulously. Though his British formations may display an excessive tactical rigidity, he conveys an essentially correct impression of a professional army well conditioned in the warfare that preceded rifled muskets and artillery, when, this battle notwithstanding, tightly disciplined lines of infantry were still useful. (*Library of Congress*)

PAWNEE COUNCIL

Aquatint by Edwin James, Account of an Expedition
from Pittsburgh to the Rocky Mountains (*1823*)

After the War of 1812, much of the Regular Army's activity was turned to exploring the vast trans-Mississippi West and opening it to settlement. Here eagle banners and other military trappings are being employed to impress Indian dignitaries. (*Library of Congress*)

FORT UNION ON THE MISSOURI

Engraving after Karl Bodmer

Fort Union, at the mouth of the Yellowstone, was still an outpost not of the Army but of the American Fur Company when the Swiss artist Bodmer painted it on his journey into the West with Prince Maximilian of Wied-Neuwied in 1833. It looked much the same when it was an Army post in the 1850s; wooden stockades like it planted the seeds of the white man's civilization all over the West. (*Courtesy New York Public Library, Rare Books Collection*)

VIEW OF WEST POINT, 1828

By George Catlin

The nursery of American military professionalism as it looked when Sylvanus Thayer was superintendent. The artillery drill occupies the Parade, with the barracks in the background; officers' and faculty quarters are to the right. (*West Point Museum Collections*)

A MILITIA DRILL IN MASSACHUSETTS IN 1832

This caricature appeared in *Harper's Monthly* in 1875 and exemplifies a staple joke of much of the century. An antidote to Jacksonian glorification of the untrained common man was useful. On the other hand, while ordinary citizens appearing at muster days might have been pretty inept, use of the word "militia" to describe both the common militia and the organized volunteer companies obscured the considerable value of the latter. (*Historical Pictures Service–Chicago*)

THE DEATH OF MAJOR RINGGOLD

"The gallant Major Ringgold" organized the Army's first battery of the new-style mobile field artillery, which had been developed in Europe during and after the Napoleonic Wars. The horse-drawn field guns were decisive on several battlefields of the Mexican War, but Ringgold died amidst their first triumph, at Palo Alto. (*Library of Congress*)

BRIGADIER GENERAL JOHN E. WOOL
AND HIS STAFF AT SALTILLO

This daguerreotype of American soldiers in Mexico is one of the first photographs to depict the United States Army or any war scene. (*The Bettmann Archive*)

THE FRONT PARAPET OF FORT PULASKI, GEORGIA, APRIL, 1862

Photograph by Timothy H. O'Sullivan

After the British seacoast raids of the War of 1812, the Corps of Engineers spent the next decades building impressive new fortifications along the Atlantic and Gulf coasts according to a plan developed largely by Simon Bernard, a graduate of the École Polytechnique. In the test of the Civil War, however, seven-and-a-half-foot solid brick walls backed with great piles of masonry crumbled before the new rifled cannons. (*Library of Congress, Brady Collection*)

CIVIL WAR INFANTRY

Company F, 114th Pennsylvania Infantry at Petersburg, Virginia, August, 1864. This spic-and-span company, still wearing the colorful Zouave uniform popular early in the war, were headquarters guards to General Meade. The riflemen are formed in two ranks as for battle. Their regiment had left Philadelphia on September 1, 1862, and had fought with the Army of the Potomac since Fredericksburg, becoming attached to Army headquarters in April, 1864. (*Library of Congress, Brady Collection*)

CIVIL WAR ARTILLERY

Photograph by George N. Bernard

Federal soldiers with a twelve-pound Napoleon smoothbore in the captured defenses of Atlanta. The picture gives a good idea of semipermanent fortifications. Note the *chevaux-de-frise* obstructing the *glacis*, that is, the forward defensive slope and another bastion, a projecting strong point, in the center distance. (*Library of Congress, Brady Collection*)

MUSTERED OUT

By A. R. Waud

One of the best of the artists who covered the Civil War for the pictorial weeklies sketched the homecoming of United States Colored Troops. Slaves had become soldiers, able to sing: "We look like *men* a-marching on." (*Library of Congress*)

UNITED STATES CAVALRYMAN

By Frederic Remington, 1890

The soldier of the western plains in his field uniform—slouch hat, blue coat, pale blue trousers, cavalry-yellow stripe, high leather boots—and armed with carbine, saber, and revolver. (*Library of Congress*)

COASTAL DEFENSES: THE LYMAN-HASKELL
MULTIPLE CHARGE ACCELERATING GUN

From *Scientific American*, 1883

After the Civil War had shown the obsolescence of the old brick-and-masonry coastal forts, improvement of the seacoast defenses became the main preoccupation of American military policy from the late years of the century until the eve of the Spanish War. This picture appeared in the year when the Gun-Foundry Board was established to make plans for the modern ordnance that in fact the United States did not possess. A few years later the Endicott Board planned modern concrete fortresses below earth level. Both projects proceeded only slowly and partially to fulfillment. (*Historical Pictures Service–Chicago*)

ENLISTED MEN,
CAVALRY AND INFANTRY, 1888

By H. A. Ogden

Ogden still ranks as the pre-eminent American painter of military uniforms. Of his seventy paintings prepared for the Quartermaster General's Department and illustrating Army uniforms from 1776 to 1907, this was one of the last of his first series, published in 1890. In it he could exercise his care for meticulous accuracy upon uniforms he observed for himself; this was the heyday of Imperial German influence upon military dress. (*U. S. Army photograph*)

FATHERS OF AMERICAN MILITARY THOUGHT

Dennis Hart Mahan, by Robert W. Weir; William Tecumseh Sherman, by L. Hart Darragh after Daniel Huntington; Emory Upton, by Frank Fowler; Arthur L. Wagner, by C. H. MacDonald. (*West Point Museum Collections*)

THE FILIPINO INSURRECTION

The sartorial splendor of an Ogden painting has given way to rumpled and dusty campaign hats. Soldiers are defending a strong point against the insurrectos; dotting the countryside with numerous fortifications was one of several means by which the Army attempted to pacify the Philippine archipelago, as its twentieth-century career of world power opened in a nasty guerrilla campaign. (*U. S. Signal Corps*)

THE HEAVILY BURDENED INFANTRYMAN OF WORLD WAR I

On the left, the pack carried in the front lines; on the right, a soldier with full equipment, at Southampton, England. In combat, everybody would have lightened his load as much as possible, but never enough, and the uniform itself was hot and uncomfortable. The overseas cap signified that the soldier was on the far side of the Atlantic. (*Culver Pictures, Inc.*)

FOUNDERS OF THE MODERN ARMY

Elihu Root, photographed by Aimé Dupont; Leonard Wood, photographed by
B. Johnston; John J. Pershing, by J. Doctoroff; Peyton C. March, photograph from
Brown Brothers. (*Culver Pictures, Inc.: Root; Historical Pictures Service–Chicago:
Wood and Pershing; Brown Brothers: March*)

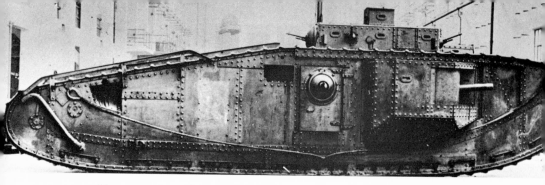

EVOLUTION
OF THE TANK

Top: the British Mark
VIII thirty-seven-ton
heavy of World War I,
which was standardized
for American production
in 1917. A few helped
form the nucleus of an
American armored force
after the war, but the
United States Army soon
neglected heavy tanks,
perhaps unduly, for light
and medium models.
Bottom: an example is the
T-2 of 1932, a light tank
armed with a 37-mm gun.
The revolving turret had
come in with the British
Mark I of 1924. (*Wide
World Photos: top; Culver
Pictures, Inc.: bottom*)

THE ARMY COMMAND TEAM OF WORLD WAR II:
HENRY L. STIMSON AND GEORGE C. MARSHALL

Both men are shown as they looked on the eve of war, in
1941. (*Culver Pictures, Inc.*)

On J
in Engla
for France
Normandy
month. Most
others have Brow
Rifles and at least
The abundant truck
one of the principal adva
the American Army in 19
1945. (*Wide World Photos*)

wit
of such mobility later in
But the beginnings
World War II were
ward. Here, northwest o
March 23, 1951, soldie
an airdropped 105-mm
(*Wide World Photos*)

VIETNAM:
GRAVESTONE SECURITY

On November 10, 1966, a soldier of the 1st Infantry Division watches from a Vietnamese cemetery as he provides cover for troops advancing across an open field. He carries an M-16 rifle and the complex communications gear of the modern battlefield. (*Wide World Photos*)

in
the
and
s of the
al Patton,
about to re-
dard medium
ermans and the
mm high-velocity
proved stabilization
accuracy of fire. Al-
Pershing tanks carrying
guns appeared late in
d War II and in Korea, only
did American troops receive
operational numbers heavy
tanks comparable to the most
powerful Russian models. (*Culver Photos, Inc.: top; United Press International Photo: bottom*)

A PERSHING MISSILE

Being launched at Cape Canaveral on February 25, 1960, the *Pershing* is a solid-fuel intermediate range ballistic missile designed for field service. (*Brown Brothers*)

of medical knowledge permitted little control of yellow fever, but the application of existing knowledge and standards of camp sanitation could have prevented the ravages of typhoid. Admittedly, it was difficult to recruit enough qualified physicians into the war Army, but Sternberg gave no great energy to the task and cooperated with the conservatives who still obstructed the recruitment of female nurses. The shortcomings of the Medical Bureau like those of the Commissariat finally provoked a scandal whose outcome vitally affected the whole Army.[17]

For the deficiencies in the staff departments reflected above all the Army's lack of a directing brain. The staff departments could go their own complacent ways in wartime as they had done through decades of peace, because they were practically autonomous branches of the War Department susceptible to coordination and energetic direction by no one.

General Shafter said of his Santiago campaign, "there was no strategy about it."[18] The same remark pretty much applies to the whole direction of the war. General Miles rightly decided that the organization of the War Department offered little opportunity for the commanding general to accomplish anything in Washington, so he sought a field command. But he believed invasion of Cuba should be postponed until most of the volunteer army could participate, since the 80,000 Spanish troops on the island were mainly veterans of warfare against the Cuban *insurrectos*. Therefore he proposed an invasion of Puerto Rico as a preliminary operation, and he spent much of the war traveling about the southern camps trying to get control of a force he might lead on that venture. He succeeded with barely enough time remaining to effect a rapid conquest before the armistice, and meanwhile he contributed little to what proved to be the main campaigns. Still, Miles's travels tried his nerves less than remaining in the War Department and were probably just as useful to the country.[19]

Secretary of War Russell Alger was at best a mediocrity and eventually became the principal scapegoat for everything that went wrong with the war. But he was hampered as much by the organizational defects of the War Department and the Army as by the limits of his own ability, and he hardly deserved the immense public obloquy that eventually descended upon him. When McKinley discovered that Alger compounded mediocrity with impulsiveness he decided that he must take on the direction of the war himself, and to the extent that central direction existed McKinley provided it. He would have had to step in to some extent because the war demanded closer and more sustained cooperation between the Army and the Navy than any previous conflict, and there was no machinery for obtaining it. The President's best efforts produced few model examples of interservice harmony. Army critics complained that McKinley was too much influenced by the maritime strategists of the Navy's War Board, and the redoubtable Alfred Thayer Mahan certainly made the board a persuasive instrument. To the extent that any Army officer had McKinley's ear, it was Adjutant General Henry C. Corbin, who probably had more influence over the course of the war than either Miles or Alger; but while Corbin was efficient he was also unimaginative and thoroughly the bureaucrat. McKinley had too many things on his mind to be a complete substitute for a good Secretary of War. By now the President was too busy to undertake so detailed a supervision of a war as Polk had conducted. McKinley's notorious aversion to hurting anybody's feelings also weakened his direction of the Army. In Washington as in the field, "there was no strategy about it," or very little.[20]

So the Spanish War was a soldiers' war, and the Cuban campaign was mostly the Regular soldiers' war. In the act of April 22, Congress authorized the formation of brigades, divisions, and corps much like those of the Civil War, three regiments to a brigade, three brigades to a division, three divisions to a corps. Seven corps were eventually activated, and the bulk of the Regular Army went into the V Corps. This corps, with two infantry divisions and one of dismounted cavalry, formed the Cuban expeditionary force and fought the campaign for Santiago. General Shafter commanded a larger body of Regulars than any American general before him, and they performed with all the valor that Emory Upton would have expected of them and as much skill as their commanders gave them opportunity to display.

The Cuban expeditionary force consisted originally of 14,412 Regulars and 2,465 volunteers, the latter in the Rough Riders and two famous National Guard regiments, the 2nd Massachusetts and 71st New York. Reinforcements arriving at the front after the principal fighting was over raised the total of volunteers to 7,443. The Rough Riders were conspicuously heroic, and for obvious reasons they received favorable publicity even out of proportion to their heroism. The Uptonians cited the conduct of several other volunteer regiments as further proof of the inferiority of citizen soldiers, especially in regiments drawn from the state militia, and Theodore Roosevelt further magnified the merits of his own regiment by joining the chorus. The 71st New York suffered the harshest criticism, because while leading the advance of the 1st Division of the V Corps toward San Juan Hill they broke under fire and refused to continue forward. But their failure occurred after they had drawn a disproportionately heavy fire to which they could not reply—or more precisely, after the fire had been drawn upon them by an American observation balloon floating overhead. Also, like all the National Guard regiments but unlike the Regulars and the Rough Riders, they faced the prospect of going into battle with the old black-powder Springfield rifles, which would betray their position with every shot.

Tactically as well as strategically, the war did not amount to much. It demonstrated the utter necessity for smokeless-powder shoulder arms and artillery; the little American artillery that got into action was badly outmatched by Spanish guns that fired smokeless powder. It did not demonstrate a way out of the infantry impasse of the Civil War. The Americans attacking the defenses of Santiago bulled ahead in frontal assaults, which won local successes against a weary and discouraged enemy but cost so many casualties that two days of serious fighting were enough to set Shafter to considering the abandonment of the whole campaign. His salvation was the demoralization of the enemy by the prospect of growing American strength after a long and frustrating insurrectionary war.[21]

If the conduct of the 71st New York was unfortunate and unheroic, it has to be balanced against the record of the National Guard regiments that happened to be assigned not to Cuba but to the VIII Army Corps which went to the Philippines. Diverted after Commodore Dewey's victory in Manila Bay, these were western organizations except for the 10th Pennsylvania Infantry, a supposedly crack eastern outfit intended to stiffen the corps. By the time they reached the Philippines, the Spanish were ready to give up and forced them into practically no real fighting. But tension developed quickly between the Americans and the Filipino independence movement, until an insurrection erupted while the Senate was debating the peace treaty. Thereupon the citizen soldiers of the VIII Corps had to fight the first round of a conflict that proved much more difficult and prolonged than the war with Spain.[22]

After the armistice with Spain, McKinley ordered the muster out of 100,000 volunteers, with priority to those who had seen action, and apportioned among the states in accordance with the numbers they had furnished; but the regiments in the Philippines had to be retained. In the end they stayed in the islands until the summer of 1899, finally to be mustered out as late as October, more than a year after their luckier comrades had gone home. During the interval they endured extremely unpleasant service in jungle warfare against Emilio Aguinaldo's Tagalogs. Much of their fighting came to be guerrilla warfare, a style the Army had had to teach itself with great difficulty against the Seminole Indians in 1835-42 and now had to teach itself again. This time there was the added complication of trying to woo the local population even while flushing out guerrillas from their midst, which ruled out Colonel Worth's old Florida method of starving everybody. Mainly the Army had to work much as General Taylor had done in Florida, creating strong points and fanning out from them methodically to subdue the surrounding countryside.

The National Guardsmen's friends at home stressed the unfairness of their prolonged service in the Philippines and called loudly for their return, and most of the men were hardly happy with their fate. But all in all they behaved with most commendable patience and soldierly courage. Elihu Root, who was Secretary of War by the time of their discharge, was much influenced by the Uptonians in his attitude toward the National Guard; but nevertheless he said of the Guardsmen in the Philippines: "This is an exhibition of sturdy patriotism which it seems to me has never been fully appreciated."[23]

Retaining the Guardsmen in the islands was anomalous, and they could not be kept indefinitely. On March 2, 1899, soon after sporadic insurrection had burst into full-fledged war, Congress voted to maintain the wartime Regular Army of 65,000 men and to enlist for terms of two years and four months "not more than 35,000 volunteers to be recruited . . . from the country at large, or from localities where their services are needed." Thus when war enthusiasm was dying and the National Guard regiments were not eager to continue in the suppression of Filipino rebellion, the Regulars secured the kind of volunteer force they had desired from the beginning of the Spanish War. The phrase about recruiting volunteers "from localities where their services are needed" meant there would be an appeal to individual Guardsmen in the Philippines, now experienced in island combat, to sign on for another hitch. Guardsmen and Guard officers might transfer to the new volunteer army in grade. In fact, two volunteer infantry regiments and some troops of cavalry were created in the Philippines, mainly from National Guardsmen already there. But the Regulars would control organization and assignments in the new volunteer army.[24]

The volunteer regiments were recruited in time virtually to full strength, and they fought very well, playing an indispensable role in the suppression of Aguinaldo's part of the Filipino rebellion.

A frequent assertion of historians of the Spanish War is that in provoking war while militarily weak, the United States failed to coordinate its foreign policy with its military policy. This view is correct only in the limited sense that the absence of both a strong military force in being and a mobilization plan compelled a hastily improvised and therefore inefficient and wasteful mobilization. The assertion is not correct in any larger sense, since the United States demonstrated that it had ample military means to support its aggressive foreign policy by whipping Spain with ease. The officials who took the country into war, whatever their faults, did not foolishly embark on an adventure beyond the capacities of American military power; they were quite correct in their confident assumption that any military problems created by Spain could be solved readily after war was declared. The Spanish might have made American military tasks more difficult than they actually did, but since they were not fools either, they refused to prolong a war they knew they must lose. As far as coordinating foreign policy with military capacity is concerned, the United States would be fortunate if its foreign policy always accorded so well with its military strength.[25]

The incidental wastefulness of an improvised war effort could be taken readily in stride, for the United States was rich and the whole nature of its industrial growth had accustomed it to wastefulness. The unplanned, helter-skelter mobilization of 1898 was consistent with the whole unplanned, helter-skelter nature of American life in the late-nineteenth-century heyday of governmental *laissez faire*.

Yet by the time of the Spanish War, the era of insouciant wastefulness, planlessness, and *laissez faire* was about to die, and public reaction to the management of the Spanish War heralded the approach of muckraking and progressivism. A middle class that would soon grow intolerant of the wasting of human lives in slums, tenements, and anthracite fields was already unwilling to tolerate a waste of lives in which its own sons were involved, as they were in the regiments of the volunteer army.

Grumbling began when word reached home of the military diet of nauseating canned beef, the widespread sickness in the southern camps, and the inadequate hospital facilities for the wounded outside Santiago. Every logistical deficiency soon appeared in the newspapers looking twice as big as life, since swarms of practitioners of the new sensational journalism hovered around the Army. A brief interlude of newspaper and public complacency accompanied the surrender of Santiago, but this calm quickly disappeared before the climactic storm of the yellow fever outbreak. General Shafter was notably unconcerned about the growing toll of fever during the leisurely negotiations for the surrender of the city. By the time the Army entered Santiago, the spread of the fever on top of its other woes had already made the V Corps, the heart of the Regular Army, a shadow of itself. Shafter belatedly awoke to its condition and began to press for its evacuation and replacement by fresh troops and especially by "immunes." The arrival of the first invalid evacuees in New York aboard two of the worst hulks of the Quartermaster's Department fleet touched off a renewed public outcry. Fear of the fever, magnified by a growing preoccupation with it, spread through Shafter's camps. Then Theodore Roosevelt and Leonard Wood initiated the famous round robin, a letter to Shafter signed by all the divisional and brigade commanders of his corps (Major General Henry W. Lawton qualified his signature with criticism of the language of the letter), asserting that the "army must be moved at once or it will perish. Persons responsible for preventing such a move will be responsible for the unnecessary loss of many thousands of lives."[26]

This extraordinary document was composed at a delicate moment in the peace negotiations with Spain, when the negotiations might have been upset by a confession of the weakness of the American Army. But Colonel Roosevelt appears to have been not at all averse to its publication, and it soon reached an Associated Press correspondent and then the world. Roosevelt followed up with a second letter of his own, asserting that his cavalry brigade was on the verge of "dying like rotten sheep."[27]

Since the attack on San Juan Hill, Roosevelt was one of the popular heroes of the war. From the round robin onward, the War Department became the scapegoat for everything that had not gone smoothly in the war, and Secretary Alger the favorite target of the journalists. McKinley continued Alger in office and shielded him as best he could, in part no doubt because he recognized the full implications of the attacks on Alger in light of his own assumption of direct leadership during the war. But retaining Alger intensified the public outcry.

The V Corps was now removed from Cuba to a healthy but isolated camp on Montauk Point, Long Island. The movement was accomplished with much dispatch, and a camp was erected with considerable speed where none had been before. But more than ever the press magnified every flaw. Though rations at Montauk were ample and some troops were smothered with edible gifts from well-wishers, reporters drew from the emaciated appearance of the men accounts of continued bad diet and ineptness in the Commissary Department. Every crowded vessel that arrived from Cuba became new evidence of deliberate callousness in the Quartermaster's Department's selection of ships.

McKinley attempted to quiet the furor by announcing an official investigation of the conduct of the war, thus offering assurance that military deficiencies would be corrected. Grenville M. Dodge, major general of volunteers in Sherman's armies during the Civil War and postwar transcontinental railroad builder, headed an investigating commission consisting of eight Union and one Confederate veterans. The Dodge Commission were gentlemen of prestige and they labored earnestly, but when they demonstrated a realistic sympathy for the War Department, the press soon led the public to the conclusion of "whitewash." The detailed report of the commission points accurately toward the basic flaws of the country's military organization, but a report that did not breathe sensation had to be, in the eyes of many, the report of an "Alger Relief Commission." So for a time the hearings of the Dodge Commission went on unspectacularly, accompanied by public restlessness.[28]

Sensation exploded again when Nelson A. Miles testified. Miles was suffering from intolerable frustration. Though he was commanding general of the Army through the war, he had somehow failed to become a popular hero. He had hoped to use the war as a springboard to the Presidency, but his part in it had fizzled into the anticlimactic Puerto Rican campaign. He was sure the cause of his plight could lie in no obtuseness of his own but rather must be the malevolent plotting of the administration. He therefore discharged his accumulated venom before the Dodge Commission, joining in the charges of War Department mismanagement and firing away most ferociously against the Commissary Department. While refusing to be either sworn or affirmed on the witness stand, he told the Dodge Commission that the canned beef had not been part of the legal ration and that its use had been some kind of experiment. But more than that, the refrigerated beef sent to the troops had been treated with secret chemicals that made it still more injurious to health. It bore an odor similar to that of a dead body treated with preservatives. It was "embalmed beef."

Miles became enamored of that phrase, the reporters took it up, and "embalmed beef" was the latest scandal. Commissary General Charles P. Eagan, called before the Dodge Commission to reply, lost control of his temper and multiplied the sensation by fulminating against Miles as a liar whose lies he would force "back into his throat covered with the contents of a camp latrine."[29] Eagan had to be tried and found guilty of conduct unbecoming an officer and gentleman, and the President felt obliged to appoint another commission to concentrate on Miles's beef charges. As it happened, Miles with customary fatuity had chosen the wrong target. He had grown so fond of the notion of "embalmed beef" that he neglected to sustain his attack on canned beef, where he might have scored a bull's-eye. The "beef court" was able to show that he had produced no serious evidence for his charges of injurious chemicals in the refrigerated beef and that in fact the troops had liked and welcomed the refrigerated product. (In light of subsequent revelations about the meat-packing industry, Miles's allegations may of course have had more weight than he could prove.)[30]

Despite the miscarriage of Miles's most serious charges, the new sensation carried McKinley to the limit of his willingness and ability to shield Secretary Alger. The 1900 elections were now approaching, and McKinley had to consider the political fortunes of his party as well as himself. When Alger in turn sought to rescue his own political fortunes by flirting with an irregular faction in Michigan Republican politics, McKinley had enough. He secured Alger's resignation and replaced him with a man of little political standing but great administrative potential demonstrated in a long legal career: Elihu Root. Alger was unfortunate; his abilities were limited, but the main problem was that he was a specimen of the late nineteenth-century age of *laissez faire* and tolerated wastefulness, carried over into a time when planlessness and wastefulness would no longer receive easy tolerance. Root proved to be a man for the new age.[31]

FOURTEEN

The New Army:
1899-1914

Really, you know, I do not need to know anything about armies and their organization, for the five reports of Elihu Root, made as Secretary of War in the United States, are the very last word concerning the organization and place of an army in a democracy.

—Lord Haldane[1]

AFTER THE GREAT Civil War, the mammoth armies of the Union dissolved, and the Regular Army reverted to little more than an Indian constabulary. The principal military reserve, the organized militia, was also neglected. Neither foreign nor domestic policy posed much need for anything else. After the lesser Spanish War, the Regular Army retained its augmented war strength and the National Guard received attention and improvement. The new role of the United States in international politics demanded a larger and better Army with a more ready reserve, and American government was adaptive enough to respond to the need.

The Spanish War was probably less a cause of the new world role of the country than an expression of it. Having become the leading industrial power during the 1890's, having completed the task of settling the North American continent, placed upon a globe shrunken by improving communications, the United States now possessed a wealth and a military potential that drew her into international political activity whether she willed it or not. Wealth and power imply responsibility, and both world wars were to demonstrate that, however vaguely, the American people sensed their responsibility and could not stand aside indefinitely in the face of global turmoil. It was a somewhat crude sense of the responsibilities implicit in wealth and power that drove the nation to intervene in Cuba in 1898. A more mature but still ill-defined awareness of the bond between power and responsibility was to shape much of President Theodore Roosevelt's foreign policy. America's growing wealth and power pushed her into an ever more active foreign policy; and though both government and people mainly sensed rather than clearly recognized, let alone controlled, the drift of events, they responded appropriately by reforming the Army for the changing demands it might encounter.

Elihu Root left a narrative of his accession to the War Department that is now well known. When an agent of President McKinley called him to offer him the department, he protested that he was a lawyer who knew nothing of war and the Army and therefore was unqualified. McKinley's agent responded that it was precisely because he was a lawyer that the President was turning to him; the principal task of the War Department would now be the administrative and legal one of governing the insular territories acquired from Spain. Root allowed himself to be persuaded on that ground, but he soon discovered that to govern the islands effectively the War Department had to transform the Army into an improved fighting force, for the Philippines at least were in open rebellion. That task in turn led Root into a general reorganization of the Army and the department.[2]

Once the reorganization began, Root took into account more than simply colonial tasks. Within a decade he was to be Secretary of State, and in that office he was to display an awareness of the relationship of power and responsibility akin to Theodore Roosevelt's. If like nearly all his countrymen he could not yet well define it, he recognized a broadening American responsibility in international politics in general, and his reforms of the Army responded to that growing general responsibility.

When he offered his first annual report in December, 1899, he dealt with the immediate problems of pacifying the Philippines and governing Cuba and Puerto Rico, but even at that early date he addressed himself also to the larger tasks of the Army. He said it was a "fundamental proposition" that "the real object of having an army is to provide for war." He observed that the Regular Army of the United States would probably never be able to fight a war alone. Therefore he proposed to seek a reserve force that could augment the Regulars effectively in war, and to ensure that the augmentation would be effective, he proposed that the reinforcement, equipment, and operations of the war Army be planned as much as possible in peace. In the existing organization, however, no one had a responsibility to plan or could do it with any assurance that plans would be implemented. To plan would require an escape from the existing headlessness of the War Department and the Army, from the division of authority between the Secretary of War and commanding general and from the independence of the bureau chiefs. Reserves, planning, and command were the essentials of a better Army.[3]

Still deeply conscious of his lack of military knowledge, Root attempted a conscientious study of foreign military organization and American reform proposals. This study soon led him to the idea of an American general staff, which could both plan for war and ease the command problem. Root studied the volumes of the Dodge Commission report on the Spanish War. He read the English military critic Spenser Wilkinson's *The Brain of an Army*, which lauded the German general staff and urged the suitability of a modified version of it in a parliamentary democracy. He opened himself to the influence of Major William H. Carter, assistant adjutant general, a military intellectual in the manner of Emory Upton and of Uptonian views, who introduced him to Upton's *The Armies of Asia and Europe*, Michie's biography of Upton, and then finally Upton's manuscript. Root was too much the civilian and had too much common sense to swallow Upton whole, but in his need for background knowledge of American military policy he found Upton an apparent salvation and grew so enthusiastic that he eventually had the manuscript published as a government document and wrote an admiring introduction for it. Significantly, however, it was less Upton's general theme that Root praised than his more detailed reform proposals, such as the three-battalion regiment, an end to the rigid seniority system of promotion, and the general staff.[4]

Root concluded that he could end the paralysis of high command by persuading Congress to drop the anomalous office of commanding general altogether and substitute a chief of the general staff. That functionary could then be chief of staff to the Secretary of War as Schofield had been informally, thus vesting authority in the civilian deputy of the President where it constitutionally belonged, but assuring the Secretary of constant expert advice. The chief of staff need no longer be chosen through mere seniority as the commanding general had been in peacetime; Congress could permit the Secretary to appoint a man in whom he had confidence.

The change of title [Root was to say] . . . would be of little consequence were it not that the titles denote and imply in the officers bearing them the existence of widely different kinds of authority. When an officer is appointed to the position of "Commanding General of the Army" he naturally expects to command, himself, with a high degree of independence. . . . The title of Chief of Staff, on the other hand, denotes a duty to advise, inform, and assist a superior officer who has command, and to represent him, acting in his name and by his authority in carrying out his policies and securing the execution of his commands. . . .[5]

The chief of staff would head a general staff that would undertake the planning function, preparing war plans for all possible contingencies and assuring the availability of all needed materials. "Our system," said Root, "makes no adequate provision for the directing brain which every army must have, to work successfully." The general staff would provide that brain. It would be neither an "executive" nor an "administrative" body but one which would plan and then see to it that plans were executed. On the German model, the general staff would work in close harmony with a war college, a higher school for the study of war. To eliminate the stultifying isolation which had enveloped the officers of the old staff bureaus, Root foresaw a regular interchange of officers between line and staff, both the general staff and the traditional staff bureaus.[6]

Root probably developed these ideas more rapidly than he announced them. In public he moved cautiously toward the general staff proposal. The scheme was bound to provoke opposition among the old bureaus whose privileges it would probably undermine, and the bureau chiefs with their long residence in Washington and their ability to distribute contracts had often cultivated influential congressmen. Root never made altogether clear what he had in mind as the ultimate relationship between the general staff and the traditional bureaus, probably in part because he was not altogether sure and in part to soften the opposition.

Preliminary soundings demonstrated that General Miles would probably regard the new plan as an assault upon his grandeur, and unless he was handled carefully he might offer another disastrous display of insubordination. Though the public had been crying for War Department reform, there was also a danger that the general staff plan might play into the hands of Democratic anti-imperialists by giving them an excuse to talk about European-style militarism.

Whatever point his thinking had reached by this time, Root contented himself in his first annual report with a proposal for an Army war college, which he said could direct the "intellectual exercise" of the Army, acquire information, and also devise plans and advise the Commander in Chief. Early in 1900 he appointed a board of officers to explore this idea. Headed by Brigadier General William Ludlow, the board suggested that the Secretary already possessed statutory authority to establish a war college by executive order, but it shied away from Root's hint that the college might include among its duties planning in the manner of a general staff. Root accepted the Ludlow Board recommendations and created a War College Board by general orders of November 27, 1901. He charged it with the advancement of Army education and the study of military policy, but he omitted general-staff-type planning.[7]

Nevertheless, the War College Board became a forerunner of a general staff. It consisted of five officers detailed for limited terms, plus the chief of engineers, the chief of artillery, the superintendent of the Military Academy, and the commanding officer of the Fort Leavenworth school. Major General Samuel B. M. Young, destined to be the first chief of staff, was its president, and Major Carter was among the officers detailed to it. It made a study of the organization and equipment that might be necessary for armies of 25,000, 50,-000, 150,000, and 250,000 men. It examined the question of improving the Army's reserves, and it helped develop further the idea of a permanent general staff.[8]

While such studies were going on, Root also busied himself with expansion of the existing Army, improvement of its equipment, and the colonial questions for whose solution he had been called to Washington in the first place. Soon after he took office, the Filipino insurrection compelled recruiting the federal volunteer regiments to their full authorization of 35,000. During 1901, efforts to saturate the countryside with strong points from which to subdue the guerrillas multiplied the outposts in the Philippines to 502. Nothing in the experience of American officers prepared them for the frustrations they met in the islands; even the Plains Indians had waged what seemed by contrast a textbook kind of war. Alternating displays of heavy force and ostentatious generosity both failed to break the Filipino insurrection. When perplexed officers invoked harsh policing of disaffected areas and harsh methods of prying information from guerrilla prisoners, the anti-imperialists attacked the Army in full cry, imperiling Root's whole program of improvements. In the end, conquest of the insurrectionists required not only hundreds of outposts but also such devices as infiltrating the enemy forces and kidnaping their leaders. Meanwhile the Filipino insurrection would evidently persist into the indefinite future, certainly beyond the expiration of the volunteers' terms in the summer of 1901.[9]

Root had to convince Congress that colonial responsibilities, if nothing else, required a permanent military expansion. In February, 1901, Congress agreed to increase the twenty-five Regular infantry regiments to 30 and the 10 regiments of cavalry to 15. The artillery regiments, so long anomalous with their mixture of field and fortress batteries, were dissolved to make way for an artillery "corps" of 30 batteries of field artillery and 126 companies of coast artillery.[10]

With three battalions of engineers, the new authorized strength of the Regular Army was 3,820 officers and 84,799 men. Not included in this total were a regiment of Philippine Scouts and a Puerto Rico regiment. Infantry companies might vary from 65 to 146 men and cavalry from 100 to 164, but the President was to maintain maximum strength until Congress voted otherwise, and he might exceed the maximum to the extent necessary to assure an adequate flow of replacements to the islands.

The expansion created 1,135 officer vacancies in the Regular Army, not less than twenty per cent of which were to be filled within a year, and the same quantity each succeeding year until the vacancies disappeared. Men not over forty could become eligible for first and second lieutenancies by receiving certification from examining boards. Enlisted men who had served for one year might take the examinations. Mostly the commissions went to outstanding volunteers, but some went also to graduates of military colleges other than West Point, such as George C. Marshall, Jr., of the Virginia Military Institute.

The reorganization act also took a step toward Root's goal of command reform, by providing that officers henceforth assigned to staff duty should serve tours of four years and not be eligible for reappointment until they had served at least two years in the line with the regiments in which they were commissioned. After the existing staff officers retired, there would be no successors so readily able to create autonomous empires. On the other hand, neither would the supply departments be managed by men grown expert in their functions; and after World War I the War Department retreated from this fairly extreme reaction against the autonomy of the bureaus.[11]

A notable weapons development program accompanied expansion and reorganization. It produced the Model 1902 three-inch field gun, using smokeless powder, firing high-explosive and shrapnel shells, and equipped with optical sights and a recoilless carriage. With subsequent variations, this gun was virtually as good as the French 75-mm and the American Army was to adopt the latter in World War I mainly because the country could not produce enough American three-inch guns fast enough. Still more important, the Army developed the Model 1903 Springfield rifle, a bolt-action magazine rifle which gave excellent service to the eve of World War II.[12]

In the administration of the new island dependencies, Root was fulfilling McKinley's high expectations. The first occupation commander in Cuba, appointed under the Alger regime, was Major General John R. Brooke, who initiated all the reforms in orderliness and sanitation for which the Cuban occupation was to be famous, and who deserved more credit that he has ever received. Brooke, however, was old and unassertive, and from the beginning public attention focused upon his subordinate in Oriente province, Leonard Wood, Roosevelt's colleague in the Rough Riders and a master of self-advertisement. Brooke was soon willing to step down, his willingness stimulated by the personality of the Oriente commander, and Root inevitably named Wood in his stead. Since Wood possessed uncommon abilities to accompany uncommon ambition, the choice was a good one. Perhaps the achievements of the American occupation were less than Root and Wood thought at the time, since like most North Americans the Secretary and the general took an indulgently paternalistic view of the islanders, and at worst American soldiers comported themselves with an arrogance toward colored colonials which bred lasting resentments. Still, the Americans surprised the Cubans and most of the rest of the world by actually pulling out when the Cubans seemed reasonably ready to govern themselves. In the meantime the Foraker Act imposed a noteworthy restraint upon American business penetration of the island (beyond anything the Cuban government itself would do before Fidel Castro), and the Army left its mark mainly in the form of schools, clean streets, and general public sanitation. In Puerto Rico and those parts of the Philippines where it was possible, the Army introduced American authority with a similar display of the better qualities of turn-of-the-century Western expansionism.[13]

As late as his annual message of 1901, Root's references to the general staff idea continued to be oblique. The War College Board went as far toward a general staff as existing law permitted, he said, and he urged further legislation without being specific about his desires. By February, 1902, he at last felt ready to have a general staff bill introduced. But his patient preparation of a path for it proved not yet enough. The staff bureaus mobilized their Congressional influence to cripple it, and General Miles not only felt himself insulted by it but conducted his campaign of opposition in such a fashion as to demonstrate that, if he was not especially intelligent, he could be shrewd and clever. He had resisted efforts by Root to consolidate Army posts throughout the country, and thereby he won the gratitude of congressmen who did not want to see an end to the business brought to their bailiwicks by scattered garrisons. He had visited the Philippines and issued a report that passed ammunition to those who claimed the Army was guilty of excessive brutality; thus he prepared a group suspicious of any improvement in the Army to align themselves with him. When he appeared before the Senate Military Affairs Committee to testify on the general staff bill, he carefully polished his Civil War record to cultivate the war veterans who dominated the committee. His principal overt line of attack against the general staff was that it was a plan most suitable for Old World monarchies.

Root astutely brought Lieutenant General John M. Schofield before the Senate Committee to try to offset Miles, Schofield bearing a war record more impressive than Miles's own. Major General Wesley Merritt, a young division commander of cavalry at the close of the Civil War and later commander of the VIII Corps in the Philippines, also brought a distinguished war record to the support of the general staff. Root himself at last devoted much of his annual report at the close of 1902 to an exposition and defense of the plan. This barrage combined with the evident weakness of the existing command system finally persuaded Congress. General Dodge had to be called on for some diligent lobbying, at which he was an old hand, and certain peripheral reforms in the staff bureaus had to be abandoned. But on February 14, 1903, Congress voted to establish a General Staff Corps, to come into existence August 15, 1903, one week after the retirement of General Miles.[14]

When the General Staff Corps appeared, the War College Board expired and gave way to an Army War College associated with the General Staff and also serving as capstone of an expanded military education system on which Root had already done much work. Before the year was over, Root also secured the participation of the Navy Department in a Joint Army and Navy Board to initiate formal cooperation and joint planning between the two services.[15]

By the time Congress passed the general staff bill, it had also reached agreement with Root on an improved reserve program, under the Militia Act of January 21, 1903, usually called the Dick Act.

Root found his professional advisers, Major Carter among the most vocal of them, eager to seize his influence to effect the closest feasible approximation of an Uptonian reserve system, a permanent federal volunteer reserve along the lines of the United States volunteer regiments of 1899. Their plan would relegate the organized militia of the states to third-line status, or perhaps to being merely a reservoir of manpower for the federal reserve. Root was sympathetic, but it was obvious that whatever his convictions he had no prestige sufficient to install such a plan without compromise; the National Guard retained too much vitality, fortified by its performance in Puerto Rico and the Philippines.[16]

Promptly upon the mustering out of most of the Spanish War volunteers in 1898, those volunteers had reorganized themselves into the National Guard regiments that they had mainly comprised. By the time Root became Secretary of War, the prewar National Guard formations were generally reconstituted and active, and once again it became impossible to ignore the National Guard if only because it was a reserve force in being, while any other kind of reserve was only hypothetical.

After Emory Upton's harsh comments on the short-service provisions of the Militia Acts of 1792 and 1795, it may seem strange that the War Department now proposed a three-month limit on the federal service of National Guard regiments. The explanation seems to be that the professionals tried to make their inevitable compromise with the Guard by agreeing to use the state formations—but only as a source of manpower, the formations themselves to lose their identity after three months' service. But Congressman Charles W. Dick of Ohio, acting as principal liaison between the National Guard Association and the Congressional military committees, was able to insist upon greater recognition for the Guard. As Root himself came into contact with Dick and representatives of the National Guard during the effort to frame an acceptable bill, his own tolerance for the Guard increased. In the end, Root and Dick were the principal architects of a fundamental revision of the militia laws, but one which preserved most of the historic state militia system. They retained a proven source of reserve manpower but promised a better trained militia more carefully coordinated with the Regular Army.[17]

The Dick Act struck at the confusion that had always surrounded the very word "militia," owing to its indiscriminate use to designate both the whole military manpower potential of the country and the organized military companies of the states. The law retained the principle of a universal military obligation, inherited from England by the first colonies. But it discarded the general enrollment and personal weapons provisions of the old militia laws, which had fallen into disuse anyway. All the able-bodied manpower of the states was declared to constitute the "Reserve Militia." If in this the Dick Act did no more than assert a principle, the preservation of the principle proved highly important during the coming world wars.

The National Guard companies and regiments were designated the "Organized Militia." Henceforth, to enhance the usefulness of the Organized Militia as a reserve for the Regular Army, the United States was to issue arms and equipment to the National Guard without charge. Annual Congressional appropriations which previously had been restricted to the purchase of arms and certain specific equipment might now be used to buy military stores generally. To maintain its status and its federal aid, a National Guard unit had to hold at least twenty-four drills or target-practice periods a year, plus a summer encampment of not less than five days in the field. The

Guard units were to undergo periodic inspection by Regular as well
as Guard officers. The Regular Army was to detail officers to the
states to instruct the Guard. Occasional joint maneuvers of Regular
and Guard formations had been held informally since the 1880's;
now Guardsmen were to receive federal pay and subsistence when
on joint maneuvers with the Regular Army. Guard officers became
eligible to attend Army schools at Fort Leavenworth or the Army
War College, and there also they might receive federal pay and subsistence.

Though not limited to merely three months, the federal service of
National Guard units was limited by the Dick Act to nine months.
However, the Dick Act provided, following the terms of the Spanish
War Act of April 22, 1898, that at the end of the nine months a
National Guard organization might volunteer as a unit for federal
service, whereupon the organization was to be accepted as a unit
with its own officers.

When the Militia Act of 1792 was drawn, the Regular Army had
been an infant, and no clear program of coordination between it and
the militia had been possible, for that and other reasons. The Dick
Act now laid a foundation for cooperation of a continually improving kind between the Regular Army and the only reserve force that
in 1903 was feasible.[18]

It was principally as a foundation for continued future improvement that Elihu Root's organizational reforms proved to serve.
Newton D. Baker, Secretary of War during World War I, was to
pay tribute to the Root reforms as indispensable to the prosecution
of that war, but at least to the eve of the war the Root reforms
remained more a promise than a fruition.

The General Staff Act gave to the General Staff Corps a chief of
staff, two other general officers, and forty-two junior officers. When
the men detailed to these positions assembled, one of them later
confessed, most of them had not the slightest idea what a general staff
was supposed to do. Their notion of staff work tended toward the
kind of specialized technical activities that had occupied the old staff
bureaus and for which those bureaus still existed. Regulations based
upon the General Staff Act attempted to clarify the duties of the staff
by means of a division of functions. They called for a War Department General Staff and the General Staff serving with the troops.
The War Department General Staff was to consist of a First Division,
dealing with administrative matters; a Second Division, responsible
for gathering military information; and a Third Division, concerned
with military education and technical matters. Root had held it essential to his notion of the general staff as "the brain of an army"

that the general staff should not entangle itself in the administration of the Army and should *plan* and *direct* but not *operate*. To that end he strengthened the traditional bureau chiefly concerned with administration, the Adjutant General's Department, by consolidating it with the Record and Pension Office. But the result of leaving administration to the old bureaus was to place the General Staff Corps in a kind of lofty vacuum, while the traditional staff bureaus remained almost as autonomous as before.[19]

To the extent that the Root reforms immediately centralized Army administration, the centralization occurred mainly in the strengthened Adjutant General's Department. There the able Henry C. Corbin, who had already made himself the most powerful professional soldier in the Army during the Spanish War, gave way in 1904 to Major General Fred C. Ainsworth. Ainsworth was an even more efficient administrator than Corbin, if perhaps less wisely able; he was also ambitious and an intriguer, and he carefully played upon Root's desire that the General Staff avoid administrative burdens to see to it that the General Staff Act omitted the Record and Pension Office from the jurisdiction of the chief of staff and made it possible for future statutes to assign increasing duties to that office.[20]

The first chiefs of staff displayed considerable uncertainty, for good reason, about how they could control and direct the Army and the staff bureaus without involving themselves in administration. Adjutant General Ainsworth pressed the natural tendencies of this situation as hard as he could while still being quiet and unobtrusive. Direction and control tended to follow administration into the Adjutant General's Office. The General Staff Corps drifted farther into limbo, its Third Division beginning to undertake some mobilization planning but to no especially visible purpose. It had inherited one of the old weaknesses of the commanding general vis-à-vis the staff bureaus: the bureaus administered the Army *now*; the General Staff Corps, like the commanding general before it, was important for a war that only *might* happen. Also, while the officers of the General Staff Corps served four-year tours of duty, the system of rotation between staff and line did not yet touch the bureau chiefs whose tenure antedated the Root reforms; Ainsworth was untouchable by virtue of having headed the Record and Pension Office before its consolidation with the Adjutant General's Department. With all these circumstances the adjutant general was well on his way to reviving the old anomalies of commanding general versus Secretary of War under new names, but with the old vitiation of planning and command.

The Dick Act did not work altogether happily either. Many Guard organizations did display a new vitality and discipline in response to

the grant of recognition and responsibilities, and some of them attracted enough public attention to secure grants from the states to
build impressive armories. But they found that despite the Dick Act,
the War Department was slow to send them up-to-date arms and
equipment. Memories of their black-powder Springfields of the Spanish War lingered on—indeed, in some organizations the Springfields
themselves did, until 1905. By the time all Guard units finally received Krag-Jorgensens, the 1903 Springfield had already replaced
the Krag among the Regulars. The War Department urged the states
to create balanced Guard divisions including cavalry and artillery as
well as infantry, but neither the federal government not the states
appropriated the funds necessary to finance the more expensive specialized arms. The National Guard remained almost entirely infantry, without their own supporting units. Absenteeism from Guard
drills tended to fall off gradually after 1903, but when Regular inspectors reported on Guard visitations, they tended to draw a discouraging picture. In part, of course, it was natural and necessary
that inspection reports should have been mainly critical; but the reports also betrayed a continued Regular Army animus toward the
Guard. Such progress as the Guard did achieve often annoyed the
Uptonians, for they did not believe that the progress could ever be
sufficient, and they feared it might encourage more reliance on the
Guard.[21]

As if to confirm such fears, in 1908 the friends of the National
Guard secured certain modifications of the Dick Act. First, the nine-
month limitation disappeared from the National Guard's federal
service. The President was to call up the Guard before asking for
other volunteers, and he was to specify the duration of the Guard's
service, provided he did not prolong an individual's term of enlistment. Second, and more important, Congress recognized the Guard
as a reserve for all wars, foreign and domestic, by stating that the
Organized Militia could be called into federal service "either within
or without the Territory of the United States." Emory Upton and
his followers consistently attempted to deprecate the state militia
by pointing to the refusal of the New York militia to cross the Niagara frontier during the War of 1812 and citing the Constitution's
failure to mention foreign service as one of the activities for which
the President could call upon the militia. Congress had now undermined that argument by explicitly authorizing militia service outside
the United States.

But was the new law constitutional? The Judge Advocate's Department of the Army soon sought an opinion on the subject from
the Attorney General, assisting him with material that suggested it
was not. If the National Guard was to be removed from any impor-

tant place in the country's military calculations, it must be proven undependable for foreign wars. In 1912 the Attorney General obliged with an opinion following the judge advocate general's suggestions, asserting that the militia could not constitutionally be obliged to perform military service outside the United States.[22]

Of his organizational innovations, only Root's improved military school system enjoyed conspicuous success from the beginning. Root's purpose here was to incorporate the older service schools and the Army War College into a coherent system. He had discovered that one-third of the officers of the Regular Army possessed no formal military education, and he believed that the Military Academy and the piecemeal schools of application could not alone equip the officers for their likely responsibilities either in the colonies or in the growing world prominence of the United States. On November 27, 1901, War Department general orders announced a reorganization of the Army's schools.

Henceforth each military post of any size was to have a school for the instruction of officers in a prescribed course of theory and practice. The men who showed special promise in the post schools were to be sent on to advanced schools of the various arms and services. These schools grew out of the ones already existing but underwent various permutations under both Root and his immediate successors. By 1910 they had evolved into the Army Service Schools at Fort Leavenworth, namely the Army School of the Line (once the Infantry and Cavalry School), the Signal School, the Army Field Engineer School, and the Army Field Service and Correspondence School for Medical Officers; plus the Mounted School at Fort Riley, the Coast Artillery School at Fort Monroe, the Engineer School at Washington, and the Medical School also at Washington. At Fort Leavenworth the old Infantry and Cavalry School had also given birth to a Staff College. The Army War College in Washington capped the system.

The War College did not so much provide academic instruction as it encouraged the officer in the study of war and of the application of his previously acquired knowledge. It worked in close cooperation with the Third Division and with a later War College Division of the General Staff, with officers assigned to the War College and the General Staff cooperating in studies that eventually included with increasing frequency mobilization planning as envisioned by Root. An officer who passed through the Army School of the Line, the Staff College, and the Army War College, or even simply the first two, was to be thoroughly prepared, Root hoped, to assume major command assignments. The other schools supplemented these three schools with more specialized training.

The schools could hardly be better than their instructors, and in Root's time the instructors still reflected much of the old Indian-fighting Army. At the post schools, instruction was likely to emphasize rote learning, and apt to concern itself with the externals of military discipline and administration, in such a way as to nurture a spit-and-polish Army but not necessarily an effective one. The curriculum of the higher schools suffered similar limitations. Nevertheless, the Fort Leavenworth schools prospered, for they had the advantage of instruction and guidance by three remarkable teachers. Arthur L. Wagner, who had cultivated high standards of military scholarship and stimulating teaching at the Infantry and Cavalry School, continued at Fort Leavenworth until 1904, when he was transferred to Washington, where he spent the last year of his life at the War College. His leadership at the Fort Leavenworth schools passed to J. Franklin Bell, who had been a lieutenant when the Spanish War broke out but who earned his brigadier's star by 1901 and was to be chief of staff by 1906. Bell (USMA, 1878) was commandant of the General Service and Staff College, one of the mutations of the original school, from 1903 to 1906. An enthusiastic champion of the schools against the indifference and skepticism of many older officers, Bell retained a close interest in them when he moved to the General Staff. Meanwhile Major John F. Morrison, (USMA 1881), took an instructorship in tactics at the Army School of the Line and introduced a method of teaching through map problems that he borrowed from the French.

Morrison required students to study tactical problems based mainly upon the French army's highly detailed maps of France's military frontier. Solutions were presented for criticism by the class, and a critique by the instructor finished each class session. "His problems were short and always contained a knockout if you failed to recognize the principle involved in meeting the situation," George C. Marshall said.[23] The best testimony to the quality of the instructors at Root's school system was perhaps their ability to select as coming men young officers who were to emerge as the leading American commanders forty years later in World War II; for Marshall, regulations were waived to permit his serving as instructor in the School of the Line while still a lieutenant.[24]

Elihu Root retired from the War Department in 1904. By then the Philippine insurrection was fading, the government of Cuba had been turned over to the inhabitants, and a workable colonial administration was functioning in Puerto Rico and the Philippines. The purposes for which Root had accepted the Secretaryship were accomplished, and the outlines of his military reform program were complete as well. Mrs. Root disliked the official social life of Washington, and the Secretary decided he could now accede in good conscience to her desire to leave. President Theodore Roosevelt, who had supported Root in carrying out the work begun under McKinley, gave the War Department to William Howard Taft, another lawyer and erstwhile civilian high commissioner in the Philippines.

Merely as an administrator, Taft may have had talents greater than Root's. But unlike Root, Taft remained interested mainly in the colonial problems of the War Department. He did not push forward the reform of the Army whose foundation Root had constructed; and since Root had been able to do little more than provide a foundation, here the Army reforms rested. Sometimes indeed there was retrogression; it was during the Taft years that Adjutant General Ainsworth built his bureau into a formidable rival of the General Staff.[25]

The next major advances in Army reform were ventured by a man who generated controversy as naturally as Root commanded respect. In part controversy was bound to attend the next advances, since they must involve a showdown between the General Staff and the Adjutant General's Department. But because he was the kind of man he was, Leonard Wood would have infuriated much of the Army if he had done no more than urge that infantrymen go on carrying rifles.

Wood became chief of staff in July, 1910. Part of his trouble was that he reached the post via an utterly unorthodox route. He was a graduate not of the Military Academy but of the Harvard Medical School. He had become a civilian contract surgeon with the Army because his means did not permit the independent struggle for practice more customary among physicians. As was common in the late nineteenth century, he moved eventually from contract status to a commission in the Medical Corps. Yet he had entered the Army through the back door; and although he distinguished himself in the campaign against Geronimo, it was decidedly through the back door that he moved into the line of the Army, receiving the colonelcy of the Rough Riders through his friendship with certain prominent Republican politicians and especially with Theodore Roosevelt.[26]

Still, it was not his unusual approach to high rank alone that made Leonard Wood an outsider to the military professionals who must cooperate in any further Army reforms. By curious happenstance, Adjutant General Ainsworth, who was to be Wood's leading rival, had come up by almost the same unusual route. He too had begun as a contract surgeon and had gone on to a commission in the Medical Corps. In fact, while Wood at least had fought in Cuba, Ainsworth had never seen action but had become chief of the Record and Pension Division of the Medical Bureau and had moved gradually to the

Adjutant General's Office on the strength of a flair for making complex records orderly and serviceable. But the old professionals of the Army did not resent Ainsworth as they resented Wood, and even those who disagreed with Ainsworth when he battled Wood seem to have felt a certain sympathy for him. Wood was overtly a political soldier as Ainsworth was not, a throwback to the Winfield Scott-type generals of the era before professionalism inoculated the officer corps against political involvements. But neither did that alone explain widespread resentment of Wood, since Ainsworth too was an uncommonly diligent cultivator of Congressional friendships.

Something more than the pattern of his career or his Republican partisanship made Leonard Wood a natural storm center to the Army. The cynical might say that, for the Army, he was too intelligent in an outspoken, obvious, and even scintillating way; he was likely to make the ordinary officer feel uncomfortable. There is some substance to that view. But the real nub of it was probably that Wood's forte was not soldiering but showmanship, and showmanship of a special kind, since there are varieties of it that blend well with a military career. Leonard Wood was a military evangelist. When he had possessed himself of a military truth, his impulse was to carry the good news not simply to his brother officers or to the War Department but to the public at large, relying on the ability to stir public enthusiasms which he knew he possessed. Whenever another officer got in Wood's way, Wood's conduct suggested that his antagonist had better remember the fate of old General Brooke, into whose place as chief of the Cuban occupation Wood had stepped by winning the newspapers and the public to his side against his commanding officer.[27]

Despite the nature of his background, Wood became chief of staff more intent than most of his more conventionally military colleagues in his dedication to the principle that the purpose of an army is to be ready to wage war, both in order to deter some wars and to fight those that cannot be avoided. He was not only a personal and political friend of Theodore Roosevelt, but he shared the Rooseveltian notions about the world power of the United States. He believed that the United States Army must be ready to fight a war with anybody, any potential enemy. With him and with Roosevelt this conviction was colored by somewhat fantastic visions of German troops landing in the Caribbean, based upon the obstreperous conduct of the German Empire during the past decade. With both, the conviction was also rooted soundly if vaguely in the belief that a nation of the wealth and power of the United States could not remain indefinitely and irresponsibly aloof from any major conflict that might erupt among the great powers.[28]

Root, a somewhat more restrained sharer in these views, had made the beginning toward fitting the Army for readiness to meet any adversary. Wood was determined to go most or preferably all of the way. He was a less patient man than Root and had large personal ambitions, including the Presidency; he apparently thought that to transform the Army into one that could hold its own in any conflict might open the White House doors. So he proposed to assemble the troops from their scattered Indian-war garrisons into a pattern that would have some connection with mobilization plans. He proposed to maneuver the troops in large bodies, at least in division strength. He proposed to improve the General Staff, to awaken it from quiescence and permit it to carry out the planning and coordinating functions that Root had envisioned for it. He was developing ideas about the reconciliation of a mass army and American democracy, to make available the ready reserve strength that would obviously be necessary if the Army was to prepare itself for any possible foe. But if he was to realize any of his grand designs, he had first to establish himself, the chief of staff, as the true professional head of the Army.

To accomplish that object required a descent from grand designs to the most petty of bureaucratic politics. For it was by controlling the day-to-day administration of the Army, however petty the details, that the special staff bureaus and especially the Adjutant General's Department had maintained their grip upon the Army itself. It was on the level of the routine and the mundane that Adjutant General Ainsworth operated, for after all, it was on that level that the Army mainly lived in peacetime. It was by fending off General Staff incursions into the day-to-day peacetime life of the Army that the staff bureaus restricted the General Staff to a lofty vacuum, and they accomplished the purpose by such small devices as refusing to pay an officer transferred to a new station by authority of the General Staff alone. On that level the power of the staff bureaus rested, and on that level Wood would have to combat them, and especially their leader Ainsworth.

The muster-roll question was to prove crucial between Wood and Ainsworth, and it was typical of the sort of issue on which Wood's grand designs had to hang. In accord with the characteristic Progressive Era desire for governmental efficiency, Congress authorized the President to establish a Committee on Economy and Efficiency to investigate the executive departments. The committee included the War Department among its primary objects of interest, and the department appointed General Ainsworth president of an investigating board of its own to cooperate with the committee. The Ainsworth Board solicited suggestions from department, post, and regimental commanders throughout the Army for improving administrative efficiency.

Among the recommendations received was one closely affecting the Adjutant General's Department. It called for a diminution of the paper work of the Army through consolidation of the muster rolls, containing service biographies of all personnel, with the returns of commands and the payrolls. The Ainsworth Board disapproved this recommendation, Ainsworth asserting that the separation of returns of commands from muster rolls was necessary to distinguish the status and history of units from the status and history of individuals. But Wood thought the recommendation a sensible one, and he had the General Staff take it and other recommendations repugnant to Ainsworth under further study. When Wood thus encroached upon the direct concerns of the Adjutant General's Department, the latent conflict between him and Ainsworth became an open and public one.

Wood next moved into direct supervision of the recruiting service, hitherto left to the adjutant general. He intervened in Military Academy matters previously in the latter's domain. Ainsworth retaliated by turning to Congress. One of his sources of strength was the ability to be of service to congressmen through his control of the pension records. He had cultivated powerful Congressional friends, who included Representative James Hay of Virginia, chairman of the House Military Committee after the Democrats won the elections of 1910. Hay had good partisan reasons for disliking Wood, and he now agreed to introduce a bill suggested by Ainsworth that would merge the General Staff with the Adjutant General's and Inspector General's Departments. The bill was so drawn as to ensure that Ainsworth would become chief of staff in the consolidated department. Since the General Staff had little opportunity to influence Congress, and congressmen tended to suspect it as an instrument of militarism, the prospects of the bill were not altogether bleak.

Wood turned to the executive branch to try to offset Ainsworth's influence with Congress. He suggested to Taft, now President, and Secretary of War Jacob M. Dickinson, that Ainsworth was a troublemaker and ought to be sent on an inspection trip, if not retired altogether. Neither Dickinson nor Taft found the ebullient Wood congenial, for reasons related to Taft's growing disenchantment with Roosevelt; but at this juncture Dickinson resigned and the War Department went to Henry L. Stimson, a protégé of Root in the legal profession and like Root a moderate Rooseveltian in military and foreign policy. Stimson and Wood were already acquainted, both were friends of Roosevelt, and Wood found the prospects of executive support newly encouraging.

In these circumstances Wood sent Ainsworth a restricted list of officers from whom the adjutant general was to select commanders of recruiting depots. He thus trespassed again on Ainsworth's customary prerogatives, and Ainsworth responded with unwise indignation. He objected to the officers nominated by Wood on the ground that they lacked the delicate combination of military and civil qualities needed in recruiting officers, and also on the ground that the chief of staff evidently desired to replace two of the present recruiters merely because they had favored Ainsworth's rather than Wood's views on the proper length of the enlistment period. Wood naturally passed this insubordinate reply on to Stimson, with appropriately acid comments on the effrontery of questioning the motives of one's superior officer. He also insisted that Ainsworth indeed was his subordinate, drawing the essential issue:

It is specifically provided in law that the Chief of Staff, under the direction of the Secretary of War, shall have supervision over The Adjutant General's Department and over all troops of the line and staff corps. . . . For him [the adjutant general] to set up standards of his own and to insist upon working for them without regard to the policy and wishes of his superiors is contrary to good order and military discipline. It was to prevent this that . . . Congress created the General Staff and made the office of the Chief of Staff the coordinating and supervisory bureau of the War Department.[29]

Stimson informed Ainsworth that he was withholding decision concerning one of Wood's recruiting officer assignments but had approved the others, and that he regretted and reprobated certain passages of Ainsworth's letter. Stimson also came to Wood's support in hearings before Congressman Hay's Military Committee on the proposed staff department consolidation and other matters of Army reorganization; the hand of Ainsworth's Congressional friends was in some measure restrained. To cap the adjutant general's discomfiture the Secretary of War presently directed him to state in detail any objections he might have to the General Staff's recommendations for consolidating the muster rolls with the company returns and with a descriptive list that would follow the soldier through his service. The implication was that Stimson was about to take Wood's view of the muster-roll question.

For three weeks Ainsworth failed to answer. Wood sent him a note prodding him on behalf of the Secretary. Still Ainsworth did nothing, and another three weeks passed. Wood sent him another reminder. Thereupon Ainsworth exploded. In a letter of February 3, 1912, he not only expressed those reasons for retaining the muster rolls that deserved consideration—including the fact that they had a recognized place in statute law—but also fulminated against those officers

so unmindful of consequences, or so uninformed as to the needs of the Government and the public with regard to the matter in question, as seriously to propose to abolish one of the most important, if not the most important, of all the records of the War Department. However, the [my] statement is submitted in the confident expectation that when other, if not wiser, counsels shall prevail, and after experience with the proposed plan or any similar plan shall have shown the inevitable evil effects thereof, this statement will receive the consideration that may not be given to it now.[30]

Wood could not have hoped for the adjutant general to play more directly into his hands. Stimson asked Judge Advocate General Enoch Crowder "whether the Army was ready to stand for the kind of language" Ainsworth had employed to his superiors, and Crowder had to agree that it could not. Stimson wanted a court-martial. Crowder held out merely for "administrative punishment." After consulting with Root and President Taft and assuring himself of their support, Stimson relieved Ainsworth from active duty. He told the President it was "good riddance."[31]

Ainsworth was unwilling to admit defeat. He continued to use his considerable influence with Congress to try to pull the teeth of the General Staff, all the way to the country's entrance into World War I. With his friend Congressman Hay he attached riders to the 1913 military appropriation bill that would have assigned thirteen officers from the Adjutant General's Office permanently to the General Staff and would have removed Wood from his office. It took considerable persuasion from Stimson to bring Taft to veto two successive appropriation bills and thus persuade Congress to drop the matter.[32]

The enemies of the General Staff did secure a reduction of the number of General Staff officers from forty-five to thirty-six. They also persuaded Congress to pass the "Manchu Law" of August, 1912, which stiffened the restrictions on detached service such as General Staff duty; now line officers below the rank of major could not in time of peace be on detached service unless they had spent two of the preceding six years with the regiment to which they were assigned.[33]

Beyond such difficulties the dismissal of Ainsworth for insubordination by no means settled the legal status of the General Staff vis-à-vis the bureaus. Nevertheless, the dismissal was a turning point in the vexed history of the Army's command. Ainsworth had led the resistance to the General Staff for a decade, and when Wood was able to remove him from the scene he scored a moral triumph for the

General Staff which henceforth had to give the bureau chiefs pause. The center of gravity of the War Department shifted from the bureaus to the General Staff. Having grasped the ascendancy, the General Staff could now move on to ensure and consolidate its leadership.

It is not so often remarked that the removal of Ainsworth was a triumph for the Secretary of War almost as much as for the General Staff. It took courage for Stimson to fly in the face of Ainsworth's Congressional influence, especially at a time when the Republican party was in disarray and Stimson, knowing Taft, could foresee the reluctance with which the President would support him when Ainsworth mounted his Congressional counterattack. But Stimson took the step because he was a Secretary of War in the image of Root, and Stimson's very presence in the War Department demonstrated President Taft's acceptance of the new importance of the department despite his misgivings in the Ainsworth affair and the inertia that had marked his own tenure as Secretary. The day when the cabinet seat for war could be regarded simply as a political reward had passed. Hitherto Calhoun, Stanton, and Root had stood virtually alone as outstanding Secretaries of War; but Stimson could lay claim to membership in their circle, and other Secretaries of stature were soon to follow. Even Presidents reluctant to take the Rooseveltian path to world power sensed the need for strong and able leadership in the War Department. The rise of the new partnership of Secretary of War and chief of staff made strong and able leadership possible.

Before the discomfiture of Ainsworth, General Wood had already moved to strengthen the General Staff through internal reform. He knew that weakness of the staff when he came to it lay partly in its own continued lack of purpose and direction. In 1911 he established a more meaningful division of labor in the staff by inaugurating Mobile Army, Coast Artillery, Militia, and War College Divisions. The first three divisions could deal with the principal segments of mobilization planning; the War College Division, in partnership with the War College, became the over-all planning agency for war and could bring together the work of the other divisions. Out of its deliberations came an outline of mobilization procedure in 1911 and general statements of manpower policy in 1912 and 1913.[34]

Wood was just as much interested in the readiness of the troops themselves. Unfortunately, in pursuing this interest he gave a trump card to Ainsworth, since he antagonized many congressmen by trying to eliminate small military posts inherited from the Indian wars but now useless, and to rearrange the Army in larger garrisons that would improve training procedures and the speed of assembly. In

1911 the average garrison comprised less than a battalion. Every Secretary of War of even moderate competence since the 1880's had attempted to do something about the "hitching post" forts. But in the face of Congressional fondness for outposts that put money into the pockets of constituents, Wood and Stimson accomplished little more improvement than their predecessors.[35]

If Wood and Stimson could not reduce the number of permanent posts, they could at least form temporary troop concentrations and improve the Army's organization on paper. When Stimson took office, Wood had already embarked on the unprecedented experiment of assembling a whole division in peacetime. The "Maneuver Division" formed around San Antonio beginning in March, 1911, the onset of the Mexican Revolution providing a convenient pretext for the effort. It took almost ninety days to concentrate fewer than 13,000 troops, to make a division that was both understrength in terms of the latest tables of organization and an organizational hodgepodge at that. Regiments throughout the country had to be skeletonized to do even that much. Officers with a knowledge of European armies blushed to imagine what the polite European military observers must be thinking.

But at least the division gave officers a tentative experience in handling large bodies of men, and especially it afforded interesting tests of new Signal Corps equipment, including telephones, wireless communications devices, and "aeroplanes" for observation and messenger service. The chief signal officer said of the latter innovation:

If there was any doubt in the minds of individuals of this command as to the utility of the aeroplane for military purposes, that doubt has been removed by aeronautical work done in this division.[36]

Meanwhile, the very shortcomings of the Maneuver Division served the purposes of the high command, permitting Wood to write in *McClure's* that the division "demonstrated conclusively our helplessness to meet with trained troops any sudden emergency," while Stimson wrote in similar vein in the *Independent*.[37]

The Secretary and the chief of staff followed up by instructing the War College to prepare a plan for the tactical reorganization of the Army, to create a permanent divisional organization. If the "hitching post" forts could not be abolished, future concentrations might be facilitated by planning the assignments of the scattered garrisons, and division commanders might coordinate the training of all their units. If divisions were created on paper, Congress might at least agree to their occasional assembly for maneuvers. Early in 1913 Stimson brought together all the general officers who were within the continental United States to present the War Department plan to them. Some of the older ones still hesitated before so drastic a departure from what they knew, but Stimson put his experience as a barrister to good use and persuaded them of the wisdom of creating the first peacetime tactical units larger than a regiment in the Army's history: four divisions.[38]

Events soon tested and confirmed that wisdom, for within a few weeks the coup against Mexican President Francisco Madero by General Victoriano Huerta touched off a spreading civil war that might lap across the Rio Grande. President Taft asked Stimson whether a strong force could quickly supplement the Army's border patrols, and Stimson was able to reply that he could accomplish it with "only a single order." On February 24, 1913, he ordered the mobilization of the 2nd Division under Brigadier General Frederick Funston at Texas City and Galveston. He dispatched only five lines to do it, compared with scores of orders that had been necessary to gather the Maneuver Division.[39]

Leonard Wood's program hardly stopped, however, with the ascendancy of the Secretary and the chief of staff and the mobilization of a single division on the Mexican border. He was among those officers embarrassed by the spectacle that the Maneuver Division had offered to European observers, for the standards by which he measured military power were European standards. To prepare the nation for responsibilities that might involve war with a first-class power, improving the command and organization of the Regular Army was only a beginning: the great question remained that of an effective reserve.

Emory Upton's pessimism about the American military future had stemmed from his observation of Germany's application of high military expertise and efficiency to a mass cadre-conscript army, in which all the manpower of the nation could be conscripted, trained, and absorbed into a thoroughly professional cadre. By conscripting men for relatively short periods of active duty and longer periods in reserve formations, the Prussians had learned to combine mass numbers with an impressive measure of professional military quality. They had dramatically demonstrated the lethal strength of the combination against Austria and France. Thereupon Germany's European neighbors, whose traditions permitted them to do so and whose locations seemed to require it, heeded their local Emory Uptons and copied the German plan. The Germans responded by enforcing conscription more stringently and drawing their mobilization plans still more finely, with their neighbors again attempting to copy them in turn.

As a result of this process, by the time Leonard Wood contemplated an American Army of European dimensions and standards, the European models had grown much more frightening than they were when they caused Upton to despair. The principal continental military rivals, the Germans and the French, were beginning the final peacetime enlargements and improvements which would give them the eighty-seven and sixty-two divisions, respectively, with which they went to war in 1914. The German army required active service of two years and maintained a peacetime army of about 800,000 men. Calling in the reserves of men recently trained would yield about 1,750,000 first-line troops, with millions more of second-class "territorial" troops behind them. The French, with their smaller population, required three years' active service, to give them a peacetime army which also numbered about 800,000. Their reserves gave them a first-line strength of about 1,500,000.[40]

The growth of such military leviathans had caused a deepening of Emory Upton's pessimism among many American officers during the years preceding Leonard Wood's tour as chief of staff. The Root reforms were encouraging, but they could not remedy the immense disparity in numbers of trained men between the United States and the European powers. So, despite the Root reforms, the first years of the twentieth century saw the mood of many of the young contributors to the professional journals at its darkest. *The Army and Navy Journal* said editorially:

We are ruled by an arbitrary and irresponsible popular opinion which, through a certain sublimated optimism which is at once benevolent and baleful, treats military service as inconsequential and renders it well-nigh impossible to maintain that vigorous discipline which is indispensable to an effective army.

Captain Matthew F. Steele, one of the better teachers at the Fort Leavenworth schools and the author of *American Campaigns*, remarking on a prize essay contest that posed the question how democracy could be effectually utilized for military purposes, said that "There is no answer."[41]

Such despair had to follow from the Uptonian premise that only soldiers as thoroughly trained as the Europeans, with their two years or more of active duty and their long hitches in the reserves, could fight effectively against a European army. But Leonard Wood was a man of too buoyant a nature to wallow in Uptonian despair. If to accept what had become the conventional thinking of the Army and echo the dicta of Emory Upton was to surrender to predictions of a hopeless military future for the United States, Leonard Wood was sufficiently unconventional to seek a new line of thought.

The nub of the question was still the quality of the citizen soldier. The United States clearly was not about to adopt a military training program of the European type, and so the country would have to go to war with a citizen army. Upton and his disciples insisted that history proved that the citizen could not be an effective soldier without prolonged training with a cadre of professionals, followed by assimilation into the professional cadre in time of war. This was the German method. Wood decided that to lift the Army from Uptonian despair he must reject Upton's view of the requirements for making a citizen soldier an effective soldier. He found the Uptonians of the Army insisting that at least two years was necessary to the making of a soldier, and even that was not really enough. Wood replied that he could train a soldier in six months.[42]

If he could do that, then the United States could quickly mobilize an army capable of facing a first-class power—if only Congress would accept a minimal program of training and organization in peacetime. Wood believed that some peacetime military training of the citizenry was essential; but unlike Upton he recognized that anything to be achieved must be tailored to the national habits and traditions:

We must also build up a system under which officers and men for our citizen soldiery can be trained with the minimum of interference with their educational or industrial careers, under conditions which will permit the accomplishment of their training during the period of youth, and once this is accomplished will permit their return to their normal occupations with the minimum of delay.[43]

This reasoning might well have led Wood into a reserve army plan that would make considerable use of the existing and traditional National Guard, which fitted so well the requirements he described. But the influence of Upton upon American military thought was so pervasive that Wood could not altogether escape it. In his writings and speeches on behalf of an enlarged citizen reserve he was to continue to recommend the reading of Upton even when he had rejected one of the most basic Uptonian premises, the inadequacy of the citizen soldier with short-term training. So Wood did not turn to the National Guard, because while he rejected the need for prolonged training, one of the basic Uptonian premises, he persisted in another, the need for assimilation of citizen soldiers into the professional cadre. He believed therefore that the citizen reserve must be a thoroughly national one, without the state influence that characterized the National Guard, and tied more closely than the Guard to the Regular Army. He also subscribed to the opinion that militia service

outside the United States, and the provisions of the Militia Act of
1908 regarding it, were unconstitutional.[44]

As chief of staff, Wood did not simply neglect the National Guard.
The Militia Division of the General Staff collected data and made
recommendations on militia mobilization. In 1912, as the reorganization of the Regular Army into tactical divisions was being initiated, the War Department also arranged the organization of the
National Guard into twelve divisions. In February, 1913, when the
2nd Division was mobilized on the Mexican border, the Taft administration also contemplated a limited National Guard mobilization,
and the War Department was able to telegraph the commander of
the Department of the East to alert a brigade of New England
Guardsmen. But the federal government still denied the Guard sufficient financial assistance to make possible balanced divisions of all
arms, and the Uptonians cited lack of balance as another count
against the Guard.[45]

Wood's acceptance of the Uptonian attitude toward the National
Guard put him in an awkward position. It deprived him of the most
cogent historical argument available to illustrate the fighting abilities
of citizen soldiers, the history of American militiamen when properly
commanded by officers who believed in them. Accordingly he had to
resort to vague references to the fighting qualities of the race, or to
point to the dubiously relevant Swiss system for tangible proof of the
merits of a citizen soldiery.

The awkwardness of Wood's position emerged all too clearly
when a close associate and disciple, Frederic L. Huidekoper, attempted to review the military history of the country in the light of
Leonard Wood's doctrines in a book called *The Military Unpreparedness of the United States* (1915). A lawyer by profession and
not a soldier, Huidekoper nevertheless was impressed by Upton's
scholarship and believed he could hardly reject his findings. He
therefore based much of his book on Upton's earlier work, quoting
from him wholesale. But because, like Wood, he wanted to argue
that citizen soldiers could be good soldiers, Huidekoper was compelled to find merits in them that seem surprising after his long quo-
tations from Upton. To reconcile the two positions, he could offer
nothing better than the lame argument that the deficiencies Upton
had castigated in the militia resulted from state organization, so that
federal control would presumably wash them away.[46]

Despite his considerable concessions to his adversaries, Wood did
reject Uptonian contempt for citizen soldiers of short-term training
and sought to revive confidence in the American military future by
restoring confidence in a citizen army. His quarrel with Ainsworth
was partly a quarrel with the extreme Uptonians of the Army, be-

cause Ainsworth championed an enlistment period of five years to assure thoroughgoing professionalism, while Wood favored a shorter enlistment. The shorter enlistment fitted one of Wood's two plans for improving the reserve: first, he would have enlistees serve only three years on active duty in the Regular Army, to be followed by three years in a reserve; second, he would create a national militia which would eventually supersede the state militias except for frontier defense. Officers for the national militia were to come from an expansion of the Military Academy, only a portion of whose graduates would henceforth go into the Regular Army, and through expansion of the military training program in the colleges.

These suggestions appeared in a supplement to the annual report of the Secretary of War for 1912, called "The Organization of the Land Forces of the United States." The General Staff prepared the supplement in consultation with Secretary Stimson. As usual, Stimson's own role was no mere passive one. He gave his ear to a junior General Staff officer, Captain John McAuley Palmer. Palmer was a 1910 graduate of the Staff College at Fort Leavenworth and thus one of the officers tapped for higher things, and he had also done an unusual amount of thinking about the problems raised by Uptonian doctrine. His personal background contributed to that thinking, for while he was a graduate of West Point, his father had been Major General John McAuley Palmer, commander of the XIV Corps in the Army of the Cumberland and not a West Pointer but one of the successful citizen soldiers of the Civil War. His father had questioned the Uptonian precepts that the younger Palmer had acquired at West Point, and the son had found himself hard put to defend them, especially the crucial idea of the expansibility of the Regular Army:

When I assumed a peacetime nucleus big enough to make a real foundation for effective expansion for a great war, I found that the American people would be saddled with a big standing army in time of peace. When I assumed a peacetime nucleus small enough to give any chance of acceptance by Congress, it would result in too small a war army— unless I also assumed a rate of expansion that would be obviously absurd.[47]

So Palmer dropped the expansible army concept as impractical, and in 1912 he was able to impress his view upon Stimson. The result was that the War Department report on "The Organization of the Land Forces of the United States" made a historic departure from the expansible army plan which had been advocated not only by Upton but by Calhoun and in embryo by Alexander Hamilton. It proposed a Regular Army not skeletonized but ready to fight immediately:

A regular army organized in divisions and cavalry brigades and ready for immediate use as an expeditionary force or for other purposes for which the citizen soldiery is not available, or for employment in the first stages of war while the citizen soldiery is mobilizing and concentrating.[48]

The War Department report could not make a permanent policy commitment, and for that reason its rejection of the Uptonian expansible army plan did not cause so much furor as might have been expected. But Palmer was to be heard from again, to challenge Uptonian doctrines not partially and tentatively as Leonard Wood was doing, but root and branch.

Attention meanwhile focused on Leonard Wood's campaign for an improved citizen reserve. On every hand Wood's ideas on the subject encountered practical difficulties. The plan to form a first-line reserve from among men passing from the Regulars into the reserve was hard to apply with the kind of small professional Army the United States possessed; in 1912 Congress authorized the furlough of men with three years' honorable service in the Regular Army into a reserve for a four-year term, but in two years this scheme produced only sixteen reservists. Wood's idea of a national militia collided with the continuing Congressional preference for the existing state militia, evidenced anew in the Volunteer Act of 1914, which sought to circumvent the Attorney General's opinion of 1912 which had disputed the constitutionality of militia service overseas. The Volunteer Act simply allowed individual militiamen to volunteer for federal service outside the United States and then required the War Department to preserve intact organized militia units three-fourths of whose members volunteered—the old and obvious expedient of the Spanish War. Wood himself had to depart the office of chief of staff in April, 1914, for at that point his term ended, and the new administration of President Woodrow Wilson had no desire to extend the term; Wood was *persona non grata* both as a partisan Republican and as an advocate of military strength in an administration that was not merely indifferent but suspicious of it.[49]

But mere practical difficulties did not repress Leonard Wood. His interest was not so much in any practical military plan, even of his own devising, as in the abstract idea of military power, to be realized through the idea of the citizen army. His departure as chief of staff actually facilitated his campaign for those ideas, since in his new post as commander of the First Military District, with headquarters at Governor's Island, he had much more time for writing and speech making, and his principal strength was his persuasiveness. He now poured into magazine articles and short books his pleas for military power and a citizen army, and to every group that would listen to him he spoke not eloquently perhaps but forcefully and earnestly. Audiences in growing numbers soon invited him and listened to him, for his new assignment only briefly preceded the outbreak of the First World War.

With Europe at war, Wood pleaded not alone but as part of a preparedness campaign joined by more and more Americans, especially those of Wood's party persuasion. And with Europe at war, a succession of frightening events from the sinking of the *Lusitania* onward gave substance to Wood's and Roosevelt's predictions that in future combats of the great powers, the United States would no longer be able to stand aloof.

FIFTEEN

Preparedness:

1914-17

National preparedness means . . . first of all, the moral organization of the people, an organization which creates in the heart of every citizen a sense of his obligation for service to the nation in time of war. . . .

—Leonard Wood[1]

IN HIS ANNUAL message for 1915, President Woodrow Wilson called on America for a continued effort to hold aloof from the European war. He also rejected any departure from the traditional limits of the American military system.

Shortly thereafter, Major General Leonard Wood dramatically repudiated the President's antipreparedness views in a speech before the Merchants' Association of New York. Soon he was cooperating openly with Stimson and other leading Republicans in organizing the American Rights Committee and the National Security League, to seek preparedness for America and intervention in the European war. With his encouragement and under the direct leadership of his friend Frederic L. Huidekoper, the Army League, of which Wood had been a leading founder in 1912, now redoubled its efforts to enlist popular support for a stronger Army.[2]

Wood's flair for calling forth influence and publicity expressed itself with special inspiration in the "Plattsburg idea." While still chief of staff, Wood had organized summer camps at which college students could receive military training if they paid their own way; in 1915 he opened a similar camp at Plattsburg, New York, paid for by private contributions, for business and professional men. The preparedness movement assured there would be volunteers; a few weeks' training under Wood's auspices assured that influential citizens would go home not only with basic military training but also with renewed enthusiasm for preparedness. The idea spread quickly, to create other camps.[3]

The European war and the preparedness campaign immensely enhanced the cogency of Wood's citizen-army gospel. His ideas had seemed wanting in practicality as well as in relevancy during peacetime, because in peacetime he could not advocate the only really feasible means of building the great-power mass army he wanted. That means was conscription. With the war, Wood could cast aside vagueness and subterfuge:

The voluntary system [he said] failed us in the past, and will fail us in the future. It is uncertain in operation, prevents organized preparation, tends to destroy that individual sense of obligation for military service which should be found in every citizen, costs excessively in life and treasure, and does not permit that condition of preparedness which must exist if we are to wage war successfully with any great power prepared for war.[4]

Wood did not fail now to demonstrate that universal military service had roots in the American military tradition, albeit in the militia system whose details he rejected. He argued that it was the principle of universal military service that Washington had endorsed when he supported Henry Knox's plan for a three-group citizen army. He could point even to a quotation from Jefferson, in which following the War of 1812 the great Virginia republican had urged "the necessity of obliging every citizen to be a soldier." And from a more ancient tradition, from Demosthenes, he quoted: "Go yourselves, every man of you, and stand in the ranks and either a victory beyond all victories in its glory awaits you, or falling you shall fall greatly, and worthy of your past."[5]

The preparedness movement took up the conscription idea, especially through the National Association for Universal Military Training, whose advisory board included both Root and Stimson. But in November, 1915, the Secretary of War asserted the administration's continuing opposition by squelching an effort by a General Staff captain to circulate among the staff officers a memorandum advocating conscription. Wood and the preparedness movement seemed only to have widened the gulf between themselves and the government.[6]

Yet there remained the war, and the pull of it upon America. Wilson might brush off the preparedness campaign as merely "good mental exercise," but he had more reason than most Americans to realize the war-making potential of the *Lusitania* episode: his decision to insist upon the letter of international law might oblige the nation to fight if the Germans did not now permanently abandon unrestricted submarine warfare. Wilson had to weigh, too, the political risks of rigid opposition to preparedness and involvement: the Republicans, Theodore Roosevelt along with Leonard Wood in the van, so dominated the preparedness movement that they might be able to pin the label of weakness on Wilson's Democratic party. Reluctantly, on July 21, 1915, Wilson asked his War and Navy Secretaries to formulate new national security programs, and he advised Congressional leaders that the administration would soon offer such programs.

The Secretary of War was Lindley M. Garrison. Though he was a Democrat, Garrison came from the same sort of eastern legal background as Wood and Stimson, and a sympathetic correspondence on War Department problems had opened between Stimson and Garrison as soon as the latter was announced as Stimson's successor. Garrison would have joined the preparedness movement earlier than Wilson, and with his encouragement the General Staff had anticipated Wilson's change of course and had already begun developing a *Statement of a Proper Military Policy for the United States*. With Wood gone, however, Uptonian attitudes were strong in the General Staff, and Garrison had to prod the officers to get them to suggest more than simply expanding the Regular Army to full war strength. Under his prodding, the *Statement* that was released in September, followed by supporting documents, advocated a program similar to Wood's suggestions before his open endorsement of conscription. The Regular Army was to be more than doubled, from 100,000 to 230,000. There was to be continued support of the National Guard; but there would also be a federal reserve of trained citizen soldiers, obviously destined for a larger role than the Guard.[7]

The General Staff had now gone a bit farther than the administration thought expedient, and Wilson agreed to support a call merely for a Regular Army of 142,000. But Garrison insisted that the country needed a ready force of 500,000, and therefore he suggested that the Regular Army be seconded by a federal force "definitely identified in personnel, provided with equipment and organization, possessed of some training, and subject to instant call," to be recruited in three annual increments of 133,000 each, and thus eventually to number 400,000. He would call it the Continental Army. He would promise the National Guard increased federal support, but he would relegate it definitely to a minor role behind the Regular Army and the ready federal reserve, the Continental Army. In support of this plan, the War Department argued that the state militia could never be subordinated to sufficient federal control to play the part envisioned for the Continental Army. At length Wilson acquiesced and endorsed the plan.[8]

The preparedness campaigners, led by the National Security League, immediately jumped to the support of Garrison's Continental Army idea, and the antipreparedness forces naturally opposed it. But to depict the prolonged and unpleasant struggle that developed over it merely as a contest about preparedness is to oversimplify grossly. The Democratic majority leader in the House of Representatives, Claude Kitchin of North Carolina, was a rural progressive with Bryanite suspicions of the war makers. With the acquiescence of Representative James Hay, once again chairman of the House Military Affairs Committee, he had seen to it that men of kindred views were conspicuous among the membership of the committee. As southerners, these men also felt misgivings about the Continental Army and the eclipse of the National Guard on states'-rights grounds. Of course the National Guard Association cultivated such misgivings. But this sort of concern also had roots in sober consideration of what was the best method of seeking military strength: Hay questioned the feasibility of recruiting the Continental Army. It was difficult enough to keep up the National Guard to an approximation of authorized strength, and in the Guard, recruits had inducements of service with their neighbors in organizations rich in local tradition. When the Army War College argued that the Continental Army plan had to be adopted because adequate federal control over the Guard was constitutionally impossible, the effect was merely to strengthen Congressional doubts by raising questions about either the honesty or the comprehension of the military command.

Hay consequently offered an alternative proposal: to strengthen the National Guard by increasing federal responsibility for it. The federal government should both equip and train the organized militia and also pay them. The federal government should curb political patronage in the Guard by reserving the right to qualify state officers for equivalent federal commissions. In return, the states should assure that federal standards would be maintained, and Guardsmen should swear an oath to respond with their entire units to federal calls for service anywhere. The latter provision would assure both federal control in wartime and the constitutionality of militia service outside the United States.[9]

Hay discussed his plan with President Wilson on January 11, 1916. The President did not drop Garrison's plan but neither did he reject the Hay plan. New to serious thought about military preparedness, Wilson had been unequipped to resist the arguments of the War Department, but now he must have recognized that the Hay plan better fitted his own concepts of constitutional government. His thoughts seem to have run to the possibility of a compromise. But the next day Garrison reacted with a vehemence that may well have startled Wilson. No compromise was possible, he said:

There can be no honest or worthy solution which does not result in national forces under the exclusive control and authority of the national government. . . . The very first line of cleavage . . . is between reliance upon a system of state troops, forever subject to constitutional limitations, . . . or reliance upon national forces, raised, officered, trained and controlled by national authority. . . .[10]

This was the voice of unreason. Garrison, like Wood, had rejected part of Emory Upton's doctrines, Upton's contempt for the citizen soldier; nevertheless he had accepted from the soldiers around him no small share of Uptonian dogmatism.

Still unsure of his own ground, Wilson was not ready to respond to Garrison's challenge by dropping his Secretary of War. At the end of the month he undertook a speaking tour to signalize his new dedication to preparedness, in which he continued to endorse the Continental Army plan. But while he addressed enthusiastic audiences in cities, he did not overcome the core of rural resistance to the drift toward European war or to the Continental Army plan that seemed part of the drift; on his return to Washington he found Garrison's opponents in Congress as strong as ever. Indeed, on February 5 Hay informed him that the Garrison plan could not be accepted, and he added a few days later that Garrison himself had become obnoxious to the Military Affairs Committee. Faced with a choice between Hay and Garrison, and between a bill of some kind and no bill, Wilson chose Hay and the National Guard. Garrison interpreted the choice as a betrayal and resigned, the Assistant Secretary of War following him. Republicans gleefully charged that the President had abandoned preparedness, and they made Garrison their latest hero, though Garrison himself was too loyal to Wilson to speak his feelings publicly.[11]

Wilson immediately offered another conciliatory gesture to Garrison's Congressional critics by appointing Newton D. Baker as Secretary of War. Baker was an outstanding progressive, mayor of Cleveland, and extremely recent convert to preparedness. Working with this congenial figure, the Democratic House leaders were able to effect rapid passage of Hay's plan through both the Military Affairs Committee and, on March 23, by a vote of 402 to 2, through the

House itself. The bill included Hay's National Guard proposals and an increase of the Regular Army to 140,000 officers and men.[12]

The next day a German submarine torpedoed the French cross-channel liner *Sussex*, with eighty casualties including two Americans. The extreme preparedness advocates and their Uptonian allies seized upon the event for a new outcry against the Hay plan, and the chairman of the Senate Military Affairs Committee, George E. Chamberlain of Oregon, was willing to cooperate with them. The Senate adopted a military bill that revived the Continental Army plan, albeit at a strength of 261,000 rather than 400,000 men. The Senate bill would also have raised the Regular Army to 250,000. Thereupon the military deadlock reappeared, this time in the House-Senate conference committee.[13]

Perhaps no legislation whatever could have emerged had not Mexico for a time replaced the European war in the newspaper headlines. There the threat of American involvement in revolution and civil war had been aggravated after Wilson's accession by the President's well intentioned but dubiously conceived efforts to hurry the Mexicans into constitutional government, Anglo-Saxon style. A naval patrol of the Mexican coast to deny the unruly Latins access to firearms had led to an unfortunate incident at Tampico, when Mexican authorities briefly incarcerated American bluejackets who had come ashore, and then to American occupation of Vera Cruz.

Following the Navy's landings at Vera Cruz, General Funston had gone there with the Fifth Brigade of the 2nd Division to command an occupying force of about 8,000, roughly half soldiers and half Marines. Since Wilson's intention was to help the Mexicans and not to provoke war with them, the occupation was embarrassing, and Washington ended it with the help of mediation by other Latin American states. Nevertheless, Vera Cruz intensified anti-American feeling in Mexico, which gave one of the contenders for power, Francisco Villa, a suitable background for raiding into the United States to express his displeasure at Wilson's support for a rival's presidential aspirations. Villa's followers shot up Columbus, New Mexico, on March 9, 1916, in the midst of the Congressional hassle over preparedness and the Hay Bill.[14]

Within a week the War Department sent about 5,000 Regulars under Brigadier General John J. Pershing across the border in pursuit of Villa. It soon became evident that whether or not Pershing caught Villa, Mexican resentment of his incursion might cause a clash with the forces of Venustiano Carranza, whom Washington now recognized as head of the Mexican government. In these dangerous circumstances, Secretary Baker tried to recruit the Regular

Army to its full authorized strength, but with little success. On April 12 Pershing's forces fought a skirmish with the Carranzistas at Parral, whereupon Carranza demanded Pershing's withdrawal. The chief of staff, Major General Hugh L. Scott, and General Funston met with Carranza's military chieftain, Álvaro Obregón, at El Paso and agreed to withdraw Pershing gradually provided Carranza controlled Villa; in simultaneous mockery of the agreement, Villa raided Glen Springs, Texas. With Carranza threatening war unless Pershing got out and the government unwilling to withdraw Pershing while Villa menaced American towns, war seemed almost inevitable. On May 9 the War Department called out the National Guard of Texas, New Mexico, and Arizona. But the militia of three states seemed hardly enough: under the pressure of events on the border and Wilson's energetic mediation, the House and Senate conferees on Army legislation at last compromised, and the National Defense Act of 1916 passed the Senate on May 17 and the House on May 20.[15]

It provided for an increase of the authorized peace strength of the Regular Army to 175,000 over a period of five years. In war the Regular Army would be expansible to 286,000, by building up the cadres of its 65 infantry regiments, 25 cavalry regiments, 21 field artillery regiments, 7 engineer regiments, 2 mounted engineer battalions, 263 coast artillery companies, 8 aero squadrons, and supporting formations. The law authorized tactical divisions and brigades, three brigades to a division, three regiments to a brigade.

The National Defense Act also embodied Hay's plan for a National Guard under increased federal supervision, with its officers and men sworn upon enlistment to obey the President and defend the Constitution of the United States. The strength of the Guard was to be increased gradually from about 100,000 to over 400,000. The federal government would provide drill pay for forty-eight armory drills a year. It would prescribe standards for Guard officers, and moreover it would prescribe the units that the Guard should maintain. Though the National Guard would clearly be the principal trained reserve, which was the essence of the Hay plan, the act did provide for a Regular Army enlisted reserve, composed of veterans of tours with the Regulars, and to be recruited with the aid of an elaborate system of bounties. The businessmen's summer camps and student military training were to be continued and placed on a firmer legal basis through an Officers' Reserve Corps and a Reserve Officers' Training Corps. An Enlisted Reserve Corps would enlist specialists for the engineer, signal, quartermaster, ordnance, and medical services.[16]

A section of the act with great potential importance reaffirmed the traditional doctrine of a universal military obligation but clearly nationalized the obligation:

The Militia of the United States shall consist of all able-bodied male citizens of the United States and all other able-bodied males who have or shall have declared their intentions to become citizens of the United States, who shall be more than 18 years of age, except as hereinafter provided, not more than 45 years of age, and said Militia shall be divided into three classes, the National Guard, the Naval Militia, and the unorganized Militia.[17]

The statute dealt comprehensively with the organization of both the Regulars and the National Guard. National Guardsmen were to enlist for six years: three in active Guard service, three in a Guard reserve. Units of the Guard were to have forty-eight drill periods a year plus fifteen days of field training, unless excused by the Secretary of War. The Regular Army would provide instructors and supplies for the Guard; discipline and supplies were to be the same as those of the Regular Army. A Militia Bureau of the General Staff would supervise the National Guard, and the Secretary of War was empowered to halt funds to those states that did not comply with federal regulations.[18]

The whole body of commentators on American military policy, Emory Upton among the rest, had strangely neglected the subject of economic mobilization. The National Defense Act, its writers influenced by the European war, at last took up the subject. It empowered the President to place orders for defense materials and to require compliance from the industries involved, on pain of government seizure; compensation was to be "fair and just" and to yield "a reasonable profit." The Secretary of War was to make a survey of all industries concerned with the manufacture of arms and ammunition. Because of the shortage resulting from German control of the synthetic nitrates industry, the President was authorized to establish government-owned nitrate plants. Following up these provisions, a rider attached to the Army appropriation act of August 29, 1916, created a Council of National Defense with an advisory commission to consider especially the problems of economic mobilization. The council was to consist of the Secretaries of War, Navy, Interior, Agriculture, Commerce, and Labor, with the Secretary of War as chairman.[19]

Slipped into the National Defense Act were much less judicious provisions conceived by the still bitter partisans of Ainsworth, with their suspicions of the General Staff. The act provided for a gradual increase of the General Staff to three general officers and fifty-two junior officers; but it provided that no more than half of the junior officers could be on duty in or near the District of Columbia. As a result, a mere nineteen officers comprised the War Department General Staff in the spring of 1917. The duties of the General Staff were declared explicitly to be limited to nonadministrative matters, which called into question again the whole issue of General Staff control over the bureaus. Secretary Baker quashed the latter issue simply by issuing an official opinion that the authority of the General Staff was unimpaired and proceeding accordingly. But the limitation on numbers badly straitened the ability of the General Staff to plan for war even as war became more surely imminent.[20]

With the same unreason that had distinguished Garrison's uncompromising stand on the Continental Army, the ardent preparedness advocates and the Uptonians denounced the National Defense Act of 1916 as a "gold brick," or far worse. The National Security League urged a veto. Theodore Roosevelt called it "one of the most iniquitous bits of legislation ever placed on the statute books." The stultifying effects of Uptonian doctrine, coupled with the overstrung nerves of a country on the edge of war, could not be more clearly demonstrated than by these incongruous reactions to the most comprehensive military legislation the American Congress had yet passed.[21]

The President called most of the National Guard into federal service under the terms of the new law before the ink was dry, and therefore before any improvements in the Guard could take effect. Pershing was still deep in Mexico with much of the Regular Army, so the border was still weak against raids and the threat of war. Two weeks after he signed the National Defense Act, Wilson called up the Guard, not as state militia but as men obligated to federal service by their oaths of enlistment, as provided in the new law. Many of them had not yet taken the new oath, but they responded.[22]

Eventually 158,664 men stood to arms in the mobilized formations of the National Guard. The Uptonians seized upon their shortcomings as vindication of opposition to the Hay Bill: the total mobilized was about 100,000 short of the full war strength of the units involved as prescribed by the new law; a disturbing number of Guardsmen were rejected for federal service because of physical deficiencies, in one division 15.5 per cent; the Guardsmen grumbled a great deal, especially as their service was prolonged into 1917 and they reflected on the comforts of their fellow citizens at home; National Guard training was not up to the level of the Regular Army, and Guard formations were still disproportionately infantry (although improvised National Guard cavalrymen seem to have applied considerable energy to the task of transforming themselves).[23]

Despite all that, it is difficult to see how else than by relying on the National Guard the United States could have begun to mobilize any comparable force of at least partially trained and equipped men. The mobilization of the National Guard in 1916 was a feeble performance compared with the European mobilizations of 1914; but to judge the former by the standards of the latter, as some military writers have done even since World War II, is to elevate military values at the expense of all others in a fashion the American people of the second decade of this century rightly were not prepared to accept. No reasonable application even of Theodore Roosevelt's or Leonard Wood's designs for America's world role demanded American mobilization tables of the European style of 1914.[24]

Still, preparation for a possible small war in Mexico imposed a sufficient strain upon the American military system to assure that many traditional American habits would have to be sacrificed if now the nation entered the great European war. The Mexican troubles also provided an unpleasant but finally useful rehearsal for larger conflict. The railroads proved incapable of handling the efficient movement of 150,000 men and their efficient supply to the Mexican border, suggesting that drastic federal controls might be necessary in a greater war to prevent repetition of the fiascoes of 1898. Supplying Pershing by motor truck and by mule wagon demonstrated to doubting supply officers the superiority of motor transport, but the maintenance of trucks in the field created a maze of new problems. Artillery shells had to be expended sparingly by guns that were few in number even for the possible demands of a Mexican war, let along the immense artillery battles of Europe. Aircraft might have been extremely valuable to Pershing's frustrating hunt for Villa, but the six with which he started out all crashed within a month, leading Congress to raise its appropriation for the Aviation Service of the Signal Corps from $300,000 to $800,000. A few of the National Guard units were better supplied with machine guns than the Regular Army, since the Regular Army had prescribed only four guns to an infantry regiment and the National Guard had been able to experiment with more; the consequent handicap of the Regulars and a glance at Europe led Congress to vote $12 million for machine-gun development.[25]

Mexico also provided a toughening of the Regulars and the National Guard and probably some measure of psychological conditioning for war throughout the country. Fortunately, the stronger of the Mexican leaders no more wanted war with the United States than Wilson wanted to fight them, since an American war might undermine their strength. Therefore neither side fanned Pershing's friction with Mexican troops into an explosion, and in early 1917 Wilson was able to pull Pershing out, his mission unaccomplished but the withdrawal accompanied by a few face-saving Mexican professions of peaceful and responsible intent. American relations with Mexico were still bad enough to lead the German foreign office into the blunder of the Zimmermann note, which intensified American war sentiment toward Germany. They were also still bad enough that an assemblage of Mexican political leaders cheered the German minister to Mexico and hissed the American soon after hearing that Germany's resumption of unrestricted submarine warfare had provoked the United States to declare war on Germany. But by that time the country and the Army were preoccupied with much larger problems than Mexico offered.

The indictment of United States policy as one of chronic unpreparedness for war fits best the First World War. On April 6, 1917, when Congress responded to Wilson's war message, the United States Army was less ready for the task ahead of it than at the opening of any previous conflict, not excepting the War of the Revolution or the War of 1812. Never before had the foe been so formidable in numbers and military skill; never before had conflict demanded so complete a mobilization of the whole nation; never before had the government faced problems of the magnitude of those posed by the decision to carry the Army to the battlefields of Europe itself. For all the contingencies of war with Germany, only the slightest preparation had been made, despite several years of preparedness agitation.

Nevertheless, an indictment of the American government and people for these military deficiencies can readily be overdrawn. It is not true that the Wilson administration was blind to the need for coordinating its diplomatic with its military policy. Until almost the moment of the delivery of his war message, the purpose of President Wilson was to avoid war. Even after Germany's resumption of unrestricted submarine warfare and the rupture of American diplomatic relations with Germany on February 1, 1917, Wilson still hoped that German policy would soften and war could be avoided. Dedicated to the preservation of peace, Wilson believed that to undertake large and vigorous military preparations for war with Germany would itself contribute to his difficulties in restraining the jingoistic part of American opinion, add to the tension between Germany and the United States, and give new weight to the tendency toward war. Whether he was right or wrong in thinking so, Wilson at least was observing considerations that deserve respect; he was not ignoring the relationship between military and foreign policy but heeding the demands of that relationship as he understood them. Underlying his caution in making military preparations was his conviction that though he was risking delays and expense at the outset of war if war came, he was not risking the vital interests of the United States, for American resources would still prove adequate to the country's military tasks. This judgment proved correct.[26]

It was naïve of Wilson, of course, to throw a fit of anger upon learning in 1916 that the General Staff was making plans for a war with Germany, since it was the normal duty of the staff to foresee any likely contingency. But it is hard to find evidence that Wilson's anger on this occasion did any particular harm. After the National Defense Act of 1916 limited the General Staff officers in Washington to nineteen, a mere eleven officers of the War College Division of the General Staff, assisted by the War College itself, carried the burden of the Army's war planning. They had to give most of their attention to Mexico. Characteristically, such thought as the General Staff accorded to war with Germany concerned mainly the possible manpower requirements; the terms of the historic American debate about military policy caused the General Staff to concentrate upon this one problem, as did almost everyone else. Such forethought about economic mobilization as was accomplished before April, 1917, was almost entirely the work of the civilian Council of National Defense and its advisory commission. Before war began, this organization was well along in designing the machinery which was later constructed to direct industrial production for war and conduct military purchasing.[27]

The United States went to war with Germany over a limited issue, the unrestricted submarine campaign. Conceivably, the United States might therefore have waged a limited war, fought merely to assure the rights of American shipping and travelers at sea. But to go to war at all evidently seemed to most Americans, including the President, to imply an effort toward complete victory. The Civil War and the Indian wars had both accustomed Americans to thinking of war in such terms. Wilson advised in his war message that Congress "take immediate steps not only to put the country in a more thorough state of defense but also to exert all its power and employ all its resources to bring the Government of the German Empire to terms and end the war."[28]

In fact, the government had not yet made a firm decision to commit a mass army to the battles of Europe. Secretary of War Baker told the House Military Affairs Committee on April 7:

. . . the plans of our military cooperation are in the making rather than having been made. . . . But if, before it is over, it is necessary to send our troops to Europe to take the places of those whose lives are lost in the struggle to which we are a part, then undoubtedly that would be done.[29]

Yet the whole tendency of events and planning was "to send our troops to Europe." From the declaration of war onward, there was never any real chance of the adoption of another policy.

The National Guard mobilization of 1916 with its failure to recruit the Guard to full strength had convinced Secretary Baker and the President of the inadequacy of volunteering to raise an army for modern war. In December, 1916, Chief of Staff Scott had requested the War College Division of the General Staff to prepare a plan for universal military training. Though this plan was intended to guide permanent policy and not simply to serve for an emergency, much of it proved useful when the war came. As early as the rupture of diplomatic relations in February, Wilson instructed Baker to have a conscription bill ready if he should have to ask for a declaration of war. The decision to commit all the power and resources of the country to Germany's defeat led to the submission of the bill to Congress immediately after the declaration.[30]

The bill became the Selective Service Act of May 18, 1917. Not all the Democrats with their rural, states'-rights traditions were so ready to adopt national conscription as Wilson and Baker. Representative S. Hubert Dent, Jr., of Alabama, who had succeeded Hay as chairman of the House Military Affairs Committee, could not go along; neither could Majority Leader Claude Kitchin. So the conscription bill had to be shepherded through the House by the ranking Republican of the Military Affairs Committee, Representative Julius Kahn of California. When it received the President's signature, it authorized him to raise the Regular Army and the National Guard to full war strength and to call the entire Guard into federal service—processes already under way under previous authorizations. It authorized him to raise 500,000 men immediately by federal draft, and then an additional 500,000 when he believed the time appropriate. Subsequent legislation granted authority for still additional increments. The recruiting of the Regular Army and the National Guard was to be by volunteering, but the draft could be invoked to remedy any deficiencies. The term of service for Regular Army, National Guard, and drafted men was to be the duration of the emergency.[31]

Scarcely two years had passed since the views of Wilson and Leonard Wood had stood almost diametrically opposed.

SIXTEEN

The First World War: 1917-18

The fact is that our officers and men are far and away superior to the tired Europeans. High officers of the Allies have often dropped derogatory remarks about our poorly trained staff and high commanders, which our men have stood as long as they can. . . . [I now have told the Allies], in rather forcible language, that we had now been patronized as long as we would stand for it, and I wished to hear no more of that sort of nonsense.

—John J. Pershing[1]

THE MONTH OF American entry into the war was also the month of France's disastrous Nivelle offensive, which cost 120,000 casualties and precipitated mutiny in fifty-four divisions, half of the French army. Only extraordinarily effective security precautions prevented still worse disaster, for by June not a single reliable French division stood between Soissons and Paris. The French general staff pleaded for the immediate dispatch of American troops, at least one division as an earnest of more to come. General Henri Philippe Pétain, the hero of Verdun called to command of the army in this dark hour, ranged billets and trenches to restore the hope and confidence of the troops, assuring them there would be no more Nivelle offensives: France would await the tanks and the Americans.[2]

In May, Marshal Joffre, the victor of the Marne, arrived in America to plead his country's desperate cause. He reiterated the call for immediate assistance—at least one division. The British, their army now forced to bear almost the whole weight of the war on the Western Front, seconded the call.

The War College Division of the General Staff had recommended that all available trained officers of the Regular Army and the National Guard be utilized to train the recruits and levies. The United States did not have enough trained soldiers to add meaningful strength to the Western Front. Therefore the whole existing force should be used to make soldiers of the new men, and only when the training of a million and a half men was complete should American forces begin to move to the battlefields. But the War Department decided that this plan omitted the moral factor and risked the collapse of the Allies before a million and a half Americans could be ready. It collected the 16th, 18th, 26th, and 28th Infantry Regiments from the Mexican border and formed them into the 1st Division, for prompt shipment to France.

Even four Regular regiments from the border were unready for European war. To bring them to war strength, hundreds of men had to be drawn from other regiments. But other hundreds of Regulars had to go to train the new armies despite the crisis of France, and when the regiments sailed they were about two-thirds recruits. Reserve officers had to fill their command staffs. The General Staff warned that the 1st Division's "new machine-gun units particularly will require organization from the ground up, as well as training of commissioned and enlisted personnel." When they embarked from New York, howitzer, mortar, and 37-mm gun crews had none of the weapons they were supposed to use and "had never even heard of them."[3]

A battalion of the 16th Infantry marched through Paris on the Fourth of July. The city cheered extravagantly for "les hommes au chapeau de cow-boy"—the soldiers still wore the broad-brimmed campaign hats designed for protection against the western sun. Experienced French soldiers were not so heartened. After the parade, the 1st Division went into intensive training at Gondrecourt, behind the front in Lorraine, beginning not with trench warfare but with elementary drill. Not until October did they seem ready for some to be attached to a French division for experience in a quiet sector of the line.[4]

So the help that America could offer in 1917 was mostly a promise. But the promise was real.

After the passage of the Selective Service Act of 1917 the United States experienced none of the brushes with catastrophe that in earlier wars had marked the quest for manpower. The great problems in creating the armies of World War I were those of equipment and training, not of recruiting. The General Staff had framed its selective service plan in light of a careful study of conscription in the Civil

War, mostly conducted by Adjutant General Enoch Crowder. Crowder enabled the Army to avoid all the worst mistakes of the earlier national draft. This time there would be no substitutes or purchased exemptions. There would be no bounties. The Army itself would not send its provost marshals knocking on doors to take a census of the eligibles, provoking resentment by their methods and presence.

Instead, each eligible person would be required to register as an obligation of citizenship or residence in the United States. In thousands of localities, local boards composed of citizens of the area would administer the draft. Though conscription would be selective, deferring those with occupations vital to industrial mobilization or with certain family obligations, it would be based upon the principle of a universal obligation to service on the part of all male citizens or friendly aliens who had declared their intent to become citizens, between the ages of twenty-one and thirty inclusive. On August 31, these ages were extended from eighteen to thirty-five.[5]

The Civil War draft had supplied directly only about six per cent of the soldiers of the Union Army. The World War I draft supplied about sixty-seven per cent of the armed forces for that war. The first inclination of the General Staff was to suspend voluntary enlistments altogether, since the selective service process could much better assure that essential civilian occupations would remain filled, while choosing the men most likely to be good soldiers. But Congress probably would not have consented to the draft had not the ancient volunteer system been preserved as well, so enlistments into the Regular Army or the National Guard continued. The draft acted as a spur to enlistments, and the enlistment rate fluctuated in response to various changes in conscription policy. As the Regular Army and the National Guard approached full strength, enlistments were curtailed. In November, 1917, the Army announced that enlistments by men in the twenty-one to thirty age bracket, those then registered for the draft, would be discontinued on December 15. On August 8, 1918, all Army enlistments were halted. In September, 1918, voluntary enlistments in the Navy and the Marine Corps also came to a stop. Thereafter conscription was the sole means of recruitment for the rest of the war.[6]

By the time the war began, the new formations authorized by the National Defense Act of 1916 had been created to the extent that the mobile line forces included thirty-eight Regular Army infantry regiments, seventeen cavalry, nine field artillery, and three engineer. About a third of these units were stationed outside the continental United States. The aggregate strength of the Regular Army, officers and men, was 127,588. The National Guard counted 80,446 officers and men in federal service and 101,174 in state service (some of the latter having just returned to the states following the Mexican border mobilization). Driblets of additional more or less ready manpower included the Regular Army Reserve, first authorized in 1912 and after its extremely slow start now grown to 4,767 men; the Officers' Reserve Corps, numbering about 2,000; the Enlisted Reserve Corps of technical specialists, numbering about 10,000; a National Guard Reserve—a sort of third line behind the National Guard, also authorized in 1916—of about 10,000; and the products of the Reserve Officers' Training Corps and its predecessor programs, of uncertain numbers.[7]

In the course of the war the Army grew from 213,557 men actually in federal service on April 1, 1917, to 3,685,458 on November 11, 1918. Thanks to a uniformly applied conscription, the stimulus it gave to voluntary enlistments, and an early stipulation that all soldiers must serve for the duration of the war, this great increase was accomplished without the tangle of discharges and reenlistments that had plagued every previous war effort. It drew upon the national tradition of a compulsory military obligation; but the success of the Selective Service Act of 1917 surely owed much also to the discipline implicit in industrial society, to the consequent immense power of the modern state, and to modern mass media of communication and publicity, on which neither George Washington nor Abraham Lincoln had been able to draw.[8]

Because of the public discipline of an industrial society, the Army could also be recruited much more in accordance with rational calculations of manpower needs than in any previous war. In all earlier American wars, estimates of manpower requirements had been haphazard, and so had the numbers of men specified in various calls for recruits. The numbers called had been based pretty much on guesses about what public sentiment would permit. But even in a democracy, by 1917 the power of government and the discipline of the population were such that the government knew it could draw men into the Army almost as long as the supply lasted and enough civilians remained to keep the economy functioning. Therefore the size of the Army could be based less upon considerations of public feeling and much more upon strategic requirements.

Estimates of those requirements naturally fluctuated with the changing fortunes of war, but the effort to build the Army according to a rationally planned pattern persisted. Three weeks before the 1st Division began arriving in France, Major General John J. Pershing, also transferred from the Mexican border, arrived there to establish an American general headquarters in Europe. He would prepare for the coming of an American Army which he would eventually command, but also he would gather information upon which the War Department could calculate the size of the Army to be sent.

After consulting with the French and the British and observing the condition of their troops, Pershing submitted a General Organization Project in July, 1917. He proposed a commitment of American troops to France probably well beyond anything Wilson had conceived of when he spoke in his war message about employing all the power of the United States: over a million men to be sent to France by December 31, 1918. Pershing argued that the United States must send a full army, of twenty divisions and their supporting troops, because such an army was "the smallest unit which in modern war will be a complete, well-balanced fighting organization." More than that, Pershing considered the French and British armies to be in dismaying condition, the French at the end of their manpower resources after Verdun, writing off their lists divisions that could not be restored to strength, and close to the end of their moral tether as well. The British were not in much better shape and were throwing their armies into the slaughter pits of their 1917 offensive. Only a large American Army could defeat the Germans, and a million men in France "should not be construed as representing the maximum force which should be sent to or which will be needed in France."[9]

The War Department developed Pershing's General Organization Project, plus his supplementary proposals for supporting troops, into a plan to place 1,372,339 men in thirty divisions with their auxiliaries in France by December, 1918. But Pershing's estimates of French and British prospects grew steadily more pessimistic, and events confirmed his fears. The British 1917 offensive smothered itself in futility with a quarter million casualties, and at the end of the year the British counted about 100,000 fewer soldiers in France than in January; they could no longer replace their losses. In November the Bolshevik Revolution assured Russia's withdrawal from the war, and Pershing estimated that in consequence Germany would be able to concentrate 250 to 260 divisions on the Western Front against 160 Allied divisions. As Germany's anticipated 1918 offensive developed, and succeeded so well that open warfare returned to the Western Front for the first time since 1914, Pershing revised his estimates to an American Expeditionary Force of 3,000,000 men, with sixty-six combat divisions, by May, 1919. He submitted that estimate on June 21, 1918, when the Germans stood poised on the Marne at Chateau-Thierry preparing for a climactic drive toward Paris, forty miles away. After a conference with Marshal Ferdinand Foch, now Allied Commander in Chief, Pershing raised his estimate again two days later: "To win the victory in 1919, it is necessary to have a numerical superiority which can only be obtained by our having in France in April 80 American divisions and in July 100 divisions."[10]

The War Department did not believe 100 large American divisions could be assembled in France by that time or would be necessary, but Pershing did receive a promise that there would be ninety-eight divisions by June, 1919, eighty of them to be in France. In place of the thirty divisions and 1,372,399 men planned for France by December 31, 1918, the increased program called for fifty-two divisions and 2,350,000 men to be with Pershing by that date. These goals led to the extension of the draft age from eighteen to forty-five.[11]

The startlingly rapid collapse of the Germans after the containment of their 1918 offensive ended the war before the "eighty-division program" could be effected. But the United States was well on its way to accomplishing the goal when the Armistice occurred. Sixty-two infantry divisions had been organized by that time, and forty-three of them were in France, totaling with their supporting troops nearly two million men.[12]

American military thought had always concentrated on the manpower problem, but in World War I the neglected subject of economic mobilization caused difficulties so severe that for a time induction of draftees had to wait upon materials to supply them. In the end the American Army had to fight with large quantities of European weapons and equipment. As the European powers had earlier discovered, the war imposed economic demands so severe that only an unprecedented mobilization of industry as well as of armies could begin to meet them. The material requirements of the Army became so large that Army supply officers alone could not cope with them, and the Army had to share with business leaders the management of the economic aspect of war. The larger the Army grew and the more enormous and complex its material needs became, the less the Army alone could direct the war effort, and the more the civilian planners had to be given influence and power rivaling that of the professional military chieftains.

The rise of civilian participation in managing the supply of military needs was hastened by the attention that the Council of National Defense gave to those needs in the last few months of peace, while the War Department was still neglecting them. On March 3, 1917, the Council established as a subsidiary body a Munitions Standards Board, composed of six industrialists, to do what its title implied, establish standards for munitions manufacturers. It soon became evident not only that standards were required but that the huge material requirements of war could be met only with excessive difficulty and at inordinate cost if the Army, the Navy, and the various supply agencies within each service competed with each other in gathering supplies, as they had done in earlier wars. Therefore two days after the declaration of war, the Munitions Standards Board gave way to a General Munitions Board, charged with the coordination of military purchasing, and composed of some twenty members including Army supply and General Staff officers.

The General Munitions Board in turn proved excessively large and unwieldy and lacking adequately defined authority; the traditional military supply agencies continued mainly to go their own separate ways. Thereupon, in July, 1917, the Council of National Defense superseded it with still another instrumentality, the War Industries Board. This seven-member body with various subcommissions at first accomplished little more than its predecessors. But when Bernard Baruch became its chairman on March 4, 1918, it took on unprecedented vigor, both through Baruch's energy and through a new grant of power from the President. Wilson now gave it genuine authority, not simply advisory functions, to determine priorities of production and purchase, to create new industrial facilities and new sources of supply, to convert existing industrial plants to new uses, and to conserve natural resources. The War Industries Board became the chief agency of economic mobilization, coordinating the activities not only of the military services but also of the other civilian war agencies which by that time had appeared.[13]

The Army was represented on the War Industries Board by Major General William Goethals, who in a variety of posts had become the Army's principal supply officer. His assistant, Brigadier General Hugh S. Johnson, was the principal active Army representative, in the process gaining the experience in industrial coordination that he was to utilize as head of the National Recovery Administration under the New Deal. The Army's liaison with civilian mobilization agencies in general was carried on largely through the War Industries Board. After March, 1918, the board quickly overshadowed its sponsor, the Council of National Defense, and soon became legally independent of it.

The Army still maintained direct contact with a few other civil mobilization agencies. Embarkation of troops for Europe demanded Army cooperation with the Shipping Board, the agency which both allocated shipping and built new tonnage. Transportation of troops and matériel inside the United States required cooperation with the Railway War Board and then the Railroad Administration. The first of these agencies attempted to accomplish voluntary coordination of the railroads somewhat in the manner of the Civil War, but the railroads became smothered in congestion and confusion that threatened a return to Spanish War conditions, and consequently the President used his authority under various defense statutes to seize them and run them through the Railroad Administration. Finally, the Army purchased foods of which there was a real or prospective shortage by receiving allocations from the Food Administration.[14]

In general, then, the Army had to secure war material and transportation by arranging with the civilian mobilization boards and especially the War Industries Board for appropriate allotments of what was available. Sometimes even the tremendous productive capacity of the United States could not assure that what was available was enough. Artillery and aviation production most conspicuously were so complexly difficult as to make the organization of mass production and the accumulation of the necessary machine tools for it a time-consuming process. In both areas, consequently, American production was just beginning to accelerate when the Armistice ended the war, and meanwhile American soldiers in France had to fire French guns and fly French and British aircraft. This fact is one of the most important reasons for saying that World War I probably found the country least prepared of any of its wars for what was expected of it.

The Army began the war with enough artillery on hand to equip divisions totaling about 220,000 men. Ammunition was in commensurate quantity. Artillery allotments per division soon had to be revised upward in accordance with European experience, to make the scarcity seem even more acute. Leonard Wood promptly suggested that French or British guns would have to be adopted. The chief of ordnance replied that "the abandonment of our arms for the inferior arms of another nation" would be "contrary to the independent spirit of our people," but he soon discovered that he had no choice. Fortunately, it is unlikely that French artillery was inferior, however damaging reliance upon it might have been to national pride. Of some 2,250 artillery pieces used by the American forces in France, only about a hundred were American guns. Similarly, the Americans had to fight with French and British tanks, when they had tank support at all; there was not a tank in the United States when the war began, and despite American possession of the world's largest automotive industry, the requirements of tank production were sufficiently specialized that no American tanks ever reached the front.[15]

The country began the war with higher hopes of developing a great military aviation industry in time to influence the outcome; the Allies received some extravagant promises of skies filled with American aircraft. But the basis for such an effort was again very small. The Aviation Section of the Signal Corps had fifty-five airplanes in flying condition, mostly obsolete. Industrial capacity of a general kind could not adjust overnight to the special requirements of producing aircraft. Those special requirements as conceived in 1917 included such peculiarities as the belief that only castor oil was a suitable lubricant for airplane motors, in accordance with which the government felt obliged to import from Java huge quantities of the beans that yielded castor oil.

Though about a billion dollars was expended in trying to push the growth of aircraft production at forced draft, in the end the United States had to settle for following the Allied advice not to try to produce fighters, because the designs changed too rapidly, but to concentrate on observation and bombing planes and more especially on engines. The 13,500 twelve-cylinder Liberty engines produced by the end of the war proved to be the principal American contribution to aviation. They were reasonably good engines for their day, especially considering that they were an all-purpose improvisation, but they were excessively likely to burst into flames under gunfire. Meanwhile, the Army Air Service grew from 75 flying officers to 11,425, and more than 5,000 fliers and observers went to France. At the time of the Armistice there were forty-five American squadrons at the front. By that time DeHaviland DH-4 observation planes were at last coming off American production lines at the rate of a thousand a month, but only a quarter of the American squadrons were flying American planes. Those that were would willingly have foregone the privilege, since the DH-4 became notorious as the "flying coffin."[16]

The country had better success with other weapons. The United States Army had been notably slow to pay attention to the machine gun, despite the work of American inventors in developing it. At the beginning of the war there were five machine guns in each of the thirty-eight infantry and seventeen cavalry regiments. Fifty-four machine-gun units in the National Guard had four guns each. The guns were of four noninterchangeable types not well suited for war as it had developed on the Western Front; most of those belonging to the National Guard were promptly reassigned to airplanes. The Tables of Organization and Equipment soon began to multiply the guns allotted even to existing regiments, and the chief of ordnance estimated that eighteen months would be required to secure a reasonably adequate supply even with the allotments relatively low. Until July, 1918, American troops in France had to be equipped with French machine guns and French automatic rifles. But the requirements for producing machine guns and automatic rifles were not quite so peculiar and complex as those of the aircraft industry, and the final record was better than expected. After July, 1918, divisions sailing for France could take with them Browning machine guns and Browning automatic rifles of American design and manufacture, and these weapons were the best of their kind in the world. But the wait for them was long, the more so since Pershing did not allow the Brownings to be used at the front until September, when enough were available to make an important impact, lest the Germans capture and copy them.[17]

The one vital weapon which occasioned no special problem was the rifle. The Model 1903 Springfield was the best of the day. The Springfield and Rock Island arsenals were manufacturing it and could step up their production. Three private plants were manufacturing Enfield rifles for the British army when the United States entered the war and had almost filled their contracts; they soon switched to manufacturing modified Enfields for the American Army, a good weapon if not quite so good as the Springfield and capable of taking the same ammunition. Rifles for 890,000 men were on hand when the war began. Since time elapsed before men could be inducted in large numbers, the accelerating supply was able to keep up with the demand. Ammunition for rifles as well as machine guns and artillery posed more difficult problems, but here a combination of increased American production with purchases abroad afforded enough.[18]

The supply of matériel other than ordnance was importantly affected by the flurry of organizational changes in the War Department which grew out of the trials of the Spanish War. In 1912 the Quartermaster and Commissary Departments, along with the Pay Department, were consolidated into a single organization to deal with most supplies other than ordnance and engineering and medical materials. To obviate the previous dependence upon hired civilian labor for much of the handling of supplies, the consolidated department became a military formation with its own enlisted personnel, the Quartermaster Corps. This service corps gradually replaced civilians with enlisted men, and by the time the National Defense Act of 1916 was passed, about 5,400 were serving with it. When the war began, the corps had 205 officers and was building toward a maximum of 369 allotted it by the National Defense Act. These numbers were few enough to undertake the supply responsibilities of the Army, but they represented a beginning toward better supply organization. One major problem not yet solved that concerned the Quartermaster Corps as well as the other supply bureaus was the degree of their subordination to the chief of staff. The Wood-Ainsworth affair had won for the chief of staff an ascendancy over the old staff departments, but it was still not clear to what extent he could direct and coordinate supply activities.[19]

During the years since the Spanish War, the Quartermaster Corps and its predecessors had brought about several changes of importance in the nature of the materials they supplied. In response both to the need for a light-weight uniform, demonstrated by campaigns in Cuba and the Philippines, and for an inconspicuous uniform in the face of modern rifles, the quartermasters adopted new Army uniforms of winter and summer weight and of olive drab and khaki coloring to replace in the field the traditional blue. The commissary service made the ration more flexible and experimented with improved emergency field rations. More important, it established the Army's first training schools for cooks and bakers, on the reasonable theory that no improvement in the components of the ration was likely to do much good if the food continued to be prepared as indifferently as it usually had been in the past. In the twilight of cavalry and horse artillery, the Quartermaster's Department found increasing difficulty in securing suitable animals for the Army and organized a Remount Service, whose functions would include breeding cavalry and artillery horses. More important than that belated improvement, the quartermasters somewhat reluctantly initiated a motor transport and maintenance service.[20]

The first great task of the Quartermaster Corps when the war began was to provide shelter for the anticipated flood of recruits. Without that, obviously nothing else could be done. Secretary of War Baker established a Cantonment Division in the corps. Colonel I. W. Littell, commander of the division, worked with a civilian Committee on Advisory Construction to draw up a plan for thirty-two cantonments, sixteen for the expanded National Guard and sixteen for the National Army, as the units of drafted men were now to be designated. The hope was to have the cantonments ready by September 1, by which date the selective service machinery was expected to be functioning in earnest and the flood of manpower beginning to arrive.

Surveys of available material and labor soon demonstrated that if the target date was to be reached, the National Guard would have to settle for tent camps, and sixteen such camps were prepared in the southern states. The wooden cantonments of the National Army were mostly located in the South, too, to facilitate year-round training, though a few concessions were made to northern local interests desirous of having soldiers' dollars in the vicinity. It was in the course of hastening cantonment construction that the Council of National Defense developed a new and controversial type of government contract designed for wide emergency application. Since there was no time for competitive bidding, especially since the work had to begin before specifications could be completed, the Council devised the cost-plus contract, with a grade scale of percentages to be paid the contractor, decreasing from ten per cent to six per cent on the cost of the work as the total cost increased.

Whatever the merits of the cost-plus system, the cantonments were ready virtually on schedule. It was a notable achievement that the Army was ready to shelter recruits faster than they could otherwise be assimilated. By October, the Cantonment Division could turn to the construction of other types of Army facilities and to the expansion of cantonments whose basic construction was complete. In that month too the War Department turned over to it all military construction in the United States, and the Cantonment Division consolidated construction work previously carried on by the Corps of Engineers, the Ordnance Department, and the Signal Corps.[21]

Assisted by the Food Administration, the Quartermaster Corps was able to feed the troops with none of the troubles and scandals of the Spanish War, a happy illustration of learning from unpleasant experiences. Clothing the Army did not go forward so well. By the middle of July, Quartermaster General Henry G. Sharpe was recommending that the assembly of the National Army be postponed from September 1 to October 1, lest he be able to clothe the men only in campaign hats and undershirts. Though not so drastically, the schedule of inductions did have to be slowed so clothing could keep pace. The calling of the National Guard in 1916 had exhausted all the reserve clothing stocks that the Quartermaster Corps had been permitted to accumulate. Remembering 1898, the corps had pleaded for years for authorization to purchase larger reserves, but Congress had persistently refused the pleas. Then the 1916 mobilization had exhausted clothing appropriations in addition to the stocks, and Congress had compounded the trouble by failing to pass a new appropriation act before it adjourned on March 4, 1917. Secretary Baker had permitted some contracting in anticipation of new appropriations, but General Sharpe still had to proceed with more caution than the situation of early 1917 made suitable.[22]

Despite all that, the Quartermaster Corps clothed 1,640,502 men by December, 1917. On a larger scale than ever before, the corps manufactured uniforms in its own establishments. But a War Department policy decision of 1915 had stipulated that government manufacturing should be sufficient only to serve as a model for and a control upon private contractors; so to a much greater extent the quartermasters turned to the private textile industry.

Still, difficulties continued. When the Council of National Defense joined with General Sharpe to study improved methods of purchasing quartermaster supplies, it concluded that to advertise for tremendous quantities in order to seek competitive bids would set off a serious price inflation. Therefore Secretary Baker ordered that contracts be placed through negotiations rather than competitive bidding, where possible arranged in cooperation with the General Munitions Board. The Quartermaster Corps accordingly contracted for clothing through a civilian Committee on Supplies. But since the Committee on Supplies was composed largely of experts from the clothing industry, this procedure tended to involve the industry's contracting with itself. Furthermore, Sharpe was probably not so assertive as he should have been in protecting the government's interests. There was unfavorable press comment, which culminated when the troops in southern camps, clothed in cotton to economize on scarce material, began shivering in the earliest and most severe winter in many years. The Senate Military Affairs Committee undertook an investigation of quartermaster activities in particular and supply and transportation problems in general, which helped precipitate a shakeup in the historic organization of Army supply.[23]

Amidst the discontent of the severe winter, Major General George W. Goethals was brought from retirement to be acting quartermaster general; he was famous as the builder of the Panama Canal. Sharpe was detailed to a War Council, headed by the Secretary of War and supposed to coordinate all the Army's supply activities. The War Council, however, was intended only as a temporary expedient, pending a reorganization of the General Staff to give that agency the coordinating power that had always been at least vaguely intended for it, but which it had never possessed as far as the supply departments were concerned. On March 4, 1918, Major General Peyton C. March returned from Europe to be chief of staff and to begin the reorganization. He would use Goethals as his principal deputy for supply, and for that purpose he took Goethals into the General Staff, naming Brigadier General Robert E. Wood acting quartermaster general.[24]

March and Goethals proposed to relieve the Quartermaster Corps of many of its traditionally diverse activities and to establish specific supply offices for specific functions. The Quartermaster Corps would become primarily a procuring and distributing agency. The two new leaders thus accelerated a tendency that had already set in. The urgency of the work of the Cantonment Division, for example, had led to its reporting directly to the Secretary of War from the beginning. When it was formally removed from the Quartermaster Corps to the General Staff and renamed the Construction Division early in 1918, the Quartermaster Corps lost little responsibility that it had not lost already. Before the war the Quartermaster Corps had controlled Army transportation in general, including the Army Transport Service, which ferried troops and supplies overseas. But arranging the shipment of American troops to France seemed to require so complete a concentration upon complex problems that the Embarkation Service was created separate from the Quartermaster Corps. Quartermaster responsibility for railroad transportation passed to an Inland Transportation Service in January, 1918. Motor transport soon went similarly to a Motor Transport Service.

On occasion, the reorganization of supply seems to have caused unnecessary confusion and excessive difficulties in morale. Though the Cantonment Division ceased to be part of the Quartermaster Corps, officers holding Quartermaster Corps commissions continued to be assigned to it, the Quartermaster Corps continued to hire most of its civilian employees, and the Quartermaster Corps still accounted for its funds and property—a rather crude division of responsibility. On the other hand, the general logic of the Goethals-March reorganization was sound. While functional departments dealt with transportation, construction, storage, and the like, purchasing for all supply bureaus moved gradually toward consolidation in a single office. A new Finance Department consolidated the accounts of the Army and led all agencies of the federal government in developing a budget system. Most important, the reorganization did effect control of supply by the chief of staff.[25]

Soon after Goethals took office as acting quartermaster general, he also became director of a Storage and Traffic Service in the Office of the Chief of Staff. In this post he coordinated the departments responsible for land and sea transport and for storage facilities in the United States. After March became chief of staff, he named Goethals director of a new Purchase, Storage, and Traffic Division of the General Staff, with the idea that here Goethals would supervise the whole supply of the Army. The Overman Act of May 20, 1918, soon gave the President authority to coordinate and consolidate executive agencies at his discretion as the war emergency demanded. This grant of power permitted a juggling of the War Department agencies to allow March and Goethals to achieve their purpose. Goethals gained control over procurement as well as transport and storage. The Quartermaster Corps lost most of the rest of its substance and responsibility, becoming merely a series of channels through which the supply office of the General Staff conducted logistical support of the Army. Substantially if not in every detail, Goethals could act as chief supply officer for the whole Army, responsible to the chief of staff.

For the first time, the Army possessed essentially a consolidated service of supply, although in achieving it there was a still further departure from Elihu Root's idea that the General Staff should plan but not administer. Goethals took more energetic control over estimates and purchasing, eliminating that excessive dependence upon interested civilian assistance for which Quartermaster General Sharpe had been criticized. Assistant Secretary of War Benedict Crowell became Goethals's immediate civilian superior, acting as civilian director of War Department mobilization activity, with the additional title of Director of Munitions. Cooperating with the civilian mobilization agencies and the War Industries Board, Crowell and Goethals accomplished the task of sending the new mass Army to Europe generally well equipped.[26]

But though well equipped, the Army could not go completely equipped. Apart from those deficiencies which American industry could not supply because the war proved too short to set up mass production, some supplies had to be found in Europe merely to relieve the burdens upon transatlantic shipping. Some supply items were obviously best secured in Europe because they were cheaper there, even if shipping had been available. Lumber for camp construction and fuel for the troops in France came from French forests, cut in cooperation with the French Forestry Service by hired civilian laborers, including many imported from Spain. Coal came from Great Britain. Where British and French textile mills had adequate capacity, it was better to purchase clothing and blankets from them than to use up shipping space. At the beginning of the war the United States Army lacked steel helmets for the Western Front, and a large quantity were bought from the British. Subsistence supplies also might most conveniently be bought in Europe when they were available, and the Quartermaster Corps set up its own plants in Europe to turn out macaroni, hard bread, and candy. As much as possible, the Army tried to find in Europe the thousands of horses that still supplemented motor transport; but French deliveries fell short of promises, shipping space had to go to the animals after all, and the supply nevertheless remained chronically short.

In August, 1917, General Pershing named Charles G. Dawes general purchasing agent for the American Expeditionary Force in Europe. Pershing continually advocated a pooling of Allied purchasing, but the British and French never agreed to more than limited cooperation. In the end, of the 18 million ship tons of material required by the A.E.F., European purchases accounted for 10 million tons.[27]

The General Staff in Washington controlled supply operations in Europe, like everything else there, only through Pershing and A.E.F. headquarters. Pershing organized the support of his forces into a Line of Communications headquarters, later redesignated the Services of Supply, under a commanding general, Services of Supply. The rear zone behind his lines, the "zone of the interior" in French terminology, he divided into several sections: eight, eventually nine, base sections grouped around the major port areas of France and England for receiving and forwarding shipments from America; an intermediate section in which the storage depots of the A.E.F. were established; and an advance section, just behind the forward zone or zone of operations, where he set up the billeting and training areas of the A.E.F. A commanding general of each section reported to the commanding general, Services of Supply. After some initial overlapping of authority, Pershing's own technical and supply staff was transferred to the staff of that officer.

As American participation in combat picked up during the summer of 1918, the War Department and the General Staff considered appointing Goethals to command the supporting troops and bases in Europe from a headquarters coordinate with Pershing's, leaving Pershing free to concentrate on the front. But Pershing wanted no diminution of his authority, and he insisted it was a traditional prerogative of the theater commander to control the support operations of his theater. To head off the War Department he transferred his first chief of staff, Major General James G. Harbord, to command of the Services of Supply, with increased authority for Harbord's headquarters; and the War Department acquiesced.[28]

The supply departments of the A.E.F. and the War Department worked out a program of automatic supply, whereby stipulated quantities of matériel would be shipped and maintained in depots in proportion to the numbers and kinds of troops in France. This system made frequent reorders unnecessary. Once the submarine threat was quieted sufficiently to give reasonable assurance in shipping schedules, the reserve supplies to be on hand in France were fixed at a forty-five-day level in the base depots, a thirty-day level in the intermediate depots, and a fifteen-day level in advance depots.

Beyond the advance depots, regulating stations made up supplies for each division in trains and sent the trains to the railheads. From there the divisions carried them forward to the front by motor and animal transport. Each combat division consumed twenty-five railroad carloads of supplies daily. To squeeze adequate service out of the railroads across France to his front, and especially to try to push the weary French railroads into shaping up to American standards, Pershing got a brigadier's commission for William W. Atterbury, general manager of the Pennsylvania Railroad, and gave him command of the A.E.F. transportation corps.[29]

Like the supply bureaus, the Medical Department of the Army entered the World War haunted by memories of its humiliation in 1898 and determined to redeem its reputation. Fortunately, on this occasion it had plenty of time to prepare itself before receiving casualties. It could set up hospitals and allocate ample numbers of beds, and it could prepare evacuation trains with Pullman berths, kitchens and dispensaries, and operating cars. It established a close cooperation with the Red Cross and other civilian health agencies. Through the Red Cross it arranged with fifty hospitals in the United States to provide the nuclei around which to build Army base hospitals. Mistakes occurred, but there was time to correct the worst of them before battle imposed a serious strain. Meanwhile, the experiences of 1898 called attention to camp sanitation and preventive medicine, and for the first time the Army went through a war with casualties from disease lower than battlefield casualties. Despite the horrendous influenza epidemic of 1918, mortality from disease in the Army was 15 per 1,000 per year, as compared with 65 per 1,000 in the Civil War.[30]

Pershing chose the part of the Western Front in which he proposed to form an American field army largely with an eye to the support requirements of his and the Allied armies. The British were sure to remain responsible for the Allies' northern flank, both for ease of supply from the home islands and to guard British strategic interests. The French ports most readily available to receive men and goods from America were those on the west coast, notably Saint-Nazaire, Bassens, and La Pallice. The French rail lines least taxed by the British and French armies were the ones reaching from those ports toward the southern Allied flank. The docks of Marseilles and the railroads north from there could supplement the western ports and railroads on that part of the front. Thus an American army could best be established and supported on the southern flank. Pershing was determined that the American Army should play primarily an offensive role; on the southern flank tempting targets awaited it: the iron fields of Lorraine, the coal basin of the Saar, the fortress and railway city of Metz, and the lateral railroad line northward from Metz through Sedan which supported the whole German front across France.[31]

Against an enemy like the Germans, trained rigorously in peace and conditioned by years on the Western Front, it was hardly enough to induct men and equip them. All soldiers agreed that, for the first time, the American Army would have to complete a systematic and thorough training program before committing its troops to battle.

But there was no universal agreement on how prolonged the training would have to be. Most officers still raised an eyebrow at Leonard Wood's notion that he could train a soldier in six months. Among most professional officers a year, or better, two years, seemed a suitable time for the making of a soldier. General Pershing was thoroughly a professional, and on this question he belonged to the Uptonian school. As American commander in France, he received authority to withhold American troops from battle until he was satisfied that their training was complete. With this authority and Uptonian convictions, he insisted upon a training program so long that for a time it appeared the Germans would prove correct in their prediction that no American army could reach the front before the French and British armies collapsed. At the end of 1917, nine months after American entry into the war, no American division had yet taken over a section of the Western Front, and Pershing's training program was such that 1918 would pass before Americans could hold any substantial portion of the line.

Of course, part of the delay resulted not from training problems per se but from the time required before large-scale inductions of draftees could begin. More than a month elapsed after the declaration of war on April 6, 1917, before Congress passed the Selective Service Act. Then the machinery to implement it was set in motion only laboriously and therefore slowly. Registration occurred July 5. The first drawing of numbers to establish priority of induction took place July 20. The first large group of draftees, 180,000, reported to cantonments in early September. By that time the building of cantonments had outpaced the time required to set up the thousands of local boards and other administrative machinery of draft selection and enforcement and to make the first selections.[32]

The delay was occasioned in part also by the necessity to provide trained officers and n.c.o.'s before assembling the recruits. In line with Uptonian doctrine the initial tendency of the General Staff was to contemplate scattering the Regular Army to form cadres for the conscripted National Army. But the limited numbers of the Regular Army left the War College Division able to allocate no more than 961 Regular Army enlisted men to each planned National Army division, and the adjutant general soon demonstrated that in fact there were not enough available Regulars to meet even that figure. The expansible army plan broke down because the Regulars, both officers and enlisted men, would have been swamped if they had been dispersed among the draftees. This fact, plus the pleas of France that at least a token force be sent quickly across the Atlantic, assured the use of the Regular Army not as Upton had proposed but as he had criticized Winfield Scott for doing.[33]

Still, there was a desperate shortage of officers and n.c.o.'s. Even while the Regular Army kept its identity, its formations and those of the National Guard were stripped dangerously thin to provide experienced soldiers to train the recruits. To provide thousands more officers, the War Department developed Leonard Wood's Plattsburg idea. The National Defense Act of 1916 authorized camps on the Plattsburg model, and upon that authorization the War Department conducted sixteen Officers' Training Camps from May 15 to August 11, 1917. Each camp was organized into a provisional training regiment of nine infantry companies, two cavalry troops, three field artillery batteries, and one engineer company. About 30,000 civilians and 7,957 Reserve Corps officers were admitted, of whom 27,341 were commissioned for active duty at the close of the course.

Other Officers' Training Camps followed on much the same pattern. For a time, after divisions were generally constituted, divisions conducted their own officers' camps. When the accelerated departure of some divisions for Europe began to disrupt that scheme, General Officers' Training Schools were created. Eventually eight such schools were organized, on a schedule that produced a class of officers per month from each of them. The original four months' course was compressed into three months. The staff departments and the Coast Artillery came to conduct separate schools for their officers. Altogether, in the course of the war 80,568 men graduated from the Officers' Training Schools into commissions.[34]

Whatever the limitations of time, officers who were to command troops did receive training for the purpose, to whatever degree was possible. In this war the Army and the War Department broke tradition and gave no commissions to leaders of fighting men on the strength of political qualifications alone. Accordingly, while "ninety-day wonders" filled the lieutenancies, and only one per cent of the company commanders in France had had a year's service, the upper ranks of the Army went to career officers and mainly to West Pointers in unprecedented proportion. Regular officers consistently praised Newton Baker, his pacifist background notwithstanding, as one of the best of all Secretaries of War, and his stout insistence on professional command was a principal reason they did so. Emory Upton himself could not have been more insistent upon trained officers than Baker was.

And surely his policy was a vast improvement over that of earlier wars. If prewar experience in a Regular commission was not the best possible preparation for the Western Front, it was the best available in America, especially with combat and administrative experience in the Philippines, Cuba, and Mexico and courses in the new Army school system as part of it. Wartime law permitted rigid seniority to give way to promotion by merit, all the way up to the grade of full general, restored as an active rank after a lapse since Sheridan's time. But Baker kept even the most potent political figures from enjoying the consequent plums. Theodore Roosevelt's Congressional friends inserted into the Selective Service Act a provision for raising four volunteer divisions, with the idea that they would be the Rough Riders of 1898 writ large, Roosevelt commanding one or all of them. But Baker ignored both Roosevelt and the power to raise such divisions. Even a merely quasipolitical figure such as Leonard Wood, ranking major general of the Army at the outset of the war, did not go on to France and higher rank. Both Pershing and Baker thought him too individualistic, undisciplined, and outspoken, and they could point accurately to his physical limitations of age and partial lameness. The same modern social disciplines that permitted the Selective Service Act also permitted this apolitical war making in a fashion not possible in earlier wars, but Baker still deserves credit for a wise policy now possible but not inevitable.[35]

One notable blunder of the officer training program has to be mentioned along with the praise. The War Department allowed the immediate need for officers to stampede it into reducing the West Point curriculum to a single year. This decision played hob with the Military Academy, inevitably creating a confused reorganization problem when the war ended, and meanwhile it added too few officers of too limited training to do any proportionate good.[36]

To assist fledgling officers in transferring to their commands lessons they had barely assimilated themselves, the War Department developed training aids on a scale far surpassing anything in earlier wars. By February 19, 1918, the War Plans Division of the General Staff was able to recommend fifty-five training and technical publications. The motion picture was utilized as a training device. The War Department approached the latter innovation in gingerly fashion, but in August, 1917, the War College Division of the General Staff secured permission to produce training films, and a year later fifty-seven reels were in circulation. They proved useful well beyond the Army's cautious anticipations.[37]

But there remained the question of how much time needed to be consumed in training the men. The War Department eventually decided that four months' training in the United States was sufficient for the infantryman before sending him to France. But in World War I, a basic training in discipline, military life, tactics, and weaponry that might have sufficed in the Civil War seemed merely a beginning. Specialists such as artillerymen had to go on to intensive training in the techniques of their arm or service. Pershing insisted that even the infantryman needed an extremely intensive and notably prolonged additional training. He must learn the techniques of trench warfare as they had developed during three years on the Western Front, and the handling of the special weapons of trench warfare, the machine gun, the hand grenade, and the mortar, plus the shovel and barbed wire.

For training in trench warfare, the American Army called upon British and French officers of long experience. But in addition, Pershing insisted that to win the war the American Army must take the offensive and drive the Germans out of their trenches, and that therefore American soldiers must go beyond the British and French preoccupation with trench warfare to learn offensive tactics suitable to open and mobile war beyond the trenches. Especially, for that purpose, Americans must learn thoroughly the use of the rifle and the bayonet, and all American soldiers must learn the marksmanship which had always been a hallmark of American Regular infantrymen. Pershing scoffed at the French tactics which had soldiers throw grenades even at Germans who were fleeing; Americans must learn to cut down their enemies with the rifle.

Finally, while they were about it, Pershing, the thoroughgoing Regular, expected his men to learn military courtesy, customs, and bearing until the dubious Regulars of the expanded Regular Army, the National Guardsmen, and the draftees all would look and dress and carry themselves like Regulars. If they did, he believed they would probably fight like Regulars.

Pershing knew that to train the American Army as he wished to train it would require time, and much time. He was a perfectionist, and he prepared to take the time. He established a lengthy training schedule for the 1st Division in France, which he proposed essentially to repeat with subsequent divisions. From the arrival of its first elements at the selected training area at Gondrecourt on July 5, 1917, the 1st Division undertook a review of basic tactical exercises which consumed a month or more. Late in August the French 47th Division of Chasseurs Alpins, the "Blue Devils," began instructing it in trench warfare and weaponry. Not until October 21 did Pershing send the division to a trial experience in the line, in a quiet sector and attached to the French 18th Division. Beginning that day, one battalion of each regiment went into line with the French for ten days, to be followed by the other battalions over a thirty-day period. At the end of November the division returned to Gondrecourt to assimilate its front-line experience in further training. Only on January 18, 1918, half a year after its arrival in France, did Pershing consider it ready for commitment on its own to another quiet sector of the front.[38]

By that time, the 2nd Division, half Regular Army and half Marines, had been in France since October. The 26th Division had begun to arrive in September—New England National Guards, appropriately the first National Guard division to cross the Atlantic, with units descended from the train bands of Massachusetts Bay, and soldiers with generations behind them in the same town companies. The 42nd Division, the Rainbow Division of National Guards from twenty-six scattered states and the District of Columbia, had begun to arrive about the end of 1917. These divisions settled into training programs patterned on that of the 1st. Since each front-line division needed another trained division to support it in a process of rotation, and since casualties in heavy action could amount to three-quarters of a division in a single day, Pershing did not want to commit any of his divisions to an active sector until all four initial divisions were ready. On this schedule, he would have an American field army late in 1918, and it would take the offensive to pry the Germans out of their trenches and win victory in open warfare in 1919. It is little wonder that the French grew impatient.[39]

In judging Pershing's program it must be noted that divisions commonly reached France filled with recent recruits, trained men having been leeched out of them to find replacements and specialists for other divisions. Not until March became chief of staff and set up specifically designated replacement divisions did Pershing begin to receive divisions that had not been reshuffled repeatedly before they joined him; and March's program came into full play only on the very eve of the Armistice.[40]

The slow arrival of Americans in France, due to shipping shortages as well as training and supply problems, and their slow additional preparation once they had arrived there encouraged the Germans to believe they could win the war with their 1918 offensive. The initial success of the blows they began delivering on March 21 suggested they might be correct. Pershing had to say, "At this moment there are no other questions but of fighting," and to offer to the Allies, "Infantry, artillery, aviation, all that we have are yours."[41] For some time before this event, growing numbers of American officers had been tending toward the conclusion that Pershing's training program was excessive, that Americans might well go into the line much earlier. Secretary Baker himself agreed with them, but he hesitated to interfere with Pershing because of the high responsibility that Pershing bore.

The practical effect of the Pershing policy [March, who did not like Pershing, was to write] was that large bodies of American troops, divisions whose morale was at the highest point, who had had from four to six months' training, and often more in camps in America, and who expected on arrival in France to be thrown into battle immediately, found the keen edge of their enthusiasm dulled by having to go over again and again drills and training which they had already undergone in America.[42]

Now, with the crisis of the German 1918 offensive, Pershing had no choice but to commit his troops without his full training program. The claims of his critics would be put to the test. But as that event occurred, another vital question regarding the fate of the American Army also reached its test: whether Pershing would be able to build and command in France independent American field armies, or whether the Americans should be shuffled into the weakened divisions of the British and the French.

Ulysses Grant in the dual role of commanding general of the United States Army and commander in the field with the Army of the Potomac had scarcely wielded fuller authority than Washington granted John J. Pershing as commander of the American Expeditionary Force. But Pershing had to fight a coalition war in which the United States was a military novice entering belatedly upon a deteriorating situation, and whether he would actually command an American army in the face of the contrary plans of the coalition partners long remained doubtful.

On May 26, 1917, Secretary of War Baker signed the order investing Pershing with his command. A Virginian by birth and the son of a Confederate army veteran, Baker accepted the idea that one of the lessons of the Civil War was that the civil government must pare its interference with military commanders to the narrowest essentials. Also, he had full confidence in Pershing. Pershing's ramrod-stiff professional integrity and dedication thoroughly impressed every statesman he ever encountered. Theodore Roosevelt had been so taken that, when he found the law would not permit him to raise Pershing from captain to major or colonel, he jumped him to brigadier general over 882 officers his senior. Pershing's uncomplaining conduct of the thankless Mexican Punitive Expedition had ensured his standing with Baker. The Secretary is said to have told him he would send him only two orders as commander of the A.E.F.: "one to go and one to return." Baker scarcely exaggerated.

Pershing received all "the authority and duties devolved by the laws, regulations, orders, and customs of the United States upon a commander of an Army in the field in time of war and with the authority and duties in like manner devolved upon department commanders in peace and war," plus "in general, . . . all necessary authority to carry on the war vigorously in harmony with the spirit of these instructions and toward a victorious conclusion." The precedents referred to had developed when there was no modern general staff and the War Department was relatively weak, while commanders in the field such as Sherman and Sheridan were strong. The distance between Washington and Pershing's headquarters in France were bound to enhance the general's authority. Pershing too was sure to push his powers to their limits: he was a headstrong, self-willed cavalry officer, brimming with a self-confidence that had been confirmed by a career of thoroughly competent performance.[43]

Specific circumstances in the government and the War Department when Pershing departed for France gave further assurance that his status would approach that of an autonomous proconsul. Though Woodrow Wilson was a strong President by almost every measurement, he felt little interest in military affairs and preferred to leave war to the generals. War repelled him, and he cared to exercise none of the careful control over military organization and strategy of a Polk or a Lincoln, or even a McKinley. His business as he saw it was the civil and diplomatic side of war and preparation for the peace. It is significant that when he went to France after the war he visited not a single battlefield where his soldiers had fought and died; some uneasiness about having led his country into war seems to have impelled him to have as little to do with the waging of the war as was possible.[44]

During the relatively short period of the war, Congress was not only controlled by the President's party but also accustomed to accepting Wilson's leadership. Efforts by Senator George E. Chamberlain, a dissident Democrat, to enhance Congressional oversight of the war, and perhaps to create a new Committee on the Conduct of the War, fell flat and resulted mainly in Chamberlain's political demise.[45]

Newton Baker was a capable Secretary of War who developed an impressive knowledge not only of military administration but of the professional aspects of command. But his policy toward command decisions in France was one of deliberate abstention. He believed his primary duty was to build an army with which Pershing could fight, and then leave Pershing to fight it.

Furthermore, for nearly a year Baker possessed inadequate professional assistance in the War Department. Because at the beginning of the war the nature of the General Staff's authority was not yet clear, the bureau chiefs all continued to report to Baker directly and to burden him with excessive detail. Baker had difficulty finding a chief of staff strong enough to develop the office into all that was implied in it and to serve as a satisfactory professional counselor. Hugh L. Scott, chief of staff when the war began, was an intelligent officer and the man who more than any other convinced Baker of the need for conscription; but Scott was neither young enough nor forceful enough to be a good wartime chief of staff. About a month after the declaration of war he departed from Washington with Elihu Root's mission to Russia, designed to try to salvage that country and its war effort.

Thereupon Major General Tasker H. Bliss, the assistant chief of staff, became acting chief. Bliss was an excellent man in many ways, widely knowledgeable in military history and theory, a linguist with literary inclinations, destined to become a talented military diplomat; but he too was not well fitted to be a wartime chief of staff. Like Scott, he was on the verge of retirement and lacking in the assertiveness to seize the potential of authority not fully defined. He lacked experience in handling large bodies of troops, and this was a handicap at least to his prestige in the officer corps. His tenure as acting chief began a year-long game of musical chairs with the post. Scott returned to his desk in August, but he retired in September (though for a time thereafter he commanded at Camp Dix). Bliss succeeded him, but in November he visited Europe, and Major General John Biddle became acting chief. Bliss returned in December but retired in January, 1918, restoring Biddle to duty as acting chief.[46]

Not until Peyton C. March was returned to Washington from command of the artillery of the A.E.F. did Baker find the chief of staff he wanted and a man to serve through the war. March took over as acting chief on March 4 and became chief of staff in his own right with the wartime rank of full general on May 25. With justice it can be said that it was March who completed the architecture of the office of chief of staff which Root had begun. Possessing in more than ample measure the forcefulness and assertiveness that Scott and Bliss had lacked, and finding in the Overman Act ample authority for any organizational changes that might otherwise have been questioned, March at last subordinated the bureau chiefs to himself, insisting that they report to the Secretary of War only through him and that they regard themselves as responsible to him. He reorganized the General Staff itself again, to multiply its effectiveness for war.

The origin of his ideas on a proper general staff is interesting, since they came in part from a study of the Japanese general staff which he had made as an observer with the Japanese during their war with Russia, knowing that the Japanese in turn had borrowed much from the Germans. By August, 1918, he had created four main General Staff divisions: Operations; Military Intelligence; Purchase, Storage, and Traffic; and War Plans. The Operations and War Plans Divisions would share the functions of the old War College Division. The duties of the former included charge over recruiting, mobilization, appointment and assignment of officers, determination of overseas priorities, selection of campsites, and preparation of tables of organization and equipment. The Operations Division also maintained liaison with the bureau chiefs. The Military Intelligence Division would take on work hitherto much neglected. At the beginning of the war, only two officers and two clerks had been concerned with gathering intelligence; March elevated the importance of this function in the structure of the General Staff and increased its personnel to 282 officers, 29 enlisted men, and 949 civilian employees. In the Purchase, Storage, and Traffic Division, Goethals oversaw the logistical support of the Army. The total personnel of the General Staff in Washington grew to 1,072.[47]

In making these changes, March had the full support of Baker, who found here the means to his own more effective over-all control of the military establishment, while he and his assistant secretaries were freed for fuller attention to Congress and the civilian mobilization agencies. Believing in the general staff principle, Baker supported March in issuing general orders that stated in broad terms the chief of staff's authority not only over the War Department but over the whole Army, including Pershing and his command:

The Chief of the General Staff is the immediate adviser of the Secretary of War on all matters relating to the Military Establishment, and is charged by the Secretary of War with the planning, development, and execution of the Army program. The Chief of Staff by law (Act of May 12, 1917) takes rank and precedence over all officers of the Army, and by virtue of that position and by authority of and in the name of the Secretary of War he issues such orders as will insure that the policies of the War Department are harmoniously executed by the several corps, bureaus, and other agencies of the Military Establishment and that the Army program is carried out speedily and efficiently.[48]

Despite this order, however, the chief of staff had to confine himself in practice mainly to the raising of the Army in the United States and to a share in the determination of which troops should go to France and when. Though Pershing was technically his subordinate, March could intervene little in the command of the A.E.F. On such an issue as the proposal to give Goethals command of the supply services in France while restricting Pershing to command of operations, the War Department acceded to Pershing's will, not March's. Secretary Baker on occasion had to act as arbiter between his two strong-willed and mutually jealous full generals, the chief of staff and the commander of the A.E.F. The truth of the relationship between them is less well reflected in Pershing's theoretical subordination than in his priority in rank over March in the Army lists; in Wilson's proposal at the close of the war that both be made permanent full generals but with Pershing the senior; and in Congress's creation for Pershing of the rank of general of the armies, while March's permanent generalship was delayed until 1930. Despite all March accomplished to complete the elevation of the office of chief of staff, Pershing continued to command in France with authority unrivalled since Grant.[49]

The order of May 26, 1917, assigning Pershing to his command clearly stipulated that he was to insist upon his American Army's taking its place beside the French and British armies as a fully equal partner, that he must not allow his troops to be absorbed permanently into French and British formations:

In military operations against the Imperial German Government you are directed to coöperate with the forces of the other countries employed against the enemy; but in so doing, the underlying idea must be kept in view that the forces of the United States are a separate and distinct component of the combined forces, the identity of which must be preserved. This fundamental rule is subject to such minor exceptions in particular circumstances as your judgment may approve.

The decision as to when your command, or any of its parts, is ready for action is confided to you, and you will exercise full discretion in determining the manner of coöperation. But until the forces of the United States are, in your judgment, sufficiently strong to warrant operations as an independent command, it is understood that you will coöperate as a component of whatever army you may be assigned to by the French Government.[50]

To carry out this section of his orders and preserve the separate and distinct identity of his American forces proved to demand all of Pershing's forcefulness and downright stubbornness. The reader of his war memoirs is likely to grow weary of the topic, since it intrudes into the memoirs continually. Pershing himself grew proportionately more weary of it, for in their efforts to bring Americans into their own thin battalions the persistence and the effrontery of the Allies were both immense. Whenever Pershing believed he had at last received firm guarantees that the British and French would support the creation of a separate American army and its assumption of control over a distinct sector of the front, the Allies would seize again upon some new crisis as a pretext for hedging the guarantees.

The British and French position was not without military reason. Their soldiers had infinitely more experience than the Americans in modern war, and they could place over the American troops officers who knew their business and staffs thoroughly practiced in the handling of large bodies of men. The Americans depended upon them for artillery, aviation, and various other kinds of support anyway. Surely the American recruits would learn war best by serving in experienced divisions, and thus some kind of integration of the

Americans into the Allied armies would best hasten the end of the war and save lives. Surely Pershing could not resist this kind of argument.

But Pershing did resist. Even if the integration of Americans into foreign armies were restricted to the insertion of whole battalions into Allied formations, rather than a distribution of companies or individuals, all kinds of practical problems were bound to make the efficiency of the arrangement less than the Allies claimed. And Pershing believed that national pride had a legitimate place in his calculations. Would Americans fight with the zeal and determination of which they were capable if they were treated with a condescension that not even the Portuguese had to bear? What would be the state of their morale if their government acquiesced in the notion that they were incapable of fighting the Germans on their own? Would not association with the war-weary French and British make the Americans war-weary and discouraged too? What influence could the United States command at the peace conference, after all her exertions, if there were no American army in the field? For good reason, Pershing's insistence that the American soldier must fight in an American army is generally accounted one of his principal achievements.

Perhaps another commander might have accomplished the same end while creating fewer bad feelings. In his best moods, Pershing was not an easy man to get along with, and he conducted his battle for a separate American army with table-thumping and harsh Anglo-Saxon words. Both the French and British governments occasionally tried to appeal over his head to wring concessions from the President, encouraged by a more conciliatory manner and by indifference and ignorance regarding military details; but they found no yielding of principle. Premier Georges Clemenceau of France repeatedly urged Marshal Foch to try to force Pershing's removal. In November, 1917, the British, French, and Italians established the Supreme War Council in Paris, where diplomatic and military representatives of the principal Allied powers would attempt to coordinate their war efforts. Tasker H. Bliss upon his retirement as chief of staff received a brevet as general and became the American military representative. Thereupon he too became a target for Allied leaders seeking American soldiers but not an American army; and being of a more obliging temper than Pershing, he sometimes gave his approval to concessions that angered the commander of the A.E.F. But Bliss, like the government at Washington, made no concession on the basic goal of a separate American army, and Pershing's unaltered instructions still gave him the decisive authority to determine American participation.[51]

The German offensive of 1918 posed the severest test for the goal

of a separate army but finally provided the means for achieving it.
Lest the Germans break through to Paris, even Pershing had to offer
the use of American troops wherever and in any way they were
needed. For the moment his goal had to be laid aside. Before the
crisis passed, some of his worst fears in placing Americans under
foreign command materialized. At the crossings of the Marne, the
French retreated on July 15 without bothering to inform four utterly
green companies of the 28th Division, the Pennsylvania National
Guard. Having been placed callously and inexplicably in a most
exposed position, these Americans had to fight their way back
through the German lines. The battle of Belleau Wood had consequences of immense benefit, but it developed out of French carelessness over the expenditure of American lives, and the French allowed
it to persist without adequate artillery or tank support.[52]

At the same time, the crisis aroused the French and British to try
to speed up the shipment of American troops to Europe. By now
men in large numbers were becoming available in the training camps
of the United States, but there was not enough shipping available to
carry them to Europe. American shipping could by no means do the
job alone, even when augmented by enemy and Dutch vessels taken
over in American ports; in the end only forty-four per cent of the
A.E.F. sailed to Europe in American ships. Until now the British
had been distinctly uncooperative about offering substantial British
tonnage to move American troops or working out a coherent shipping program. They had been preoccupied with their losses to submarines and the consequent threat to their vital supplies, and they
had been skeptical of the utility of bringing a separate American
army to France. But with Sir Douglas Haig's B.E.F. falling back in
sorry defeat from the Passchendaele Ridge for which it had expended
so much blood the year before, and his divisions extending their
fronts because replacements were not to be had, the British now
offered enough additional shipping to transport to Europe 120,000
Americans a month, provided they were all combat troops and
would fight with British divisions.

This British admission that they could muster the shipping to accelerate American troop movements, plus the growing desperation of
the Allied situation as the German advance continued, gave the
Americans opportunity to bargain in order to get the British shipping
yet not sacrifice the American army program. Pershing, March, the
War Department, and even to a degree the President were to become
embroiled in a controversy whether superfluous concessions were
extended to the British, and if so by whom, and the British evidently
experienced some misunderstanding about what the Americans finally agreed to send. Essentially, however, the British promised to

provide ships to boost the total of Americans moving to France to 120,000 a month. The Americans agreed that they would dispatch in May the infantry, engineer, and Signal Corps troops, with their unit headquarters, of six divisions to train with and thus reinforce the British army. Any excess shipping would transport the artillery of these divisions, which would train with the French. When the stipulated combat troops had all been shipped, their necessary support troops would follow; and when these had arrived and the combatants had been trained, American divisions were to be assembled and used as Pershing wished. Presently the American concession of granting priority to infantry, engineer, and Signal Corps troops was extended into June.[53]

Though Pershing had to fend off still more demands for shipping infantry and machine gunners only and postponing indefinitely the creation of a separate American army, this agreement broke the worst of the shipping shortage. With losses to submarines decreasing and tonnage becoming more readily available, there opened a period of vigorous British cooperation with the American Embarkation Service. Ultimately, 49.9 per cent of the A.E.F. sailed in British vessels. The shipping schedule of the spring of 1918 was actually exceeded: 244,407 Americans sailed in May; 277,894 in June; a peak of 306,302 in July; 281,454 in August; and 252,100 in September. By the end of that month Marshal Foch, named Allied Commander in Chief during the crisis of the German offensive, assured the War Department that estimates could be revised downward: forty American divisions should be enough to assure Germany's defeat. In July the German offensive had halted, stopped with the aid of Americans thrown into the French armies at the crossings of the Marne. Into their offensive the Germans had poured their last energies. With their failure, and the arrival of enough Americans to turn the numerical balance, the tide flowed at last with the Allies.[54]

Foch shifted the Allies in turn to the attack, "Tout la monde a la bataille!" his war cry. At Soissons and across the Ourcq and the Vesle to the Aisne, American divisions fought in the first counterstrokes still as part of French corps and armies.[55] But their numbers, and the proof of Belleau Wood and Soissons that the Americans could fight, and the new good fortune of the situation permitted Pershing to insist on the final preparations for erecting an American field army with its own sector of the front. Headquarters, American I Corps, Major General Hunter Liggett, took over the Belleau Wood–Chateau-Thierry Sector in July. The headquarters had been intended to become active in the spring, but the German drive had delayed it. Pershing suggested that an American army might now be built around the I Corps front at Chateau-Thierry. But for political, logistical, and strategic reasons he and Foch reverted to the original plan for an American army on the Allied southeastern flank in Lorraine.

There they decided, again reconfirming an earlier tentative understanding, that the American Army would undertake its first offensive against the Saint-Mihiel salient, an arrowhead in the Allied lines on the path to Metz and astride the flank of any advance through the Argonne Forest toward Sedan.[56]

On July 24 Pershing issued his formal orders for the creation of the United States First Army, effective August 10. The assembling of the army from divisions hitherto scattered along the Western Front and in reserve took place during August. On September 12 the army opened its Saint-Mihiel attack.

It consisted then of three American corps of fourteen divisions, a total of about 550,000 American troops, plus 110,000 French soldiers. Its artillery comprised 3,010 guns, none of them of American manufacture and 1,329 of them manned by French personnel. It possessed 267 light tanks, all of them of French manufacture and 113 manned by the French. Supporting it were nearly 1,400 airplanes, under the command of Colonel William Mitchell of the American Air Service, but including the British Independent Bombing Squadrons under Major General Sir Hugh Trenchard, and a French air division of 600 planes.[57]

The composition of the First Army thus reflected both the rapid growth of American manpower in France and the persisting limitations of American equipment. These features continued to mark the American war effort through the three remaining months of conflict. On October 12 there were sufficient American troops to permit Pershing to organize a Second Army, which took over the front south of the First Army and was to drive toward the Briey-Longwy iron fields, while the First Army continued an offensive it had opened September 26 on a line from the Argonne Forest to the Moselle River. Pershing became an army group commander. Hitherto he had received his orders from Foch through Pétain as part of the latter's group of armies; now he was coequal with Pétain and Sir Douglas Haig. Hunter Liggett and Robert Lee Bullard, soon to be commissioned lieutenant generals, commanded the First and Second Armies, respectively.[58]

By November 1, the A.E.F. counted seven corps and forty-one divisions, some of the latter depot or replacement divisions and a few still scattered among the armies of the Allies. This number of American divisions proved enough to assure German defeat, fulfilling Foch's prophecy of early October. In part this was true because forty

American divisions were equivalent to about eighty divisions of any of the other great powers. French, British, and German divisions formally numbered about 12,000 combatants each, and when Marshal Joffre visited the United States immediately after the declaration of war he recommended the same size: European officers believed that 12,000 combatants represented the maximum number that one general and his staff could handle. Actually, French and British divisions were often down to as few as 5,000 combatants. In a debatable decision, however, Pershing fixed an American division at 979 officers, 27,082 men, with support troops making a total of about 40,000. His purpose was to achieve a capacity for sustained battle which would ensure that American divisions would not falter short of their objectives as British and French divisions so often had done. For the warfare of the Western Front, where rapid and flexible maneuver was not at a premium, Pershing's judgment may have been right.

The American infantry division consisted of two brigades of infantry, one of field artillery (two regiments of 75-mm guns, one of 155-mm guns), a regiment of engineers, a division machine-gun battalion, a signal battalion, and the division supply and sanitary trains. Each infantry brigade in turn comprised two infantry regiments, each including three battalions and a machine-gun company. The battalion numbered four companies of 6 officers and 250 men each; the strength of a regiment was 112 officers and 3,720 men. The Tables of Organization and Equipment allotted to an infantry division 72 artillery pieces, 260 machine guns, and 17,666 rifles. The division was the basic, self-contained unit and could be shifted readily from one corps to another or from one part of the front to another.

Corps and armies were not Table of Organization units; their strength varied according to needs. A corps, primarily a command and administrative organization with certain permanently attached artillery, engineer, signal, and supply components, comprised two to six divisions. An army consisted of three to five corps.[59]

The divisions at first fell into three categories based on their origins: Regular Army (1st through 8th Divisions), National Guard (26th through 42nd), and National Army (76th through 93rd). Regimental designations distinctively indicated these three categories. Regimental numerals under 100 were reserved for the old Regular Army organizations and the new Regular formations raised for the war. The National Guard was so thoroughly federalized, its service no longer based on a Presidential call to the states but upon the individual's enlistment oath, that in federal service the regiments lost their historic state numerals. All National Guard regiments received numerals in the 100's, the famous old 7th New York Regiment becoming the 107th United States Infantry, the Irish 69th New York the 165th Infantry, and so on. National Army infantry regiments, the new formations based on the Selective Service Act, had numbers over 300. This regimental numbering system remained through the war and still persists; but on August 7, 1918, General March issued orders otherwise erasing the distinctions among Regular Army, National Guard, and National Army, amalgamating all into the United States Army with common administration, command, and insignia. Thereby he recognized the mixing of personnel which had long since vitiated the official distinctions.[60]

Not least among the reasons why the Allies viewed the creation of an American field army with something less than enthusiasm was their concern that inexperienced American commanders and especially staffs would not be able to manage large numbers of men and complicated logistical problems. The Americans themselves had to acknowledge that such concern was hardly groundless.[61] Pershing established schools of staff and line in France for officer training supplementary to that given by the Army school system in America. Corps schools trained both unit commanders and noncommissioned officers. Still other schools trained instructors for the corps schools. There were special schools for each staff and supply department and every branch of the service, such as the artillery school occupying the quarters of the historic French cavalry school at Saumur. The apex of the A.E.F. school system was the General Staff School at Langres, ably organized by Major General James W. McAndrew, who went on to succeed Harbord as Pershing's chief of staff. None of these schools had the capacity or time to train as many officers as thoroughly as Pershing would have liked, but they did what they could at forced draft.[62]

The Army school system in America had attained a degree of maturity too recently and had graduated too few for Pershing to feel complacent about his officers. The war did produce conspicuous examples of American command failures, notably the breakdown of much of the 26th Division's upper echelon in the counteroffensive against the Marne salient, a case of too many insufficiently trained National Guard officers wilting under pressures for which they had not been prepared.[63]

But Pershing's own misgivings proved greater than necessary, and the deeper misgivings of the French and British certainly were excessive. If the Regular Army's schools had trained too few officers, the war demonstrated that those few had been wisely selected and well instructed; they sustained a respectable level of ability and skill. American staff work was sometimes remarkably good and by 1918 well able to stand comparison with French and British. Pershing constructed at General Headquarters, A.E.F., a kind of miniature war department, with a general staff that was far better than the General Staff at Washington had ever been before the war. Its organization was to serve as a model for a reorganization of the War Department General Staff that fixed the outlines of that body into World War II. The staff work of armies, corps, and divisions rivaled that of General Headquarters with surprising frequency.

The greatest single achievement of American staff work in France was the one often cited in recent years because of George C. Marshall's part in it. This was the preparation and realization of a complex of plans for the attack on the Saint-Mihiel salient, a shift westward from the Saint-Mihiel area to the Meuse-Argonne, and the initial attack in the latter area. The principal staff planners involved were Colonel Fox Conner, chief of the Operations Section of GHQ, known as one of the most brilliant students of warfare in the American Army, and the primary initiator of the plans; Colonel Hugh A. Drum, chief of staff of the First Army; and Colonel Marshall and Colonel Walter S. Grant, both also of the Operations Section of GHQ. When Foch opened the Allied counterattacks of 1918, German weakness proved to be much worse than anticipated. The Allied advance pushed eastward so rapidly that the elimination of the Saint-Mihiel salient, planned so long as the first American offensive, seemed to Foch now to be a diversion from the main business of pressing forward where the Germans were already giving way. He suggested the abandonment of the Saint-Mihiel offensive, and did so in a manner that suggested a new effort to scuttle independent American operations along with it. Pershing insisted on the offensive, both because he had long planned it as a set piece to demonstrate American prowess and because he still believed in the strategic value of eliminating the German salient. Foch then consented that the Saint-Mihiel attack might proceed on September 12, provided that the First Army also open an offensive toward Sedan between the Argonne Forest and the Heights of the Meuse, sixty miles from Saint-Mihiel, on September 26.

Therefore the Saint-Mihiel offensive had to be so planned as to be carried out under meticulous control. Furthermore, fifteen divisions had to be on the Meuse-Argonne front in time for the offensive there, nine of them to participate in the first phase of the Meuse-Argonne. To that end infantry and supporting troops to the number of 600,000 had to move into position on the Meuse-Argonne while the Saint-Mihiel offensive was still in progress, at least 400,000 of them coming from the Saint-Mihiel sector. At the same time, some 220,000 French and Italian troops had to be moved out of the Meuse-Argonne to make way for the Americans. Three thousand guns had to go into line on the new front, with 40,000 tons of ammunition. All these movements across the rear of the army attacking at Saint-Mihiel must occur at night without lights, in order to conceal Allied intentions from the enemy. Pershing as well as Foch doubted that the shift could be accomplished. Doing it was the special responsibility of Colonel Marshall. It was done.[64]

So much was the war one that demanded intricate planning and logistical arrangements that the achievements of the staffs often seem more impressive than those of the line commanders, whose control over combat was at best severely limited once their troops were committed. Because of the rigid seniority system in prewar promotion, Pershing found many of the division commanders relatively old and therefore unfit for physical reasons, since trench warfare presented unusual hazards to health and demanded high stamina and vigor. He ruthlessly weeded out those who did not meet his standards, in these or any other respects. Perhaps he was too ruthless and too impatient. It is hard to perceive the justice of his removal of Major General William L. Sibert from command of the 1st Division in December, 1917. Sibert was at his best as an administrator and had won his reputation in governing the Panama Canal Zone. Pershing wanted a more aggressive warrior type to lead the first American division in action and chose Robert Lee Bullard in Sibert's stead. But Sibert was never given a real chance to prove himself as a war leader, and Pershing's carping about how he handled the division's training suggests a man looking for pretexts for an action he had already decided to take. Other dismissals raise similar questions.

But with determined pruning, sending misfits to "blooey"—the reassignment center at Blois—Pershing gave the A.E.F. the competent leadership he wanted. By the summer of 1918 he had grown disillusioned with the method of training his divisions by assigning them temporarily to the French or British. With the Allies, Americans simply drank up pessimism, and they learned only trench warfare. "The fact is that our officers and men are far and away superior to the tired Europeans," Pershing decided. "I have had to insist very strongly . . . to get our troops out of leading strings."[65]

If the war produced no American general of recognizable genius, it offered little opportunity for the display of genius. The design of operations had become largely a committee process; the conduct of operations afforded little room for qualities other than dogged persistence.

Of the top generals, Hunter Liggett proved fully equal to the tactical demands of both corps and army command. He was a fat man and at first had a hard time convincing Pershing that he met the latter's high physical standards and had "no fat above the neck."

Eventually, Pershing promoted him as rapidly as he could and consistently used him in the most critical sectors. He and his excellent staff planned the American offensive of November 1, 1918, an admirable scheme for opening the German center in Napoleonic fashion and then maneuvering against the newly cleared flanks. It may not be only because Pershing had too many things to do that the First Army performed better after Pershing relinquished its direct command to Liggett.

Bullard, organizer of A.E.F. infantry schools, was an able division and corps leader, who probably possessed a capacity for army command beyond anything he had a chance to display during the short life of the Second Army. James G. Harbord was an aggressive division commander as well as an outstanding staff and supply officer. Perhaps the most original American tactician was Major General Charles P. Summerall. An artilleryman already famous for his part in breaching the walls of Peking, he commanded the 1st Division artillery at Cantigny, a brigade of the 2nd Division at Soissons, the 1st Division at Saint-Mihiel, and the V Corps in the Meuse-Argonne. He developed with thoroughness unexampled even on the Western Front the communications network which linked advancing troops with their supporting artillery; so that when his troops were held up they could be sure as no others in the Army of summoning an artillery fire that would hit where it was supposed to and eliminate the obstacles before them. More than that, he sent many of his 75's forward in direct contact with the infantry.[66]

Much the same thing can be said of Pershing himself as of most of his principal subordinates: he was able but he never displayed the qualities of a transcendently great captain. His most important single achievement was the construction of the American armies in Europe for whose integrity he fought so long. Closely related to his insistence upon an American field army was his conviction that the French and British had grown too exclusively wedded to the tactics of trench warfare, that open warfare must return when the Germans at last retreated, and that therefore American soldiers must learn offensive tactics appropriate to open warfare. He probably envisioned a return to open warfare more complete than ever occurred; the Germans retired stubbornly from one prepared position to another, and always their machine guns were skillfully placed and tenaciously employed. Still, Pershing was right in his insistence that soldiers must not be allowed to expect the constant protection of trenches. His insistence upon the rifle and bayonet training appropriate to warfare outside the trenches paid off when his men threaded their way through Belleau Wood and the Argonne Forest.

The American Army was unique in its requirement that the infantryman shoot for record and that he practice marksmanship under simulated battle conditions as well as on the firing range. Even the British regular army, whose marksmanship astonished the Germans at the beginning of the war, had shot simply on the "cone of fire" principle, while other armies emphasized fire by volleys. In suitable circumstances the skill with the rifle cultivated by the American Army since the Indian wars could still work an awesome effect on the battlefield.

Yet automatic-fire infantry weapons became ever more prominent, more and more reshaping battlefield tactics. Against defending machine guns, infantry tended to advance only a part of a platoon at a time. The other part would try to pin down the defenders with fire, while their advancing comrades scampered from shelter to shelter. Though water-cooled machine guns were themselves too bulky to accompany the forward edge of an attack, automatic rifles were especially useful for delivering the attackers' covering fire. American rifle companies by 1918 included sixteen automatic rifles along with 235 Springfields, both weapons firing the same .30-caliber cartridge. The automatic rifles were British Lewis guns, French Chauchats, or, toward the close of the war, the new and very superior American Browning Automatic Rifle.

Pershing's stress on rifle and bayonet tactics suggests a somewhat conservative approach to war, and significantly so. "Open warfare" of the traditional kind was destined never to appear again, and it is by no means clear how well Pershing recognized the fact. The machine gun had sealed the ascendancy of the defense over attacking infantry which had developed as early as the American Civil War. Improved artillery, firing shrapnel shells and better keyed in on its targets, gave the attackers an asset they had not possessed in the Civil War, but it was insufficient to offset the machine guns. Field telephones were much employed in the World War, especially to coordinate infantry and artillery, but without field radio the attackers still faced insoluble problems of battlefield communications. Unless attackers enjoyed a large numerical preponderance over exhausted and demoralized troops, as the Allies did in the final months of the war, infantry and artillery alone could no longer break well prepared defensive positions.

To reopen battlefields required the intervention of the tank on a scale far beyond its employment in World War I, and of the airplane beyond the capacities of World War I craft. Pershing's interest in the tank, however, was small in proportion to its importance. American attacks were conducted with light French tanks rather than the heavy tanks of the British, or often with no tanks at all. No American tanks were available. Hunter Liggett's First Army began its final offensive on November 1 with nineteen light tanks—one per 35,000 troops. Mainly, Pershing could not help it, but the absence of tanks does not appear to have bothered him as it would a less traditionalist general. In contrast, as an old cavalryman he was one of those generals who still hoped the horse cavalry might somehow be turned loose on retreating German armies. As late as August, 1918, and in the face of persisting shipping problems, he still asked the War Department to send him eight mounted cavalry regiments.[67]

Pershing's conservatism appeared also in his cautiously prolonged training program. Of course, he bore a heavy responsibility for American lives, but he might have given more consideration to the chance that more lives might be saved and the war shortened if he committed American troops to battle with a less perfectionist insistence on complete training. In the face of the German 1918 offensive, and then to create an American Army to participate in the Allied counterstrokes, Pershing finally had to use his divisions on the offensive before they underwent the full training and seasoning program he had envisioned. The results must have surprised him, and they roundly confuted Uptonian ideas about what is required to make a soldier.

During the Saint-Mihiel battle, the 42nd Division, the National Guard "Rainbow" Division, received some 9,000 replacements fresh from America. Major General Charles T. Menoher was reluctant to use them because of Pershing's ideas on prolonged training. But Menoher's chief of staff, the brilliant young Brigadier General Douglas MacArthur, urged him to try the men anyway, arguing that they were ready enough, especially to fight beside troops who were now seasoned. Menoher yielded, and the replacements fought very well. MacArthur later found that one soldier of conspicuous merit had had less than two months' training in the United States.[68]

Pershing's original training program ignored certain points suggested by Secretary Baker in July, 1918:

We have just discovered two things about training in this country which apparently nobody knew or thought of before we went into the war. First, that while it may take nine months or a year to train raw recruits into soldiers in peace time, when there is no inspiration from an existing struggle, it takes no such length of time now, when the great dramatic battles are being fought, and men are eager to qualify themselves to participate in them. We are certainly able to get more training into a man now in three months than would be possible in nine months of peace time training. And second, we have learned that to keep men too long in training camps in this country makes them grow stale and probably does as much harm by the spirit of impatience and restlessness aroused as it does good by the longer drills. . . . I think you will find that men who have had four months' training here are pretty nearly ready for use in association with your veterans and experienced troops, and that no prolonged period of European training, for Infantry at least, will be found necessary.[69]

The American armies that fought in the final battles of the war were not polished military machines. Often men went into battle without much skill even in Pershing's *sine qua non*, the school of the rifle; and no one would argue that the men should not have had at least the four months' training that Baker proposed but which sometimes they did not get. The Germans still affected a condescending attitude toward the American Army generally, using expressions such as those of Hindenburg in his memoirs, when he said that the Americans "were not yet quite up to the level of modern requirements in a purely military sense."[70] Thoughtful Americans themselves had to concede that they got away with mistakes and ineptitudes that would have caused severe trouble against a less exhausted enemy.[71] American casualties were disproportionately high, in large part because Americans were not battle wise like the French, the British, and the enemy. On the other hand, American casualties were high also because the American Army displayed an aggressiveness and a confidence that no other army in Europe any longer possessed, and the victories that can be won by such troops may well compensate for the costs of amateurishness by hastening final triumph.

The Germans may have affected condescension toward the Americans, but their reports from Belleau Wood onward betray their real attitudes. They had believed their own propaganda pronouncements that the Americans would never be able to send large numbers of uniformed men to Europe, and that even if the men arrived the Americans could not form them into a modern army soon enough. When Americans nevertheless began to arrive at a rate of 250,000 or more a month in the summer of 1918 it was disturbing. When Americans were met in combat and showed strength and élan despite their lack of a strong national martial tradition and despite their diverse ethnic backgrounds, the Germans did not know what to make of it. When the Americans continued to arrive in mounting numbers and continued to go into battle with the dash of the Regulars of the 1st Division or the Marines of the 2nd Division, German calculations were so upset that the high command went into a funk from which it never emerged, except to importune the civil government to make peace.

The American citizen soldiers thoroughly erased the misgivings of their own conservative and completely professional commander. As Pershing said to Baker in July, 1918:

The fact is that our officers and men are far and away superior to the tired Europeans. High officers of the Allies have often dropped derogatory remarks about our poorly trained staff and high commanders, which our men have stood as long as they can. . . . [I now have told the Allies], in rather forcible language, that we had now been patronized as long as we would stand for it, and I wished to hear no more of that sort of nonsense.[72]

Or as, in his memoirs, he described the climactic American battle:

The Meuse-Argonne battle presented numerous difficulties, seemingly insurmountable. The success stands out as one of the great achievements in the history of American arms. Suddenly conceived and hurried in plan and preparation; complicated by close association with a preceding major operation; directed against stubborn defense of the vital point of the Western Front; attended by cold and inclement weather; and fought largely by partially trained troops; this battle was prosecuted with an unselfish and heroic spirit of courage and fortitude which demanded eventual victory.[73]

The pride of Pershing and the officers around him in the victorious American Army was to affect profoundly the Army's postwar attitudes toward the role of the citizen soldier.

SEVENTEEN

Between Two Wars:
1918-39

In many cases there is but one officer on duty with an entire battalion; this lack of officers has brought Regular Army training in the continental United States to a virtual standstill.

—Douglas MacArthur[1]

ELIHU ROOT, Theodore Roosevelt, Leonard Wood, and a handful of other Americans had in some measure foreseen that world power might impel the United States to dispatch mass armies to fight across the ocean. They had not foreseen clearly enough and the nation had not sufficiently shared their vision to prepare the country and the Army for the burdens that fell upon them in 1917 and 1918. When the guns fell silent on November 11, 1918, and the A.E.F. began to turn homeward, the Army's leaders had to reckon with the possibility of a future war of a similar kind, and to try to ensure that the United States would be better prepared for a recurrence of such war, despite a military tradition of looking mainly to the defense of the continental homeland.

It was not easy to prepare a viable military policy at the close of World War I, especially a policy which must make departures from established peacetime habits. Woodrow Wilson was more indifferent to military matters than ever, as he planned a League of Nations that would put an end to war, and exhausted his health in pleading for America to support it. Wilson's followers joined him in resting their hopes for future world security upon the League. Those Americans who did not follow him sought mainly to turn aside from all foreign entanglements; most of them rejected the notion of future American participation in overseas war just as they rejected the League.

The laws authorizing the wartime Army entitled nearly all who served in it to prompt discharge, and the soldiers returned to the United States and to their homes in a rush that dwarfed the Civil War demobilization: 2,608,218 enlisted men and 128,436 officers received discharges by June 30, 1919. By January 1, 1920, only 130,000, mainly the Regular Army, stood under arms to maintain the token American occupation of Germany at Coblenz and to carry on the normal peacetime duties of the Regulars.[2]

While the wartime Army disintegrated and national attention focused upon Wilson's journey to Paris and its aftermath, Congress began considering the legislative foundations of future military policy. To make the circumstances still less auspicious for the Army, Congress simultaneously awoke from its wartime acquiescence in all the military undertakings of the executive and, with hostile Republicans in control, began a critical investigation of the conduct of the war. A Select Committee on Expenditures in the War Department, under the chairmanship of Representative William J. Graham of Illinois, spent a year and a half ferreting out all the flaws it could find in the hastily improvised mobilization. When the Republicans took over the executive branch on March 4, 1921, and there were no longer Democrats in the War Department to be annoyed, the investigation abruptly ended. With much reason, the Democratic minority of the Graham Committee said of the majority report: "If half of what the majority of the sub-committee says in its report is true, the United States could have played no effective part in the prosecution of the war, but we know that it is not true."[3]

The talents of the chief of staff did not include sensitivity to public policy. March and the General Staff misjudged the signs of the times and decided that the vivid memory of the war made an Uptonian military organization at last possible. They proposed to Congress a permanent Regular Army of 500,000 men, that is, five times the force that had preceded the National Defense Act of 1916. They proposed to organize this force as an expansible army, so it would serve as the half-strength skeleton of a field army of five corps. To fill out the Regular Army cadres in war, they presumably would have drawn upon reserves formed by a proposed system of universal military training. The General Staff planners would have suggested an eleven months' conscription term. General March, who was closer to Leonard Wood than to the thoroughgoing Uptonians on the amount of training required to make a soldier—he had criticized Pershing's lengthy training program—cut the suggested term of universal military service to three months. The General Staff plan relegated the

National Guard to third rank, behind the expansible Regular Army and its conscripted reserves.

Not surprisingly, Congress boggled at March's plan, and hearings on it continued inconclusively for months after its submission in January, 1919. The only Army legislation passed by Congress that year was an act of February 28, to maintain a stopgap by authorizing resumption of enlistments in the Regular Army under the National Defense Act of 1916.[4]

Congress nearly despaired of getting a useful military bill, since the Army clung stubbornly to Emory Upton while the legislators would not yield to him. Republican Senator James W. Wadsworth of New York, chairman of the Senate Military Affairs Committee and no enemy of reasonable military preparedness, thought it peculiarly inappropriate that the Army should now be offering a military program that with its large Regular cadres and conscript reserves so strongly suggested the German system.

In October, 1919, Wadsworth's committee at last heard a professional officer who tendered an alternative to Emory Upton. The officer was Colonel John McAuley Palmer, whose rejection of Uptonian ideas had earlier impressed Stimson and influenced Stimson's report on "The Organization of the Land Forces of the United States." Since that time Palmer had been close to Pershing, as a member of the original general staff of the A.E.F. His war career had been interrupted by bad health, but he had returned to duty in time to command the 58th Infantry Brigade of the 29th Division in action east of the Meuse. At the close of the war Pershing sent him to represent the A.E.F. in the General Staff's deliberations on postwar military policy, but the General Staff had already formulated its plan by the time he arrived. Nevertheless, the protraction of Congressional hearings enabled certain young officers who found Palmer persuasive to urge Senator Wadsworth to hear him, and Wadsworth agreed.

Palmer was now less enchanted with Emory Upton than before, since as he saw it the effective work of American citizen soldiers in France had refuted the old belief that the making of a soldier required at least a year or preferably two. Why then must there be so much emphasis on the Regular Army that the General Staff should insist upon a force far beyond any strength that Congress would accept, while proposing to skeletonize the Regular organization so it would not be ready to fight anyway? In his testimony and subsequent elaborations of it, Palmer suggested a much smaller Regular Army, whose formations would not be skeletonized but essentially complete. Such a Regular Army could be ready to serve immediately in any military emergency short of one requiring mass mobilization, and meanwhile Palmer proposed that much of its peacetime energy be devoted to training the citizen army that must be the nation's reliance in major war.

The citizen army should be recognized candidly as the main American Army. As a model for America, Palmer proposed the Swiss citizen army, with its professional soldiers mainly the trainers of citizen formations. Companies, regiments, and divisions should be organized in peace to prepare for war, but they should be mostly citizen-army formations, not Regular Army units in which citizen soldiers would be absorbed and submerged.[5]

Palmer had decided even before World War I:

If American citizen armies, extemporized after the outbreak of war, could do as well as Washington's Continentals and as well as the citizen armies of Grant and Lee, what might they not do if organized and trained in time of peace?

Furthermore, he had concluded that only a military policy based upon a citizen army could be "in harmony with the genius of American institutions." The General Staff plan was not in harmony with those institutions. By contemplating the thorough absorption of citizen soldiers into the Regular cadres, it recalled Upton's belief that military policy should be delegated altogether to professional control. That plan was derived from the German plan, and under it the German government had allowed so free a rein to its military commanders that "the extent and direction of its political aims were determined by the possibilities of military success." As Palmer was later to put it:

The forms of military institutions must be determined on political grounds, with due regard to national genius and tradition. The military pedant may fail by proposing adequate and economical forces under forms that are intolerable to the national genius.[6]

Palmer so impressed the Wadsworth Committee that it asked the War Department to release him to assist in preparing a new military law. Reluctantly and disclaiming responsibility for his views, the department agreed. With the assistance of Lieutenant Colonel John W. Gulick, an officer of similar opinions, Palmer spent the next ten months working with the committee.

Palmer carried greater weight because testimony in support of his came from the newly commissioned general of the armies, John J. Pershing. Pershing remained the complete professional soldier, and he still regretted that he had not been able to give his divisions the thorough training he desired, especially in open warfare, before he sent them into battle. But he could not dismiss the merits of a citizen soldiery after watching his draftees and National Guardsmen break the German line where the enemy fought hardest to defend it. The battle for the Argonne Forest and the heights of Montfaucon and Romagne had assured a new assent to Palmer's views from Pershing and the protégés he had gathered and would gather around him, including his new aide, Colonel George C. Marshall.[7]

Palmer did much to shape the National Defense Act of June 4, 1920, which emerged from the Congressional deliberations. He failed to secure universal military training for the citizen army, which he proposed but which Congress would not accept in any form, either as the War Department had proposed it or as Palmer had suggested it in a modification of the Swiss system. But the War Department proposal for the Regular Army was cut nearly in half, to 280,000 men, and the principal military reliance of the country was to be placed forthrightly upon citizen soldiers. Those soldiers were to be prepared for war through both the National Guard and an Organized Reserve, the latter the counterpart of the National Army of 1917.[8]

The National Guard was restored, in fact, to a somewhat larger control over its own affairs, through a reorganization of the Militia Bureau of the War Department which placed the bureau under the direction of a Guardsman. The President was authorized to use the National Guard only when Congress approved a call of troops in excess of the Regular Army. Citizen officers, especially for the Organized Reserve, were to come from an expanded Reserve Officers Training Corps in the colleges and from Citizens Military Training Camps on the Plattsburg model. The Regular Army was to devote much of its energy to training both the National Guard and the Organized Reserve, but increasingly the citizen forces were to be led and trained by their own officers, as such officers became available. Nonprofessional officers were to be granted tours of duty on the General Staff itself, and they were to join with the General Staff in drawing the plans to implement the new law.[9]

These last provisions were in line with one of Palmer's most drastic departures from Emory Upton: he believed that the army of a democracy must rely not only upon citizen soldiers but as much as possible upon citizen officers. His enthusiasm for the Swiss system was based partly on its officer corps, which was composed mainly of citizen soldiers even in its highest ranks. He argued that American history amply demonstrated the value of citizen officers:

There will always be a place for professional soldiers such as Grant and Lee, Sherman and Stonewall Jackson and Pershing, but the door must not be closed to civic leaders with native military talent such as Washington and Greene, Andrew Jackson and John A. Logan.[10]

The utilization of citizen officers was essential also to Palmer's belief that a democratic state required as democratic as possible an army:

A free state cannot continue to be democratic in peace and autocratic in war. . . . An enduring government by the people must include an army of the people among its institutions.[11]

The new law abandoned the old territorial division of the United States into military administrative departments and provided instead for a peacetime tactical as well as administrative organization. Under the plans drawn by the General Staff in consultation with the citizen reserves to implement the law, the country would be divided into nine corps areas, assigned to the headquarters of three armies. Each corps area would contain one Regular Army division, two National Guard divisions, and three Organized Reserve divisions. The Regular division and an additional training staff would train the citizen formations of the corps area. But the Regular divisions would be as complete as possible, not skeletonized, in accord with the abandonment of the expansible army plan.

The law gave the four combat arms, infantry, cavalry, coast artillery, and field artillery, administrative headquarters in the War Department on a level with the traditional service bureaus. New arms and services, the Air Service, Chemical Warfare Service, and Finance Department, received the same status. Among the duties of the combat arms headquarters was the development of tactical doctrine for their arms, responsible to the General Staff. The autonomy of the old bureaus was again curtailed, meanwhile, by the establishment of a single promotion list to replace the separate branch lists.[12]

Altogether, the law laid impressive foundations. As the critically minded Pershing succeeded March as chief of staff, he allowed himself unwonted expressions of enthusiasm for it. ". . . the new law," he said, "simply provides that our traditional citizen army be organized in time of peace instead of being extemporized, as in the past, after danger has actually come."[13]

But America in the 1920's was dedicated not only to the dream that wars had ended forever, but even more strongly to the more prosaic fetish of economy in government. The goals of the National Defense Act of 1920 broke down because Congress and the executive gave them lip service but little practical support. As early as 1921 Congress reduced the Regular Army to 150,000. The next year it decreed a further reduction to 137,000, and more than a thousand "surplus" Regular officers were discharged. In 1927 a further cut, to 118,750, occurred. Activities and equipment even for the reduced establishment were forced into narrow budgetary limitations. The Budget and Accounting Act of 1921 created the Bureau of the Budget and a unified budget for the executive departments. This measure was generally a sound one, but for the Army in the 1920's it meant that requests for appropriations had to undergo tailoring by a frugal Bureau of the Budget before they could be transmitted to Congress, where the Budget and Accounting Act required all executive officers to support only the official budget.[14]

The application of the Congressional and budgetary axe prevented completion of the nine Regular divisions planned under the National Defense Act of 1920. Palmer thereupon urged that some of the divisions be abandoned altogether, to permit filling as many as possible. But the Uptonian tradition prevailed, and the General Staff departed from Palmer's plan of a Regular Army in readiness to maintain all nine divisions in skeletonized form. Financial pressure was also offered as a reason for eliminating the nine corps training detachments, that is, the Regulars who were to be detailed to devote themselves exclusively to training citizen soldiers; they were incorporated into the skeletonized Regular divisions.

Citizen formations fared no better. Skimpy appropriations to the National Guard, which depended on federal drill pay, helped ensure that Guard formations rarely reached half the 435,000-man strength contemplated in 1920. The ROTC courses did maintain a pool of reserve officers, but the Organized Reserve of the 1920's consisted usually of an Officers' Reserve Corps of about 100,000 and an Enlisted Reserve Corps that was practically nonexistent because there were no means of recruiting it. The reserve officers haphazardly kept themselves in touch with military knowledge. Congress would not appropriate enough money to permit requiring them to train periodically, so some volunteered for occasional training, some took correspondence courses, and others allowed their military usefulness to wither away.[15]

The National Guard did manage an important legislative achievement in 1933. There was no immediate practical improvement, but the Guard secured added assurance that its formations would serve in war as units. Technically the Guard had entered federal service in 1917 through the drafting of its members as individuals, a system which might permit dispersing the individuals to every corner of the Army. In 1933 Congress responded to the wishes of the National Guard Association by amending the National Defense Act of 1916 to give the Guard a new kind of dual status: the Guard units would henceforth be both the militia of the states, under the militia clauses of the Constitution, and a permanent reserve component of the United States Army, under the army clause of the Constitution. Itself in the doldrums and with the Guard an ally in the quest for minimal defense funds, the Regular Army did not stand in the way of this change.[16]

For the most part, however, the early 1930's saw the condition of the Army go from bad to worse. Though naturally there were thoughts of using the Army to absorb some of the unemployed of the Great Depression, and of including military projects among public works, the initial reaction of the government to the Depression was to curtail expenditures to maintain its own fiscal soundness. By this time the antiwar sentiment which had earlier spawned the quest for a League of Nations had shifted to a gloomy, negative kind of pacifism, automatically hostile to any measure which might improve the Army. The late 1920's and the early 1930's were the heyday of popular antiwar literature, Ernest Hemingway's *A Farewell to Arms*, Robert Sherwood's *The Idiot's Delight*, John Dos Passos's *U.S.A.*, the English translation and the film version of *All Quiet on the Western Front*, Laurence Stallings's *The First World War—A Photographic History*, and the rest. The Depression only hardened the pacifist mood by deepening its gloom, and by putting the business community in bad odor the Depression made all the more acceptable the growing idea that wars are caused by greedy munitions makers and that the Great War of 1914–18 had been a prime example of the fact.

The Regular Army's role in breaking up the camps of the Bonus Army did nothing to enhance its popular standing. With the advent of Franklin D. Roosevelt's administration, Army construction did share slightly in Depression relief projects, but offsetting that were the hearings of the Gerald P. Nye Committee, enhancing still more the public distrust of anything military. Sometimes the Army's share in organizing and maintaining the Civilian Conservation Corps is cited as a beneficial experience, both in its aspect as a kind of small-scale mobilization and in its exposure of thousands of young men to an approximation of military training; but the disruption of the Army's already feeble formations and its diversion from military tasks probably more than erased any advantage.[17]

Altogether, despite the encouraging possibilities raised by the National Defense Act of 1920, the Army during the 1920's and early 1930's may have been less ready to function as a fighting force than at any time in its history. It lacked even the combat capacity that the Indian campaigns had forced on it during the nineteenth century and the pacification of the Philippines had required early in the twentieth century. As anything more than a small school for soldiers the Army scarcely existed. In 1936 the General Staff reviewed its mobilization plan with a realistic eye to what it could actually accomplish. Its planners decided that the only troops they could count on early in a mobilization were the 110,000 of the Regular Army, who were not in combat-ready units. They doubted that much of the National Guard could be readied for any meaningful duty in short order. They believed they could feed, clothe, transport, and shelter such troops as could be mustered during the first thirty days of mobilization. But as for supply, they said those troops

Can be supplied with required equipment from storage or procurement *except for airplanes, tanks, combat cars, scout cars, antiaircraft guns, searchlights, antiaircraft fire control equipment, .50 caliber machine guns, ponton equipment*, and possibly *organizational motor equipment*. There will be shortages in the stocks on hand of *gas masks, radio and telephone equipment*, and *equipment for medical regiments*. For reconditioning and preparation for shipment to troops of artillery material, a period of 90 days will be required.[18]

Writing his war memoirs about this time, General March commented that the United States on its own initiative had rendered itself more impotent than Germany under the military limitations of the Treaty of Versailles.[19]

Yet the Army of the twenties and the early thirties had new resources of strength that in time would permit it to overcome grave weakness. The National Defense Act of 1920 had further bolstered the Root reforms in the instruments of planning and command.

In part the act merely incorporated into the permanent organization of the Army changes first made under the wartime Overman Act. Gas warfare had prompted the improvisation of a Chemical Warfare Service, and now the duties of that service were defined and personnel assignments allotted it. The Finance Department created by General March was to remain as the central fiscal agency. A permanent office of chief of chaplains was instituted, to give order and direction to a historic service that until now had been only vaguely authorized and required to involve itself in a miscellany of nonreligious functions. Most important among such matters, Congress confirmed the separation of the Air Service from the Signal Corps and its status as a separate combat arm.[20]

But the act went on to assure and strengthen the Root reforms. Secretary Baker had observed that the war could not have been won without the General Staff, and Congress was sufficiently convinced that it ceased the raids which had nearly crippled the staff on the eve of war. The National Defense Act of 1920 gave the General Staff a reasonably adequate complement of officers: the chief of staff, four assistants, and eighty-eight other officers not below the rank of captain would comprise the War Department General Staff. Congress gave it broad duties of a general planning nature and charged it to concentrate upon those broad duties and not to become entangled in the essentially routine work of the special staff departments. The General Staff was

to prepare plans for national defense and the use of the military forces for that purpose, both separately and in conjunction with the naval forces, and for the mobilization of the manhood of the Nation and its material resources in an emergency, to investigate and report upon all questions affecting the efficiency of the Army of the United States, and its state of preparation for military operations; and to render professional aid and assistance to the Secretary of War and the Chief of Staff.[21]

The National Defense Act of 1920 included also the first permanent assignment of responsibility for planning for industrial mobilization. The Assistant Secretary of War was charged with supervising the procurement of all military supplies and with assuring that there would be "adequate preparation for the mobilization of material and industrial organizations essential to war-time needs." In part this provision stemmed from Benedict Crowell's able performance along these lines as Assistant Secretary during the war. The law did not make clear where the boundary lay between the mobilization functions of the General Staff and of the Assistant Secretary of War, and consequently a board appointed to study the proper organization of the War Department General Staff was asked in 1921 to comment on the issue. This board, headed by Pershing's former A.E.F. chief of staff and supply officer, James G. Harbord, recommended that the General Staff prepare estimates of required materials and the Assistant Secretary of War then plan how the materials were to be acquired. Roughly, the Harbord report would have ensured the retention of all strictly military aspects of mobilization planning in the General Staff, while the Assistant Secretary would plan for the business and industrial aspects of war.[22]

Following the National Defense Act, Pershing's accession as chief of staff in 1921 further elevated that office and the General Staff it headed. Pershing's personal prestige was an important asset, and the ambiguous relationship between Pershing and March came to an end. More tangibly, Pershing strengthened the General Staff in an unexpected direction. The experiences of the war, with its autonomous A.E.F., combined with the limited effectiveness of the General Staff before the war, created among many officers a ready assumption that in war the General Staff would confine itself to building the Army at home, leaving overseas operations to autonomous theater commanders. But the Harbord Board recommended that instead the General Staff should hereafter concern itself vigorously with the coordination of combat operations, and in his new vantage point Pershing agreed. He set up and developed the War Plans Board for operations planning, and in doing so he prepared the way for the General Staff to play a much different and larger role in World War II than in the war just past. In the 1940's General Marshall was to make the General Staff the command center for combat operations around the globe.[23]

The Harbord report and Pershing together determined also that the War Department General Staff should organize itself permanently not so much along the lines designed by General March as in accord with the organization of the A.E.F. general staff. The General Staff was to be divided into five main sections: the Personnel Division, first division or G-1; the Military Intelligence Division, second division or G-2; the Operations and Training Division, third division or G-3; the Supply Division, fourth division or G-4; and the War Plans Division. The division heads each received the title of assistant chief of staff. Within this organization, G-3 and the War Plans Division would share major responsibility for strategic planning for war.[24]

The wartime dependence of the Army upon the Navy to support its overseas operations prompted a postwar revival of the Army and Navy Joint Board, first organized in 1903 to foster interservice cooperation under the similar impetus of the Spanish War and the Philippine Insurrection but since fallen into a state of torpor. In a reorganized Joint Board the Army would be represented by the chief of staff, the assistant chief of staff G-3, and the chief of the War Plans Division. Through the Joint Board the two services sought to prepare coordinated war plans, the "color" plans for possible future wars with each of the great powers, each possible enemy designated by a color. Such strategic planning, however, interested the Navy more than the Army. Through the twenties and into the thirties, the only color plan that carried any immediate prospect of being invoked was Plan Orange for a war against Japan, and naturally this plan contemplated a larger and more dramatic role for the Navy than for the Army. At least until the Washington Disarmament Conference, naval planners also toyed in fascination with the Red-Orange Plan for war against Great Britain and Japan combined, a plan rendered hypnotically engrossing not by its contact with political realities but by the immense problems posed by its hypothetical enemy combination.[25]

Less involved than the Navy in the most interesting of the color plans, the Army in the twenties and early thirties paid more attention to mobilization planning than to strategic planning. There developed a series of General Staff mobilization plans, principally those of 1923, 1924, 1928, 1933, and 1936. How much the mobilization plans were to be tailored to fit the color plans was a question never quite resolved. Furthermore, perhaps because industrial mobilization planning was within the province of the Assistant Secretary of War, General Staff mobilization planning still displayed the old preoccupation with manpower rather than logistical issues. The official historians of War Department mobilization planning remark that

By 1927–28, it appeared that a preponderance of planners on the War Department General Staff could still remember vividly the large armies of World War I, but that they were tending to forget how dependent on the complex elements of supply those armies had been.[26]

The mobilization plans of the 1920's were Uptonian both in their preoccupation with manpower and in their adoption of a skeletonized Regular Army as a foundation for expansion. But when Douglas MacArthur became chief of staff in 1930, he was troubled by one of the same aspects of the latter approach that had worried Palmer: a Regular Army skeletonized in order to be expansible provided no force for prompt readiness even to meet relatively small emergencies. MacArthur believed that mobilization planning should provide for a moderate-sized mobile force ready to be committed to action whenever it might be needed. He set the planners on the new tack of working up an Instant Readiness Force.

As a step in that direction, he also moved to create field army headquarters in peacetime. The three army headquarters projected in 1920 had never appeared, but MacArthur now divided the country into four army areas, with the senior corps commander in each designated for the time being as the army commander.

Army commanders [his directive announced] are tactical commanders immediately available to command their armies in field operations and are so distinguished from corps area commanders whose functions are primarily administrative.[27]

For instant readiness, MacArthur also arranged an elaborate plan whereby each officer of the Regular Army was designated beforehand to fill a specific slot upon mobilization. When mobilization occurred, the chief of staff himself would become commanding general of the field forces, and the War Plans Division would become the nucleus of the general staff, GHQ field forces.[28]

MacArthur hoped to transform several divisions into instant readiness units, and to strengthen several National Guard divisions to afford something with which to back them up. Unfortunately, to effect this idea and to provide simultaneously a semblance of adequate garrisons for the outlying possessions of the United States seemed to the General Staff to require an increase of the Regular Army to at least 165,000 men. During the early 1930's MacArthur made several appeals for such an increase, but neither the executive nor Congress was ready to respond.

Still, MacArthur did manage to bring the mobilization plans closer to realism than they had been before, and he inaugurated the first of what was intended to be a series of "Six-Year Programs" for research, development, and reequipment, making a beginning toward overcoming the General Staff's neglect of supply.[29]

Meanwhile, the office of the Assistant Secretary of War somewhat compensated for that neglect. The duties assigned it by the National Defense Act ensured that the Assistant Secretary's office would keep memories of the tremendous logistical problems of World War I alive. In 1921 the Assistant Secretary established within his office a Planning Branch to concern itself with industrial mobilization planning. This agency was to cooperate with the seven special staff departments concerned with supply, which by this time included the Quartermaster Corps, the Corps of Engineers, the Signal Corps, the Ordnance Bureau, the Chemical Corps, the Medical Department, and the Air Corps. Together the Planning Branch and the supply departments would decide how and where to procure military material. Together with the General Staff the supply departments were supposed to decide what kinds of material should be procured.

To prepare its personnel for their job, the Planning Branch required that all officers assigned to it read the records of the mobilization agencies of World War I, especially of the War Industries Board. Out of this practice grew the Army Industrial College, established by Secretary of War John W. Weeks in 1923 on the recommendation of Assistant Secretary Dwight F. Davis, and intended to educate officers in industrial mobilization problems. From an initial student body of nine officers and an initial course of five months, the school grew in scope and prestige until by the middle 1930's it had become in its field a complement to the Army War College. Navy, Marine Corps, and Army line as well as staff officers came to be included in student quotas. Prominent business leaders participated in the school's programs, and its students' papers were put to immediate use by the Planning Branch.[30]

In 1922 the War and Navy Departments also created an interservice industrial planning agency, the Army and Navy Munitions Board. Until well into the thirties, however, the Navy showed little interest in joint planning for industrial mobilization. Even after naval interest grew with the world tensions of the 1930's, the Navy's attitude was fundamentally different from the Army's. The Navy intended as much as possible to fight a war with the fleet in being at the outset of the war. The Army expected a vast expansion of matériel after mobilization; the Navy did not anticipate an expansion nearly so great.[31]

During the 1920's the Planning Branch concerned itself mainly with procurement planning in a strict and limited sense. It was only toward the end of the decade that it turned to the larger implications of industrial mobilization, including such problems as assurance of labor supply, mobilization of management, and the extent and means of wartime government control over the economy in general. By the beginning of the 1930's the growing popular belief in the villainy of munitions makers as sponsors of war gave a somewhat surprising stimulus to industrial mobilization planning. President Herbert Hoover signed a resolution creating a War Policies Commission, to study whether the Constitution should be amended to make possible stringent federal economic controls in wartime, including seizure of private property. The War Policies Commission then studied an Industrial Mobilization Plan prepared by the War Department, as well as a set of recommendations on the subject from Bernard Baruch. In consequence the War Department received the benefit of a high-level civilian review of its ideas, and the department could then proceed with greater assurance that its planning would prove useful. The Nye Committee gave a similar review to a revised Industrial Mobilization Plan in 1933, and the plan pretty well passed muster with that hypercritical body.[32]

The Planning Branch continued to vacillate on several important issues, such as whether to seek Congressional authorization for mobilization agencies and policies before an emergency or simply to have drafts of bills on hand. As events turned out, furthermore, the next emergency produced less civilian support for its ideas than it had come to anticipate, since President Franklin D. Roosevelt saw in them both excessive centralization of power below the Presidential level and excessive military power. Nevertheless, the War Department approached World War II with much preliminary thought accomplished concerning the raw materials it would need, the productive capacity that must be allocated to it, and the agencies through which industrial mobilization should be directed.[33]

Despite all that, the main thrust of American plans for future war remained in manpower planning. The Army itself, not merely a parsimonious Congress and executive, must share the blame for neglecting study and development of the new weapons introduced during the Great War which gave hope of breaking the battlefield stalemate, along with instruments wherewith a defender might counter them.

America moved out of the Great War into a social revolution generated by the internal combustion engine, and under the circumstances a natural object of American military experiment might have been the tank. But just as the United States had neglected motor transport before the war, and just as the Americans had left to the British the development of the best tanks of the war—at a cost of many American lives—so in the postwar years the Americans remained indifferent, while the British led the way in fashioning better tanks and a doctrine of armored warfare for their employment.

Pershing's interest in tanks had never been conspicuous, but he had been sufficiently convinced of their value on the Western Front to initiate the American Tank Corps under Colonel S. D. Rockenbach, organized January 26, 1918. A flamboyant young cavalryman, Major George S. Patton, Jr., was chosen to command the Tank Center at Langres, France, and then to lead the 304th Tank Brigade at Saint-Mihiel, the first American tank battle. But after the war these organizations expired. The National Defense Act of 1920 allowed the Tank Corps and its equipment to revert to the infantry. There were 23,405 tanks on order at the end of the war. Only 1,115 survived with the American Army into the postwar years: 15 three-ton Ford baby tanks, 100 heavies modeled on the British Mark VIII, and 1,000 six-ton light tanks modeled on the French Renault. Except for a handful of experimental types, these tanks remained the only ones in the American Army until 1930.[34]

In Great Britain more than in the United States or France or Russia, the tank program was nourished by cavalrymen. There were distinct advantages in the consequent British tendencies to emphasize the tank's speed and its potential as a weapon of exploitation. Furthermore, the British possessed in J. F. C. Fuller and B. H. Liddell Hart two of the most astute military writers of the day, both of them caustically critical of World War I commanders who had tried no means of breaking the tactical deadlock save the sacrifice of hundreds of thousands of lives, both foreseeing as a remedy a new mobile warfare in which the tank would be mated with motorized reconnaissance, motorized infantry, and motorized supply, the whole coordinated by radio, to restore power to the offensive and decision to the battlefield. Fuller, a founder of the Royal Tank Corps, was instrumental in preserving three cadre tank battalions when the war ended. In 1923 the British introduced the Mark I Vickers medium tank, much faster than its predecessors and featuring a revolving turret, the prototype of the tanks of World War II. In 1926 they organized the Experimental Mechanized Force, to apply the tactical theories of combined motorized arms.[35]

Secretary of War Dwight F. Davis witnessed a demonstration of the Experimental Mechanized Force at Aldershot the next year. He was impressed, and he asked the American General Staff to undertake similar experiments. Summerall was now chief of staff, and he complied with a simple order to G-3 to organize a mechanized force. So in the summer of 1928 the 16th and 17th Tank Battalions and the 2nd Platoon, 4th Tank Company, with their creaky, unreliable vehicles, were joined at Camp Meade, Maryland, by the Army's only armored cavalry troop, a battalion of infantry, a battalion of artillery, a company of engineers, a signal company, a medical detachment, an ammunition train, and a squadron of observation planes to form the prototype of American armored forces. Happily, the G-3 officer under whose wing the project fell was Major Adna Romanza Chaffee, son of the early chief of staff of the same name and an imaginative cavalry officer already interested in tanks. Chaffee became the principal contributor to the report on the Camp Meade experiment, and he recommended forming completely mechanized regiments of tanks, motorized infantry, and motorized guns. He saw the tank now as potentially neither an infantry nor a cavalry weapon but the core of a new arm, capable of striking with the speed and shock power of cavalry, but with some of the staying force of infantry as well.

The chief of staff and the Secretary of War accepted Chaffee's armored force recommendations in principle, but only with painful slowness was anything done. Another primitive mechanized force was hardly assembled before Douglas MacArthur, the new chief of staff, ordered a restudy of the whole mechanization question, out of which came a decision to let each arm develop its own possibilities for mechanization separately. The cavalry could now have its own tanks, called "combat cars" to evade the provisions of law which assigned tanks to infantry, and Chaffee could pursue some of his ideas as executive officer and eventually commander of the 7th Cavalry Brigade (Mechanized), slowly assembled at Fort Knox, Kentucky. The brigade became a hodgepodge of light tanks, armored cars, infantry-carrying half-tracks, and truck-drawn 75-mm guns; but with the infantry simultaneously resuming its own tank development, and much of the cavalry brass hostile to anything but the horse, an armored force of combined arms languished.[36]

So did development of the tank itself. By the 1930's the Army was ready to order a few new ones, but it treated the experiments of the remarkable tank designer J. Walter Christie, a civilian nearly seventy years old, with relative indifference. Partly to conform to an arbitrary limit of seven and a half tons imposed by standard Army bridging equipment (which had to be abandoned when war came), the Army concentrated on light tanks to the exclusion of mediums and heavies. Out of the light tanks of the 1930's evolved the General Stuart or "Honey" of World War II, maneuverable but too lightly armed and armored for general usefulness. Not until the lessons of the Spanish Civil War were digested in 1939 did the Army hastily begin developing the medium tanks that were to be indispensable. Christie's tank of the early 1930's traveled 42½ miles an hour on tracks compared with the 18 miles an hour of contemporary Ordnance Department tanks; it was well armored and performed spectacularly well over fields and across hills. But when completely equipped it would weigh fifteen tons, too much by the accepted standards. It remained for the Russians to develop out of the two Christies they received the tank family that led to the T-34, and the United States went all through World War II without a heavy tank comparable to the Russians' and the Germans'.[37]

The nurture of armored force doctrine passed into other hands, too. In the economy-bound 1930's, even the British abandoned their Experimental Mechanized Force. As so often happens, it was the power that lost the war that responded most readily to the new possibilities of the next war. Implementing the ideas of Fuller, Liddell Hart, and Chaffee on more than a miniature scale fell to the Germans; the first armored divisions to go into battle neither as cavalry nor infantry but as a new arm combining cavalry and infantry features with new strengths of its own, were the German Panzers on the plains of Poland.

The military airplane received much more attention than the tank in the United States during the twenties and thirties. But here too there was neglect of the "tactical" possibilities in support of ground troops, destined to be the airplane's most useful military employment in World War II. Especially it fell to the Germans again to develop cooperation between mechanized and armored ground forces and aircraft. In the United States, the Army, the government, and the public spent their energies in debate over claims that aircraft could do something far grander, namely, transfer the decisive phase of war away from the traditional and bloody battlefield altogether, through "strategic" employment of airplanes against the enemy's factories, commerce, and cities.

For man to take flight was intoxicating, and the intoxicating qualities of flight must surely go far to explain the inflated claims for the capacities of military aircraft that began to circulate among aviators while the planes themselves were still feeble contraptions of wood, canvas, and wire, drawn along by habitually stalling engines. Mainly for administrative reasons the British as early as 1918 established an Air Ministry parallel to the War Office and the Admiralty, and with it an "independent" Royal Air Force parallel to the army and navy. In doing so, the British government can scarcely have recognized all the implications of its decision, which included the immediate encouragement of Major General Sir Hugh Trenchard in his ideas about an air power as independent of the ground forces as the navy. The RAF quickly began setting up Independent Bombing Squadrons under Trenchard, with the "strategic" mission of carrying war beyond the enemy armies to the population and resources that supported them. Brigadier General William Mitchell, the American combat air commander at Saint-Mihiel and the Meuse-Argonne, came into contact with Trenchard and began to propose the same innovations for the United States, an independent air force employed in the independent exertion of "air power."

During the 1920's Trenchard's and Mitchell's ideas of independent "air power" grew into a full-fledged military doctrine, chiefly in the writings of the Italian theorist Giulio Douhet. This doctrine, and American receptiveness to it, may have owed something to William T. Sherman's method of waging war against the civil population and resources of the South and his subsequent rationalizations of it, for the doctrine proposed by aerial bombing not only to destroy the enemy's factories and communications but to terrorize his people and government and thus overcome his will to fight. Air power enthusiasts claimed that this evidently barbarous method of warfare would in fact make war more humane by shortening it, and thus make war cheaper as well. To effect it, however, the American air power enthusiasts insisted they must be liberated from the control of ground soldiers, through establishment of an independent air force.[38]

A deliberatory board headed by Assistant Secretary of War Benedict Crowell did propose a separate air force in 1919. But a more comprehensive report in 1923, by a board headed by Major General William Lassiter, urged caution. It pointed to the two varied types of air force operations, the support of ground forces and attack of areas remote from the ground forces. It recommended air units attached to ground commands for the first purpose, and "a large, semi-independent unit" for the second. It urged long-range efforts to build up pilot strength, organization, and an expansible aviation industry.[39]

Despite the Lassiter report, Billy Mitchell propagandized for the doctrines of air power and the independent air force with increasing vehemence through the early 1920's—and with increasing insubordination as well, until he charged the War Department and the General Staff with criminal negligence and "almost treasonable" conduct, and thus obliged them to bring him before a court-martial. The court convicted him of charges of insubordination, suspended him for two and a half years, and provoked his resignation from the service. His methods of pursuing his goals were akin to those of Leonard Wood, but Wood had possessed enough balance to remain on the safe side of court-martial offenses. Mitchell has enjoyed a latter-day reputation as a prophet, having predicted so many things about the future of the airplane that advancing technology was bound to make some of the predictions come true. But World War II did not vindicate his prophecies about the decisiveness of air power in the next war, and in the 1920's his theories were utterly disproportionate to the military aircraft available.[40]

Mitchell's court-martial stirred up a sufficient furor that President Calvin Coolidge appointed a board under the New York banker Dwight W. Morrow to investigate the air power claims. The Morrow Board confined itself to recommending a minor increase in military aviation, not an independent air force. In 1926, the year after the court-martial, Congress did give the airmen the sop of somewhat greater prestige by transforming the Air Service into the Army Air Corps, and creating the post of Assistant Secretary of War for Air, destined to be suspended in an economy effort in 1933.

The airmen of course continued their agitation, and in 1933 a new board under Major General Hugh A. Drum recommended a compromise whereby the Air Corps would be detached from the command of the regional corps areas and placed directly under a General Headquarters, Air Force, responsible to the General Staff. This plan clearly would grant considerable autonomy. Before it could be effected, President Roosevelt undertook the experiment of circumventing allegedly monopolistic commercial airline holding companies by canceling their contract to carry air mail and turning the air mail over to the Army Air Corps. The result was a famous fiasco, in which the Air Corps demonstrated that it had been neglected so much that it could barely fly at all. Five Air Corps pilots were killed, six injured, and eight planes wrecked in the first week of carrying the mail. Billy Mitchell could proclaim the need for drastic changes to be proven; and still another board, under former War Secretary Baker, reiterated the recommendation for a GHQ Air

Force to control operations, not supply and training, in the Air Corps. On March 1, 1935, it was established.

The air mail experiment had shown that improved Army aviation was needed indeed, but it is not altogether clear that the creation of GHQ Air Force improved the ability of military aviation to fight the war that was to come. GHQ Air Force concentrated all the energy it could upon developing a heavy bomber to fit the theories of strategic air power. Both Congress and the General Staff tried to restrain this tendency, Congress out of misgivings over the aggressive nature of heavy bombers and the General Staff out of an interest in "tactical," ground-support aircraft. Despite their efforts, Air Corps infatuation with the heavy bomber and strategic air power took the United States into World War II with a reasonably good bomber, the B-17 Flying Fortress, but without similarly adequate fighters and attack planes to support surface battles, and with a capacity to coordinate ground force and its air support that appears to have remained inferior to the Germans' throughout the war. When the war in Europe was months along, the United States still lacked the air as well as the ground component of the armor-aircraft team with which the Germans introduced the Blitzkrieg.[41]

Other weapons development was as slow. Congress apparently thought World War I weapons should be used until they wore out, so the Army limped along with them into the early thirties, when they were literally wearing out as well as obsolescent. Caliber-.50 machine guns were still expected to perform as both antitank and antiaircraft weapons. World War I pieces were still the standard trench mortars. Before the war was over, Summerall had recommended that the 105-mm gun replace the 75 as the standard divisional artillery piece, and World War II was to bring an urgent need for such replacement; but through the thirties the modified French 75 kept its old place. When a worker in the Ordnance Department developed the semiautomatic Garand rifle, the Army was reluctant to give up the modified Model 1903 Springfield, of which large quantities were still on hand. The Army's equipment as well as its manpower and appropriations reached a nadir while Douglas MacArthur was chief of staff. MacArthur's report for 1934 showed only twelve post-World War I tanks in service. Available equipment generally, he said, was "inadequate even for limited forces . . . and, such as they are, manifestly obsolescent." As late as 1939 only $5,000,000, 1.2 per cent of the Army budget, went into research and development, to contribute to improved weapons.[42]

Industrial mobilization planning in the thirties did not include taking tangible steps toward relieving equipment shortages rapidly in case of war. From 1929 onward the Army sought permission to grant limited "educational contracts" to private industry, whereby manufacturers could be induced to secure the necessary machine tools and set up procedures for fashioning military matériel. Not until 1938 did Congress permit the expenditure of $2,000,000, transferred from other Army funds, for this purpose. Similarly, the Army failed until 1940 to persuade Congress to permit the accumulation of stockpiles of "critical and strategic materials" not sufficiently available in the United States. By then it was very late, and the war was to pose severe problems in finding substitutes and synthetics.[43]

On October 2, 1935, General Malin Craig replaced MacArthur as chief of staff. Craig had been chief of staff of the I Army Corps in the closing months of the Great War, and he was a Pershing protégé, with qualities of hardheaded realism and determination reminiscent of Pershing himself. Since the war he had been chief of cavalry, assistant chief of staff G-3, a corps commander, and commandant of the Army War College. A chief of staff less publicly conspicuous than MacArthur, he carried forward various projects that Mac-Arthur had inaugurated to bring more realism into both manpower and logistical planning, and he accomplished more than MacArthur toward preparing the Army for war. He could do so partly because of growing international tensions during his term and an increasingly sympathetic President. But he accomplished much at a time when he still had little support, and mainly he was a success because he was uncommonly foresighted and capable. He retired in 1939 and is little remembered now, but it is questionable whether any soldier did more than he to make possible American military accomplishments in World War II.[44]

When he took office Craig was most disturbed by the highly theoretical nature of existing General Staff planning and its lack of relation to the feeble Army which must be the foundation of anything to be attempted in war.

The problem encountered on my entry into office was the lack of realism in military war plans. . . . [They] comprehended many paper units, conjectural supply, and a disregard of the time element which forms the main pillar of any planning structure.[45]

He immediately ordered a study of the mobilization plans to determine whether the forces and logistical support they contemplated could actually be mustered in the time proposed, and the study had to conclude that they could not. He thereupon set the General Staff to preparing a new Protective Mobilization Plan which would set attainable goals and which would make the most of the limited military resources available to secure the strongest possible force at the outset of war. He returned to that basic idea of the National Defense Act of 1920, that the Army should prepare to train recruits but must also be ready to fight. His thinking was appropriate to the darkening years of the late thirties.

Time [he said] is the only thing that may be irrevocably lost, and it is the thing first lost sight of in the seductive false security of peaceful times. . . . The sums appropriated this year will not be fully transformed into military power for two years. Persons who state that they see no threat to the peace of the United States would hesitate to make that forecast through a two-year period.[46]

A good example both of the nature of Craig's approach and of the problems that beset him appears in his support of a G-4 statement of October 30, 1936, suggesting a reduction in weapons research expenditures and personnel. Such expenditures were already extremely small, and Craig certainly was not hostile to research. But he believed the weapons of the Army were so few, so worn, and so often obsolete that for the moment the Army must concentrate not on developing the best possible weapons but on securing serviceable ones in reasonably adequate quantities. Unless new weapons were ordered now, the lag of two years, or more, of which Craig spoke would mean that the Army would still be practically unable to fight at all for two years in the future, a condition too perilous to be tolerated. So research on a rapid-fire antiaircraft gun was curtailed, and the Army ordered guns of the Swedish Bofors 40 designs. Research on antitank guns was curtailed, and the Army placed orders for 37-mm guns of German design. The 37-mm gun was later to prove too small, but it was better than the machine guns that had to be used until it could be delivered. The whole program of slowing research soon evaporated under new international pressures and new appropriations, but Craig still hewed to his basic policy: in an uncertain world, the Army could not depend upon plans that would require years to be realized; the Army must be as ready as possible to fight.[47]

By 1936 and 1937 there was just enough renewed Congressional interest in the Army to give Craig some small encouragement. His predecessor MacArthur would have conceded the absence of realism in much of the staff planning of his tenure; he did so when he and his General Staff concluded that without an increase of the Regular Army to 165,000 men there could be no realistic plans, even for an initial protective force. But in response to his prodding, Congress did authorize for fiscal 1935 an enlisted strength of 165,000, up from 118,570. The President released only enough of the appropriation to go to 147,000. But in response to renewed pleas from Craig, Congress again authorized 165,000 for fiscal 1938, and the President now seemed in a more receptive mood.[48]

The cause was evident. A rapidly rearming Germany was assuming more threatening attitudes toward its neighbors, Japan was touching off the "China Incident," and Craig's warnings about time lags were acquiring a more obvious pertinence. Staff planners remembering World War I had always envisioned a sudden thrust of American rearmament following "M day"—mobilization day—in the manner of 1917. The restoration of American military power was now about to begin, but in a different way, as a slowly accelerating process.

President Roosevelt had initiated a naval rebuilding program as early as 1934, after Japan withdrew from the Washington and London naval limitations agreements. Roosevelt's tastes were nautical, and perhaps partly for that reason he was much slower to sympathize with Army requests for rebuilding. The initial Army increases of the middle thirties took place despite the advice of the President and the Bureau of the Budget. Roosevelt's message to Congress of January 28, 1938, is often cited as the beginning of rearmament, for on that occasion he took somber note of the activities of the Rome-Berlin-Tokyo Axis and said, "Our national defense is inadequate for purposes of national security and requires increase." But the President's emphasis was still on naval rearmament; he recommended an appropriation of about $28 million for that purpose for the next year, and only about $17 million for the Army, largely for new antiaircraft guns, educational orders for new weapons, and $2 million for the beginning of an ammunition reserve.[49]

The President multiplied these estimates late in the year, after the Munich crisis and the humiliation of Czechoslovakia had followed hard upon Germany's *Anschluss* with Austria. He offered a new rearmament program on November 14, but this time his emphasis was mainly on air power. He had learned from British and French spokesmen that they saw their principal inferiority to Germany in their deficiency of modern aircraft, and to try to right the balance in favor of the democracies Roosevelt now proposed a $500 million program for 10,000 planes.

The War Department was to work out the details. Both Assistant Secretary Louis A. Johnson, for the time being Acting Secretary, and the General Staff proceeded as though the President's rearmament calls implied a rounded rearmament, building balanced armed forces that could maintain the national defense in its every aspect. But this effort was not what Roosevelt had in mind. Indeed, it is still unclear how much he intended to expand even the Army Air Corps. His request for airplanes did not include requests for the pilots, crews, organization, ground service, and maintenance facilities that must join with planes to make an air force. He was not pleased when the War Department planned large expenditures for air bases and air training. Evidently he intended in large part that planes should be built for Great Britain and France. Evidently much of his purpose, too, was to make a propaganda gesture, an earnest of American support for the European democracies that he hoped would cause Germany and Italy to pause.[50]

Nevertheless, with the support of Assistant Secretary Johnson, the General Staff tried to convince Roosevelt that the only sound way to undertake military countermeasures against the dictators was to construct balanced forces, not only a complete air force rather than simply airplanes, but also ground forces balanced and capable of combat. A War Plans Division study, "The Most Serious Weaknesses in Our National Defense System," argued that with Germany mustering ninety divisions, Italy forty-five, and Japan employing fifty on the China mainland alone, it was intolerable that the United States should remain without a single combat division. After much persuasion, Roosevelt agreed to cut his goal in airplanes to 6,000, to support the creation of a balanced air force, and to divert some funds to procuring ground forces equipment. But he did not agree to seek additional manpower for the ground forces. Under the budget law the Army remained forbidden to ask Congress for appropriations not sought by the President; but Deputy Chief of Staff George C. Marshall prepared information on the Army's acute ground needs which officers might transmit to Congressional committees if they were asked.[51]

During the early months of 1939 the immediate goals of the General Staff came to be the procurement of sufficient matériel to equip an initial protective force of 730,000 men, to be formed from the eventual full recruitment of the Regular Army and the National Guard, and a prompt increase of personnel to raise five infantry divisions to full peace strength. Many writers believe that by this time public opinion was ahead of both President and Congress in willingness to rearm and to support Great Britain and France. The Gallup polls of the period support this view, that by now President Roosevelt was overestimating isolationist and pacifist opinion and showing excessive caution before it. On the other hand, Congress was still capable of making trouble for a foreign policy of support for the democracies, as evidenced by Roosevelt's failure to secure modification of the neutrality laws in the summer of 1939. Still, on rebuilding the Army, Congress ran ahead of Roosevelt; in a supplemental appropriations act passed during the summer, it removed the 165,000-man ceiling on the twelve months' average number of enlisted men and appropriated additional funds for paying the Army. The effect was to permit an increase to 210,000, without more specific authorization.[52]

In midsummer, on the eve of a new European war which might engulf the United States at an unpredictable time and under unpredictable circumstances, the Army stood somewhat stronger than it had during the early thirties; but at best it was not only a small Army but one still attuned to the combat styles of 1918 rather than to the war of armor and aircraft that the Germans were about to unleash. The total strength of the Regular Army, officers and men, was approaching 190,000. More than a quarter of that strength, however, was dispersed through the outlying possessions. The approximately 140,000 within the United States were still scattered in a fashion remarkably reminiscent of the days of Indian war, among 130 posts chiefly of battalion size. Field army commands scarcely existed except in theory; the corps headquarters had long since come to function mainly as administrative headquarters in the fashion of the old geographical departments, rather than as the tactical commands the National Defense Act of 1920 intended them to be. Of the nine infantry divisions supposedly in existence, only the 1st, 2nd, and 3rd had even the framework of a divisional organization, while the other six were merely understrength brigades. The 1st and 2nd Cavalry Divisions also existed, about 1,200 men each under peace strength and of uncertain value even by the standards of 1918. There were also the 7th Cavalry Brigade (Mechanized) and a few oddments of regiments not included in any division.[53]

The infantryman of 1939 had not yet received his semiautomatic Garand rifle and therefore still carried the modified 1903 Springfield. The infantry still used also the inaccurate three-inch Stokes mortar of the Great War, though superior 81-mm and 60-mm mortars had been developed. The .50-caliber machine gun was still the basic anti-tank weapon; as late as February, only one 37-mm gun was available. The basic field artillery weapon remained the 75-mm gun; there were now plans to replace it with the more versatile and altogether superior 105-mm howitzer, but these were plans for the eventual, not the immediate future. Gradually the 75-mm guns on hand were being altered to permit a higher angle of fire; generally they and the 155-mm howitzers had been modified to permit rapid hauling over highways.[54]

The National Guard numbered about 200,000 men. As usual, professional soldiers expressed deep skepticism about its value because it did not possess training at all comparable to the Regulars'. Customarily, it drilled forty-eight nights a year and took two weeks of field duty annually. Its equipment was of the same antique vintage as the Regulars' and generally in short supply even for understrength formations. Opportunities for combined exercises with the Regular Army had been far fewer than the framers of the National Defense Act of 1920 had hoped. But the Guard did offer at least partially trained cadres of eighteen divisions.[55]

In one important respect the Army was further along in 1939 than ever before in peacetime: in planning for both its own and industrial mobilization. The strengthening of the General Staff during and after World War I, and more particularly the realistic planning upon which Malin Craig had insisted since 1936, had given the Army a capacity for directed growth that was to permit its expansion with about as little confusion as a fluid world situation and uncertain national purposes permitted. For example, when in mid-April, 1939, Craig called for a War Plans Division preliminary study of "steps to be taken in the event that war develops in Europe and that the President adopts a policy of preparedness," the WPD was able to present the preliminary study by the end of the month. By May 5, G-4 was able to produce from the preliminary study a program for first-priority items of supply.[56]

About the same time, operations planning took a new direction. An exchange of letters among Army and Navy planning chiefs activated the Joint Army and Navy Board. That agency instructed its planning arm, the Joint Planning Committee, to draw up in place of the color plans a series of plans contemplating war with a likely coalition of hostile powers. The Joint Planning Committee, made up of the war plans chiefs of both services and their assistants, then set to work on what became the Rainbow plans, five plans which set forth varying goals ranging from defense of the Western Hemisphere to the sending of American expeditionary forces against the homelands of a hostile coalition. The most ambitious of them, Rainbow 5, was destined to be the basis of American strategy in the next war.

EIGHTEEN

The Army and the Arsenal of Democracy: 1939-45

In our unity, in our American unity, we will pursue two obvious and simultaneous courses; we will extend to the opponents of force the material resources of this nation and, at the same time, we will harness and speed up the use of those resources in order that we ourselves in the Americas may have equipment and training equal to the task of any emergency and every defense.

—Franklin D. Roosevelt[1]

BY A NOTABLE coincidence, Malin Craig's term as chief of staff ended in August, 1939, and his successor was formally installed on September 1. This circumstance has helped obscure Craig's contributions to preparing the United States Army for World War II. It was also, however, a circumstance of fine historical fitness, for it brought to his post in time to run the whole course the general who became the principal military architect of the Western democracies' ultimate victories over the Axis powers.

George C. Marshall, Jr., had shown himself a superb staff officer with the Operations Section of Pershing's GHQ in France, and he had gone on after the Great War to become a military aide to Pershing. Even before that, he had collected a remarkable file of fitness reports, including Lieutenant Colonel (later Major General) Johnson Hagood's reply in 1916 to the question whether he would like to have Marshall under his command: "Yes, but I would prefer to serve *under his command.*" Despite achievements and praise, the interwar years had been mainly frustrating ones for Marshall. Hagood had said in 1916 that Marshall ought to be made a brigadier general without delay: ". . . every day this is postponed is a loss to the Army and the nation." But Marshall did not actually win his star until 1936, when he was fifty-six years old, and by then his age made his prospects for a second star very uncertain. Meanwhile he moved through a series of unpromising training and administrative assignments with both Regulars and National Guards. Except for a tour at the Infantry School at Fort Benning, he had perhaps less opportunity to distinguish himself than in his assignments before 1917.[2]

If John J. Pershing is to be counted one of the great American soldiers, his claim is less that of a battle captain than of an architect of the Army. His A.E.F. was not only the first modern American combat army but the nursery of much good to follow. The War Department General Staff of the interwar years grew directly out of the general staff of the A.E.F. Recognizing the merit of John Mc-Auley Palmer's non-Uptonian ideas on military policy, Pershing, through his support of Palmer, helped make the National Defense Act of 1920 a better foundation for a permanent military policy than the United States had ever had. Not least, Pershing recognized the potential of George C. Marshall and never forgot it. He labored through the middle 1930's to secure Marshall's brigadiership before it was too late for Marshall to rise higher. He helped ensure that Marshall came to the attention of Malin Craig, another of his protégés, when in 1938 Craig was looking for a chief of the War Plans Division who could suitably rise within the year to replace Major General Stanley D. Embick as deputy chief of staff. Marshall received these posts, but it required Pershing's direct persuasion of the President to elevate the recently commissioned general over numerous seniors to become chief of staff in 1939. "He is in a position where he will make a great name for himself and prove a great credit to the American Army and the American people," Pershing wrote of Marshall at that time. Except for the old general of the armies, it would not have happened.[3]

In 1917 and 1918 Pershing had overshadowed the chiefs of staff. Marshall in contrast was to retain in his office the undisputed professional leadership of the Army. In part the command arrangements of the new war had to differ from those of 1917–18. The former war had been fought on a single front, and the role of the War Department was to transmit troops and supplies to the responsible commander in the only theater of operations. But in the new war each theater commander was to be only one of several, and a Washington command post had to coordinate strategy on many fronts spanning the globe. Marshall transformed the office of the chief of staff into that command post, and he filled the office with a consistency and fullness of success unmatched by any other commander of the American Army in any previous war. He mastered both the grand strategy of the war and, to an extraordinary degree, the details of staff planning, including those of industrial mobilization and logistical support. He won and held the confidence of both the President and Congress. With an impulsive President who delighted to have a hand in the conduct of the war, Marshall was patient in restraining Roosevelt's wayward impulses, and strong and generous in encouraging and implementing his sound decisions. With Congress he was respectful and cooperative, a lucid guide to the complexities of global war. He was an excellent judge of the capacities of soldiers, and he selected his subordinates with a wisdom that permitted the Army to go through a long war with fewer important command upheavals than ever before. Commanding an army of citizen soldiers, Marshall displayed a respect for their qualities reminiscent of John McAuley Palmer, whom he called from retirement to lay plans for the Army of the next postwar period.

The greatest of men cannot altogether transcend the institutions that nourish them. When Marshall committed errors of judgment, his principal mistakes were not wholly his own but implicit in the history of the United States Army, which had grown up defending a continent it could dominate completely, but which was still new to the military perplexities of the world at large.

In September, 1939, most Americans probably felt and feared that the new war would not end without their country's involvement. The memory of World War I was the main root of that feeling, and so recollections of 1914–17 contributed to immediate acceleration of the effort to ensure that war would not find America so unprepared as it had twenty-odd years before. But on this issue the memory of the earlier war cut both ways; misgivings about America's participation in it, and disillusionment over Wilson's failure to achieve his noble peace aims, created a special resistance to involvement in Europe's troubles, causing Roosevelt to move very cautiously toward preparedness. During the interval between the European declarations of war and American entry, the country prepared for war more purposefully and with less need of preparedness propagandizing than in 1914–17; but less was accomplished before Pearl Harbor than might have been had it not been for a still vocal antipreparedness opinion and the President's perhaps excessive concern for it.

Before September, Roosevelt had allowed the Army to believe

that war in Europe would lead at once to recruitment of the 280,000 men authorized by the National Defense Act of 1920. His actual response was more cautious. On September 8 he declared a limited national emergency, the meaning of which was not altogether clear. The same executive order raised the Regular Army by 17,000 men to 227,000 and authorized a National Guard increment to 235,000. It also permitted expansion of the officer corps through assignment of reserve officers to active duty, and it allowed a few emergency expenditures, notably $12 million for motor transportation.[4]

Though the General Staff found the order disappointing, the 17,000-man increase was not without value. Enough corps troops could now be assembled to establish several tactical corps headquarters, and enough army troops to create a functioning field army headquarters. There followed, in April, 1940, the first full-fledged corps maneuvers since 1918, and in May, corps-versus-corps maneuvers, with the first tests of new weapons and tactics in the light of early reports of German methods. Along with the establishment of corps and army headquarters, General Marshall also ordered a basic reorganization of the Regular infantry, in line with staff studies carried out under Craig and earlier. The four-regiment "square" division gave way to the smaller three-regiment "triangular" division, to afford greater maneuverability and flexibility. The contraction of the division would also permit transforming the three operational square divisions of 1939 into five triangular divisions. After the triangular divisions passed their field test in the spring, 1940, maneuvers, the Army moved to reorganize all its divisions, including those of the National Guard.[5]

In early 1940 Roosevelt allowed an Army budget of $853 million to be submitted to Congress. This amount was well over twice the usual budgets of the middle thirties and $2 million more than the expanded fiscal 1940 budget. But it was still small in terms of the possible needs of war and the estimates which the General Staff could not offer publicly. It was small in relation to the comment with which Marshall defended it against threats of Congressional cutbacks: "If Europe blazes in the late spring or early summer, we must put our house in order before the sparks reach the Western Hemisphere."[6]

Nevertheless, the House passed a bill granting about 9½ per cent less than the President requested. But before the Senate acted, Europe did blaze. On April 9 the Germans began the conquest of Denmark and Norway. The President then allowed a request for an additional $8 million for critical equipment, especially airplane detectors and warning devices. On May 7 the Supply Division of the General Staff gave Marshall preliminary suggestions on equipping a protective mobilization force expanded to 1,166,000 men. Three days later the Germans invaded the Low Countries and France. During the startling events of the next few weeks, the fiscal caution of Congress gave way to fears for the Western Hemisphere itself—for the fall of France suggested that the French and perhaps soon the British fleet might pass into German control.

The Senate Appropriations Committee urged Roosevelt to offer new defense estimates. He responded with a personal appearance before Congress asking supplemental appropriations of $732 million. This sum would raise the Regular Army to 255,000 and purchase equipment for a protective mobilization force of 755,000. The Senate raced ahead with a bill to raise the Regular Army to full peacetime strength, 280,000. The House readily concurred. Before the bill reached Roosevelt's desk, Congress was hearing still further appeals from General Marshall, and in response to his new requests for 335,000 Regulars, voted 375,000. The same legislation raised total War Department appropriations to nearly $3 billion, including substantial amounts to expand industrial capacity for military production both by immediate orders and by creation of new facilities.[7]

Meanwhile Roosevelt was beginning to implement industrial mobilization plans for agencies to coordinate civilian and military efforts. During the frenzied month of May he created an Advisory Commission to the old Council of National Defense, which the appropriations act of 1916 had authorized. The Council itself remained in limbo, but the Advisory Commission began an active career. As its specialist in production planning it borrowed William S. Knudsen from General Motors. Knudsen soon informed the War Department that he could not plan production for the Army unless he knew how large and in what ways the Army expected to grow. The department responded to this advice against the background of no longer imminent but actual French collapse and British evacuation of the continent. It presented to Knudsen the first clear statement of the long-range needs anticipated by the General Staff in the growing world crisis: a combat army of a million men by October 1, 1941, of two million by January 1, 1942, and of four million by April 1, 1942. By the latter date it hoped for an annual productive capacity of 36,000 airplanes.[8]

Manpower projections of this sort obviously called for conscription. All through the twenties and thirties a Selective Service branch of G-1 had been keeping the details of a conscription plan up to date. It had been impossible for the Army to doubt that a new war would require a new draft; officers of both the Emory Upton and John McAuley Palmer schools would have favored compulsory service in peacetime had they dared to advocate it. Nevertheless, despite the fall of France, the peril of Britain, and the manpower estimates given to Knudsen, the General Staff felt reluctant to call for conscription in the summer of 1940. It continued to assume that conscription would become possible only after a declaration of war. It feared that to propose a draft now would so arouse isolationist and antipreparedness forces as to endanger other requests now meeting generous acceptance in Congress. Anyway, the General Staff told itself, the Regular Army would have a hard time absorbing large numbers of draftees, so it might be more efficient to wait until voluntary enlistments had reached their limits.

Roosevelt shared the staff's misgivings about asking for conscription. But in the summer of 1940 public and Congressional sentiment so outran the President and the Army that conscription was enacted without their leadership. It happened that 1940 marked the twenty-fifth anniversary of Leonard Wood's Plattsburg camp. On the very eve of Europe's "blazing" in early May, leaders of the Civilian Military Training Camps Association met in New York to plan appropriate observance of the anniversary. Grenville Clark, one of the surviving leaders of 1915, suggested that the most appropriate observance would be a new civilian campaign for preparedness. To pursue this idea a dinner was scheduled for late May. When it occurred, France was in rapid process of collapse. The guests, who included Henry L. Stimson, Elihu Root, Jr., and Brigadier General John McAuley Palmer (Retired), decided that what ought to be done was to call for draft legislation. Palmer carried this decision to Washington and to his friend Marshall.

The chief of staff believed he could not respond favorably. After several other probing efforts in the War Department and the executive branch failed, the leaders of the Civilian Military Training Camps Association turned to a direct effort in Congress. They persuaded Senator Edward R. Burke, Democrat of Nebraska, to sponsor a selective service bill in the Senate, and James W. Wadsworth, Republican of New York, to do the same in the House. This was the Wadsworth who had been so impressed with Palmer's military ideas in 1920, and he had remained in touch with Palmer ever since. Congress promptly displayed surprising support for the Burke-Wadsworth bill, and from the beginning it seemed likely to pass.[9]

The executive's restraint may well have been wise; a conscription proposal from the Army itself would have provoked charges of militarism and very possibly brought a less favorable response. Once the Burke-Wadsworth bandwagon began rolling, however, Roosevelt and the War Department were happy to jump on. Significantly, Roosevelt announced in June that he had selected Henry L. Stimson to return to his old post as Secretary of War; his call to Stimson came the day after Taft's former Secretary had delivered a radio speech on behalf of conscription. From his renewed eminence Stimson was able to strike a few well-placed blows for selective service even before he took office. With Roosevelt's approval, Marshall threw all his persuasiveness to the support of the Burke-Wadsworth bill, as he had evidently been waiting and preparing to do.[10]

The prospect of conscription compelled the War Department to think about mobilizing the National Guard. In retrospect the reasons for beginning its mobilization in 1940 seem overwhelming. It would provide its partially trained cadres of eighteen divisions. Though it was short of equipment, the material it did possess would be an invaluable addition to the Army's limited supply. The uncertain future of the French fleet and German motions in the direction of Latin America were causing Marshall to consider the dispatch of an expeditionary force to South America; that force would have to come from the Regular Army and would deplete its training capacity perhaps irreparably unless the National Guard could supply training cadres to compensate for the loss. Conversely, some Guard formations might soon be far enough along in their own training to be able to move into potential combat zones themselves, freeing Regulars for instructional tasks; this was to occur with the dispatch of National Guards to the Philippines in 1941. So accustomed were the Regulars to regarding the Guard with skepticism, however, that the original plan of 1940 was for only a very limited Guard mobilization. Only when the Burke-Wadsworth bill raised questions about the inequity of conscription unaccompanied by mobilization of the Guard did the General Staff decide to call out the Guard.[11]

On August 27 Congress passed a joint resolution authorizing the President to call the National Guard and other reserves to active duty for one year. On September 16 it passed the Burke-Wadsworth bill, providing selective service for one year. Both measures limited the employment of troops raised under them to the Western Hemisphere and the possessions of the United States. Both were passed awkwardly late in the year if training was to get started while good weather remained.[12]

The Army was glad to have the draft, and subsequent events confirmed that it came none too soon for the national safety. But reflections on the difficulty of training a large conscript army, with which officers had consoled themselves before a draft law seemed possible, now became highly pertinent. The General Staff had hoped that somehow they might apply the ideal training scheme they had worked out in their planning, whereby recruits would get a thorough basic training and then only gradually be welded into larger and larger units, in which the tactics of platoons, companies, battalions, regiments, divisions, and armies would be learned step by step, with the officers themselves gradually gaining experience in larger and larger commands until at last the leaders of divisions, corps, and armies would be chosen only after they were thoroughly grounded in the handling of smaller units. Hardly anything of the kind occurred during the first year and more of mobilization. For some months recruits moved directly into Regular Army divisions to raise them to full peace strength, and in the process Regular formations found themselves engaged in basic training and advanced exercises simultaneously. Major General Lesley McNair came away from a visit to one division in September, 1940, with an impression of "blind leading the blind, and officers generally elsewhere."[13]

The National Guard cadres did prove useful for their organizational structure and their officers and men of at least some training. But the training of many of the men was extremely minimal, and many of the officers themselves knew so little that they had to be learning their own business while trying to teach their men at the same time. As in World War I, the Regulars deemed many Guard officers physically or otherwise unqualified for the rigors of modern combat, and the Regulars also decided that many Guard units required a wholesale reshuffling to break up local officer cliques.[14]

One very encouraging factor was the availability of Reserve officers, mainly products of the college ROTC programs. The qualities of these men proved to be remarkably high; the Army soon concluded that they were already sufficiently disciplined and trained that they needed only conditioning in the increasingly rigorous training camps before they stepped promptly into instructional roles themselves. In December, 1940, G-1 estimated that 106,000 of them were eligible for active service, and this pool seemed more than ample for the Army expansion then contemplated for the following year and even beyond. So ample did the supply appear that the General Staff was reluctant to set up officer candidate schools, which at length began to function only in July, 1941, when Marshall insisted they were necessary for the morale of the draftees as a promise that a draftee could hope to become an officer. By the end of 1941 the Officer Candidate Schools had graduated only 1,389. Meanwhile, the Reserve officers won Marshall's accolade as "probably our greatest asset during this present expansion."[15]

With that asset, the War Department was not tempted to repeat its World War I mistake of virtual abandonment of the Military Academy at West Point. In accord with interwar General Staff plans, however, it did drastically curtail the Army school system, sometimes perhaps unwisely. The Army War College and the Army Industrial College were suspended in June, 1940. Before the end of the war the consequent interruption of the supply of officers educated for the highest staff and command responsibilities became an embarrassment. The Command and General Staff School turned to much abbreviated courses, which graduated officers qualified for leadership up to the division level. Inevitably, the various service schools offered greatly accelerated basic courses, with special emphasis on training National Guard and Reserve officers in such a way as to help them pass on their new knowledge to others. Later the service schools resumed more advanced officer courses, while also offering special one-month programs for the officers of divisions about to be activated. An Armored School, Tank Destroyer School, and Antiaircraft Artillery School joined the older service schools.[16]

To create a unified command over the training of the new Army, the General Staff brought out a plan first conceived just after World War I and revitalized while MacArthur was chief of staff. It provided that when mobilization occurred, an operational general headquarters was to be set up on the model of Pershing's GHQ, A.E.F., with the chief of staff to assume Pershing's place as commanding general, Field Forces. Accordingly, General Headquarters was activated on July 26, 1940, and Marshall became commanding general, Field Forces, as well as chief of staff. Marshall found, however, that in practice his new role had to remain chiefly a formal one, and active direction of GHQ was vested in the chief of staff, GHQ, General McNair, until now commandant of the Command and General Staff School. The idea was that as Pershing had trained the A.E.F., so now Marshall, or in fact McNair, was to train the Field Forces. GHQ became a headquarters superior to the four field armies and directing their training activities.[17]

The jurisdiction of GHQ, however, included tactical units only, and its direct authority did not extend to selective service recruits in basic training. Once both the Regular and National Guard units had been pretty well filled and the construction of camps permitted, by about April, 1941, recruits no longer were sent from reception centers directly into tactical units, but to Replacement Training Centers for thirteen weeks' basic training. GHQ developed a program whereby upon the completion of basic training the soldier would proceed systematically through three additional phases of training: small-unit training; combined training, that is, training in the coordination of the various weapons of the regiment and the division; and large-unit maneuvers. During 1940 and 1941 McNair and his staff worked out the details of this course to frame a program that could be retained through the war and which gave the soldier of World War II a much better preparation for combat, especially in proportion to training time consumed, than any of his predecessors.

McNair's program included proficiency tests at every step of the way; an emphasis on elementary training and general proficiency, with frequent review, as a prerequisite to specialist training; an effort to maintain the integrity of tactical units once they were organized; and a preference for free, not rigorously controlled, maneuvers, with realistic simulation of battle conditions, meticulous umpiring, and immediate critiques.[18]

General McNair believed that the analogy between his command and Pershing's ought to be carried to the point of regarding GHQ as a theater of operations headquarters. Then, the corps area headquarters would be limited to strictly administrative functions; GHQ and the tactical armies, corps, and divisions under it would operate as though they were overseas, with GHQ enjoying the plenitude of power that such a situation would imply. In part the General Staff agreed with this view and tried to implement it; but they did not agree completely, and in consequence there was a somewhat indefinite quality about McNair's authority. In training matters the army commanders were clearly responsible to him; but the corps area commanders remained in charge of their own supply systems, responsible to G-4, General Staff. With rather uncertain authority McNair also had to start his work with only seven officers assigned to GHQ, and even by June, 1941, he had only twenty-three, before a more rapid growth began.

To complicate the situation further, on July 3, 1941, GHQ became an operations as well as a training command, which meant principally that it took over the defense planning responsibility for the North American continent. The War Plans Division could then concentrate on global strategic planning and on planning for operations overseas, but the purpose and authority of GHQ became more clouded. Nevertheless, despite these handicaps and those implicit in a rapid mobilization, McNair through uncommon energy ensured that training was much more systematic and thorough than in any previous emergency, and fully justified the creation of GHQ.[19]

For all that, the forced-draft mobilization which got under way during the collapse of France and drove the country to its first peacetime national conscription was plainly losing some of its momentum by the end of the year. The growth and reequipping of the Army did move forward through 1941, but not so rapidly as the General Staff wished or as post-Pearl Harbor hindsight would have justified. By December 7, 1941, the Army was not so strong as it might have been after nearly a year and a half of partial mobilization. A host of blighting factors, some of them the fault of various government agencies and some not, made late 1940 and most of 1941 a time of troubles for the Army, with progress always seeming slow in relation to the dangers of the hour.

A relatively small, though not negligible, fiasco in preparing to enforce selective service set the unhappy pace for much of what was to come. Despite all the mobilization planning of the interwar years, the Army had failed to give much thought to the creation of training camps suitable for the formation and thorough training of whole divisions. Planning based on the experiences of 1917–18 had envisioned only brief preliminary training in American camps, followed by final training overseas, such as Pershing had conducted in France. The need to train expanded Regular divisions, National Guards, and new divisions provided by selective service all within the United States, retaining them at least a year, had gone largely unanticipated. A divisional camp required 40,000 to 100,000 acres. A hasty preparation of training camps began, so hasty that sometimes the sites were chosen without surveys, yet unavoidably so time-consuming that inductions had to be delayed.

The requirements for camps and for reasonably orderly training slowed the calling of both National Guardsmen and draftees. In August, 1940, the General Staff planned to call 55,000 Guardsmen in mid-September, 55,000 in mid-October, 65,000 in mid-November, and 40,000 in December. They planned on 75,000 selective service inductees in October, 115,000 in November, 115,000 in December, and 95,000 in January. Both schedules had to be stretched out, especially the one for draftees.[20]

When troops were inducted, equipment for training them remained acutely short all through 1941. More than anything else, industrial mobilization in late 1940 and 1941 witnessed a loosening of resolves formed at the fall of France, and a smaller achievement than there might have been. For a combination of good reasons and less persuasive ones, and especially because he desired neither military nor strongly centralized control of the economy, Roosevelt paid little attention to the Army's much discussed industrial mobilization plans and tried to improvise a set of agencies for economic preparation for war. In succession and in various patterns of combination, a War Resources Board, an Office of Emergency Management, the Advisory Commission to the Council of National Defense, an Office of Production Management, and subordinate agencies with uncertain lines of authority all tried to coordinate industrial mobilization. Not until after Pearl Harbor did the administration return in some desperation to one of the essentials of the Army's industrial mobilization plans, a superagency with truly extensive powers. This was the

War Production Board. But its chairman, Donald M. Nelson, proved insufficiently decisive and aggressive, and confusion persisted well into the war itself.[21]

More fundamentally, once the first shock of the French collapse had passed, Roosevelt continued to hesitate before a fully candid commitment either to the support of Germany's surviving opponents or to the rearmament of the United States. He still feared the political consequences, and therefore the long-run consequences for all his purposes, of too overt a challenge to isolationism. Lest he strengthen the isolationists, he feared also too abrupt a redirecting of the national economy and normal life. So he conjoined phrases about constructing an "arsenal of democracy" with actual policies that allowed peacetime consumer goods to flow from factories in nearly undiminished volume. After half a year of supposed rearmament, industrial output at the end of 1940 included no medium tanks (partly because the Army had been so slow to develop them), none of the new 105-mm howitzers, no heavy caliber antiaircraft guns, and practically no heavy artillery. In January, 1941, preparation of four antiaircraft regiments for an expeditionary force within the Western Hemisphere raised the prospect that to give those four regiments full equipment allowances, thirty-seven other regiments, with twenty per cent equipment allowances, would have to be stripped even of the guns they needed for training. A landing of the 1st Division and the 1st Marine Division in the Azores, planned for June, would have exhausted all stocks of certain critical types of ammunition, including three-inch antiaircraft and 37-mm antitank. In 1941 the greatest automotive industry in the world still poured forth motor cars and prepared the 1942 models, while the Army remained desperately short of tanks. Americans were shocked by photographs of mock-up weapons used in the Louisiana maneuvers of September, 1941, but the troops retained the mock-ups, while department stores were full for the Christmas season of 1941.[22]

Interwar mobilization planning had failed to foresee another obstacle to equipping the American Army, the diversion of much American arms production to foreign powers. Roosevelt decided after the fall of France that the United States must assist in keeping in the field Great Britain and any other effective enemies of the Axis, even at the expense of American rearmament. Apart from the loftier moral and political motives for this policy, he believed that the woeful military weakness of the country in 1940 could better be remedied by a relatively slow buildup behind a British shield than by a frenzied buildup in the face of a Germany completely victorious in Europe. So he sought a nice balance between bolstering the British with American arms and pushing the rearmament of the American forces themselves. Congress, more intent upon the readiness of the American Army, voted on June 28, 1940, that no Army or Navy munitions could be transferred to foreign nations unless the chief of staff or the chief of naval operations certified that they were not essential to the defense of the United States. But Roosevelt prevailed upon Marshall to declare as surplus those weapons that were such only in anticipation of deliveries scheduled for the uncertain future. The General Staff was unhappy with the policy, but Marshall believed he must yield gracefully to the higher national aims which the military had enlisted to serve.[23]

The Air Corps especially groaned under the program of aiding Britain. In September, 1940, Roosevelt directed that bomber production henceforth be divided evenly with the British; although no such fixed formula was actually followed, by the end of the year diversions to Britain were causing the Air Corps to cut its pilot training programs in half. The General Staff gave somewhat hesitant endorsement to the lend-lease plan, which would ensure continued if not increasing division of production with other armies, which would reverse even the minimally effective Congressional prohibition against export of essential weapons, and which eventually turned out to bring the Soviet Union into a share of American industrial production.

Under lend-lease, for example, a schedule drawn up in September, 1941, called for a sharing of aircraft production anticipated by June, 1942, whereby the Army would receive 4,189 tactical planes, Great Britain 6,634, Russia 1,835, China 407, and other nations 109. With such sharing and with output falling below expectations, plans drawn about the same time in late 1941 foresaw an army of 1,820,000 men only seventy per cent equipped as late as June, 1942. Lend-lease obligations soon reduced even that anticipation; virtually all immediately scheduled medium tank production, for example, was soon slated for Britain and Russia.[24]

In the sequel, Pearl Harbor found the United States Army still largely fitted out with worn or obsolete equipment. Pearl Harbor then touched off a program for the rapid creation of new divisions, which made equipment shortages still more acute. The Army suffered with the shortages well into 1943. The General Staff had to devise a priority program of A, B, and C divisions and nondivisional units, with still finer gradations within each of the three main categories. Only units of A priority were to receive complete issues of authorized equipment; only units due for prompt shipment into combat zones normally received A priority. B and C units were "training units" not scheduled for prompt combat. B units received fifty per cent of their authorized equipment or, if they were nondivisional, still less. C units received a still lower quota. Sometimes units got an A priority so briefly before their transfer overseas that they never had time to acquaint themselves with complicated equipment before taking it into battle. One of the authors of the Army's own mobilization history recounts his experiences with the 3rd Division, which opened its crates of bazookas only on shipboard bound for the North African invasion, and puzzled out for itself what the contraptions were.[25]

For a time in 1941 manpower as well as weapons caused the General Staff concern, since both the National Guard and the selectees were serving under Congressional authorization of only a one-year term. Among the expressions of a more relaxed national attitude which developed as British resistance persisted into 1941 was a growing Congressional disinclination to extend that term. The Selective Service Act of 1940 had hardly been passed before the General Staff had to consider what it would do when the one-year term ended, and through the spring of 1941 there was increasing reason to include plans for getting along without the selectees. Roosevelt himself was slow again to ask for General Staff recommendations to extend Guard and selectee service. In a famous vote, the House at last concurred with the Senate in extending service, 203 to 202. The squeak was probably not so narrow as the tally implies, since several other affirmative votes apparently could have been had if necessary; nevertheless the margin was much too close for comfort, and again General Marshall's patience and skill in presenting the Army's case to Congress had probably been indispensable.[26]

That hurdle had scarcely been cleared before a threat to manpower expansion came from another and unexpected source, the President. In the fall of 1941 Roosevelt reacted to the persistent equipment shortages by suggesting that the Army might be reduced, to make more supplies available for friendly forces already in combat. The chief of staff failed to dissuade him, and the General Staff had to look for a scheme that would reduce the forces in being with minimum damage to the capacity to grow again. It prepared a plan for gradual demobilization of the best trained National Guard divisions, which could remain together as units and maintain at least part of their training edge. Eighteen Guard divisions were to begin being deactivated in February, 1942; Pearl Harbor naturally canceled the plan.[27]

Presidential and Congressional vacillations on military policy in 1941 reflected a larger uncertainty of national policy. Roosevelt seems to have persisted almost to December, 1941, in the hope that with sufficient American material help, Great Britain, Russia, and China could defeat the Axis powers without an American declaration of war. Yet he tried to cling to that hope while recognizing the dangers both that the Axis might force American entry into combat through direct attack, or that direct American involvement might become the only alternative to Axis victory. If the latter possibility should materialize, furthermore, Roosevelt was not sure he could persuade Congress and the country to follow him into war; so he continued to behave cautiously in order to retain the closest possible rapport with what he took to be the caution of public opinion.

With Roosevelt thus hesitating among conflicting goals and hopes in shaping his foreign policy, his military policy could hardly escape some inconsistency. At the very time he was preparing to reduce the Army, in the fall of 1941, he was also talking about dispatching American expeditionary forces to overseas bases, to stand beside those already occupying Greenland and Iceland. In addition, the increased commitment to the British implicit in lend-lease was taken to require a General Staff study of the amount of manpower and resources that would have to be applied if Hitler and his partners were finally to be beaten. This study produced, about the same time that plans for reduction of the Army in 1942 were also jelling, the so-called Victory Program, which contemplated an American army of 8,795,658 men. Major Albert C. Wedemeyer, charged with drawing up the Victory Program, pointed out that he had to proceed from "a more or less nebulous national policy, in that the extent to which our Government intends to commit itself with reference to the defeat of the Axis Powers has not yet been clearly defined." Thus handicapped, he assumed that defeat of the Axis would in fact require a maximum American mobilization, and he attempted to calculate first the number of men available to the Army if the needs of the other services, industry, and civilian life were met, and to go on from there to a calculation of the matériel required for such an army. His forecast of the total army to be mobilized approximated strikingly the total actually mobilized by May 31, 1945, when the Army numbered 8,291,336 officers and men.[28]

But when the Japanese struck Pearl Harbor, the realization of any such program seemed almost a chimerical undertaking. A kind of mobilization had been proceeding for a year and a half, but the hesitancies and doubts of late 1940 and 1941 had prevented it from creating an army proportionate to the demands now brutally thrust forward. The thirty-six divisions existing in December, 1941, included no more infantry divisions than had existed in some form in the peacetime Army. Though many of those divisions had come a long way during the growth of the Army to 1,638,086 men, only a single division and one antiaircraft artillery regiment were on a full war footing. By February, 1942, eight divisions were expected to be trained and equipped with essentials, but adequate ammunition for combat would be available for only two of them.

The United States still lacked military strength to do anything more than stand on the defensive for many months, and that with the loss of many outlying positions, including the Philippines. The first peacetime army-versus-army maneuvers had recently been completed, the Louisiana maneuvers pitting the Second against the Third Army, but they had revealed numerous deficiencies among the troops in basic soldierly skills and among their officers in basic command skills; so the 1,600,000-odd men of the Army still had to be rated as of very uneven military proficiency. The circumstances of the Japanese attack on Pearl Harbor, furthermore, exposed serious shortcomings in military alertness, carried over from the easygoing peacetime years, and in the kind of Army-Navy cooperation that would be essential to winning the global war now begun.

Still, the existence of detailed manpower and industrial mobilization plans, the activation of the National Guard, the inauguration of selective service, and the introduction of large-scale peacetime maneuvers permitted the Army to enter World War II in infinitely better condition than in 1917. Industry had at least completed much of its tooling up for war. The failures at Pearl Harbor notwithstanding, in its attitudes the Army had already gone a long way across the bridge from its peacetime doldrums to the firmness of war.

On the day before Pearl Harbor, GHQ estimated that the United States would need 200 divisions before opening major offensive operations against the Axis powers. Major Wedemeyer's Victory Program, as modified by the General Staff, foresaw an army of 213 divisions by June, 1944. It set an immediate objective of seventy-one divisions by the end of 1942. With only thirty-six divisions available, the immediate effort of the Army following Pearl Harbor concentrated upon the rapid mobilization of additional divisions.

The War Department worked out a plan calling for the activation of three or four divisions a month beginning in March, 1942. New divisions were to be created through a cadre system, whereby a quota of experienced officers and enlisted men would be withdrawn from a parent division to form the organizing and training nucleus of a new division. These officers and men would undergo special training at the service schools (the division commander and his staff at the Command and General Staff School) to prepare them for their heavy burden as the divisional cadre. Most of the officers for the new division then would come from officer candidate schools. Over the objections of General McNair, who believed that divisions should be built upon men who had completed their basic training, the plan called for enlisted men to be shipped to the new division direct from reception centers. The War Department envisioned ten to twelve months as the time necessary to carry a new division from activation to combat readiness: seventeen weeks for establishing initial organization and accomplishing the thirteen-week basic training program; thirteen weeks of unit training up to and including the regimental level; fourteen weeks of combined training, to include at least one division-versus-division maneuver. In its essentials this procedure merely continued and built upon McNair's 1941 training program, and in its essentials it continued through the war.[30]

By mid-1942 the Army began to meet severe difficulties in attempting to hold to its schedule for creating new divisions. Equipment shortages caused divisions to be activated without enough weapons for adequate and realistic training. Manpower shortages were appearing and quickly growing acute. The formation of combat divisions had to compete with the manpower demands of the Navy and the Army's air arm, and both geography and the need to fight in some fashion while the Army's divisions were forming demanded a heavy emphasis on American sea and air power. The Army's own services of supply also competed with the combat divisions for men, and the supply requirements of an army mechanizing and attempting to maintain its soldiers in an approximation of the affluent American standard of living constantly outran prewar plans.

To maintain the activation schedule, selective service inductions had to be accelerated. As 1942 went on, it became evident that there must be a postponement of the original hope for an Anglo-American expedition to recapture a foothold in western Europe before the year ended, and soon indeed a postponement beyond 1943. This realistic postponement reduced the immediacy of the need for ground combat forces. Revised shipping estimates, more realistic than their predecessors, reduced the numbers of men who could be transported overseas by 1944. Revised estimates by the War Production Board questioned the feasibility of equipping the huge Army originally planned. The 1942 divisional program was carried forward despite the obstacles, and during the year thirty-seven new divisions were created, to yield a total of seventy-three by the end of December. But in the face of the obstacles, the troop basis—the blueprint for Army expansion —was modified downward during the fall of 1942, to project only a 100-division army by the close of 1943. In January of the new year, continued competing manpower demands of the air and supply services caused a postponement of twelve of the 1943 divisions into 1944.

These two latter decisions proved to be crucial ones in a series of decisions that finally prevented the Army from attaining anything resembling the 213-division combat strength envisioned in the Victory Program of 1941. Though twelve divisions were postponed from 1943 to 1944, inductions continued at the rate previously scheduled, and the men who would have filled those twelve divisions went into other branches, most of them thus lost forever from the combat divisions. Experience brought continually reinforced evidence that American standards for mechanization and completeness of supply would not permit 213 divisions to be formed from the 8,000,000 or so men expected to be available to the Army; too many would have to be diverted to air and support forces, and the industrial requirements of both the United States and its allies would not permit enlargement of the Army manpower pool. Anyway, the continued resistance of Russia tied up most of the German army and made it likely that the United States would not have to face so many German soldiers as originally anticipated. The upshot of all these factors was that the Army's ground combat manpower never advanced much beyond the level attained at the end of 1942. Through 1942 the Army had persisted in concentrating on the formation of new divisions and finding manpower to fill them; after 1942 the main effort turned to improving the support and sustaining the efficiency of the existing divisions.

At the close of 1942 the total strength of ground combat units was 1,917,000 men. By the spring of 1945 and the close of the European war, this number grew only to slightly over 2,000,000. While some 2,000,000 men were added to the Army during 1943, only 365,000 of them went into the ground combat forces, and many of those were replacements for the combat losses of the year. During 1944 and early 1945 the number of men allotted to the ground combat forces was actually reduced by 241,000. The divisions added after 1942 were established largely by reducing divisional tables of organization and diverting men from nondivisional into divisional combat forces.

The Army thus mobilized not 213 divisions during World War II but only ninety-one. Eighty-nine divisions existed at the end of the European war, the 2nd Cavalry Division having been twice demobilized in part or in whole to account, somewhat oddly, for the other two divisions in the total of ninety-one.[31]

One of the outstanding organizational successes of the Army in World War II was its ability to maintain as effective combat units all eighty-nine divisions that it raised and desired to maintain. Of the fifty-eight divisions shipped to France in World War I, only forty-two were effective combat units at the end of the war, the rest having had to be stripped for replacements or diverted to other purposes. The World War II divisions were kept up despite the fact that three months of intensive combat on the average cost an infantry regiment

100 per cent casualties. By early 1945 forty-seven infantry regiments in nineteen divisions had suffered from 100 to over 200 per cent casualties. But the Army substantially replaced these losses.[32]

To have raised and maintained only eighty-nine divisions, however, was not so impressive an achievement, for this strength barely matched the demands placed upon it. In contrast, Germany mobilized some 300 divisions, Russia about 400, and Japan about 100. Every American division had to be committed to combat. At the time of the German surrender, over ninety-six per cent of American ground combat forces were overseas. When the Germans staged their counteroffensive in the Ardennes in December of 1944, the last divisions in the United States had been hurried to Europe, and no more were forming. The Army had committed its last combat reserves to the theaters of operations. No important uncommitted reserve remained within those theaters. In 1944 the need for infantry divisions became so great and the number available proportionately so small that seven divisions had to be sent into battle without participating in the division-versus-division maneuvers that McNair had prescribed for complete training, and ten participated in such maneuvers with only thirty to sixty per cent of the men they took overseas.

Though the divisions were maintained, the thinness of ground combat strength required that, through 1944, divisions still in training had to be stripped of men periodically for replacements for the divisions overseas and then had to be shipped overseas themselves often with nearly half or more of their personnel recent additions. Worse than that, the lack of reserve divisions required that those in the line remained there too long. The individual soldier had to feel he would fight until he became a casualty, and the strain, fatigue, and attrition of excessive time in combat surely multiplied casualties.[33]

To have tried to muster as many divisions as Germany did would have been foolish, since Russia pinned down many of the German divisions; and even had that not been true, American sea and air power would have given the American Army a flexibility enabling it to strike in superior force at points of its choosing. Furthermore, as the chief supplier of matériel for the coalition opposing the Axis, the United States had to retain much of its manpower in the industrial economy, so that other nations might maintain their divisions in the field.

But to raise no more divisions than the Army did was almost certainly to raise too few. Many ranking officers believed so, but no one ever devised a means of solving the problem in the seemingly evident way: to bring into combat units a greater proportion of the supporting forces of the Army. In the spring of 1945, in an Army of almost 8,300,000, only slightly over 2,000,000 were in ground combat units. Some 2,354,210 of the remainder formed the Army Air Forces. The rest were in the service forces, noncombat units of the ground forces, and "overhead," the latter including especially the pipelines of replacements going toward the front, men in replacement and reassignment depots, and furloughed men and others going away from the front—as McNair despairingly called it, "the invisible horde of people going here and there but seemingly never arriving." As early as 1942, when the proportion of ground combat troops was still considerably higher than later, the chief of staff of the Army Ground Forces wrote:

. . . from the general information at hand, it appears that over-all production of services to combat forces is grossly excessive; and some definitive measures to control the dissipation of manpower to these non-combatant functions must be instituted at once.[34]

But the measures were never instituted or even discovered. Excluding aviation and antiaircraft artillery, the combat troops of the Army numbered only about 300,000 more in 1945 than in 1918. Making allowances for the proportionately lesser need for combat soldiers owing to mechanization, the conclusion seems inescapable that the effort to maintain an approximation of the American standard of living in the Army and even in the combat zones diverted an excessive amount of manpower away from the essential combat units of the Army. On one hand, the War Department and the General Staff very nicely calculated and mobilized nearly the precise number of combat troops needed to win the war. On the other hand, it might have been better—if a way could have been found—to pay more heed to the maxim that in war not economy but an excess of means is desirable. A final economy in time and lives would probably have been the result of providing a larger margin of ground combat troops. As the Army's official history puts it, ". . . some commanders, like General McNair, fought to keep the Army lean and simple. In World War II they lost this fight."[35]

The Harbord Board of 1921 and the interwar planners in general had built upon Elihu Root's reforms and the experience of World War I to give the Army, by 1941, arrangements for wartime high command superior to those carried into any previous war. But lacking the gift of prophecy, they built what would have been a model command system for World War I, which fell short of the requirements of a very different World War II. Since the many fronts of World War II prevented the anticipated and relatively simply transformation of GHQ into an expeditionary force headquarters on the model of Pershing's GHQ, A.E.F., requiring General Marshall instead to make the chief of staff's office a central command post over numerous theater commands, the onset of war left GHQ in a kind of limbo, with an uncertain future. Even before Pearl Harbor, the effort to combine operations and training responsibilities in GHQ had not worked altogether well. Nevertheless, McNair had made of GHQ a training headquarters of unprecedented value not to be lightly dispensed with.

Not only was the place of GHQ uncertain as the Army moved into a war of numerous theater commands, but the problem of command of the air arm persisted unsettled from peace into war. The air power advocates had never ceased in their call for an independent air force. The Army's own top air officers inclined to soft-pedal that call once war was near, for they recognized that the air service would be hard put to construct all the administrative and supporting echelons of an independent service in time to be ready for the war. But while not so insistently calling for independence, those officers did seek increasing autonomy within the Army. After Pearl Harbor, the necessity to fight in the air and at sea, if the United States was to fight at all while the Army assembled its ground forces, gave new cogency to air power arguments.

The onset of war seemed also to call for a single officer in charge of supporting the Army, with powers comparable to those Goethals had held in World War I. In the existing arrangement the supply bureaus were at last clearly responsible to the chief of staff, but reporting to him, they overburdened his office. G-4, the supply division of the General Staff, had become a huge operating agency with an officer personnel of more than 200, and its planning duties were neglected while it grappled with operational detail. To the extent that GHQ sought to fulfill its original design on the model of Pershing's headquarters, its efforts to assume logistical functions clashed with both the old supply bureaus and G-4.

All these circumstances suggested a basic reorganization of the Army's command system almost immediately after war was declared. In fact, a special War Department committee, headed by Major General Joseph T. McNarney, had begun considering such a reorganization in August, 1941. On December 18, 1941, Congress gave suitable authority for reorganization in a measure similar to the Overman Act of World War I, the First War Powers Act. Upon this foundation, the President carried out the sweeping War Department reorganization of March 9, 1942, largely designed by the McNarney Committee, and implemented under Executive Order 9082 of February 28, 1942.[36]

The air service had already taken several new steps toward autonomy in March, 1939, October, 1940, and June, 1941. On the first date the chief of the Air Corps was given direct command of both GHQ Air Force and all other air activities (unless any such activities were specifically exempted by the Secretary of War). Thus, for the first time a single officer under the General Staff held direct control of everything the Army did in the air. On the second date Major General H. H. Arnold moved up from the office of chief of the Air Corps into the new post of acting deputy chief of staff for air; this was a step toward an air force general staff under the deputy chief of staff, who would report directly to the chief of staff, not the General Staff, and thus free the air force from direct supervision by the ground-oriented General Staff. In the meantime it gave the air service a voice at the highest command level to supplement its status as a bureau (the Air Corps) and a combat command (the Air Force).

The reorganization of October, 1940, was a compromise of air and ground objectives, and it also included a concession by the air service: GHQ Air Force was removed from the control of the chief of the Air Corps and subordinated to GHQ, with a view to wartime operational control by a theater commander. But this concession created both dissatisfaction among the airmen and puzzling lines of command, and it gave way on June 20, 1941, to a new Army regulation creating the Army Air Forces. The deputy chief of staff for air would command the AAF, an Air Staff would continue to develop under him, and he would coordinate the office of chief of the Air Corps, an Air Force Combat Command which succeeded GHQ Air Force, and all other air units and activities.[37]

The Army reorganization of March 9, 1942, carried the logic of earlier air reorganizations to the conclusion of an Army Air Forces command altogether separate from the ground forces, with its own Air Staff and its own chief, who was directly responsible to the chief of staff. General Arnold became chief of the AAF. At the same time, the reorganization looked to the other principal and related command problems. GHQ would cease to exist, but its training functions would pass to the Army Ground Forces, of which General McNair would be the chief, and which would supervise all training in the United States, with the ground combat troops within the United States subordinate to it. The offices of the chiefs of the combat arms, initiated in 1920, were abolished, and their functions as formulators of tactical doctrine were assumed by the Army Ground Forces. All support and logistical functions in the United States would pass meanwhile to a Services of Supply. The offices of the chiefs of the supporting services and arms, including the Engineers and the Signal Corps, would continue to exist, but subordinate to the chief of the

Services of Supply, Lieutenant General Brehon B. Somervell. To the three coordinate commands, Ground Forces, Services of Supply, and Air Forces, the General Staff delegated operating duties concerned with administration, supply, and training within the United States. These commands were to provide the troops, equipment, and supplies and the means of transporting them, for and to the overseas theaters.[38]

With the creation of the Army Ground Forces, the responsibility of GHQ for planning and control of operations returned to the General Staff. The General Staff then became the central command post for operations in all theaters of war. To assist the chief of staff in his central command role, the War Plans Division shortly gave way to an expanded agency called the Operations Division (OPD) of the General Staff. OPD developed as both the principal war planning agency and the central operations command post that GHQ had hoped to be. It not only planned, but it was also the arm of the chief of staff through which he controlled the "strategic direction of military forces in the theater of war." Its responsibilities grew so large that it assumed the shape of an inner general staff within the official General Staff.

OPD stood especially close to one of the principal purposes of the reorganization. Throughout, General McNarney had been guided by the conviction that "The magnitude of the Army and the nature of operations preclude adequate supervision by the Chief of Staff of the activities of the Army through the General Staff as now organized." McNarney hoped to strengthen the ability of the chief of staff to control and coordinate a complex variety of forces fighting a coalition war all across the globe. To do so he employed both negative and positive means. Negatively, he would free the chief of staff of much detailed activity concerned with raising, training, and equipping troops, so he would be freer to concentrate on the fighting fronts. Therefore, as McNarney put it:

Except for the basic decisions which must be made by the Chief of Staff, the functions of mobilization and preparation of forces for war are to be performed by three separate and autonomous commands, the Army Air Forces, the Army Ground Forces and the Services of Supply. Each of these commands will be under its own responsible and authoritative commanding general.[39]

Positively, McNarney would give the chief of staff an effective machinery through which to coordinate the fighting fronts. General MacArthur had remarked when he was chief of staff that "The War Department has never been linked to fighting elements by that net-

work of command and staff necessary to permit the unified functioning of the American Army." OPD was to provide the necessary
links.[40]

Supporting those fighting fronts around the world was a task that
dwarfed even the logistical operations of World War I, and one
which prewar planning, shaped so much by the example of World
War I, had not adequately anticipated. Because of the hesitancies
that had marked the year and a half of partial mobilization preceding
Pearl Harbor, when war came the equipment on hand and soon to be
on hand was far from enough, and arrangements for transporting
supplies and equipment to the fronts and bases now to be opened
were, if anything, even less adequate. Those arrangements, and hasty
improvisations built upon them, suffered further from the reverses
inflicted on American forces in the Pacific after Pearl Harbor, reverses which persistently outran American anticipations and caused
continual disruption of supply and troop movement schedules. The
Germans' destructive extension of their submarine campaign to the
American coast and the Caribbean disarranged supply schedules
only slightly less. Well into 1942 the enemy's continued possession of
the initiative, combined with the unparalleled breadth of the war,
kept in confusion the dispensing of supplies that were nowhere in
sufficient quantity anyway.

It was a considerable achievement for the Army's supply management as well as for American productivity and American and
Allied shipping that American and Allied forces got enough support
to fend off every disaster except those that were utterly beyond pre-
vention, such as the fall of the Philippines; that enough equipment
reached such critical fronts as the British lines in Egypt to sustain
them; and that withal the means were gathered to open counteroffen-
sives in the Pacific and North Africa before the end of 1942.

Though the shape and scope of the war far outran logistical planning based on the model of World War I, the logistical organization
that eventually carried the Army nevertheless reflected strongly the
experience of 1917–18, and especially the arrangements developed by
Pershing for the A.E.F. G-4 and therefore principal supply officer of
the General Staff at the beginning of the war was General Somervell. His thinking ran toward centralized supply management within
the General Staff, through the establishment there of a post similar to
Goethals's of World War I. In the reorganization of March 9, 1942,
however, logistical command went instead to the commanding general, Services of Supply, an office given to Somervell himself. Beyond
the various other influences which led to the creation of SOS, this
organization was in the image not of Goethals's office in 1918 but of

Pershing's organization in France. As Pershing had eventually concentrated support and administrative duties in an A.E.F. Services of Supply under Harbord, subordinate to his own General Headquarters A.E.F. but leaving the latter free to concentrate on strategy, so now Somervell's SOS would support all the American armies as Harbord's had supported the A.E.F., and the General Staff would act mainly as a strategic command post for all the armies as had Pershing's General Headquarters for the A.E.F.

Somervell's rejected plan for a Goethals-type post within the General Staff reflected the belief that the General Staff should shape strategy and logistics coordinately, with the main working responsibility for both within the General Staff. The creation of the SOS reflected Marshall's belief, following Pershing's, that the strategic command post should concentrate on strategy, with logistical support to be developed in subordination to strategy, not coordinate with it. Therefore, working command of logistical support was removed from the strategic command post, the General Staff.[41]

Marshall of course knew that strategy and logistics must be interdependent, but in the 1942 reorganization he may nevertheless have overestimated the extent to which logistics could be subordinated to strategy. Under the pressure of events, strategy and logistics subsequently came to be shaped coordinately in the General Staff after all. As the War Plans Division of the General Staff evolved into the Operations Division, and OPD became the key instrument for central direction of the war and as such an inner general staff within the General Staff, OPD increasingly concerned itself with logistics and developed its own staff of specialists in logistics. The Theater Group of OPD was the control center for the various theater commands; standing between the theater commands and other echelons of the War Department, it naturally concerned itself with the theaters' logistical needs. Especially, it developed a Troop Movements Section which coordinated troop movements overseas. Meanwhile, the Resources and Requirements Group of OPD, later called simply the Logistics Group, dealt with over-all logistical problems with a view to coordinating the logistical requirements of all theaters and balancing requirements and assets. The Logistics Group worked through SOS and was dependent upon SOS even for logistical information; but at the same time it was aware of strategic plans as SOS was not. In consequence, through these constituent groups of OPD, OPD within the General Staff became in practice the highest logistical planning agency of the Army. SOS found its judgments and actions subject to a constantly growing supervision and scrutiny from OPD, even in matters that might have been regarded as routine.[42]

These developments generated a certain friction between OPD and SOS. But they did not prevent SOS from becoming an extremely powerful agency. The growth of OPD notwithstanding, SOS sometimes moved into policy making to a greater extent than its original conception might have implied. The history of SOS fully justified its eventual redesignation as the Army Service Forces, with that title's implications of fully equal status with the Army Ground Forces and the Army Air Forces. The SOS, later ASF, was the operating agency for all supply within the United States and to the overseas theaters, with the exception of supplies peculiar to the Air Forces. Under the commanding general, SOS, were the traditional supply agencies and the newer ones prompted by technological change: the Quartermaster Corps, Ordnance Department, Chemical Warfare Service, Medical Corps, Signal Corps, Corps of Engineers, and Transportation Corps. The corps area commands created by the National Defense Act of 1920, which had always been mainly administrative and supply rather than tactical units, now became service commands under SOS.

In addition to its large responsibilities for supply, SOS-ASF carried a great miscellany of administrative functions, receiving practically all the administrative burdens of the Army in the United States that were not directly related to combat and preparation for combat. Incorporated into it were the Adjutant General's Office and, under a chief of administrative services, such traditional agencies as the Judge Advocate General's Department, the Office of the Provost Marshal General, the Finance Department, the Corps of Chaplains, and the National Guard Bureau.

In theory the Under Secretary of War, succeeding the Assistant Secretary of War, and G-4 retained their prewar responsibilities for the support of the Army. General Somervell as commander of SOS was in theory subordinate to the Under Secretary with respect to supply procurement and to G-4 with respect to supply requirements and distribution. But so much of the staffs of both the Under Secretary and G-4 moved to SOS, depriving the former of expertise and information, that this subordination was largely nominal, especially as far as G-4 was concerned. In fact, Somervell moved deep into the former policy-making activities of G-4 and, to a lesser degree, the Under Secretary. His ability to do so was the more assured because he was also designated direct adviser to Marshall in matters of supply. Furthermore, SOS received large responsibilities for administering Army lend-lease supplies, and these responsibilities led also into what amounted to a policy-making role in the crucial area of sharing American military supplies with the Allies.[43]

The agglomeration of agencies thrown together in SOS-ASF did not make for a notably coherent or even harmonious organization. Though the primary commitment of SOS-ASF was to that complex of supporting functions now lumped under the vague word "logistics" (a term but recently come into general Army usage and still of imprecise meaning), the administrative agencies thrown into it had but the loosest connection with any ordinary concept of logistics. In a war in which transportation was more difficult and more critical than in any previous conflict, futhermore, friction developed between the supply and the transportation branches of SOS-ASF.

There is a basic incongruity between the purposes of supply officers, to have the most ample quantities of the right kinds of matériel available to the troops at the right time and place, and of transportation officers, to keep means of transport flowing as smoothly and uninterruptedly as possible. This incongruity had been apparent in earlier wars, but never so much as the delicate balance among numerous theaters and supply lines made it now. In World War I there had been logistical help from the Allies to ease the problem, but that help was much more limited now. The vast distances of the Pacific badly strained transportation resources. Transportation officers labored to keep all shipping filled to maximum cargo and moving with maximum dispatch; supply officers sought specialized cargoes that did not always lend themselves to maximum use of capacity, and they sought delivery at times not always appropriate to prearranged schedules. So disputes rather than harmony often prevailed between Brigadier General LeRoy Lutes, chief of the SOS Operations Division (the command center of SOS supply much as the Operations Division of the General Staff was the command center of the whole Army), and Major General Charles P. Gross, chief of transportation. Their disputes centered upon the issue of control of the ports whence overseas shipment departed, and resulted in a shifting distribution of authority between supply and transportation officers in the ports. Meanwhile Somervell conducted a similar contest outside SOS with the War Shipping Administration, to assure to the Army what he considered an adequate allocation and control of scarce troop transports and cargo vessels.[44]

After Pearl Harbor, scarce shipping and supplies still had to be shared with the Allies, since lend-lease continued and America's now direct stake in the war made it more obviously essential to keep in the field those Allied forces already fighting the Axis. At the Arcadia Conference of British and American civil and military leaders which occurred in Washington in January, 1942, the two powers agreed to create a combined Munitions Assignments Board to allocate military supplies from, it was hoped, a common British-American production pool. Determining a formula for allocations was much harder than creating the MAB. The British proposed allocations to theaters of operations on a schedule of strategic priorities. But the Americans objected to that system on several grounds: that it would favor the British, because their troops were already in action in many theaters, and those theaters would naturally tend to get high priorities; that it would be excessively rigid, since the shifting fortunes of war would upset prearranged priorities; that it would tend to divert excessive quantities of supplies to relatively inactive theaters such as India, because the mere existence of a theater command would tend to act as a magnet on supplies when theater commands served as the basis for distribution. The Americans at first developed no clear counterproposal of their own, but their increasingly firm insistence was upon allocations based first not upon strategy but upon a realistic appraisal of production capacity, that capacity then to be shared to meet basic national needs, but beyond that to be shared with the greatest possible flexibility.[45]

Though the combined Munitions Assignments Board was supposed to be a high-level agency responsible to the Anglo-American Combined Chiefs of Staff, Somervell's SOS-ASF achieved considerable working control over it. Somervell himself became a member in August, 1942. The chairman and secretariat of the MAB committee for ground forces equipment came from an International Division established within SOS-ASF. Recommendations from the committee were based on SOS-ASF studies, and in ninety-five per cent of its pertinent decisions MAB followed those recommendations. More than that, the basic arrangement for division of Army supplies between Americans and British came to be the Weeks-Somervell Agreement, worked out by Somervell and Lieutenant General Sir Ronald Weeks in November, 1942. By that time it was evident that American production, mammoth though it was, would not achieve the programs fashioned in the first flush of the war spirit at the beginning of the year, and that accordingly allocations to all Allied armies would have to be scaled down. The Weeks-Somervell Agreement set the pattern for a whole series of agreements to deal with other varieties of supply, and the pattern it set was the American one of beginning with realistic estimates of production, guaranteeing basic needs, but avoiding a direct attempt to tie supply allocations to rigid strategic and operational plans.[46]

As the organization of SOS-ASF to support the whole Army followed the example of Pershing's support organization for the A.E.F., so the support arrangements of the various theaters of operations followed the same example. SOS-ASF saw to the initial equipment of the troops that it shipped overseas. The Navy was to see to it that troops and equipment could cross the oceans safely. At the port of destination, the support organization of the theater took over. Each theater commander possessed an autonomy analogous to Pershing's —though not fully equal to Pershing's, owing to the demands of global war—and that autonomy extended to his rear area organization. Like Pershing's Services of Supply (and parallel to SOS-ASF), the theater rear area organization handled all administrative and technical as well as supply services for the theater. As Pershing had conceded in 1918 when the War Department suggested a rear area commander independent of and coequal with him, the rear area commander had direct access to War Department logistical agencies. This direct access to SOS-ASF permitted the conduct of more or less routine logistical functions without the intervention of the theater commander. But theater policy making remained in the theater commander's hands.

Even the structural pattern of his rear area services was left to the theater commander. In 1942 Somervell tried to compel the rear area organization of the European theater to parallel the organization of the War Department SOS in detail, so each SOS officer in Washington could deal with an equivalent officer in Europe. But the theater command protested this effort at control from Washington, and the theater was allowed to continue with its own arrangements, in which the European rear area organization followed the old General Staff "G" structure more than the structure of SOS. So the conduct of Army supply overseas was decentralized. But the War Department, and SOS-ASF as its operating agency, coordinated supply among the various theaters, determined theater priorities and adjusted supply to strategic needs, and allocated shipping and scarce materials.[47]

Needless to say, not the least of the ways in which the Services of Supply–Army Service Forces became a very important organization was in the number of men they absorbed. It was against the mushroom growth of service personnel that McNair continually inveighed in his effort to keep the Army lean and simple. But the service forces' side of their argument with McNair lay in the rueful observation of General Staff G-3 that "unless we will be satisfied with an Army like the Japanese, wherein every soldier can carry a week's supply of rice, it will not be possible to greatly reduce the size of the services."[48]

G-3 may have exaggerated the starkness of the dilemma. Nevertheless, the effort to keep quantities of supply lavish and the troops reasonably comfortable steadily removed men from combat units planned in the early troop bases into service formations. For a brief period in 1942, the emphasis on rapid multiplication of combat divisions kept McNair relatively content, while Somervell complained that the development of SOS was "completely hamstrung." But once a minimum number of combat divisions approached readiness, the emphasis swung in the opposite direction. On the eve of Pearl Harbor, service forces constituted only 26.3 per cent of the Army's total manpower. By September, 1942, the logistical complexities of global war had already pushed them up to 34.4 per cent of the Army. By the end of the war, the manpower of service forces, including Ground Forces service units as well as ASF proper, almost equaled the manpower of combat units: 2,041,000 in combat units, 1,558,000 in service units.[49]

In one important area the functions of ASF diminished rather than grew during the war. The establishment of the Army Air Forces in the 1942 reorganization opened the way to the Air Forces' development of their own logistical services, as rapidly as they could free themselves from dependence on SOS-ASF. This development had not been wholly the intent of the reorganization, which had recognized important distinctions between air and ground supplies and an already considerable Air Forces logistical autonomy, but which had contemplated generally a single administration of all supply systems, under SOS. Instead, the Air Forces moved steadily toward a separate and parallel logistical system of their own, and their autonomy was already such that an SOS officer had to remark, "I don't believe there is anything we can do about it."[50]

To follow Army mobilization in earlier wars often gives the impression that everything learned in one war was forgotten by the time of the next. But this is not true of World War II; the mobilization experiences of 1917–18 were not forgotten, and enough study and planning based upon them persisted through the twenties and thirties to permit the Army of the 1940's to reproduce many of its earlier successes and avoid many of its earlier mistakes.

The experience of 1917–18 and the interwar planners did not, however, and largely could not, prepare the Army for the extent to which its mobilization for World War II had to be merely one part of a mobilization of half the world, supported everywhere in some measure by the United States. Every aspect of the Army's mobilization for World War II was shaped and limited by America's simultaneous industrial and military contributions to its coalition partners. World War II introduced the American Army to an era of interdependence with other armies, which remains and is likely to remain as long as the Army itself.

NINETEEN

Global War:

1941-45

On the way back to our headquarters we passed the equipment of an American armored division drawn up alongside the road. It included tanks and light armored vehicles and must have extended for about three miles. Commodore Schade said the Russians were much impressed by it.

—James Forrestal[1]

SECRETARY OF WAR Henry L. Stimson had been close to the Root reforms. He himself had done much to assure them during the Leonard Wood–Fred Ainsworth controversy. He believed strongly that their underlying principles must guide American military organization. Therefore he was much disturbed by one feature of the March, 1942, reorganization, which he took to threaten if not directly contravene those principles.

Article 6 of Executive Order 9082 disturbed Root's balance between the chief of staff and the Secretary of War. It read:

The Secretary of War is authorized and directed to prescribe such functions, duties, and powers of the commanders of the various forces and commands of the Army of the United States and the agencies of the War Department and to issue from time to time such detailed instructions regarding personnel, funds, records, property, routing of correspondence, and other matters as may be necessary to carry out the provisions of this order. Such duties by the Secretary of War are to be performed subject always to the exercise by the President directly through the Chief of Staff of his functions as Commander-in-Chief in relation to strategy, tactics, and operations.[2]

Stimson feared that this section carried the War Department a long way back toward the days of Winfield Scott and Nelson Miles, and the old, unhappy dual authority of Secretary and commanding general, by returning the Secretary to merely administrative functions and removing him from the operational chain of command. He resisted the full application of the order and continued to insert himself into deliberations on strategy and operations as much as he could. He believed he did so rightly, for a mere executive order could not deprive him of what he believed to be his constitutional function as civilian deputy to the civilian Commander in Chief.

Fortunately, his insistence caused no serious friction, because he and Marshall trusted and respected each other, and Marshall continued to give him opportunities to discuss purely military matters. Both Secretary and chief of staff determined that between their two offices there should be a "door that was always open."[3] But the executive order, the complexities of the war, and Stimson's advanced age nevertheless pushed the Secretary of War toward the periphery of military decisions. In the turmoil of war, few except Stimson seem to have paid much attention to the shifting balance of civil and military power.

Apart from the larger implications, and in terms of tangible issues of the conduct of the war, when he was able to inform himself Stimson remained often a valuable influence even in technical questions. He pushed Marshall toward more rapid development of radar, and he prodded Admiral Ernest J. King of the Navy to exploit the potential of the Army's aircraft in antisubmarine war. The old lawyer was often more receptive to new military technologies than the younger but more rigid professionals. Mainly, however, Stimson had to confine himself to the civil aspects of War Department activities, guarding, for example, the adequacy of the Army's allotments of raw materials, industrial production, and manpower, in the process feuding with Donald Nelson of the War Production Board, and seeking unsuccessfully to keep the selective service agency completely separate from the civilian manpower agency and to secure larger manpower quotas for the Army.

Among Stimson's major accomplishments was his part in bringing civilian deputies of uncommonly high caliber to the department. Robert Patterson, with a background in corporation law akin to Stimson's and service in the federal judiciary, came as Assistant Secretary and became Under Secretary; to him Stimson gave an increasingly free hand in industrial procurement, still a large work despite the growth of SOS-ASF.[4] From backgrounds similar to Patterson's came John J. McCloy, Assistant Secretary after April, 1941, and Robert A. Lovett, Assistant Secretary of War for Air. In line with the growing independence of the Army Air Forces, Lovett was in effect Secretary of the Air Forces in a position parallel to Stimson's, despite his theoretical subordination.[5]

McCloy acted as general deputy for Stimson, overseeing a variety of onerous tasks, which included the relocation of the Japanese from the West Coast,[6] Army Intelligence, and military government in occupied territories. In the latter area, he brought about the creation of a Civil Affairs Division of the General Staff. He also led in creating the State-War-Navy Coordinating Committee in December, 1944, an agency designed to coordinate the activities of the three departments involved where military and foreign policies increasingly intermingled. McCloy was the War Department's principal representative on SWNCC, sitting with the Assistant Secretaries of State and the Navy; both the Operations and the Civil Affairs Division of the General Staff were represented on subcommittees.[7]

In part, the new definition of the place of the Secretary of War embodied in the 1942 reorganization was merely a confirmation of practice already adopted by President Roosevelt. Roosevelt's character and inclinations demanded that he be a Commander in Chief not on the model of Wilson, turning his back on all but the most formal and needful military responsibilities, but on the model of Lincoln and even of Polk, intimately concerned with strategy as well as with military administration. Roosevelt had insisted upon direct and constant communication with his chief of staff from his first turning toward foreign and military questions. The basic command decisions of the global war had to be his own, and he required the military information and the direct hand on the military machine with which to make and implement them.

Sometimes Roosevelt's delight in the direct exercise of his powers as Commander in Chief brought trials to his military subordinates. For one thing, though Roosevelt hoped to unite foreign and economic policy with the military direction of the war through his own person, he had no adequate staff of his own to assist him or even to record Presidential decisions and instructions. Consequently there always seemed to be loose ends of incomplete decisions and incompletely shared information. One of Stimson's functions was to act as a link between the War Department and cabinet- and agency-level civil decisions, but he could not keep himself well enough informed to perform this function fully. Marshall urged the construction of Presidential staff machinery comparable to that available to the British Prime Minister for the coordination of policy, but Roosevelt's administrative habits perpetuated loose arrangements in which "details supposedly decided upon" were "left in the air or subject to varying interpretations." To a degree, the growing staff machinery of the Joint Chiefs of Staff offered a remedy as the war progressed, but that machinery could not venture too far into diplomatic and economic policy.[8]

A perhaps worse difficulty of the President's military activity, at least from the viewpoint of his military counselors, was his impulsive and intuitive method of reaching decisions, especially when influenced by the British Prime Minister. Winston Churchill exceeded even Roosevelt in his determination to retain for himself the principal military direction of his country's war effort. Thus the grand strategy of the Western Allies was the product of the frequent personal meetings and constant communication of the President and the Prime Minister.

Churchill fancied himself a born strategist, and he brought to his leadership of the war firm strategic preconceptions rooted in memories of the Western Front and Gallipoli and in his island's peculiar military strengths and weaknesses. Impulsive and intuitive in Roosevelt's own manner, he often bent the President away from military judgments that American military chieftains considered sound, toward adventures that the latter believed wasteful, dangerous, and in sum irresponsible.[9]

Specifically, the central theme of all the strategic deliberations of the Western Allies until June 6, 1944, was the running debate between the American military's insistence on the cross-channel invasion of Europe and Churchill's preference for a multitude of smaller assaults on the whole periphery of Germany's empire. The American military leaders regarded the cross-channel invasion as the sound and certain means to defeat Germany. Churchill believed his schemes would restrict the possibility of another Western Front and the concomitant bleeding of limited British manpower and resources, vindicate the Gallipoli strategy of a generation earlier, and perchance bring valuable political byproducts in the postwar distribution of power with the Soviet Union. Repeatedly Churchill seemed to be diverting Roosevelt from the American strategy of the cross-channel invasion, and continually a major effort of the Army high command was to hold the President firm in support of his own military advisers' plans. Marshall and to a still greater extent Stimson remained the undeviating champions of the attack that began in the planning offices as Operation Bolero and emerged at last as Operation Overlord, until General Dwight D. Eisenhower's troops actually crossed the Normandy beaches in 1944.[10]

For all that, it is important not to exaggerate Churchill's influence over Roosevelt or the President's deviation from the advice of his military deputies on any point. Roosevelt's interest in the military side of the war was not only active but intelligent, his relations with

Marshall were both close and harmonious, and he deserves a share of credit for the astute selection of commanders which eventually marked the Army's participation in the war. Woodrow Wilson's indifference had created an unfortunate precedent, suggesting the erosion of all but the most formal aspects of the President's role as Commander in Chief under the complexities of modern war. Roosevelt's activity honorably restored the office to its constitutional estate.

The long tug of war of the American Army command with the British over the cross-channel invasion underlined still other problems of the American command structure. When American military chieftains met their British counterparts for combined strategic planning, through nearly the first half of the war the British could argue for their strategic designs with greater forcefulness than the Americans, simply because they had superior interservice command arrangements and superior organization for the kind of interservice strategic planning that had to underlie a global war. World War II, not only demanding unprecedented cooperation of the Army with the Navy but adding air power as well, required a new level of American military command above and coordinating the Army and the Navy in a way that the civilian Commander in Chief and prewar interservice committees could not accomplish. In the end, the war turned the American armed forces decisively toward unified command, which had been discussed with growing frequency at least since the Root reforms, but was never before urgently needed. Yet it was the necessity for greater interservice unity in order to deal effectively with the British that served as the immediate precipitant of new interservice arrangements.

Winston Churchill was better served organizationally than Franklin Roosevelt by both civilian and military staffs. He not only presided over a War Cabinet, the highest executive authority in his government, but as Minister of Defence as well as Prime Minister he exerted immediate supervision of the war effort through a defense committee including the Foreign Secretary, the Minister of Production, the civilian heads of the War Office, Admiralty, and Air Ministry, and the chiefs of Great Britain's three military services. The latter three professional military men not only sat within the defense committee; as a group they themselves had a formal corporate existence as the Chiefs of Staff Committee. As such they not only represented their individual services but jointly headed an array of interservice staffs responsible to the Chiefs of Staff Committee.[11]

The Joint Army-Navy Board that had existed for most of the years since 1903 was not a means of permitting the American armed services to present a common front to the British or of engaging in common planning that would bind all parties. Roosevelt had strengthened it in 1939 by directing it to function under the immediate supervision of the Commander in Chief, but its decisions had only such force of authority as the individual service heads chose to give them within their commands, except in rare cases when Roosevelt gave the decisions his formal approval. Early in 1941 the Army and the Navy undertook an increasingly close liaison with the British armed forces, including formal strategic discussions as early as January, known as the ABC-1 conversations. The growing intimacy of these discussions pointed up the difficulties of the divided American services' attempting to deal with the unified British military command, and the Argentia meeting between Roosevelt and Churchill further displayed the American problem. There Marshall, the chief of naval operations, and, somewhat anomalously, General Arnold of the Army Air Forces, met with the British chiefs of staff but did not bring to the conference nearly the background of interservice planning that the British could offer.

Just after Pearl Harbor the American and British chiefs of staff met again, when Churchill brought his retinue to Washington to discuss America's new role as a full partner in war. Here the British took the initiative in combined strategic planning and often overrode American ideas—already the priority of a cross-channel invasion became a bone of contention—through the sheer weight of their interservice preparations. Henceforth the division of the American services vis-à-vis the united British services would become intolerable, furthermore, because the British rightly proposed continuous Anglo-American military consultation for the rest of the war. The two countries established the Combined Chiefs of Staff, which grew to be the principal interallied headquarters. The British Chiefs of Staff left permanent representatives in Washington, through whom they kept in touch with the deliberations of the American service chiefs, and through whom British and American strategy was coordinated. Periodically the American and British chiefs of staff met each other directly, to agree on major strategic decisions, but henceforth their conversations were prepared for by the Combined Chiefs of Staff in Washington, and the Combined Chiefs of Staff carried on the day-to-day direction of interallied strategy.

The Combined Chiefs of Staff first met on January 23, 1942. The CCS was an indispensable instrument, but its formation did require immediate tightening of American interservice cooperation. The United States was represented in the first CCS meetings by Marshall, Arnold, and for the Navy, Admiral Harold R. Stark, chief of naval operations, and Admiral Ernest J. King, commander in chief, United States Fleet. Stark soon moved on to other duties, and King assumed both naval offices. Meanwhile Roosevelt had taken one step toward remedying the staff deficiencies of the Commander in Chief by appointing Admiral William D. Leahy chief of staff to the President. Presently Leahy joined Marshall, King, and Arnold and presided as chairman of their meetings, thus crystallizing for the rest of the war what now came to be known as the Joint Chiefs of Staff.[12]

The American and British commands clarified the responsibilities of the Combined Chiefs and of the American and British Joint Chiefs in March, 1942. The CCS was responsible for "formulation of policies and plans" for the "strategic conduct of the war" and for priorities and allocations in production and overseas movements. Under CCS, the world was divided into three major strategic spheres. The American Joint Chiefs of Staff would have principal responsibility for the Pacific area, including Australia, and for China. The British would have similar responsibility for the Middle and Far East except China. The CCS would exercise more direct control over the Atlantic-European area.[13]

Both the CCS and the JCS developed more and more elaborate committee support as the war went on. The growth of the supporting machinery for the JCS was especially marked, for here the Americans continued to feel frustrated by insufficient interservice machinery to prepare them for confrontations with the British long after the JCS itself was established. Through 1942 joint Army-Navy decisions continued to be pretty much the agreements that Marshall and King could thrash out themselves. As late as the Casablanca Conference of January, 1943, the British showed up with some ten times as many interservice planners as the Americans and with superior interservice preparation. The result, as Brigadier General Albert Wedemeyer put it, was that "We lost our shirts and . . . are now committed to a subterranean umbilicus operation in midsummer," meaning that efforts which the Americans would have applied to hastening and strengthening the cross-channel attack were diverted to the invasion of Sicily.[14]

Staff machinery to support the JCS therefore proliferated greatly during 1943, including a strengthened Joint Planning Staff supported by an active Joint War Plans Committee to carry on day-to-day planning, a Joint Logistics Committee, and a Joint Administrative Committee. In consequence, the later interallied conferences of the year, culminating in the Cairo and Teheran meetings, found the JCS able to present a united American service front to the British and the other Allies, supported by adequate staff planning, and thus to assure that American strategic designs would stand or fall more nearly on their merits, and not be discarded through having been insufficiently prepared. Moreover, more adequate interservice staffs gave a new authoritative quality to JCS decisions, whereby the

American war effort became more truly one under interservice command, rather than merely a series of compromises among rival Army, Navy, and Air Force strategies. Nevertheless, it must be emphasized that the CCS and JCS both operated under the rule of unanimity, and a certain amount of compromise and in general a committee-like quality inevitably characterized their decisions. If the strategic choices open to the Allies in World War II had been more numerous than they were, or if the CCS-JCS machinery had had to confront more dramatic crises than it ever did, it is not sure that command by committee would have emerged so successfully from the war.[15]

The growth of the CCS-JCS machinery greatly accelerated the Army Air Forces drive toward autonomy, since the adoption of the British pattern in the CCS and JCS brought General Arnold into a position coequal with Marshall and King on the highest level of combined and joint planning. On that pattern also, Air Forces representatives sat coordinately with those of the War Department General Staff on all the principal agencies of the JCS and thus of the CCS. In October, 1943, Marshall yielded to the logic of this situation by permitting the Air Forces to take recommendations to the JCS committee system without first passing them through his War Department offices. Increasingly, too, the Air Forces took upon themselves the direct implementation of JCS decisions that concerned them, without waiting for directives to pass through the War Department machinery.[16]

The relationship of the individual services and their own command and planning organizations to the CCS-JCS structure was never altogether clear, and a measure of mutual forbearance and discretion was essential to the functioning of the joint command. General Marshall, for example, continued to draw upon the strategic planning of both the Joint War Plans Committee, in his capacity as a member of JCS, and the Operations Division of the War Department General Staff, in his capacity as chief of staff of the Army. There was no clear delineation between the kinds of planning the two agencies conducted, although as it grew in stature and experience the JWPC naturally took on more of the most critical and least routine strategic problems. Close liaison was assured, since Army representatives on the JCS committees came largely from OPD, and the Army members of JWPC met frequently with OPD, eventually on a regular schedule. One defect of the JCS committee structure was the remoteness of its members from operations, a matter in which OPD enjoyed a distinct advantage. Conversely, overseas commanders and staffs were handicapped by lack of familiarity with the JCS machinery.[17]

That unfamiliarity of the JCS machinery helped assure that OPD would continue to be the most important link between the command structure in Washington and the theaters overseas. It was through OPD planning and directives, furthermore, that the Army undertook to implement its share of CCS-JCS decisions. Under the 1942 reorganization, General Marshall commanded the Army, directly under the President; and the instrument through which he exercised his unprecedented command over a multitude of theaters was OPD. As he developed the implications of the 1942 reorganization, OPD came to resemble a theater commander's general staff, but with the whole world as its theater. Increasingly it overshadowed the old "G" divisions of the War Department General Staff, reduced as G-1, G-3, and G-4 were to a handful of officers each, and charged mainly as they were with advising the zone of interior activities of the three Army commands. The "G" divisions carried on even these activities largely in accord with OPD strategic decisions. G-2 continued with a larger staff in its work of collecting and evaluating information about the enemy, but it too proceeded largely as an agency serving OPD.

OPD both planned and controlled the operations of the Army. The 1942 reorganization charged it with "formulation of plans and the strategic direction of military forces in the theater of war." General McNarney, the principal architect of the 1942 reorganization, said:

By the creation of the Air Forces, Ground Forces and SOS the Chief of Staff gains time to give most of his attention to war operations. The War Plans Division, WDGS [which presently became OPD], is the headquarters General Staff through which the Chief of Staff, plans, supervises, and directs operations. His decisions are implemented by the Air Forces and Ground Forces who provide the trained forces, by the Service of Supply which provides supplies (except items peculiar to the Air Forces and provided by them) and moves them to the theaters of operations, and by the commanders of the various theaters of operations, and task forces who actually control combat operations in their respective areas of responsibility.[18]

Colonel William K. Harrison, Jr., explained OPD further to the Senate Military Affairs Committee:

In this war, we are fighting on many fronts . . . we have the great question of the use of our means in different places. So that right here—under the Chief of Staff—we have to centralize the direction of operations so that this War Plans Division now, not only makes war plans, that is, future plans, but it necessarily must control and direct the operations under the Chief of Staff.[19]

OPD could become an inner general staff inside the War Department General Staff, doing things that the old General Staff itself had not been able to do, because officially and from its beginning it was oriented toward operations as well as planning, and because it worked unimpeded by procedural traditions that had developed in the General Staff during its long years of doubtful authority. As its organization evolved, OPD came to be divided into four major "groups," each subdivided into "sections." The Executive Group was the secretariat of OPD. The Strategy and Policy Group mainly carried out the strategic planning functions of the agency. The Theater Group contained a section for each of the theaters of operations, plus a Troop Movements Section, and was more closely concerned with operations. The section of the Theater Group responsible for each theater of war acted as a kind of general staff for the theater commander far behind his front. It kept itself informed of his efforts to carry out his mission, and it acted within OPD to ensure him the necessary resources. Through the theater sections, OPD monitored the efforts of the theater commanders to comply with JCS and War Department decisions. The Pearl Harbor attack had demonstrated that this monitoring function was of incalculable importance; the Pearl Harbor disaster had occurred partly because the Hawaiian commanders had failed to act upon directives from Washington and the War Department had failed to inform itself whether they were acting. Meanwhile, the Logistics Group of OPD sought to ensure that the Army as a whole as well as the theater commanders in particular would receive the logistical support necessary to carry out the planning and operational decisions of OPD's other groups and sections.[20]

The OPD organization chart listed the most important of its many tasks: "Preliminary studies, estimates, and plans for potential theaters of operations"; "Preparation of directives to commanders of theaters or other task forces"; "combined and joint planning"; "central control agency for operations"; "War Department Command Post for field operations"; "coordination of all ground, air, and service activities required to effectuate War Department decisions pertaining to the organization and operations of task forces, theaters, defense commands, overseas possessions, and leased bases."[21]

The career of General Dwight D. Eisenhower is another mirror of the importance of OPD. Just after Pearl Harbor, Eisenhower became deputy chief of WPD for the Far East and the Pacific, largely because of his acquaintance with the area gained while he was an assistant to MacArthur in the Philippines from 1935 to 1940. He proved willing to assume responsibilities and to make decisions, thereby pleasing Marshall, and the chief of staff elevated him to assistant chief of staff, WPD, on February 16, 1942, when Brigadier General Leonard T. Gerow left the post. In the transition from WPD to the larger tasks of OPD, Eisenhower became the first assistant chief of staff, OPD. He did much to fashion OPD and to make it an efficient working organization. He supervised the drafting of the strategic plans which from the first aimed the American war effort toward the cross-channel invasion of Europe. In the spring of 1942, in response to a visit of Marshall to London, the British formally accepted the invasion as the basis of combined planning, though with the reservations out of which were to grow subsequent American disappointments. In an effort to stimulate preparations in England, Eisenhower traveled there in May. When he returned to the United States in June, he criticized the lack of punch behind even the American side of preparations in England. His experience in OPD became an important asset in his relations with the War Department during his tenure as commanding general, European Theater of Operations.[22]

General Lesley McNair's design to keep the Army lean and simple approached success in the organization of the ground combat forces, over which McNair could preside as commander of AGF. He shaped the basic infantry division and its supporting arms to achieve the best possible combination of fighting power with flexibility and maneuverability, in the maximum possible number of divisions that he could squeeze from what he thought the all too limited supply of ground combat manpower.

Immediately after World War I ended, the Army had begun a reexamination of the huge infantry division of that war. The 1917–18 division had possessed the great staying power that Pershing expected of it, but it was also a cumbersome division difficult to maneuver and support. Pershing himself was willing after the war to study a smaller, more nimble division, better suited to the open warfare which he himself so strongly emphasized, and to be supported with completely motorized transport. Out of the consequent studies came the plan for the triangular division of three regiments, with brigade organization omitted, to replace the square division of four regiments in two brigades. The new organization was approved in principle in 1935, and in 1937 and 1939 the model of the new division was developed through field tests, perhaps the most elaborate of their kind ever conducted in peacetime in the United States.

McNair himself did the main work of transforming the new division from theory to actuality as chief of staff of the test division. Out of the tests came a report recommending a triangular division of 10,275 men to replace the 22,000-man square division. The War

Department did not approve quite so drastic a reduction even though it approved the principal organizational patterns that emerged from the tests; it adopted a division of 14,981 men. During the interval when McNair was chief of staff, GHQ, he lost direct connection with infantry reorganization, and in his opinion fat began to accumulate in the division anew. When he became commander of AGF, he created a study group to trim down the infantry division again, from its then authorized strength of 15,500 men.

> The triangular division was initiated some five years ago [he said] with the primary purpose of streamlining the organization and rendering it more effective in combat. Since the reorganization there has been a steady succession of changes, all in the direction of returning to the cumbersome and impracticable organization of the old square division. It is felt mandatory that every proposal which increases overhead must be resisted if the division is to be effective in combat.[23]

Once more, McNair failed to establish a division altogether as lean and simple as he would have liked, but his comments did express the basic philosophy upon which he was able to build the World War II division.

McNair believed that the division must contain within it only such elements as it needed to be able to advance against average resistance. It must not be overburdened with an elaborate hierarchy of headquarters; they merely created a flood of orders, wasted men, and impeded the flexibility of the division. It must not be burdened with numerous defensive weapons; its purpose was to attack and advance, and in an emergency its stock of weapons could be supplemented from reserve pools. It must not be burdened with equipment of any kind that it would not ordinarily need. If a division carried all the defensive armament it might need to withstand a heavy attack, or all transport and transport maintenance it would need to move in the most difficult terrain, or all the medical services it would need when unusually heavily engaged, it would be immobilized by its own impedimenta. Furthermore, if the division possessed all the equipment it would need for any emergency, much of that equipment would be lying wastefully idle much of the time. And some equipment is most effective when not tied to one division: if a certain sector of a front faces an especially heavy attack, artillery should be concentrated there from all along the line.

Upon the basic principle, then, that the division should include only those elements it would normally need to advance against average resistance, McNair pared down the division by the complementary processes of streamlining and pooling. He streamlined the division by trying to remove all superfluous elements, extending the principle on which brigade headquarters had disappeared. Largely this meant that he expected soldiers not to be excessively specialized but instead to take on a variety of tasks. Rather than have specialized antitank crews and guns forward with the rifle companies at all times, he preferred to assign rocket launchers to the ordinary weapons platoon of the infantry company, letting the men defend themselves first with those instruments and also with their grenades and with improvised weapons. Rather than support a multitude of Signal Corps specialists, he preferred that infantrymen and artillerists operate their own radios and telephones. Infantrymen could drive trucks as well as quartermasters. Infantrymen did not need engineers for rudimentary mine detection. Infantry regiments could haul supplies in their own trucks if given direct access to the sources, and so McNair laid down the rule that "Division and corps are not in the channel of supply except in emergencies."[24]

With less success, McNair also pushed his conviction that officers could serve several functions. A division's artillery commander, for example, could also be artillery officer on the staff of the division commander, and the commanding officer of the divison medical battalion could also be the chief surgeon. It was characteristic of McNair that he believed most people do not work as hard as they can and could perform more tasks than they normally do.

While streamlining the division, McNair furthered the de-fatting process by pooling specialists and special equipment in nondivisional units that could be assigned flexibly whenever a division might need them. Massed enemy tanks or aircraft could not threaten all divisions simultaneously, so specialized antitank and antiaircraft units could be pooled to go to the aid of whatever divisions were especially threatened. A tank attack too heavy to be handled by the infantrymen with their rocket launchers, or even by the divisional antitank guns and artillery, could be countered by a mobile force of tank destroyers. Transport maintenance such as the forward units could not provide for themselves could best be afforded by pools serving several divisions. Elaborate bridging equipment did not need to be carried by the divisional engineer battalion but could come out of a pool when needed. The same general arrangement could be used for all the special combat support and logistical services not required every day.

McNair would have cut the 1942 division by something over 2,000 men. The Tables of Organization and Equipment eventually approved by the War Department cut it by only 1,250. Even this saving permitted the eventual organization of sixty-six infantry divisions from men who would otherwise have made up only sixty, no small thing in the pinch for divisions that developed late in the war.[25]

The infantry division which emerged in 1943 from McNair's work and which remained the basic division of World War II was built around twenty-seven rifle companies totaling 5,184 men. Each rifle company consisted of three rifle platoons and a weapons platoon. The rifle platoon consisted of three rifle squads of twelve men each, armed with ten M-1 (Garand) rifles, one automatic rifle, and one Model 1903 Springfield rifle. The weapons platoon contained two .30-caliber light machine guns, three 60-mm mortars, three antitank rocket launchers, and one .50-caliber machine gun primarily for antiaircraft defense.

Three rifle companies were grouped with a heavy weapons company to form an infantry battalion. The heavy weapons company numbered 162 officers and men and carried six 81-mm mortars, eight .30-caliber heavy machine guns, seven antitank rocket launchers, and three .50-caliber machine guns. Attached to the battalion headquarters company was an antitank platoon armed with three 37-mm antitank guns (until the much superior 57-mm guns came along). The headquarters company also had three .30-caliber machine guns, one .50-caliber machine gun, and eight antitank rocket launchers. Three infantry battalions plus a headquarters company (which included six 105-mm howitzers), a service company, and an antitank company (twelve antitank guns plus one .50-caliber and four .30-caliber machine guns) made up the infantry regiment.

The three divisional artillery battalions included one 155-mm howitzer battery and two 105-mm howitzer batteries each, firing a total of twelve of the former and thirty-six of the latter guns. There was also a headquarters and service battery. Three infantry regiments plus the three artillery battalions comprised the combat elements of a division, supported by division engineer, signal, ordnance, quartermaster, medical, and military police units, with a headquarters company and a mechanized reconnaissance troop.[26]

McNair recognized that the standard division would have to be modified in various theaters to meet various situations, and the theater commanders were the more free to make *de facto* modifications in the constituents of a division because of the flexibility afforded by pooling the support elements. In practice, the infantry division came to operate usually with a tank battalion and other supporting elements in quasipermanent attachment, so that a division commander generally controlled somewhat more than 15,000 men. The regiment often operated with tanks, engineers, and perhaps additional support attached to form a regimental combat team. But McNair was vindicated in his belief that the Army should concentrate upon forming standard divisions, rather than attempt to create in the United States a variety of specialized divisions for the varying combat theaters; and the standard division of which he was the principal architect served admirably well, especially considering that it had to be fashioned without benefit of much American combat experience in the new warfare of tanks and airplanes.[27]

The division was a standardized unit, made up of constituent standardized units, each with its officers, men, and equipment prescribed in Tables of Organization and Equipment. But McNair decided that units larger than the division should not be standardized but rather that corps and armies should be "task forces," each assembled from standardized parts with a view to its specific mission. At the beginning of 1942 there still existed Troop Lists describing the "type" army and the "type" corps in terms of a formal structure for each. The type corps consisted of three divisions plus specified corps troops. The type army consisted of three corps plus specified army troops. But on September 21, 1942, McNair proposed that the type army and type corps be abandoned. He pointed to German success in using a more flexible tactical organization of task forces built for specific missions. Though the War Department never formally accepted his full proposal, in effect his plan was followed. Just as he wanted no resources frozen in divisions if they could not normally be used every day, so he wanted no resources fixed in corps and armies if they were not strictly necessary.

Consequently, armies and corps were stripped of all organic elements except headquarters and allied formations needed to exercise command. All troops not organized into divisions, and in effect all divisions as well, became part of a GHQ reserve, to be attached to corps or armies or detached again at will.[28]

To ensure the flexibility of this plan, McNair proposed that all troops not organized into divisions should be formed into permanent units of the smallest size compatible with efficiency. Then such small, interchangeable units could be shuttled into and out of corps and armies in just the quantity that any situation demanded. For nondivisional combat troops, the Army Ground Forces decided that the smallest unit compatible with efficiency was the battalion. Therefore fixed brigades and regiments mostly disappeared outside the infantry, and supporting combat troops were organized into battalions, pooled in GHQ reserve and attached to corps and armies as needed. For service troops, the still smaller company was chosen as the smallest unit compatible with efficiency, and it was companies of service troops that could be assigned as needed.

If an occasion arose to use a large mass of nondivisional combat

troops, three or four battalions could be brought together in a
"group." But the group was a tactical organization only, each battalion was supposed to remain self-sufficient in administration and
supply, and the group was not a permanent formation. Occasionally,
groups of antiaircraft, field artillery, or tank destroyer battalions
were united in a "brigade." But like the group, the new brigade was
only an impermanent, tactical arrangement; its constituent groups
and battalions were not organic to it, and in fact it was infrequently
used. On a similar pattern, service companies might be grouped into
a battalion, but among service troops even a battalion was an impermanent *ad hoc* arrangement. Nondivisional combat battalions
and service companies were standardized parts, with formal
Tables of Organization; but they could be assigned to armies and
corps in any combination. In practice, the corps was a tactical unit,
and nondivisional combat battalions were mainly attached to it. The
army was an administrative as well as a tactical unit, and service
companies were mainly attached to the army. Always flexibility and
economy were McNair's watchwords.[29]

Many observers both inside and outside the Army believed in
1939 and 1940 that the new technology of war, with its tanks, tank
destroyers, self-propelled artillery, tactical air support, and airborne
troops, would demand a variety of specialized divisions, tailored not
only to specific theaters of combat but to the employment of specific
weapons. The spectacle of the German Panzer divisions rolling
across Poland and France seemed to confirm this impression. But
McNair as usual was skeptical about highly specialized formations,
and again his caution came to be vindicated. His procedure in the
development of such new instruments of war as armored, antitank,
and antiaircraft forces was to grant them a status somewhat analogous to that of the old combat "arms"—infantry, cavalry, artillery—
and with it a considerable autonomy in the development of their
doctrine and tactics; but once they had reasonably well thought·out
and tested their mission, to reabsorb them into a team of all the
combat forces.

Thus the new quasiarms were given their own headquarters for
training and development, through the creation of various "forces,"
such as the Armored Force; "commands," such as the Antiaircraft
Command; and "centers," such as the Tank Destroyer Center. The
autonomy of the Armored Force went far enough, under the impressions left by the first German campaigns of the war, that armored
commanders began to dream of an independent development parallel to that of the Air Forces, and distinctive armored divisions and
armored corps were created. But as McNair had anticipated, increased experience deflated the autonomist aspirations of all the new

"arms," so that only armor took divisions of its own into battle, the other new "arms" were organized into formations no higher than battalions, and an increasingly close association with the traditional combat arms had to be developed when combined training of all ground combat forces became an evident necessity. Adequate combined training eventually posed some of the most difficult obstacles to readying the Army for battle, since bringing sufficient diverse equipment together at appropriate stages of training was not easily done, especially in the early days of the war when all kinds of equipment were scarce.[30]

The German Blitzkrieg prompted estimates that as many as fifty or sixty American armored divisions would be necessary for the United States to win the war. As late as May 22, 1942, the projected troop basis drawn up by OPD called for forty-six armored divisions. In the wake of the German conquest of France, American armored commanders envisioned armored corps and divisions sweeping deep into the enemy's country, striking the vital blows of the war, while conventional infantry contented itself with mopping-up operations. The chief of the Armored Force said as late as July, 1942:

The triangular division has its place in the scheme of affairs to protect lines of communication, to hold ground, to assist the armored units in supply and the crossing of obstacles such as rivers, defiles, etc. They do not carry the spearhead of the fight and never will when tanks and guns are present.[31]

But the British campaigns against the Germans in the Western Desert, and then the Russian campaigns, were already unveiling increasingly effective antitank tactics and weapons, including both antitank guns and mines, and the tanks found themselves increasingly in need of infantry support. McNair, unlike the armored commanders, conceived of the tank as a weapon of exploitation akin to the old cavalry, useful for penetrating the enemy's country and pursuing him *after* his main positions had been broken; but to break well-prepared positions was, he believed, work for the traditional infantry-artillery team, albeit with tank and air support. Once the armies developed improved defenses against the tank, the war moved closer to McNair's conception than to the armored force zealots'.

Therefore the tank would have to work in close cooperation with infantry. The design of armored formations themselves changed to incorporate a growing proportion of infantry, to assist in taking as well as to hold ground. As designed in 1940–42, American armored divisions numbered 14,620 men, with 4,848 in tank units, 2,389 in armored infantry, and 2,127 in armored artillery. There were two tank regiments of three battalions each, one armored infantry regiment of three battalions, and three artillery battalions. The armored infantry was equipped to move in lightly armored half-tracks. In 1943, however, the armored division was remodeled to comprise an equal number of infantry and tank battalions, three of each, plus the three artillery battalions.

Regiments now disappeared from the armored division, in pursuit again of McNair's goal of flexibility. With no fixed regimental formations present in the division anyway, additional battalions of tanks, infantry, or artillery could readily be added or detached in any combination as any situation required. To handle these flexible arrangements, armored division headquarters included two "combat commands," each a subheadquarters to which the division commander might assign such task forces as he chose. "Although the division organically probably will aggregate something like 11,000," McNair said, "you may make it 20,000 if you so desire, simply by adding armored or infantry battalions."[32]

In practice, the armored division did not become quite that flexible. Usually there was no pool of infantry battalions from which to draw, since the need for infantry divisions forced the incorporation of virtually all battalions into the divisions. Usually there was no pool of tank battalions either; while the reduction of the organic tank strength of each armored division seemed to create a pool, the requirements of infantry-tank cooperation drew practically all tank battalions out of it into more or less permanent attachment to infantry divisions.

The necessity for infantry-tank coordination to break strongly defended positions naturally reduced the quantity of armored divisions even while it reduced the tank strength within those divisions. From the originally planned fifty or sixty, the number of armored divisions actually organized fell to sixteen. McNair questioned the wisdom of maintaining even that number. On several occasions during the European campaign of 1944 when infantry divisions were acutely needed and in short supply, keeping up sixteen armored divisions did seem a kind of luxury.

McNair wrote: "An armored division is of value only in pursuit or exploitation. For plain and fancy slugging against an enemy who is unbroken or at least intact the tank battalion or group is adequate."[33] The war proved to be much more a war of the old infantry-artillery team than the German campaigns of 1939 and 1940 had suggested. Once good antitank weapons had been developed and their tactics well planned, tanks alone could not force a breakthrough. What they could do well was to join tactical aviation in cooperating with the infantry as a sort of superartillery. In this role they did break at last the tactical deadlock which had gripped the battlefield for nearly a hundred years.

But the return to mobile warfare that distinguished the Second from the First World War was due no more to this facilitation of the breakthrough by means of armor and air assistance to the infantry-artillery team, than to the possibility of mobile exploitation after the breakthrough. Even with limited or nonexistent tank support, the infantry of 1914–18 had occasionally managed to open a gap in the enemy's lines; certainly the Germans had done it repeatedly in their 1918 offensive, with virtually no tanks at all. The critical problem of World War I involved not only forcing the breakthrough but also inability to exploit the breakthrough once it did occur. There had been no means of pressing the advance fast enough and long enough to prevent the enemy's reforming his lines. In World War II, however, mechanized movement, including tanks but including also thoroughly motorized infantry, made it possible to push through a gap in the enemy's lines with enough sustained force and speed to keep him reeling, until he entered fresh defenses far to the rear or until the attacker outran his fuel supply. American corps in the European theater usually combined one armored division with two infantry divisions; when the possibilities for exploiting a breakthrough existed, maintaining enough armored divisions for such a ratio no longer appeared a luxury.[34]

Improved battlefield communication was another prerequisite to escape from the century-old tactical deadlock, and in World War II, field radios at last permitted swift movement scattered over wide areas, combined with reasonably good contact among troops and their officers. There were still complex difficulties to plague communication of tanks and airplanes with infantry and artillery; the Germans began to master them more quickly than their opponents. To the end of the war, aircraft sometimes bombed the ground forces they were supposed to be protecting, and tanks and infantry found it hard to stay in touch. But battlefield communication was infinitely better than it had ever been before.[35]

Aided by improved communications, the infantry-artillery team remained essential to effecting the breakthrough. So the infantry division, with tank, artillery, and aircraft support, remained the basic combat unit of the Army. Other specialized divisions contemplated early in the war had even less success than the armored division in retaining their specialized identities.

The armored division was originally intended to serve in armored corps, each of which would also include a motorized infantry division. The motorized infantry division was to be provided with enough motor transport to move all its elements simultaneously. But when motorized divisions were created, they proved to be so elaborately equipped, and more specifically so demanding of shipping space to be carried overseas, that theater commanders did not want them, preferring to receive greater numbers of standard formations carried to them by an equal amount of shipping. The standard division included motor transport for all its elements except infantry anyway, and six quartermaster truck companies from an army pool could motorize that as well. In fact, the 18th Infantry Division discovered during the rush across northern France that it could move more than thirty miles a day without even requisitioning quartermaster trucks; it simply piled its infantry on its howitzers, tanks, and tank destroyers. Other divisions promptly made the same discovery. The motorized divisions were reconverted to standard infantry divisions, and the motorized division disappeared from the troop basis.

Special desert and mountain divisions met the same fate. The project to create such divisions led to experiments with "light" divisions, which had all the parts of standard infantry divisions, except with smaller numbers, but which were intended to move in countries without roads and thus unassisted by motor transport. Organic transportation consisted of handcarts, or toboggan sleds for mountain divisions in cold weather, along with pack mules and possibly quarter-ton trucks for the field artillery. But the theater commanders were dubious about light divisions from the start, and maneuvers of the 71st and 89th Light Divisions in the mountains of California confirmed their doubts; the divisions, understrength already, were incapable of sustaining themselves in fighting condition. They were reconverted to standard infantry divisions. The 10th Light Division (Pack, Alpine) did remain a specialized division, but with its strength increased to approximate that of a standard division, whereupon it was designated the 10th Mountain Division.

Even the airborne divisions generally came to approximate standard infantry divisions, except in the means by which they reached the scene of combat. They began like the light divisions as smaller parallels of standard divisions, but as understrength formations they had trouble sustaining combat. In Europe four of them were enlarged from 8,500 to 12,799 men, with two parachute regiments, a glider regiment almost identical to a standard infantry regiment, and a battalion of 105-mm howitzers. Only the one airborne division in the Pacific retained thoroughly peculiar Tables of Organization.

After disbanding the 2nd Cavalry Division for a second and final time, the Army did retain one cavalry division, the 1st, throughout the war. It continued to be an old-style square division, and in theory it was not mechanized but horse cavalry. Curious anachronism though it was, it carved itself a splendid battle record in the Southwest Pacific, fighting dismounted but perpetuating some of the most famous old regiments of the Army, including Custer's 7th Cavalry. If maintaining it was partly a bow to tradition, then there was something to be said for this exception in a war in which seemingly overriding practical necessities submerged the identity of historic Regular Army and National Guard formations perhaps all too often.[36]

Altogether, the experience of the war confirmed that suspicion of excessive specialization with which General McNair began the war. The standard triangular infantry division proved a suitable instrument for all the theaters in which American ground forces fought, in a war whose tactics ultimately departed less than had been anticipated from traditional infantry-artillery combat. Perhaps McNair pruned the standard division too much, since tank and engineer and other supporting troops beyond those called for in the T/O&E's had to be attached more or less permanently. But McNair's pooling system made such attachments possible with a minimum of difficulty. The shaping of the standard infantry division, before there could be much American combat experience on which to draw, was a notable achievement of American military organization.

Infantry assault doctrine of World War II was based on the covering-fire tactics of the final phase of World War I. Each twelve-man rifle squad was to have a two-man scout section, a four-man fire section, and a five-man maneuver and assault section. The squad leader and the scout section would locate the enemy, and the leader would then call upon the second section's fire, which included the squad's Browning Automatic Rifle. Under that fire, the third section would advance.

Unfortunately, this method brought only a fraction of the squad's power to bear fully in the climactic advance; and too often the squad leader was pinned down with the scout section. Often, the infantry turned for help to the tanks. Partly for this reason, tanks became habitually assigned to all sizable infantry formations. A favorite method of attack came to be one in which a team of three to seven, or possibly more, tanks combined with an infantry company. Sometimes the tanks advanced first, sometimes they advanced with an infantry skirmish line, sometimes the infantry rode them. In any case, the tanks took on centers of resistance, while the infantry eliminated antitank weapons.

A seemingly more old-fashioned method of advance also found growing favor and proved effective especially in General Patton's commands. Patton liked the power of a "marching fire offensive," wherein casualties might be great but results could be too. All the infantry moved forward together in a thick skirmish line, generally with close tank support. Browning Automatic Rifles and light air-cooled machine guns went with them. Everybody fired at every possible center of resistance within reach. All the large weapons that could be mustered laid down a supporting fire. Once again as in older armies, every man drew psychological support from the mass of his comrades, and once again the enemy felt the psychological shock of seeing a fearsome mass move against him. If the method was old-fashioned, automatic weapons, tanks, and modern artillery coordination could once again make it effective.

Perhaps the most questionable element in American ground fighting power was the American tank. During the European campaigns, the principal tank in the Anglo-American arsenal was the M-4 medium, the General Sherman, mounting a 75- and later a 76-mm gun. It had superseded the M-3 General Grant and the light Honey, but it was inferior to the German Panther as well as to the heavier Tiger in almost every respect save endurance, including armament and defensive armor. On the Eastern Front, the Germans were hard put to keep up with the power, armor, and maneuverability of the Russians' T-34's, T-34/85's, and Stalins; in the West, German tanks outgunned American and were so stoutly armor-plated that their hulls long seemed almost indestructible. The American mediums were hastily developed, largely after the beginning of the war. Once having abandoned light tanks to concentrate on mediums, however, the Army Ground Forces overrode the Ordnance Department and many armored force men to refuse to develop, until too late to do much good, heavier tanks comparable to the German Tigers and Panthers, let alone the Royal Tiger or the Russian Stalin. McNair's headquarters insisted on mediums out of respect for manueverability and speed; but after the invasion of France the Shermans had to receive heavier armor and guns if they were to battle the Panthers and Tigers on any approximation of reasonable terms, and then the ratio of weight to engine power and balance was so upset that the Shermans could often be outmaneuvered as well as outgunned. The one clear superiority of American tanks was in their durability. This quality was of great value in the long, fast pushes across Europe after the breakthroughs in Normandy and on the Rhine. But it was an asset that could be overdeveloped, when a tank was likely to be knocked out by enemy fire before it traveled the 3,000 miles its engine was supposed to run without major overhaul, and when durability helped cause the sacrifice of fighting qualities.

For American tanks combatting Panthers and Tigers, it was fortunate to begin receiving, belatedly in the fall of 1944, hypervelocity armor-piercing (HVAP) shells for their 76-mm guns; they could now penetrate German tank armor except in front. Even now, they had to depend on superior numbers to permit their working their way to the enemy's flanks, and many Shermans had to be expended in the process. To American armored soldiers it was small consolation when the M-26 General Pershing heavy tank, with a 90-mm gun, at last went into mass production—at the end of the war.[37]

With American tanks afflicted by marked shortcomings, and the tank in general proving less to supplant the infantry-artillery team than to join as a new partner with it, perhaps the outstanding element in the American arsenal was the artillery. To both the tank-and-infantry team and the marching fire advance, artillery support was essential. For this war, unlike the war of 1917–18, the Army had available an excellent American weapon for divisional artillery, ready for mass production, the 105-mm howitzer. As early as World War I, gunners such as Summerall had felt the need for a more powerful weapon at least to supplement the 75, and the 155-mm howitzer had been pressed into service as divisional artillery along with the 75. But the 155-mm howitzer was insufficiently mobile and suffered from other drawbacks as well. After the war the Ordnance Department agreed that the standard field gun should be of about 105-mm, and the Army achieved great success with field tests of captured German 105's. Tests of an American 105, of a split-trail carriage for it, and of better recoil mechanisms, continued through the interwar years, to produce the gun that became "the work-horse of the Army" in 1941–45, a howitzer capable of firing thirteen different kinds of shell at a rate of twenty rounds a minute, with a maximum range of 12,000 yards.

For heavier work, the 105 was supplemented with 155-mm guns ("Long Toms"), 8-inch howitzers, 240-mm howitzers, and 8-inch guns. Increasingly, there were also self-propelled guns. The Armored Force had earlier championed their development as tank destroyers: field guns mounted on a tank chassis but with thinner armor and an open turret, designed to hit and run against tanks. The Ordnance Department had gladly speeded their development, foreseeing more diverse uses for them. So it proved; self-propelled 76-mm, 3-inch, and 90-mm guns were among the most important tactical innovations of the war, moving as assault guns in direct support of infantry and armor. So valuable were they that Long Toms and 8-inch howitzers were mounted on tank chassis in time to participate in breaking the Siegfried Line, and by the time Japan surrendered, 8-inch guns and 240-mm howitzers were being set on heavy tank chassis to go to the Pacific.

Whatever guns were at hand, excellence in employing them had become one of the most consistent traditions of the American Army since the days of Henry Knox and Sam Ringgold, and the artillery of

World War II maintained the tradition. Continuing the developments in which Summerall had played such an outstanding part during World War I, and which he had nourished when he was chief of staff, American artillery surpassed its rivals especially in the perfection of its fire-direction centers. The Americans stressed aggressive use of the guns close to the front of the infantry, extensive employment of forward spotters in the infantry and tank advance and in liaison aircraft overhead, and the best possible communications network to link every gun not only with its battery and battalion headquarters but with all appropriate command posts back to corps and army. The guns became proficient in concentrating overwhelming fire on chosen targets almost instantaneously on call.[38]

Their bombardment, combined with bombardment from the air and, in coastal invasions, naval bombardment from offshore, frequently left defenders stunned and befuddled before an attack began. By this means, and by moving forward along with tanks to give infantry heavy firepower throughout an advance, the artillery joined with armor to permit once again the breaking of even strong enemy defenses; the ability then of tanks, self-propelled guns, and motorized infantry to exploit the breakthrough restored mobility to war.

"I do not have to tell you who won the war," General George S. Patton, Jr., was to say. "You know our artillery did."[39] And Marshall wrote:

We believe that our use of massed heavy artillery fire was far more effective than the German techniques and clearly outclassed the Japanese. Though our heavy artillery from the 105-mm. up was generally matched by the Germans, our method of employment of these weapons has been one of the decisive factors of our ground campaigns throughout the world.[40]

If the artillery and infantry and their new partners, the tanks and "tactical" aircraft, proved capable of breaking the battlefield deadlock, the extreme prophecies about the decisiveness of "strategic" air power went unfulfilled. The failure of the German air force to crack the British will and ability to fight during 1940 and 1941 cannot be taken readily as a refutation of Trenchard, Douhet, and Mitchell, because the *Luftwaffe* was not designed to attempt the winning of a war alone, but rather for tactical cooperation with the ground forces. With mounting intensity, however, the British and American air forces did undertake the strategic bombing of Germany's centers of industry, communications, and population in the Trenchard-Douhet-Mitchell manner, and largely with aircraft designed for the purpose, especially the American B-17. At most, the question of the impact upon the enemy remains moot. The main demonstrable value of air power was in support of the ground forces. No other triumph of air power contributed so evidently to winning the war as the sealing off of the Normandy invasion zone from German reinforcement and support before and during the Allied landings.[41]

The limitations of "strategic" air power and the usefulness of "tactical" air power suggested questions about the autonomy accorded the Army Air Forces. Fortunately, in the combat theaters air power was generally assigned to the theater commander, who could do much to assure its coordination with the ground forces. But the Air Forces waged their increasingly successful drive for a unique freedom from direct responsibility to OPD, and they secured a limited autonomy even in relation to the theater commanders. The Strategic Air Forces in Europe were placed under the immediate command first of Royal Air Force headquarters and then jointly of the RAF and General Arnold in Washington. Similarly, the Strategic Air Forces in the Pacific came under Arnold's direct command. In the sequel, however, the dramatic enhancement of strategic air power revealed at Hiroshima and Nagasaki diverted questions about air force command arrangements by making all previous experience seem already obsolete.

At the close of World War II the United States Army was the mightiest in the world. Only the Russian army exceeded it in numbers; and in weaponry (except tanks), strategic mobility, and logistic capacities the Russian army was markedly inferior. In every theater the American Army had faced enemies long trained in war and had speedily overcome them. The world admired this "prodigy of organization," as Winston Churchill called it, "an achievement which the soldiers of every other country will always study with admiration and envy."[42]

The achievement was possible because, small and ill-equipped though the Army was as late as 1939, the forces of American history, military and otherwise, combined to fit America admirably to wage the kind of war that World War II proved to be. World War II was a war of mass armies. The large American population and the tradition of an armed citizenry springing to the country's need, a tradition tested and proved for modern war during 1917–18, permitted the creation of a mass army. Mass armies could be organized, maintained, and fought effectively only by leaders possessing highly developed management skills; the United States Army had cultivated an officer corps with such skills through Elihu Root's General Staff and school systems and their extensions, nourished by the more generalized management skills of a complex industrial society. Perhaps most important, World War II was a "gross national product war," in which sheer quantities of weapons, supplies, and transport could decisively outweigh an enemy; America's industrial leadership fitted it preeminently to wage such a war.

In 1940 the military leaders of the country turned to recruiting the citizenry into a mass army with few of the misgivings that had marked American thought about citizen soldiers during the time of Emory Upton's greatest influence. World War I had given the United States a workable system of conscription, drawn from the lessons of the Civil War experiment in conscription; and the 1917 system could be invoked again. More than that, World War I had demonstrated to even the most thoroughly professional of soldiers, such as Pershing, the speed with which the American citizenry could be transformed into soldiers capable of facing any in the world. Pershing's aide John McAuley Palmer had spelled out that lesson of World War I in his copious military writings, and George C. Marshall had felt the influence and shared the conclusions of both Pershing and Palmer. A citizen army could be recruited swiftly and sent into battle, not under the cloud of the old Uptonian pessimism, but in confidence born of the memories of Chateau-Thierry and the Argonne.

The Second World War confirmed the lesson of the First, that American citizen soldiers could be sent confidently onto any battlefield after a relatively brief, intensive training. Training methods were better refined in World War II than they had been in 1917, and the unavoidable delays that preceded the cross-channel invasion of Europe saved the American Army from a pressure toward rapid commitment so overpowering as that of 1918. Nevertheless, the speed with which citizen soldiers could be prepared to compete with an enemy's veterans was striking in its confirmation of the wisdom of the Palmers in their old debates with the Uptons. Any division, however thoroughly trained, of course requires a period of seasoning in combat before it can be one of the best. As early as April, 1943, however, Brigadier General Thomas Handy, then head of OPD, was highly impressed by the 1st, 9th, 34th, and 1st Armored Divisions after their brief blooding in North Africa:

. . . We can feel sure of the Divs in line—There had been some doubt as to 34th [National Guard] Div—But while I was there this Div took Hill 609 which was really the key point of German position. . . .

General opinion US Troops has changed most markedly since moved to North [of Tunisian front]—not much expected as terrain extremely difficult but they did [advance] and are advancing—The fact that [the British] 8th Army was stopped by same type of terrain has tended to raise very much the opinion of all concerned re our troops—[43]

By 1944 Major General James M. Gavin's 82nd Airborne Division was something of an elite formation. Nevertheless, there was an element of tribute to all American soldiery in the compliment when Lieutenant General Miles Dempsey of the British Second Army said to Gavin after Operation Market Garden: "I am proud to meet the commander of the greatest division in the world today."[44]

A citizen army with a background like the American brought certain distinct advantages to World War II. Since the war was so much a war of equipment, and especially of mechanical equipment, the acquaintance of Americans with the gadgetry of American life gave them a decided edge in handling the paraphernalia of modern war. General McNair could cut down on the maintenance forces of the infantry division knowing that every rifle squad would contain men with mechanical knowledge and aptitudes to permit an improvised maintenance of almost any kind of equipment. At least as important, Americans went into mechanized war with a psychological assurance, a confidence born of familiarity with the machine age, and this assured confidence doubtless contributed to the vigor with which Americans kept their tanks, trucks, and guns rolling aggressively forward across the plains of northern France and the *Autobahnen* of Germany whenever the opportunity for mobile, fluid war opened before them. Significantly, the most marked difference between the American Army and any of its adversaries was its immense advantage in mobility.

To administer an organization such as the American Army of more than 8,000,000 men would have been a task requiring a high order of ability even without the pressures of war. To command this Army in a multifront war, as well as to administer and maintain it, demanded leadership and managerial qualities of an exceptional kind. The Army rose to the occasion by throwing forward leaders who were indeed exceptional in their skills, as well as in character and decisiveness: Marshall; MacArthur, vain and flamboyant but as close an approximation of the old-fashioned Napoleonic style of the brilliant chieftain as the war produced; Eisenhower, the master of coalition command and military diplomacy, and also a much stronger and more decisive military personality than he is sometimes recognized to have been; and Bradley, an army and army group commander of the first rank.

Yet it was not the abilities of such individuals, however outstanding, that was most impressive about military command in World War II. It was the extent to which command had to become a work of staffs and committees, since no individual could hope to hold together in his own mind all the details of supply, movement, order of battle, terrain and climate, and strategic and tactical problems to enable him to command alone even a single theater, let alone the whole war effort. The war was commanded and the Army managed by a committee system: the CCS and JCS, each with its rule of unanimity, and all the network of supporting staffs of both the combined and joint commanders and the War Department and Army, plus the complex staffs of the theater commanders. The war itself was too complex to be managed in any other way. But for all the staff and committee machinery to mesh properly, the human beings involved had to be men of skill and ability trained in common principles of management and leadership and able to communicate with each other clearly through a preestablished common vocabulary. The Army staff and school system had produced a remarkable supply of such men, of proven ability and proven capacity to cooperate. Not only did the officer corps of the Regular Army afford a wealth of leadership skill, but furthermore the Army had succeeded in imparting its leadership methods to the reserve officers who proved so indispensable in its expansion, and then also to the newly recruited and trained officers of the war emergency.

Even those officers of high rank who enjoyed a fairly large scope for the exercise of their individual abilities reflected the qualities of the prewar staff and school system. For most of them had long since been selected by their chiefs and by the instructors in the schools as men who would exercise the highest responsibilities if war should come. Not only did the staff and school system train a corps of management and command experts; the system and the chiefs of staff who presided over it, most notably Pershing, had succeeded also in recognizing men of more than routine competence and selecting and grooming them early. The Eisenhowers, Bradleys, and Pattons did not catapult to the top of the Army by accident; their potential had been perceived and cultivated when they were still junior officers.[45]

Without millions of men to fill the ranks and competent officers to organize and command, American productive capacity turned to military purposes would have done little good. But with those assets, American war production became decisive. Though the quality of American military equipment was generally high, the advantages of the American Army were more in superior quantity than in superior quality. The severe limitations on funds for research and development between the wars helped cause a lag in the quality of some American equipment when the war began. The National Defense Research Committee, organized under Dr. Vannevar Bush during the flurry of activity following the fall of France, accelerated development by bringing about an unprecedentedly close and harmonious cooperation between soldiers and civilian scientists, to go along with increased funds for research. Even in the straitened period between the wars, the United States Army had pioneered in the development of radar, though not so rapidly as the British. Subsequent developments of American military technology included the proximity fuse, shaped charges, bazookas and recoilless rifles, improved landing craft for amphibious war and the DUKW truck that could move cross-country or on water as well as over roads, and mobile flexible fuel pipelines. The intensive American development of high frequency radio was indispensable to the fire control that made American artillery outstanding. Despite these impressive qualitative advances, however, the American emphasis remained on quantity of materials.[46]

In large part this emphasis represented a deliberate decision, to sacrifice sometimes the possibility of creating the very best matériel in order to get weapons and equipment into prompt mass production. The quantity of American weapons, then, overwhelmed enemies with sheer weight of firepower. The lavish quantity of American equipment and transport gave American forces assured logistical support in any theater of war. Lavish quantity in transport and supplies also gave American forces their immense advantage in strategic and tactical mobility.

If there was justification for the risk of mobilizing only eighty-nine divisions, much of the justification must be that the divisions could be shifted wherever they were needed with a promptness that no other army could match. In combat, too, they could move with unparalleled rapidity. Always they confirmed the wisdom of Pershing and others who had moved toward completely motorized transport immediately after World War I. The movement of German infantry divisions was hobbled by what Americans regarded as an astonishing dependence on horse transport. The Germans in turn were less pleasantly astonished by the mobility of the motorized American divisions. After the Germans had failed to credit American troops with much aggressiveness in the fighting among the Normandy hedgerows, it was most unsettling to encounter the combination of aggressiveness and speed with which they advanced once the battle became fluid, with devastating effect on German resistance and morale.[47]

Though American strategic mobility made a variety of strategies possible for the United States, the overwhelming quantity of American firepower and logistical capacity made the strategy consistently pursued by American commanders during the war the logical and appropriate strategy: to concentrate first upon the destruction of the strongest enemy power, and to seek to meet and defeat him in his very heartland. Multiple attacks against the periphery of Axis power might have worn down the enemy in time, but to strike at Germany by the direct cross-channel route was the sure road to victory, and American material strength made the choice of that road possible and right.

World War II called for the very ingredients of military power that American history had best prepared: the mass army that could be drawn from the citizen soldiery of American tradition; the skilled officer corps that the small American Regular Army had cultivated since Dennis Mahan's day, reinforced now by general American management skills; the lavish military equipment that American productive capacity could supply in unrivaled profusion. Psychologically, too, the war at least seemingly was one for which Americans' history had prepared them. In the way in which Americans mainly regarded it, it was a kind of Indian raid writ large: the enemy fell treacherously upon the community's outer defenses, whereupon the community set aside everything else for the duration of the emergency to take up arms, punish the assailant, and break his military power. The aggressor repulsed and beaten, the community could return to the ways of peace.

Altogether, World War II presented demands for which American history had prepared the country so well that the war sometimes seemed a climax toward which American history had been fatefully moving. This sense of a climax prepared for is reflected, for example, in the writings of one school of historians who justify or at least palliate the abuses of the country's late nineteenth-century industrialization on the ground that forced-draft industrialization proved a necessary preparation for the military salvation of democracy in the twentieth-century wars.[48]

But if World War II seemed an appropriate climax to much of the history of the American Army and nation, it may prove to have been a climax too in the sense of a last act of a drama now closed. For the military problems of the period following the war proved to be of a new order, for which neither the Army nor the country was well prepared by the past.

Already World War II had offered disturbing suggestions of new dimensions of war, to which accustomed American methods of war adjusted only uneasily. For one thing, the Axis powers made unprecedented use of disloyalty and subversion as instruments of war. World War II was the war of "the fifth column." So much and so effectively did the Axis seem to employ subversion, espionage, and sabotage in the early years of the war that their enemies came to regard their fifth-column techniques with awe and to overestimate their prowess. An obsession with the threat of sabotage helped cause the Pearl Harbor disaster, since the Army commander in Hawaii became so preoccupied with the idea of sabotage that he guarded against the wrong danger, neglecting preparations against attack by air. The obsession with the fifth column led also to that disturbing invasion of civil liberties, the forced evacuation of Japanese-Americans as well as Japanese aliens from the Pacific Coast.[49]

Still more disturbing were the indications that a military response of the kind that had been habitual since the Indian wars—an all-out concentration on solving the military problems at hand—was no longer enough. The United States poured its energies into the quest for military victory over the Axis powers, submerging all other purposes for the time being. In the world that emerged from the war, the Axis powers had been rendered impotent, but Western democracy faced an at least equal threat in Soviet Communism, whose capacity to imperil the West had been enhanced by the West's very success against the Axis. Winston Churchill and certain other leaders, both Allied and American, had warned against this danger during the war, and had sought to shape the conduct of the war in such a way as to mitigate it. They had failed to dissuade President Roosevelt and the American military chieftains that the war should be fought with important regard for no consideration except the military defeat of the Axis.

There seems little reason to believe that any different strategy could have altered substantially the distribution of power that emerged from the war. Churchill's designs against the "soft underbelly" of Europe, for example, made insufficient allowance for the geographic hardness of the underbelly. Nevertheless, the political implications of strategy suggested by Churchill deserved the most serious consideration, and the American tendency to view strategy in a narrowly military light was a characteristic encouraged by American history but destined no longer to suffice.

World War II almost certainly would have ended a military era in any case, for under any circumstances the postwar Communist threat to American security would almost certainly have taken more subtle and sophisticated forms than any previous threat, whether posed by Mohawk or Nazis. The coming of the atomic bomb foreclosed any doubt that the epoch which had thus far shaped American military history was gone. The War Department had cultivated the Manhattan District Project within the Army, under Major General Leslie R. Groves, but sealed off from most of the Army. When another agency of the War Department or the Army occasionally brushed against the Manhattan District Project, there was wonder at the high priorities accorded its mysterious activities, but few officers even in the inner reaches of the General Staff knew its purpose. Though he considered his office diminished by the 1942 reorganization, the Secretary of War was one of the few who did know; and as events had it, it was Stimson who first passed word of the atomic bomb to the new President who was to bear the responsibility of deciding to use it.[50]

☆ PART FOUR ☆

Since 1945

For the course of war . . . of itself contriveth most things upon the occasion. Wherein he that complies with it with most temper standeth the firmest, and he that is most passionate oftenest miscarries.

—Thucydides[1]

TWENTY

Postwar and Cold War:

1945-50

The world is not static, and the status quo is not sacred. But we cannot allow changes in the status quo in violation of the charter of the United Nations by such methods as coercion, or by such subterfuges as political infiltration.

—Harry S Truman[1]

DURING THE MONTHS that first followed the surrenders in the schoolhouse at Reims and on the deck of the *Missouri*, the Army like the nation did not direct its conduct mainly to the new dangers posed by Soviet power and the unleashing of the atom. All hoped that life would now proceed into the broad uplands that Prime Minister Churchill had once promised as the reward awaiting effort, and that four years of wartime partnership with the West would yet prove to have changed the outlook of the Communist dictatorship.

The Army took up, and on the whole with intelligence and success, a far vaster work of military government than it had ever confronted before. Under General Joseph T. McNarney and General Lucius D. Clay, the American occupying forces helped to breathe life again into Germany. General of the Army Douglas MacArthur fashioned for himself new laurels as American proconsul in Japan.[2] Beyond that, the Army turned, as though World War II had indeed been merely an Indian raid writ large, to its accustomed postwar tasks of demobilization and reorganization for peace. The unexpectedly prompt surrender of Japan forced the scrapping of elaborate plans for merely partial demobilization and for the shifting of the main bulk of American strength from Europe to the Pacific to invade the home islands.

The War Department was sensitive enough to Soviet ambitions to desire a generally cautious demobilization even after Japan's surrender. But Congress and the new administration of President Harry S Truman felt obliged to yield to the public cry that, after the longest American war since the Revolution, citizen soldiers should be returned swiftly to their homes. In many areas soldiers themselves demonstrated for prompt discharge. The War Department had planned discharges according to a point system, worked out before the Japanese defeat, to reward length and arduousness of service; but soon after Japan's surrender it announced that the point system would be submerged and all men with two years' service would be released forthwith.

The President announced that the Army would be reduced to 1,950,000 men by June, 1946. That figure was soon cut by 400,000, and by the spring of 1946 the announced goal was an Army, including the Air Forces, cut to 1,070,000 officers and men by July 1, 1947. At the request of the President and in response to the disturbing slowness of the world's return to the broad uplands of tranquility, Congress did agree to temporary extensions of the Selective Service Act to March 31, 1947, but with the 1,070,000-strength for July 1, 1947, written into the law as a limitation. On March 31, 1947, no further extension having been legislated, the Selective Service Act of 1940 and its extensions ceased to operate.[3]

The United States planned to retain the largest peacetime Army in its history, but a ground Army of some 600,000 was likely nevertheless to prove small in relation to new national responsibilities.

During the war the usual professional notion of dissolving the National Guard once the war ended had enjoyed a certain currency in the War Department and the General Staff. By the close of the war, however, there was no doubt that both utility and expediency would require reestablishment of the Guard on substantially its prewar footing. It would be somewhat enlarged over the Guard of the 1930's, and it would be supplemented by an Organized Reserve patterned after it but wholly federal in organization. Uptonian contempt for the citizen soldier was dying among the Regular officer corps, but not necessarily Uptonian distaste for the Guard with its dual federal-state loyalties. Nevertheless, the Guard divisions had been invaluable during the mobilization of 1940; they had fought creditably, requiring reorganization but not so long a preparation as divisions created wholly anew; and to anger the Guard might still carry some political risk.

The War Department drew up a postwar National Guard troop

basis calling for twenty-seven infantry divisions and, for the first time, two armored divisions, plus twenty-one additional regimental combat teams, thirty-three tank battalions, fifteen mechanized cavalry battalions, and a variety of other units designed to add up to a reasonably balanced force. An Air National Guard was added to the Army National Guard. The War Department offered a terminal promotion to the next higher grade to all officers under the rank of colonel who entered one of the Organized Reserve formations upon separation from the service. Though Congress did not appropriate enough funds in the postwar years nor military interest sustain itself sufficiently to build the 1946 troop structure to full strength, 324,-761 ground forces Guardsmen were serving in 4,597 units by June, 1950. By that time there were 68,785 officers and 117,756 men in 10,629 activated units of the Organized Reserve. An additional 390,-961 officers and men were carried on the rolls of the Organized Reserve but were not in active training units.[4]

As the wartime Army shrank to peace strength in more or less accustomed fashion, its reorganization too proceeded less as an attempt to meet new kinds of international perils than as a conventional postwar effort to assimilate the lessons of the war just ended. Even the unification of the armed forces in 1947 bore this aspect, of looking less to present and future dangers than to the experiences of the late war.

Some aspects of postwar reorganization, in fact, are difficult to interpret even as responses to World War II, but appear more simply as preparations for a hoped-for tranquil peacetime. One of the principal purposes of the 1942 reorganization and of the development of OPD to its wartime prominence had been to reduce the number and variety of agencies reporting to and directly responsible to the chief of staff, in order to save him from an impossibly diverse burden of concern for numerous agencies and to channel more effectively his direction of the whole Army. But reorganization in 1946 reduced the scope of what had been OPD; restored the prewar structure of five coequal General Staff divisions, which it had been difficult for the chief of staff to coordinate; and finally left twenty-nine individual staffs or divisions reporting directly to the chief of staff or his deputy. The rationale of the reorganization was the restoration of central control over the whole ground Army through elimination of ASF and a change in the status of AGF; but the method of pursuing this goal made effective exercise of central control difficult.[5]

The reorganization was announced in War Department Circular 138 of May 14, 1946, following upon the recommendations of a board headed by Lieutenant General Alexander M. Patch, a canvassing of Army opinion on those recommendations, the recommendations of a new board under Lieutenant General William H. Simpson which surveyed the expressions of opinion, and Presidential approval of the final scheme. Under Circular 138 the Army Ground Forces and Army Air Forces continued as separate commands, with a general awareness that the Air Forces were likely soon to be removed from the Army altogether. The Army Ground Forces would continue as the headquarters through which the General Staff would command the ground troops within the United States. Under AGF, the old corps area and wartime field force organizations gave way to six army areas in the continental United States. With the disappearance of the Army Service Forces, the traditional administrative and technical agencies, along with some new ones, returned as separate divisions of the War Department.[6]

Within the General Staff, the allocation of officers to the five divisions reflected the end of OPD ascendancy and the restoration of substantial equality: Personnel and Administration Division, formerly G-1, 100 officers; Intelligence, formerly G-2, 250; Organization and Training, formerly G-3, 60; Service, Supply and Procurement, formerly G-4, 200; Plans and Operations, formerly OPD, 82. Most of the coordination of logistical functions that had been attempted in wartime by the Army Service Forces was to be lodged in the Service, Supply and Procurement Division of the General Staff. But the "command functions" of ASF reverted to the administrative and technical branches. The Logistics Group of OPD was transferred to Service, Supply and Procurement. A short-lived Research and Development Division of the General Staff also passed into Service, Supply and Procurement in 1947.[7]

Concerned about the problems of controlling the complex mechanisms of the Army, the Patch and Simpson Boards grappled long with the old question of the extent to which, in order to control, the General Staff should involve itself in "operating." The Patch Board announced that "The old theory that a staff must limit itself to broad policy and planning activities has been proved unsound in this war." Nevertheless, Circular 138 went far toward reasserting Elihu Root's position. It avoided any form of the verb "to operate" in describing the functions of the General Staff. It instructed the General Staff to *plan, direct, coordinate,* and *supervise.* It did make clear that the General Staff was to follow up, that is, to make sure its directions were heeded, as it had not done in the preliminaries to Pearl Harbor, but as OPD had learned to do. Mainly, it stipulated:

No function will be performed at the general or special staff level of the War Department which can be decentralized to the major commands, the Army areas, or the administrative and technical services without loss of adequate control of operations by the General and Special Staffs.

To some degree, moreover, Circular 138 implied a restoration of responsibility to the Secretary of War, beyond the administration of the War Department. But command of the Army remained clearly and specifically with the chief of staff:

The Chief of Staff is the principal military adviser to the President and to the Secretary of War on the conduct of war and the principal military adviser and executive to the Secretary of War on the activities of the Military Establishment. The Chief of Staff has command of all components of the Army of the United States . . . and is responsible to the Secretary of War for their use in war and plans and preparations for their readiness for war.[8]

The broad reorganization of national defense under the National Security Act of July 26, 1947, which "unified" the armed forces, did not at once greatly affect the internal organization of the Army under Circular 138. This was true partly because the National Security Act did not so much unify the armed forces, though the Army had been seeking substantial unity, as federate them.

Proposals to unite the armed forces in a single defense establishment had circulated periodically through most of the twentieth century. From the beginning of America's career as a world power, in the Spanish War, the military expression of American power had required thrusts across the waters and the cooperation of sea and ground forces. Geography dictated that such was likely to be the continued condition of American power. From the Spanish War onward, furthermore, it was evident that separate and differently organized War and Navy Departments could impede the coordination that overseas war required.

Nevertheless, the Army at first opposed unification, especially when the Frank Willoughby report of 1921, the work of a kind of forerunner of the post-World War II Hoover Commission, recommended it. The Army recognized that the principal civilian support for unification at that time came from those who hoped to use unification to assist the economy-in-government drive of the period, and the Army feared that unification would be simply a screen for further reduction of an already straitened budget. Also, any extended discussion of the question might well aggravate the growing air power controversy, at a time when most generals wanted to keep the air arm firmly within the Army's control. Significantly, John McAuley Palmer deviated from most of the Army on this issue during the twenties; just as he preceded most of his comrades in urging the merits of the citizen soldier, so he preceded them again in favoring a single Department of National Defense.[9]

World War II brought a change of mind. Now the need for Army-Navy cooperation was greater than ever, and again the cooperation achieved in war failed to match the need. One of the many causes of disaster at Pearl Harbor was the absence of coordination and even communication between the services in Hawaii. A plague to Pacific operations through the war was friction between the Pacific Ocean Area Command, under Admiral Chester W. Nimitz of the Navy, and the Southwest Pacific Area Command, under General MacArthur. Controversies between these two commands sometimes drove a wedge between Army and Navy representatives on the JCS. As the war approached its close, the problem grew worse; until the defeat of Germany, the Army had acquiesced in a secondary role in the Pacific while the Navy accepted a similar role in the Atlantic, but in the summer of 1945 the Army was shifting its center of gravity toward the Pacific.[10]

The movement of the Air Forces toward independence introduced a third service. Many of the most unpleasant interservice disputes in the wartime JCS involved the air arm, as for example a controversy over the allocation of air power for submarine warfare between the Army Air Forces and the Navy. The creation of the Twentieth Air Force and then the United States Strategic Air Forces in the Pacific under the direct command of JCS through General Arnold added a third Pacific command and threatened to turn the war against Japan into three separate wars under Nimitz, MacArthur, and General Carl A. Spaatz of the Strategic Air Forces. During the 1920's the Army had feared a fundamental defense reorganization lest it lose its control of the air arm. By the 1940's the Air Forces were sure to win a divorce from the Army anyway, and the Army had to consider how it could retain a close enough association to afford some assurance of essential tactical air support. The Army rightly believed it would be intolerable to fight in the future with no greater assurance of cooperation from the Air Force than it had had from the Navy in the past. On a less elevated but vital level, too, the Army could foresee that in any post-World War II economy drive the more glamorous Air Force and Navy were likely to fare better than the Army; the closer an approach to a single service the Army could secure, and thus the greater military control of the allocation of defense funds, the better off the Army might be.[11]

General Marshall endorsed the principle of unification as early as 1941. The wartime JCS soon impressed Marshall and a growing number of Army leaders as an inadequate unifying device, with its requirement of unanimity and inherent slowness of decision. When reorganization of JCS was being contemplated at the beginning of 1943, the Army members of the Joint United States Strategic Committee and the Joint Planning Staff, both agencies of JCS, recommended a "United States General Staff." In June of the same year, a Post-War Policy Committee of JCS recommended, under Army initiative, the same proposal, including a single chief of staff for the services. In October an Army Service Forces study recommended a single department of defense, and Marshall approved the recommendation. In the spring of 1944, similar Army suggestions were submitted to a House of Representatives special Committee on Post-War Military Policy and published for the first time.[12]

To this point, the Navy either went along with Army proposals or kept silence. The more the Navy thought about the proposals, however, the less were Navy men inclined to agree with them. The Navy believed it had a peculiar strategic mission and peculiar strategic and technical problems which were not likely to receive adequate recognition in a unified command, wherein an Army–Air Force partnership might well overrule the Navy. Furthermore, having already engaged in acrimonious controversy with the Army Air Forces over air power above the sea, the Navy feared loss of its own air arm to the Air Force. Conceivably, unification might also mean loss of the Navy's landing force, the Marine Corps, to the Army.

Secretary of the Navy Frank Knox nevertheless told Stimson that for his part, he favored a single military department. But when Knox died in May, 1944, and James Forrestal succeeded him, the Navy Department passed to a man who shared many of the misgivings of the admirals. Forrestal persuaded Stimson to agree that the Army would cease its efforts toward unification until after the war, with the implied threat that otherwise the Navy would openly attack unification. Meanwhile a JCS committee headed by Admiral J. O. Richardson proceeded with a survey already begun and prepared a report which included a degree of compromise between Army and Navy attitudes but which again proposed a single defense department and a single chief of staff. But Admiral Richardson himself dissented from the report, and in 1945 Forrestal opened a counteroffensive by trying to formulate "constructive recommendations" of the Navy's own. He engaged Ferdinand Eberstadt, an old friend from the investment banking field and a former member of the War Production Board and other agencies that had dealt with both services, to study the unification issue for him.[13]

The resulting Eberstadt Report has often been praised, and it was indeed a carefully drawn document that was perceptive in its emphasis on the idea that unification involved larger matters than the armed services had yet accorded much discussion. Eberstadt contended that the major problem was not coordination of the services but coordination of military policy with national policy in general. At the same time, however, he expressed more confidence in JCS and the joint command arrangements of World War II generally than experience warranted. The JCS had never met, and might well not have passed, any test requiring rapid decision of a crucial question on which the services disagreed; but the reader of the Eberstadt Report would hardly know it. While too readily praising JCS, the Eberstadt Report with even more excessive readiness blackened the Army's unification proposals by comparing them with German, Japanese, and Italian institutions, a tactic of proven effectiveness dating from the earliest charges that Elihu Root's reforms would Prussianize the American Army.[14]

In the face of the shrewdly persuasive Eberstadt Report, the Army made the mistake of compromising its own proposals to try to accommodate the critics. The Collins Report, the latest expression of Army opinion, prepared under Lieutenant General J. Lawton Collins, no longer called for a single chief of staff but for a projection of JCS into a five-man United States Chiefs of Staff, to include the three service chiefs plus the Secretary of Defense and his principal military adviser. The issue became further muddied when Collins and Marshall gave differing expositions of the latest plan to the Senate Military Affairs Committee, with Marshall suggesting greater command and operating authority for the Chiefs of Staff than did Collins.[15]

By now President Truman was in the White House, and he was inclined toward a strong unification program with a single chief of staff. But the Congressional hearings developed a considerable sympathy for the Navy's misgivings, and the Army's own abandonment of the single chief of staff undercut the remaining strength of that proposal. The President also abandoned the single chief of staff, and legislation took shape in Congress as a grafting of Eberstadt's and Forrestal's ideas about coordination of national and military policy upon the Collins Report. Forrestal had accomplished much toward preserving the separate services by turning attention to the broader issues of policy coordination. To combine the Eberstadt and Collins proposals had the appearance of compromise. But the Congressional adaptation of the Collins Report essentially kept the wartime JCS, and that was a far cry from genuine unification. The Navy professed to regard even the preservation of JCS as a concession on its part, but "unification" now took place mainly on the Navy's terms.[16]

The Army's management of its proposals had not been especially skillful; but in the immediate postwar years and in fact ever since, the Congressional and public fear that unified armed forces mean militarism has been strong enough to make acceptance of a single chief of staff highly unlikely.

The National Security Act of 1947 provided for a "National Military Establishment" consisting of three military departments, Army (successor to the War Department), Navy, and Air. A Secretary of Defense headed the Military Establishment as the President's principal assistant in national security matters. The Secretary of Defense together with the Secretaries of Army, Navy, and Air and the service chiefs made up a War Council. The three service chiefs, plus a chief of staff to the President when he appointed one, continued as the Joint Chiefs of Staff, that institution now receiving its first statutory recognition. The Joint Chiefs were authorized to have a joint staff of not more than 100 officers, with the three services represented in approximately equal numbers. One of Marshall's principal concerns was that the Joint Chiefs should continue to enjoy the direct access to the President that had developed during the war. The National Security Act did not specifically so provide—as it could not, since the President can hardly be forced to take advice; but it did imply continued access, and the Joint Chiefs continued in practice to have it. Meanwhile, other interservice agencies authorized by the National Security Act were a Munitions Board and a Research and Development Board.[17]

To link the National Military Establishment to the formulation of national policy at large, three agencies recommended by Eberstadt and Forrestal were included in the act. The National Security Council, composed of the President, the Secretary of Defense, and other principal defense and foreign policy officials, was envisioned as determining a single, coherent national military policy, coordinated with broader national purposes. The Central Intelligence Agency would coordinate the intelligence activities of various government departments and report and make recommendations to the National Security Council. The National Security Resources Board would concern itself with the coordination of military and civilian mobilization.[18]

The Army's historic experience with both divided authority, under a Secretary of War and a commanding general, and unified authority, under the Secretary of War in partnership with a chief of staff, had led it to seek unified authority similar to its own for the National Military Establishment. The working of the National Security Act of 1947 seemed to show that Army misgivings about divided authority were thoroughly justified. The National Security Act was a disappointment. Forrestal, as much as any one person its architect, became the first Secretary of Defense; and as he approached the end of a year and a half in the office he acknowledged his own disappointment and called for a stronger Secretary of Defense. The Secretary described by the act of 1947 lacked a staff of his own to give him the knowledge essential to strength, and he could not develop with the JCS collectively the kind of intimate relation of mutual confidence that had grown up between Army chiefs of staff and Secretaries of War to help generate the strength of the Secretaries.

The JCS remained the committee that it had always been, with the inherent weaknesses of a committee. Neither the Secretary of Defense nor JCS was equipped to develop a coherent and positive military program. The National Security Council proved incapable of doing its job of providing the policy guidelines upon which a military program might be built. The NSC was misconceived from the beginning. Forrestal had favored it largely because he had been impressed by the British War Cabinet and saw the NSC as an American counterpart. But the British War Cabinet could be an effective body thanks mainly to the British cabinet rule of collective responsibility, while in the United States the NSC could not share the indivisible responsibility of the President for national policy. President Truman dramatized that fact by pointedly refraining from attending NSC meetings for three years. But meanwhile JCS remained pretty much without guidance on the broader national policy that the Military Establishment was to serve.[19]

In short, the National Security Act split off the Air Force from the Army, but it failed to provide the insurance of interservice cooperation that the Army had believed must accompany that step. The Secretary of Defense emerged as scarcely more than a mediator between the President and the services and among the services, especially in working out compromises on budget matters. Forrestal did bring the service chiefs together to reach understandings about their respective missions and roles, but although the consequent Key West and Newport agreements have been much discussed, they neither changed nor clarified much. In them, the services agreed to recognize each other's obvious primary functions—land, sea, and air warfare—and agreed that their secondary missions might overlap, but that none was to develop weapons and capabilities that could serve it only in a secondary mission. More specifically the understandings meant that the Navy might retain an air arm and even develop a "super" aircraft carrier but must not encroach upon the Air Force monopoly of strategic air power.[20]

Not only did Forrestal decide accordingly that in regard to defense organization "my position on the question has changed," but so also did Eberstadt. The latter became chairman of a Task Force on National Security Organization of the Hoover Commission on government reorganization, and its report deplored the curtailment of

Presidential authority by the statutory position of the NSC, the weakness of the Secretary of Defense, and the military autonomy which resulted from the weakness and confusion of authority among the civilian leaders of the Military Establishment.[21]

In response to the recommendations of both Forrestal and the Hoover Commission, and in line with his own consistent attitude, President Truman recommended the amendment of the National Defense Act. He did not seek and surely could not have secured a reversal of the basic compromise that had shaped the law of 1947, but he did secure a somewhat clearer definition of responsibility and power. By a new law of August 10, 1949, the National Military Establishment was transformed into a Department of Defense, an executive department of the government. The Departments of the Army, Navy, and Air Force lost their status as executive departments and became "military departments" within the Department of Defense. The Secretary of Defense would have the enhanced authority of the head of an executive department, with an appropriate staff to assist him. In an effort to improve the effectiveness of JCS, a chairman was authorized who was not to represent any single service. The Joint Staff was increased from 100 to 210 officers. On the other hand, Congress explicitly prohibited the creation of a single chief of staff over the armed forces or an armed forces general staff.[22]

A federated rather than genuinely unified interservice system permitted statutory recognition of the organization of the Army itself substantially as it had been since 1946. Congress passed a new organic law, the Army Reorganization Act of July 20, 1950, generally accepting the Department of the Army and the Army itself as they had been reshaped by executive action under wartime emergency legislation. While considering the bill, congressmen voiced some of their long-standing suspicions of the General Staff system, but those suspicions were reflected in the law only in a stipulation reaffirming the pre-World War II position of the Secretary vis-à-vis the chief of staff, by declaring the latter "directly responsible to the Secretary" in operational matters. This provision could not change much. The Secretary of the Army was subordinate to the Secretary of Defense, and as one of that official's advisers in JCS, the chief of staff in a sense stood above as well as below the Secretary of the Army. Through JCS, the chief of staff both in theory and practice was closer to policy making than the service Secretary.

The old limits on the size of the General Staff disappeared, the Secretary of the Army being empowered to determine its total size and its composition. Henceforth Congress would abandon the traditional practice of appropriating funds to each of the technical services and would appropriate directly to the Secretary of the Army; consequently the office of Comptroller of the Army was established to unify Army fiscal activities under a single head, responsible to the Secretary. The Secretary of the Army was to have the aid of a deputy, called the Under Secretary, and in addition he has had three (since 1958) or four (before 1958) Assistant Secretaries.

Under the new law, the Secretary of the Army was to determine the number and relative strengths of the arms and services. For the present, three combat arms received statutory recognition: infantry, artillery, and armor. Field artillery, coast defense, and air defense (until 1947 called antiaircraft) artillery merged into a single arm, the fixed coastal guns having lost their importance, and air defense artillery being often employed in ground combat. The "mechanized cavalry" that still existed was incorporated into armor. For the present, too, the Department of the Army recognized fourteen services: the Chemical Corps; the Corps of Engineers; the Military Police Corps, made a permanent entity by a law of June 28, 1950, after wartime Military Police in both world wars took the place of the earlier and interwar practice of detailing such men as were needed to the provost marshal general; the Ordnance Corps; the Quartermaster Corps; the Signal Corps; the Transportation Corps, now receiving permanently the former transportation duties of the Quartermaster and Engineer Corps; the Adjutant General's Corps; the Finance Corps; the Women's Army Corps, permanently established by Congress on June 12, 1948, to retain the World War II corps of women clerks and specialists; the Army Medical Service; the Chaplains; the Inspectors General; and the Judge Advocate General's Corps.[23]

Though strictly speaking it is neither an arm nor a service, Army Aviation maintained and expanded itself after World War II as a quasiarm, including divisional aviation companies for combat support, observation, liaison, and communications; transport aviation battalions assigned to field armies for rapid movement of troop detachments and supplies; helicopter ambulance units; and sky cavalry battalions to perform reconnaissance for missile commands. Most of these units included both fixed-wing and helicopter aircraft. In the late 1940's their potential was only beginning to be perceived.[24]

The historic preoccupation of the Army's thought in peacetime has been the manpower question: how, in an unmilitary nation, to muster adequate numbers of capable soldiers quickly should war occur. At the close of World War II the Army's thoughts about its role and mission returned to that historic preoccupation.

But they did so with old controversies happily close to resolution. World War II assured the triumph of the John McAuley Palmer school of thought, confident that the citizen soldier could be a good soldier, over the Emory Upton school. At the close of World War I the American battles in France seemed to have refuted Upton, but the German army had been so well along toward defeat before Americans met it that there could still be cause for doubt, and the General Staff's proposals for national defense policy in 1919 had called for a swollen Regular Army of the Uptonian expansible type. In World War II, however, the citizen soldiers had bested fresher and more tenacious adversaries than in 1918, and Uptonian arguments scarcely seemed tenable any longer. The officer corps at last looked with confidence to the employment of citizen soldiers in any future wars.

But there would still remain the problems of recruiting citizen soldiers and readying them for battle as quickly as possible in an emergency. Therefore, though the officer corps was now willing to accept forthrightly its probable dependence on armed citizens, it looked for a plan to speed their absorption into the service. Marshall knew that John M. Palmer had long been thinking in such terms and respected his thinking. During the war he put Palmer in charge of preparing a plan to cultivate the military potential of the citizenry. Recalled to active duty in 1941 at the age of seventy-one, Palmer continued as special assistant to the chief of staff until 1946. His work helped assure the future of the National Guard and the Organized Reserves. He also prepared for Marshall the policy statement which the chief of staff issued as War Department Circular 347 on August 24, 1944, and which became the basis of Army manpower recommendations through the rest of the 1940's.

In it Marshall and Palmer proposed universal military training. They supported the proposal with arguments that may have been excessively historical in nature, but whose nature is understandable in light of Palmer's long debate with the Uptonians. They spoke of two methods of drawing upon the whole potential military manpower of a nation: the system of Germany and Japan, in which "a special class or caste of professional soldiers" dominates "leadership in war and the control of military preparations and policy," and in which "only the brawn of a people is prepared for war," since the military professionals reserve all leadership for themselves; and second, a system in which "organized units drawn from a citizen army reserve, effectively organized in time of peace," form the war army, but with "full opportunity for competent citizen soldiers to acquire practical experience through temporary active service and to rise by successive steps to any rank for which they can definitely qualify."

They proposed a universal military training program which should keep the door of advancement open to citizen soldiers in the latter fashion, so that the United States would be able to call forth in war a mass army but one thoroughly in harmony with the whole nation and its democratic institutions. "This is the type of army," they said, "which President Washington proposed to the first Congress as one of the essential foundations of the new American Republic."[25]

Though Marshall endorsed the virtues of a citizen soldiery, he argued that experience proved that the National Guard, the Reserve Officers' Training Corps, and the Citizens' Military Training Camps had not provided a large enough reserve of citizen soldiers. For this reason he urged a military training program universally applied: "Only by universal military training can full vigor and life be instilled into the Reserve system."[26]

Not only was the officer corps eager to endorse universal military training, but the Marshall-Palmer emphasis on a citizen army attuned to democratic institutions was much more congenial to non-military opinion than any Uptonian plan had been. For this reason, and as long as World War II continued and kept military manpower problems in the foreground of national thought, unprecedented harmony within the Army on the manpower question was matched by unprecedented public support for the Army's long-run manpower proposals.

More than a year before War Department Circular 347 appeared, Palmer's old Congressional associate Representative James W. Wadsworth became cosponsor of the Gurney-Wadsworth bill to prescribe one year of military training for all young men sometime between the ages of eighteen and twenty-one, to be followed by four years in a reserve. Palmer helped prepare the bill. About the same time, in 1943, President Roosevelt began to endorse the universal training of youth. A Gallup poll in November, 1943, showed popular support of about two-to-one for some kind of universal training. A group of prominent educators, including the presidents of Yale, Dartmouth, the Massachusetts Institute of Technology, Amherst, and Lafayette addressed a letter to the President urging immediate consideration of such a program, to assure it before any postwar reaction could set in. On July 5, 1945, the Post-War Military Policy Committee of the House of Representatives endorsed the principle of universal military training.[27]

When Harry S Truman became President, universal military training received clearer and more enthusiastic White House support than Roosevelt had given it. On September 26, 1945, Truman called for extension of selective service and promised also that he would soon present a universal military training program. He did so before a joint session of Congress on October 23. His plan would have required one year of military training for all males when they became eighteen or finished high school, with all to take the training before they turned twenty. He emphasized anew the idea of universality; even those not physically fit for active military service would receive such training as was appropriate. After the year of training, young men would move into a General Reserve for six years, after which they would pass into a secondary reserve.[28]

Despite this uncommon array of military and civil support, the universal military training idea went nowhere. Congress extended selective service, eventually to March 31, 1947, but set universal military training aside. The War Department thereupon offered a more detailed set of proposals that included elements of compromise. Under a plan announced on October 2, 1946, the department would have provided six months in special training centers for every young man, to be followed by various optional programs which included enlistment in the National Guard or the Organized Reserve. The training units would now be separated from the armed forces; in the special training camps, the trainees would not be subject to the Articles of War but to a "Code of Conduct" prepared for the occasion. There would be nonmilitary phases of the training, supervised by a civilian advisory board appointed by the President. In December, Truman also attempted to invigorate the project, by appointing a President's Advisory Commission on Universal Training headed by Karl T. Compton, president of M.I.T. The Advisory Commission's report, issued May 29, 1947, proposed a six-month training program with much the same types of options thereafter as the War Department had suggested. A civil commission was to have general charge of the training program.[29]

Nonmilitary training, now increasingly emphasized in an effort to cultivate Congressional support, had been included in Roosevelt's and Truman's programs from the beginning, and from the beginning the inclusion of this idea had been a symptom of weakness. Truman was to go so far as to say that "The military phase was incidental to what I had in mind." He claimed that his main interest was in the improvement of youth:

. . . to develop skills that could be used in civilian life, to raise the physical standards of the nation's manpower, to lower the illiteracy rate, to develop citizenship responsibilities, and to foster the moral and spiritual welfare of our young people.[30]

Such proclaimed objectives all too obviously seemed hedges against anticipated objections to peacetime military conscription.

(Truman also claimed that universal training was not really conscription.)[31] To offer them as goals may well have weakened rather than strengthened the program in Congress, where legislators showed a healthy skepticism about military training as the most convenient means of fostering citizenship and moral and spiritual values.

Universal military training continued to languish despite the attempted sugar-coating. No doubt the postwar reaction against which the educators had warned Roosevelt had something to do with the decline of Congressional and public enthusiasm. But more than the ordinary postwar reaction worked against universal military training. Ironically, the officer corps had come to general agreement on how to prepare a mass army of citizen soldiers only when the plan on which they agreed was coming to seem irrelevant to the national needs.

Universal military training was a program for developing a mass army of the type required in the two world wars. After the explosion of the atomic bombs over Hiroshima and Nagasaki, however, many thoughtful Americans questioned whether the era of mass armies had not ended. Though publicly committed to universal military training, the Army and the Truman administration must have wondered about the same question. Post-1945 proved to be no ordinary postwar period, and there were soon menaces enough to America's security to dilute any ordinary postwar reaction against the military. But America's principal military safeguard against those menaces was the atomic bomb, and a new war seemed likely to be an atomic war; so it was difficult for many to foresee how a mass army produced by universal military training might be needed.

Significantly, Congress took some sort of positive action on universal military training only after its irrelevance became, at least temporarily, complete. After the beginning of the Korean War, Truman himself recommended that Congress postpone universal military training until the immediate crisis could be dealt with. The Korean War demanded a renewal and intensification of selective service, but it did not demand the mass armies of universal military training, and it left the Army too busy to handle a universal training program. In 1951, however, after the President had announced that universal military training was shelved for the time being, Congress passed the Universal Military Training and Service Act, which among other things endorsed universal military training in principle. It did so when there was no prospect that the principle would be implemented, and it has never done anything more.[32]

Probably the issues of defense reorganization and universal military training would have been handled much as they were during the late 1940's if the Soviet Union had never existed, for thinking about them bore remarkably little relation to the postwar problems of intransigent Communism. Both service unification and the universal military training idea were products of the American military past, not of the immediate world situation. Despite the opening of the Cold War, the American Army faded to near impotence after World War II, at least in relation to the country's responsibilities, and scarcely recovered before the invasion of South Korea in June, 1950.

For to most Americans, including most of the government, the Army in the late 1940's seemed almost irrelevant to the Communist challenge. So pervasive was this attitude that the Army itself appears to have suffered increasingly under a sense of its own irrelevance, with consequent damage to energy and efficiency. To the extent that Americans saw the Communist threat as a military threat, their answer to it was simply the American atomic monopoly. If the Communists should—incredibly—resort to overt military force, the sequel, Americans assumed, must be full-scale war; and the United States would win such a war with air-atomic power.

There was a small renewal of interest in traditional forms of military power after Communist advances in the eastern Mediterranean and the withdrawal of British power from that area brought the announcement of the Truman Doctrine in the spring of 1947. The Army supplied advisers and equipment for the Greek army's contest against Communist guerrillas. When a Communist coup captured Czechoslovakia in February, 1948, the consequent national alarm included some small notice that the Army's effective combat strength was down to two and one-third divisions. Total Army and Marine Corps ground troops numbered only 631,000 men. Since at this juncture too the Key West conference of the Joint Chiefs made a slight increase in ground strength a politic concession to the Army, to accompany concessions to the Air Force and Navy, the Joint Chiefs now recommended a return to selective service, and Secretary Forrestal called on Congress to increase Army and Marine ground strength by 250,000 men.

Congress did pass the Selective Service Act of June, 1948, to be in effect for two years. But a long and complex budget struggle netted the Army an increase of only about 100,000 men. Only some 300,-000 were drafted under the new Selective Service Act before the Korean War. Government and public still envisioned war almost exclusively in terms of air-atomic power, and the Army still seemed irrelevant. The Berlin blockade led to the North Atlantic Treaty of mutual assistance in August, 1949; but air power sufficed to overcome the crisis, directly through the air lift and indirectly, it was thought, through the dispatch of two B-29 bomber groups to Britain as an earnest of American determination.[33]

In 1949, American military policy was so fixedly based on air power and atomic weapons that the unexpectedly early Soviet explosion of an atomic weapon in September brought little change. The United States responded to the loss of its monopoly merely by hastening the design of the more powerful hydrogen bomb.

By that time Louis Johnson was Secretary of Defense. An ambitious man, the more so since his ambitions for higher office had once been disappointed in the War Department, Johnson judged now that the results of the 1948 Presidential election had only obscured but had not overcome the popular postwar desire to economize in government and especially in the defense establishment. Apparently he decided that a policy of military economy would best serve the Truman administration and his own ambitions. Air-atomic power would make his policy safe. So he cut military expenditures below the $15 billion ceiling that Truman had already set. The Army was on the sidelines during the subsequent "war of the admirals," the Navy's spectacular protests against cancellation of its supercarrier; but Army strength also receded.

On January 9, 1950, President Truman presented a defense budget reduced to $13.5 billion. Congress cut the authorized strength of the Army from 677,000 to 630,000 men. By June, actual strength was down to 591,487 men.[34]

This Army of 1950 was very much a postwar Army, shaped less by military doctrine looking to a future war, to which this Army so often seemed irrelevant, than by the past, by the last war, of whose massive armies it was the remnant. Under the shadow of atomic power, development of nonatomic weapons had lagged, and procurement had lagged still more, so the weapons of the Army remained those of World War II, developed as long ago as the period from World War I through the mid-1930's, and now often warworn: the M-1 rifle, the Browning Automatic Rifle, .30- and .50-caliber machine guns, 60- and 81-mm and 4.2-inch mortars, 75-mm bazookas, and 105-mm howitzers. Though Pershing tanks had made limited appearances on World War II battlefields, available tanks were still mainly Shermans, despite their shortcomings. With World War II weaponry, the Army was geared for World War II tactics.

The combat strength of the Army resided in ten divisions, a division-size European Constabulary, and nine separate regimental combat teams. According to the T/O&E's, the infantry division was essentially the "redeployment division" of World War II, a reorganization of the 1943 division, incorporating elements which General McNair had consigned to corps or army pools but which had proved to be necessities of normal combat conditions; these included principally a tank battalion and an antiaircraft artillery battalion. Except for the 1st Infantry Division in Germany, however, economies had caused the Army to skeletonize its divisions. The infantry regiments had two rather than three battalions, and the artillery battalions had two rather than three batteries. These reductions were serious handicaps in a tactical system that assumed three-battalion regiments; in combat, a regimental commander would have to fight with a single battalion if he desired a reserve, or put both battalions into line and fight without a reserve. Furthermore, the divisions generally lacked their organic armor. The active infantry battalions were short one rifle company. No division had its wartime complement of weapons. Ammunition reserves were severely limited; the divisions in Japan had a forty-five days' supply. Supporting units were weaker than the divisions themselves.

The best officers and men were World War II veterans, a dwindling but still large group. Newer infusions included both enlistees and the draftees of the 1948 Selective Service Act. After 1945, when no immediate ground combat seemed in prospect and the whole American nation hoped to relax from the prolonged rigors of depression and war, the government had sought to extend some of the amenities of the affluent society to the Army; when the draft had lapsed, doing so had seemed essential to inviting enlistments. Several civilian and military boards had therefore reexamined the code of military justice, partly with a view to softening some of its harsher outlines. In response, Congress established the new Uniform Code of Military Justice of May 5, 1950, applicable to all the armed forces. The Uniform Code did ease to a degree the severities of military discipline, obedience, and responsibility; notably, dismissal from the service was no longer the inevitable result of an officer's conviction by court-martial for conduct unbecoming his station. Many professional officers saw in the relaxing of military justice the cause of a gradual blunting of the Army's combat edge, and they were to blame the new code for many of the shortcomings of American soldiers in 1950.

More likely, those shortcomings derived mainly from broader impediments to discipline and combat readiness. The divisions were chiefly stationed on occupation duty in Germany, Austria, and Japan, and the administrative chores of occupation interfered with training and conditioning programs. Peacetime training in general was much less rigorous than that of the war years; especially it lacked combat simulation, which would have posed dangers distasteful to postwar public opinion. The four divisions in Japan simply lacked ground for extensive training exercises. The familiar economies of the time discouraged any programs that might be expensive. The drive for economy went so far as to send 1950 graduates of the Military Academy direct to their assignments without the now customary interval in service schools of their branches.[35]

Neither enlistees—often lured into the Army by promises of preparation for skilled careers—nor draftees, nor most of the officers, nor certainly the government expected the Army to serve soon as a combat army, and weapons, organization, and state of mind all reflected this fact.

TWENTY-ONE

The Impact of Korea:
1950-61

There can be, I think, no quick and decisive solution to the global struggle short of resorting to another world war. The cost of such a conflict is beyond calculation. It is therefore our policy to contain Communist aggression in different fashions in different areas without resorting to total war. . . . The application of this policy has not always been easy or popular. . . .

—George C. Marshall[1]

WHEN THE Communist North Korean army invaded South Korea in 1950, it was quickly evident that the Communist purpose was not to force an ultimate showdown with the West but simply to overrun all of Korea. If the Communists were not going to force the final showdown, neither could the United States and the other Western powers persuade themselves to initiate atomic holocaust and destroy much of civilization in a disproportionate effort to save Korea. But the Truman administration also decided promptly that it could not simply sacrifice Korea to a Communist display of force, because to do so would be not only to abandon a ward of the United States but also to invite successive small invasions by the Communists elsewhere. Receiving the support of the United Nations Security Council, President Truman resolved to commit to Korea whatever American military strength was necessary to turn back the Communist invaders.

The Communists had almost certainly miscalculated by failing to foresee the American response. The Americans had certainly miscalculated by failing to include small wars on the periphery of the

Communist empire within their serious military planning. The Army and the Joint Chiefs themselves were delinquent in neglecting the possibility, though a larger delinquency belonged to the policy makers who gave them no indication that the country would involve itself in such wars. Communists and Americans both thus found themselves in a limited war which neither had foreseen, but neither of them were willing to extend the war beyond Korea, with all the risks that such a move implied. Both therefore contented themselves with fighting a war limited to Korea and with limited objectives, the conquest of South Korea on the part of the Communists, the salvation of the South and perhaps—only perhaps—the recapture of the North on the part of the Americans.

Thus the Korean War became a contest not unlike those limited wars for territorial prizes that the European powers were accustomed to waging in the era of the birth of the American Army, before the wars of the French Revolution loosed democratic passions and mass armies upon Europe to open the modern age of total war. The seventeenth- and eighteenth-century era of limited war had emerged after the wars of religion had become so devastating that rival faiths and states had learned they must rein in their hatreds and coexist with each other, restricting their armed conflicts to peripheral areas and questions, lest European civilization be destroyed. Similarly, after the two world wars and then the appearance of the atomic bomb had raised expectations that the next war, if it came, must be an apocalypse, the very apocalyptic nature of those expectations now held back the Korean contestants and persuaded them to limit their warfare.

At first the American government anticipated a war so limited that American participation could be confined mainly to air, sea, and logistical support, leaving the ground combat to the Republic of Korea. This anticipation was consistent with the assumption, strongly if only half-consciously developed among many Americans since 1945, that infantry warfare was a thing of the past for Americans. An American military advisory mission of five hundred men was already with the ROK Army, and to facilitate reliance on that army, the mission was now placed under the command of General Douglas MacArthur, who in his Tokyo headquarters became United Nations Commander as well as United States Commander in the Far East. But the Army of the Republic of Korea had no tanks or heavy weapons, and the Soviet Union had supplied the North Koreans with both. Out of this weakness and the faulty generalship of an inexperienced high command, many ROK formations, including whole divisions, went out of existence in the first few days of the war. When observers sent by MacArthur and then MacArthur himself visited

Korea, they soon concluded that only American ground troops could halt the North Koreans short of the ocean. Truman accepted Mac-Arthur's judgment. As yet, no one foresaw how deep a ground commitment would be necessary.[2]

But once Americans began to fight, perception of the difficulties grew daily. The North Koreans proved to be skillful, tough, and numerous. American troops hastily shuttled to Korea from the occupation army in Japan were unready for them physically, psychologically, and even in equipment. The two-battalion regiments were too thin for sustained resistance on fluid battlefields on which the enemy had captured momentum before they arrived. The poorly conditioned American troops sagged under combat gear in hundred-degree temperatures on the steep Korean hills. Nothing had prepared them mentally for an ugly ground war in a remote country of whose very existence they had hardly been aware. The North Koreans came on with Soviet T-34 tanks, off the sides of which American 75-mm bazooka rockets bounced harmlessly—even when the rockets exploded, which was not always, because they were often too old to explode properly. There was not enough ammunition for the 105-mm guns that had to kill the tanks the bazookas could not kill. No antitank mines were available in Japan. Sherman tanks had to make the long trip from America, because Japanese bridges had restricted MacArthur's occupation force to light tanks.[3]

A disproportionate number of American officers became front-line casualties, including the commander of the first division to be committed, Major General William F. Dean of the 24th Division, captured while trying to make his way back into his lines. In part, inadequate leadership at lower levels compelled generals and colonels to play the roles of lieutenants and sergeants. In part, commanding officers could often maintain contact with their front only by being there, and then not well enough, because communications continually broke down. Telephone wire would be lost during successive retreats, and radios kept going dead because they also dated from World War II and were too old for the job.[4]

So the American Army itself was soon hard pressed to prevent the Communists from driving them into the sea, and a partial mobilization became necessary in the United States.

For American industry, partial mobilization posed no problems of excessive difficulty. Productive capacity was so immense that there was no question of procuring ample quantities of war matériel while still producing generously for the home market. Qualitatively, it was enough to send the forces in Korea the final products of the development program of World War II; the North Koreans had good Soviet equipment but not the very latest and best. Though the 75-mm bazooka failed, for example, its larger brother, the 3.5-inch rocket launcher, could penetrate the T-34.

A partial mobilization of manpower posed problems that were less readily soluble. Perplexing from the beginning, manpower problems became especially intractable after November, 1950, when the Chinese Communists entered the war and substantial forces became necessary for the indefinite future.

Ultimately, the Army mobilized 2,834,000 men and twenty divisions. Eight Army divisions and one Marine Corps division were committed to Korea; the rest served as a reserve pool and guarded against the possibility, much feared by the Truman administration, that the Soviets might take advantage of American preoccupation with Korea to launch other military adventures elsewhere.

Obviously such a mobilization of American manpower did not approach total mobilization or the dimensions of World War II. But herein lay much of the perplexity. The Army faced larger responsibilities than could be borne by Regulars alone. Citizen soldiers had to be called on and citizens' lives disrupted, in considerable numbers. Yet since there was no need for all the country's manpower, who was to be called? How could the burdens of the war be distributed fairly? How could they be distributed and not cause a political outcry that might undermine the Truman administration and the whole war effort with it?

These questions were never answered satisfactorily. The distribution of the burdens of the war was hardly fair, and consequent dissatisfaction not only contributed to the political undoing of the administration but at least complicated and confused the waging of the war.

On the very eve of war, Congress extended the Selective Service Act.[5] When war began, Congress also extended expiring enlistments. In the first crisis of the war, the retreat through South Korea toward the sea, the Army cannibalized all its formations not intended for commitment to Korea to bring the units in or bound for combat to war strength. Directly and by stimulating enlistments, the Selective Service Act permitted replenishment and strengthening of the cannibalized units.

Initial failure to halt the North Korean advance convinced the Joint Chiefs and the administration that they might need additional organized formations very promptly. The Selective Service Act empowered the President to order reserve components of the armed forces to active federal service for not more than twenty-one months. But while the Army thought it needed some, it did not need all the National Guard and Reserves. In July it ordered two National

Guard divisions, the 40th (California) and 45th (Oklahoma) to alert status, and they were federalized on September 1 and their formations filled with drafted men. Two additional divisions, the 28th (Pennsylvania) and 43rd (Connecticut, Rhode Island, and Vermont) were federalized a few days later.

After the Chinese joined the war, four more Guard divisions entered federal service: the 31st (Alabama and Mississippi), the 37th (Ohio), the 44th (Illinois), and the 47th (Minnesota and North Dakota). The two Guard divisions first called, the 40th and 45th, were shipped to Korea. The 28th and 43rd went to strengthen the Allied line in Germany. The remaining four federalized Guard divisions became personnel and training stations, into and out of which trainees were shuttled. Eventually three additional regimental combat teams of the Guard and 714 company-size units were mobilized, aggregating 138,600 officers and men and some thirty-four per cent of the Army National Guard. The Army Reserve eventually contributed still more, some 244,300 officers and men in addition to 43,000 Reserve officers who were on active duty when the war began.[6]

In June, 1951, Congress again extended the draft. Indeed, it took advantage of the mood of war to pass the Universal Military Training and Service Act, decreeing an obligation to military service for all male citizens.[7]

But despite the name of the law, the fulfillment of John McAuley Palmer's and George C. Marshall's program of universal service was put off to an undetermined future time by the law itself. Perhaps Congress could now accept the principle of universal service because to be able to apply it would have been comfortingly simple; it would have eliminated unfairness. But to attempt its application in 1951 would only have disrupted the Korean war effort for which universal service was not required, and so inequities persisted. The law also extended the existing selective service and reserve systems. Hundreds of thousands of men became selectees, but still more of the same ages avoided service through various deferments, exemptions, and disabilities—essentially because the armed forces would not have known what to do with all of them. Some National Guardsmen continued on federal service while others escaped, with the very geography of Guard unit distribution adding to the inequities. Since the Regulars and the Guard afforded sufficient organized units, Reserves were called to federal service largely from among the inactive Reservists, officers and men who had not been undergoing unit training. These men were especially apt to wonder why they should be in Korea while thousands of active Reservists were still at home; but the Army wanted individual replacements for units already mobilized, while units still in America remained there as a strategic reserve against a bigger war that might come.

The best plan that the Army believed itself able to employ to minimize the inequities of an unfair mobilization system was the rotation program. This program was invoked in 1951 when it became evident that the war might well last indefinitely. Under it, men drafted or called to active duty from the National Guard and the Reserves were dispatched to Korea for relatively short terms, then rotated back to formations not in combat and eventually out of the active Army and into the reserve pool. Rotation was based on a point system. A soldier who had earned thirty-six points rotated out of Korea. A man received four points a month for service in the battle line, three a month for service anywhere in a combat zone, and two a month anywhere in Korea. By rotation the Army not only distributed the burden of Korean service but also built a steadily growing pool of manpower that not only was trained but possessed combat experience. This pool would be invaluable if the Communists should provoke a larger war.

The rotation system rotated individuals, not military units, a method which kept increasingly experienced headquarters staffs in Korea, prevented whole units from being idle in the pipeline, and altogether held to a minimum the number of formations committed to the Korean battlefront while keeping as many as possible free for other possible service elsewhere.

The great defect of the system was that the eight Army divisions in Korea and their constituent and attached formations experienced so rapid a shuttling of manpower in and out of their ranks that they never achieved much internal cohesion. Enlisted men and junior officers spent their time counting the days until they would be rotated out. They did not develop a sense of unit. Constantly shifting personnel could not learn the teamwork essential to creating fully effective squads, platoons, and companies. Least of all could they acquire *esprit de corps*, a unit pride of the sort that might in part have compensated for the listlessness that grew from lack of understanding of the kind of war being fought. The enemy did not rank American soldiers high in aggressiveness or in stamina under pressure. If the Americans had been fighting a more modern enemy army, with firepower and logistical support comparable to their own, the relatively incohesive formations of the rotation system might not have been able to win.[8]

Again in Korea as in World War II, the Army was hard put to maintain a ground combat strength that seemed commensurate with the numbers in uniform. To maintain twenty divisions with a strength of about sixteen thousand each, the Army mobilized almost three million men. The apparatus of logistical support for the combat divisions became more elaborate than that of 1941–45. In part the cause was the distance to the Korean front and the immense difficulty of supporting troops in a mountainous and road-poor country. But in part too the lavishness of the supporting establishment was another product of the nation's psychological unpreparedness for the war. In an effort to maintain reasonably high morale among soldiers called to fight in a distant land, under a dubious system of selection and without the drive for total victory that was familiar to Americans, the Army made a heroic effort to approximate the American standard of living among the Korean mountains. With ample provision of warm clothing when winter came, Thanksgiving turkey dinners near the Yalu River, Cokes, and cigarettes (though free beer gave way to public protest), the Army came about as close as possible to succeeding in that impossible task. But along with the accomplishment went rifle companies sometimes fighting at twenty-five per cent of authorized strength, long after the first crisis. Some estimates held that after the Chinese intervention the ratio of Communist to UN men in uniform in Korea was 6 to 5 but Communist superiority in fighting men was at least 5 to 1.[9]

The inequities of mobilization and the problems of lavish supply compounded the larger problem of the Korean War, that it was not a war that Americans could readily understand and therefore not one that they could wholeheartedly support. The Korean War somewhat resembled the limited wars of the seventeenth and eighteenth centuries. But those wars had remained limited largely because they were fought in the absence of democratic public opinion and so were not fanned by popular passions into national crusades. The Korean War, in contrast, had to be fought under the pressures of American public opinion. That opinion was unprepared for any costly ground war when the Korean conflict began. It was also conditioned by the whole of American history—and this was true of much opinion in the Army itself—in which war had been regarded as an unlimited enterprise, in which the enemy whose conduct had been so rude, unlawful, and immoral as to shatter American tranquility should be crushed as punishment for his crime and as warrant for future security.

If the Indian campaigns did not altogether fit that description, their outcome was nevertheless the virtual destruction of the enemy. Those of them that were not all-out wars but limited punitive expeditions could usually be handled by the Regular Army, and as long as the Regulars did the fighting and citizen soldiers did not need to be called up, the public was not likely to become sufficiently aroused to demand unlimited victory. But the Korean War did demand the calling of citizen soldiers, and under a system of such manifest inequities as to aggravate any public tendencies toward discontent.

The Korean War resembled the wars of Frederick the Great in the limited objectives to which the contending governments attempted to confine it. But it could not be fought in the strikingly passionless climate of Frederick's wars, and the resulting stresses not only injured the morale of the American fighting man but shook the very high command of the American Army and its relation to the civil power.

Until April 11, 1951, General of the Army Douglas MacArthur ruled over the Korean War with a plenitude of power such as no American commander had possessed since John J. Pershing and such as few have possessed in any era. This condition was the result both of MacArthur's formidable stature, political as well as military, and of the effort to control his conduct from Washington through the Joint Chiefs of Staff, which demonstrated the inevitable weaknesses of a corporate body in attempting to deal with a strong individual. MacArthur's power in the Pacific was diluted by no such diffusion of command as had limited him during World War II, when he shared command of the Pacific theater with Admiral Nimitz. MacArthur was now Commander in Chief, Far East, over all American armed forces in the area. When the United Nations sanctioned the military effort in Korea, President Truman designated him Commander in Chief, United Nations Command, as well. Because World War II had not officially ended, MacArthur was also Supreme Commander for the Allied Powers in the Far East. Furthermore, though it was the only active war occurring in which American forces were involved, Korea remained for the Joint Chiefs a peripheral war, because Washington concentrated consistently on the danger of a greater global war. So MacArthur became a colossus bestriding Korea, enforcing his own sometimes intuitive command decisions even when his interservice planning staff objected, or even when the Joint Chiefs demurred, until the nemesis of power at last overtook him.[10]

The Joint Chiefs had agreed in 1948 that in supervising any theater command, they would exercise their authority through the branch of service primarily involved in that theater. Thus JCS directives were dispatched to MacArthur through the chief of staff of the Army, General J. Lawton Collins, acting as executive agent of the JCS. The place of the Secretary of Defense in the command structure was very unclear, but the Joint Chiefs nevertheless submitted their directives to him for his approval. His role became more influential

after September 12, 1950, when the President dropped Louis Johnson, upon whose policies Korea threw an especially embarrassing
light, and appointed George C. Marshall. Not even Marshall's prestige and character, however, nor Truman's respect for him as "the
greatest living American," could altogether retrieve the weakness of
the Secretary's position in matters of strategy and command. On
those matters his office was not much stronger than the assertive
commanding generals of the past would have liked the Secretary of
War to be.[11]

The Secretary of Defense passed the Joint Chiefs' directives on to
the President for his approval, significantly doing so through the
agency of the chairman of the Joint Chiefs, General Omar Bradley.
Bradley met with the President every morning. Some directives were
submitted also to the National Security Council. The President not
only bore the usual final responsibility assigned to him by the Constitution but was also the channel through which the United Nations
sent any directives to MacArthur. Meanwhile the delicate problems
of diplomatic policy posed by Korea led to an unwonted but healthy
closeness of consultation between the military and the State Department. A State-JCS meeting occurred weekly, attended by the Joint
Chiefs, the Deputy Secretary of State, and usually the chairman of
the State Department Policy Planning Staff and the Assistant Secretary of State for Far Eastern Affairs. Also significantly, although
initially owing to a misunderstanding, no representative of the Secretary of Defense attended the meetings until the summer of 1951.[12]

All such apparatus notwithstanding, MacArthur long retained his
very free hand. The Joint Chiefs deferred to his experience, rank,
and reputation, to his intense emotional involvement in the Far East,
an involvement they did not share, and to his unmeasured but possibly dangerous political potency as a man cultivated and admired by
Republican party leaders. The Navy and Marine Corps objected to
MacArthur's plan for the September, 1950, landing at Inchon. But
although those services mainly would have to execute the plan, and
they had good reasons for misgivings about a two-phased landing
between immense tides leading not to a beach but a sea wall, Mac-
Arthur had his way. This was true although two of the Joint Chiefs,
Collins of the Army and Admiral Forrest Sherman of the Navy,
visited the Far East shortly before the landings, and Sherman was
exposed to his service's misgivings on the scene.

MacArthur continued to have his way in relatively small things
and large. The Joint Chiefs objected to his sponsoring a ceremonial
return to the Korean capital at Seoul in the company of President
Syngman Rhee, because the United States did not want to identify
itself too closely with that despotic old gentleman; nevertheless, Mac-

Arthur participated in combined ceremonies with Rhee. More importantly, a JCS directive of September 27, 1950, for operations north of the thirty-eighth parallel, enjoined employing non-Korean troops in the provinces adjacent to China and the Soviet Union. The purpose, obviously, was to try to avoid provoking an intervention by the major Communist powers. But MacArthur acted otherwise and got away with it.

Thereafter the Joint Chiefs felt growing doubts about the wisdom of MacArthur's troop dispositions in North Korea. Their misgivings increased over a period of weeks before the Chinese attacks of November, 1950, finally confirmed them. But so reluctant were they to interfere with MacArthur on a matter of military judgment that they urged Secretary of State Dean Acheson to intervene with the President, so that Truman might instruct MacArthur to consolidate his forces.[13]

The principal headquarters through which MacArthur directed the Army forces of his joint command was that of the Eighth United States Army in Korea (EUSAK). The Eighth Army had been the organization occupying Japan. On July 13, 1950, its commander, Lieutenant General Walton H. Walker, a veteran of Patton's campaigns, transferred his headquarters to Korea. Through the "Taejon Agreement" Walker also directed the Republic of Korea Army through its chief of staff. The ROK Army never became officially part of the Eighth Army (although in a not very successful effort to reinforce American units, individual Korean soldiers were for many months assigned directly to the American forces). Other United Nations troops were attached to the Eighth Army.[14]

At the climax of the war, from the Inchon landings through the Chinese intervention, some American ground forces in Korea were not part of the Eighth Army. The Inchon landings were a project upon which MacArthur determined from his first visit to Korea after the Communist invasion in June, 1950. They were designed to produce a Cannae victory that would destroy the North Korean army, and their planning received MacArthur's special interest. The Inchon plan was developed by a Special Planning Staff that grew up within the Joint Strategic Plans and Operations Group, MacArthur's principal interservice planning agency. To command the landings, MacArthur chose no less an officer than his chief of staff for the Far Eastern Command, a member of his personal inner coterie, Major General Edward Almond. A new headquarters, the X Corps, was created to conduct the landings, and Almond received the X Corps while remaining chief of staff. The staff of the X Corps emerged mainly from the Special Planning Staff. The X Corps would not be part of the Eighth Army but would be rather a sort of strategic reserve for the Far East Command, directly under Mac-Arthur. As such it carried out the landings, and as such it campaigned until its evacuation by sea from Hungnam and Wonsan. It accomplished MacArthur's Cannae victory at Inchon, but its deployment in North Korea as a separate command was a dubious arrangement that may have contributed to the disasters of November and December, 1950. General Almond remained theoretically chief of staff, Far Eastern Command, until after MacArthur himself departed.[15]

Although MacArthur enjoyed his considerable autonomy in the Far East and Korea, he was not alone in making the decision to carry the war north beyond the thirty-eighth parallel. The Joint Chiefs, the National Security Council, and the President all contributed to the decision, on the ground that final destruction of the North Korean army was a military necessity. The General Assembly of the United Nations joined in, lured by the attractive idea that if Mac-Arthur entered North Korea, the root cause of the war would be eliminated; North and South Korea could be reunited.

Unfortunately, by the time MacArthur's forces crossed the thirty-eighth parallel, the Chinese Communist government was already uttering dire warnings that it could not stand idly by while the banners of imperialism advanced to the Manchurian frontier. At first the warnings were generally interpreted as a bluff. But as MacArthur's advance continued, and his supply lines grew longer and more vulnerable, and North Korean geography caused him to scatter his forces beyond mutual supporting distances in mountainous terrain, growing numbers of observers in Washington and elsewhere began to take the continuing Chinese warnings seriously. A brief interval of euphoria gave way to increasing unease.

In the fall of 1950, that unease mounted rapidly everywhere except in MacArthur's headquarters. President Truman met with the general on Wake Island on October 15 and raised the possibility of Chinese intervention, but MacArthur assured him there was no danger of it. In late November, MacArthur announced a post-Thanksgiving offensive to win the war by Christmas. He ignored the misgivings implicit in the Joint Chiefs' current directives as he had already ignored their specific injunction against sending non-Koreans to the Chinese border. After October 25, Chinese soldiers were encountered on the battlefront with alarming frequency, but the Joint Chiefs could not bring themselves to do anything forceful about either their unease or MacArthur's scattered deployment. MacArthur knew that everyone else was apprehensive, but lesser men had questioned his judgment and intuition before, and he believed he had always been vindicated.[16]

This time his inner certainty failed him. His intelligence service failed him, too. Chinese troop concentrations south of the Yalu which almost certainly would not have gone undetected by the American aerial reconnaissance service of 1944 or 1945 passed unnoticed, another indication of the lapse of American military skills during the postwar years. On November 28, the day after MacArthur launched his final attack, Chinese armies of more than 300,-000 men struck him a totally unexpected counterblow. Although the Americans that they hit fought well, the United Nations forces were not properly aligned to receive the attack, the South Korean II Corps collapsed, widening the gulf between the Eighth Army and the X Corps, and MacArthur's command had to retreat. After MacArthur's headquarters had repeatedly assured him that the Chinese would not intervene, the appearance of large numbers of Chinese forces was so demoralizing that the retreat soon resembled a flight and carried the United Nations forces south below the parallel again and eventually even below Seoul.[17]

The disaster unnerved most of America's allies and caused the Truman administration to change its mind about the objects of the war. The administration would now be content merely to hold South Korea. It would fight with all determination to achieve at least that much, despite the Chinese, but to try to reconquer the North after Chinese intervention seemed to pose costs and risks too great.

But both personal and political considerations impelled MacArthur to reject a limited war fought for negative aims. The old warrior could hardly bear to see his illustrious career close with an ignominious defeat, as it would if the action against the Chinese Communists on the Chongchon River in North Korea proved to be his last major battle. Politically—and his years as American proconsul in Japan had confirmed him in the habit of consulting his political as well as military convictions—he believed that the Far East was the cockpit of the world struggle against Communism, and that the Communists must be beaten decisively here or become the winners of the game throughout the world. Philosophically, he professed the popular revulsion against limited war. "War's very object is victory . . . ," he was to say. "In war, indeed, there can be no substitute for victory."[18]

MacArthur was an extremely self-centered man who had always been conspicuous in the Army not only for his brilliance but for an individualism that reached maverick proportions. During World War II the Joint Chiefs had been sufficiently wary of his ego to allow him his own way in certain matters denied to other theater commanders. He had little to lose by challenging the administration; he had already possessed every honor likely to be open to him except the

Presidency itself. He had been chief of staff of the Army when other generals of the 1950's had been captains or majors, if that. He decided to challenge the new war policy of the administration.[19]

Opening a debate against the Joint Chiefs' directives, he insisted that Chinese intervention required that the war now be carried to China itself. China must be attacked by air and by sea, and Chiang Kai-shek's Kuomintang army must be employed on the battlefields of the Asian mainland. Failure to defeat China now would result in ultimate failure to defeat Communism around the globe. While the Eighth Army retreated, MacArthur warned that all Korea would be lost if his proposals were not adopted. When the Eighth Army halted the Chinese advance after all, he warned that intolerably expensive attrition was the only alternative to his plans. When his debate with the Joint Chiefs brought no change in administration policy, he turned from private to public debate: he would appeal over the heads of his military superiors and the government to the opposition party and the people.

Already he had engaged in sufficient public airing of his policy views that on December 6 the President issued an executive order to all theater commanders to clear their public statements with the Defense or State Department; the order was aimed clearly at MacArthur. Nevertheless, MacArthur chose an especially delicate hour to issue an important public statement without clearance. When he learned in March that the administration was about to send out peace overtures, he forestalled them, issuing on March 24 his own offer to meet with the Communist commander on the field of battle to end the war, but coupling his offer with threats of disaster for China itself if his terms were not accepted. General Bradley reminded MacArthur of the order of December 6. Nevertheless, MacArthur allowed Representative Joseph Martin, Republican leader in the House, to read to Congress a letter in which MacArthur endorsed Martin's and the opposition's view that the Korean War should be carried to China and rejected the administration's restraint.[20]

No government could allow its military deputy thus to undermine its foreign policy, consort with the domestic opposition, and impress its allies with the uncertainty of its program. Since MacArthur had already acted as well as spoken in defiance of JCS directives, there could be no assurance that he would not extend the war to China on his own initiative. Not to discipline MacArthur would be to allow the conduct of American foreign policy to pass from the White House to the Dai-Ichi. "If I allowed him to defy the civil authorities in this manner," President Truman said, "I myself would be violating my oath to uphold and defend the Constitution."[21]

Fortunately, there was an alternative leadership already available in the Far East: Lieutenant General Matthew B. Ridgway's. General Walker had been killed when his jeep overturned on December 23, and Ridgway, an outstanding leader of airborne troops in World War II, had replaced him. Early in 1951 Washington became so alarmed over MacArthur's warnings that none of Korea could be held without extending the war that General Collins and Air Force Chief of Staff Hoyt Vandenberg went to the Far East to see for themselves. They discovered that the new commander of the Eighth Army disagreed with MacArthur's prognostications, and more than that, they stayed to observe while Ridgway began to fulfill his own more confident predictions. Consequently, from January onward the Joint Chiefs often bypassed MacArthur, to send directives straight to Eighth Army headquarters in Korea. In effect, as early as January, MacArthur ceased to hold direct control over the Eighth Army.[22]

On April 6 Truman took the question of MacArthur's dismissal to his four most intimate advisers: Secretary of State Acheson, Averell Harriman, Marshall, and Bradley. He did not reveal that he had already decided upon dismissal. Harriman and Bradley favored dismissal; Acheson and Marshall inclined toward caution. During the day, however, Marshall reviewed the files on MacArthur, and the next morning he agreed with what Harriman had already said: that MacArthur had been insubordinate so long that he had deserved to be removed two years before. Bradley then took the question to the Joint Chiefs. They recommended MacArthur's recall not only out of concern for the principle of civilian supremacy but also because they believed the Far Eastern commander must be "more responsive to control from Washington."[23]

There followed the mass emotional demonstrations accompanying MacArthur's return to the United States and so frightening to the administration. But there also followed, despite lengthy Congressional hearings, MacArthur's strikingly rapid fading away into relative obscurity. The public was happy to welcome a war hero who expressed their frustrations over limited war; but it was another thing to accept his remedy for frustration, with its risk of all-out war.

The MacArthur crisis is not likely to be paralleled soon, nor does it appear to signify a permanent impairment of the Army's subordination to the civil power. MacArthur's personal combination of achievement and egotism was essential to the crisis. That combination is not likely soon to reappear, and it is not a combination encouraged by American military institutions. But there remains the issue which MacArthur exploited—America's misgivings over limited war —and if not the MacArthur incident alone, then the whole frustrating Korean War proved, in the Presidential election of 1952, the political undoing of the administration that sponsored that war.

Ridgway now moved to MacArthur's place at the Dai-Ichi in Tokyo, and Lieutenant General James Van Fleet succeeded to the command of the Eighth Army. Ironically, Van Fleet was a believer in MacArthur's affirmation that there is no substitute for victory. Perhaps more significant of the Army's general condition, he was a better disciplined soldier than MacArthur, and he fought the war in accordance with his orders.[24]

When the United States Army first marched onto European battlefields in 1917–18, a history of combat mainly against such enemies as Indians and Filipinos made questionable its capacity for fighting European-style war against a first-rate European power. It had to learn much about European war from its allies, the British and French. By 1950, in contrast, the Army had become so adjusted to European war that it had to struggle to cope with Korean and Chinese methods that would often have seemed familiar to its Indian-fighting forebears but that now seemed strange.

The Asian Communists, their tactics conditioned by guerrilla warfare, placed great emphasis on penetration of weak points and encirclement of detachments. The Korean terrain facilitated their encircling tactics. The Americans, accustomed to the relatively neat linear battlefields of Europe, never wholly adjusted to a chaotic sort of warfare in which the enemy continually insinuated himself into flanks or rear and in which attacks repeatedly came from several directions at once. The Americans never wholly adjusted to an enemy who not only infiltrated their lines by stealth and at night but who usually attacked at night. The old Indian-fighting Army had habituated itself to fluid tactics with elements of guerrilla-style war; the Army of 1950 had long since forgotten the tactics of the Indian wars. The Army of 1950 had become roadbound, while the North Koreans and Chinese could move across roadless hills that the Americans customarily thought impenetrable. The Army had become dependent upon artillery support that could not always be available in the Korean hills. The Army had become dependent on elaborate radio and telephone communications that could not always function in the Korean mountains. Its habituation to European war sometimes put the American Army in Korea approximately in the condition of Braddock's Regulars on the Monongahela.

Nevertheless, deficiencies in training, toughness, unit cohesion, and psychological readiness were graver weaknesses in Korea than the tactical deficiencies resulting from an unaccustomed style of war. The retreat to the Naktong River in the summer of 1950 was less a display of faulty tactical conceptions than of faulty execution by troops who were too lightly trained, too loosely disciplined, and too lacking in motivation to match the determination of the enemy. The victories at Inchon and the breakout from the Naktong Perimeter were victories of matériel and numbers against a North Korean army that had been badly worn by months of combat and had overextended itself. When the Chinese came in, the American defeat at Kunu-ri exemplified many of the same shortcomings as the earlier defeats of the summer; the American Army even yet had not developed a toughness and cohesion equal to its foes'.[25]

A somewhat disproportionate amount of national and intra-Army soul-searching and hand-wringing has occurred over collaboration with their captors by some of the American soldiers who fell into Communist hands. Many proved unable to bear the physical and mental strains of Communist prisoner of war camps, and a few even defected to the enemy. In the light of American performance on the early Korean battlefields, lack of toughness and stamina in prisons should not have been surprising. Soldiers unprepared for battle, as the first to reach Korea were, naturally were also unprepared for the rigors of prison camps. Yet American weaknesses in the prisons have attracted much more attention than the closely related shortcomings in battle.

Of course, defeat in battle had been suffered before, while collaboration with the enemy by American prisoners was something new. But it is hardly remarkable that American prisoners in Korea collaborated with the enemy in ways unknown during any other war; it was only in the Korean War of all American wars that the enemy applied unconventional pressures upon his captives to cooperate with him. Occasional bestial behavior by prisoners whose treatment had reduced them to the level of animals was not unprecedented; it had occurred in the Civil War prison camps. Simple "bugging out" of a war was not unprecedented; it had often happened when conditions favored it, as in Washington's Revolutionary armies. Other soldiers captured by Communists and subjected to their indoctrination had also sometimes defected; the Germans have not been accused of weakness in their national backbone because defections occurred among their soldiers in Russian POW camps. Few American captives of the Communists behaved like heroes. Also, very few behaved like traitors. Most resisted their captors only passively and therefore went along to a degree with Communist indoctrination sessions; whole populations behind the Iron Curtain cooperate at least to this extent and no comment is occasioned, since most men are not heroes and will usually do what seems necessary to survive. On the diet and in the living conditions of Communist POW camps, mere survival was no small problem. But the best evidence indicates that few prisoners cooperated with the enemy beyond the general extent to which any prisoner always must cooperate with his captors in order to live.

Significantly, the prisoners who most often behaved badly were those captured during the early months of the war. Once American soldiers had accepted the existence of the unpleasant war in Korea, whether they liked it or not; once they had campaigned long enough to become seasoned and disciplined warriors; and once they had been provided with warnings and instructions on how to behave and maintain discipline if captured, their Communist captors found them less malleable. The Communists chose to segregate later American prisoners from those taken early in the war.[26]

Improved conduct by POW's paralleled the fighting improvement of the Army. Such improvement did follow upon experience. It became evident especially after the accession of General Ridgway to command of the Eighth Army. His predecessor Walton Walker was a good officer, but Ridgway was more than that: he was an inspirational battle captain in the manner of George Patton, Philip Sheridan, or Stonewall Jackson. He managed to impress a fighting spirit upon his corps and division commanders and thence downward through the army as Walker had never done. Ridgway rallied the Eighth Army after the Chinese had sent it scurrying out of North Korea, found it reluctant even to make contact with the enemy, restored its confidence in itself, and sent it northward to defeat the Chinese and push them back across the thirty-eighth parallel. He accomplished these things partly through his own example of confidence, displayed on many tours of the front. He did it also by insisting upon very high standards of discipline, whereby he in time gave the Eighth Army professional qualities such as few American forces of comparable size have sustained and which survived even the hazards of the rotation system.

Ridgway also made useful tactical adjustments. Part of what he did was simple; he required better patrolling and tighter security. But while Walker had preferred to concentrate American forces in the relatively good tank country of the valley invasion routes, Ridgway increasingly committed his troops to the mountains. He made the Americans learn to fight there in what had been the enemy's chosen ground, and thus he minimized the possibility of deep Chinese penetrations like the one that had put them into the ridges between the Eighth Army and the X Corps in the North. His tactical system called for the maximum exploitation of firepower, including air and artillery, to soften up the enemy in methodical attacks, in place of the swift but vulnerable movements of mechanized columns that had approached the Yalu. In the idiom of his troops, he introduced the tactics of the meat grinder, to chew up Chinese manpower at a rate even the Chinese could not afford.

Once experience and Ridgway's ability to command had made the Eighth Army skillful and determined in war, the tactical deficiencies unveiled by unaccustomed Communist methods of war could be overcome, for the military deficiencies of the Chinese were much graver than those of the Americans. The Chinese could still infiltrate through American lines, cut off American detachments at least temporarily, and throw wave after wave of brave infantry against them until sometimes they opened gaps in the American defenses. But if they opened gaps, they could not well exploit them. Moving on foot and by foot cart, oxcart, and camel, they lacked sufficient mobility to pour through a gap before it could be sealed. Though their ability to communicate by means of flares, bugles, and other simple devices was an advantage when the Americans' radio communications would not work, flares and bugles were inadequate to coordinating swift mass movement to seize tactical advantages. The immensely superior firepower of the Americans meant also that when the Communists did win a tactical advantage, it was at the expense of casualties so high that the attackers were left bleeding and exhausted by the time there arose any opportunity to exploit a breakthrough. Americans learned in time also that Chinese tactics were mechanical and repetitive and therefore could be anticipated.

Altogether, the Korean War demonstrated that the great numbers of Chinese manpower cannot alone defeat moderate numbers of reasonably determined opponents if the opponents are a modern army and the weapons and logistics of the Chinese display shortcomings similar to those in Korea. The war especially demonstrated that Chinese power cannot yet assert itself effectively at any distance from China's borders as long as Chinese military transport remains primitive. The mere stretching of Chinese communications to some two hundred miles from the Yalu proved almost fatally crippling.[27]

The American superiority of firepower resided in infantry weapons, in an artillery in the proud American tradition of that arm, and in tactical air support which always controlled the skies. Though the Air Force had neglected preparation for tactical support, and though better preparation and especially more planes better designed for tactical support might have improved the Korean balance of power, the Army could not have stood firm in Korea without the tactical air support it did receive.[28]

American firepower superiority was achieved through quantity, variety, and skillful employment of weapons, since on both sides the weapons themselves remained chiefly those of World War II. The principal exceptions were jet aircraft and helicopters, the potential of the latter just beginning to be realized in reconnaissance, air rescue work, and small troop movements. Along with the 3.5-inch bazooka, the 105-mm recoilless rifle was added to 57-mm and 75-mm pieces in the infantryman's arsenal of artillery. Several antiaircraft weapons of World War II were no longer effective when they had to cope with jets, but they became useful antipersonnel weapons; this was true of the half-tracked Quad .50, a vehicle mounting four .50-caliber machine guns that could fire as a unit, and of the fully tracked Dual 40, mounting two 40-mm Bofors guns. The artillery workhorses remained the 105's, 155's, and 8-inchers of World War II. Though the M-26 Pershing tank with its 90-mm gun made an appearance, the maneuverability of the old Sherman proved useful in the Korean hills, especially since the tank was mounted with a new high-velocity 76-mm gun.[29]

Matthew Ridgway's stiffening of the Eighth Army was all the more important because it shortly preceded a change in the conflict which made the Korean War still more incomprehensible to the American public and much of the soldiery. Since the American government had abandoned the aim of conquering North Korea, once the Chinese advance was halted in the early months of 1951 and Ridgway's army began counterattacking, the United States and United Nations sent out peace feelers. The Communists were slow to respond. The Chinese evidently desired another attempt at complete victory for their side. But their efforts to that end were no more successful than MacArthur's corresponding ones had been; in March, April, and May of 1951 the UN forces battered huge numbers of Chinese while repelling thrust after thrust at the UN line. The Chinese efforts so exhausted their authors that by the end of May the initiative clearly belonged to the Eighth Army again. Thereupon the chief Soviet delegate to the United Nations suggested that the Communists were willing to discuss a truce, and truce negotiations began at Kaesong on July 10.[30]

Having failed to win complete victory on the battlefield, however, the Communists proceeded to milk the truce negotiations for every conceivable propaganda advantage that might create the appearance of their having won the war. The negotiations settled into a dreary round of acrimony that often seemed likely to prove endless, and in fact they were to last more than two years. Thus the Eighth Army had to maintain the war, probing the enemy if only to keep itself in fighting condition, rectify its lines, and sustain a certain pressure against the enemy. But to Americans at home and to many men in the ranks the fighting now seemed utterly pointless. Any small patch of ground gained was as likely as not to return to the enemy when the final cease-fire line was drawn. In November, 1951, indeed, the negotiators virtually assured that the cease-fire line would be the battle line of that date, no matter what happened in combat between then and the truce.[31]

By now both sides had dug deep into their hills, and networks of trenches, foxholes, and obstacles resembled the battlefields of World War I. Both sides relied increasingly on artillery fire, both because of the strength of the defensive positions and on the UN side in an effort to relieve the burdens and casualties of the infantry. The Chinese brought up even more guns than the Americans, though American fire coordination still gave the Eighth Army artillery superiority. Artillery fire became even more intense than in World War I; more shells were fired in Korea than in all of World War II. Yet artillery alone could not win ground battles.

Neither could air power. The Air Force tried to break the deadlock by depriving the enemy's front of support from the rear. Efforts to interdict enemy communications alternated with efforts to force him to give up the war through bombardment of such strategic targets as were available in North Korea. But no complete interdiction of the front proved possible, and none of the Air Force's efforts brought decisive results.

The American government believed that whatever the apparent futility of ground battles for outpost hills, the ground battles had to be won if Communist prestige and power were to suffer sufficiently to force the Communist truce negotiators to a cease-fire. Therefore the American infantry still had to fight, the hill battles continued, and American casualties persisted at a rate of thirty thousand a year. All this occurred while the American rotation system came into full effect. But throughout the period of the truce negotiations and the tactical stalemate, the Eighth Army seems to have received consistently high marks from Chinese intelligence officers.[32]

While the front-line troops fought a war strange in both methods and purpose, behind the lines the Army also found itself fighting a strange battle, in its prisoner of war camps. After the November agreement on a cease-fire line, the truce negotiations themselves focused on what happened there. The United States Army had not often handled large numbers of prisoners of war. During the Civil War, both Confederate and Union prison camps were abominations, blotting the records of both armies. In World War I, prisoners taken by the Americans were turned over to the British and French, whose prison systems had long since been going concerns. In World War II few prisoners came into American hands until 1943, and then the American prison system was simply modeled on the British. Few

Japanese ever became prisoners, so the American Army had to deal in any large numbers only with captives of its own cultural background.[33] In Korea, however, the Army had to cope with more than 100,000 Orientals, and under especially delicate circumstances. It soon became evident that thousands of the prisoners would not return to Communism voluntarily, and the United States concluded that it could not in honor force them to return. But as soon as the Communists discovered the reluctance with which many of their erstwhile soldiers contemplated repatriation, they turned all their ingenuity to disrupting the whole UN prison system to obscure the loss of face they seemed about to suffer.

The Army thus found itself embarrassed by the Koje Island prison riots, and by the captivity of one of its brigadiers by his own captives. Every effort to quell prison demonstrations set off by hard-core Communist POW's was hampered by the sensibilities of a host of neutral observers. Fortunately, the Army sufficiently neglected those sensibilities to restore command of Koje Island, and a general overhaul of the prison discipline system was then accomplished by Brigadier General Haydon Boatner, before the Communists were able to stage the mass prison break they were planning. In the end, the Army's embarrassments passed into the background, and the Communists had to swallow the humiliation of the refusal of some 50,000 prisoners out of 132,000 to go home.[34]

In the end, too, for all its frustrations the Korean War gave a new sense of purpose to the Army, and made possible a sort of Army renaissance. If the war was not glorious, it did hold the line against Communist expansion, which was the best that most reasonable men thought American foreign and military policy could do without excessive risk of Armaggedon. Without the strengthening of the Army, even that modest aim could not have been fulfilled in Korea.

These facts were blurred for a time by the effects of the war upon American domestic politics. The unpopularity of the war certainly contributed largely to the results of the 1952 elections. The new administration of President Dwight D. Eisenhower was therefore not only eager to secure a prompt cease-fire in Korea, which it contrived to do partly by threatening to turn atomic cannon against the Chinese infantry masses, but also anxious to avoid involvement in any similar limited war. Therefore the administration tried to give the impression that it would simply refuse such involvement and would immediately invoke nuclear weapons in any crisis that threatened the security of the United States. Secretary of State John Foster Dulles announced a "new look" in American military policy, replacing limited war with "massive retaliation."[35]

But the "new look" of "massive retaliation" was in fact the old look of the Truman administration's pre-Korean policy of reliance on the atomic deterrent alone. If air-atomic power had failed to deter a Communist adventure on the military frontier in 1950, because the threat of atomic war was not credible in a peripheral crisis, the nuclear deterrent alone was hardly likely to be more successful in the mid-1950's, now that the Soviet Union had acquired a substantial nuclear arsenal of its own.

Behind the screen of rhetoric, therefore, the Eisenhower administration had to retain much of the increase in ground strength created during the Korean War. It sufficiently cut back the Army to provoke periodic expressions of dismay and even resignations from Army officers who feared that the nation was reverting to the Army weakness that had invited attack in Korea. The resignations included those of Matthew Ridgway and Maxwell Taylor, both one-time commanders of the Eighth Army in Korea and then chiefs of staff of the Army. Lieutenant General James M. Gavin, director of research and development and one of the most promising of American officers, also resigned, and he, Ridgway, and Taylor all quickly vented their misgivings in books.[36]

In the election campaign of 1960 the Democratic Presidential candidate took up the Ridgway-Taylor-Gavin charge that the nation was imperiled by a policy that neglected conventional forms of military power and relied unduly upon nuclear bombs. By now the electorate had sufficiently digested the experience of the Korean War so that the idea may have carried some political weight. In any case, when John F. Kennedy took office, he and Secretary of Defense Robert S. McNamara set out to reorganize all the armed forces, and to strengthen the Army especially, in order to ensure a capacity to respond appropriately to Communist military challenges anywhere on the spectrum of violence, with nuclear power if need be but also with conventional ground forces or with specialized counterinsurgency forces.[37]

In doing so, Kennedy and McNamara were confirming and decisively strengthening a trend that had already set in during the later years of the Eisenhower administration. Even at the height of the Dulles era, there had been more of rhetoric than of substance in "massive retaliation." No one could forget that in Korea the Army had been essential; no responsible man could doubt that for all the foreseeable future it would continue to be so.

TWENTY-TWO

The Army of the 1960's

. . . For we can seek a relaxation of tensions without relaxing our guard.
—John F. Kennedy[1]

SECRETARY OF DEFENSE Robert McNamara believed that the doctrine of "massive retaliation" not only dangerously restricted the ability of the United States to respond to a variety of hostile challenges, but that for all its bluster it sprang from fear and a want of national self-confidence. He believed that the nation had turned to an exclusively nuclear deterrent in part because Americans had come to believe that they and their allies could not rival the military power of the Communist bloc in conventional weapons and on the ground. Upon taking office, he set out first to demonstrate that this belief was false, and then having generated confidence that American power could counter any Communist military challenge, to build armed forces that would assure the fulfillment of such confidence.

In November, 1963, four days before the abrupt and tragic close of the Kennedy Presidency, McNamara felt able to assure the American people that a long familiar world picture was now obsolete: a Communist military Goliath no longer faced an American David whose only reliance was his nuclear slingshot. The United States confronted the Soviet Union with balanced military power. As far as Army ground power was concerned, McNamara had entered office with the Army fallen back from its Korean strength to eleven combat divisions. But it now counted sixteen combat-ready divisions. American troops in Europe along with those of the European allies actually outnumbered the forces the Eastern powers held under arms. Though the Russians and their allies could rapidly mobilize greater numbers in Europe in a crisis of the first order, any large-scale mobilization would bring nuclear weapons into the picture to strike still a different kind of balance. Meanwhile Europe was secure against Communist probing adventures. While Western ground power thus permitted a firm diplomacy in Europe, the United States Army possessed a new mobility and, with sixteen divisions, a sufficient ready strength to intervene quickly in any trouble spot around the world. Operation Big Lift had just demonstrated the ability of the United States, unprecedented in military history, to airlift an entire division from one continent to another. American airlift capacity had risen seventy-five per cent since the beginning of 1961, and was scheduled to rise four hundred per cent by 1967. The strong and mobile United States Army was also increasingly versatile; with its Special Forces leading the way, it was confident of its capacity to fight not only limited wars of the Korean type but all sorts of unconventional wars as well.[2]

As always, Secretary McNamara kept at hand still more facts and statistics to support his optimistic conclusions. But the world of nuclear deterrence and brush-fire wars remains a far different world from that for which American experience before 1945 prepared the country and its Army, and the perplexities of military policy remained greater than the Defense Secretary's ebullient confidence sometimes implied. In 1963 he offered hopes about the unconventional war in Vietnam that the next few years certainly did not fulfill. When Vietnam betrayed his confidence about the armed forces' ready ability to cope with unconventional war, it also reintroduced for the Army persistent perplexities about manpower, the selective service system, and the reserves, as well as about the adjustment of weapons and tactics to the Communists' latest variations on the theme of brush-fire war.

The Army of the 1950's and 1960's has consisted of five major categories of forces: those concerned with continental defense and with training in the United States; those deployed overseas; the strategic reserve in the United States for the reinforcement of overseas areas; the reserve components, National Guard and Army Reserves; and military assistance detachments in allied and friendly nations.

On February 1, 1955, the Continental Army Command was created to direct the activities of the forces within the United States. It took the place of the Office of the Chief of Army Field Forces, the post-World War II zone of the interior ground command, and by 1956 it represented something of a return to the ideas embodied in GHQ on the eve of the global war. That is, it combined some of the features of the wartime Army Ground Forces with those of a theater command. Until 1956 it chiefly supervised training. After early 1956 it became responsible also for the continued improvement and development of the Army, coordinating the studies, experiments, and plans out of which new organization, weapons, and doctrine emerged. In addition, it commanded the six field armies within the continental United States and the Military District of Washington, through the field armies preparing for the ground defense of the United States and giving logistical support to the National Guard and Army Reserves.

The Continental Army Command delegated the Army's share in continental air defense to the Army Air Defense Command. Created in 1950, this organization was responsible directly to the chief of staff of the Army for its administrative and training activities, and for operations it formed a part of the interservice North American Air Defense Command. It included National Guard and Reserve units with air defense missions.

Until the growth of a third Army concentration in Vietnam in the middle 1960's, the principal Army forces overseas were the Seventh Army in Germany and the Eighth Army in Korea. The Seventh Army was consistently the heart of the ground forces of the North Atlantic alliance. Along with lesser units of the European Command, it comprised about one quarter of active Army forces during the early 1960's. The Eighth Army stood behind the cease-fire line in Korea as the principal guarantor of the truce there and of the free world's ability to confront land-based military challenges throughout the adjacent area. In the early 1960's it included two American divisions plus Korean troops.

Based in the United States were the Strategic Army Corps, the nucleus of a strategic reserve ready to move to trouble spots around the globe. In the 1960's there were two such corps, the III and the XVIII Airborne. They were joined with the operating squadrons of the Air Force's Tactical Air Command and with their supporting airlift to form the unified STRIKE Command, under an Army general with an Air Force lieutenant general as his deputy. The strategic reserve came to be regarded as including also designated high-priority National Guard and Reserve forces which might replenish it if its Regular Army units were committed. Its history is thus intertwined with that of the National Guard and the Army Reserve.[3]

The reserve components standing behind the Regular Army were reshaped by several laws of the Korean and immediate post-Korean periods. The Universal Military Training and Service Act of 1951 decreed that all male citizens between the ages of eighteen and a half and twenty-six who joined or were inducted into the armed forces also incurred an obligation to military reserve service. The Armed

Forces Reserve Act of 1952 established three categories to which obligated persons might be assigned: the Ready Reserve, the Standby Reserve, and the Retired Reserve. The Ready Reserve would comprise the units and the individuals with the requisite military occupation specialties to fill out the Army, National Guard, and Reserve forces called to active duty in a limited emergency or early in a general mobilization. The President was empowered to call up a million Ready Reservists in case of national emergency without further recourse to Congress. The Standby Reserve would consist of individuals having an active status in the Reserves but for various reasons not subject to an involuntary call to active duty except by action of Congress. The Retired Reserve would consist of individuals now retired but of course subject to Congressional call.[4]

After the Korean cease-fire, President Eisenhower recommended further assurances that the Army could count on a strong citizens' reserve. Congress produced the Reserve Forces Act of 1955, projecting an enlargement of the Ready Reserve to 2,900,000 men by 1970. Though this goal proved illusory, the act remains the foundation of reserve practices. To curb the recalling of combat veterans for second or third hitches, which had caused much resentment during the Korean War, it provided that the Ready Reserve should consist of persons who entered the active forces after the Korean cease-fire, except for veterans who might volunteer for Ready Reserve status. To stimulate reserve recruitment, men were given the options of fulfilling their military obligation with a six-year term, two years in the active Army and four in the Reserves, or with an eight-year term, only one-half year of which would be devoted to active-duty basic training, followed by seven and a half years in the Ready Reserve.[5]

As events turned out, these efforts to use the selective service system for leverage wherewith to fill the reserve components proved all too often merely to stock the Reserves with men of doubtful value and did not produce reserve components ready for call. President Eisenhower spent his final years in office calling for smaller, not larger, Reserve forces, for cutbacks not from any figure resembling the 1970 goal but from the 700,000 for whom Congress was actually appropriating funds. Reserve units harbored men without appropriate military occupation specialties and kept men despite poor attendance records. While the unit rosters looked reassuringly full, the country spent money—Eisenhower estimated over $80,000,000 a year—for excess reserve strength of little or no military value.[6]

McNamara soon offered a more penetrating critique. He found the whole reserve system lacking a satisfactory rationale. He found no reasoned justification for the size of the reserve components, either for their existing numbers or for the size to which Eisenhower would have cut them; both sets of numbers seemed merely fortuitous. He found no clear idea of what function the reserves were supposed to serve. When he took office, the strategic reserve composed of active ground forces consisted of six Army and two Marine divisions. Three of the Army divisions, however, were not combat-ready. Thus any emergency such as combat in Southeast Asia would quickly consume the active Army's strategic reserve. If the National Guard and Army Reserves were to be worth their expense, surely they should be available to replenish the strategic reserve in this kind of situation; to do so must logically be one of their major purposes. But the principal combat units of the National Guard and the Army Reserve, McNamara discovered, would require some four to nine months to reach combat readiness, and so they could not serve so obvious a major function.[7]

The Berlin crisis of 1961 soon illustrated this defect. In the summer of the first year of the Kennedy administration, the Soviet Union embarked upon a new round of diplomatic pressure and military threats to pry the Western powers out of the former German capital. Kennedy and McNamara wanted to reduce the necessity of relying on Dulles-style nuclear brinkmanship to counter this effort, and so they resolved to build up the Army's combat-ready conventional strength. On July 25 the President went before the television cameras to warn of an acute danger of war implicit in the Soviet pressure and, assuring that he was in earnest, to call for the mobilization of 150,000 reservists. In consequence, some 46,000 Ready Reservists were ordered to report for active duty in late September, and in October the call was extended to the 32nd Infantry Division (Wisconsin), the 49th Armored Division (Texas), and the 150th Armored Cavalry Regiment (West Virginia) as well as scores of smaller units of the National Guard. The immediate purpose was to permit replacement of the 4th Infantry and 2nd Armored Divisions in the strategic reserve should those formations be committed to Europe. Unfortunately, recent budgets had set a ceiling of about seventy per cent of war strength for the Guard units, and in general they were months away from combat readiness. Individual Ready Reservists were posted to them to complete their components, supposedly being chosen according to military occupation specialties; but even this operation turned out to be an affair of vast confusion, with the specialty indices proving considerably less than reliable. The whole was accompanied by the usual questions about the fairness of the selections for service, with Congress among the questioners.[8]

The administration and the Army were satisfied that the mobilization helped stabilize the Berlin crisis. But the incident also confirmed

McNamara's belief that the Army must have both a stronger active strategic reserve and National Guard and Army Reserve units really prepared for quick reinforcement of the active Army. He announced a plan that would cut the National Guard to 467,000 men and the Army Reserve to 375,000, the outer limits to which his studies indicated the reserve forces were in fact likely to be recruited. He would eliminate four National Guard and four Reserve divisions plus hundreds of smaller units, while thoroughly reorganizing what remained. The National Guard would consist of twenty-three combat divisions, seven brigades, and some 1,743 other units, the Army Reserve of six combat divisions, thirteen training divisions, four brigades, two maneuver area commands, and 2,155 other units. Six divisions would become high-priority units, to be maintained at seventy-five to eighty per cent of full war strength and with priorities for equipment and for specialists from the Ready Reserve reinforcement pool. The highest priority units were to be capable of deployment with the active Army in four weeks. Other units were to be developed into sufficient readiness to permit deployment within eight weeks, until two-thirds of the reserve personnel were brought into the high-priority categories. Under this system the Army could increase its strategic reserve by sixty per cent within eight weeks, and the United States would become capable, McNamara said, of fighting two fairly large limited wars simultaneously, or impressively augmenting the ground forces of Europe.

Despite opposition in Congress and the state houses over the loss of units, McNamara substantially completed this "realignment" in 1963. He went on also to establish stricter standards for reserve personnel, including maintenance of Army physical and mental qualifications, enforcement of attendance requirements, and insistence that ninety per cent of the personnel of every unit be qualified in their appropriate military occupation specialties.[9]

Yet the restless Defense Secretary continued to regard the reserve components with disquietude. Addicted to cost accounting procedures and to insistence upon efficiency, he found much that was irrational in the parallel structures of National Guards and Army Reserves, two distinct reserve components requiring two administrative structures but overlapping in functions. Historically, the Army Reserves were a product of the Army's distrust of state influence in the National Guard, the fruition of the old Uptonian campaign for a completely federal Army reserve. But in the post-World War II era, was not federal control of the National Guard sufficient to render outmoded the old Army fears of dual federal and state control? McNamara thought so, and in 1964 he announced his intention of carrying out another realignment of the reserve components which would eliminate still more Army Reserve units and place all the remaining ones in the National Guard, thus in effect consolidating the two types of reserves into one. President Lyndon B. Johnson accepted the plan and incorporated it into his annual defense message to Congress at the beginning of 1965. He promised a saving of $150 million a year through the elimination of units for which there was no military need, and a still further advance in the efficiency of the consolidated National Guard.

By now communities across the country had acquired economic and political stakes in Army Reserve units akin to those that had always made the National Guard so politically sensitive an organization, and congressmen raised an outcry to dwarf the considerable one that had greeted the realignment of 1963. The protest was sufficient to obstruct the implementation of McNamara's plan. Whatever the immediate fate of the proposals, however, the eventual consolidation of the reserve components into a single structure would seem assured. The arguments for a separate Army Reserve paralleling the National Guard were always tenuous; when several decades of experience since World War II have shown the Guard at least as efficient and responsive as the Army Reserves, those arguments are hard to find.[10]

Yet deeply rooted in the country's history as is a system of citizen reserves, the impediments to its military efficiency seem to keep its relationships with the Army constantly troubled ones. After all McNamara's efforts to heighten the readiness of the National Guard and the Army Reserves, and evidence of their considerable success, when an apparently appropriate hour struck, the Secretary of Defense hesitated to call upon them. By the middle 1960's the American military involvement in Vietnam made far greater demands upon the Army's strategic reserve than the Berlin crisis of 1961 had done, the very sorts of demands for which McNamara's improvements in the readiness of Guards and Reserves would seem to have been designed. With the arrival of elements of the 4th Infantry Division in Vietnam in the summer of 1966, all or substantial parts of five Army and two Marine divisions were there. American troop strength in the country reached 320,000 men and was scheduled to advance beyond 400,000. Simultaneously the Army maintained the equivalent of six divisions in Germany and two in Korea. The strategic reserve of the active Army was ground exceedingly thin. McNamara had described the purpose of the reserve components as to "Provide the Active Army with the quick reinforcement it needs to meet sudden crises while retaining the present capability to support a general mobilization";[11] but the war in Vietnam grew larger and the reserves were not called.

The danger did not lie simply in depleting the active Army's strategic reserve. To make the Regular Army as much as possible a fighting army, the Regulars by now had been designed to look to the reserve components for logistical and training support in any operations as large as those in Vietnam. The Regular Army was not organized to fight a war on the scale of Vietnam without mobilization of some reserve units and specialists. By 1966, other Regular Army units had been virtually stripped of logistical support and especially military construction units for Vietnam. The United States hired large numbers of Vietnamese, and became commensurately dependent on them, to build and maintain harbors, airports, warehouses, barracks, roads, and pipelines. Nevertheless, the provision of logistical support lagged behind the requirements of the fighting forces. Meanwhile, Army divisions remaining in the United States became clogged with trainees, and a backlog developed of more than 100,000 men enlisted in the reserves but unable to be assigned to training centers, because the Army had swelled beyond its capacity to train recruits without the federalization of reserve divisions for training purposes.[12]

When reserve units were mobilized for the Berlin crisis, Secretary McNamara had not been impressed by them. Despite his efforts to improve them, he may still have harbored doubts. The 1961 mobilization, furthermore, had provoked discontent not only among the reservists called but extensively throughout their states and among their congressmen. The Secretary now labored under a President intent upon preserving a consensus of popular support for his administration and the Vietnam war. For whatever reasons, these and possible others, the reserves remained unmobilized, and the Vietnam War strained the Regular Army as the architects of the Army and its citizen reserves had not intended.

While the reserves remained uncalled, the selective service system provided replacements for the active Army. As long as possible, the Army fought the Vietnam War mainly with enlistees, not draftees, again stripping units in noncombat zones around the globe to find men for the fight. But by 1966 it was no longer enough to send draftees to fill the units outside the combat area; increasingly they had to go to Vietnam as well. They did so, paradoxically, while other young men long since trained and shifted into reserve components remained safe at home. As during the Korean War, so now a host of inequities in the selective service system became apparent and were accentuated.

Selective service came under its sharpest attack since World War II. Opponents of the Vietnam War seized upon its discrepancies as a convenient bludgeon with which to thump the war, the Army, and the government. Again as in Korea, all young men were theoretically liable for service but fewer than half were called, and the selections of the system seemed full of injustices. Again universal military training was sometimes suggested to eliminate the injustices, but universal service would have given the Army more men than it knew how to use. Others suggested a lottery as somehow mysteriously fairer than human choice as a means of determining who should bear arms. Ever since Korea, there had been a current of interest, in the Army and outside, in the idea of making enlistment in the Regular Army attractive enough, in pay and perquisites, that the Regulars alone could fight most of the country's limited wars, as they had fought most of the Indian wars of the past. The advantages in extending the Army's capacity to fight small wars while minimizing public outcry were obvious. In 1962 an Assistant Secretary of Defense spoke publicly and wistfully about enhancing the prestige of military service, so "we could probably throw away the draft in short order and build the kind of volunteer-professional force we seek."[13] The attempt was probably worth making; but selective service could hardly be abandoned until success was assured, and success did not really seem likely.

When the Army went into new brush-fire wars in the 1960's, it did so much better prepared in training, weapons, and doctrine as well as in numbers of combat-ready divisions than it had been when the Communists invaded South Korea. Experience in Korea of course helped make it so, and even at the height of the "massive retaliation" period, the memory of Korea worked against utter neglect of the ground Army. It is true that during the Dulles era the Army for a time had to fend off obscurity by interesting itself especially in ground-to-air missiles, the replacements for antiaircraft artillery in defending against a potential enemy's nuclear delivery systems; and when intercontinental ballistic missiles became an imminent possibility, the Army often expressed enthusiasm for developing antimissile missiles, thus giving itself a prominent national security role. But during the 1950's one aspect of the nuclear infatuation itself restored the Army's prominence in national security policy.

This was the introduction of tactical nuclear weapons. By the early 1950's, nuclear technology had created warheads sufficiently small and of sufficiently limited radioactive fallout that it became possible to contemplate their employment as tactical weapons on the battlefield. The United States developed these small nuclear packages before the Russians, and for a time some Americans hoped that here was a new American nuclear monopoly: the Russians might have heavy nuclear bombs, but they did not have nuclear weapons fit for use by ground forces. When this delusion quickly passed, upon the Russians' prompt development of their own nuclear weapons for land war, there still remained the hope that tactical nuclear weapons might aid the defense much more than an attacking army, and that consequently they would offset the Communists' numerical strength and give Western ground forces a new lease on life, especially in Europe.

Thus the 1950's witnessed a remarkable enthusiasm for the idea of tactical nuclear war, and the Army naturally seized upon an enthusiasm that brought it back into the mainstream of strategic planning. The Army itself and national security agencies and students of all kinds turned to exploring the probable nature of tactical nuclear war. The California Institute of Technology received a contract for Project Vista, a study of tactical nuclear weapons, and reported that the battle could now be brought back to the battlefield. Henry A. Kissinger's *Nuclear Weapons and Foreign Policy*, one of the decade's most widely read books on national security issues, dealt largely with the prospects for tactical nuclear war.[14]

The Army's own policy research organs were stimulated. In 1948 the Air Force had sponsored the Rand Corporation as an autonomous but subsidized nonprofit organization to conduct informed study and thought about national security questions. The Army followed suit the same year by establishing the Operations Research Office in conjunction with the Johns Hopkins University. The ORO dealt not only with the Army's peculiar concerns but with the largest national security issues, including the implications of the economic and political as well as military systems of the rival power blocs. But the Army did determine the general course of ORO work—enough to cause growing dissatisfaction among its civilian leaders—and thus the new possibilities for ground warfare became a special object of its interests.[15]

Studies of tactical nuclear war tended to enhance the sophistication of the Army's thought about tactical problems in general, since they had to pay some attention to all the latest weaponry of ground warfare, conventional as well as nuclear. They seem to have encouraged weapons research and development in general, too. Certainly there was a mutually stimulating effect between the development of tactical nuclear weapons and consideration of how to use them. The atomic cannon that President Eisenhower sent to Korea to pressure the Chinese into accepting a cease-fire was a cumbersome 280-mm artillery piece of limited mobility. It was soon joined by much more flexible carriers of nuclear warheads, a family of missiles that included Honest John and its successor Little John, fired from lightweight launching equipment that could be carried by helicopters and having a range of fifteen miles; and the Corporal and its successor the Sergeant, ballistic guided missiles with a range of seventy-five miles. Developed somewhat later were the Pershing, a solid-fuel missile with a range of four hundred miles; a nuclear shell for 8-inch guns; and Davy Crockett, a nuclear-armed mortar that could be carried and operated by two or three men. Tactical nuclear weapons could carry conventional warheads and thus generally enhance the Army's firepower in conventional as well as nuclear war; while more prosaic weapons such as rifles and tanks also had to undergo continued rapid improvement to prepare them for the possibilities of the nuclear battlefield.

By 1956 interest in nuclear war on the ground had grown strong enough to cause fundamental changes in the organization of the infantry division, to adjust to the presumed requirements of nuclear tactics. During that year and the next, all Regular Army infantry and airborne divisions became "pentomic," an awkward designation that was supposed to indicate the supersession of the triangular division by a five-sided formation for atomic war. The three regiments of the triangular division gave way to five "battle groups." With five basic constituent units, the division could assume a pentagonal formation and thus face in all directions at once, since it was assumed that tactical nuclear weapons would be so destructive that divisions would often be isolated and have to fight much like wagon trains in the defensive circles of the Indian wars. Nuclear war was believed likely to create so chaotic a battlefield situation that its tactical fluidity was described also by analogy with the tactics of ships at sea, with divisions or their battle groups playing the parts of the ships.

The battle group was smaller than a regiment but larger than a battalion. It consisted of four rifle companies and one mortar company in the infantry division, or five rifle companies in the airborne division. Because of the need both for dispersing under atomic attack and alternately concentrating several divisions when facing the massed numbers of the enemy, the pentomic division would depend upon reserve pools for most of its supporting units. Thus when the regiment disappeared from the division T/O&E, the regimental tank companies were withdrawn from the division altogether. The infantry division did retain a divisional armored battalion, an armored cavalry squadron, a 105-mm howitzer battalion of five firing batteries, and a composite artillery battalion of gun and missile batteries capable of firing atomic weapons. But with the emphasis on pooling of supporting units, the numerical strength of the division fell to 13,748 officers and men, including a higher proportion of combat infantry than in the Korean War division.[16]

All this interest in tactical nuclear weapons assured the Army's vitality and prestige during the otherwise inauspicious middle and late 1950's. But the flurry of enthusiasm proved short-lived. Not only did tactical nuclear weapons fail to remain an American monopoly for more than an instant, but it soon became highly doubtful even that they would assist a defending more than an attacking army. In fact, "doubtful" described almost everything about their employment. To commence tactical nuclear war would be to risk unfathomed perils, and consequently other restraints in addition to moral ones might prevent the United States from being the first power to use them. Furthermore, it seemed highly questionable whether once a war crossed the nuclear threshold the employment of nuclear weapons could be restrained from escalating into full-scale nuclear war. Especially did exchanges of missiles seem likely to escalate, as missiles of more and more weight and range would probably rise into the nuclear fray. If Pershings bombarded an enemy's marshalling yards from four hundred miles away, could the enemy be persuaded there was a difference in kind between this sort of attack and assault by intermediate range ballistic missiles such as the Jupiter and Thor? Some of the early writers to have seen positive implications in tactical nuclear war, including Henry A. Kissinger, avowed second thoughts based on such considerations. Senator John F. Kennedy said: "Inevitably, the use of small nuclear armaments will lead to larger and larger nuclear armaments on both sides, until the world-wide holocaust has begun."[17]

After Kennedy became President, his Secretary of Defense was not quite so categoric in his opposition to tactical nuclear weapons, but McNamara obviously preferred to escape reliance on them as much as possible. He would not rule out their use, especially in the defense of Europe. He perceived that the United States might in some situation find it advisable to make controlled and limited use of them to affirm its determination and to warn an adversary not to push too hard. But it was to minimize reliance on tactical as well as strategic nuclear weapons that McNamara turned to building up the conventional forces and their reserves.

The Army and its capacity for conventional war were the chief beneficiaries, so the passing of the tactical nuclear weapons enthusiasm did not injure but rather enhanced the Army's renewed importance in American defense planning. In 1961 McNamara called for an increase of the Army from some 875,000 to about a million men, with a more than proportionate increase in combat-ready divisions. He mapped the course that soon increased the combat-ready divisions from eleven to sixteen, with six high-priority reserve divisions behind them. He sought 129 of the most modern troop- and equipment-carrying aircraft as a first step toward an eventual four hundred per cent increase in airlift capacity. He went on to stockpile equipment and supplies for two additional divisions in Europe, to await the divisions should they be airlifted there. He similarly "prepositioned" equipment in the Far East and aboard "floating depot" ships. By 1963 he had improved Army procurement sufficiently to set about stockpiling enough matériel to permit the sixteen active Army and six high-priority reserve divisions to fight for an indefinite time from the stockpiles, so that in a large-scale emergency the Army's combat capacity would remain high until full war production could be expected to be well under way.

During the 1950's the Defense Department and Congress had sometimes opposed this sort of strengthening of the Army on the ground that Russia's conventional strength was so overwhelming that whether the United States Army counted eleven or sixteen divisions made little difference. The Soviet army was customarily depicted as mustering 150 divisions. But to justify his quest for additional conventional power, McNamara also sponsored a new study of Soviet ground strength. The Soviet army numbered about 2,200,000 men, and McNamara found it difficult to believe that the Russians could squeeze 150 divisions out of those numbers when a million Americans yielded only sixteen divisions. American intelligence reexamined the Soviet order of battle, the composition of Soviet divisions, and Soviet logistical problems. The conclusion was that given the length of the Soviet supply line to the Iron Curtain in Germany, the complexity of modern logistical support, and the need for the Soviets to divert some of their troops to their Asian frontiers and on internal security missions, the Soviet army could not and did not maintain anything like the overwhelming superiority in Europe that the 150-division shibboleth suggested. They might indeed be able to throw about sixty divisions against western Europe, but division for division these units were not equal to their Western counterparts. The strength of the Soviets and their East European allies certainly was not sufficiently superior to guarantee their success if they attacked well-equipped and determined adversaries in Europe. Improving the Army's capacity for conventional war was surely not an exercise in futility.[18]

Thus the Army shifted away from plans that called for the automatic use of nuclear weapons against an attack in Europe. The details of the Army's subsequent thinking about the balance between nuclear and conventional weapons and tactics are not clear, in part because it was characteristic of McNamara to distrust any dogma and to discourage predictions about the shape some unspecified future crisis might take. Each emergency should be met on its own terms, he believed, and they could not well be foreseen in detail.

What he desired was sufficient military strength on every level so that the United States could respond to any emergency with the highest appropriate response but without having to fly to nuclear arms when they were not appropriate.

Nevertheless, one consequence of the passing of the nuclear enthusiasm was another reorganization of the Army's divisions. Field maneuvers showed the pentomic division better suited to standing on the defensive than to generating power in the attack. Especially did it seem ill-designed for an aggressive role, including an aggressive defensive, in a nonnuclear war. The battle groups were not big enough for sustained offensive power. Furthermore, the wide variety of missions the Army might be obliged to perform along the whole spectrum of nuclear and nonnuclear wars suggested that the division ought to be a more flexible and adaptable instrument. The outcome of these considerations was the "Reorganization Objectives Army Division," thence, the "ROAD division."

To a degree the Army returned to the triangular pattern that had served it well in World War II and Korea. The ROAD division consisted of three brigades plus a headquarters and organic and assigned supporting units. The brigades, however, were not brigades in the sense that that term had had in the old square division, but in the sense employed in World War II supporting-arms brigades. They were flexible formations, headquarters adapted to commanding as many battalions as any situation might require, in any mixture of infantry, mechanized, armored, and airborne battalions plus companies or platoons of supporting arms and services. The ROAD division could readily mix nuclear and conventional arms, if required to do so. Armored as well as infantry and airborne divisions could readily fit the new form, since indeed the flexibility of the new brigades was modeled on the combat commands which had characterized armored divisions since World War II. Though the possibility of a great variety of strengths was the essence of the new division, usually a division again numbered about fifteen thousand men, heavier than the pentomic division. In summary, the ROAD division was in basic structure a triangular division. But the division itself was no longer a T/O&E unit; its headquarters were the combat commands for flexible task forces.

The division headquarters included two assistant division commanders with the rank of brigadier general, one to direct the activities of the maneuver elements and one to direct logistical support activities. In addition to the headquarters and headquarters company, the division base comprised: (1) an armored cavalry squadron of three armored cavalry troops equipped with tanks, armored personnel carriers, and self-propelled mortars, plus an air cavalry troop using armed troop-carrying helicopters; (2) a signal battalion of three companies equipped with telephones, teletypes, and long-range radios; (3) an engineer battalion of five companies, one of them a bridge company; (4) an aviation battalion with a headquarters company, an aviation company (general support) with airplanes and helicopters for reconnaissance and liaison, and an airmobile company of three airlift platoons of eight troop-carrying aircraft each, plus a service platoon; (5) a military police company; (6) a division support command which brought all technical and supply elements into a composite unit organized not by separate technical branches but along functional lines. The organic division artillery consisted of three battalions of 105-mm (or heavier) howitzers, eighteen to the battalion; a composite battalion of 155-mm and 8-inch howitzers; and a missile battalion. Finally, the division had its three brigade headquarters, ready to absorb varying numbers and types of battalions.

The infantry battalion consisted of three rifle companies (180 officers and men each) and a headquarters company (290). The latter included a reconnaissance platoon, a 4.2-inch mortar platoon, and an antitank platoon. The rifle company consisted of a headquarters platoon of twelve officers and men, three rifle platoons of forty-four each, and a weapons platoon of thirty-six. Each rifle platoon had a headquarters of three, three rifle squads of ten men each, and a weapons squad of eleven men. The rifle squad was divided into two five-man fire teams, each team having one automatic rifle. The other eight men carried six rifles and two grenade launchers. The weapons squad had two light machine guns and two 90-mm recoilless rifles; four of its men, primarily assigned to these weapons, also carried pistols, and the rest had rifles. Tactical doctrine still stressed the value of covering fire for advances in open ground, and the organization of the rifle squad permitted leapfrog movements by the fire teams. The infantry also learned, however, to advance by Patton's marching fire tactics.

A mechanized battalion was an infantry battalion equipped with armored personnel carriers as organic transportation. An airborne battalion as usual had lighter and fewer vehicles than a standard infantry battalion. An armored battalion included reconnaissance and self-propelled mortar platoons plus three tank companies of eighteen tanks each. In the middle 1960's the tanks were mainly fifty-one-ton M-60's firing 105-mm guns, heavy tanks of the sort that had been so conspicuously lacking in World War II.

For budgetary and planning purposes, a ROAD infantry division usually included eight infantry and two armored battalions; an armored division, six armored and five mechanized battalions; an airborne division, nine airborne infantry battalions plus an airborne gun battalion. There were also mechanized divisions, usually of seven mechanized and three armored battalions.[19]

The reemphasis on conventional strength was designed partly to permit the defense of Europe in some measure without resort to nuclear arms, if only to postpone the day when nuclear arms might be fired and thus to buy time for the settlement of a crisis. The reemphasis was based also, however, on the Kennedy administration's belief that the most likely form of combat in which the Army might be engaged was a local, limited war at least roughly on the Korean model. The Army's strategic reserve and airlift capacity were especially suitable for such wars.

During the 1950's, however, it had become evident that the Communists, having been once burned in Korea, were twice shy about open aggression of the kind they had practiced there. Their violent means of extending their power were now more likely to be various mixtures of subversion and guerrilla war, often just below or just above the threshold of what Westerners were accustomed to recognize as war, and therefore creating puzzles for the United States about how to respond in order to check Communism without escalating borderline situations into open war and thereby handing the Communists a propaganda advantage as well as suffering other penalties. Premier Khrushchev made this tendency of Communist policy an avowed one on January 6, 1961, just before the Kennedy administration took office, when he stated that Communists were opposed to both world wars and local wars but that they fully and unreservedly supported "wars of national liberation." By the 1960's, furthermore, China was the more aggressive of the major Communist powers, and wars of national liberation, mixing subversion and guerrilla tactics, held a special historic appeal for Chinese Communism and Mao Tse-tung. Thus President Kennedy, Secretary Mc-Namara, and the Army turned their attention not only to nuclear and "conventional" war but also to the "unconventional" war of subversion and guerrillas.[20]

Unconventional war had become prominent especially in Southeast Asia, in the Philippines, Malaya, and Indochina, and when the Kennedy administration took office it was smoldering in Laos and South Vietnam. When the United States felt obliged to assist a state threatened by Communist subversion and guerrillas, Kennedy and McNamara believed, it would not be wise to respond by dispatching large numbers of American troops. The alien presence of those troops might well merely aggravate the political discontent and economic dislocations which nourished subversion. Furthermore, a principal element of the strength of subversives and guerrillas was their ability to melt into the local population, and Americans would not be well equipped to counter that tactic in exotic lands. The Kennedy administration therefore concluded that the best service the United States could give to friendly governments beset by subversion and guerrilla war was to aid them with supplies and with advice and training in the techniques of counterinsurgency struggle. "We recognize the inadequacy of their forces to cope with outright invasion," McNamara said of the countries on the fringe of the Communist empire, "yet with our assistance we count on their courage and ability to deal with large-scale guerrilla warfare."[21]

The Army entered this picture with its Special Forces. This organization had originated during the 1950's, when a faculty concerned with special war had moved out of the Army General School at Fort Riley in 1952 to become part of the Psychological Warfare Center at Fort Bragg, and then had grown into the Special Warfare School, officially established on May 1, 1957. At the beginning of 1961 the Special Forces who had been or were being instructed at the school numbered slightly under a thousand men, and their principal concern was preparing for activity behind enemy lines amidst the chaos of a nuclear war.

In the Army lexicon of the 1960's, "special war" encompasses psychological warfare, counterinsurgency operations, and unconventional warfare, the latter of which includes subversion, escape and evasion, and guerrilla warfare. Confronted with the problems of Laos and Vietnam, President Kennedy and Secretary McNamara soon decided that the Special Forces should concern themselves with the whole gamut of these types of war, and especially with guerrilla operations of the sort prevalent in Southeast Asia. They ordered the Special Warfare School to expand its curriculum accordingly. In the first twenty-one months of the administration, they increased the size of the Special Forces by 150 per cent, the beginning of an almost geometric progression in the following few years. Kennedy especially became fascinated by guerrilla war. Over Army opposition based on a long-standing suspicion of elite forces within yet set apart from the Army, he authorized the Special Forces to wear the green beret to symbolize that they were also special in status.

The Special Forces were now to perfect the techniques of unconventional warfare and then to impart those techniques to the armies and internal security agencies of countries threatened by subversion and guerrillas, both by training foreign students at the Special Warfare School and by dispatching Special Forces groups to threatened areas. The men in the green berets would fight alongside the soldiers of the countries to which they were assigned, but they would mainly be advisers and would not constitute an American military presence large enough to stir up undue animosity. The green berets were all volunteers for their mission—doubly so, since parachute operations loomed large in their doctrine, and they volunteered first for airborne assignment, then for the Special Forces. They received intensive training in guerrilla-type operations, intelligence, weapons, engineering, demolition, and communications. They trained in high-altitude free-fall parachute jumps, a favored means of entering an area of operations, in SCUBA diving, and in hand-to-hand combat. They became specialists in medical aid, including sanitation and preventive medicine. They were chosen for personal qualities that ought to inspire confidence in the foreign soldiers and peoples among whom they would work, and they were trained in order to accentuate those qualities. All of them became language specialists, and all learned to communicate their knowledge to persons with little or no command of English and little or no military background.

In addition to the Special Warfare Center at Fort Bragg, Special Forces centers were established in Okinawa, Vietnam, Panama, and Germany. By 1966 the Special Forces comprised some 10,500 men in seven Special Forces groups around the world. By that time the largest and most prominent of them had long been the Fifth Group in Vietnam. Unhappily, in that country the Kennedy-McNamara theory of counting on local "courage and ability to deal with large-scale guerrilla warfare," merely assisted by the United States, failed to work.[22]

By the beginning of 1965 the South Vietnamese government came perilously close to losing its war against the Viet Cong guerrillas. The Johnson administration reacted by accelerating the buildup of American troops which reached 320,000 by the autumn of 1966. The buildup was commenced with misgivings; all the considerations which had caused Kennedy and McNamara to prefer native forces against "wars of national liberation" still applied, and the more so because Vietnam was haunted by remembrance of the French army's defeat there a decade before.

To some extent the Army hoped to avoid repetition of France's disasters by extending as many as possible of the skills of the Special Forces to all its troops in Vietnam. The Special Forces, who in John Kennedy's lifetime had pushed their elite status almost to autonomy —sometimes serving under CIA rather than Army directives—were brought back under normal Army command, and the Fifth Special Forces became an integral part of the larger Army commitment in Vietnam. The conventional divisions sent to Vietnam set up their own intensive training programs in the peculiarities of Vietnamese combat, such as the "ambush academy" of the 25th Division.[23]

More important, having decided that a large buildup was necessary, the Johnson administration and the Army hoped to make a virtue of necessity and overwhelm the Viet Cong by sheer weight of numbers and firepower. Specifically, they hoped to succeed where the French had failed by drawing upon the immense logistical apparatus of the American Army for superior intelligence, superior mobility, and tremendously superior firepower. These three qualities were to make the weight of the American Army tell against the guerrillas despite their light-footed agility. By the summer of 1966 they were doing so.

This was possible partly because the guerrillas were not always so agile as they seemed. Like the Chinese in Korea, the Viet Cong and their North Vietnamese supporters proved to be somewhat mechanical and repetitive in their tactics. To combat the large conventional forces of the Americans, their preferred method was to use their knowledge and control of much of the countryside to prepare elaborate ambushes. They might consume a month in painstaking preparation of a trap, massing ammunition and supplies and digging intricate networks of dugouts and underground connecting passages. Then finally they would maneuver to provoke their opponents into the trap.

The Army in turn came to rely upon painstaking intelligence surveys to discover such traps in the making. The Americans used Vietnamese informers for this purpose, but they relied heavily and characteristically also on methodical aerial and ground reconnaissance using the most modern electronic detection devices. When they discovered a trap in the making, they either forestalled the enemy with a spoiling attack, or they waited to allow him to draw them into the trap, upon which they would throw enough force against him to turn the tables. Especially the latter technique required the utmost mobility and firepower. For mobility, the helicopter came into its own in Vietnam as a heavy-duty troop carrier, joining with airplanes and going where airplanes could not go to permit concentrating troops with a rapidity far beyond the enemy's ability to match. A new kind of division appeared, the 1st Cavalry (Air Mobile) Division, equipped with a full complement of transport for movement by air and expressly outfitted to be "sky cavalry." But so much did other divisions also become "air mobile" that the new 1st Cavalry seemed likely to follow the course of the motorized divisions of the early days of World War II; it would simply hasten the process by which all divisions geared themselves for rapid movement.

It was a historic axiom of guerrilla warfare that if during a guerrilla attack, the enemy found time to reload his weapons, the attack had failed and should be abandoned.[24] The American Army in

Vietnam sought to nullify this old rule by maintaining in instant readiness reserves of firepower so great that reloading in the guerrillas' presence would not be required.

Not surprisingly, the weapons developed and issued during the interval since Korea sometimes fell short of expectations in Vietnam. Sometimes, too, Vietnam raised fundamental questions about the kind of firepower most appropriate for the foot soldier in modern war. The standard infantry rifle was no longer the M-1 but the M-14. This weapon fired a 7.62-mm cartridge, which the NATO powers had adopted as standard for their light weapons so that ammunition would be interchangeable. Its characteristics represented a compromise between the old American Army tradition of single-shot marksmanship, firing a heavy slug accurately over long distances, and a newer tendency toward light rapid-fire weapons firing bursts of smaller rounds at short range. The M-14 featured both accuracy at long range and a switch to convert it quickly into an automatic-fire rifle. But compromises are often less than satisfactory, and this one proved to have produced a weapon that performed erratically and was difficult to handle as an automatic rifle. Furthermore, Vietnam did not afford many opportunities for careful aiming at long distances.

Some troops there received a different rifle, the M-16, a much lighter .223-caliber automatic rifle that with 120 rounds of ammunition weighed no more than the M-14 empty. The M-16 sprayed volleys of small, high-velocity, steel-jacketed bullets so shaped that on impact they would spin end over end to increase the damage they inflicted. Its lightness and its qualities as a rapid-fire weapon made it so much more satisfactory than the M-14 in Vietnam that the Army decided to issue it to all combat units there. Its success also complicated the Army's thinking about rifles for the future and clouded the NATO decision for 7.62-mm weapons. Significantly, the Army meanwhile shifted its rifle training from the historic emphasis on firing at fixed distant bull's-eyes, to firing at pop-up targets at short range.[25]

Whichever rifle was used, however, the varied arsenal of American ground and tactical air weapons afforded ample firepower to outshoot the enemy in Vietnam. The American intelligence services seemed adequate, and mobility and firepower so indisputably superior, that the American buildup soon appeared safe against a recurrence of the French army's downfall. In the middle 1960's the most satisfactory way of dealing with wars of national liberation remained a reliance upon indigenous troops, merely assisted by Special Forces and other American aid. But where indigenous forces did not suffice, the Army believed it had disproved the Communists' theories about the vulnerability of large conventional armies to guerrilla warfare. Maoist theory expected Communist guerrilla tactics to wear down conventional adversaries until at last the Communists themselves could shift to open war against an already emasculated foe. The Army believed it had demonstrated in Vietnam that, instead, a conventional Army properly alert and mobile could exploit its superiority in armaments to wear down a guerrilla adversary, forcing him either to come into open battle prematurely and thus play his enemy's game, or eventually to fade away. With due allowance for a thousand changes in war, the Army's old Indian campaigns had led to similar conclusions.

By 1966, then, the Army seemed immune to military defeat in Vietnam. Whether it could one day pacify the country was more questionable. It hoped to do so by combining retribution against the Viet Cong in the manner just described with redevelopment of a secure and viable society and economy in the manner of Ramón Magsaysay's successful campaign against the Huk guerrillas of the Philippines. While the Army could contribute to redevelopment, however, most of that work would have to be done by other American agencies and the Vietnamese. Whether American patience would suffice to see the job through was one aspect of what was questionable. Though American opinion understood limited war better than in 1950–53, it did not accept such war easily; and altogether the Vietnamese conflict raised political issues that appeared infinitely more complex and disturbing than those of Korea. The outcome of the Army's effort would finally turn on the resolution of those largely nonmilitary issues.

In 1965 and 1966 General William C. Westmoreland commanded the American forces in Vietnam, subordinate to the joint Southwest Pacific Command of Admiral Ulysses Grant Sharp. Like Korea, Vietnam required an intimate cooperation among the Army and supporting Air Force and Navy elements, and like Korea it tested the Defense Department's arrangements for interservice command. Various questions could be and were raised about the Vietnam command system. A very important one concerned the absence of a supreme allied commander, without whom the South Vietnamese forces did not always cooperate with the Americans as closely as they might have. In another important respect, however, the American command system was considerably stronger than it had been in Korea: the Southwest Pacific Command was under the firm and direct control of the Secretary of Defense; no Army, Navy, or Air Force headquarters interposed to impair its qualities as a joint, interservice, functional command. These arrangements implied for the

Army and the other individual services a future much different from their past.

The command difficulties of the Korean War had prompted a series of studies and reports, notably those of the committee headed by Nelson Rockefeller in 1953, which generally proposed to strengthen the authority of the Secretary of Defense over both the individual services and the joint commands. President Eisenhower first moved cautiously in that direction with his Reorganization Plan No. 6, submitted to Congress at the end of April, 1953. Congress not acting to the contrary, the President reduced the secretaries of the individual military departments to the status of "operating managers" for the Secretary of Defense. For joint commands, the Joint Chiefs would no longer be the authority to designate one of their number as executive agent to act for them in supervising a joint command. Instead, the Secretary of Defense would name the service chief who was to be executive agent, and the chain of command would then run from the President through the Secretary of Defense, and from the Secretary of Defense to the appropriate service department. The Secretary thus gained operational power at the expense of the Joint Chiefs. There remained, however, the cumbersome interposition of one of the service departments between the supreme military authority and the joint commands.[26]

The next and more decisive effort to improve defense organization came in late 1957, occasioned by the Russians' orbiting of the first earth satellite. President Eisenhower now asserted that the links in the chain of command to the overseas theaters were excessively numerous, and that the armed forces must become more genuinely unified in those theater commands that made up "the cutting edge of our military machine." He proposed that authority should flow directly from the President through the Secretary of Defense to the joint commands. The secretaries of the military departments and the individual chiefs of staff should disappear from the chain of operational command. With the Secretary of Defense directly responsible for the joint commands, however, the Joint Chiefs should act as his military staff. Their advice and assistance to the Secretary of Defense should become the primary duties of the Joint Chiefs. Major portions of their responsibilities for the individual services should be delegated to their vice chiefs of staff. Meanwhile the moribund Key West agreements on division of functions among the services should be pushed aside, and the Secretary of Defense should be empowered to transfer, reassign, abolish, or consolidate functions within his department.[27]

Congress watered down these proposals. Fearful of the creation of a single armed service, it expressly reaffirmed its intent to retain the three separate services. Thus it also diluted the President's plan to permit reassignment of service functions. It merely empowered the President, in a national emergency, to transfer, reassign, or consolidate service functions, but not to abolish any function assigned by law to one of the armed forces. Any transfer would remain in effect only until the end of the emergency that had permitted it.

Nevertheless, Congress did acquiesce in the President's proposal that the Secretary of Defense should direct the joint commands, with no other agency intervening, and with the Joint Chiefs as his staff for the purpose. To ensure the command authority of the Secretary of Defense, Congress abolished the command status that the chief of naval operations and the chief of staff of the Air Force had possessed by statute. Thanks to the legacy of Elihu Root, the chief of staff of the Army had never held such statutory command authority. Henceforth all the individual service chiefs could be bypassed while members of their services fell under the direction of unified theater commanders responsible to the Secretary of Defense. Here was a far greater shift of power than had occurred in any previous readjustment within the Defense Department.[28]

Service units not assigned to unified commands, however, would remain subject to the customary authority of their own military department and chief of staff. The Department of the Army through the Secretary of the Army and the Army chief of staff would continue to recruit, train, and support Army troops. Within a unified command, the Department of the Army would continue to be responsible for the administration of Army forces. Logistical support to unified commands would be delegated by the Secretary of Defense to one or more of the services. On the other hand, interservice procurement of common supply items was already established in the Defense Department and was extended by Secretary McNamara, and weapons development became increasingly a responsibility of the Defense Department.[29]

Under the new arrangements the Army and the other services functioned in the defense establishment in a way not dissimilar to the activities of the Army Ground Forces and Army Service Forces in the Army of World War II. As AGF and ASF had raised, trained, administered, and equipped troops which they then turned over to the theater commands, AGF and ASF acting as huge procurement agencies and supply depots for those commands, so now the Army itself, along with the Navy and Air Force, would train, administer, and equip formations to be turned over to the unified commands, the Army itself becoming a huge procurement agency and supply depot for the unified commands. Henceforth, the mission of the Army is to develop land forces for sustained combat, while the unified commands under the Secretary of Defense direct and control operations.

As part of the McNamara reforms, the Army itself reorganized in 1962 and 1963, the better to carry out its newly defined mission. Since 1946, the logistical and research and development activities so prominent in that mission had again spread out among a congeries of technical services. McNamara preferred a return to consolidated functional commands resembling the AGF and ASF of World War II. So beside the Continental Army Command, which retained control over training, the Army erected two other major functional commands, the Army Matériel Command and the Combat Developments Command. The first of these was to design, improve, procure, and supply weapons and equipment. Five subordinate field commands of the Army Matériel Command developed and procured various specialties: the Missile Command, the Munitions Command, the Weapons Command, the Mobility Command, and the Electronics Command. Another field command, the Test and Evaluation Command, was responsible for final acceptance and for maintaining uniform standards. A final field command, the Supply and Maintenance Command, received, stored, and shipped weapons and equipment.

Meanwhile the Combat Developments Command was to plan the evolution of the Army, its tactics, organization, and doctrine. Its subordinate headquarters included the Combined Arms Group, concerned with the main combat arms of the field army; the Combat Service and Support Group, concerned with logistical support of combat armies; the Special Doctrine and Equipment Group, concerned with special war and tropical and Arctic warfare; the Office of Special Weapons Development, concerned with the development of doctrine for tactical nuclear war; and the Combat Development Experimentation Center, a field laboratory concerned with acting out problems of future warfare.

The redefinition of the Army's mission within the Defense Department and the consequent reorganization of the Army itself left the Army General Staff virtually free of operational functions. Thus the changing nature of the Army returned the General Staff at last to its original role as an over-all planning and policy-making body. The General Staff therefore underwent another reorganization also, into eight main offices. With the inauguration of the new functional commands, the Special Staff departments, which were the descendants of the old War Department bureaus, similarly lost their operational functions; and in a kind of belated affirmation of Leonard

Wood's triumph over Fred Ainsworth, most of the Special Staff departments were subordinated to various offices of the General Staff, whence they dispensed technical advice in their respective fields.

Under the deputy chief of staff, personnel, fell the offices of the provost marshal, the chief of chaplains, the adjutant general, and the surgeon general. The deputy chief of staff, military operations, received the chief signal officer as one of his subordinates. The deputy chief of staff, logistics, inherited the traditional engineer, support services, and transportation headquarters. The remaining General Staff offices were those of the secretary of the General Staff; comptroller of the Army; assistant chief of staff, intelligence; chief of reserve components; and chief of research and development. Among the Special Staff departments, the inspector general, the judge advocate general, and the chief of information continued to report directly to the chief of staff.[30]

Withal, the weight of tradition and shared memories in each of the services bears heavily against their full amalgamation. Here the history of interservice and Army education since World War II is characteristic as well as important in itself.

Even before the creation of the Defense Department, the interservice commands of World War II suggested interservice schools to prepare officers for such commands. Therefore the Army War College, suspended in 1940, did not reopen at the end of World War II, but instead the Army made the historic building of the War College at Washington Barracks (now Fort Lesley J. McNair), where it had resided since 1907, available for a National War College. Here officers of all the services together, the men tapped to hold in the future the highest command responsibilities, would study jointly the great problems of war and national policy. Similarly, the Army Industrial College was reconstituted at Fort McNair in 1946 as the Industrial College of the Armed Forces "to further prepare selected military and civilian personnel for important policy making, command and staff assignments within the national and international security structure." In 1946 there was created also the Armed Forces Staff College to educate selected officers in joint and combined operations. These three schools are under the direct control of the Joint Chiefs of Staff; the first two were intended to form together the interservice apex of the military school systems.[31]

But the eclipse of the schools of the individual services proved temporary. The Navy reopened its own War College, the Air Force established one, and in 1950 the Army War College resumed, first at Fort Leavenworth and since 1951 at Carlisle Barracks, Pennsylvania. In theory the interservice colleges cap the school systems, but in fact the war colleges of the several services remain avenues to the highest responsibilities at least equal in importance and prestige to the National War College and the Industrial College of the Armed Forces. The importance of the older war colleges reflects larger issues. The individual services still regard officers posted to the joint staff apparatus of the Joint Chiefs as representatives of the interests of their respective services. The joint agencies find it difficult to cultivate interservice attitudes and loyalties. The several services prefer to elevate officers conditioned by their own school systems, and the Army feels misgivings about National War College courses that it does not feel about the Army War College.[32]

Within the Army schools themselves, of course, interservice activities have received growing attention since World War II. Classes and faculty at the Army War College have long included representatives of the other services and of the Department of State. The Army War College course of instruction has concerned "The United States and Its National Strategy" and "Military Doctrine, Strategy, and Readiness," with the academic year culminating in a National Strategy Seminar.

The Command and General Staff College at Fort Leavenworth retains an influence and prestige barely second to the Army War College. Below these two there remain a variety of branch schools, including such post-World War II innovations as the Army Civil Affairs and Military Government School, the Army Command Management School, the Army Information School, the Army Intelligence School (established 1941), the Army Language School, the Army Special Warfare School, and the Army Strategic Intelligence School.

The Military Academy is still the foundation-stone of Army education for professional officers, its graduates being intended to set standards and serve as models for officers drawn from other sources. This has remained true though fewer than forty per cent of the commissioned officers on active duty have been Regulars, and the ROTC has become the principal source of commissioned personnel. After World War II, a board of consultants under the chairmanship of Dr. Karl T. Compton reviewed the Military Academy curriculum with an eye to the new responsibilities of Army officers in national policy and worldwide diplomacy. The recommendations of the board led to a limited revision of the curriculum, with an extension of liberal arts and scientific subjects at the expense of more strictly professional and technical ones. Already Colonel Lucius Holt and Colonel Herman Beukema had initiated a notable strengthening of the history and social science offerings, Holt's work beginning as early as 1910.

The post-World War II curriculum has devoted about half its course hours to "scientific and engineering" subjects, one-fourth to "social and humanistic" studies, and one-fourth to "professional" studies. Civilian critics and some inside the Army nevertheless raise questions periodically about the heavy emphasis on engineering and closely related subjects, which has persisted essentially unchanged since the founding of the Academy. There have also been questions about the extent to which the Academy still adheres to Sylvanus Thayer's system of small classes with daily recitation, with the critics arguing that the system promotes rote memorization rather than reflective thought. Numerous small classes also keep the Academy dependent on an inbred faculty with many junior officers.[33]

Yet the intellectual activity of several Army officers in the post-Korean years suggests that the Army and its educational system do manage to stimulate the mind and thought of the officers, despite evident and inherent handicaps. The books on military policy written by Generals Ridgway, Gavin, and Taylor during the 1950's are cogent appraisals of the weaknesses of the massive retaliation doctrine and of the need for flexible military power, and they helped to ensure a return to a national security policy of flexible response. In the long run, however, the importance of the books may lie less in their specific criticisms of transient policies, the criticisms themselves made transient by changing circumstances and technologies, than in the evidence they offer of broad and constructive thought within the officer corps and especially among men who have reached or approached its summit. They attest to the continuance of a respect for thoughtfulness and study, not always easily compatible with military stresses upon discipline and action but a part of the American Army's inheritance from Dennis Mahan through Sherman, Emory Upton, and John McAuley Palmer to the present.

It is not surprising that of the three services, the Army should have adapted most readily to the demands of the nuclear age for military policies of flexible response. Limited warfare doctrine gave the Army a renewed sense of purpose when many Americans had thought ground armies obsolete. Nevertheless, even the Army's acceptance of limited war has not been easy, for in the United States the officer corps has been sufficiently attuned to general national attitudes to share much of the popular attitude toward war. Though Bradley and Marshall became champions of limiting war to accord with political ends during the Korean conflict, they themselves excluded political considerations from war making as recently as World War II. More of the officers who held high rank in Korea shared MacArthur's views about that conflict than Marshall's, Bradley's, and Ridgway's.

For the Army to have produced as thoughtful a rationale for limited war and flexible response as that of Ridgway, Gavin, and Taylor during the 1950's remains one of the most striking evidences for Professor Morris Janowitz's conclusion in his study of *The Professional Soldier* in America, that of the three services, the Army stands out as the one that has most encouraged a thoughtful and innovative approach in its officer corps.[34]

This generalization of Janowitz's fits into a larger one that he draws from his survey of the composition and attitudes of the officer corps. It has not been likely in the twentieth-century United States Army, he argues, that a man will rise to the highest ranks merely by being competent and staying out of trouble. The careerist who chooses to advance by conforming without deviation to a standard Army pattern, doing everything the Army's way, may become a brigadier or even a major general. But he is not likely to become an army commander or chief of staff. The chiefs of staff have with remarkable consistency been in some measure extraordinary men. Consistently they have displayed originality of thought and independence of character. Consistently their careers in the junior and middle ranks have deviated somewhat from a stereotyped line and staff career. Eisenhower and Ridgway, for example, both believed their careers were injured by failure to see combat in World War I; but both became involved in the Army's relations with the civil power and diplomacy between the wars, and such involvement proved a much more important preparation and stepping-stone to the highest rank than a junior officer's combat experience. General Marshall certainly fostered the careers of innovative and thoughtful men during his long tenure as chief of staff. Though Janowitz's exploration of the phenomenon does not reach so far into the past, it is possible to surmise that an Army tradition of respect for originality and even a measure of unconventionality may have been encouraged in potential commanding generals and chiefs of staff from the time of those unconventional commanding generals, Ulysses Grant and William Tecumseh Sherman.[35]

If the Army has contrived to remain adaptable and thoughtful despite all the contrary pressures of military discipline, these qualities constitute a prime assurance of its ability to serve the country adequately in the uncertain future. It has become a cliché to say, with Abraham Lincoln, that "the dogmas of the quiet past are inadequate to the stormy present. As our case is new, so we must think anew, and act anew." The Army's adjustment to the age of nuclear power and cold war, like everyone's, must be a continuing process.

The adjustment must not only be strategic and tactical. With the passing of America's old-time international security and the coming of constant military responsibilities across the world, a conventional neat division between civil and military affairs will no longer suffice to preserve the constitutional subordination of the military to the civil power. That subordination won an old-fashioned kind of vindication in President Truman's dismissal of General MacArthur. But there remain the much more complex problems of civil-military relations posed by constant conscription of manpower, constant readiness at least for limited war, and the weight economic and otherwise of the military-industrial complex created by modern arms requirements, of whose dangers President Eisenhower warned in his farewell testament.

Maintaining an Army of about a million men, with tens of thousands of citizens passing through it annually, and through its reserves, makes the Army an immense social force. This fact can be exploited consciously to effect desired social change. One of the most important pressures favoring integration of the races in America has been the military's nondiscrimination policy invoked by President Truman's Executive Order No. 9981 of July 26, 1948: "It is the declared policy of the President that there shall be equality of treatment and opportunity for all persons in the armed services without regard to race, color, religion or national origin." The motives for this policy were military as well as social. In the mid-nineteenth century, when simply to be treated as a man was a new thing for the American Negro, Negroes could take pride in being accepted as soldiers at all, and the Negro regiments with their mainly white officers, especially the 9th and 10th Cavalry, were good fighting outfits with distinguished records through the War with Spain. But with the twentieth century's higher standards of justice and equality, it was no longer enough for the Negro that he be allowed to be a soldier in segregated units; to be recognized truly as a man now seemed to demand acceptance into any military formation. Negro outfits no longer felt the pride that had once characterized the "buffalo soldiers" of the old Regular Army Negro formations. On the contrary, conscious that confinement to a Negro unit implied a stigma, Negro soldiers understandably did not always fight well. The poor performance of some Negro units in Korea helped hasten the implementing of President Truman's order. When the order was carried out, the military results proved to be the ones hoped for. The social results are immeasurable. When the color line disappears on Army property even in the deepest South, the environs of that property can hardly remain unaffected.[36]

The integration of the Negro follows upon the Army's twentieth-century transformation into an instrument of social mobility for other American minority groups. During the nineteenth century, the

officer corps had been a socially conservative preserve of the Anglo-
Saxon Protestant middle and upper classes, with a tendency toward
aristocratic, Episcopalian, and old southern values. There were
strong reasons, rooted in English as well as American history, why
this should have been so. But the twentieth century created still
stronger pressures for more varied social origins. The World Wars
and then the Cold War and Korea made competence the overriding
criterion for military advancement as it had not needed to be in the
old years of security. After 1933, official federal policy favored the
use of the government as a force for social equality and mobility in
every possible area. So the twentieth-century officer corps tended to
become one of the most conspicuous avenues of ascent open to
Americans who lacked the credentials of the historic Anglo-Saxon
Protestant establishment.[37]

To use—and restrain—its immense social, economic, and political influence wisely and effectively, the Army obviously must hold
itself in close rapport with the people. To secure military success in
so complex and difficult a war as the one in Vietnam, it must also
depend upon its rapport with the people. Unless the people decide
that the war in Vietnam is in truth their war, the Army must finally
fail. American professional soldiers have often found the citizen soldier troublesome, but throughout the country's history the citizen
soldier has served the professional well, not least by linking him,
even in spite of himself, to the nation at large. The United States
emerged from the two world wars with both of its dual military
traditions strengthened by a new mutual respect between professional and citizen soldiers. Yet there is at least a suggestion of a neo-
Uptonian outlook in the Defense Department's reluctance to call
upon citizen reserves for the war in Vietnam. Let us hope it is no
more than a suggestion. Let us hope that the perplexities of brush-
fire wars do not injure the partnership between professional and
citizen soldiers sealed in 1917–18 and 1941–45.

The duality of the American military tradition has given the
United States Army both many of its historic perplexities and its best
qualities too. At once an expert army and a people's army, it has
served as the nation's sword without endangering the nation's democracy. Troublesome as the dual military tradition has sometimes
been, the very duality of the American military past is an inheritance
to be guarded jealously.

☆ APPENDIX ☆

Secretaries of War and of the Army

SECRETARIES OF WAR

1. Henry Knox, Sept. 12, 1789–Dec. 31, 1794
2. Timothy Pickering, Jan. 2, 1795–Dec. 10, 1795
3. James McHenry, Jan. 27, 1796–May 13, 1800
4. Samuel Dexter, May 13, 1800–Jan. 31, 1801
5. Henry Dearborn, Mar. 5, 1801–Mar. 7, 1809
6. William Eustis, Mar. 7, 1809–Jan. 13, 1813
7. John Armstrong, Jan. 13, 1813–Sept. 27, 1814
8. James Monroe, Sept. 27, 1814–Mar. 2, 1815
9. William H. Crawford, Aug. 1, 1815–Oct. 22, 1816
10. John C. Calhoun, Oct. 8, 1817–Mar. 7, 1825
11. James Barbour, Mar. 7, 1825–May 23, 1828
12. Peter B. Porter, May 26, 1828–Mar. 9, 1829
13. John H. Eaton, Mar. 9, 1829–June 18, 1831
14. Lewis Cass, Aug. 1, 1831–Oct. 5, 1836
15. Joel R. Poinsett, Mar. 7, 1837–Mar. 5, 1841
16. John Bell, Mar. 5, 1841–Sept. 13, 1841
17. John C. Spencer, Oct. 12, 1841–Mar. 3, 1843
18. James M. Porter, Mar. 8, 1843–Jan. 30, 1844
19. William Wilkins, Feb. 15, 1844–Mar. 4, 1845
20. William L. Marcy, Mar. 6, 1845–Mar. 4, 1849
21. George W. Crawford, Mar. 8, 1849–July 23, 1850
22. Charles M. Conrad, Aug. 15, 1850–Mar. 7, 1853
23. Jefferson Davis, Mar. 7, 1853–Mar. 6, 1857
24. John B. Floyd, Mar. 6, 1857–Dec. 29, 1860
25. Joseph Holt, Jan. 18, 1861–Mar. 5, 1861
26. Simon Cameron, Mar. 5, 1861–Jan. 14, 1862
27. Edwin M. Stanton, Jan. 20, 1862–May 28, 1868
28. John M. Schofield, June 1, 1868–Mar. 13, 1869
29. John A. Rawlins, Mar. 13, 1869–Sept. 6, 1869
30. William W. Belknap, Oct. 25, 1869–Mar. 2, 1876
31. Alphonso Taft, Mar. 8, 1876–May 22, 1876
32. James Donald Cameron, May 22, 1876–Mar. 3, 1877
33. George W. McCrary, Mar. 12, 1877–Dec. 10, 1879
34. Alexander Ramsey, Dec. 10, 1879–Mar. 5, 1881

35. Robert T. Lincoln, Mar. 5, 1881–Mar. 5, 1885
36. William C. Endicott, Mar. 5, 1885–Mar. 5, 1889
37. Redfield Proctor, Mar. 5, 1889–Nov. 5, 1891
38. Stephen B. Elkins, Dec. 17, 1891–Mar. 5, 1893
39. Daniel S. Lamont, Mar. 5, 1893–Mar. 5, 1897
40. Russell A. Alger, Mar. 5, 1897–Aug. 1, 1899
41. Elihu Root, Aug. 1, 1899–Jan. 31, 1904
42. William H. Taft, Feb. 1, 1904–June 30, 1908
43. Luke E. Wright, July 1, 1908–Mar. 11, 1909
44. Jacob M. Dickinson, Mar. 12, 1909–May 21, 1911
45. Henry L. Stimson, May 22, 1911–Mar. 4, 1913
46. Lindley M. Garrison, Mar. 5, 1913–Feb. 10, 1916
47. Hugh L. Scott (*ad interim*), Feb. 11, 1916–Mar. 8, 1916
48. Newton D. Baker, Mar. 9, 1916–Mar. 4, 1921
49. John W. Weeks, Mar. 5, 1921–Oct. 13, 1925
50. Dwight F. Davis, Oct. 14, 1925–Mar. 5, 1929
51. James W. Good, Mar. 6, 1929–Nov. 18, 1929
52. Patrick J. Hurley, Dec. 9, 1929–Mar. 3, 1933
53. George H. Dern, Mar. 4, 1933–Aug. 27, 1936
54. Harry H. Woodring, Sept. 25, 1936–June 20, 1940
55. Henry L. Stimson, July 10, 1940–Sept. 21, 1945
56. Robert P. Patterson, Sept. 27, 1945–July 18, 1947
57. Kenneth C. Royall, July 19, 1947–Sept. 17, 1947

SECRETARIES OF THE ARMY

1. Kenneth C. Royall, Sept. 17, 1947–Apr. 27, 1949
2. Gordon Gray, June 20, 1949–Apr. 12, 1950
3. Frank Pace, Jr., Apr. 12, 1950–Jan. 20, 1953
4. Robert T. Stevens, Feb. 4, 1953–July 21, 1955
5. Wilber M. Brucker, July 21, 1955–Jan. 20, 1961
6. Elvis T. Stahr, Jr., Jan. 23, 1961–July 5, 1962
7. Cyrus R. Vance, July 5, 1962–Jan. 20, 1964
8. Stephen Ailes, Jan. 20, 1964–June 18, 1965
9. Stanley R. Resor, June 30, 1965–

SENIOR OFFICERS OF THE ARMY TO 1821

During the Revolutionary War, George Washington served as Commander in Chief of the Continental Army by act of Congress of June 15, 1775, being installed in the office on June 17. After Washington's resignation, practice varied as to whether the senior officer of the Army was formally designated as its commanding officer, until May 28, 1798, when Congress explicitly provided for the appointment of a Commanding General of the Army. Emerging from retirement, Washington held this position from July 13, 1798, until his death, December 14, 1799. Thereafter no officer was again designated formally to command the Army until 1821. Commanders of geographical departments as well as heads of War Department bureaus customarily reported directly to the Secretary of War.

1. General George Washington, June 17, 1775–Dec. 23, 1783
2. Major General Henry Knox, Dec. 23, 1783–June 20, 1784
3. Captain John Doughty, June 20, 1784–Aug. 12, 1784
4. Lieutenant Colonel Josiah Harmar, Aug. 12, 1784–Mar. 4, 1791
5. Major General Arthur St. Clair, Mar. 4, 1791–Mar. 5, 1792
6. Major General Anthony Wayne, Apr. 13, 1792–Dec. 15, 1796
7. Brigadier General James Wilkinson, Dec. 15, 1796–July 13, 1798
8. Lieutenant General George Washington, July 13, 1798–Dec. 14, 1799
9. Major General Alexander Hamilton, Dec. 14, 1799–June 15, 1800
10. Brigadier General James Wilkinson, June 15, 1800–Jan. 27, 1812
11. Major General Henry Dearborn, Jan. 27, 1812–June 15, 1815
12. Major General Jacob Brown, June 15, 1815–June 1, 1821

COMMANDING GENERALS OF THE ARMY

Under the act of Congress reducing the Army in 1821, Jacob Brown formally became Commanding General of the Army on June 1, 1821. Despite the anomalies of this office discussed in the text, it continued in existence until the retirement of Nelson A. Miles on August 8, 1903, with the exception of two fairly extended periods when it was vacant: (1) November 24, 1846, until May 11, 1849. When Winfield Scott departed from Washington to lead the invasion of Mexico, he was restricted to control over his immediate command. When he returned to the United States, the political jealousies of President Polk's Democratic administration limited him to command of the Eastern Division, until President Taylor restored him to command of the Army. (2) March 11, 1862, until July 23, 1862. President Lincoln removed George B. McClellan from command of the Army on the former date; Henry W. Halleck at length took over the office on the latter date.

1. Major General Jacob Brown, June 1, 1821–Feb. 24, 1828
2. Major General Alexander Macomb, May 29, 1828–June 25, 1841
3. Brevet Lieutenant General Winfield Scott, July 5, 1841–Nov. 1, 1861
4. Major General George B. McClellan, Nov. 1, 1861–Mar. 11, 1862
5. Major General Henry W. Halleck, July 23, 1862–Mar. 9, 1864
6. General Ulysses S. Grant, Mar. 9, 1864–Mar. 4, 1869
7. General William T. Sherman, Mar. 8, 1869–Nov. 1, 1883
8. General Philip H. Sheridan, Nov. 1, 1883–Aug. 5, 1888
9. Lieutenant General John M. Schofield, Aug. 14, 1888–Sept. 29, 1895
10. Lieutenant General Nelson A. Miles, Oct. 5, 1895–Aug. 8, 1903

CHIEFS OF STAFF OF THE ARMY

1. Lieutenant General Samuel B. M. Young, Aug. 15, 1903–Jan. 8, 1904
2. Lieutenant General Adna R. Chaffee, Jan. 9, 1904–Jan. 14, 1906
3. Major General John C. Bates, Jan. 15, 1906–Apr. 13, 1906
4. Major General J. Franklin Bell, Apr. 14, 1906–Apr. 21, 1910

5. Major General Leonard Wood, Apr. 22, 1910–Apr. 20, 1914
6. Major General William W. Wotherspoon, Apr. 21, 1914–Nov. 15, 1914
7. Major General Hugh L. Scott, Nov. 16, 1914–Sept. 21, 1917
8. Major General Tasker H. Bliss, Sept. 22, 1917–May 18, 1918
9. General Peyton C. March, May 19, 1918–June 30, 1921
10. General of the Armies John J. Pershing, July 1, 1921–Sept. 13, 1924
11. Major General John L. Hines, Sept. 14, 1924–Nov. 20, 1926
12. General Charles P. Summerall, Nov. 21, 1926–Nov. 20, 1930
13. General Douglas MacArthur, Nov. 21, 1930–Oct. 1, 1935
14. General Malin Craig, Oct. 2, 1935–Aug. 31, 1939
15. General of the Army George C. Marshall, Sept. 1, 1939–Nov. 18, 1945
16. General of the Army Dwight D. Eisenhower, Nov. 19, 1945–Feb. 7, 1948
17. General of the Army Omar N. Bradley, Feb. 7, 1948–Aug. 16, 1949
18. General J. Lawton Collins, Aug. 16, 1949–Aug. 16, 1953
19. General Matthew B. Ridgway, Aug. 16, 1953–June 30, 1955
20. General Maxwell Taylor, June 30, 1955–June 30, 1959
21. General Lyman Lemnitzer, June 30, 1959–Sept. 31, 1960
22. General George H. Decker, Sept. 31, 1960–Oct. 1, 1962
23. General Earle G. Wheeler, Oct. 1, 1962–July 6, 1964
24. General Harold K. Johnson, July 6, 1964–

Expenditures of the War Department and the Department of the Army Since 1789

(in thousands of dollars)

Year	Amount	Year	Amount	Year	Amount
1789–91	633	1831	4,842	1871	35,800
1792	1,101	1832	5,446	1872	35,372
1793	1,130	1833	6,704	1873	46,323
1794	2,639	1834	5,696	1874	42,314
1795	2,481	1835	5,759	1875	41,121
1796	1,260	1836	12,169	1876	38,071
1797	1,039	1837	13,683	1877	37,083
1798	2,010	1838	12,897	1878	32,154
1799	2,467	1839	8,917	1879	40,426
1800	2,561	1840	7,097	1880	38,117
1801	1,673	1841	8,806	1881	40,466
1802	1,179	1842	6,612	1882	43,570
1803	822	1843	2,957	1883	48,911
1804	875	1844	5,179	1884	39,430
1805	713	1845	5,753	1885	42,671
1806	1,224	1846	10,793	1886	34,324
1807	1,289	1847	38,306	1887	38,561
1808	2,901	1848	25,502	1888	38,522
1809	3,346	1849	14,853	1889	44,435
1810	2,294	1850	9,400	1890	44,583

1811	2,033	1851	11,812	1891	48,720
1812	11,818	1852	8,225	1892	46,895
1813	19,652	1853	9,947	1893	49,642
1814	20,351	1854	11,734	1894	54,568
1815	14,794	1855	14,774	1895	51,805
1816	16,012	1856	16,948	1896	50,831
1817	8,004	1857	19,262	1897	48,950
1818	5,623	1858	25,485	1898	91,992
1819	6,506	1859	23,244	1899	229,841
1820	2,630	1860	16,410	1900	134,775
1821	4,461	1861	22,981	1901	144,616
1822	3,112	1862	394,368	1902	112,272
1823	3,097	1863	599,299	1903	118,630
1824	3,341	1864	690,792	1904	165,200
1825	3,660	1865	1,031,323	1905	126,094
1826	3,943	1866	284,450	1906	137,326
1827	3,939	1867	95,224	1907	149,775
1828	4,146	1868	123,247	1908	175,840
1829	4,724	1869	78,502	1909	192,487
1830	4,767	1870	57,656	1910	189,823
1911	197,199	1931	486,142	1951	8,635,939
1912	184,123	1932	476,305	1952	17,452,710
1913	202,129	1933	434,621	1953	17,054,333
1914	208,350	1934	408,587	1954	13,515,388
1915	202,160	1935	487,995	1955	9,450,383
1916	183,176	1936	618,587	1956	9,274,301
1917	377,941	1937	628,104	1957	9,704,788
1918	4,869,955	1938	644,264	1958	9,775,877
1919	9,009,076	1939	695,256	1959	10,284,059
1920	1,621,953	1940	907,160	1960	10,293,993
1921	1,118,076	1941	3,938,943	1961	11,102,621
1922	457,756	1942	14,325,508	1962	12,425,939
1923	397,051	1943	42,525,563	1963	11,499,000
1924	357,017	1944	49,438,330	1964	12,050,000
1925	370,981	1945	50,490,102		
1926	364,090	1946	27,986,769		
1927	369,114	1947	9,172,139		
1928	400,990	1948	7,698,556		
1929	425,947	1949	7,862,397		
1930	464,854	1950	5,789,468		

SOURCE: *Historical Statistics of the United States*

For 1789–1842, years ending December 31; 1844–present, June 30; 1843 figure is for Jan. 1–June 30.

ORGANIZATION OF THE WAR DEPARTMENT
SEPTEMBER 4, 1792*

```
                    ┌─────────────────────┐
                    │      PRESIDENT      │
                    │  George Washington  │
                    └─────────────────────┘
                               │
                    ┌─────────────────────┐              ┌──────────────────────────┐
                    │  SECRETARY OF WAR   │              │  COMMANDING OFFICER OF THE│
                    │     Henry Knox      │              │  TROOPS IN THE SERVICE OF THE│
                    └─────────────────────┘              │       UNITED STATES       │
                               │                         │   Maj. Gen. Anthony Wayne │
                                                         └──────────────────────────┘
                                                                      │
   ┌────────────────┬──────────────┬──────────────┬──────────────┐
   │                │              │              │              │
┌─────────┐  ┌──────────┐  ┌──────────┐  ┌──────────┐     ┌──────────────────────┐
│ADJUTANT │  │QUARTER-  │  │PHYSICIAN │  │PAYMASTER │     │THE LEGION OF THE      │
│AND      │  │MASTER    │  │GENERAL   │  │OF THE    │     │UNITED STATES          │
│INSPECTOR│  │GENERAL   │  │James Craik│ │ARMY      │     └──────────────────────┘
│-GENERAL │  │James     │  │          │  │Caleb Swan│
│Lieut.   │  │O'Hara    │  └──────────┘  └──────────┘
│Henry    │  └──────────┘
│DeButts, │
│4th      │
│Infantry │
└─────────┘
```

*The date on which Anthony Wayne formed the Legion of the United States.

PRESIDENT
James Monroe

COMMANDING GENERAL
Maj. Gen. Jacob Brown

SECRETARY OF WAR
James C. Calhoun

ADJUTANT
GENERAL
Lt. Edmund Kirby
(Acting)

INSPECTOR
GENERAL
Col. James
Gadsden

JUDGE
ADVOCATE
S. A. Storrow

QUARTERMASTER
GENERAL
Brig. Gen. Thomas
S. Jesup

COMMISSARY OF
PURCHASES
Callender
Irvine

SURGEON
GENERAL
Joseph Lowell

PAYMASTER
GENERAL
Daniel Parker

CHIEF
ENGINEER
Col. Alexander
Macomb

TOPOGRAPHICAL
ENGINEER
Bvt. Maj.
John Anderson

THE ARMY

*The effective date of the reorganization act of March 2, 1821.

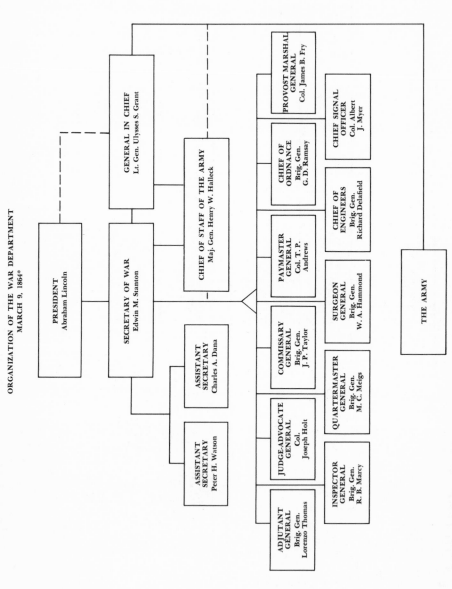

ORGANIZATION OF THE WAR DEPARTMENT
MARCH 9, 1864*

PRESIDENT
Abraham Lincoln

GENERAL IN CHIEF
Lt. Gen. Ulysses S. Grant

SECRETARY OF WAR
Edwin M. Stanton

CHIEF OF STAFF OF THE ARMY
Maj. Gen. Henry W. Halleck

ASSISTANT SECRETARY
Charles A. Dana

ASSISTANT SECRETARY
Peter H. Watson

ADJUTANT GENERAL
Brig. Gen. Lorenzo Thomas

JUDGE-ADVOCATE GENERAL
Col. Joseph Holt

INSPECTOR GENERAL
Brig. Gen. R. B. Marcy

QUARTERMASTER GENERAL
Brig. Gen. M. C. Meigs

COMMISSARY GENERAL
Brig. Gen. J. P. Taylor

SURGEON GENERAL
Brig. Gen. W. A. Hammond

PAYMASTER GENERAL
Col. T. P. Andrews

CHIEF OF ENGINEERS
Brig. Gen. Richard Delafield

CHIEF OF ORDNANCE
Brig. Gen. G. D. Ramsay

CHIEF SIGNAL OFFICER
Col. Albert J. Myer

PROVOST MARSHAL GENERAL
Col. James B. Fry

THE ARMY

*On this date Grant received his commission as lieutenant general and General in Chief.

PRESIDENT
Woodrow Wilson

SECRETARY OF WAR
Newton D. Baker

ASSISTANT SERETARY
William M. Ingraham

CHIEF OF STAFF
General Hugh L. Scott

GENERAL STAFF

CHIEF OF MILITIA BUREAU
Brig. Gen.
Wm. A. Mann

INSPECTOR GENERAL
Brig. Gen. J. L. Chamberlain

CHIEF OF BUREAU OF INSULAR AFFAIRS
Brig. Gen.
Frank McIntyre

SURGEON GENERAL
Maj. Gen.
Wm. C. Gorgas

CHIEF OF ORDNANCE
Brig. Gen.
Wm. Crozier

PANAMA CANAL

CHIEF OF COAST ARTILLERY
Brig. Gen.
Erasmus Weaver

ADJUTANT GENERAL
Brig. Gen.
H. P. McCain

JUDGE ADVOCATE GENERAL
Brig. Gen.
Enoch H. Crowder

QUARTERMASTER GENERAL
Maj. Gen.
Harry G. Sharpe

CHIEF OF ENGINEERS
Brig. Gen.
Wm. H. Black

CHIEF SIGNAL OFFICER
Brig. Gen.
Geo. C. Squire

THE ARMY

Strength of the Active Army Since 1789

Year	Total	Officers	Enlisted
1789	718	46	672
1794	3,813	235*	3,578
1801	4,051	248	3,803
1802	2,873	175	2,698
1803	2,486	174	2,312
1804	2,734	216	2,518
1805	2,729	159	2,570
1806	2,653	142	2,511
1807	2,775	146	2,629
1808	5,712	327	5,385
1809	6,977	533	6,444
1810	5,956	441	5,515
1811	5,608	396	5,212
1812	6,686	299	6,387
1813	19,036	1,476	17,560
1814	38,186	2,271	35,915
1815	33,424	2,272	31,152
1816	10,231	735	9,496
1817	8,446	647	7,799
1818	8,155	697	7,458
1819	8,506	705	7,801
1820	10,554	696	9,858
1821	5,773	547	5,226
1822	5,358	512	4,846
1823	6,117	525	4,053*
1824	5,973	532	5,441
1825	5,903	562	5,341
1826	5,989	540	5,449
1827	5,885	546	5,339
1828	5,702	540	5,162
1829	6,332	608	5,724
1830	6,122	627	5,495
1831	6,055	613	5,442
1832	6,268	659	5,609
1833	6,579	666	5,913
1834	7,030	669	6,361
1835	7,337	680	6,657
1836	9,945	857*	9,088*
1837	12,449	873	11,576
1838	9,197	717	8,480
1839	10,691	749	9,942
1840	12,330	789	11,541
1841	11,319	754	10,565
1842	10,780	781	9,999
1843	9,102	805	8,297

Year	Total	Officers	Enlisted
1844	8,730	813	7,917
1845	8,509	826	7,683
1846	27,867	2,003*	25,864*
1847	44,736	2,863*	41,873*
1848	47,319	2,865	44,454
1849	10,744	945	9,799
1850	10,929	948	9,981
1851	10,714	944	9,770
1852	11,376	957	10,419
1853	10,572	961	9,611
1854	10,894	956	9,938
1855	15,911	1,042	14,869
1856	15,715	1,072	14,643
1857	15,918	1,097	14,821
1858	17,678	1,099	16,579
1859	17,243	1,070	16,173
1860	16,215	1,080	15,135
1861	186,845	†	†
1862	637,264	†	†
1863	918,354	†	†
1864	970, 905	†	†
1865	1,000,692	†	†
1866	57,072	†	†
1867	57,194	3,056	54,138
1868	51,066	2,835	48,231
1869	36,953	2,700	34,253
1870	37,240	2,541	34,699
1871	29,115	2,105	27,010
1872	28,322	2,104	26,218
1873	28,812	2,076	26,736
1874	28,640	2,081	26,559
1875	25,513	2,068	23,445
1876	28,565	2,151	26,414
1877	24,140	2,177	21,963
1878	26,023	2,153	23,870
1879	26,601	2,127	24,474
1880	26,594	2,152	24,442
1881	25,842	2,181	23,661
1882	25,811	2,162	23,649
1883	25,652	2,143	23,509
1884	26,666	2,143	24,519
1885	27,157	2,154	25,003
1886	26,727	2,102	24,625
1887	26,719	2,200	24,519
1888	27,019	2,189	24,830
1889	27,759	2,177	25,582
1890	27,373	2,168	25,205

Year	Total	Officers	Enlisted
1891	26,463	2,052	24,411
1892	27,190	2,140	25,050
1893	27,830	2,158	25,672
1894	28,265	2,146	26,119
1895	27,495	2,154	25,341
1896	27,375	2,169	25,206
1897	27,865	2,179	25,686
1898	209,714	10,516	199,198
1899	80,670	3,581	77,089
1900	101,713	4,227	97,486
1901	85,557	3,468	82,089
1902	81,275	4,049	77,226
1903	69,595	3,927	65,668
1904	70,387	3,971	66,416
1905	67,526	4,034	63,492
1906	68,945	3,989	64,956
1907	64,170	3,896	60,274
1908	76,942	4,047	72,895
1909	84,971	4,299	80,672
1910	81,251	4,535	76,716
1911	84,006	4,585	79,421
1912	92,121	4,775	87,346
1913	92,756	4,970	87,786
1914	98,544	5,033	93,511
1915	106,754	4,948	101,806
1916	108,399	5,175	103,224
1917	421,467	34,224	387,243
1918	2,395,742	130,485	2,265,257
1919	851,624	91,975	759,649
1920	204,292	18,999	185,293
1921	230,725	16,501	214,224
1922	148,763	15,667	133,096
1923	133,243	14,021	119,222
1924	142,673	13,784	128,889
1925	137,048	14,594	122,454
1926	134,938	14,143	120,795
1927	134,829	14,020	120,809
1928	136,084	14,019	122,065
1929	139,118	14,047	125,071
1930	139,378	14,151	125,227
1931	140,516	14,159	126,357
1932	134,957	14,111	120,846
1933	136,547	13,896	122,651
1934	138,464	13,761	124,703
1935	139,486	13,471	126,015
1936	167,816	13,512	154,304
1937	179,968	13,740	166,228

Year	Total	Officers	Enlisted
1938	185,488	13,975	171,513
1939	189,839	14,486	175,353
1940	269,023	18,326	250,697
1941	1,462,315	99,536	1,362,779
1942	3,075,608	206,422	2,869,186
1943	6,994,472	579,576	6,414,896
1944	7,994,750	776,980	7,217,770
1945	8,267,958	891,663	7,376,295
1946	1,891,011	267,144	1,623,867
1947	991,285	132,504	858,781
1948	554,030	68,178	485,852
1949	660,473	77,272	583,201
1950	593,167	72,566	520,601
1951	1,531,774	130,540‡	1,401,234
1952	1,596,419	148,427	1,447,992
1953	1,533,815	145,683	1,388,182
1954	1,404,598	128,208	1,276,390
1955	1,109,296	121,947	987,349
1956	1,025,778	118,364	907,414
1957	997,994	111,187	886,807
1958	898,925	104,716	794,209
1959	861,964	101,690	760,274
1960	873,078	101,236	771,842
1961	858,622	99,921	758,701
1962	1,066,404	116,050	950,354
1963§	975,155	107,769	867,386
1964§	972,445	110,276	862,169
1965§	963,273	110,450*	852,823*
1966§	953,094	110,740*	842,354*

SOURCE: *Historical Statistics of the United States*

* Estimate.
† Reliable figures not available.
‡ Includes 178 Navy medical officers on duty with the Army.
§ Excludes personnel paid for by agencies other than the Department of Defense.

☆ NOTES ☆

INTRODUCTION

1. Leonard D. White in his preface to Louis Smith, *American Democracy and Military Power: A Study of Civil Control of the Military Power in the United States* (Chicago: University of Chicago Press, 1951), p. xi. This book is the best institutional study of American civil-military relations, and its reflection of Upton's influence is unfortunate but only incidental to its main purpose. In general its attitudes are thoroughly civilian. On Smith's topic, see also Pendleton Herring, *The Impact of War: Our American Democracy Under Arms* (New York: Farrar and Rinehart, 1941); and for the years since 1930, Walter Millis, with Harvey C. Mansfield and Harold Stein, *Arms and the State: Civil-Military Elements in National Policy* (New York: Twentieth-Century Fund, 1958).

    Upton's book is *The Military Policy of the United States from 1775* (Washington: Government Printing Office, 1904). The two standard histories of the United States Army both draw their interpretations from Upton: William A. Ganoe, *History of the United States Army* (New York: Appleton-Century, 1936) and Oliver Lyman Spaulding, *The United States Army in War and Peace* (New York: Putnam, 1937). Though both reflect a somewhat narrowly military viewpoint and stray from the history of the Army as an institution to refight battles and campaigns, both represent indispensable spadework from which every writer on Army history must benefit. C. Joseph Bernardo and Eugene H. Bacon, *American Military Policy: Its Development Since 1775* (Harrisburg: Stackpole, 1955) is larger in scope and also very useful, but it is another book whose viewpoint is thoroughly military and whose themes are largely Uptonian. T. Harry Williams, *Americans at War: The Development of the American Military System* (Baton Rouge: Louisiana State University Press, 1960) is a thoughtful work by a civilian historian but is very brief. The most satisfactory general history of American military policy, a most stimulating book, is Walter Millis, *Arms and Men: A Study in American Military History* (New York: Putnam, 1956). Walter Millis, ed., *American Military Thought* (Indianapolis: Bobbs-Merrill, 1966) is a good collection of documents, as is Raymond G. O'Connor, *American Defense Policy in Perspective: From Colonial Times to the Present* (New York: Wiley, 1965).

    An interesting example of Uptonian distortion of the vision of a civilian professional historian is Fred A. Shannon's well-known study of *The Organization and Administration of the Union Army* (2 vols., Cleveland: Clark, 1928), especially the section on "The State-Rights Principle Applied to the Army."

2. 82nd Congress, 1st Session, Hearings before the Committee on

Armed Services and the Committee on Foreign Relations, *Military Situation in the Far East* (Washington: Government Printing Office, 1951), p. 45. MacArthur was a complex and a sophisticated man, despite appearances to the contrary, and he may very well not have believed this sort of thing; but the argument was useful for explaining away his insubordination, and his followers were mostly willing to accept it. See John W. Spanier's comments in *The Truman-MacArthur Controversy and the Korean War* (Norton Library ed., New York: Norton, 1965), pp. 12–13, 233–36.

CHAPTER ONE

1. The Assize of Arms (1181). David C. Douglas and Charles W. Greenaway, eds., *English Historical Documents* (12 vols. projected, London: Eyre and Spottiswoode, 1953–   ), II, 416.
2. See Michael Powicke, *Military Obligation in Medieval England* (Oxford: Clarendon Press, 1962), and Allen French, "The Arms and Military Training of Our Colonizing Ancestors," *Massachusetts Historical Society Proceedings*, LXVII (1941–44), 3–21. John W. Fortescue, *A History of the British Army* (13 vols., London: Macmillan, 1899–1930) is the classic in its field. It deals with the pre-seventeenth-century backgrounds in I, 1–190.
3. Darrett B. Rutman, "A Militant New World, 1607–1640," Ph.D. thesis, University of Virginia, 1959, and Herbert L. Osgood, *The American Colonies in the Seventeenth Century* (3 vols., New York: Macmillan, 1904–7), I, chaps. iii, xiii; II, chap. xv, survey the beginnings of the colonial military system. On the fort at Jamestown, Charles E. Hatch, Jr., *Jamestown, Virginia: The Town Site and Its Story* (National Park Service Historical Handbook Series Number Two, Washington: The National Park Service cooperating with The Association for the Preservation of Virginia Antiquities, 1952), pp. 7–8. Richard L. Morton, *Colonial Virginia* (2 vols., Chapel Hill: University of North Carolina Press, 1960) embodies recent scholarship on the founding of the colony but says little about military affairs.
4. Quoted in Hatch, *op. cit.*, p. 16.
5. Philip Alexander Bruce, *Institutional History of Virginia* (2 vols., New York: Putnam, 1910), II, Part IV, esp. pp. 3–14, 123–226; Osgood, *op. cit.*, II, 384–86. Louis Morton, "The Origins of American Military Policy," *Military Affairs*, XXII (1958–59), 75–82, is a convenient introduction to military regulations imposed in the colonies. A brief but uncommonly perceptive discussion of colonial military institutions is Part Thirteen of Daniel J. Boorstin, *The Americans: The Colonial Experience* (New York: Random House, 1958). Arthur Vollmer, *Background of Selective Service*, Monogr. No. 1, Vol. II, *Military Obligations: The American Tradition* (Washington: Government Printing Office, 1947) prints various records of the colonial assemblies' activity in military matters.
6. Studies of the colonial military systems include: Arthur E. Buffinton, "The Puritan View of War," *Colonial Society of Massachusetts Publications*, XXVIII (Transactions, 1930–33), 67–86; Clarence P. Clendenen, "A Little Known Period of American Military History," *Mili-*

tary Affairs, XIX (1955), 37–38; Douglas E. Leach, "The Military System of Plymouth Colony," *New England Quarterly*, XXIV (1951), 342–64; Jack S. Radebaugh, "The Militia of Colonial Massachusetts," *Military Affairs*, XVIII (1954), 1–18; Louis Dow Scisco, "Evolution of Militia in Maryland," *Maryland Historical Magazine*, XXXV (1940), 166–77; Morrison Sharp, "Leadership and Democracy in the Early New England System of Defense," *American Historical Review*, L (1945), 244–60; E. Milton Wheeler, "Development and Organization of the North Carolina Militia," *North Carolina Historical Review*, XLI (1964), 307–23.

For an interesting eighteenth-century proposal for the strengthening of the militia, see Fred K. Vigman, "A 1775 Plan for . . . a National Militia in Great Britain and . . . America," *Military Affairs*, IX (1945), 355–60. A general survey of the history of the American citizen soldier is John K. Mahon, "The Citizen Soldier in National Defense," Ph.D. thesis, University of California (Los Angeles), 1950. John W. Shy, *Toward Lexington: The Role of the British Army in the Coming of the American Revolution* (Princeton: Princeton University Press, 1965), pp. 9–14, points out that the militia became much better established in New England and Virginia, with their homogeneous populations, than in the more heterogeneous Middle Colonies and South Carolina. The military history of Georgia differs from that of the other colonies in that Georgia was intended as a military settlement, and James Oglethorpe's ideas included that of an American army which would be neither militia nor imported British regulars; *ibid.*, pp. 31–33.

7. Leach, *op. cit.*, pp. 351–57; Morton, *op. cit.*, pp. 79–80; Radebaugh, *op. cit.*, pp. 2–8. For the seventeenth-century antecedents of contemporary Massachusetts regiments, see Department of the Army, *The Army Lineage Book*, II, *Infantry* (Washington: Government Printing Office, 1953), p. 520, and Mark M. Boatner III, *Military Customs and Traditions* (New York: McKay, 1956), p. 66. On the 182nd Infantry, "Histories of Old American Regiments," *Military Affairs*, XIII (1949), 208; *ibid.*, p. 222 for Virginia's 176th Infantry.

8. W. Packer Clark, *Official History of the Militia and the National Guard in Pennsylvania* (3 vols., Philadelphia: Handler, 1909); Robert L. D. Davidson, *War Comes to Quaker Pennsylvania* (New York: Columbia University Press, 1937); *Pre-Revolutionary Military Service in Pennsylvania* (Pennsylvania Historical and Museum Commission, Division of Public Records, Information Leaflet No. 2); Carl Van Doren, *Benjamin Franklin* (New York: Viking, 1952), pp. 183–87.

9. Jim Dan Hill, *The Minute Man in Peace and War: A History of the National Guard* (Harrisburg: Stackpole, 1963) points out the looseness with which many writers have employed the catchall term "militia" and draws distinctions among the various types of militia, pp. 1–4, 26–31. For the growth of different types of military organizations under the common term "militia," see Howard H. Peckham, "Speculations on the Colonial Wars," *William and Mary Quarterly*, third series, XVII (1960), 463–72, and John W. Shy, "A New Look at Colonial Militia," *ibid.*, XX (1963), 181–84. Also see again Mor-

ton, *op. cit.*, pp. 78–80, and Radebaugh, *op. cit.*, pp. 2–8. Justin H. Smith edited *The Historie Booke* for the Ancient and Honorable Artillery Company (Boston, 1903).

10. There is a wealth of material on weapons in the colonial period: W. Y. Carman, *A History of Firearms from Earliest Times to 1914* (London: Routledge and Paul, 1955); John G. W. Dillin, *The Kentucky Rifle* (3rd ed., New York: Ludlum and Beebe, 1946); Charles Ffoulkes, *Arms and Armament: An Historical Survey of the British Army* (London: Harrap, 1945); James E. Hicks, "United States Military Shoulder Arms, 1795–1935," Parts 3 and 4, *Journal of the American Military History Foundation*, II (1938), 36–42; Horace Kephart, "The Rifle in Colonial Times," *Magazine of American History*, XXIV (1890), 179–91; Harold L. Peterson, *Arms and Armor in Colonial America: 1526–1783* (New York: Bramhall House, 1956), an especially useful and well-illustrated work, and "Military Equipment of the Plymouth and Massachusetts Bay Colonies," *New England Quarterly*, XX (1947), 197–208; Felix Reichmann, "The Pennsylvania Rifle: A Social Interpretation of Changing Military Techniques," *Pennsylvania Magazine of History and Biography*, LXX (1945), 3–14; Carl P. Russell, *Guns on the Early Frontier: A History of Firearms from Colonial Times Through the Years of the Western Fur Trade* (Berkeley: University of California Press, 1957); Leroy D. Satterlee and Arcadi Gluckman, *American Gun Makers* (Buffalo, New York: Ulbrich, 1940); Charles W. Sawyer, *Firearms in American History: 1600 to 1800* (Boston: the author, 1910) and *Our Rifles* (Boston: Williams Book Store, 1946); Philip B. Sharpe, *The Rifle in America* (New York: Morrow, 1938); Townsend Whelen, *The American Rifle* (New York: Century, 1918); Norman B. Wilkinson, "The Pennsylvania Rifle," *American Heritage*, I (Summer, 1950), 3–5, 64–66. See also Donald E. Worcester, "The Weapons of American Indians," *New Mexico Historical Review*, XX (1935), 227–38.

11. Douglas E. Leach, *Flintlock and Tomahawk: New England in King Philip's War* (New York: Macmillan, 1958), pp. 67, 70–71, 80–81, 87–88, 152–54, 167, 197, 216–17, 220, 228–29. John K. Mahon has written on the general problems of Indian warfare, "Anglo-American Methods of Indian Warfare, 1676–1794," *Mississippi Valley Historical Review*, XLV (1958), 254–75.

12. John C. Fitzpatrick, ed., *The Writings of George Washington* (39 vols., Washington: Government Printing Office, 1931–44), I, 302, 305.

Although the recession of the frontier eroded frontier military skills, the town life of New England, as Shy (*Toward Lexington*, pp. 6–14) points out, was much more conducive to maintaining a militia than the plantation society of Virginia with its scattered population. Thus King Philip's War did not confront New England with quite the crisis of defense policy that came out of the simultaneous Indian troubles in Virginia; Wilcomb E. Washburn, *The Governor and the Rebel: A History of Bacon's Rebellion* (Chapel Hill: University of North Carolina Press, 1957) depicts Bacon's rebellion mainly as an outcome of the historic militia's failure to deal with the Indians to the satisfaction of settlers on the frontier.

13. Douglas Southall Freeman, *George Washington* (7 vols., New York:

Scribner, 1948–57), II, 150, with a brief bibliographical note on Bland's *Tactics*.

CHAPTER TWO

1. Robert Dinwiddie to James Abercromby, Aug. 15, 1754, in *The Official Records of Robert Dinwiddie, Lieutenant-Governor of the Colony of Virginia, 1751–1758* . . . , with an introduction and notes by R. A. Brock (2 vols., Richmond: Virginia Historical Society, 1883), I, 286.

2. Douglas Southall Freeman, *George Washington* (7 vols., New York: Scribner, 1948–57), II, 8. Francis Parkman, *France and England in North America* (9 vols., Boston: Little, Brown, 1865–92), the classic account of the struggle with France, remains not only stirring but generally reliable. A reading of Parkman should be supplemented with the appropriate volumes of the modern survey, Lawrence H. Gipson, *The British Empire Before the American Revolution* (12 vols., Caldwell, Idaho: Caxton, and New York: Knopf, 1936–65). A brief account is Howard H. Peckham, *The Colonial Wars, 1689–1762* (Chicago: University of Chicago Press, 1964). A popular account by the director of the Fort Ticonderoga restoration is strongest in its handling of the northern campaigns: Edward P. Hamilton, *The French and Indian Wars: The Story of Battles and Forts in the Wilderness* (Garden City: Doubleday, 1962).

3. Virginia's military troubles are followed in copious detail in Freeman, *loc. cit.* See especially II, 172–74, 182, 189–92, 200–201, 218, 253–254. Note again John W. Shy's argument that the troubles were partly inherent in a rural society with a scattered population, *Toward Lexington: The Role of the British Army in the Coming of the American Revolution* (Princeton: Princeton University Press, 1965), pp. 8–14, 17–18.

4. Gipson, *op. cit.*, VII, 231–32; Stanley Pargellis, *Lord Loudoun in North America* (New Haven: Yale University Press, 1933), pp. 11–12. The latter account of the British commander in chief in 1756–1757 is indispensable, the best military monograph on the French and Indian War.

5. John C. Fitzpatrick, ed., *The Writings of George Washington* (39 vols., Washington: Government Printing Office, 1931–44), II, 97.

6. Pargellis's account of the thinking of the British government on the post of commander in chief in North America is, as usual, the most satisfactory; *op. cit.*, pp. 5–30. On the British command system in general there is Julian S. Corbett, *England in the Seven Years' War: A Study in Combined Strategy* (2 vols., London: Longmans, 1907). C. E. Carter, "The Office of Commander in Chief, A Phase of Imperial Unity on the Eve of the Revolution," in Richard B. Morris, ed., *The Era of the American Revolution* (New York: Columbia University Press, 1939) deals with a later phase in the history of the office, as he does in "The Significance of the Military Office in America, 1763–1775," *American Historical Review*, XXVIII (1923), 475–88. There is bibliographical information in Henry P. Beers, "The Papers of the British Commanders-in-Chief in North America, 1754–1783," *Military Affairs*, XIII (1949), 79–94.

7. Lee McCardle, *Ill-Starred General: Braddock of the Coldstream Guards* (Pittsburgh: University of Pittsburgh Press, 1958) is a sympathetic biography.

8. Pargellis, *op. cit.*, pp. 15–34; Stanley Pargellis, ed., *Military Affairs in North America, 1748–1765: Selected Documents from the Cumberland Papers in Windsor Castle* (New York: Appleton-Century, 1936), pp. 34–39, 45–48, 53–54. For a brief survey of the generally unhappy earlier experiments with independent companies of the regular establishment stationed in America, including the island colonies, see Shy, *op. cit.*, pp. 20–44; also Stanley Pargellis, "The Four Independent Companies of New York," in *Essays in Colonial History Presented to Charles McLean Andrews by His Students* (New Haven: Yale University Press, 1931), pp. 96–123.

9. Pargellis, *Lord Loudoun*, pp. 41, 61–66, 108–9. Lewis Butler, *The Annals of the King's Royal Rifle Corps* (5 vols., London: Murray, 1913–32) is the history of the regiment descended from the Royal Americans; Volume I concerns the original regiment.

10. Pargellis, *Lord Loudoun*, p. 121.

11. *Ibid.*, pp. 119, 121.

12. The Mutiny Act was both the legal foundation of the British army and specifically of its discipline and a principal means of assuring Parliamentary supremacy over the military. First enacted in 1689 following the Glorious Revolution, it authorized the trial of soldiers by courts-martial for one year only. Without yearly renewal, the Crown would have no legal foundation upon which to discipline the army. This measure, together with the practice of granting army appropriations for one year only, prevented the king's ruling for an indefinite period without calling Parliament, in the manner of Charles I. Originally brief, the Mutiny Act in time grew lengthy and complex. For a good discussion of its application to America, see Shy, *op. cit.*, esp. pp. 163–85.

13. Pargellis, *Lord Loudoun*, pp. 105–19, 121–30.

14. *Ibid.*, pp. 67–109.

15. Introductions to European war in the eighteenth century include: A. F. Becke, *An Introduction to the History of Tactics* (London: Rees, 1909); Walter L. Dorn, *Competition for Empire, 1740–1763* (New York: Harper, 1940), pp. 80–102; Edward Mead Earle, ed., *Makers of Modern Strategy: Military Thought from Machiavelli to Hitler* (Princeton: Princeton University Press, 1943), pp. 26–74; John U. Nef, *War and Human Progress* (Cambridge: Harvard University Press, 1950), pp. 147–328; Hoffman Nickerson, *The Armed Horde* (New York: Putnam, 1940), pp. 19–63; Richard A. Preston, Sydney F. Wise, and Herman O. Werner, *Men in Arms: A History of Warfare and Its Interrelationships with Western Society* (New York: Praeger, 1956), pp. 129–46; Robert S. Quimby, *The Background of Napoleonic Warfare: The Theory of Military Tactics in Eighteenth-Century France* (New York: Columbia University Press, 1957); Theodore Ropp, *War in the Modern World* (Collier ed., New York: Collier Books, 1962), pp. 40–59; and Alfred Vagts, *A History of Militarism* (rev. ed., New York: Meridian, 1959), pp. 77–96. Selections from several of these works and other pertinent material can be found in Gordon B. Turner, ed., *A History of Military Affairs in Western Society Since the Eighteenth Century* (3 vols., Princeton:

Advisory Committee of the Princeton University Military History Project, 1952). For a work on the background of eighteenth-century war, see Michael R. Roberts, *The Military Revolution, 1560–1660* (Belfast: Boyd, 1956).

16. Quoted in Daniel J. Boorstin, *The Americans: The Colonial Experience* (New York: Random House, 1958), p. 346.

17. Vagts, *op. cit.*, chap. 1. For a discussion of the purchase system that is pertinent and penetrating though focused on a later period, see Cecil Woodham-Smith, *The Reason Why* (New York: McGraw-Hill, 1953), pp. 21–26; also Arvel B. Erickson, "Abolition of Purchase in the British Army," *Military Affairs*, XXIII (1959), 65–76.

18. On Indian warfare see George T. Hunt, *The Wars of the Iroquois* (Madison: University of Wisconsin Press, 1940); John Tebbel and Keith Jennison, *The American Indian Wars* (New York: Harper, 1960); Henry Holbert Turney-High, *Primitive War, Its Practice and Concepts* (Columbia, S.C., 1949). The impact of Indian warfare on European tactics is discussed in Louis Morton, "The End of Formalized Warfare," *American Heritage*, VI (August, 1955), 12–19, 95.

19. Deputy Quartermaster General Sir John St. Clair, quoted in Pargellis, *Military Affairs in North America*, p. 94.

20. Pierre Claude Pecaudy de Contrecoeur, quoted *ibid.*, p. 129.

21. A thorough study revising the traditional harsh judgments on Braddock's expedition is in Gipson, *op. cit.*, VI, 62–98. See also McCardle, *op. cit.*, pp. 240–72. A modern analysis reaching more critical conclusions is Stanley Pargellis, "Braddock's Defeat," *American Historical Review*, XLI (1936), 253–69. The long familiar conclusion that the defeat was a triumph of Indian methods over European formalized war is restated in Don Higginbotham, *Daniel Morgan, Revolutionary Rifleman* (Chapel Hill: University of North Carolina Press, 1961), p. 5. Charles Hamilton, ed., *Braddock's Defeat* (Norman: University of Oklahoma Press, 1959) prints several contemporary narratives.

22. For Bouquet, see E. Douglas Branch, "Henry Bouquet, Professional Soldier," *Pennsylvania Magazine of History and Biography*, LXII (1938), 41–51; Butler, *op. cit.*, I, 102–7; S. K. Stevens, Donald H. Kent, and Autumn Leonard, eds., *The Papers of Henry Bouquet* (16 vols., Harrisburg: Pennsylvania Historical and Museum Commission, 1951); Dale Van Every, *Forth to the Wilderness: The First American Frontier, 1754–1774* (New York: Morrow, 1961), pp. 85–90, 97, 99.

23. Pargellis, *Lord Loudoun*, pp. 256–57, 301.

24. *Ibid.*, pp. 301–3.

25. John R. Cuneo, *Robert Rogers of the Rangers* (New York: Oxford University Press, 1959) is a laudatory biography offering disappointingly little on Rogers's tactics. Pargellis, *Lord Loudoun*, pp. 303–4, 309, is much less enthusiastic, as is Burt B. Loescher, *History of Rogers' Rangers: The Beginnings, 1755–1758* (San Francisco, 1946).

26. Pargellis, *Lord Loudoun*, pp. 304–5. On Gage, see John Richard Alden, *General Gage in America* (Baton Rouge: Louisiana State University Press, 1948) and C. E. Carter, ed., *Correspondence of General Thomas Gage* (2 vols., New Haven: Yale University Press, 1931–33).

27. Pargellis, *Lord Loudoun*, pp. 61–67, 299–300, 316–18; *Military Affairs in North America*, pp. 292–93, 327–30, 335–41; Freeman, *op. cit.*, II, 312–13.
28. See note 22, above.
29. Alfred Proctor James, ed., *Writings of General John Forbes Relating to His Service in North America* (Menasha, Wis.: The Collegiate Press, 1938), p. 125.
30. Edward E. Curtis, *The Organization of the British Army in the American Revolution* (New Haven: Yale University Press, 1926), pp. 4–5; J. F. C. Fuller, *British Light Infantry in the Eighteenth Century* (London: Hutchinson, 1925); Eric Robson, "British Light Infantry in the Eighteenth Century: The Effect of American Conditions," *Army Quarterly*, LXII, No. 2 (1950), 209–22.
31. Much obstructive underbrush is cleared away from this question by Peter Paret, "Colonial Experience and European Military Reform at the End of the Eighteenth Century," *Bulletin of the Institute of Historical Research*, XXXVII (May, 1964), 47–59.
32. Fitzpatrick, *op. cit.*, II, 114.

CHAPTER THREE

1. John C. Fitzpatrick, ed., *The Writings of George Washington* (39 vols., Washington: Government Printing Office, 1931–44), VI, 380.
2. Worthington C. Ford *et al.*, eds., *Journals of the Continental Congress, 1774–1789* (34 vols., Washington: Government Printing Office, 1934–37), II, 89–90. One of the best accounts of the founding of the Continental Army is in Douglas Southall Freeman, *George Washington* (7 vols., New York: Scribner, 1948–57), III. The history of the Continental Army can be traced in Randolph G. Adams and Howard H. Peckham, *Lexington to Fallen Timbers, 1775–1794* (Ann Arbor: University of Michigan Press, 1942). A popular account is Lynn Montross, *Rag, Tag, and Bobtail: The Story of the Continental Army* (New York: Harper, 1952). On the creation of the Army, see also Allen French, *The First Year of the American Revolution* (Boston: Houghton Mifflin, 1934).
3. Ford *et al.*, *op. cit.*, II, 91–94.
4. *Ibid.*, p. 111–23. The American Articles of War incorporated features of both the Parliamentary Mutiny Act and the royally decreed Articles of War.
5. Fitzpatrick, *op. cit.*, III, 309.
6. Ford *et al.*, *op. cit.*, II, 100–101.
7. Charles K. Bolton, *The Private Soldier Under Washington* (New York: Scribner, 1902), pp. 6–9; Louis Clinton Hatch, *The Administration of the American Revolutionary Army* (New York: Longmans, Green, 1904), pp. 1–2; Willard M. Wallace, *Appeal to Arms: A Military History of the American Revolution* (New York: Harper, 1951), pp. 4–5; Christopher Ward, *The War of the Revolution* (2 vols., New York: Macmillan, 1952), I, 20–21. Bolton's work and Hatch's are still the best in their fields. On the private soldier, interesting observations appear also in John C. Fitzpatrick, *The Spirit of the Revolution* (Boston: Houghton Mifflin, 1924); and modern printings of firsthand accounts both of enlisted men and of officers

are innumerable. The Wallace and Ward books, along with John Richard Alden, *The American Revolution, 1775–1783* (New York: Harper, 1954) and Howard H. Peckham, *The War for Independence: A Military History* (Chicago: University of Chicago Press, 1958) are the best recent general surveys of the battles and campaigns. Francis Vinton Greene, *The Revolutionary War and the Military Policy of the United States* (New York: Scribner, 1911) attempts to explore the influence of the Revolutionary campaigns on later military policy; written by a National Guard officer, it was an early effort to liberate the subject from Emory Upton's heavy hand. Marvin A. Kreidberg and Merton G. Henry, *History of Military Mobilization in the United States Army, 1775–1945* (Washington: Department of the Army, 1955) is fullest on the twentieth century and Uptonian throughout. For firsthand accounts of all American wars to 1918, see William Matthews and Dixon Wecter, *Our Soldiers Speak, 1775–1918* (Boston: Little, Brown, 1943).

8. Oliver Lyman Spaulding, *The United States Army in War and Peace* (New York: Putnam, 1937), p. 30; Ward, *op. cit.*, I, 54–56. In fact, Steuben later reported that American regiments ranged from three to twenty-three companies; practice seems to have been much more irregular than theory. William A. Ganoe, *History of the United States Army* (New York: Appleton-Century, 1936), p. 4. Greene's experiences in the Kentish Guards appear in Theodore Thayer, *Nathanael Greene: Strategist of the American Revolution* (New York: Twayne, 1960).

9. Fitzpatrick, *Writings of Washington*, III, 329–30; Freeman, *op. cit.*, III, 492–93.

10. Freeman, *op. cit.*, III, 509.

11. *Ibid.*, p. 577.

12. For Washington's expectations of a short war, see *ibid.*, *passim*, esp. pp. 417, 451–52, 515.

13. Spaulding, *op. cit.*, pp. 38–39; Fitzpatrick, *op. cit.*, III, 142, 173, 265; Ward, *op. cit.*, I, 208–10.

14. The crisis of December, 1775, can be followed in all the standard histories, especially Freeman, *op. cit.*, III, chap. xxii. For the general problem of morale see Allen Bowman, *Morale of the American Revolutionary Army* (Washington: American Council on Public Affairs, 1943).

15. Fitzpatrick, *Writings of Washington*, IV, 211.

16. Freeman, *op. cit.*, IV, 6–8, 27, 103–4, 125, 146–48, 151.

17. Technically, a "flying camp" was a small mixed force of infantry and cavalry constantly in motion. In the Revolutionary army, the term was used to mean a mobile reserve. Freeman, *op. cit.*, IV, 103 n.

18. George Otto Trevelyan, *The American Revolution* (4 vols., New York: Longmans, Green, 1909–12). Part II, Vol. II, 17, quoted in Ward, *op cit.*, I, 276. Washington's comments on the "disgraceful and dastardly" conduct of his militia at Kip's Bay are in Fitzpatrick, *Writings of Washington*, VI, 58. There are stories that Washington, observing the flight of his troops, exclaimed, "Are these the men with which I am to defend America?" and, "Good God, have I got such troops as those?" Freeman, *op. cit.*, IV, 194 n. For a sampling of Washington's similar comments, see Fitzpatrick, *Writings of Washington*, VI, 63, 81, 95–96, 110–12.

19. Ford *et al.*, *op. cit.*, V, 762–63, 788, 853, 855–56; VI, 1045–46; Freeman, *op. cit.*, IV, 206–10; Ward, *op. cit.*, I, 320. Bernhard Knollenberg, *Washington and the Revolution, A Reappraisal: Gates, Conway, and the Continental Congress* (New York: Macmillan, 1940), pp. 122–28, argues that, contrary to the impression given by Upton in his disparagement of Congress, Washington himself had misgivings about the wisdom of seeking long-term enlistments.

20. Ford *et al.*, *op. cit.*, VI, 856, 920–21; Freeman, *op. cit.*, IV, 238.

21. Freeman, *op. cit.*, IV, 268, 273.

22. Fitzpatrick, *Writings of Washington*, IV, 398.

23. Freeman, *op. cit.*, V, 294–97.

24. Ford *et al.*, *op. cit.*, VI, 1043–46.

25. Freeman, *op. cit.*, IV, 332–35.

26. Fitzpatrick, *Writings of Washington*, VII, 350; North Callahan, *Henry Knox: General Washington's General* (New York: Rinehart, 1958), p. 100; Freeman, *op. cit.*, IV, 404–5; Thayer, *op. cit.*, p. 154.

27. Freeman, *op. cit.*, IV, 530–33.

28. Fitzpatrick, *Writings of Washington*, X, 366.

29. Freeman, *op. cit.*, IV, 583–84. Various aspects of attempts to enforce compulsory militia service are discussed in three articles by Arthur J. Alexander: "How Maryland Tried to Raise Her Continental Quotas," *Maryland Historical Magazine*, XIII (1947), 193–95; "Pennsylvania's Revolutionary Militia," *Pennsylvania Magazine of History and Biography*, LXIX (1945), 15–25; "Service by Substitute in the Militia of Lancaster and Northampton Counties (Pennsylvania) During the War of the Revolution," *Military Affairs*, IX (1945), 278–82. See also Orville T. Murphy, "The American Revolutionary Army and the Concept of Levee en Masse," *ibid.*, XXIII (1959–60), 13–20.

30. Ford *et al.*, *op. cit.*, X, 199–203; Freeman, *op. cit.*, IV, 585–86; Ward, *op. cit.*, II, 594, 883.

31. Fitzpatrick, *Writings of Washington*, XX, 114.

CHAPTER FOUR

1. Quoted in John C. Fitzpatrick, ed., *The Writings of George Washington* (39 vols., Washington: Government Printing Office, 1931–1944), VI, 109.

2. On Washington and the choice of officers, see Douglas Southall Freeman, *George Washington* (7 vols., New York: Scribner, 1948–57), V, 171–72, 226–27. Jennings B. Sanders, *The Evolution of the Executive Departments, 1774–1789* (Chapel Hill: University of North Carolina Press, 1935) reviews the first Congressional experiments in executive and administrative machinery; chaps. v and vi deal with the administration of the war. Harry M. Ward, *The Department of War, 1781–1789* (Pittsburgh: University of Pittsburgh Press, 1962) touches briefly on the earlier background. Also see Elizabeth Cometti, "The Civil Servants of the Revolutionary Period," *Pennsylvania Magazine of History and Biography*, LXXV (1951), 159–69.

3. Worthington C. Ford *et al.*, eds., *Journals of the Continental Congress, 1774–1789* (34 vols., Washington: Government Printing Of-

fice, 1934–37), V, 434–35; Page Smith, *John Adams* (2 vols., Garden City: Doubleday, 1962), I, 267, 292–94, 298; Ward, *op. cit.*, pp. 2–3.

4. Ford *et al., op. cit.*, VIII, 563; Freeman, *op. cit.*, IV, 549.

5. Freeman, *op. cit.*, IV, 558–60, 582–83, 585, 596–98, 607–10, 629; Ward, *op. cit.*, pp. 3–5.

6. Ford *et al., op. cit.*, XIX, 133.

7. There is a sketch of Lincoln by Clifford K. Shipton in George Athan Billias, ed., *George Washington's Generals* (New York: Morrow, 1964), pp. 193–211.

8. Quoted in Freeman, *op. cit.*, V, 405; see also Ward, *op. cit.*, pp. 17–19.

9. Ward, *op. cit.*, pp. 11–20.

10. Freeman, *op. cit.*, is especially good on Washington's staff. There is an excessively laudatory biography of Gates by Samuel W. Patterson, *Horatio Gates, Defender of American Liberties* (New York: Columbia University Press, 1941). Gates is sketched by the editor in Billias, *op. cit.*, pp. 79–108. On Reed there is an old work, William B. Reed, *The Life and Correspondence of Joseph Reed* (2 vols., Philadelphia, 1847), and John F. Roche, *Joseph Reed: A Moderate in the American Revolution* (New York: Columbia University Press, 1957). On Tilghman, Oswald Tilghman, *Memoir of Lieutenant Colonel Tench Tilghman* (Albany, 1876). Among the many Hamilton biographies, relatively full accounts of Hamilton's wartime service can be found in John C. Miller, *Alexander Hamilton: Portrait in Paradox* (New York: Harper, 1959) and Broadus Mitchell, *Alexander Hamilton* (2 vols., New York: Macmillan, 1957). On Pickering, Octavius Pickering and Charles W. Upham, *The Life of Timothy Pickering* (4 vols., Boston, 1867–73).

11. On Washington and Conway, Freeman, *op. cit.*, IV, chap. xxiii, generally follows Washington's view of the affair, while Bernhard Knollenberg, *Washington and the Revolution, A Reappraisal: Gates, Conway, and the Continental Congress* (New York: Macmillan, 1940), pp. 37–92, is unusual in its sympathy for Conway (and strains to make the point).

12. The best account of quartermaster supply in the Revolution is Erna Risch, *Quartermaster Support of the Army: A History of the Corps* (Washington: Department of the Army, 1962), chaps. i and ii. This volume includes the commissariat, for which see also Victor L. Johnson, *The Administration of the American Commissariat During the Revolutionary War* (Philadelphia: University of Pennsylvania, 1941). On medicine in the Continental Army, see Howard Lewis Applegate, "The Medical Administrators of the American Revolutionary Army," *Military Affairs*, XXV (1961–62), 1–10, and Robert Courtney Hall, "The Beginnings of American Military Medicine," *Annals of Medical History*, IV (1942), 122–31.

13. Risch, *op. cit.*, pp. 3–8. Mifflin's biography is Kenneth R. Rossman, *Thomas Mifflin and the Politics of the American Revolution* (Chapel Hill: University of North Carolina Press, 1952).

14. Risch, *op. cit.*, pp. 13–15.

15. Quoted *ibid.*, p. 16.

16. *Ibid.*, pp. 19–22.

17. Ford *et al., op. cit.*, III, 323, quoted in Risch, *op. cit.*, p. 9. On the history of the Army ration, see John R. Merlin, "Critique of the Army

Ration, Past and Present," *Military Surgeon*, X (1922), 38–60, 163–187. See also Christopher Ludwig, "Christopher Ludwig, Baker-General of the Army of the United States During the Revolutionary War," *Pennsylvania Magazine of History and Biography*, XVI (1892), 343–48. The reader can study a specialized aspect of the early ration in "Classics of Alcohol Literature, Early Medical and Official Views on Rations of Spirits in the Army and Navy of the United States," *Quarterly Journal of Studies on Alcohol*, IV (March, 1944), 606–34.

18. Risch, *op. cit.*, pp. 8–21. On Moylan, Martin I. J. Griffin, *Stephen Moylan* (Philadelphia: privately printed, 1909) quotes extensively from Moylan's correspondence.

19. Risch, *op. cit.*, pp. 23–24.

20. *Ibid.*, pp. 26–29; Freeman, *op. cit.*, III, 583; IV, between pp. 241–42, 438–47.

21. Edmund C. Burnett, "The Continental Congress and Agricultural Supplies," *Agricultural History*, II (1928), 111–28; Freeman, *op. cit.*, IV, 452, 573–76, 639–42.

22. Fitzpatrick, *op. cit.*, X, 192–96.

23. Dr. Waldo's journal is the most frequently quoted firsthand narrative of Valley Forge: "Valley Forge, 1777–78: The Diary of Surgeon Albigence Waldo of the Continental Line," *Pennsylvania Magazine of History and Biography*, XXI (1897), 299–323. See also William Shainline Middleton, "Medicine at Valley Forge," *Annals of Medical History*, II (1941), 461–86.

24. Risch, *op. cit.*, p. 36.

25. Freeman, *op. cit.*, IV, 578.

26. Risch, *op. cit.*, pp. 1, 40–48.

27. Fitzpatrick, *op. cit.*, XVII, 273.

28. Quoted in Risch, *op. cit.*, p. 56.

29. Freeman, *op. cit.*, IV, 144–47, 151–55.

30. Risch, *op. cit.*, pp. 44–48.

31. Fitzpatrick, *op. cit.*, XVI, 387–88. On Revolutionary uniforms, see Charles M. Lefferts, *Uniforms of the American, British, French, and German Armies in the War of the American Revolution, 1775–1783* (New York: New-York Historical Society, 1926). Not altogether accurate but still probably the best source on American uniforms are the paintings by H. A. Ogden published by the Quartermaster General's Office in 1890, with accompanying text by Henry Loomis Nelson, and with later supplements, recently republished as *Uniforms of the United States Army* (2 vols., New York: Yoseloff, 1959–60). See also Frederick P. Todd, *Soldiers of the American Army, 1775–1954* (Chicago: Regnery, 1954), with drawings by Fritz Kredel.

32. Risch, *op. cit.*, pp. 41–66.

33. Freeman, *op. cit.*, V, 181–85, 189–90, 193–95, 202, 204, 211–13, 220, 223.

34. The standard account of the mutiny is Carl Van Doren, *Mutiny in January* (New York: Viking, 1943).

35. Freeman, *op. cit.*, V, 244–49; Van Doren, *op. cit.*, pp. 204–7.

36. Risch, *op. cit.*, pp. 59–66.

37. Merrill Jensen, *The New Nation: A History of the United States During the Confederation* (New York: Knopf, 1950), p. 34.

38. Freeman, *op. cit.*, V, 405–6, 412; Victor L. Johnson, "Robert Morris

and the Provisioning of the American Army During the Campaign of 1781," *Pennsylvania History*, V (1938), 7–20; Risch, *op. cit.*, pp. 66–73. Nathanael Greene's southern army continued to be supplied by requisitions upon the states until late 1782, when Greene arranged for a contractor to provide first clothing and then provisions. Louis Clinton Hatch, *The Administration of the American Revolutionary Army* (New York: Longmans, Green, 1904), pp. 119–20.

39. Freeman, *op. cit.*, III, 577; IV, 92, 125; Hugh Jameson, "Equipment for the Militia of the Middle States, 1775–1781," *Military Affairs*, III (1939), 26–38. Dorothy C. Barck, "A List of 500 Inhabitants of New York City in 1775 . . . ," *New-York Historical Society Quarterly Bulletin*, XXIII (1939), 23–31, touches on seizures of British muskets at the outbreak of the war.

40. Freeman, *op. cit.*, III, 509; IV, 22, 82, 125; Orlando W. Stephenson, "The Supply of Gunpowder in 1776," *American Historical Review*, XXX (1925), 271–81.

41. North Callahan, *Henry Knox: General Washington's General* (New York: Rinehart, 1958), pp. 19–20, 76–77, 142, 162; Freeman, *op. cit.*, IV, 17. See also William E. Birkhimer, *Historical Sketch of the Organization, Administration, Matériel and Tactics of the Artillery, United States Army* (Washington: Chapman, 1884).

42. William A. Ganoe, *History of the United States Army* (New York: Appleton-Century, 1936), pp. 7–12; Oliver Lyman Spaulding, *The United States Army in War and Peace* (New York: Putnam, 1937), pp. 29–30, 35–40; Christopher Ward, *The War of the Revolution* (2 vols., New York: Macmillan, 1952), I, 117. There is information on Continental tactics in John W. Wright, "Some Notes on the Continental Army," *William and Mary Quarterly*, second series, XI (April–July, 1931), 81–105, 185–209; XII (April, 1932), 79–103.

43. Ford *et al.*, *op. cit.*, III, 321–24; V, 762; XVIII, 893–97; Ganoe, *op. cit.*, pp. 17–18, 21, 29, 31–32, 35; Spaulding, *op. cit.*, pp. 38–40, 57–58, 69–71; Willard M. Wallace, *Appeal to Arms: A Military History of the American Revolution* (New York: Harper, 1951), p. 227; C. Ward, *op. cit.*, I, 117–18; II, 594.

44. See Knollenberg, *op. cit.*, chap. xi, "Flogging in the American Army"; also Maurer Maurer, "Military Justice Under Washington," *Military Affairs*, XXVIII (1964–65), 8–16.

45. Steuben's tactical manual has its most recent reprinting in Joseph R. Riling, *Baron von Steuben and His Regulations for the Order and Discipline of the Troops of the United States* (Philadelphia: Riling Arms Books, 1966). The best biography of Steuben is easily John McAuley Palmer, *General von Steuben* (New Haven: Yale University Press, 1937), which is both full of praise for him yet reasonably restrained in its estimates of his accomplishments, and the work of one of America's most perceptive military writers. Also available are Friedrich Kapp, *The Life of Frederick William von Steuben* (New York: Mason Bros., 1859); Joseph B. Doyle, *Frederick William von Steuben and the American Revolution* (Steubenville, Ohio: Cook, 1913); and Rudolph Cronau, *The Army of the Revolution and Its Organizer* (New York: Cronau, 1913).

46. Quoted in George Washington Greene, *The Life of Nathanael Greene* (3 vols., New York: Putnam, 1867), I, 336. A judicious summation of Washington's role and importance as commander in chief is in

Freeman, *op. cit.*, V, 487–501. See also Thomas G. Frothingham, *Washington, Commander-in-Chief* (Boston: Houghton Mifflin, 1930). Billias, *op. cit.*, is the best introduction to the generalship of Washington's principal subordinates and contains suggestions for further reading. See also "Washington's Opinion of General Officers," *Magazine of American History*, III (1879), 82–83. A manual on the duties of a Revolutionary officer is Thomas Simes, *The Military Guide for Young Officers* (2 vols., Philadelphia, 1776).

47. Quoted in Freeman, *op. cit.*, V, 482.

48. Fitzpatrick, *op. cit.*, XV, 274; Freeman, *op. cit.*, IV, 100; V, 482.

49. Fitzpatrick, *op. cit.*, XIX, 189. See John W. Wright, "The Rifle in the American Revolution," *American Historical Review*, XXIX (1924), 293–99, and "The Corps of Light Infantry in the Continental Army," *ibid.*, XXXI (1926), 454–61. Eric Robson, *The American Revolution in Its Political and Military Aspects: 1763–1785* (New York: Oxford University Press, 1955) offers stimulating observations on the methods of both sides in fighting the war. See also Durand Echeverria and Orville T. Murphy, "The American Revolutionary Army: A French Estimate in 1777," *Military Affairs*, XXVII (1963–64), 1–7, 153–62. For weapons, see also James E. Hicks, "United States Military Shoulder Arms, 1795–1935. Part 3. The French Infantry Musket of the Models of 1763 and 1766. Part 4. The United States Musket Model of 1795," *Military Affairs*, II (1938), 36–42.

50. Charles J. Stillé, *Major-General Anthony Wayne and the Pennsylvania Line in the Continental Army* (Philadelphia: Lippincott, 1893) is still generally the most useful work on Wayne's exploits.

51. A number of the essays in Billias, *op. cit.*, take up the issue of the Revolutionaries' possible employment of unconventional war. John W. Shy on Charles Lee, pp. 25–53, is outstanding; see also Don Higginbotham on Daniel Morgan, pp. 291–313, which emphasizes the topic more than does Higginbotham's *Daniel Morgan: Revolutionary Rifleman* (Chapel Hill: University of North Carolina Press, 1961); also Marcus Cunliffe on George Washington, pp. 3–17, which emphasizes the conservatism of Washington's generalship.

Jac Weller, "Irregular But Effective: Partizan Weapons Tactics in the American Revolution," *Military Affairs*, XXI (1957–58), 118–31, and "The Irregular War in the South," *ibid.*, XXIV (1960–1961), 124–36, deal with the southern partisans. In addition to works already mentioned, see John R. Alden, *The South in the Revolution, 1763–1789* (Baton Rouge: Louisiana State University Press, 1957); Robert D. Bass, *Gamecock: The Life and Campaigns of General Thomas Sumter* (New York: Holt, Rinehart and Winston, 1961); North Callahan, *Daniel Morgan: Ranger of the Revolution* (New York: Holt, Rinehart and Winston, 1961); Chalmers G. Davidson, *Piedmont Partisan: The Life and Times of Brigadier-General William Lee Davidson* (Davidson, N.C.: Davidson College, 1951); James Graham, *The Life of General Daniel Morgan of the Virginia Line of the Army of the United States* (New York: Derby & Jackson, 1856); Anne King Gregorie, *Thomas Sumter* (Columbia: University of South Carolina Press, 1931); Henry Lee, *Memoirs of War in the Southern Department* (2nd ed. New York: University Publishing Co., 1869); Robert C. Pugh, "The Revolutionary Militia in the Southern Campaigns, 1780–1781," *William and Mary Quarterly*, third series, XIV (1957), 154–75; M. F. Treacy, *Prelude to Yorktown: The Southern Campaigns of Nathanael Greene, 1780–1781* (Chapel Hill: University of North Carolina Press, 1963). On the British side, see Robert D. Bass, *The Green Dragoon: The Lives of Banastre Tarleton and Mary Robinson* (New York: Holt, 1957); John Graves Simcoe, *A Journal of the Operations of the Queens Rangers from the End of the Year 1777 to the Conclusion of the Late American War* (Exeter, 1787); Banastre Tarleton, *A History of the Campaigns of 1780 and 1781 in the Southern Provinces . . .* (London, 1787).

52. Callahan, *Knox* contains much information on the Continental artillery. A good study of the artillery in a campaign in which it figured prominently is Jac Weller, "Guns of Destiny: Field Artillery in the Trenton-Princeton Campaign," *Military Affairs*, XX (1956), 1–15. Fairfax Downey, *Sound of the Guns: The Story of American Artillery from the Ancient and Honorable Company to the Atom Cannon and Guided Missile* (New York: McKay, 1956) is a popular history; see also Birkhimer, *op. cit.* For an introduction to artillery, there is Albert Manucy, *Artillery Through the Ages: A Short Illustrated History of Cannon, Emphasizing Types Used in America* (Washington: Government Printing Office, 1949).

53. W. F. Heavey, "The Corps in the Days of the Revolution," *Military Engineer*, XXXI (Nov.–Dec., 1939), 410–15; Elizabeth S. Kite, *Brigadier-General Louis Lebègue Duportail* (Baltimore: Johns Hopkins Press, and Philadelphia: Dolphin, 1933).

54. Charles Francis Adams, *Studies Military and Diplomatic* (New York: Macmillan, 1911), pp. 59–113, presents a critical essay on Washington's use of cavalry. Some information is gathered in a popular history, John K. Herr and Edward S. Wallace, *The Story of the U.S. Cavalry, 1775–1942* (Boston: Little, Brown, 1953). See also "Selections from the Correspondence of Col. Stephen Moylan, of the Continental Cavalry," *Pennsylvania Magazine of History and Biography*, XXXVII (1911), 341–61; Harold L. Peterson, *The American Sword, 1775–1945* (New Hope, Pennsylvania: Halter, 1954); John H. Stutesman, Jr., "Colonel Armand and Washington's Cavalry," *New York Historical Quarterly*, XLV (1961), 5–42.

55. The volumes listed in note 51 above deal with mounted operations in the South.

56. Quoted in Wallace, *op. cit.*, p. 273.

CHAPTER FIVE

1. Number 41. See Jacob E. Cooke, ed., *The Federalist* (Middletown, Conn.: Wesleyan University Press, 1961), p. 271.

2. John C. Fitzpatrick, ed., *The Writings of George Washington* (39 vols., Washington: Government Printing Office, 1931–44), XX, 49–50.

3. *Ibid.*, VI, 112.

4. Quoted in Merrill Jensen, *The New Nation: A History of the United States During the Confederation* (New York: Knopf, 1950), p. 29.

5. The best account of this affair is *ibid.*, pp. 28–36, 67, 69–70. See also Edmund C. Burnett, *The Continental Congress* (New York:

Macmillan, 1941), pp. 553–67; Forrest McDonald, *E Pluribus Unum: The Formation of the American Republic, 1776–1790* (Boston: Houghton Mifflin, 1965), pp. 23–27; Clarence L. Ver Steeg, *Robert Morris, Revolutionary Financier* (Philadelphia: University of Pennsylvania Press, 1954).

6. Quoted in Jensen, *op. cit.*, p. 79.
7. The Newburgh Addresses are printed in Worthington C. Ford *et al.*, eds., *Journals of the Continental Congress, 1774–1789* (34 vols., Washington: Government Printing Office, 1934–37), XXIV, 294–98. See John Richard Alden, *The American Revolution, 1775–1783* (New York: Harper, 1954), p. 266; Douglas Southall Freeman, *George Washington* (7 vols., New York: Scribner, 1948–57), V, 429–33, 436 n; Jensen, *op. cit.*, pp. 68–72, 76–77; McDonald, *op. cit.*, pp. 27–28; Willard M. Wallace, *Appeal to Arms: A Military History of the American Revolution* (New York: Harper, 1951), pp. 265–66.
8. Freeman, *op. cit.*, V, 433–37; Jensen, *op. cit.*, pp. 76–77; McDonald, *op. cit.*, pp. 28–30; Ver Steeg, *op. cit.*, pp. 178–86; Wallace, *op. cit.*, pp. 266–67.
9. Quoted in Jensen, *op. cit.*, p. 79.
10. Wallace Evan Davies, *Patriotism on Parade: The Story of Veterans and Hereditary Organizations in America, 1783–1900* (Cambridge: Harvard University Press, 1955), chap. i; Jensen, *op. cit.*, pp. 262–265.
11. Fitzpatrick, *op. cit.*, XXVI, 288, 350.
12. Burnett, *op. cit.*, pp. 575–80; Wallace, *op. cit.*, pp. 267–68; Harry M. Ward, *The Department of War, 1781–1789* (Pittsburgh: University of Pittsburgh Press, 1962), pp. 28–30.
13. On demobilization, see Louis Clinton Hatch, *Administration of the American Revolutionary Army* (New York: Longmans, Green, 1904), chaps. viii–ix. In large part, the officers and men never saw the money promised them. When peace was established and the Army disbanded, the states regretted the promise of pensions for officers. They were unable to agree upon permitting Congress to raise a revenue for this or other purposes. Many officers became obliged to sell the certificates attesting to their pension rights at depreciated rates, to obtain ready cash. After 1790 the government of the Constitution arranged for ultimate payment in full, but only to the actual holders of certificates; those who had sold were ignored. Occasional measures thereafter provided for needy veterans, but not until 1828 did Congress agree to provide for Revolutionary veterans in general by voting full pay for life, though not exceeding a captain's pay, to all officers who in 1780 had been entitled to half pay for life, and by granting similar pensions to all enlisted men who had been promised a bounty of eighty dollars. Thereafter, as the surviving veterans grew fewer, Congress grew correspondingly generous to them and their widows. *Ibid.*, pp. 193–95.
14. This theme is developed in Curtis P. Nettels, *George Washington and American Independence* (Boston: Little, Brown, 1951).
15. Ward, *op. cit.*, p. 5.
16. Quoted in Jensen, *op. cit.*, p. 82.
17. Fitzpatrick, *op. cit.*, XXVI, 360, 374–98. See Russell F. Weigley, *Towards an American Army: Military Thought from Washington to*

Marshall (New York: Columbia University Press, 1962), pp. 10–14.

18. Henry Cabot Lodge, ed., *The Works of Alexander Hamilton* (12 vols., New York: Putnam, 1904), VI, 463–83.

19. Ford *et al.*, *op. cit.*, XXVII, 524; James Ripley Jacobs, *The Beginning of the U.S. Army, 1783–1812* (Princeton: Princeton University Press, 1947), p. 14; Ward, *op. cit.*, p. 42.

20. Ward, *op. cit.*, pp. 40–41, 44–46.

21. Mark M. Boatner III, *Military Customs and Traditions* (New York: McKay, 1956), pp. 70–74. From 1783 to June 2, 1784, about 700 men had remained under arms. They consisted mainly of Henry Jackson's Regiment of Foot and Major Sebastian Bauman's two companies of the Corps of Artillery. As will develop, Congress voted on June 3, 1784, to call up 700 militia; the Army was reduced to eighty men for only one day. Apparently it was hoped that the militia could be used more cheaply than the remaining Continentals. Also, Jackson's and Bauman's Continentals were mainly Massachusetts and New Hampshire men stationed in New York, where Yankees were not overly beloved.

22. Ford *et al.*, *op. cit.*, XXVII, 530–31.

23. Jacobs, *op. cit.*, pp. 18–20; John K. Mahon, "Pennsylvania and the Beginnings of the Regular Army," *Pennsylvania History*, XXI (1954), 33–44.

24. J. F. Callan, *The Military Laws of the United States* (Philadelphia: Childs, 1863), p. 78; Jacobs, *op. cit.*, pp. 23–24; Ward, *op. cit.*, pp. 56–58.

25. Reginald Horsman, "American Indian Policy in the Old Northwest, 1783–1812," *William and Mary Quarterly*, third series, XVIII (1961), 35–53; Jacobs, *op. cit.*, pp. 18–39; Ward, *op. cit.*, pp. 60–74.

26. Jacobs, *op. cit.*, pp. 13–39; Erna Risch, *Quartermaster Support of the Army: A History of the Corps* (Washington: Department of the Army, 1962), pp. 76–77; Ward, *op. cit.*, pp. 53–54, 59–60, 83–84, 89.

27. Jacobs, *op. cit.*, pp. 35–39; Risch, *op. cit.*, pp. 76–81.

28. Ward, *op. cit.*, p. 75.

29. Ford *et al.*, *op. cit.*, XXXI, 891–92; Ward, *op. cit.*, pp. 75–81.

30. William A. Benton, "Pennsylvania Revolutionary Officers and the Federal Constitution," *Pennsylvania History*, XXXI (1964), 419–35.

31. Quoted in Louis Smith, *American Democracy and Military Power: A Study of Civil Control of the Military Power in the United States* (Chicago: University of Chicago Press, 1951), p. 27. A history of American antimilitarism, and of distrust and suspicion of the military from colonial times, is Arthur A. Ekirch, Jr., *The Civilian and the Military* (New York: Oxford University Press, 1956).

32. *Pennsylvania Packet*, Sept. 23, 1787, quoted in Benton, *op. cit.*, pp. 423–24.

33. Smith, *op. cit.*, pp. 19–20.

34. Quoted in Benton, *op. cit.*, pp. 422–23.

35. Quoted in Smith, *op. cit.*, p. 19.

36. Cooke, *op. cit.*, pp. 20–21. Smith, *op. cit.*, offers an excellent discussion of the military provisions of the Constitution. See also Clarence A. Berdahl, *War Powers of the Executive in the United States* (Urbana: University of Illinois Press, 1921).

37. Number 25. Cooke, *op. cit.*, pp. 161–62.

38. *Ibid.*, p. 271.
39. *American State Papers, Military Affairs* (7 vols., Washington: Gales and Seaton, 1832–61), I, 5–6; Callan, *op. cit.*, p. 87; Jacobs, *op. cit.*, pp. 41–42; Ward, *op. cit.*, pp. 101–4. An older history is L. D. Ingersoll, *A History of the War Department of the United States, with Biographical Sketches of the Secretaries* (Washington: Francis D. Mohun, 1880).
40. *American State Papers, Military Affairs*, I, 6–13.
41. Callan, *op. cit.*, pp. 89–90; Jacobs, *op. cit.*, pp. 46–50; Ward, *op. cit.*, pp. 103–6. Frederick Phisterer, *Statistical Record of the Armies of the United States* (New York: Scribner, 1883) is the most convenient source on Army strength into the late nineteenth century.
42. Randolph G. Adams, "The Harmar Expedition of 1790," *Ohio Archaeological and Historical Quarterly*, L (1941), 60–62; Jacobs, *op. cit.*, chap. iii; Basil Meek, "General Harmar's Expedition," *Ohio Archaeological and Historical Quarterly*, XX (1911), 74–108; Howard H. Peckham, "Josiah Harmar and His Indian Expedition," *ibid.*, LV (1946), 227–41. For Army posts in the West, see Francis Paul Prucha, *A Guide to the Military Posts of the United States, 1789–1945* (Madison: State Historical Society of Wisconsin, 1965).
43. Callan, *op. cit.*, pp. 90–91; Jacobs, *op. cit.*, pp. 118–19.
44. Jacobs, *op. cit.*, pp. 76–84; Risch, *op. cit.*, pp. 88–100; Ward, *op. cit.*, pp. 133–35.
45. Jacobs, *op. cit.*, chap. v; William H. Smith, *The Life and Public Services of General Arthur St. Clair* (2 vols., Cincinnati: Clark, 1882); Frazer Wilson, *Arthur St. Clair* (Richmond: Garrett and Massie, 1944).
46. Callan, *op. cit.*, pp. 92–93; Jacobs, *op. cit.*, p. 125; Ward, *op. cit.*, pp. 143–44.
47. For the origin of the "Legion of the United States," see Jacobs, *op. cit.*, pp. 130–31; for its organization, *American State Papers, Military Affairs*, I, 40–41. Fletcher Pratt, *Eleven Generals: Studies in American Command* (New York: Sloane, 1949) has a useful discussion of the legionary organization in its chapter on Anthony Wayne and the Fallen Timbers campaign.
48. Richard C. Knopf, *Anthony Wayne, A Name in Arms: The Wayne-Knox-Pickering-McHenry Correspondence* (Pittsburgh: University of Pittsburgh Press, 1960) assembles much documentary material on Wayne's campaign. Knopf has written a number of articles on the campaign, of which one is especially pertinent to the institutional history of the Army: "Crime and Punishment in the American Legion, 1792–1793," *Bulletin of the Historical and Philosophical Society of Ohio*, XIV (1956), 232–38.
49. Callan, *op. cit.*, pp. 95–100.

PART TWO

1. Dennis Hart Mahan, *An Elementary Treatise on Advanced Guard, Outpost, and Detachment Service of Troops . . .* (Rev. ed., New York: Wiley, 1864), p. 36.

Chapter Six

1. From the First Inaugural. James D. Richardson, ed., *Compilation of the Messages and Papers of the Presidents* (10 vols. and supplements, Washington: Government Printing Office, 1899–1903), I, 323.

2. J. F. Callan, *The Military Laws of the United States* (Philadelphia: Childs, 1863), pp. 100–105; William A. Ganoe, *History of the United States Army* (New York: Appleton-Century, 1936), pp. 112–13; James Ripley Jacobs, *The Beginning of the U.S. Army, 1783–1812* (Princeton: Princeton University Press, 1947), pp. 370–81; Marshall Smelser, *The Congress Founds the Navy* (Notre Dame: University of Notre Dame Press, 1959), and "The Passage of the Naval Act of 1794," *Military Affairs*, XXII (1958–59), 1–12.

3. Callan, *op. cit.*, pp. 111–13, 118–19; B. C. Steiner, *The Life and Correspondence of James McHenry* (Cleveland: Burrows, 1907), pp. 291–95.

4. Callan, *op. cit.*, pp. 192–222; Carlos Emmor Godfrey, "Organization of the Provisional Army of the United States in the Anticipated War with France, 1789–1800," *Pennsylvania Magazine of History and Biography*, XXXVIII (1914), 129–82.

5. Douglas Southall Freeman, *George Washington* (7 vols., New York: Scribner, 1948–57), VII, 521–24, 528–34; Bernhard Knollenberg, "John Adams, Knox and Washington," *American Antiquarian Society Proceedings*, LVI (Oct., 1946), Part II, pp. 207–38; Stephen G. Kurtz, *The Presidency of John Adams: The Collapse of Federalism, 1795–1800* (Philadelphia: University of Pennsylvania Press, 1957), pp. 325–27; Page Smith, *John Adams* (2 vols., Garden City: Doubleday, 1962), II, 973–74, 980–83.

6. Quoted in Kurtz, *op. cit.*, p. 308.

7. Quoted in Smith, *op. cit.*, II, 983.

8. The best recent work is Jacob E. Cooke, "The Whiskey Insurrection—A Re-Evaluation," *Pennsylvania History*, XXX (1963), 316–346, which calls into question much previous interpretation. The standard account has been Leland Baldwin, *Whiskey Rebels* (Pittsburgh: University of Pittsburgh Press, 1939). See also Freeman, *op. cit.*, VII, chap. vii, and Bennett M. Rich, "Washington and the Whiskey Insurrection," *Pennsylvania Magazine of History and Biography*, LXV (1941), 334–52.

9. Quoted in Kurtz, *op. cit.*, pp. 309–10.

10. Quoted *ibid.*, pp. 315–16.

11. Quoted *ibid.*, pp. 314–15.

12. Quoted in Leonard D. White, *The Federalists: A Study in Administrative History* (New York: Macmillan, 1956), p. 275.

13. Kurtz, *op. cit.*, p. 330.

14. Quoted in Smith, *op. cit.*, II, 983.

15. Quoted *ibid.*, 1004, 1006–7, 1033–34.

16. *American State Papers*, *Military Affairs* (7 vols., Washington: Gales and Seaton, 1832–61), I, 139–41; Ganoe, *op. cit.*, p. 108; Jacobs, *op. cit.*, p. 236.

17. Quoted in Harry M. Ward, *The Department of War, 1781–1789* (Pittsburgh: University of Pittsburgh Press, 1962), pp. 132–33.

18. Julian P. Boyd, ed., *The Papers of Thomas Jefferson* (17 vols. to date, Princeton: Princeton University Press, 1950–   ), VII, 106; Richardson, *op. cit.*, I, 323.

19. Samuel P. Huntington, *The Soldier and the State: The Theory and Politics of Civil-Military Relations* (Vintage ed., New York: Vintage Books, 1964), pp. 196–97. See also Sidney Forman, "Thomas Jefferson on Universal Military Training," *Military Affairs*, XI (1947), 177–78; Leonard D. White, *The Jeffersonians: A Study in Administrative History, 1801–1829* (New York: Macmillan, 1959), pp. 212–213. The Huntington book is an outstanding work on its subject.

20. Callan, *op. cit.*, pp. 148–49. I was privileged to read and make use of the manuscript of Stephen E. Ambrose's new history of West Point, which supersedes its predecessors: *Duty, Honor, Country: A History of West Point* (Baltimore: Johns Hopkins Press, 1966). See also Sidney Forman, *West Point: A History of the United States Military Academy* (New York: Columbia University Press, 1950). For Hamilton's and Secretary of War McHenry's suggestions, see *American State Papers, Military Affairs*, I, 133. There is much information about the founding of the Military Academy in Norman B. Wilkinson, "The Forgotten 'Founder' of West Point" (Louis Tousard), *Military Affairs*, XXIV (1960–61), 177–88; also Edward Holden, "Origins of the United States Military Academy, 1777–1802," in *The Centennial History of the United States Military Academy at West Point, 1802–1902* (2 vols., Washington: Government Printing Office, 1904), I, 201–22.

21. Callan, *op. cit.*, pp. 148–49.

22. Huntington, *op. cit.*, pp. 195–200, is perceptive on the growth of "technicism" in the officer corps under the auspices of Jefferson and West Point. See Samuel Tilman, "The Academic History of the Military Academy, 1802–1902," *Centennial History*, I, 223–438.

23. The best work on Army exploration is William H. Goetzmann, *Army Exploration in the American West, 1803–1863* (New Haven: Yale University Press, 1959). Elliott Coues, ed., *The Expeditions of Zebulon Montgomery Pike, to the Headwaters of the Mississippi River, Through Louisiana Territory, and in New Spain, During the Years, 1805–6–7* (3 vols., New York: Francis P. Harper, 1895) is superseded by Donald Jackson, ed., *The Journals of Zebulon Montgomery Pike, With Letters and Related Documents* (2 vols., Norman: University of Oklahoma Press, 1966). See also Bernard DeVoto, *The Course of Empire* (Boston: Houghton Mifflin, 1952) and ed., *The Journals of Lewis and Clark* (Boston: Houghton Mifflin, 1953); E. B. Drewry, "Episodes in Western Expansion as Reported in the Writings of James Wilkinson," Ph.D. thesis, Cornell University, 1935; W. E. Hollon, *The Lost Pathfinder: Zebulon Montgomery Pike* (Norman: University of Oklahoma Press, 1949) and "Zebulon Montgomery Pike's Mississippi Voyage, 1805–1806," *Wisconsin Magazine of History*, XXXII (1949), 445–55; Donald Jackson, "How Lost Was Pike?" *American Heritage*, XVI (Feb., 1965), 10–15, 75–80; Milo M. Quaife, ed., *The Southwestern Expedition of Zebulon M. Pike* (Chicago: Donnelly, 1925).

24. See Jacobs, *op. cit.*, *passim*, esp. pp. 245–46, 383.

25. The colorful Wilkinson has inspired a voluminous literature. Much of it takes its cue from Frederick Jackson Turner's judgment that he

was "the most consummate artist in treason that the nation ever possessed" (*American Historical Review*, III [1898], 652). Despite Wilkinson's seemingly compulsive deviousness, this verdict is probably too harsh; Francis S. Philbrick effectively defends Wilkinson in the specific incident of the Burr conspiracy in *The Rise of the West, 1754–1830* (New York: Harper and Row, 1965), pp. 234–52. Wilkinson published his own *Memoirs of My Own Times* (3 vols. and atlas, Philadelphia: Small, 1816). The biographies include Thomas Robson Hay and M. R. Werner, *The Admirable Trumpeter* (Garden City: Doubleday, 1941); James Ripley Jacobs, *Tarnished Warrior* (New York: Macmillan, 1938); and R. O. Schreve, *The Finished Scoundrel* (Indianapolis: Bobbs-Merrill, 1933). See also P. W. Christian, "General Wilkinson and Kentucky Separatism, 1784–1798," Ph.D. thesis, Northwestern University, 1935; I. J. Cox, "General Wilkinson and His Latin Intrigues with the Spaniards," *American Historical Review*, XIX (1914), 794–812, and "Wilkinson's First Break with the Spaniards," *Biennial Report*, Department of Archives and History of the State of West Virginia, 1911–12, 1913–14; Thomas Robson Hay and M. R. Werner, "General Wilkinson—The Last Phase," *Louisiana Historical Quarterly*, XIX (1936), 407–35, and "Some Reflections on the Career of General James Wilkinson," *Mississippi Valley Historical Review*, XXI (1934–35), 471–94.

26. Scott is quoted in Charles Winslow Elliott, *Winfield Scott, the Soldier and the Man* (New York: Macmillan, 1937), p. 37. For the Butler case, Jacobs, *Beginning of the U.S. Army*, pp. 261–64, and *Tarnished Warrior*, pp. 199–201.

27. Quoted in Jacobs, *Beginning of the U.S. Army*, pp. 307–8, and White, *Jeffersonians*, p. 253.

28. Jacobs, *Beginning of the U.S. Army*, pp. 225–29; Erna Risch, *Quartermaster Support of the Army: A History of the Corps* (Washington: Department of the Army, 1962), pp. 75–84, 111–29; White, *Jeffersonians*, pp. 215, 224–28.

29. *American State Papers, Military Affairs*, I, 139–41, 156; Callan, *op. cit.*, pp. 141–49; Jacobs, *Beginning of the U.S. Army*, pp. 192, 236, 252–53.

30. Callan, *op. cit.*, pp. 150–51, 200–203; White, *Jeffersonians*, pp. 213, 531–35.

31. Henry Adams, *History of the United States During the Administrations of Jefferson and Madison* (9 vols., New York: Scribner, 1889–1901), IV, 249–88; Walter Wilson Jennings, *The American Embargo, 1807–1809* (Iowa City: University of Iowa, 1921); Louis Martin Sears, *Jefferson and the Embargo* (Durham: Duke University Press, 1927); White, *Jeffersonians*, pp. 461, 464–68.

32. On the continuing complexities of brevet rank, see Ganoe, *op. cit.*, pp. 121, 153, 167, 200–201, 219, 230, 308, 337.

33. Fairfax Downey, *Sound of the Guns: The Story of American Artillery from the Ancient and Honorable Company to the Atom Cannon and Guided Missile* (New York: McKay, 1956), pp. 63–66; J. F. C. Fuller, *A Military History of the Western World* (3 vols., New York: Funk and Wagnalls, 1954–56), II, 350, 414–18; Francis B. Heitman, *Historical Register and Dictionary of the United States Army* (2 vols., Washington: Government Printing Office, 1903), I, 51; Jacobs, *Beginning of the U.S. Army*, pp. 273–76.

34. Irving Brant, *James Madison* (6 vols., Indianapolis: Bobbs-Merrill, 1941–61), V, 123–29; Richardson, *op. cit.*, I, 478.
35. Brant, *op. cit.*, V, 437; Jacobs, *Beginning of the U.S. Army*, pp. 342–43, 383.
36. Callan, *op. cit.*, pp. 217–29; Risch, *op. cit.*, pp. 135–44; White, *Jeffersonians*, pp. 225–26. Raphael P. Thian, *Legislative History of the General Staff of the Army of the United States* (Washington: Government Printing Office, 1901) reprints the basic laws governing the staff departments.
37. Jacobs, *Beginning of the U.S. Army*, pp. 344–53, and *Tarnished Warrior*, pp. 247–60.
38. Elliott, *op. cit.*, pp. 30–36; Jacobs, *Beginning of the U.S. Army*, pp. 353–54, and *Tarnished Warrior*, pp. 261–62.
39. Callan, *op. cit.*, pp. 212–16, 220–21; Richardson, *op. cit.*, I, 494; Brant, *op. cit.*, V, 396–401.

CHAPTER SEVEN

1. Henry Adams, *History of the United States During the Administrations of Jefferson and Madison* (9 vols., New York: Scribner, 1889–1901), VIII, 45.
2. J. F. Callan, *The Military Laws of the United States* (Philadelphia: Childs, 1863), pp. 212–30; Marvin A. Kreidberg and Merton G. Henry, *History of Military Mobilization in the United States Army, 1775–1945* (Washington: Department of the Army, 1955), pp. 44–47.
3. Callan, *op. cit.*, pp. 236–38; C. Joseph Bernardo and Eugene R. Bacon, *American Military Policy: Its Development Since 1775* (Harrisburg: Stackpole, 1955), p. 126; Kreidberg and Henry, *op. cit.*, pp. 44–47.
4. *American State Papers, Military Affairs* (7 vols., Washington: Gales and Seaton, 1832–61), I, 385–88, 432; Kreidberg and Henry, *op. cit.*, p. 46. For Madison as a war leader, see the essay by Marcus Cunliffe in Ernest R. May, ed., *The Ultimate Decision: The President as Commander in Chief* (New York: Braziller, 1960), pp. 23–53.
5. Marguerite M. McKee, "Service of Supply in the War of 1812," *Quartermaster Review*, VI (Jan.–Feb., 1927), 6–19, (Mar.–Apr., 1927), 45–55; Erna Risch, *Quartermaster Support of the Army: A History of the Corps* (Washington: Department of the Army, 1962), pp. 136–62; Leonard D. White, *The Jeffersonians: A Study in Administrative History, 1801–1829* (New York: Macmillan, 1959), pp. 224–229.
6. On the campaigns of the War of 1812, Harry L. Coles, *The War of 1812* (Chicago: University of Chicago Press, 1965) is a recent, brief, scholarly survey of military as well as diplomatic and political aspects of the war. In many ways Henry Adams's work remains the best military history; its military passages have been published separately as *The War of 1812*, H. A. DeWeerd, ed. (Washington: Infantry Journal, 1944). Francis F. Beirne, *The War of 1812* (New York: Dutton, 1949) is good; Glenn Tucker, *Poltroons and Patriots: A Popular Account of the War of 1812* (2 vols., Indianapolis: Bobbs-

Merrill, 1954) is readable and includes some incidents that other works skim over lightly. The Uptonian outlook of Bernardo and Bacon, *op. cit.*, accounts for their extended treatment of the failures of militia to obey orders or to serve at all, pp. 118–22, 130–32.

7. Callan, *op. cit.*, pp. 237–40; Kreidberg and Henry, *op. cit.*, pp. 48–51.

8. Callan, *op. cit.*, pp. 247, 249, 250–52; Oliver Lyman Spaulding, *The United States Army in War and Peace* (New York: Putnam, 1937), pp. 131, 135.

9. Armstrong's apologia is John Armstrong, *Notices of the War of 1812* (2 vols., New York: Wiley and Putnam, 1840). A neglected account of the Washington-Baltimore campaign of 1814 is Neil H. Swanson, *The Perilous Fight* (New York: Farrar and Rinehart, 1945).

10. Callan, *op. cit.*, pp. 242–47; White, *op. cit.*, pp. 237–38. The same legislation provided for a physician and surgeon general and an apothecary general, to be civilians and not members of the General Staff.

11. The posts of adjutant and inspector general (created March 3, 1791), quartermaster general (recreated March 28, 1812), commissary general of ordnance (July 2, 1812) and paymaster had all existed previously, but with shifting administrative apparatus and without the fixed status now accorded the War Department General Staff. See Raphael P. Thian, *Legislative History of the General Staff of the Army of the United States* (Washington: Government Printing Office, 1901).

11. Irving Brant, *James Madison* (6 vols., Indianapolis: Bobbs-Merrill, 1941–61), VI, 68, 167, 261.

12. Kreidberg and Henry, *op. cit.*, pp. 54–59; Risch, *op. cit.*, pp. 152–77 (pp. 176–77 for the quotation from Brown); White, *op. cit.*, pp. 229–31.

13. White, *op. cit.*, pp. 225–28.

14. Brant, *op. cit.*, VI, 47–50.

15. *Ibid.*, pp. 340–45.

16. *American State Papers, Military Affairs*, I, 514–21; Bernardo and Bacon, *op. cit.*, pp. 138–40; Brant, *op. cit.*, VI, 26, 132, 226, 229, 235, 239, 337, 349, 359–60; Kreidberg and Henry, *op. cit.*, pp. 53–56.

17. Charles Winslow Elliott, *Winfield Scott, the Soldier and the Man* (New York: Macmillan, 1937), *passim*, esp. pp. 36–37, 101. See also James Barnes, *The Giant of Three Wars: A Life of Gen. Winfield Scott* (New York: Appleton, 1903).

18. Quoted in Theodore Ropp, *War in the Modern World* (Collier ed., New York: Collier Books, 1962), pp. 129–30. For the tactics of the French Revolutionary and Napoleonic wars, see especially *ibid.*, pp. 102–39. C. W. C. Oman, *Wellington's Army* (London: Longmans, Green, 1912), based on the same writer's *History of the Peninsular War* (7 vols., Oxford: Clarendon Press, 1902–30), is the best work on the British army of the period. Jay Luvaas, *The Education of an Army: British Military Thought, 1815–1940* (Chicago: University of Chicago Press, 1965) has a chapter on "The Peninsular Tradition" of Wellington's army and its great contemporary historian, Sir William Napier. John W. Fortescue, *The County Lieutenancies and the*

Army, 1803–1814 (London: Macmillan, 1909) deals with the British use of militia in recruiting during the Napoleonic era.

19. Elliott, *op. cit.*, pp. 146–53. Benson J. Lossing, *The Pictorial Field-Book of the War of 1812* (New York: Harper, 1869) made use of a "Memoir of the Campaign of Niagara," in which Major Thomas S. Jesup of the 25th Infantry described his training of the regiment under Scott's direction, p. 802 n.

20. Fletcher Pratt, *Eleven Generals: Studies in American Command* (New York: Sloane, 1949) has a good chapter on Jacob Brown and his battles on the Niagara frontier. In addition to the campaign histories listed earlier, see Louis L. Babcock, *The War of 1812 on the Niagara Frontier* (Buffalo, New York: Buffalo Historical Society, 1927) and Ernest Cruikshank, *The Battle of Lundy's Lane* (Welland, Ont.: Lundy's Lane Hist. Soc., 1893).

21. For the battle of the Thames, Beirne, *op. cit.*, pp. 213–20; Tucker, *op. cit.*, I, 339–343. Swanson, *op. cit.*, is unusually appreciative of the virtues of the citizen soldiers at Baltimore, if somewhat romantically so. For the New Orleans campaign, see Marquis James, *Andrew Jackson, The Border Captain* (Indianapolis: Bobbs-Merrill, 1933).

22. Henry Adams, ed., *The Writings of Albert Gallatin* (3 vols., Philadelphia: Lippincott, 1879), I, 700.

23. Charles M. Wiltse, *John C. Calhoun, Nationalist, 1782–1828* (Indianapolis: Bobbs-Merrill, 1944), pp. 138–39.

24. *Ibid.*, pp. 149, 248. The edition of Calhoun's works currently in progress goes to July, 1818, and has not yet reached the most important period of his tenure as Secretary of War; Vol. II does not print in full most documents previously printed: Robert L. Meriwether and W. Edwin Hemphill, eds., *The Papers of John C. Calhoun* (2 vols. to date, Columbia: University of South Carolina Press, 1959–   ). Calhoun's principal reports can be found in the old *Works of John C. Calhoun* (6 vols., New York: Appleton, 1855), as well as in *American State Papers, Military Affairs*.

25. *Works of Calhoun*, V, 30.

26. Risch, *op. cit.*, pp. 181–88; White, *op. cit.*, pp. 238–40, 246–50. For the surgeon general, see P. M. Ashburn, *A History of the Medical Department of the United States Army* (Boston: Houghton Mifflin, 1929); Charles W. Ayars, "Some Notes on the Medical Service of the Army, 1812–1839," *Military Surgeon*, L (1922), 505–24; Harvey E. Brown, compiler, *The Medical Department of the United States Army from 1775 to 1873* (Washington: Government Printing Office, 1873). L. D. Ingersoll, *A History of the War Department of the United States, with Biographical Sketches of the Secretaries* (Washington: Francis D. Mohun, 1880), is good on the early bureaus of the department.

27. Quoted in White, *op. cit.*, pp. 240–44. For Calhoun's conception of the relationship between staff and line, see also Elliott, *op. cit.*, pp. 217–24; Wiltse, *op. cit.*, p. 171.

28. Quoted in White, *op. cit.*, p. 245.

29. Samuel Flagg Bemis, *John Quincy Adams and the Foundations of American Foreign Policy* (New York: Knopf, 1950), pp. 313–16, 326; James, *op. cit.*, pp. 307–19; Wiltse, *op. cit.*, pp. 155–63, 177–79.

30. Bernardo and Bacon, *op. cit.*, p. 152; William H. Carter, *Creation*

of the American General Staff, 68th Congress, 1st Session, Senate Documents, II (serial 8254), no. 119; Elliott, op. cit., pp. 426–28. For the varying military districts of the nineteenth century, see Raphael P. Thian, Notes Illustrating the Military Geography of the United States, 1813–1880 (Washington: Government Printing Office, 1881).

31. Callan, op. cit., pp. 266–67.
32. William A. Ganoe, History of the United States Army (New York: Appleton-Century, 1936), pp. 146–47; Spaulding, op. cit., pp. 145, 147–48, 480–83. For histories of the old regiments of the Army see Theophilus F. Rodenbaugh and William L. Haskin, eds., The Army of the United States: Historical Sketches of Staff and Line (New York: Merrill, 1896).
33. Works of Calhoun, V, 25–40.
34. Ibid., p. 82.
35. Ibid., p. 83.
36. Ibid., pp. 84, 87.
37. Ibid., p. 92.
38. Ibid., pp. 88–91.
39. Ibid., p. 84.
40. On March 2, 1821, Congress adopted a much limited version of the expansible army plan while reducing the Army from 12,664 men to 6,183. Callan, op. cit., pp. 306–9.

CHAPTER EIGHT

1. Henry W. Halleck, Elements of Military Art and Science (3rd ed., New York: Appleton, 1863), pp. 144–45. First published in 1846.
2. Scott told Benson Lossing the story of the gray uniforms. Lossing, The Pictorial Field-Book of the War of 1812 (New York: Harper, 1869), p. 806 n.
3. J. F. Callan, The Military Laws of the United States (Philadelphia: Childs, 1863), pp. 201, 225.
4. Works of John C. Calhoun (6 vols., New York: Appleton, 1855), V, 54–57, 72–80; Leonard D. White, The Jeffersonians: A Study in Administrative History, 1801–1829 (New York: Macmillan, 1959), p. 256.
5. Joseph Gardner Swift, The Memoirs of Gen. Joseph Gardner Swift, LL.D., U.S.A., First Graduate of the United States Military Academy, West Point, H. Ellery, ed. (Worcester, Mass.: Blanchard, 1890); Lester A. Webb, Captain Alden Partridge and the United States Military Academy, 1806–1833 (Northport, Ala.: American Southern, 1965).
6. There is much information on Thayer, presented with admiration, in R. Ernest Dupuy, Where They Have Trod: The West Point Tradition in American Life (New York: Stokes, 1940), esp. pp. 62–182, 205–27.
7. American State Papers, Military Affairs (7 vols., Washington: Gales and Seaton, 1832–61), II, 76–80; III, 375; Sidney Forman, West Point: A History of the United States Military Academy (New York: Columbia University Press, 1950), pp. 36–60; North American Review, XXIII (1826), 269–73; White, op. cit., pp. 257–59.

8. On the rise of military schools, see Henry Barnard, *Military Schools and Courses of Instruction in the Science and Art of War* (Philadelphia: Lippincott, 1862); Gordon A. Craig, *The Politics of the Prussian Army, 1640–1945* (New York: Oxford University Press, 1956), pp. 45–46; Edward Mead Earle, *Makers of Modern Strategy: Military Thought from Machiavelli to Hitler* (Princeton: Princeton University Press, 1943), pp. 172–74; Samuel P. Huntington, *The Soldier and the State: The Theory and Politics of Civil-Military Relations* (Vintage ed., New York: Vintage Books, 1964), pp. 39–50. On Jomini, see Earle, *op. cit.*, pp. 77–92, and the bibliography, pp. 524–25; John R. Elting, "Jomini: Disciple of Napoleon?" *Military Affairs*, XXVIII (1964–65), 17–26. There are various editions of Jomini's works, including an English translation of *Précis de l'art de la guerre*, G. H. Mendell and W. P. Craighill, tr., *Summary of the Art of War* (Philadelphia: Lippincott, 1864).

9. William Duane, *The American Military Library* (2 vols., Philadelphia, 1807–9), on which see also Fred K. Vigman, "William Duane's American Military Library," *Military Affairs*, VIII (1944), 321–26; Maurice Saxe, *Mes Rêveries* (2 vols., Amsterdam and Leipzig, 1757) and English translation, *Reveries, or Memories upon the Art of War* (London, 1757); Jon Manchip White, *Marshal of France: The Life and Times of Maurice, Comte de Saxe* (Chicago: Rand-McNally, 1962), pp. 260–74.

10. Craig, *op. cit.*, pp. 37–65; Walter Goerlitz, *History of the German General Staff, 1657–1945*, tr. Brian Battershaw (New York: Praeger, 1952), pp. 13–47; William O. Shanahan, *Prussian Military Reforms, 1786–1813* (New York: Columbia University Press, 1945). The leading German work is Gerhard Ritter's monumental *Staatskunst und Kriegshandwerk: Das Problem des "Militarismus" in Deutschland* (3 vols. to date, Munich: Oldenbourg, 1954–   ), I.

11. Dennis Hart Mahan, *An Elementary Treatise on Advanced Guard, Out-Post, and Detachment Service of Troops . . .* (Rev. ed., New York: Wiley, 1864). First published in 1847. For Mahan's career, see Dupuy, *op. cit.*, pp. 228–40, and *Men of West Point: The First 150 Years of the United States Military Academy* (New York: Sloane, 1951), pp. 12–24; Russell F. Weigley, *Towards an American Army: Military Thought from Washington to Marshall* (New York: Columbia University Press, 1962), pp. 42–53.

12. Mahan, *op. cit.*, pp. 217–18.

13. *Ibid.*, pp. 32–34.

14. See note 1 above. A good biography is Stephen E. Ambrose, *Halleck, Lincoln's Chief of Staff* (Baton Rouge: Louisiana State University Press, 1960).

15. Halleck, *op. cit.*, pp. 144–47, 149, 324.

16. Huntington, *op. cit.*, pp. 217–20; Max L. Marshall, "A Survey of Military Periodicals," M. A. thesis, University of Missouri, 1953; Benjamin Blake Minor, *The Southern Literary Messenger, 1834–1864* (New York: Neale, 1905).

17. *Works of Calhoun*, V, 79.

18. Oliver Lyman Spaulding, *The United States Army in War and Peace* (New York: Putnam, 1937), p. 154; L. D. White, *op. cit.*, pp. 258–59.

19. William A. Ganoe, *History of the United States Army* (New York: Appleton-Century, 1936), p. 166.
20. Quoted in John William Ward, *Andrew Jackson, Symbol for an Age* (Galaxy ed., New York: Oxford University Press, 1962), p. 46.
21. *American State Papers, Military Affairs,* IV, 285, 683; V, 307, 347; VI, 988; VII, 1–3, 89; Huntington, *op. cit.,* p. 205; Leonard D. White, *The Jacksonians: A Study in Administrative History* (New York: Macmillan, 1954), pp. 208–12. See also Richard L. Watson, "Congressional Attitudes Towards Preparedness, 1829–1835," *Mississippi Valley Historical Review,* XXXIV (1947–48), 611–36.
22. Forman, *op. cit.,* pp. 49–51.
23. White, *Jacksonians,* pp. 210–12.
24. Huntington, *op. cit.,* pp. 203–4. Ward, *op. cit.,* pp. 13–57, is an extended discussion of the Jacksonian attitude toward the militia and the Jacksonian distrust of military education and training, as part of Jacksonian confidence in nature and the "natural" man. On the militia obligation, see Lena London, "The Militia Fine, 1830–1860," *Military Affairs,* XV (1951), 133–44.
25. James D. Richardson, *Compilation of the Messages and Papers of the Presidents* (10 vols. and supplements, Washington: Government Printing Office, 1899–1903), IV, 438.
26. Reports of the Secretary of War, 1837–40; C. Joseph Bernardo and Eugene R. Bacon, *American Military Policy: Its Development Since 1775* (Harrisburg: Stackpole, 1955), pp. 158–59; Walter Millis, *Arms and Men: A Study in American Military History* (New York: Putnam, 1956), p. 100; J. Fred Rippy, *Joel R. Poinsett, Versatile American* (Durham: Duke University Press, 1935), pp. 175–77; Henry H. Simms, *The Rise of the Whigs in Virginia, 1824–1840* (Richmond: William Byrd Press, 1929), pp. 144–45.
27. John Hope Franklin, *The Militant South, 1800–1861* (Beacon ed., Boston: Beacon Press, 1964), pp. 172–86, vividly describes the musters and activities of the militia companies. Franklin writes of the South, and his theme is the special flourishing of organized militia there as an evidence of southern militance; but what he says of the volunteer companies was true on only a slightly lesser scale in the North as well. See also John K. Mahon, "A Board of Officers Considers the Condition of the Militia in 1826," *Military Affairs,* XV (1951), 85–94; Paul T. Smith, "Militia in the United States from 1846 to 1860," *Indiana Magazine of History,* XV (1919), 20–47.
28. *Works of Calhoun,* V, 25–54, 139–47; Charles M. Wiltse, *John C. Calhoun, Nationalist, 1782–1828* (Indianapolis: Bobbs-Merrill, 1944), pp. 167–68, 182–85, 203–5, 214–16. The romance of the Old West has helped inspire numerous works on the advance of the military frontier. Among those concerning this period are: Henry P. Beers, "Military Protection of the Santa Fe Trail to 1843," *New Mexico Historical Review,* XII (1937), 113–33, and "The Western Military Frontier, 1815–1846," Ph.D. thesis, University of Pennsylvania, 1935; William L. Evans, "The Military History of Green Bay," *Proceedings of the State Historical Society of Wisconsin,* 1899 (Madison, 1900), pp. 128–46; Grant Foreman, *Advancing the Frontier* (Norman: University of Oklahoma Press, 1958); Marcus L. Hansen, *Old Fort Snelling, 1819–1858* (Iowa City: State Historical

Society of Iowa, 1918); Arthur P. Hayne, "Report of Inspection of the Ninth Military Department, 1819," ed. by Lester B. Shippee, *Mississippi Valley Historical Review*, VII (1920–21), 261–74; Elvid Hunt, *History of Fort Leavenworth, 1827–1937* (2nd ed., Fort Leavenworth: Command and General Staff School Press, 1937); Fred S. Perrine, "Military Escorts on the Santa Fe Trail," *New Mexico Historical Review*, II (1927), 175–93, 269–304; Francis Paul Prucha, *Broadax and Bayonet: The Role of the United States Army in the Development of the Northwest* (Madison: State Historical Society of Wisconsin, 1953), "The Settler and the Army in Frontier Minnesota," *Minnesota History*, XXIX (Sept., 1948), 231–246, and ed., "Fort Ripley: The Post and the Military Reservation," *ibid.*, XXVIII (Sept., 1947), 205–24; Mendell Lee Taylor, "The Western Service of Stephen Watts Kearny, 1815–1848," *New Mexico Historical Review*, XXI (1946), 169–84; Andrew Jackson Turner, "The History of Fort Winnebago," *Wisconsin Historical Society Collections*, XIV (1898), 65–102; United States National Park Service, *Soldier and Brave: Indian and Military Affairs in the Trans-Mississippi West, Including a Guide to Historic Sites and Landmarks* (New York: Harper and Row, 1963); Jacob Van der Zee, "Forts in the Iowa Country," *Iowa Journal of History and Politics*, XII (April, 1914), 163–204; Edgar Bruce Wesley, *Guarding the Frontier: A Study of Frontier Defense from 1815 to 1825* (Minneapolis: University of Minnesota Press, 1935), and "Life at a Frontier Post. Fort Atkinson, 1823–1826," *Military Affairs*, III (1939), 203–9; Otis E. Young, *The First Military Escort on the Santa Fe Trail, 1829; from the Journal and Reports of Major Bennet Riley and Lieutenant Philip St. George Cooke* (Glendale, Cal.: Clark, 1952). A brief popular history of the Indian campaigns up to the Civil War is Fairfax Downey, *Indian Wars of the U.S. Army (1776–1865)* (Derby, Conn.: Monarch Books, 1964).

29. On the formation of the 1st Dragoons see Callan, *op. cit.*, pp. 325–26, 329–30; Albert G. Brackett, *History of the United States Cavalry from the Formation of the Federal Government to June 1, 1863* (New York: Harper, 1865); Dwight L. Clarke, *Stephen Watts Kearny: Soldier of the West* (Norman: University of Oklahoma Press, 1961), pp. 55–58; Louis Pelzer, *Henry Dodge* (Iowa City: State Historical Society of Iowa, 1911); Spaulding, *op. cit.*, pp. 160–61.

30. Clarke, *op. cit.*, Philip St. George Cooke, *Scenes and Adventures in the Army; or, Romance of Military Life* (Philadelphia, 1859); James Hildreth, *Dragoon Campaigns to the Rocky Mountains; Being a History of the Enlistment, Organization, and First Campaigns of the Regiment of United States Dragoons* (New York: Wiley and Long, 1836); Louis Pelzer, ed., "A Journal of Marches by the First United States Dragoons, 1834–1835," *Iowa Journal of History and Politics*, VII (July, 1909), 331–78, and *Marches of the Dragoons in the Mississippi Valley* (Iowa City: State Historical Society of Iowa, 1917); Valentine M. Porter, ed., "Journal of Stephen Watts Kearny," *Missouri Historical Collections*, III (1908), 8–29, 99–131; Otis E. Young, *The West of Philip St. George Cooke, 1809–1895* (Glendale, Cal.: Clark, 1955).

31. Samuel E. Cobb, "The Florida Militia and the Affair at Withlacoochee," *Florida Historical Quarterly*, XIX (Oct., 1940), 128–39;

Charles Winslow Elliott, *Winfield Scott, the Soldier and the Man* (New York: Macmillan, 1937), pp. 288–310, 322–31; Ethan Allen Hitchcock, *Fifty Years in Camp and Field*, W. A. Croffut, ed. (New York: Putnam, 1909); John K. Mahon, "Two Seminole Treaties: Payne's Landing, 1832, and Fort Gibson, 1833," *Florida Historical Quarterly*, XLI (1962), 1–21; James W. Silver, "Edmund Pendleton Gaines and Frontier Problems," *Journal of the Southern Historical Association*, I (1935), 320–44; John T. Sprague, *The Origin, Progress, and Conclusion of the Florida War* (New York: Appleton, 1847); John B. B. Trussell, "Seminoles in the Everglades: A Case Study in Guerrilla Warfare," *Army*, XII (Dec., 1961), 41–45.

32. Callan, *op. cit.*, pp. 336–37; Theo. F. Rodebaugh, *From Everglade to Cañon with the Second Dragoons* (New York: Van Nostrand, 1875); Spaulding, *op. cit.*, pp. 162–63.

33. Callan, *op. cit.*, pp. 341–49.

34. Holman Hamilton, *Zachary Taylor, Soldier of the Republic* (Indianapolis: Bobbs-Merrill, 1941), pp. 122–41.

35. William A. Ganoe, *History of the United States Army* (New York: Appleton-Century, 1936), pp. 188–89; Edward S. Wallace, *General William Jenkins Worth: Monterey's Forgotten Hero* (Dallas: Southern Methodist University Press, 1953).

36. Callan, *op. cit.*, pp. 358–59, 364.

37. Grant Foreman, *Indian Removal* (Norman: University of Oklahoma Press, 1932); Prucha, *Broadax and Bayonet;* Dale Van Every, *Disinherited: The Lost Birthright of the American Indian* (New York: Morrow, 1966).

38. Samuel R. Bright, "Coast Defense and the Southern Coasts Before Fort Sumter," M.A. thesis, Duke University, 1958, despite its title has much to say about coastal fortifications in general up to the Civil War. See also *Works of Calhoun*, esp. V, 44–46; John G. Barnard, *Notes on Sea-Coast Defense* (New York, 1861); John M. Hammond, *Quaint and Historic Forts of North America* (Philadelphia: Lippincott, 1915); White, *Jeffersonians*, pp. 260–61; Wiltse, *op. cit.*, pp. 153, 164, 199.

39. Frank Barnes, *Fort Sumter National Monument, South Carolina* (National Park Service Historical Handbook Series Number Twelve, Washington: Government Printing Office, 1952); Quincy A. Gilmore, *The Siege and Reduction of Fort Pulaski* (New York, 1862); Ralston B. Lattimore, *Fort Pulaski National Monument, Georgia* (National Park Service Historical Handbook Series Number Eighteen, Washington: Government Printing Office, 1954).

40. Russell F. Weigley, *Quartermaster General of the Union Army: A Biography of M. C. Meigs* (New York: Columbia University Press, 1959), pp. 31–112.

41. *Works of Calhoun*, V, 40–54, 139–47.

42. E. G. Campbell, "Railroads in National Defense, 1829–1848," *Mississippi Valley Historical Review*, XXVII (1940–41), 361–78; Harry E. Cole, "The Old Military Road" (from Green Bay to Prairie du Chien), *Wisconsin Magazine of History*, IX (Sept., 1925), 47–62; Forest G. Hill, *Roads, Rails, and Waterways: The Army Engineers and Early Transportation* (Norman: University of Oklahoma Press, 1957); Arthur A. Maass, *Muddy Waters: The Army Engineers and the Nation's Rivers* (Cambridge: Harvard University Press, 1951);

Prucha, *Broadax and Bayonet;* White, *Jeffersonians,* pp. 261–63.
43. Weigley, *Quartermaster General,* pp. 102–4.
44. Quoted in R. Ernest Dupuy, *The Compact History of the United States Army* (New York: Hawthorn, 1956), p. 74. Henry P. Beers, "A History of the U. S. Topographical Engineers, 1813–1863," *Military Engineer,* XXXIV (1942), 287–91, 348–52; Allan Nevins, *Frémont, Pathmarker of the West* (new ed., New York: Longmans, Green, 1955); Carl I. Wheat, *Mapping the Transmississippi West* (San Francisco: Institute of Historical Cartography, 1958); Richard G. Wood, *Stephen Harriman Long, 1784–1864* (Glendale, Cal.: Clark, 1966).
45. Bernardo and Bacon, *op. cit.,* pp. 163–65; R. E. Dupuy, *op. cit.,* pp. 86–88; Edward J. Nichols, *Zach Taylor's Little Army* (Garden City: Doubleday, 1963), p. 33; Francis Paul Prucha, ed., *Army Life on the Western Frontier: Selections from the Official Reports Made Between 1826 and 1845 by Colonel George Croghan* (Norman: University of Oklahoma Press, 1958). The San Patricio Battalion of the Mexican army, formed from among American deserters, gives some indication of the ethnic composition of the American Army. It is famous as an organization of Irish-Americans, but of 113 San Patricios captured at Churubusco, only 34 were Irish, while 54 were American by birth, 17 German, and 1 each Nova Scotian, French, and Polish. Elliott, *op. cit.,* pp. 528–29.
46. 21st Congress, 1st Session, House Rep. 166 (serial 199), Committee on Military Affairs, "Ardent Spirits to Soldiers"; 22nd Congress, 1st Session, House Rep. 63 (serial 224), Committee on Military Affairs, "Desertion in the Army"; Alexander Macomb, "Army—Enlistment of Minors," 22nd Congress, 2nd Session, House Doc. 16 (serial 233); Bernardo and Bacon, *op. cit.,* pp. 163–65; White, *Jacksonians,* pp. 202–5.
47. Ganoe, *op. cit.,* pp. 179–80; Marvin A. Kreidberg and Merton G. Henry, *History of Military Mobilization in the United States Army, 1775–1945* (Washington: Department of the Army, 1955), p. 71 n; White, *Jacksonians,* pp. 196–202.
48. Elliott, *op. cit.,* pp. 241–49; White, *Jacksonians,* pp. 191–94.
49. Scott offers his own florid version of his controversies in *Memoirs of Lieut.-General Scott, LL.D., Written by Himself* (2 vols., New York: Sheldon, 1864), Scott's tactical manuals include *Infantry Tactics, or Rules for the Exercises and Maneuvers of the United States Infantry* (3 vols., New York: Harper, 1861). See also Schuyler Hamilton, "Anecdotes of General Winfield Scott," *Southern Historical Association Publications,* IV (May, 1900), 187–98.
50. Robert Anderson, tr., *Instruction for Field Artillery, Horse and Foot* (Philadelphia, 1839); Stanley L. Falk, "Artillery for the Land Service: The Development of a System," *Military Affairs,* XXVIII (1964–1965), 97–110; Daniel Tyler, tr., *A System of Exercise and Instruction of Field Artillery* (Philadelphia, 1826); Fairfax Downey, *Sound of the Guns: The Story of American Artillery from the Ancient and Honorable Company to the Atom Cannon and Guided Missiles* (New York: McKay, 1956), p. 86; Spaulding, *op. cit.,* p. 165.
51. William E. Birkhimer, *Historical Sketch of the Organization, Administration, Matériel and Tactics of the Artillery, United States*

Army (Washington: Chapman, 1884), pp. 50–51; Downey, *op. cit.*, p. 88; Millis, *op. cit.*, pp. 96–97; Spaulding, *op. cit.*, pp. 165–66.

52. J. F. C. Fuller, *The Conduct of War, 1789–1961: A Study of the Impact of the French, Industrial, and Russian Revolutions on War and Its Conduct* (New Brunswick: Rutgers University Press, 1961), pp. 88–89; Millis, *op. cit.*, p. 92; Nichols, *op. cit.*, p. 38.

CHAPTER NINE

1. U. S. Grant, *Personal Memoirs of U. S. Grant*, E. B. Long, ed. (Cleveland: World, 1952), p. 84.
2. Holman Hamilton, *Zachary Taylor, Soldier of the Republic* (Indianapolis: Bobbs-Merrill, 1941), pp. 156–80; Edward J. Nichols, *Zach Taylor's Little Army* (Garden City: Doubleday, 1963), pp. 35–71; Justin H. Smith, *The War with Mexico* (2 vols., New York: Macmillan, 1914), I, 138–64. Smith's book is still the outstanding history of the war. More recent military accounts are Robert Selph Henry, *The Story of the Mexican War* (Indianapolis: Bobbs-Merrill, 1950) and Otis A. Singletary, *The Mexican War* (Chicago: University of Chicago Press, 1960), and on Taylor's campaigns, Nichols, *op. cit.*
3. Grant, *op. cit.*, p. 84.
4. *Ibid.*, p. 26; Hitchcock quoted in Nichols, *op. cit.*, pp. 18–19.
5. Dwight L. Clarke, *Stephen Watts Kearny: Soldier of the West* (Norman: University of Oklahoma Press, 1961), pp. 92–96.
6. Quoted in Leonard D. White, *The Jacksonians: A Study in Administrative History* (New York: Macmillan, 1954), pp. 56–57. For Polk as Commander in Chief, see *ibid.*, pp. 50–66; Charles Winslow Elliott, *Winfield Scott: the Soldier and the Man* (New York: Macmillan, 1937); Hamilton, *op. cit.*, esp. pp. 218–23; Louis Smith, *American Democracy and Military Power: A Study of Civil Control of the Military Power in the United States* (Chicago: University of Chicago Press, 1951), pp. 41–42, 48–49, 187; J. H. Smith, *op. cit.* Bernard DeVoto, *The Year of Decision, 1846* (Boston: Houghton Mifflin, 1942) pours acid on Polk. Polk poured acid on his contemporaries in his *Diary of James K. Polk During His Presidency*, Milo Milton Quaife, ed. (4 vols., Chicago: McClurg, 1910). See also Eugene I. McCormac, *James K. Polk: A Political Biography* (Berkeley: University of California Press, 1922) and Charles A. McCoy, *Polk and the Presidency* (Austin: University of Texas Press, 1960). For the evolution of Presidential war powers, see Clarence A. Berdahl, *War Powers of the Executive in the United States* (Urbana: University of Illinois Press, 1921).
7. Polk, *op. cit.*, III, 31. On Marcy, see White, *op. cit.*, pp. 51, 53–61, 63–64.
8. White, *op. cit.*, pp. 61–62.
9. Quoted in Elliott, *op. cit.*, pp. 425–27.
10. *Ibid.*, pp. 423–44; J. H. Smith, *op. cit.*, I, 198–200, 283, 350–54. See also K. Jack Bauer, "The Vera Cruz Expedition of 1847," *Military Affairs*, XX (1956), 162–69.
11. Quoted in Erna Risch, *Quartermaster Support of the Army: A History*

of the Corps (Washington: Department of the Army, 1962), p. 237. On supply in the Mexican War, see *ibid.*, pp. 237–99; Marvin A. Kreidberg and Merton G. Henry, *History of Military Mobilization in the United States Army, 1775–1945* (Washington: Department of the Army, 1955), pp. 77–80; Ivor Spencer, "Overseas War—in 1846!" *Military Affairs*, IX (1945), 306–13; White, *op. cit.*, pp. 57–59.

12. Risch, *op. cit.*, pp. 248–50.

13. Hamilton, *op. cit.*, pp. 199–201; Nichols, *op. cit.*, pp. 128–34; Risch, *op. cit.*, pp. 263–73. Taylor's own record is *The Letters of Zachary Taylor from the Battlefields of the Mexican War*, William H. Samson, ed. (Rochester: Genesee Press, 1908).

14. Scott's military reputation has remained consistently high despite his personal foibles. Taylor's has fluctuated abruptly. His own subordinates assessed him variously, and so have modern historians. J. H. Smith and DeVoto are highly critical, DeVoto caustically so; more recent historians have undertaken a rehabilitation, especially Holman Hamilton, Edward Nichols, and Brainerd Dyer, *Zachary Taylor* (Baton Rouge: Louisiana State University Press, 1946). On the division and brigade commanders, see John F. H. Claiborne, *The Life and Correspondence of John Anthony Quitman* (New York: Harper, 1860); Clarke, *op. cit.;* Edward S. Wallace, *General William Jenkins Worth: Monterey's Forgotten Hero* (Dallas: Southern Methodist University Press, 1953).

15. J. F. Callan, *The Military Laws of the United States* (Philadelphia: Childs, 1863), pp. 367–87; Kreidberg and Henry, *op. cit.*, pp. 70–77; J. H. Smith, *op. cit.*, I, 190–96.

16. Callan, *op. cit.*, pp. 379–82; William A. Ganoe, *History of the United States Army* (New York: Appleton-Century, 1936), p. 217; J. H. Smith, *op. cit.*, II, 363–64; Oliver Lyman Spaulding, *The United States Army in War and Peace* (New York: Putnam, 1937), pp. 211–12.

17. Jim Dan Hill, *The Minute Man in Peace and War: A History of the National Guard* (Harrisburg: Stackpole, 1963), pp. 22–25; Kreidberg and Henry, *op. cit.*, pp. 74–78; J. H. Smith, *op. cit.*, I, 190–96; II, 319–21, 512–13.

18. Quoted in Nichols, *op. cit.*, p. 84.

19. Quoted *ibid.*, p. 231.

20. Quoted in George W. Cullum, *Biographical Register of the Officers and Graduates of the United States Military Academy* (3 vols., Boston: Houghton Mifflin, 1891), I, 11. Most memoirs and biographies of Civil War leaders include chapters on their protagonists' youthful activities in Mexico. Lloyd Lewis, *Captain Sam Grant* (Boston: Little, Brown, 1950) is outstanding. See also Robert Anderson, *An Artillery Officer in the Mexican War, 1846–47: Letters of Robert Anderson, Captain 3rd Artillery, U.S.A.* (New York: Putnam, 1911); George B. McClellan, *The Mexican War Diary of George B. McClellan*, William Starr Myers, ed. (Princeton: Princeton University Press, 1917); E. Kirby Smith, *To Mexico with Scott: Letters of Captain E. Kirby Smith to His Wife* (Cambridge: Harvard University Press, 1917).

21. Douglas Southall Freeman, *R. E. Lee* (4 vols., New York: Scribner, 1934), I, chap. xv; J. H. Smith, *op. cit.*, II, 49–51, 408; T. Harry

Williams, *P. G. T. Beauregard: Napoleon in Gray* (Baton Rouge: Louisiana State University Press, 1955), pp. 27–30, and ed., *With Beauregard in Mexico: The Mexican War Reminiscences of P. G. T. Beauregard* (Baton Rouge: Louisiana State University Press, 1956).

22. Elliott, *op. cit.*, p. 455; Freeman, *op. cit.*, I, 226–27, 247–48; J. H. Smith, *op. cit.*, II, 366.

23. On the training of Taylor's volunteers, Emory Upton, *The Military Policy of the United States from 1775* (Washington: Government Printing Office, 1904), p. 208; Grant's comment is from his *Memoirs*, p. 84.

24. There is a considerable literature on Doniphan's march: Ralph P. Bieber, ed., *Journal of a Soldier Under Kearny and Doniphan, 1846–1847* (Southwest Historical Series, III, Glendale, Cal.: Clark, 1935); William E. Connelley, *Doniphan's Expedition and the Conquest of New Mexico and California* (Topeka: Bryant & Douglas Book & Stationery Co., 1907); Frank S. Edwards, *A Campaign in New Mexico with Colonel Doniphan* (Philadelphia, 1847); John T. Hughes, *Doniphan's Expedition; Containing an Account of the Conquest of New Mexico* (Cincinnati, 1847; reprinted, Chicago: Rio Grande Press, 1962); William H. Richardson, *Journal of William H. Richardson, a Private Soldier in Col. Doniphan's Command* (Baltimore, 1847); Adolphus Wislizenus, *Memoir of a Tour to Northern Mexico, Connected with Col. Doniphan's Expedition, in 1846 and 1847* (Washington, 1848). Short accounts can be found in Ray Allen Billington, *The Far Western Frontier, 1830–1860* (New York: Harper, 1956), pp. 185–88; DeVoto, *op. cit.*, pp. 388–420.

25. Quoted in Elliott, *op. cit.*, p. 448.

26. *Ibid.*, pp. 553–56, 563–65; J. H. Smith, *op. cit.*, II, 163–68, 226–30, 252, 459–61; Spaulding, *op. cit.*, pp. 223–24; Edward S. Wallace, "The United States Army in Mexico City," *Military Affairs*, XIII (1949), 158–66. See also Theodore Grivas, *Military Governments in California, 1846–1850; With a Chapter on Their Prior Use in Louisiana, Florida, and New Mexico* (Glendale, Cal.: Clark, 1963).

27. Callan, *op. cit.*, p. 363; Ganoe, *op. cit.*, pp. 192–93; Samuel P. Huntington, *The Soldier and the State: The Theory and Politics of Civil-Military Relations* (Vintage ed., New York: Vintage Books, 1964), pp. 205–7; White, *op. cit.*, p. 208.

28. *Army and Navy Journal*, II (1864–65), 27.

29. Callan, *op. cit.*, pp. 393–94, 397, 399–403, 408–9; Ganoe, *op. cit.*, pp. 192, 228–29, 231.

30. Callan, *op. cit.*, pp. 435–36; Ganoe, *op. cit.*, p. 238; Hudson Strode, *Jefferson Davis, American Patriot, 1808–1861* (New York: Harcourt, Brace, 1955), pp. 245–80.

31. On Davis and the civil works in the capital, see Russell F. Weigley, *Quartermaster General of the Union Army: A Biography of M. C. Meigs* (New York: Columbia University Press, 1959), pp. 65–77; 58th Congress, 2nd Session, House Rep. 646 (serial 4585), *Documentary History of the Construction and Development of the United States Capitol Building and Grounds;* Glenn Brown, *History of the United States Capitol* (2 vols., Washington: Government Printing Office, 1900–1903); W. B. Bryan, *A History of the National Capitol* (2 vols., New York: Macmillan, 1914–16); Charles E. Fairman, *Art*

and Artists of the Capitol of the United States . . . (Washington: Government Printing Office, 1927).

For the Army in the West during Davis's tenure, see: Louise Barry, "The Fort Leavenworth-Fort Gibson Military Road and the Founding of Fort Scott," *Kansas Historical Quarterly*, XI (1942), 115–29; Averam B. Bender, *The March of Empire: Frontier Defense in the Southwest, 1848–1860* (Lawrence: University of Kansas Press, 1952), and "The Soldier in the Far West, 1848–1860," *Pacific Historical Review*, VIII (1939), 159–78; M. L. Crimmins, "Colonel J. K. F. Mansfield's Report of the Inspection of the Department of Texas in 1856," *Southwestern Historical Quarterly*, XLII (1938–39), 122–48, 215–57, 351–87; John Van Deusen DuBois, *Campaigns in the West, 1851–1861: The Journal and Letters of Colonel John Van Deusen DuBois, with Pencil Sketches by Joseph Heger*, George P. Hammond, ed. (Tucson: Arizona Pioneers Historical Society, 1949); Carolyn Thomas Foreman, "Colonel James B. Many, Commandant at Fort Gibson, Fort Towson and Fort Smith," *Chronicles of Oklahoma*, XIX (June, 1941), 119–28; Robert W. Frazer, ed., *Mansfield on the Condition of the Western Forts, 1853–54* (Norman: University of Oklahoma Press, 1963); Kate L. Gregg, "The History of Fort Osage," *Missouri Historical Review*, XXXIV (1940), 439–88; Risch, *op. cit.*, pp. 301–32; Edward S. Wallace, *The Great Reconnaissance: Soldiers, Artists and Scientists on the Frontier, 1848–1861* (Boston: Little, Brown, 1955); Raymond L. Welty, "Supplying the Frontier Posts," *Kansas Historical Quarterly*, VII (1938), 154–69; Walker D. Wymans, "The Military Phase of Santa Fe Freighting, 1846–1865," *ibid.*, I (1932), 415–28.

32. Ganoe, *op. cit.*, pp. 236–37.

33. Albert Manucy, *Artillery Through the Ages: A Short Illustrated History of Cannon, Emphasizing Types Used in America* (Washington: Government Printing Office, 1949), pp. 14–16; Walter Millis, *Arms and Men: A Study in American Military History* (New York: Putnam, 1956), pp. 93–94.

34. Richard Delafield, *Report on the Art of War in Europe in 1854, 1855, and 1856* (Washington: Bowman, 1860); George B. McClellan, *The Armies of Europe* (Philadelphia: Lippincott, 1861); Alfred Mordecai, *Military Commission to Europe in 1855 and 1856: Report* (Washington: Bowman, 1861).

35. Ganoe, *op. cit.*, p. 236. For the camel experiment, see Will C. Barnes, "Camels on Safari," *Quartermaster Review*, XVI (Jan.–Feb., 1937), 7–13, 68–72; Risch, *op. cit.*, pp. 319–320; Wallace, *Great Reconnaissance*, pp. 230–66.

36. E.g., Report of the Secretary of War, 1853, pp. 7–14, 29–32.

37. C. Joseph Bernardo and Eugene R. Bacon, *American Military Policy: Its Development Since 1775* (Harrisburg: Stackpole, 1955), p. 252; Elliott, *op. cit.*, pp. 426–28; White, *op. cit.*, pp. 191–93.

38. Elliott, *op. cit.*, pp. 648–58; Dunbar Rowland, ed., *Jefferson Davis, Constitutionalist: His Letters, Papers and Speeches* (10 vols., Jackson: Mississippi Department of Archives and History, 1923), II, 472–73, 475–76, 481, 488, 508–11, 542–44, 548, 550; III, 1, 10–11, 36; White, *op. cit.*, pp. 195–96.

39. Allan Nevins, *The Emergence of Lincoln* (2 vols., New York: Scribner, 1950), II, 199–200, 372–75; Roy F. Nichols, *The Disruption of*

American Democracy (New York: Macmillan, 1948), pp. 190, 258, 264, 329–30, 553–54, 557; Weigley, *op. cit.*, pp. 78–112.

40. Nels Anderson, *Desert Saints: The Mormon Frontier in Utah* (Chicago: University of Chicago Press, 1942); Billington, *op. cit.*, pp. 214–17; M. Hamlin Cannan, "Winfield Scott and the Utah Expedition," *Military Affairs*, V (1941), 208–10; LeRoy R. Hafen and Ann W. Hafen, *The Utah Expedition, 1857–1858* (Glendale, Cal.: Clark, 1958); E. Cecil McGavin, *U. S. Soldiers Invade Utah* (Boston: Meador, 1937); Nevins, *op. cit.*, II, 478–80; Richard D. Poll and Ralph W. Hansen, "Buchanan's Blunder: The Utah War, 1857–1858," *Military Affairs*, XXV (1961–62), 121–31.

41. R. F. Nichols, *op. cit.*, p. 478.

CHAPTER TEN

1. John A. Logan, *The Volunteer Soldier of America* (Chicago and New York: Peale, 1887), p. 464.

2. *The War of the Rebellion: A Compilation of the Official Records of the Union and Confederate Armies* (4 series, 70 vols. in 128 vols., Washington: Government Printing Office, 1880–1901), ser. IV, vol. I, pp. 115–17, 126–31, 302, 310, 326–27, 537, 825–26, 1095–97; hereafter cited as *O.R.* See also E. Merton Coulter, *The Confederate States of America, 1861–1865* (Baton Rouge: Louisiana State University Press, 1950), pp. 313–28; Marvin A. Kreidberg and Merton G. Henry, *History of Military Mobilization in the United States Army, 1775–1945* (Washington: Department of the Army, 1955), pp. 134–37; Albert B. Moore, *Conscription and Conflict in the Confederacy* (New York: Macmillan, 1924), pp. 1–26.

3. *O.R.*, ser. III, vol. I, 67–68; Kreidberg and Henry, *op. cit.*, pp. 91–93. Fred A. Shannon, *The Organization and Administration of the Union Army* (2 vols., Cleveland: Clark, 1928), I, 15–52, 259–94, is harshly critical of the methods used to raise troops in 1861. Kenneth P. Williams, *Lincoln Finds a General: A Military Study of the Civil War* (5 vols., New York: Macmillan, 1950–59), I, 60–62, 64–66; II, 796–97, cogently sets forth the necessities for those methods and refutes the criticisms of both Shannon and Emory Upton.

On numbers in the Civil War armies, Frederick Phisterer, *Statistical Record of the Armies of the United States* (New York: Scribner, 1883) is supplemented by Thomas L. Livermore, *Numbers and Losses in the Civil War in America, 1861–65* (Boston: Houghton Mifflin, 1901).

4. For Lincoln's address of July 4, 1861, see Roy P. Basler, ed., *The Collected Works of Abraham Lincoln* (9 vols., New Brunswick: Rutgers University Press, 1953), IV, 421–41; the quoted phrases appear on p. 438. For defections of officers of the Regular Army, see *Messages and Documents, War Department, 1865–1866, Part Three*, I, 6–7. For the distribution of the Regular Army in 1861, see William A. Ganoe, *History of the United States Army* (New York: Appleton-Century, 1936), pp. 244–45; Francis Paul Prucha, "Distribution of Regular Troops before the Civil War," *Military Affairs*, XVI (1952), 169–73. On Twiggs and the Department of Texas, *O.R.*, ser. I, vol. I, 521–79.

5. A. Howard Meneely, *The War Department, 1861: A Study in Mobilization and Administration* (New York: Columbia University Press, 1928). For the return of West Point graduates, see Kreidberg and Henry, *op. cit.*, pp. 115–16. Lincoln increased the Regular Army by proclamation on May 3 (*O.R.*, ser. III, vol. I, 145–46), and Congress subsequently validated his action (J. F. Callan, *The Military Laws of the United States* [Philadelphia: Childs, 1863], pp. 473–76).

6. *O.R.*, ser. III, vol. I, 303–4; Williams, *op. cit.*, I, 114–16.

7. *O.R.*, ser. III, vol. I, 380–84, 455–56; Williams, *op. cit.*, I, 114–15, 118, 399–400.

8. Williams, *op. cit.*, I, 120–21.

9. Basler, *op. cit.*, IV, 432.

10. *O.R.*, ser. III, vol. I, 39, 42–43, 902–5. Shannon, *op. cit.*, I, 107–48, surveys "The Problem of Munitions" at length.

11. Coulter, *op. cit.*, pp. 200, 206; Clement Eaton, *A History of the Southern Confederacy* (New York: Macmillan, 1954), pp. 82–83, 131–32, 265; Claud E. Fuller and Richard D. Stuert, *Firearms of the Confederacy* (Huntington, W. Va.: Standard Publications, 1944); Allan Nevins, *The War for the Union* (2 vols. to date, New York: Scribner, 1959–   ), I, 114–16; 359–61; Theodore Ropp, *War in the Modern World* (Collier ed., New York: Collier Books, 1962), p. 190 n; Samuel B. Thompson, *Confederate Purchasing Operations Abroad* (Chapel Hill: University of North Carolina Press, 1935); Frank E. Vandiver, *Ploughshares into Swords: Josiah Gorgas and Confederate Ordnance* (Austin: University of Texas Press, 1952).

12. Mark Mayo Boatner III, *The Civil War Dictionary* (New York: McKay, 1959), p. 767; Ganoe, *op. cit.*, pp. 264–65; *O.R.*, ser. III, vol. V, 1042; Shannon, *op. cit.*, I, 107–50. Nevins, *op. cit.*, I, 342–69, has an excellent discussion of "The Firepower of the North" in the early part of the war.

13. *O.R.*, ser. III, vol. I, 42–43; vol. V, 1042; Boatner, *op. cit.*, p. 121; Ropp, *op. cit.*, p. 183 n; Shannon, *op. cit.*, I, 126; Jennings Cropper Wise, *The Long Arm of Lee: The History of the Artillery of the Army of Northern Virginia* (2 vols., Lynchburg, Va.: Bell, 1915), I, 37–42.

14. 37th Congress, 3rd Session, *Report of the Committee on the Conduct of the War*, I, 139. See William B. Hesseltine, *Lincoln and the War Governors* (New York: Knopf, 1948), pp. 146–92; Kreidberg and Henry, *op. cit.*, pp. 123–26; Nevins, *op. cit.*, I, 67–91; Erna Risch, *Quartermaster Support of the Army: A History of the Corps* (Washington: Department of the Army, 1962), pp. 338–61; Cyril B. Upham, "Arms and Equipment for the Iowa Troops in the Civil War," *Iowa Journal of History and Politics*, XVI (1918), 27–51; Russell F. Weigley, *Quartermaster General of the Union Army: A Biography of M. C. Meigs* (New York: Columbia University Press, 1959), pp. 182–206.

15. Jacob D. Cox, "War Preparations in the North," in Robert Underwood Johnson and Clarence Clough Buel, eds., *Battles and Leaders of the Civil War* (4 vols., New York: Century, 1884–88), I, 84–98; Kreidberg and Henry, *op. cit.*, pp. 97–99; Bell Irvin Wiley, *The Life of Billy Yank: The Common Soldier of the Union* (Indianapolis: Bobbs-Merrill, 1951), pp. 17–44, 50–53. Bruce Catton's various works offer much perceptive observation of the Civil War citizen

soldier; see especially *America Goes to War* (Middletown, Conn.: Wesleyan University Press, 1958), pp. 48–67. T. Harry Williams, *Hayes of the Twenty-third: The Civil War Volunteer Officer* (New York: Knopf, 1965), based mainly on the diary of Rutherford B. Hayes, is the best account of a volunteer officer's experiences from the raising of his regiment through the war, set in the context of Williams's broad study of American military problems, free of Uptonian bias, and judiciously sympathetic to the citizen soldier. For Fred Shannon's views on the raising of the army, see in addition to his book his "States Rights and the Union Army," *Mississippi Valley Historical Review*, XII (1925–26), 51–71. William J. Roehrenbach, *The Regiment That Saved the Capital* (New York: Yoseloff, 1961) concerns New York's famous 7th Regiment.

16. Michael Fitch of the 6th Wisconsin is quoted in Henry Steele Commager, ed., *The Blue and the Gray: The Story of the Civil War As Told by Participants* (2 vols., Indianapolis: Bobbs-Merrill, 1950), I, 76, which includes a number of selections on the first gathering of the Union armies, pp. 69–76.

17. Moore, *op. cit.*, pp. 356–57. Robert Preston Brooks, "Conscription in the Confederate States of America," *Bulletin of the University of Georgia*, XVII (March, 1917), 441, concludes, in contrast, that conscription provided only twenty-five per cent of the Confederate army's manpower. See also *O.R.*, ser. IV, vol. I, 1081, 1095–97; vol. II, 160; vol. III, 11, 178, for the legislation. Bell Irvin Wiley, *The Life of Johnny Reb: The Common Soldier of the Confederacy* (Indianapolis: Bobbs-Merrill, 1943) discusses conscription, pp. 124–26, 132, 142–143, 245, 341–42.

18. *O.R.*, ser. III, vol. I, 699, 722–23; C. Joseph Bernardo and Eugene R. Bacon, *American Military Policy: Its Development Since 1775* (Harrisburg: Stackpole, 1955), p. 196; Kreidberg and Henry, *op. cit.*, pp. 101–2.

19. *O.R.*, ser. III, vol. II, 2–3, 28–29, 180, 187–88, 198–205, 225–26. On Stanton, Benjamin P. Thomas and Harold M. Hyman, *Stanton: The Life and Times of Lincoln's Secretary of War* (New York: Knopf, 1962) supersedes all earlier biographies, including George C. Gorham, *Edwin M. Stanton* (2 vols., Boston: Houghton Mifflin, 1899); Frank A. Flower, *Edwin McMasters Stanton* (Akron: Saalfield, 1905); and Fletcher Pratt, *Stanton, Lincoln's Secretary of War* (New York: Norton, 1953). On the functioning of the War Department, see Roscoe Pound, "Bureaus and Bureau Methods in the Civil War," *Massachusetts Historical Society Proceedings*, LXVII (1941–1944), 420–35.

20. William T. Sherman, *Personal Memoirs of W. T. Sherman* (2 vols., New York: Webster, 1892), II, 388; Bruce Catton, *Mr. Lincoln's Army* (Garden City: Doubleday, 1951), pp. 189–90; Armin Rappaport, "The Replacement System during the Civil War," *Military Affairs*, XV (1951), 95–106.

21. Callan, *op. cit.*, p. 531; *O.R.*, ser. III, vol. II, 291, 334.

22. *O.R.*, ser. III, vol. II, 188; vol. IV, 72–73; Hesseltine, *op. cit.*, pp. 201–3.

23. *O.R.*, ser. III, vol. IV, 128–33; *United States Statutes at Large*, XII, 731–37; Carl R. Fish, "Conscription in the Civil War," *American Historical Review*, XXI (1915–16), 100–103.

24. Neil C. Kimmons, "Federal Draft Exemptions, 1863–1865," *Military Affairs*, XV (1951), 25–33; Kreidberg and Henry, *op. cit.*, pp. 104–9, 112–13. See also Edward N. Wright, *Conscientious Objectors in the Civil War* (Philadelphia: University of Pennsylvania Press, 1931).

25. Bruce Catton, *A Stillness at Appomattox* (Garden City: Doubleday, 1953), pp. 33–36, and *This Hallowed Ground: The Story of the Union Side of the Civil War* (Garden City: Doubleday, 1956), pp. 317–19; Thomas and Hyman, *op. cit.*, p. 298.

26. Bernardo and Bacon, *op. cit.*, pp. 206–8; Kreidberg and Henry, *op. cit.*, pp. 109–11; Shannon, *op. cit.*, esp. I, 69–71; II, 53–55, 80. The problem of desertion was closely related to the bounty system; see Ella Lonn, *Desertion During the Civil War* (New York: Century, 1928).

27. Catton, *Stillness at Appomattox*, p. 234. Early accounts of the Negro's participation in the Union war effort include William Wells Brown, *The Negro in the American Rebellion* (Boston, 1867); James M. Guthrie, *Camp-Fires of the Afro-American* (Philadelphia, 1889); George Washington Williams, *A History of Negro Troops in the War of the Rebellion* (New York: Harper, 1888); and Joseph T. Wilson, *Black Phalanx* (Hartford, 1888). Thomas Wentworth Higginson, *Army Life in a Black Regiment* (Boston: Lee and Shepard, 1890) is a classic work by a white organizer and officer of a Negro regiment. John Hope Franklin, ed., *The Diary of James T. Ayers* (Springfield: State of Illinois, 1947) concerns the recruiting of Negro soldiers. In the early years of the twentieth century, Fred A. Shannon's interest in the Union Army led him to write "The Federal Government and the Negro Soldier," *Journal of Negro History*, XI (1926), 570–80; and leftist interest in the Negro was reflected in Herbert Aptheker's *The Negro in the Civil War* (New York: International Publishers, 1938). Post-World War II concern about the Negro's place in America has brought a rash of works: Herbert Aptheker, "Negro Casualties in the Civil War," *Journal of Negro History*, XXXII (1947), 10–80; Frederick M. Binder, "Pennsylvania Negro Regiments in the Civil War," *ibid.*, XXXVII (1952), 383–417; Dudley Taylor Cornish, *The Sable Arm: Negro Troops in the Union Army* (New York: Longmans, Green, 1956); Robert C. McConnell, ed., "Concerning the Procurement of Negro Troops in the South During the Civil War," *Journal of Negro History*, XXXV (1950), 320–35; James M. McPherson, *The Negro's Civil War: How American Negroes Felt and Acted During the War for the Union* (New York: Pantheon, 1965), a collection of documents, and *The Struggle for Equality: Abolitionists and the Negro in the Civil War and Reconstruction* (Princeton: Princeton University Press, 1964), pp. 192–220; Benjamin Quarles, *The Negro in the Civil War* (Boston: Little, Brown, 1953); L. D. Reddish, "The Negro Policy of the United States Army," *Journal of Negro History*, XXXIV (1949), 9–29. Willie Lee Rose, *Rehearsal for Reconstruction: The Port Royal Experiment* (Indianapolis: Bobbs-Merrill, 1964) touches on the raising of Negro troops, especially reviewing the origins of the 1st South Carolina Volunteers, the first Negro regiment officially authorized by the War Department. See also Thomas and Hyman, *op. cit.*, pp. 229–50, 256–57, 259–65, 371–75.

28. Jim Dan Hill, *The Minute Man in Peace and War: A History of the*

National Guard (Harrisburg: Stackpole, 1963), pp. 84–90, discusses the emergence of various types of United States volunteers. For the sharpshooters, see Charles A. Stevens, *Berdan's United States Sharpshooters in the Army of the Potomac* (St. Paul: Price-McGill, 1892).

29. *O.R.*, ser. III, vol. III, 170–72; vol. IV, 188; Hill, *op. cit.*, p. 86; Kreidberg and Henry, *op. cit.*, p. 115.

30. Frederick Phisterer, *New York in the War of the Rebellion* (6 vols., Albany: Lyon, 1912) deals with the New York militia. Many writers have been critical of Stanton's plans for raising emergency troops without perhaps crediting sufficiently his desire to escape the historic problems of state reserve forces by moving toward a federal reserve. W. S. Nye, *Here Come the Rebels!* (Baton Rouge: Louisiana State University Press, 1965), pp. 64, 149–62, is an example, although in general this is an excellent history of the emergency preparations to defend the North before Gettysburg and offers much information about the states' military forces midway in the Civil War. Edwin B. Coddington, "Pennsylvania Prepares for Invasion, 1863," *Pennsylvania History*, XXXI (1964), 157–75, is the most perceptive account of the emergency troops problem. See also Thomas and Hyman, *op. cit.*, pp. 271–74.

31. Robert S. Chamberlain, "The Northern State Militia," *Civil War History*, IV (1958), 105–18.

32. D. Alexander Brown, *The Galvanized Yankees* (Urbana: University of Illinois Press, 1963); Harold M. Hyman, "Civil War Turncoats: A Commentary on a Military View of Lincoln's War Prisoner Utilization Program," *Military Affairs*, XXII (1958–59), 134–38.

33. *O.R.*, ser. III, vol. V, 717–19; *Messages and Documents, War Department, 1865–1866, Part Three*, I, 44, 56, 199, 212; Kreidberg and Henry, *op. cit.*, pp. 108–9; Glenn Tucker, *Hancock the Superb* (Indianapolis: Bobbs-Merrill, 1960), pp. 264–65.

34. Sherrod E. East, "Montgomery C. Meigs and the Quartermaster Department," *Military Affairs*, XXV (1961–62), 183–98; Risch, *op. cit.*, pp. 333–38, 389–94; Weigley, *op. cit.*, pp. 183–84, 217–36, 318–20.

35. Quoted in Weigley, *op. cit.*, p. 165.

36. Risch, *op. cit.*, pp. 337, 427–40; Weigley, *op. cit.*, pp. 167, 219–20, 222–23.

37. Risch, *op. cit.*, pp. 345–48; Weigley, *op. cit.*, pp. 234–35.

38. *O.R.*, ser. III, vol. II, 802–3.

39. Risch, *op. cit.*, pp. 348–61, 444–46.

40. *Ibid.*, pp. 374–79; Weigley, *op. cit.*, pp. 255–60, 317–18, 331.

41. *Revised Regulations for the Army of the United States, 1861* (Philadelphia, 1861), p. 243; Risch, *op. cit.*, pp. 447–50.

42. Harold A. Small, ed., *The Road to Richmond: The Civil War Memoirs of Major Abner R. Small of the Sixteenth Maine Volunteers. Together with the Diary which he kept when he was a Prisoner of War* (Berkeley: University of California Press, 1939), pp. 196–97. There is much often amusing material on the soldier's view of subsistence in John D. Billings, *Hardtack and Coffee, or, The Unwritten Story of Army Life* (Boston: Smith, 1887), one of the best of the memoirs of soldier life. See also Commager, *op. cit.*, chaps. viii, ix, xii, xiii, and Wiley, *Billy Yank*, pp. 224–46.

43. Sherman, *op. cit.*, II, 392.

44. Risch, *op. cit.*, pp. 368–73, 405–19; Weigley, *op. cit.*, pp. 222, 234, 243–44, 248–50, 312–15; also Theodore R. Parker, "William J. Kountz, Superintendent of River Transportation under McClellan, 1861–62," *Western Pennsylvania Historical Magazine*, XXI (1938), 237–54.

45. Festus P. Summers, *The Baltimore and Ohio in the Civil War* (New York: Putnam, 1939), p. 165, quoted in Risch, *op. cit.*, p. 403.

46. E. G. Campbell, "The United States Military Railroads, 1862–1865. Part I. War Time Operation and Maintenance," *Journal of the American Military History Foundation*, II (1938), 70–89; Risch, *op. cit.*, pp. 361–66, 394–404; George Edgar Turner, *Victory Rode the Rails* (Indianapolis: Bobbs-Merrill, 1953); Thomas Weber, *The Northern Railroads in the Civil War* (New York: King's Crown Press, 1952). For the relationship of transportation and strategy, see John G. Moore, "Mobility and Strategy in the Civil War," *Military Affairs*, XXIV (1960–61), 68–97.

47. Risch, *op. cit.*, pp. 373–74, 420–26; Weigley, *op. cit.*, pp. 166, 234, 268, 270.

48. George Worthington Adams, *Doctors in Blue: The Medical History of the Union Army in the Civil War* (New York: H. Schuman, 1952); Stewart Brooks, *Civil War Medicine* (Springfield, Ill.: Charles C Thomas, 1966); S. W. Mitchell, "The Medical Department in the Civil War," *Journal of the American Medical Association*, LXII (May 9, 1914), 1445–50; Richard A. Shryock, "A Medical Perspective on the Civil War," *American Quarterly*, XIV (1962), 160–73. On the Sanitary Commission, William Quentin Maxwell, *Lincoln's Fifth Wheel: The Political History of the United States Sanitary Commission* (New York: Longmans, Green, 1956).

49. *O.R.*, ser. III, vol. I, 151–54; Boatner, *op. cit.*, pp. 612–13; K. P. Williams, *op. cit.*, II, 777.

50. *O.R.*, ser. III, vol. I, 145–46.

51. A War Department order of July 19, 1861, spoke of "Corps d'Armée," Lincoln ordered the Army of the Potomac divided into corps in March, 1862, but not until July 17, 1862, did Congress authorize the President to form army corps at his discretion. Boatner, *op. cit.*, pp. 610–13; K. P. Williams, *op. cit.*, II, 780–81. For the records of Civil War organizations, see Frederick H. Dyer, *A Compendium of the War of the Rebellion* (3 vols., New York: Yoseloff, 1959).

52. Boatner, *op. cit.*, pp. 37–38. The badges are illustrated in the *Atlas* to *O.R.*

53. Boatner, *op. cit.*, pp. 25–26, 611. There are brief histories of the armies and sketches of their commanders in Francis Trevelyan Miller, ed., *The Photographic History of the Civil War* (10 vols., New York: Review of Reviews, 1912), X, 166–84.

54. Boatner, *op. cit.*, pp. 234–35, 610–11. The *Atlas* of *O.R.* maps the shifting departmental boundaries.

55. Oliver Lyman Spaulding, *The United States Army in War and Peace* (New York: Putnam, 1937), pp. 243–44; Emory Upton, *The Military Policy of the United States from 1775* (Washington: Government Printing Office, 1904), pp. 238–39.

56. Callan, *op. cit.*, pp. 470, 484–89; *O.R.*, ser. III, vol. I, 349; Kreidberg and Henry, *op. cit.*, pp. 117–19; K. P. Williams, *op. cit.*, I, 118. For officers appointed from civil life, see Guy V. Henry, *Military*

Record of Civilian Appointments in the United States Army (2 vols., New York: Carleton, 1869).

57. *O.R.*, ser. III, vol. II, 214–17; vol. IV, 455; Kreidberg and Henry, *op. cit.*, pp. 119–23; T. H. Williams, *op. cit.*, pp. 19–38.

58. *O.R.*, ser. III, vol. I, 229–30; Kreidberg and Henry, *op. cit.*, p. 120.

59. K. P. Williams, *op. cit.*, I, 147–49, discusses with his usual pungency the apologies for McClellan's interminable training program. In general, military histories of the Civil War say little about training the troops. See Fenwick Y. Hedley, "The School of the Soldier," in Miller, *op. cit.*, VIII, 180–88; Kreidberg and Henry, *op. cit.*, pp. 121–22; Wiley, *Billy Yank*, pp. 45–55; T. H. Williams, *op. cit.*, *passim*.

60. Catton, *Stillness at Appomattox*, pp. 31–33, 135–36; Wiley, *Billy Yank*, pp. 128–29, 192–94, 218–23, 293; K. P. Williams, *op. cit.*, I, 118.

CHAPTER ELEVEN

1. *United Service Magazine*, III (1865), 375.

2. M. C. Meigs to Charles D. Meigs, Oct. 14, 1865, M. C. Meigs Papers, Library of Congress, quoted in Russell F. Weigley, *Quartermaster General of the Union Army: A Biography of M. C. Meigs* (New York: Columbia University Press, 1959), p. 336.

3. Richard Delafield, *Report on the Art of War in Europe in 1854, 1855, and 1856* (Washington: Bowman, 1860), p. 110; Editors of the *Army Times*, *A History of the U. S. Signal Corps* (New York: Putnam, 1961), pp. 22–25, 30–37, 40–55; Erna Risch, *Quartermaster Support of the Army: A History of the Corps* (Washington: Department of the Army, 1962), pp. 366–68, 458; Kenneth P. Williams, *Lincoln Finds a General: A Military Study of the Civil War* (5 vols., New York: Macmillan, 1950–59), I, 117–18.

4. Mark Mayo Boatner III, *The Civil War Dictionary* (New York: McKay, 1959), pp. 576–77, 761–62; *History of the U.S. Signal Corps*, pp. 11–55. On battlefield communications and their difficulties, see T. Harry Williams, *Hayes of the Twenty-third: The Civil War Volunteer Officer* (New York: Knopf, 1965), pp. 35–38; Prentice G. Morgan, "The Forward Observer," *Military Affairs*, XXIII (1959–60), 209–12; George Raynor Thompson, "Civil War Signals," *ibid.*, XVIII (1954), 188–201.

5. Francis A. Lord, *They Fought for the Union* (Harrisburg: Stackpole, 1960) contains much material on weapons and tactics. See also William A. Albaugh and Edward N. Simmons, *Confederate Arms* (Harrisburg: Stackpole, 1957); Boatner, *op. cit.*, pp. 522, 766–68, 860–61; Robert V. Bruce, *Lincoln and the Tools of War* (Indianapolis: Bobbs-Merrill, 1956); *Civil War Ordnance*, I (Washington: American Ordnance Association, 1961); Jack Coggins, *Arms and Equipment of the Civil War* (Garden City: Doubleday, 1962); Claud E. Fuller and Richard D. Stuert, *Firearms of the Confederacy* (Huntington, W. Va.: Standard Publications, 1844); Claud E. Fuller, *The Rifled Musket* (Harrisburg: Stackpole, 1958); Arcadi Gluckman, *United States Muskets, Rifles and Carbines* (Harrisburg: Stackpole, 1948); James E. Hicks, *Notes on United States Ordnance* (2 vols.,

Mount Vernon, N.Y.: James E. Hicks, 1946); Berkeley R. Lewis, *Small Arms and Ammunition in the United States Service* (Washington: Smithsonian Institution, 1956); Joseph W. Shields, *From Flintlock to M1* (New York: Coward-McCann, 1954).

6. See *U.S. Infantry Tactics* (Philadelphia: Lippincott, 1861). Among discussions of Civil War tactical developments, see Stephen E. Ambrose, *Upton and the Army* (Baton Rouge: Louisiana State University Press, 1964), pp. 28–34, 56–60; A. F. Becke, *An Introduction to the History of Tactics* (London: Rees, 1909), pp. 57–108; Bruce Catton, *Mr. Lincoln's Army* (Garden City: Doubleday, 1951), pp. 191–99; J. F. C. Fuller, *The Conduct of War, 1789–1961: A Study of the Impact of the French, Industrial, and Russian Revolutions on War and Its Conduct* (New Brunswick: Rutgers University Press, 1961), pp. 103–7; John K. Mahon, "Civil War Infantry Assault Tactics," *Military Affairs*, XXV (1961–62), 57–68; Theodore Ropp, *War in the Modern World* (Collier ed., New York: Collier Books, 1962), pp. 175–84.

   The Civil War was studied acutely by the English military writer G. F. R. Henderson, not only in his great biography *Stonewall Jackson and the American Civil War* (authorized American ed., New York: Grosset and Dunlap, 1945), but also in his shorter works, collected by Jay Luvaas, ed., *The Civil War: A Soldier's View, A Collection of Civil War Writings by Col. G. F. R. Henderson* (Chicago: University of Chicago Press, 1957). See also Jay Luvaas, *The Education of an Army: British Military Thought, 1815–1940* (Chicago: University of Chicago Press, 1965), pp. 216–47, and *The Military Legacy of the Civil War: The European Inheritance* (Chicago: University of Chicago Press, 1959).

7. See *Instructions for Field Artillery* (Philadelphia: Lippincott, 1861) and John Gibbon, *The Artillerist's Manual* (2nd ed., New York: Van Nostrand, 1863). Also Fairfax Downey, *Sound of the Guns: The Story of American Artillery from the Ancient and Honorable Company to the Atom Cannon and Guided Missile* (New York: McKay, 1956), pp. 118–72; Francis Trevelyan Miller, eds., *The Photographic History of the Civil War* (10 vols., New York: Review of Reviews, 1912), V, *Forts and Artillery;* L. Van Loan Naisawald, *Grape and Canister: The Story of the Field Artillery of the Army of the Potomac, 1861–1865* (New York: Oxford University Press, 1960); K. P. Williams, *op. cit.*, II, 713–15, 722–24; Jennings Cropper Wise, *The Long Arm of Lee: The History of the Artillery of the Army of Northern Virginia* (Lynchburg, Va.: Bell, 1915).

8. Fairfax Downey, *The Guns at Gettysburg* (New York: McKay, 1958); K. P. Williams, *op. cit.*, II, 713–15.

9. On the breechloader controversy, see especially Fred A. Shannon, *The Organization and Administration of the Union Army* (2 vols., Cleveland: Clark, 1928), I, 128–42, and K. P. Williams, *op. cit.*, I, 118–20; II, 782–85.

10. Michael Howard, *The Franco-Prussian War: The German Invasion of France, 1870–1871* (New York: Macmillan, 1962), pp. 36, 118; Ropp, *op. cit.*, p. 163.

11. The Spencer carbine was the standard Union cavalry arm by 1864 (though not yet in use at Gettysburg, a durable myth to the contrary notwithstanding). It fired a .52-caliber copper rim-fire cartridge. A

tubular magazine containing seven cartridges was inserted in the butt of the stock, whence a spring fed the cartridges to the breech. Ten extra magazines could be carried in a special box. The cartridge was the first self-contained metallic cartridge to come into practical use, but it contained only forty-five grains of black powder, and consequently the Spencer carbine lacked range and power. An infantry version firing a more powerful cartridge was used for a time, but it had to be abandoned because its heavier cartridge broke down the breech mechanism. On cavalry, in addition to the works on weapons and tactics cited earlier, see: William H. Carter, *Horses, Saddles and Bridles* (Baltimore: Lord Baltimore Press, 1902); Philip St. George Cooke, *Cavalry Tactics* (2 vols., Philadelphia: Lippincott, 1862); Fairfax Downey, *Clash of Cavalry: The Battle of Brandy Station, June 9, 1863* (New York: McKay, 1959); Miller, *op. cit.*, IV, *The Cavalry;* Charles D. Rhodes, *History of the Cavalry of the Army of the Potomac* (Kansas City: Hudson-Kimberly, 1900); John W. Thomason, *Jeb Stuart* (New York: Scribner, 1934); Arthur L. Wagner, ed., *Cavalry Studies from Two Great Wars* (Kansas City: Hudson-Kimberly, 1896).

12. Augustus Buell, quoted in Bruce Catton, *Never Call Retreat* (*The Centennial History of the Civil War*, III, Garden City: Doubleday, 1965), p. 96. To accept this observation of Buell's seems safe enough despite the revelations of his untrustworthiness in Milton W. Hamilton, "Augustus C. Buell: Fraudulent Historian," *Pennsylvania Magazine of History and Biography*, LXXX (1956), 478–92.

13. K. P. Williams, *op. cit.*, remains the best study of the problems and evolution of Union Army, corps, and division command. See also E. J. Stackpole, "Generalship in the Civil War," *Military Affairs*, XXIV (1960–61), 57–67.

14. William Gilmore Beyer, *On Hazardous Service: Scouts and Spies of the North and South* (New York: Harper, 1912); George H. Casamajor, "The Federal Secret Service," in Miller, *op. cit.*, VIII, 266–84; W. S. Nye, *Here Come the Rebels!* (Baton Rouge: Louisiana State University Press, 1965), *passim*, esp. p. 29; K. P. Williams, *op. cit.*, esp. I, 255–56.

15. A study of Civil War staff work is a desideratum. For preliminary work toward such a study, see Stephen E. Ambrose, *Halleck: Lincoln's Chief of Staff* (Baton Rouge: Louisiana State University Press, 1960), and "The Union Command System and the Donelson Campaign," *Military Affairs*, XXIV (1960–61), 78–86. The writings of Major General Andrew A. Humphreys, chief of staff of the Army of the Potomac from July 12, 1863, are often neglected but especially worth exploring: *From Gettysburg to the Rapidan* (New York: Scribner, 1883) and *The Virginia Campaign of '64 and '65: The Army of the Potomac and the Army of the James* (New York: Scribner, 1883). For a biography of Grant's principal staff officer, a citizen soldier, by an excellent professional officer, see James Harrison Wilson, *The Life of John Rawlins* (New York: Neale, 1916).

16. Bruce Catton's phrase, in *Never Call Retreat*, chap. iii.

17. For the Prussian staff system, see the works cited in Chap. 8, note 10 above. There has been considerable discussion of the influence of Jomini on Civil War generalship; see especially David Donald, *Lincoln Reconsidered: Essays on the Civil War Era* (New York: Knopf,

1956), "Refighting the Civil War." Discussions of this sort tend to exaggerate the theoretical bent and the bookishness of the leaders of the Union Army.

18. Roy P. Basler, ed., *The Collected Works of Abraham Lincoln* (9 vols., New Brunswick: Rutgers University Press, 1953), V, 98; *O.R.*, ser. I, vol. VII, 533.

19. Dennis Hart Mahan, *An Elementary Treatise on Advanced Guard, Out-Post, and Detachment Service of Troops* . . . (Rev. ed., New York: Wiley, 1864), pp. 32–34.

20. T. H. Williams, *op. cit.*, esp. pp. 24–25.

21. Bruce Catton, *Terrible Swift Sword* (*The Centennial History of the Civil War*, II, Garden City: Doubleday, 1963), pp. 135–37, 142, 332–34; K. P. Williams, *op. cit.*, I, 223–24, 228–31.

22. Basler, *op. cit.*, V, 346.

23. On Lincoln as a military leader, see Colin R. Ballard, *The Military Genius of Abraham Lincoln* (Cleveland: World, 1952); Richard N. Current, *The Lincoln Nobody Knows* (New York: McGraw-Hill, 1958), chap. vi; T. Harry Williams, *Lincoln and His Generals* (New York: Knopf, 1952). For McClellan's relations with Lincoln until the Presidential War Orders, K. P. Williams, *op. cit.*, I, 125–59. "The bottom is out of the tub" is from M. C. Meigs's interesting account of "The Relations of President Lincoln and Secretary Stanton to the Military Commanders in the Civil War," *American Historical Review*, XXVI (1920–21), 285–303. For an aspect of Lincoln's control of the armies, see David Homer Bates, *Lincoln in the Telegraph Office* (New York: Century, 1907).

24. As usual, K. P. Williams, *op. cit.*, I, chap. vii, is perceptive. Emory Upton, *The Military Policy of the United States from 1775* (Washington: Government Printing Office, 1904), pp. 293–95, is predictably contemptuous in treating Lincoln's foray into direct military command. Lincoln's principal biographer among professional historians, James G. Randall, regrettably reflects the judgments of the Uptonians and the admirers of McClellan; *Lincoln the President* (4 vols., New York: Dodd, Mead, 1946–55), II, chap. xix.

25. Ethan Allen Hitchcock, *Fifty Years in Camp and Field*, W. A. Croffut, ed. (New York: Putnam, 1909), esp. pp. 437–46; Benjamin P. Thomas and Harold M. Hyman, *Stanton: The Life and Times of Lincoln's Secretary of War* (New York: Knopf, 1962), pp. 214–17.

26. Basler, *op. cit.*, VI, 31; Thomas and Hyman, *op. cit.*, pp. 217, 255–56.

27. Stephen E. Ambrose, "Lincoln and Halleck: A Study in Personal Relations," *Journal of the Illinois State Historical Society*, LII (1959), 208–24, and *Halleck: Lincoln's Chief of Staff* (Baton Rouge: Louisiana State University Press, 1962), pp. 64–93; Thomas and Hyman, *op. cit.*, pp. 296–98; Williams, *Lincoln and His Generals*, pp. 302–3.

28. There are charts depicting War Department organization during the Civil War in Kreidberg and Henry, *op. cit.*, pp. 130–33. See Raphael P. Thian, *Legislative History of the General Staff of the Army of the United States* (Washington: Government Printing Office, 1901); *History of the U.S. Signal Corps;* George James Stansfield, "A History of the Judge Advocate General's Department, United States Army (Part I)," *Military Affairs*, IX (1945), 219–37.

29. U. S. Grant, *Personal Memoirs of U. S. Grant*, E. B. Long, ed. (Cleveland: World, 1952), pp. 191–92.

30. William T. Sherman, *Personal Memoirs of W. T. Sherman* (2 vols., New York: Webster, 1892), II, 227. For Sherman and his strategy, there are two excellent biographies: Lloyd Lewis, *Sherman, Fighting Prophet* (New York: Harcourt, Brace, 1958); B. H. Liddell Hart, *Sherman: Soldier, Realist, American* (New York: Praeger, 1958).

31. Adam Badeau, *Military History of Ulysses S. Grant, from April, 1861, to April, 1865* (3 vols., New York: Appleton, 1882), III, 642–644.

32. James M. McPherson, *The Struggle for Equality: Abolitionists and the Negro in the Civil War and Reconstruction* (Princeton: Princeton University Press, 1964), pp. 67–68.

33. Bruce Catton, *Terrible Swift Sword* (*The Centennial History of the Civil War*, II, Garden City: Doubleday, 1963), pp. 188–93; T. Harry Williams, "Investigation: 1862," *American Heritage*, VI (Dec., 1954), 16–21.

34. *Ibid.;* Thomas and Hyman, *op. cit.*, pp. 260–62.

35. See 37th Congress, 3rd Session and 38th Congress, 2nd Session, *Reports of the Committee on the Conduct of the War* (4 vols. for each session); William W. Pierson, Jr., "The Committee on the Conduct of the War," *American Historical Review*, XXIII (1917–18), 550–576. Truman writes of the committee in *Memoirs by Harry S Truman* (2 vols., Garden City: Doubleday, 1955–56), I, 168.

36. Bruce Catton, *A Stillness at Appomattox* (Garden City: Doubleday, 1953), pp. 19–21, 230–31; Bell Irvin Wiley, *The Life of Billy Yank: The Common Soldier of the Union* (Indianapolis: Bobbs-Merrill, 1951), pp. 109–23.

37. A. H. Carpenter, "Military Government of Southern Territory, 1861–1865," *American Historical Association Annual Report, 1900*, I, 465–498; Frank Freidel, "General Orders 100 and Military Government," *Mississippi Valley Historical Review*, XXXII (1945–46), 541–56; Robert F. Futrell, "Federal Military Government in the South, 1861–1865," *Military Affairs*, XV (1951), 181–91; Wilton P. Moore, "The Provost Marshal Goes to War," *Civil War History*, V (1959), 62–71, and "Union Army Provost Marshals in the Eastern Theater," *Military Affairs*, XXVI (1962–63), 120–26; Thomas and Hyman, *op. cit.*, pp. 306–7, 408.

38. Harold M. Hyman, *To Try Men's Souls: Loyalty Tests in American History* (Berkeley: University of California Press, 1959), pp. 166–198; Basler, *op. cit.*, VII, 50–53.

39. Basler, *op. cit.*, V, 259–60, 342–43, 462–63; Eric L. McKitrick, *Andrew Johnson and Reconstruction* (Chicago: University of Chicago Press, 1960), pp. 126–27; Thomas and Hyman, *op. cit.*, p. 307.

40. McKitrick, *op. cit.*, pp. 120–33; Thomas and Hyman, *op. cit.*, pp. 357–58, 402–3, 438–39, 448–49.

41. George R. Bentley, *A History of the Freedmen's Bureau* (Philadelphia: University of Pennsylvania Press, 1955); John A. Carpenter, *Sword and Olive Branch: Oliver Otis Howard* (Pittsburgh: University of Pittsburgh Press, 1964), a biography of the general who became commissioner of the Freedmen's Bureau; Oliver Otis Howard, *Autobiography* (New York: Baker and Taylor, 1907); McPherson, *op. cit.*, pp. 178–91; Thomas and Hyman, *op. cit.*, pp. 460–61.

42. Harold M. Hyman, "Johnson, Stanton, and Grant: A Reconsideration of the Army's Role in the Events Leading to Impeachment,"

American Historical Review, LXVI (1960), 85–100; this article and Thomas and Hyman, *op. cit.*, broke ground in approaching the study of the Army's role in Reconstruction. James E. Sefton, "The Army and Reconstruction," Ph.D. thesis, University of California (Los Angeles), 1965, is the first comprehensive study of the topic; it challenges Thomas and Hyman on the extent to which the Radicals did or believed they had to limit Johnson's control of the Army. The interpretation of Reconstruction followed herein is that developed by McKitrick; by LaWanda and John H. Cox, *Politics, Principle, and Prejudice, 1865–1866: Dilemma of Reconstruction America* (New York: Free Press of Glencoe, 1963); and by W. R. Brock, *An American Crisis: Congress and Reconstruction, 1865–1867* (New York: St. Martin's Press, 1963); and summarized briefly by Kenneth M. Stampp, *The Era of Reconstruction, 1865–1877* (New York: Knopf, 1965). On Reconstruction historiography, see Bernard Weisberger, "The Dark and Bloody Ground of Reconstruction Historiography," *Journal of Southern History*, XXV (1959), 427–47.

On the militia of the Johnson governments, see Otis A. Singletary, *Negro Militia and Reconstruction* (Austin: University of Texas Press, 1957), pp. 3–6.

43. Hyman, "Johnson, Stanton, and Grant," pp. 88–92; Thomas and Hyman, *op. cit.*, pp. 474–77.

44. Thomas and Hyman, *op. cit.*, pp. 477–79.

45. Hyman, "Johnson, Stanton, and Grant," pp. 91–93.

46. *Ibid.*, pp. 93–94; Thomas and Hyman, *op. cit.*, pp. 484–94.

47. Adam Badeau, *Grant in Peace* (Hartford, 1887); Hyman, "Johnson, Stanton, and Grant," pp. 96–97; Thomas and Hyman, *op. cit.*, pp. 497–530. The "Command of the Army Act" was in fact a proviso attached to the Army appropriation act; *Statutes at Large*, XIV, 486–87.

48. *Statutes at Large*, XV, 14; Hyman, "Johnson, Stanton, and Grant," pp. 96–98; Thomas and Hyman, *op. cit.*, pp. 533–47.

49. David M. DeWitt, *The Impeachment and Trial of Andrew Johnson* (New York: Macmillan, 1903); McKitrick, *op. cit.*, pp. 486–509; Thomas and Hyman, *op. cit.*, pp. 547–613.

50. Report of the Secretary of War, 1865, I, 1, 19, 21; 1866, pp. 3–6; 1867, p. 416; *Statutes at Large*, XIV, 332; William A. Ganoe, *History of the United States Army* (New York: Appleton-Century, 1936), p. 307; McKitrick, *op. cit.*, pp. 448–85; John McAllister Schofield, *Forty-six Years in the Army* (New York: Century, 1897); Thomas and Hyman, *op. cit.*, pp. 614–40.

51. *Statutes at Large*, XV, 318; XVI, 317; Singletary, *op. cit.*

52. Singletary, *loc. cit.*, and "The Negro Militia During Radical Reconstruction," *Military Affairs*, XIX (1955), 177–86.

53. Quoted in Russell F. Weigley, *Quartermaster General of the Union Army: A Biography of M. C. Meigs* (New York: Columbia University Press, 1959), pp. 336, 341.

Chapter Twelve

1. *Statutes at Large*, XIV, 332; William A. Ganoe, *History of the United States Army* (New York: Appleton-Century, 1936), pp. 306–9.

2. *Statutes at Large*, XV, 318; C. Joseph Bernardo and Eugene H. Bacon, *American Military Policy: Its Development Since 1775* (Harrisburg, Stackpole, 1955), pp. 237–40; Ganoe, *op. cit.*, pp. 324–30; Marvin A. Kreidberg and Merton G. Henry, *History of Military Mobilization in the United States Army, 1775–1945* (Washington: Department of the Army, 1955), p. 141.

3. Robert G. Athearn, *William Tecumseh Sherman and the Settlement of the West* (Norman: University of Oklahoma Press, 1956); R. Ernest Dupuy, *The Compact History of the United States Army* (New York: Hawthorn, 1956), p. 151; Ganoe, *op. cit.*, pp. 331, 350.

4. Again, the literature on any phase of the Army's Indian-fighting years is extensive. For Indian policy, see Robert G. Athearn, *High Country Empire: The High Plains and the Rockies* (New York: McGraw-Hill, 1960), and *Sherman and the Settlement of the West;* James C. Malin, *Indian Policy and Westward Expansion* (Bulletin of the University of Kansas Humanistic Studies, II, No. 3, Nov., 1921); Walter Prescott Webb, *The Great Plains* (New York: Ginn, 1931).

   Among general surveys of the post-Civil War Indian wars: Fairfax Downey, *Indian-Fighting Army* (New York: Scribner, 1941), one of Downey's better books, which seems to capture the flavor of the Indian-fighting Army; Paul I. Wellman, *Death on Horseback: Seventy Years of War for the American West* (Philadelphia: Lippincott, 1947); Sidney E. Whitman, *The Troopers: An Informal History of the Plains Cavalry, 1865–1890* (New York: Hastings, 1962). There is vast material on battles and campaigns, especially the Custer fight. On weapons, see the works cited in Chap. 11, note 5, above. On the breechloader, also see again Kenneth P. Williams, *Lincoln Finds a General: A Military Study of the Civil War* (5 vols., New York: Macmillan, 1950–59), I, 118–20; II, 782–85.

5. For Army life on the trans-Mississippi frontier, the best general work is Don Rickey, Jr., *Forty Miles a Day on Beans and Hay: The Enlisted Soldier Fighting the Indian Wars* (Norman: University of Oklahoma Press, 1963). See also: John Bourke, *On the Border with Crook* (New York: Scribner, 1891); Francis Courtney Carrington, *My Army Life and the Fort Phil Kearny Massacre* (Philadelphia: Lippincott, 1910); Edward M. Coffman, "Army Life on the Frontier, 1865–1898," *Military Affairs*, XX (1956), 193–201; James H. Cook, *Fifty Years on the Old Frontier* (New Haven: Yale University Press, 1923); Louis F. Crawford, *Rekindling Camp Fires* (Bismarck, N.D.: Capital Book Co., 1926); Phillippe Regis de Trobiand, *Military Life in Dakota* (St. Paul: Alvord Memorial Commission, 1957); John F. Finerty, *War-Path and Bivouac* (Chicago: Donohue and Heineberg, 1890); George A. Forsyth, *Thrilling Days of Army Life* (New York: Harper, 1902); Edward E. Hardin, "An Army Lieutenant in Montana, 1874–76," *Military Affairs*, XXIII (1959–60), 85–90; Frazier and Robert Hunt, *I Fought with Custer: The Story of Sergeant Windolph, Last Survivor of the Little Big Horn* (New York: Scribner, 1947); Charles King, *Campaigning with Crook; And Stories of Army Life* (New York: Harper, 1890); Edward J. McClernand, "Service in Montana, 1870 and 1871," *Military Affairs*, XV (1951), 192–98; Don Rickey, Jr., "The Enlisted Man of the Indian Wars," *ibid.*, XXIII (1959–60), 91–96; Frances Roe, *Army Letters from an Officer's Wife, 1871–1888* (New York: Appleton, 1909); Alvin

H. Sydenham, "The Diary Journal of Alvin H. Sydenham: Part I," *Bulletin of the New York Public Library*, XLIV (1940), 113–16, 529–36; Homer D. Wheeler, *Buffalo Days* (Indianapolis: Bobbs-Merrill, 1923).

On various Army posts in the West: Thomas E. Blades and John W. Wike, "Fort Missoula," *Military Affairs*, XIII (1949), 29–36; D. A. Brown, *Fort Phil Kearny: An American Saga* (New York: Putnam, 1962); Charles P. Elliott, "An Indian Reservation Under General Crook," *ibid.*, XII (1948), 91–102; LeRoy R. Hafen and Francis M. Young, *Fort Laramie and the Pageant of the West, 1834–1890* (Glendale, Cal.: Clark, 1938); David J. Hieb, *Fort Laramie National Monument, Wyoming* (National Park Service Historical Handbook Number Twenty, Washington: Government Printing Office, 1954); John H. Nankiwell, "Fort Garland, Colorado," *Colorado Magazine*, XVI (Jan., 1939), 13–28; W. S. Nye, *Carbine and Lance: The Story of Old Fort Sill* (Norman: University of Oklahoma Press, 1937); G. Hubert Smith, "The Archives of a Military Post," *Minnesota History*, XXII (1941), 297–301 (on Fort Ridgely, Minn.); Jerome Thomases, "Fort Bridger: A Western Community," *Military Affairs*, V (1941), 177–88; Robert M. Utley, *Fort Union National Monument, New Mexico* (National Park Service Historical Handbook Number Thirty-five, Washington: Government Printing Office, 1962).

Erna Risch, *Quartermaster Support of the Army: A History of the Corps* (Washington: Department of the Army, 1962), pp. 468–507, deals with the supply of the western frontier Army. For remarks on desertion, see Bernardo and Bacon, *op. cit.*, pp. 241–42.

6. John Pope, address to the Army of the Tennessee, Oct. 16, 1873, copy in W. T. Sherman Papers, Library of Congress, XXXVI, 4722–4723.

7. John A. Logan, *The Volunteer Soldier of America* (Chicago and New York: Peale, 1887).

8. Samuel P. Huntington, *The Soldier and the State: The Theory and Politics of Civil-Military Relations* (Vintage ed., New York: Vintage Books, 1964), pp. 222–26, discusses "business pacifism" and supplies bibliographical references. See also Merle Curti, *Peace or War: The American Struggle, 1636–1936* (New York: Norton, 1936), a general history of American pacifism.

9. Oliver Lyman Spaulding, *The United States Army in War and Peace* (New York: Putnam, 1937), p. 369; C. Vann Woodward, *Reunion and Reaction: The Compromise of 1877 and the End of Reconstruction* (Boston: Little, Brown, 1951), pp. 8–9.

10. Pope, *loc. cit.*

11. *The Centennial History of the United States Military Academy at West Point, 1802–1902* (2 vols., Washington: Government Printing Office, 1904), *passim;* Huntington, *op. cit.*, pp. 237–39; T. Bentley Mott, *Twenty Years as a Military Attaché* (New York: Oxford University Press, 1937), pp. 41–42.

12. Huntington, *op. cit.*, pp. 230–32; Russell F. Weigley, *Towards an American Army: Military Thought from Washington to Marshall* (New York: Columbia University Press, 1962), pp. 79–89.

13. Major General Charles D. Herron, quoted in Forrest C. Pogue, *George C. Marshall: Education of a General, 1880–1939* (New York:

Viking, 1963), pp. 94–95. On the postgraduate school system: Ganoe, *op. cit.*, pp. 363, 422–23; Huntington, *op. cit.*, pp. 239–41; Kreidberg and Henry, *op. cit.*, pp. 147–48; John W. Masland and Laurence I. Radway, *Soldiers and Scholars: Military Education and National Policy* (Princeton: Princeton University Press, 1957), pp. 80–81; Ira L. Reeves, *Military Education in the United States* (New York: Free Press Printing Co., 1914), pp. 213–33; Henry Shindler and E. E. Booth, *History of the Army Service Schools* (Fort Leavenworth: Staff College Press, 1908); Morris Swett, "The Forerunners of Sill," *Field Artillery Journal*, XXVIII (Nov.–Dec., 1938), 453–63; Eben Swift, "An American Pioneer in the Cause of Military Education," *Journal of the Military Service Institution of the United States*, XLIV (Jan.–Feb., 1908), 67–72.

    Arthur L. Wagner's works include *The Campaign of Königgrätz* (Fort Leavenworth, 1889); *Elements of Military Science* (Kansas City: Hudson-Kimberly, 1898); *Organization and Tactics* (New York: Westermann, 1895); *The Service of Security and Information* (Washington: Chapman, 1893).

14. Donald N. Bigelow, *William Conant Church and the Army and Navy Journal* (New York: Columbia University Press, 1952); J. B. Fry, "Origin and Progress of the Military Service Institution of the United States," *Journal of the Military Service Institution*, I (1879), 20–32; Huntington, *op. cit.*, pp. 243–44; "The Journal's First Half Century," *Combat Forces Journal*, V (Oct., 1954), 17–20.

15. John Bigelow, Jr., *The Campaign of Chancellorsville: A Strategic and Tactical Study* (New Haven: Yale University Press, 1910), *Mars-la-Tour and Gravelotte* (Washington: Government Printing Office, 1884), and *The Principles of Strategy* (rev. ed., Philadelphia: Lippincott, 1894); Weigley, *op. cit.*, pp. 93–99.

16. Stephen E. Ambrose, *Upton and the Army* (Baton Rouge: Louisiana State University, 1964), esp. pp. 60–66; Emory Upton, *Infantry Tactics: Double and Single Rank* (New York: Appleton, 1874). To harmonize with his infantry tactics, Upton also developed an *Artillery Tactics* (New York: Appleton, 1875) and a *Cavalry Tactics* (New York: Appleton, 1874).

17. Quoted in Peter Smith Michie, *Life and Letters of General Emory Upton* (New York: Appleton, 1885), pp. 386–87.

18. Emory Upton, *The Armies of Asia and Europe* (New York: Appleton, 1878); Ambrose, *op. cit.*, pp. 85–150.

19. Ambrose, *op. cit.*, pp. 151–59; Weigley, *op. cit.*, pp. 137–61.

20. Emory Upton, *The Military Policy of the United States from 1775* (Washington: Government Printing Office, 1904), *passim*, esp. p. 9.

21. *Ibid.*, esp. pp. 149, 416–17, 426–27. The "truly democratic doctrine" of conscription is from p. 85.

22. *Ibid.*, p. 4.

23. *Ibid.*, pp. 280, 423.

24. *Ibid.*, p. 323.

25. *Ibid.*, p. 258.

26. *Ibid.*, p. 144. Hancock set forth his contrary views when he testified in 1878, as did Sherman and Upton, before the Burnside Committee on the reorganization of the Regular Army. See 45th Congress, 1st Session, Senate Reports, I (serial 1837), no. 555.

27. Upton, *Military Policy*, p. 336. Upton's ideas are discussed at greater length in Weigley, *op. cit.*, pp. 100–126.
28. James S. Pettit, "How Far Does Democracy Affect the Organizaton and Discipline of Our Armies, and How Can Its Influence Be Most Effectually Utilized?" *Journal of the Military Service Institution*, XXXVIII (1906), 2.
29. *Ibid.*, p. 38.
30. *American Federationist*, VI (1899), 40, quoted in Leonard D. White, *The Republican Era, 1869–1901: A Study in Administrative History* (New York: Macmillan, 1958), p. 136. For the traditional liberal interpretation of the use of the Army in strikes, see Matthew Josephson, *The Politicos, 1865–1896* (Harvest ed., New York: Harcourt, Brace and World, 1963), pp. 255, 563, 566–67, 574–87. Robert V. Bruce, *1877: Year of Violence* (Indianapolis: Bobbs-Merrill, 1959) offers an interpretation of the Railroad Strike of 1877 somewhat more sympathetic to the federal government's employment of military force. A comprehensive history is Marlin S. Reichley, "Federal Military Intervention in Civil Disturbances," Ph.D. thesis, Georgetown University, 1939. See also Elwell S. Otis, "The Army in Connection with the Labor Riots of 1877," *Journal of the Military Service Institution*, V (1884), 292–323.
31. William H. Riker, *Soldiers of the States: The Role of the National Guard in American Democracy* (Washington: Public Affairs Press, 1957), pp. 41–66, depicts a militia renaissance in the late years of the nineteenth century. Jim Dan Hill, *The Minute Man in Peace and War: A History of the National Guard* (Harrisburg: Stackpole, 1963), pp. 128–32, is skeptical of this notion, and argues, reasonably, that "The vituperative, emotion-burdened and confused issues [of labor disturbances] were no asset to the National Guard's progress and development." For the founding of the National Guard Association, see Martha Derthick's history of the association, *The National Guard in Politics* (Cambridge: Harvard University Press, 1965), pp. 15–16. For the increase in militia appropriations, *Statutes at Large*, XXIV, 401–2; Bernardo and Bacon, *op. cit.*, pp. 247–51. For the designation "National Guard," Francis V. Greene, "The New National Guard," *Century*, XXI (Feb., 1892), 483–98, esp. p. 486 n.
32. *Statutes at Large*, XII, 504; XIV, 336; XVI, 373; XIX, 74; XXVIII, 7; Kreidberg and Henry, *op. cit.*, pp. 145–46; Gene M. Lyons and John W. Masland, *Education and Military Leadership: A Study of the ROTC* (Princeton: Princeton University Press, 1959).
33. See note 26 above.
34. 48th Congress, 1st Session, House Executive Documents (serial 2204), no. 97, Report of the Gun-Foundry Board; *Statutes at Large*, XXII, 472; Walter Millis, *Arms and Men: A Study in American Military History* (New York: Putnam, 1956). pp. 150–51.
35. 49th Congress, 1st Session, House Executive Documents, XXVIII (serial 2395–2396), no. 49, Report of the Endicott Board; Report of the Secretary of War, 1886, pp. 32–33; *Statutes at Large*, XXIII, 434; Millis, *op. cit.*, pp. 151–52.
36. Report of the Secretary of War, 1887, pp. 118–21, 123–24; 1889, pp. 68–74; 1890, pp. 5–7; 1892, pp. 17, 46.
37. *Revised Regulations for the Army of the United States, 1895*, p. 26.
38. Benjamin P. Thomas and Harold M. Hyman, *Stanton: The Life and*

Times of Lincoln's Secretary of War (New York: Knopf, 1962), *passim*, esp. pp. 547–71, 610–11.

39. William H. Carter, *Creation of the American General Staff*, 68th Congress, 1st Session, Senate Documents, II (serial 8254), no. 119, pp. 2, 19–20, 33–35; Lloyd Lewis, *Sherman, Fighting Prophet* (New York: Harcourt, Brace, 1958), pp. 601–2; John M. Schofield, *Forty-six Years in the Army* (New York: Century, 1897), pp. 406–10, 420–23, 468–76; William T. Sherman Papers, Library of Congress, XXVII, 3570, 3789; XXVIII, 3798–3800; William T. Sherman, *Personal Memoirs of W. T. Sherman* (2 vols., New York: Webster, 1892), II, 441–43, 450–54, 463; White, *op. cit.*, pp. 141–42.

40. Sherman, *Memoirs*, II, 444.

41. Lewis, *op. cit.*, pp. 608, 615, 622; B. H. Liddell Hart, *Sherman: Soldier, Realist, American* (New York: Praeger, 1958), pp. 412–13, 417–19.

42. Liddell Hart, *op. cit.*, p. 419; White, *op. cit.*, pp. 138–39, 142–43.

43. Bernardo and Bacon, *op. cit.*, pp. 255–56.

44. Kreidberg and Henry, *op. cit.*, pp. 144–45; Risch, *op. cit.*, pp. 511–512; Upton, *Military Policy*, p. 159; Weigley, *op. cit.*, pp. 138, 166–167; White, *op. cit.*, p. 144.

45. Schofield, *op. cit.*, pp. 420–21.

46. *Ibid.*, pp. 410, 536–39; Weigley, *op. cit.*, pp. 168–73.

47. Weigley, *op. cit.*, pp. 173–74. For Miles, see Virginia Weisel Johnson, *The Unregimented General: A Biography of Nelson A. Miles* (Boston: Houghton Mifflin, 1962); Nelson A. Miles, *Personal Recollections* (Chicago: Werner, 1896), and *Serving the Republic* (New York: Harper, 1911).

48. Bernardo and Bacon, *op. cit.*, pp. 245–46; Ganoe, *op. cit.*, pp. 365, 370; Kreidberg and Henry, *op. cit.*, pp. 147–48, 168; Report of the Secretary of War, 1898, I, Pt. I, 253; 56th Congress, 1st Session, Senate Document 221 (serial 3859), *Report of the Commission Appointed by the President to Investigate the Conduct of the War Department in the War with Spain* (8 vols.), I, 196–98 (hereafter cited as *Dodge Commission Report*).

49. Ganoe, *op. cit.*, pp. 262, 280, 366; Huntington, *op. cit.*, p. 207.

50. *Dodge Commission Report*, I, 197, 277, 442–43; Kreidberg and Henry, *op. cit.*, p. 168; Risch, *op. cit.*, p. 524.

51. Ganoe, *op. cit.*, the title of chap. ix.

PART THREE

1. Howard K. Smith, *The State of Europe* (New York: Knopf, 1950), pp. 69–70.

CHAPTER THIRTEEN

1. Finley Peter Dunne, *Mr. Dooley in Peace and in War* (Boston: Small, Maynard, 1899), "On War Preparations," p. 9.

2. *Statutes at Large*, XXX, 261; William A. Ganoe, *History of the United States Army* (New York: Appleton-Century, 1936), p. 371; Walter Millis, *The Martial Spirit* (Boston: Houghton Mifflin, 1931), p. 152. Millis's irreverent history, in the debunking manner of the

1920's, is still a good survey of the war. For a recent popular history, richly illustrated, see Frank Freidel, *The Splendid Little War* (Boston: Little, Brown, 1958). A standard older history is Frank Ensor Chadwick, *The Relations of the United States and Spain: The Spanish-American War* (New York: Scribner, 1911). George C. Reinhardt and William R. Kintner, *The Haphazard Years: How America Has Gone to War* (Garden City: Doubleday, 1960) is a history of mobilization that begins with the Spanish War.

3. *Statutes at Large*, XXX, 361–66; Margaret Leech, *In the Days of McKinley* (New York: Harper, 1959), pp. 198–201; Marvin A. Kreidberg and Merton G. Henry, *History of Military Mobilization in the United States Army, 1775–1945* (Washington: Department of the Army, 1955), pp. 153–56; Millis, *op. cit.*, pp. 151–60.

4. *Statutes at Large*, XXX, 361–63, 405; Kreidberg and Henry, *op. cit.*, p. 162; Theodore Roosevelt, *The Rough Riders* (New York: Scribner, 1899).

5. James D. Richardson, ed., *Compilation of the Messages and Papers of the Presidents* (20 vols., New York: Bureau of National Literature, 1897–1911), XIV, 6473–74; Jim Dan Hill, *The Minute Man in Peace and War: A History of the National Guard* (Harrisburg: Stackpole, 1963), pp. 157–60; Franklin F. Holbrook, *Minnesota in the Spanish-American War and the Philippine Insurrection* (St. Paul: Minnesota War Records Commission, 1923); Kreidberg and Henry, *op. cit.*, pp. 156–59.

6. Richardson, *op. cit.*, XIV, 6477.

7. *Dodge Commission Report*, I, 254 (see Chap. 12, note 48 above); Kreidberg and Henry, *op. cit.*, pp. 163–64.

8. *Dodge Commission Report*, esp. I, 202–22; Kreidberg and Henry, *op. cit.*, pp. 165–69; Erna Risch, *Quartermaster Support of the Army: A History of the Corps* (Washington: Department of the Army, 1962), pp. 513–40.

9. *Statutes at Large*, XXX, 274; Kreidberg and Henry, *op. cit.*, pp. 167–168; Risch, *op. cit.*, pp. 516, 520–23.

10. *Dodge Commission Report*, I, 197; Leech, *op. cit.*, pp. 293–95; Risch, *op. cit.*, pp. 516–40.

11. Risch, *op. cit.*, pp. 535–56, esp. p. 535 on the wagons.

12. John D. Miley, *In Cuba with Shafter* (New York: Scribner, 1899), chaps. ii–iii (Miley was an aide to Shafter); Millis, *op. cit.*, pp. 241–248; Risch, *op. cit.*, pp. 539–45; Roosevelt, *op. cit.*, pp. 54–62.

13. The Quartermaster's Department was more fortunate in the ships it could find on the Pacific Coast, and the transportation of troops to the Philippines was accomplished much more satisfactorily than the first movement to Cuba, despite the immense distance involved. Risch, *op. cit.*, pp. 550–51.

14. *Ibid.*, pp. 545–55.

15. Leech, *op. cit.*, pp. 242–44, 246; Millis, *op. cit.*, pp. 260–78.

16. 56th Congress, 1st Session, Senate Document 270 (serial 3870–72), *Food Furnished by Subsistence Department to Troops in the Field* (3 vols.); Leech, *op. cit.*, pp. 297–300; Risch, *op. cit.*, pp. 528–34; Louis L. Seaman, "The U. S. Army Ration and Its Adaptability for Use in Tropical Climates," *Journal of the Military Service Institution*, XXIV (1899), 375–97, and "The Soldier's Ration in the Tropics—Its Use and Its Abuse," *ibid.*, XXVIII (1900), 83–95.

17. Leech, *op. cit.*, pp. 300–304.

18. Quoted *ibid.*, p. 249.

19. Virginia Weisel Johnson, *The Unregimented General: A Biography of Nelson A. Miles* (Boston: Houghton Mifflin, 1962), pp. 316–20, 330–41.

20. Leech, *op. cit.*, is good on the President's direction of the war. See also H. Wayne Morgan, *William McKinley and His America* (Syracuse: Syracuse University Press, 1963), and Ernest R. May's essay in May, ed., *The Ultimate Decision: The President as Commander in Chief* (New York: Braziller, 1960), pp. 93–107. The Secretary of War offered his own excuses: Russell A. Alger, *The Spanish-American War* (New York: Harper, 1901).

21. The most detailed account of military operations is Herbert H. Sargent, *The Campaign of Santiago de Cuba* (3 vols., Chicago: McClurg, 1907). An uncommonly useful soldier's view of the war is Charles Johnson Post, *The Little War of Private Post* (Boston: Little, Brown, 1960). The intelligent military writer John Bigelow, Jr., wrote his *Reminiscences of the Santiago Campaign* (New York: Harper, 1899). For the 71st New York, see John E. Elmendorf, ed., *Memorial Souvenir: The 71st Regiment New York Volunteers in Cuba* (New York, 1899).

 For one of the newer tactical features of the war, see John Henry Parker, *History of the Gatling Gun Detachment, Fifth Army Corps, at Santiago* (Kansas City: Franklin Hudson, 1898).

22. On the Philippine campaign see Uldarico S. Baclagon, *Philippine Campaigns* (Manila: Graphic House, 1952); Frederick Funston, *Memories of Two Wars: Cuban and Philippine Experiences* (New York: Scribner, 1914); James A. LeRoy, *The Americans in the Philippines: A History of the Conquest and the First Years of Occupation* (2 vols., Boston: Houghton Mifflin, 1914); William T. Sexton, *Soldiers in the Sun: An Adventure in Imperialism* (Harrisburg: Military Service Publishing Co., 1939); Leon Wolff, *Little Brown Brother: How the United States Purchased and Pacified the Philippine Islands at the Century's Turn* (Garden City: Doubleday, 1961).

23. Quoted in Hill, *op. cit.*, p. 162, which deals with the National Guard units sent to the Philippines, pp. 162–64.

24. *Statutes at Large*, XXX, 977; Hill, *op. cit.*, pp. 175–78.

25. Emory Upton's criticisms of American military policy were projected into the Spanish War era by Frederick L. Huidekoper, *The Military Unpreparedness of the United States: A History of the American Land Forces from Colonial Times Until June 1, 1915* (New York: Macmillan, 1915).

26. Alger, *op. cit.*, pp. 265–73; Leech, *op. cit.*, pp. 274–76; Roosevelt, *op. cit.*, pp. 203–4.

27. Leech, *op. cit.*, p. 276.

28. *Dodge Commission Report*. The conclusions appear in I, 107 ff. See also Leech, *op. cit.*, pp. 304–16.

29. Quoted in Leech, *op. cit.*, p. 318.

30. *Dodge Commission Report*, esp. VII, 3255–61; Leech, *op. cit.*, pp. 316–22; Risch, *op. cit.*, pp. 533–34.

31. Philip C. Jessup, *Elihu Root* (2 vols., New York: Dodd, Mead, 1938); Leech, *op. cit.*, pp. 366–78.

Chapter Fourteen

1. Quoted in Philip C. Jessup, *Elihu Root* (2 vols., New York: Dodd, Mead, 1938), I, 240.

2. *Ibid.*, pp. 215–18, 242–54. For Theodore Roosevelt's conception of foreign and military policy, see especially William Henry Harbaugh, *Power and Responsibility: The Life and Times of Theodore Roosevelt* (New York: Farrar, Straus and Cudahy, 1961). Howard K. Beale, *Theodore Roosevelt and the Rise of America to World Power* (Baltimore: Johns Hopkins Press, 1956) is more critical of Roosevelt. On Root, see also Richard W. Leopold, *Elihu Root and the Conservative Tradition* (Boston: Little, Brown, 1954); Philip L. Semsch, "Elihu Root and the General Staff," *Military Affairs*, XXVII (1963–64), 16–27. Root's statements of policy are found in Robert Bacon and James B. Scott, *The Military and Colonial Policy of the United States: Addresses and Reports by Elihu Root* (Cambridge: Harvard University Press, 1924). Elihu Root, *Five Years of the War Department* (Washington: Government Printing Office, 1904) collects Root's annual reports.

3. Report of the Secretary of War, 1899, pp. 44–45.

4. Stephen E. Ambrose, *Upton and the Army* (Baton Rouge: Louisiana State University Press, 1964), pp. 155–56; William H. Carter, *Creation of the American General Staff*, 68th Congress, 1st Session, Senate Documents, II (serial 8254), no. 119, pp. 1–2, 15, 31–32, 35–36; Jessup, *op. cit.*, I, 242–43; Jay Luvaas, *The Education of an Army: British Military Thought, 1815–1940* (Chicago: University of Chicago Press, 1965), p. 285.

5. Report of the Secretary of War, 1903, p. 46.

6. *Ibid.*, 1902, pp. 42–49, esp. p. 43; Jessup, *op. cit.*, I, 240–64.

7. Report of the Secretary of War, 1899, p. 49; 1901, pp. 21–25; Marvin A. Kreidberg and Merton G. Henry, *History of Military Mobilization in the United States Army, 1775–1945* (Washington: Department of the Army, 1955), pp. 176–77.

8. Reports of the Secretary of War, esp. 1901, p. 25; Kreidberg and Henry, *op. cit.*, p. 177.

9. William A. Ganoe, *History of the United States Army* (New York: Appleton-Century, 1936), pp. 399–413; for the Philippines see also Chap. 13, note 22, above.

10. *Statutes at Large*, XXXI, 748–58. A subsequent artillery reorganization in 1907 created separate Coast Artillery and Field Artillery Corps. The Coast Artillery was fixed at 170 companies, while the Field Artillery returned to a regimental organization, with six regiments of six four-gun batteries, two of them mountain or pack artillery regiments and one a horse artillery regiment. *Statutes at Large*, XXXIV, 861–64. See also A. C. M. Azoy, "Great Guns: A History of the Coast Artillery Corps," *Coast Artillery Journal*, LXXXIV (1941), 426–34; Ganoe, *op. cit.*, pp. 412–13.

11. Ganoe, *op. cit.*, pp. 412, 417; Forrest C. Pogue, *George C. Marshall: Education of a General, 1880–1939* (New York: Viking, 1963), pp. 62–67; Bacon and Scott, *op. cit.*, pp. 375, 377–78.

12. Clark S. Campbell, *The '03 Springfield* (Beverly Hills, Cal.: Fadco, 1960); Walter Millis, *Arms and Men: A Study in American Military History* (New York: Putnam, 1956), p. 178.

13. On Wood, there is Hermann Hagedorn's uncritical biography, *Leonard Wood, A Biography* (2 vols., New York: Harper, 1931). The reports of the Cuban, Puerto Rican, and Philippine occupation commanders are printed in the Reports of the Secretary of War. See also Jessup, *op. cit.*, I, 221–22, 285–388; Margaret Leech, *In the Days of McKinley* (New York: Harper, 1959), pp. 300–407.

14. Carter, *op. cit.*, pp. 31–32, 35–36, 47–50; Jessup, *op. cit.*, I, 251–53.

15. Root, *op. cit.*, pp. 333–34; Kreidberg and Henry, *op. cit.*, p. 177.

16. Carter set forth his views on the Army and its reserves in "The Organized Militia—Its Past and Future," *United Service*, third series, III (Feb., 1903), 789–94, and later in "The Militia Not a National Force," *North American Review*, CXCVI (July, 1912), 130–31, and *The American Army* (Indianapolis: Bobbs-Merrill, 1915). See also Elbridge Colby, "Elihu Root and the National Guard," *Military Affairs*, XXIII (1959–60), 20, 28–34, for Root's misgivings about the National Guard, and Martha Derthick, *The National Guard in Politics* (Cambridge: Harvard University Press, 1965), pp. 22–25. Carter's estimate of Root appears in his "Elihu Root—His Services as Secretary of War," *North American Review*, CLXXVIII (Jan., 1904), 110–21.

17. Bacon and Scott, *op. cit.*, pp. 121–29, 139–52, 349–478; Derthick, *op. cit.*, pp. 24–27; Jim Dan Hill, *The Minute Man in Peace and War: A History of the National Guard* (Harrisburg: Stackpole, 1963), pp. 180–89; Jessup, *op. cit.*, I, 240–68.

18. *Statutes at Large*, XXXII, 775–80.

19. The best history of the early years of the General Staff is Otto L. Nelson, Jr., *National Security and the General Staff* (Washington: Infantry Journal Press, 1946), pp. 58–186; this book reprints many documents. For an assessment of the Root reforms, see Paul Y. Hammond, *Organizing for Defense: The American Military Establishment in the Twentieth Century* (Princeton: Princeton University Press, 1961), pp. 10–48; also Hammond's "The Secretaryships of War and the Navy: A Study of Civilian Control of the Military," Ph.D. thesis, Harvard University, 1953, and Samuel P. Huntington, *The Soldier and the State: The Theory and Politics of Civil-Military Relations* (Vintage ed., New York: Vintage Books, 1964), pp. 251–253. For background, there is J. D. Hittle, *The Military Staff: Its History and Development* (Harrisburg: Military Service Publishing Co., 1944). For an early chief of staff, see William H. Carter, *The Life of Lieutenant General Chaffee* (Chicago: University of Chicago Press, 1917).

20. On the Adjutant General's Office, which passed through several metamorphoses in the Root period, and on Ainsworth, see Mabel E. Deutrich, *Struggle for Supremacy: The Career of Fred C. Ainsworth* (Washington: Public Affairs Press, 1962), and Siert F. Riepma, "Portrait of an Adjutant General," *Journal of the American Military History Foundation*, II (1938), 26–35.

21. Rutherford Bingham, "A Brief Study of Some of the Conditions Responsible for the Inefficiency of the Organized Militia and Their Cure," *Journal of the Military Service Institution*, XLV (1911), 358–67; Derthick, *op. cit.*, pp. 27–32; Hill, *op. cit.*, pp. 191–95; A. W. A. Pollock, "The 'National Guard': A Hint from the United States," *Nineteenth Century*, XLVI (1909), 910–20.

22. *Statutes at Large*, XXXV, 399–403; Report of the Secretary of War, 1912, I, 24.

23. Pogue, *op. cit.*, p. 99.

24. On the Army schools in Root's day, see C. Joseph Bernardo and Eugene H. Bacon, *American Military Policy: Its Development Since 1775* (Harrisburg: Stackpole, 1955), pp. 308–13; Kreidberg and Henry, *op. cit.*, pp. 202–5; John W. Masland and Laurence I. Radway, *Soldiers and Scholars: Military Education and National Policy* (Princeton: Princeton University Press, 1957), pp. 83–86; Pogue, *op. cit.*, pp. 93–108; Ira L. Reeves, *Military Education in the United States* (New York: Free Press Printing Co., 1914).

25. Jessup, *op. cit.*, I, 411–12; Henry F. Pringle, *The Life and Times of William Howard Taft* (2 vols., New York: Farrar and Rinehart, 1939), I, 251–55.

26. Hagedorn, *op. cit.;* Huntington, *op. cit.*, pp. 279–82; Eric F. Wood, *Leonard Wood: Conservator of Americanism* (New York: Doran, 1920). For the attitudes of the officer corps toward the America of their day, see Richard C. Brown, "Social Attitudes of American Generals, 1898–1940," Ph.D. thesis, University of Wisconsin, 1951.

27. Millis, *op. cit.*, p. 200, calls Wood "a military evangelist." For Wood and Brooke, see Leech, *op. cit.*, pp. 390–93.

28. Leonard Wood wrote prolifically; e.g., "Training for War in Time of Peace," *Outlook*, XC (1909), 976–89; "Why We Have No Army," *McClure's*, XXXVIII (1912), 677–83; "The Army's New and Bigger Job," *World's Work*, XXVIII (1914), 75–84; *The Military Obligation of Citizenship* (Princeton: Princeton University Press, 1915); *Our Military History: Its Facts and Fallacies* (Chicago: Reilly and Britton, 1916).

29. 62nd Congress, 1st Session, House Report 508 (serial 6131), Relief of the Adjutant General from the Duties of His Office, p. 19. The Wood-Ainsworth controversy can be followed in Archibald W. Butt, *Taft and Roosevelt: The Intimate Letters of Archie Butt, Military Aide* (2 vols., New York: Doubleday, 1930), II, 763–64, 780–83; Deutrich, *op. cit.*, chap. viii; Hagedorn, *op. cit.*, II, chap. v; Elting E. Morison, *Turmoil and Tradition: A Study of the Life and Times of Henry L. Stimson* (Boston: Houghton Mifflin, 1960), pp. 150–61; Nelson, *National Security and the General Staff*, pp. 109–66; Henry L. Stimson and McGeorge Bundy, *On Active Service in Peace and War* (New York: Harper, 1947), pp. 33–37.

30. 62:1 House Rep. 508, pp. 6–13.

31. Deutrich, *op. cit.*, p. 121; Morison, *op. cit.*, pp. 158–59.

32. Bernardo and Bacon, *op. cit.*, pp. 305–7; Deutrich, *op. cit.*, pp. 123–127; Morison, *op. cit.*, pp. 161–67.

33. *Statutes at Large*, XXXVII, 571, 594; Bernardo and Bacon, *op. cit.*, p. 323.

34. Hagedorn, *op. cit.*, II, 99–100.

35. Report of the Secretary of War, 1912, I, 15–18; Deutrich, *op. cit.*, p. 124; Morison, *op. cit.*, pp. 167–68.

36. Quoted in Pogue, *op. cit.*, p. 114. On the Maneuver Division, see *ibid.*, pp. 112–14; Ganoe, *op. cit.*, pp. 439–40; Millis, *Arms and Men*, pp. 202–3.

37. Wood, "Why We Have No Army," *loc. cit.*, pp. 677–83; Henry L.

Stimson, "What Is the Matter with Our Army?" *Independent*, LXXII (Apr. 18, 1912), 827–28.

38. Report of the Secretary of War, 1912, I, 15–18; Morison, *op. cit.*, pp. 167–69; John McAuley Palmer, *America in Arms: The Experience of the United States with Military Organization* (New Haven: Yale University Press, 1941), pp. 138–39.

39. Morison, *op. cit.*, p. 169.

40. S. L. A. Marshall, *The American Heritage History of World War I* (New York: American Heritage Publishing Co., 1964), pp. 35–37; Theodore Ropp, *War in the Modern World* (Collier ed., New York: Collier Books, 1962), pp. 199–200.

41. Quoted in *Journal of the Military Service Institution*, XXXVIII (1906), 358, 368; Russell F. Weigley, *Towards an American Army: Military Thought from Washington to Marshall* (New York: Columbia University Press, 1962), pp. 144–61.

42. Millis, *op. cit.*, p. 201.

43. Leonard Wood, "What the War Means to America," in P. F. Collier and Son's *The Story of the Great War* (8 vols., New York: Collier, 1916–20), I, 12.

44. E.g., Wood, *Our Military History*, pp. 177–78.

45. Bernardo and Bacon, *op. cit.*, p. 316; Hill, *op. cit.*, pp. 200–204, 209–10; Kreidberg and Henry, *op. cit.*, pp. 186–87.

46. Frederick L. Huidekoper, *The Military Unpreparedness of the United States: A History of the American Land Forces from Colonial Times Until June 1, 1915* (New York: Macmillan, 1915), esp. pp. 222–28.

47. Palmer, *op. cit.*, p. 136; Weigley, *op. cit.*, pp. 225–29.

48. Report of the Secretary of War, 1912, I, 128; the report on "The Organization of the Land Forces" occupies pp. 69–128.

49. *Statutes at Large*, XXXVII, 590–91; XXXVIII, 347–51; Report of the Secretary of War, 1913, p. 21; 1914, p. 11; Hagedorn, *op. cit.*, II, 146–47.

CHAPTER FIFTEEN

1. Leonard Wood, *Our Military History: Its Facts and Fallacies* (Chicago: Reilly and Britton, 1916), p. 185.

2. Russell F. Weigley, *Towards an American Army: Military Thought from Washington to Marshall* (New York: Columbia University Press, 1962), pp. 144–61, 204, 208. Wood's friendly biographer wrote a history of the preparedness movement; see Hermann Hagedorn, *The Bugle That Woke America* (New York: John Day, 1940). For scholarly treatment, see Edward H. Brooks, "The National Defense Policy of the Wilson Administration, 1913–1917," Ph.D. thesis, Stanford University, 1950; Arthur S. Link, *Wilson: Campaigns for Peace and Progressivism* (*Wilson*, V, Princeton: Princeton University Press, 1965), and *Woodrow Wilson and the Progressive Era, 1910–1917* (New York: Harper, 1954), pp. 174–96; William W. Tinsley, "The American Preparedness Movement," Ph.D. thesis, Stanford University, 1939. For Wood's Merchants' Association speech, see Hermann Hagedorn, *Leonard Wood, A Biography* (2 vols., New York: Harper, 1931), II, 151–53.

3. Ralph Barton Perry, *The Plattsburg Movement* (New York: Dutton, 1921).

4. Leonard Wood, *The Military Obligation of Citizenship* (Princeton: Princeton University Press, 1915), pp. 33–34.

5. Leonard Wood, "What the War Means to America," in P. F. Collier and Son's *The Story of the Great War* (8 vols., New York: Collier, 1916–20), I, 9.

6. Marvin A. Kreidberg and Merton G. Henry, *History of Military Mobilization in the United States Army, 1775–1945* (Washington: Department of the Army, 1955), pp. 201–2; Elting E. Morison, *Turmoil and Tradition: A Study of the Life and Times of Henry L. Stimson* (Boston: Houghton Mifflin, 1960), pp. 225–26.

7. C. Joseph Bernardo and Eugene H. Bacon, *American Military Policy: Its Development Since 1775* (Harrisburg: Stackpole, 1955), pp. 340–344; Link, *Wilson and the Progressive Era*, pp. 179–87; Walter Millis, *Arms and Men: A Study in American Military History* (New York: Putnam, 1956), pp. 217–18; John McAuley Palmer, *Washington, Lincoln, Wilson: Three War Statesmen* (Garden City: Doubleday, 1930), pp. 315–17.

8. War Department General Staff, *Statement of a Proper Military Policy for the United States* (Washington: Government Printing Office, 1916), pp. 1–21.

9. Bernardo and Bacon, *op. cit.*, pp. 341–43; Martha Derthick, *The National Guard in Politics* (Cambridge: Harvard University Press, 1965), pp. 33–44; Link, *Wilson and the Progressive Era*, pp. 183–184.

10. Quoted in Millis, *op. cit.*, p. 223; see Bernardo and Bacon, *op. cit.*, pp. 343–44; Link, *Wilson and the Progressive Era*, p. 186.

11. John Dickinson, *The Building of an Army* (New York: Century, 1922), pp. 43–44; Link, *Wilson and the Progressive Era*, pp. 184–186.

12. C. H. Cramer, *Newton D. Baker: A Biography* (Cleveland: World, 1961), pp. 76–82; Link, *Wilson and the Progressive Era*, pp. 186–187.

13. Link, *Wilson and the Progressive Era*, pp. 187–88.

14. *Ibid.*, pp. 107–36.

15. Jim Dan Hill, *The Minute Man in Peace and War: A History of the National Guard* (Harrisburg: Stackpole, 1963), pp. 221–22; Link, *Wilson and the Progressive Era*, pp. 137–40, 188.

16. *Statutes at Large*, XXXIX, pt. 2, 166–217.

17. *Ibid.*, p. 197.

18. *Ibid.*, pp. 197–213.

19. *Ibid.*, pp. 213–16, 649–50.

20. *Ibid.*, pp. 167–69.

21. Derthick, *op. cit.*, p. 39; William Henry Harbaugh, *Power and Responsibility: The Life and Times of Theodore Roosevelt* (New York: Farrar, Straus and Cudahy, 1961), p. 482; Link, *Wilson and the Progressive Era*, pp. 188–89.

22. War Department General Staff, *Report on Mobilization of the Organized Militia and National Guard of the United States* (Washington: Government Printing Office, 1916).

23. *Ibid.*; Hill, *op. cit.*, pp. 230–43.

24. Cf. Kreidberg and Henry, *op. cit.*, pp. 200–201.

25. Roger Batchelder, *Watching and Waiting on the Border* (Cambridge: Harvard University Press, 1917); Millis, *op. cit.*, pp. 228–232; Frank Tompkins, *Chasing Villa* (Harrisburg: Military Service Publishing Co., 1934).

26. For Wilson's purposes, see especially Link, *Wilson: Campaigns for Peace and Progressivism.*

27. Grosvener B. Clarkson, *Industrial America in the World War* (Cambridge: Harvard University Press, 1923), esp. pp. 24–30. For Wilson's anger over the General Staff's war plans, Frederick Palmer, *Newton D. Baker: America at War* (2 vols., New York: Dodd, Mead, 1931), I, 40–41.

28. Henry Steele Commager, ed., *Documents of American History* (6th ed., 2 vols. in 1, New York: Appleton-Century-Crofts, 1958), II, 310.

29. Quoted in Kreidberg and Henry, *op. cit.*, p. 292.

30. Cramer, *op. cit.*, pp. 96–97; Kreidberg and Henry, *op. cit.*, pp. 236–243.

31. *Statutes at Large*, XL, 76–83; Cramer, *op. cit.*, pp. 96–97. Frederic L. Paxson, *American Democracy and the World War* (3 vols., Boston: Houghton Mifflin, 1936) remains the best general survey of the American war effort.

CHAPTER SIXTEEN

1. John J. Pershing, *My Experiences in the World War* (2 vols., New York: Stokes, 1931), II, 189–90.

2. On the French army mutinies of 1917, see Corelli Barnett, *The Swordbearers: Supreme Command in the First World War* (Signet ed., New York: New American Library, 1965), pp. 200–237; Paul-Marie de la Gorce, *The French Army* (New York: Braziller, 1963), pp. 119–29; Alistair Horne, *The Price of Glory: Verdun, 1916* (New York: St. Martin's, 1963), pp. 319–25; Richard M. Watt, *Dare Call It Treason* (New York: Simon and Schuster, 1963).

3. Pershing, *op. cit.*, I, 15–40; Forrest C. Pogue, *George C. Marshall: Education of a General, 1880–1939* (New York: Viking, 1963), pp. 142–44; Society of the First Division, *History of the First Division During the World War, 1917–1919* (Philadelphia: Winston, 1922); United States Army, 1st Division, *World War Records, First Division, AEF* (25 vols., Washington: Government Printing Office, 1928–31).

4. Pershing, *op. cit.*, I, 150–56, 264–65.

5. Marvin A. Kreidberg and Merton G. Henry, *History of Military Mobilization in the United States Army, 1775–1945* (Washington: Department of the Army, 1955), pp. 253–77, gives a detailed description of the operations of the selective service system. See also the observations of the provost marshal general, who was both the principal author and administrator of the system, Enoch H. Crowder, *The Spirit of Selective Service* (New York: Columbia University Press, 1920), and a biography, David A. Lockmiller, *Enoch Crowder* (Columbia: University of Missouri Press, 1955). Also Peyton C. March, *The Nation at War* (Garden City: Doubleday, 1932), chap. xviii.

6. Kreidberg and Henry, *op. cit.*, pp. 227–28, 246–53.

7. *Ibid.*, pp. 221–27; for numbers in World War I, see Leonard P.

Ayers, *The War with Germany: A Statistical Summary* (Washington: Government Printing Office, 1919).

8. Kreidberg and Henry, *op. cit.*, pp. 277–80.

9. *Ibid.*, pp. 296–98; Pershing, *op. cit.*, I, 94–102, and *passim*. The growth of the American commitment in Europe can be traced in Department of the Army, *The United States Army in the World War* (17 vols., Washington: Government Printing Office, 1948), I, *Organization of the American Expeditionary Forces*. See also Thomas G. Frothingham, *The American Reinforcement in the World War* (Garden City: Doubleday, 1927).

10. Kreidberg and Henry, *op. cit.*, pp. 298–304; Pershing, *op. cit.*, II, 104–24, and *passim*.

11. Kreidberg and Henry, *op. cit.*, pp. 304–6; March, *op. cit.*, pp. 250–255; Pershing, *op. cit.*, II, 233–36, and *passim*.

12. Kreidberg and Henry, *op. cit.*, pp. 306–7.

13. On economic mobilization see: American Academy of Political and Social Science, *Mobilizing America's Resources for the War* (Philadelphia, 1918); Arthur Bullard, *Mobilizing America* (New York: Macmillan, 1917); Grosvener B. Clarkson, *Industrial America in the World War* (Cambridge: Harvard University Press, 1923); Benedict Crowell, *America's Munitions, 1917–1918* (Washington: Government Printing Office, 1919), and with Robert F. Wilson, *The Armies of Industry* (2 vols., New Haven: Yale University Press, 1921), and *The Giant Hand* (New Haven: Yale University Press, 1921); Randall B. Kester, "The War Industries Board, 1917–1918: A Study in Industrial Mobilization," *American Political Science Review*, XXXIV, (1940), 655–84; Franklin H. Martin, *Digest of the Proceedings of the Council of National Defense During the World War* (Washington: Government Printing Office, 1934).

14. C. H. Cramer, *Newton D. Baker: A Biography* (Cleveland: World, 1961), chap. viii; Kreidberg and Henry, *op. cit.*, pp. 336–43; Erna Risch, *Quartermaster Support of the Army: A History of the Corps* (Washington: Department of the Army, 1962), pp. 628–36.

15. Crowell, *America's Munitions;* H. A. DeWeerd, "American Adoption of French Artillery, 1917–1918," *Military Affairs*, III (1939), 104–116.

16. The trials and perplexities of American aviation in World War I can be followed in a thoughtful book, which sets the problem into the context of weapons development at large and points out the revolutionary impact of the constant improvements in aviation which made one day's superior aircraft obsolete six months later (at first the Americans thought they could adopt the French SPAD as they adopted the 75-mm gun, but the two situations proved not comparable): I. B. Holley, Jr., *Ideas and Weapons: Exploitation of the Aerial Weapon by the United States During World War I; A Study in the Relationship of Technological Advance, Military Doctrine, and the Development of Weapons* (New Haven: Yale University Press, 1953). Arthur Sweetser, *The American Air Service* (New York: Appleton, 1919), and Edgar S. Gorrell, *The Measure of America's World War Aeronautical Effort* (Northfield, Vt.: Norwich University, 1940) are also useful.

17. Crowell, *America's Munitions*, p. 161; Kreidberg and Henry, *op. cit.*, pp. 232–33; Pershing, *op. cit.*, I, 131; II, 7, 374.

18. Kreidberg and Henry, *op. cit.*, p. 320; Pershing, *op. cit.*, I, 26.
19. Risch, *op. cit.*, chap. xiii.
20. *Ibid.*, pp. 574–80, 584–89, 593–97.
21. *Ibid.*, pp. 605–9; Kreidberg and Henry, *op. cit.*, pp. 311–18.
22. Risch, *op. cit.*, pp. 577–80.
23. *Ibid.*, pp. 615–28.
24. *Ibid.*, pp. 629–33; Edward M. Coffman, "The Battle Against Red Tape: Business Methods of the War Department General Staff 1917–1918," *Military Affairs*, XXVI (1962–63), 1–10; March, *op. cit.*, pp. 187–88.
25. Albert Gleaves, *A History of the Transport Service, 1917–1919* (New York: Doran, 1921); Risch, *op. cit.*, pp. 630–44.
26. Kreidberg and Henry, *op. cit.*, pp. 336–44; Risch, *op. cit.*, pp. 630–644.
27. Pershing, *op. cit.*, *passim*, esp. I, 104–5, 147–49, 179–80, 267, 291–292, 336–37, 397–99; II, 57–59, 85–87, 110, 169, 229, 329; Risch, *op. cit.*, pp. 666–82.
28. Johnson Hagood, *The Services of Supply: A Memoir of the Great War* (Cambridge: Harvard University Press, 1927); James G. Harbord, *The American Army in France* (Boston: Little, Brown, 1936), pp. 339–404, 486–510; March, *op. cit.*, pp. 193–96; Pershing, *op. cit.*, esp. II, 180–91; Risch, *op. cit.*, pp. 645–53; William J. Wilgus, *Transporting the A.E.F. in Western Europe* (New York: Columbia University Press, 1931).
29. Risch, *op. cit.*, pp. 665–66.
30. Cramer, *op. cit.*, pp. 98–99; Kreidberg and Henry, *op. cit.*, pp. 287–289.
31. Pershing, *op. cit.*, I, 79–86.
32. Kreidberg and Henry, *op. cit.*, pp. 262–67.
33. *Ibid.*, pp. 294–95.
34. *Ibid.*, pp. 281–83.
35. Cramer, *op. cit.*, pp. 109–16; March, *op. cit.*, chap. v.
36. Sidney Forman, *West Point: A History of the United States Military Academy* (New York: Columbia University Press, 1950), pp. 172–174. Douglas MacArthur tells of his difficulties in restoring the Academy as its first postwar superintendent in his *Reminiscences* (New York: McGraw-Hill, 1964), pp. 77–83. There is extensive treatment of the MacArthur reforms in Stephen E. Ambrose, *Duty, Honor, Country: A History of West Point* (Baltimore: Johns Hopkins Press, 1966), pp. 261–302.
37. Kreidberg and Henry, *op. cit.*, pp. 289–90.
38. Pershing's views on training are discussed frequently in his *Experiences*. There is an excellent discussion of "The First Division in France" in Pogue, *op. cit.*, chap. ix.
39. New York Historical Commission, *The Second Division* (New York: Second Division Association, 1927); Henry J. Reilly, *Americans All—The Rainbow at War* (Columbus, Ohio: Heer, 1936). The 26th Division and its first commander, Major General Clarence Edwards, became the subjects of much controversy after Pershing decided Edwards was not his kind of general; see Harry A. Benwell, *History of the Yankee Division* (Boston: Cornhill, 1919); Frank P. Sibley, *With the Yankee Division in France* (Boston: Little, Brown, 1919);

Emerson Gifford Taylor, *New England in France, 1917–1918* (Boston: Houghton Mifflin, 1920).

40. March, *op. cit.*, p. 7; Pershing, *op. cit.*, I, 380; II, 122; Laurence Stallings, *The Doughboys: The Story of the AEF, 1917–1918* (New York: Harper and Row, 1963), p. 145.

41. Pershing, *op. cit.*, I, 305.

42. March, *op. cit.*, p. 258.

43. Pershing, *op. cit.*, I, 38–40. For "one to go and one to return," Frederick Palmer, *Newton D. Baker: America at War* (2 vols., New York: Dodd, Mead, 1931), p. 180. On Pershing, in addition to his reminiscences, see Frederick Palmer, *John J. Pershing, General of the Armies* (Harrisburg: Military Service Publishing Co., 1948), the best personal portrait, by his press officer, and Richard O'Connor, *Black Jack Pershing* (Garden City: Doubleday, 1961). Scholarly biographies by Frank E. Vandiver and Donald Smythe are in preparation.

44. On Wilson as a war leader, see the essay by Ernest R. May in May, ed., *The Ultimate Decision: The President as Commander in Chief* (New York: Braziller, 1960), pp. 111–31.

45. The relations of the War Department with Congress are reviewed briefly in Cramer, *op. cit.*, pp. 145–54. See also Louis Smith, *American Democracy and Military Power: A Study of Civil Control of the Military Power in the United States* (Chicago: University of Chicago Press, 1951), pp. 207–11.

46. On Baker, see the biographies by Frederick Palmer and C. H. Cramer. Frederick Palmer's writings also include a biography of Bliss, a most interesting figure: *Bliss, Peacemaker: The Life and Letters of General Tasker Howard Bliss* (New York: Dodd, Mead, 1934). Hugh L. Scott wrote *Some Memories of a Soldier* (New York: Century, 1928).

47. March, *op. cit.*, pp. 34–56, 226.

48. Quoted *ibid.*, pp. 49–50.

49. The rivalry between March and Pershing shows up plainly in the memoirs of both and can be followed there. March wrote *The Nation at War* as a sort of rebuttal to Pershing's *Experiences*. At this writing, Edward M. Coffman is about to publish a biography of March.

50. Quoted in Pershing, *op. cit.*, I, 38–39.

51. Palmer, *Bliss*, pp. 199 ff.; Pershing, *op. cit.*, I, 253, 304–10; David F. Trask, *The United States in the Supreme War Council: American War Aims and Inter-Allied Strategy, 1917–1918* (Middletown, Conn.: Wesleyan University Press, 1961).

52. Stallings, *op. cit.*, is a recent account of the American participation in the fighting, written with Stallings's usual verve, and especially good on Belleau Wood, chaps. v and vi. On the 28th Division at the Marne, see *ibid.*, pp. 119–21, 123–25; also the division's history, H. G. Proctor, *The Iron Division* (Philadelphia: Winston, 1919).

53. Benedict Crowell and Robert F. Wilson, *The Road to France* (2 vols., New Haven: Yale University Press, 1921); Edward N. Hurley, *The Bridge to France* (Philadelphia: Lippincott, 1927); Pershing, *op. cit.*, esp. chaps. xxvii–xxix.

54. Kreidberg and Henry, *op. cit.*, pp. 324–36.

55. I Corps headquarters was organized on January 20, 1918; II Corps, February 24; III Corps, March 30. See Historical Section, Army

War College, *Order of Battle of the United States Land Forces in the World War (1917–19); Headquarters, Armies, Army Corps, Services of Supply, and Separate Forces* (Washington: Government Printing Office, 1931).

56. Pershing, *op. cit.*, chaps. xli and xlii.

57. Alfred T. Hurley, *Billy Mitchell: Crusader for Air Power* (New York: Watts, 1964), p. 35; Pershing, *op. cit.*, pp. 260–66.

58. Pershing, *op. cit.*, II, 335–36.

59. *The Army Almanac: A Book of Facts Concerning the United States Army* (Harrisburg: Stackpole, 1959), pp. 632–33; Historical Section, Army War College, *Order of Battle of the United States Land Forces in the World War (1917–19); American Expeditionary Forces, Divisions* (Washington: Government Printing Office, 1931), and *Order of Battle . . . ; Zone of the Interior* (Washington: Government Printing Office, 1949), pp. 637–41.

60. Department of the Army, *Army Lineage Book*, I, *Infantry* (Washington: Government Printing Office, 1953); Jim Dan Hill, *The Minute Man in Peace and War: A History of the National Guard* (Harrisburg: Stackpole, 1963), pp. 265–67; Oliver Lyman Spaulding, *The United States Army in War and Peace* (New York: Putnam, 1937), p. 410.

61. Not the least reason was that through nearly three years of European war before April 6, 1917, European censorship and Wilsonian horror of any sort of involvement had combined to keep a great deal of information about new methods of war from reaching American officers who would have studied them had they been able. Stallings, *op. cit.*, p. 387, points out Hunter Liggett's comments on the subject.

62. Pershing, *op. cit.*, I, 150–56, 173, 208, 259, 344.

63. For discussion, see the works on the 26th Division cited in note 39 above; Stallings, *op. cit.*, pp. 156–57.

64. Pogue, *op. cit.*, pp. 171–79.

65. Pershing, *op. cit.*, II, 189–90.

66. Hunter Liggett, *Commanding an American Army: Recollections of the World War* (Boston: Houghton Mifflin, 1925), and *A.E.F.: Ten Years Ago in France* (New York: Dodd, Mead, 1928); Robert Lee Bullard, *Personalities and Reminiscences of the War* (Garden City: Doubleday, 1925), *Fighting Generals* (Ann Arbor: Edwards, 1944), and with Earl Reeves, *American Soldiers Also Fought* (New York: Longmans, Green, 1936); Joseph T. Dickman, *The Great Crusade: A Narrative of the World War* (New York: Appleton, 1927). There is a sketch of Summerall in Fletcher Pratt, *Eleven Generals: Studies in American Command* (New York: Sloane, 1949).

67. On World War I tactics, see especially "Infantry in Battle," *Infantry Journal* (Washington: Infantry Journal, 1939); Douglas W. Johnson, *Battlefields of the World War* (New York: Oxford University Press, 1921), and *Topography and Strategy* (New York: Holt, 1917); Pascal Marie Henri Lucas, *L'évolution des idées tactiques en France et en Allemagne pendant la guerre de 1914–1918* (Paris: Berger-Levrault, 1924). On the infantry rifle, Clark S. Campbell, *The '03 Springfield* (Beverly Hills, Cal.: Fadco, 1957). On the machine gun, C. D. Baker-Carr, *From Chauffeur to Brigadier* (London: Benn, 1930), by a British officer who pushed the use of the machine gun; George M. Chinn, *The Machine Gun* (2 vols., Washington:

Government Printing Office, 1951); William Crozier, *Ordnance and the World War* (New York: Scribner, 1920).

On artillery, see Harry G. Bishop, *Field Artillery, The King of Battles* (Boston: Houghton Mifflin, 1935); Edward S. Farrow, *American Guns in the War with Germany* (New York, 1920); P. H. Ottosen, *Trench Artillery, A.E.F.* (Boston: Lothrop, Lee and Shepard, 1931); William J. Snow, *Signposts of Experience: World War Memoirs* (Washington: Field Artillery Association, 1941), and "The First Chief of Field Artillery," *Field Artillery Journal*, XXX (1940), 3–14, 97–106, 163–65, 249–60, 341–45.

On tanks, see Victor W. Germains, *On the Mechanization of War* (London: Sifton Praed, 1927); Ralph E. Jones, *The Fighting Tanks Since 1916* (Washington: National Service Publishing Co., 1933); B. H. Liddell Hart, *The Tanks: The History of the Royal Tank Regiment and Its Predecessors; Heavy Branch Machine-Gun Corps, Tank Corps, and Royal Tank Corps, 1914–1945* (2 vols., New York: Praeger, 1959); Richard M. Ogorkiewicz, *Armor: A History of Mechanized Forces* (New York: Praeger, 1960); Sir Ernest D. Swinton, *Eyewitness* (Garden City: Doubleday, 1933).

On aircraft, Army War College, *The Signal Corps and the Air Service, 1917–1918* (Washington: Government Printing Office, 1922); Andrew Boyle, *Trenchard* (London: Collins, 1962); John M. Bruce, *British Aeroplanes, 1914–1918* (London: Putnam, 1957); Gorrell, *op. cit.;* Mason M. Patrick, *The United States in the Air* (Garden City, Doubleday, 1928); Sir Walter A. Raleigh and H. A. Jones, *The War in the Air* (6 vols., Oxford: Clarendon Press, 1922–1937); William C. Sherman, *Air Power and Armies* (London: Oxford University Press, 1936); James M. Spaight, *The Beginnings of Organized Air Power* (London: Longmans, Green, 1927), and *British Aeroplanes, 1914–1918* (London: Longmans, Green, 1925); Oliver Stewart, *The Strategy and Tactics of Air Fighting* (London: Longmans, Green, 1925); Harry A. Toulmin, *Air Service, American Expeditionary Force, 1918* (New York: Van Nostrand, 1927). On technology and doctrine, Holley, *op. cit.*, is again valuable.

On the limited cavalry action of the war, see Cavalry School, *Cavalry Conflict* (Harrisburg: Telegraph Press, 1937).

68. March, *op. cit.*, pp. 259–60.
69. Quoted in March, *op. cit.*, pp. 258–59; Pershing, *op. cit.*, II, 183–84.
70. Marshal von Hindenburg, *Out of My Life*, tr. F. A. Holt (London: Cassell, 1933), p. 284. See George S. Viereck, *As They Saw Us: Foch, Ludendorff and Other Leaders Write Our War History* (Garden City: Doubleday, 1929).
71. See for example George C. Marshall, "Profiting by War Experiences," *Infantry Journal*, XVIII (Jan., 1921), 34–37.
72. Pershing, *op. cit.*, II, 189–90.
73. *Ibid.*, p. 391.

CHAPTER SEVENTEEN

1. Quoted in C. Joseph Bernardo and Eugene H. Bacon, *American Military Policy: Its Development Since 1775* (Harrisburg: Stackpole, 1955), p. 388.

2. *Ibid.*, pp. 381–82; Benedict Crowell and Robert F. Wilson, *How America Went to War—Demobilization* (New Haven: Yale University Press, 1921); Peyton C. March, *The Nation at War* (Garden City: Doubleday, 1932), chap. xxii.

3. Quoted in March, *op. cit.*, p. 353.

4. *Statutes at Large*, XL, 1211; Report of the Secretary of War, 1919, pp. 480–81; March, *op. cit.*, pp. 330–33.

5. 65th Congress, 1st Session, Senate Committee on Military Affairs, *Reorganization of the Army: Hearings Before the Subcommittee of the Committee on Military Affairs, United States Senate, Sixty-fifth Congress, First Session, on . . . S.2715 . . .* ; John McAuley Palmer, *America in Arms: The Experience of the United States with Military Organization* (New Haven: Yale University Press, 1941), pp. 101–3, 136–47, 168–70; James W. Wadsworth in his introduction to John McAuley Palmer, *Statesmanship or War* (Garden City: Doubleday, 1927), pp. ix–xv; Russell F. Weigley, *Towards an American Army: Military Thought from Washington to Marshall* (New York: Columbia University Press, 1962), pp. 226–39.

6. Palmer, *America in Arms*, pp. 136–37, 141, and *Statesmanship or War*, p. 29.

7. Pershing's testimony is in *Reorganization Hearings, S.2715*, II, 1571–1704. See also John J. Pershing, "Our National Defense Policy," *Scientific American*, CXXVII (1922), 83, 142, and Pershing's introduction to John McAuley Palmer, *Washington, Lincoln, Wilson: Three War Statesmen* (Garden City: Doubleday, 1930). For Marshall, see William Frye, *Marshall: Citizen Soldier* (Indianapolis: Bobbs-Merrill, 1947), pp. 174–78, and Forrest C. Pogue, *George C. Marshall: Education of a General, 1880–1939* (New York: Viking, 1963), pp. 204–10.

8. *Statutes at Large*, XLI, 759–812.

9. See interpretations of the act in 69th Congress, 2nd Session, House of Representatives Committee on Military Affairs, *The National Defense: Historical Documents Relating to the Reorganization Plans of the War Department and to the Present National Defense Act;* Palmer, *Statesmanship or War*, pp. 167–76, including the interpretations of Pershing and Secretary of War John W. Weeks, and *Washington, Lincoln, Wilson*, pp. 362–70.

10. Palmer, *America in Arms*, p. 104.

11. Palmer, *Statesmanship or War*, p. 74.

12. *Statutes at Large*, XLI, 759–61, 766, 768–75; Leo P. Brophy, "Origins of the Chemical Corps," *Military Affairs*, XX (1956), 217–26. The first chief of chaplains was also appointed in 1920; see Roy J. Honeywell, *Chaplains of the United States Army* (Washington: Department of the Army, 1958).

13. Pershing, "Our National Defense Policy," *loc. cit.*, p. 83.

14. For fiscal policy and the Army, see Elias Huzar, *The Purse and the Sword* (Ithaca: Cornell University Press, 1950).

15. Bernardo and Bacon, *op. cit.*, pp. 387–89; Palmer, *America in Arms*, pp. 187–90; *Statesmanship or War*, pp. 164–66; *Washington, Lincoln, Wilson*, pp. 367–70; Pogue, *op. cit.*, pp. 219–21.

16. *Statutes at Large*, XLVIII, 153–61; Martha Derthick, *The National Guard in Politics* (Cambridge: Harvard University Press, 1965), pp. 50–51.

17. John W. Killigrew, "The Army and the Bonus Incident," *Military Affairs*, XXVI (1962–63), 59–65; Marvin A. Kreidberg and Merton G. Henry, *History of Military Mobilization in the United States Army, 1775–1945* (Washington: Department of the Army, 1955), pp. 461–63; Pogue, *op. cit.*, pp. 274–80, 308–11; Arthur M. Schlesinger, Jr., *The Coming of the New Deal (The Age of Roosevelt*, II, Boston: Houghton Mifflin, 1959), pp. 338–40.

18. Quoted in Kreidberg and Henry, *op. cit.*, p. 468.

19. March, *op. cit.*, pp. 341–43.

20. For the Chemical Warfare Service, Leo P. Brophy *et al.*, *The Chemical Warfare Service* (2 vols., *United States Army in World War II: The Technical Services*, Washington: Department of the Army, 1959–61). On the Air Service, Army Air Forces Historical Studies, No. 25, *Organization of Military Aeronautics, 1907–1935* (Washington: Government Printing Office, 1944); Alfred Goldberg, ed., *A History of the United States Air Force, 1907–1957* (Princeton: Van Nostrand, 1957).

21. *Statutes at Large*, XLI, 763.

22. *Ibid.*, p. 764; 69:2 *Historical Documents Relating to the Reorganization Plans*, pp. 580–83; Harold W. Thatcher, *Planning for Industrial Mobilization, 1920–1940* (Quartermaster Corps Historical Studies, No. 4, Washington: Government Printing Office, 1943); Harry B. Yoshpe, "Economic Mobilization Planning Between the Two World Wars," *Military Affairs*, XV (1951), 199–204; XVI (1952), 71–96.

23. Roy S. Cline, *Washington Command Post: The Operations Division (United States Army in World War II: The War Department*, Washington: Department of the Army, 1951), pp. 20–21; Mark S. Watson, *Chief of Staff: Prewar Plans and Preparations (United States Army in World War II: The War Department*, Washington: Department of the Army, 1950), pp. 62–64.

24. Cline, *op. cit.*, pp. 20–21; Watson, *op. cit.*, pp. 72–78.

25. On the Joint Board and the "color" plans: Maurice Matloff and Edwin M. Snell, *Strategic Planning for Coalition Warfare, 1941–1942 (United States Army in World War II: The War Department*, Washington: Department of the Army, 1953), pp. 1–10; Louis Morton, "Germany First," in Kent Roberts Greenfield, ed., *Command Decisions* (Washington: Department of the Army, 1960), pp. 12–20; Watson, *op. cit.*, pp. 79–81, 97–102. On mobilization planning, R. Elberton Smith, *The Army and Economic Mobilization (United States Army in World War II: The War Department*, Washington: Department of the Army, 1959), chaps. i–iii.

26. Kreidberg and Henry, *op. cit.*, p. 417.

27. Quoted *ibid.*, p. 432.

28. This plan plainly reflected the experience of World War I and anticipated a similar war, in which major operations would be confined to a single front. The chief of staff would step into Pershing's wartime role, to be replaced in Washington by a new chief who would be a secondary figure, like March. In line with such thinking, in 1936 the Army Regulations were revised to declare that the chief of staff "is in peace, by direction of the President, the Commanding General of the Field Forces and in that capacity directs the field organization and the general training of the several armies, of the overseas forces, and of the G.H.Q. units." Watson, *op. cit.*, p. 64.

29. Kreidberg and Henry, *op. cit.*, pp. 424–61; Watson, *op. cit.*, pp. 26–29.

30. Kreidberg and Henry, *op. cit.*, pp. 493–98.

31. *Ibid.*, pp. 499–502.

32. 72nd Congress, 1st Session, House Document 163 (serial 9538), War Policies Commission Report; Kreidberg and Henry, *op. cit.*, pp. 502–524.

33. Harold J. Tobin and Percy W. Bidwell, *Mobilizing Civilian America* (New York: Council on Foreign Relations, 1940). For Roosevelt's aversion to centralization of mobilization power below the Presidential level, see William L. Langer and S. Everett Gleason, *The Challenge to Isolation, 1937–1940* (New York: Harper, 1951), pp. 472–480.

34. Mildred Harmon Gillie, *Forging the Thunderbolt: A History of the Development of the Armored Force* (Harrisburg: Military Service Publishing Co., 1947), chaps. i–ii.

35. B. H. Liddell Hart, *The Liddell Hart Memoirs, Vol. I, 1895–1938* (New York: Putnam, 1966), and *The Tanks: The History of the Royal Tank Regiment and Its Predecessors; Heavy Branch Machine-Gun Corps, Tank Corps, and Royal Tank Corps, 1914–1945* (2 vols., New York: Praeger, 1959); Jay Luvaas, *The Education of an Army: British Military Thought, 1815–1940* (Chicago: University of Chicago Press, 1965), pp. 331–424; G. leQ. Martel, *In the Wake of the Tank* (London: Sifton Praed, 1931). Also Eugene M. Emme, "Technological Change and Western Military Thought, 1914–1945," *Military Affairs*, XXIV (1960–61), 6–19.

36. Gillie, *op. cit.*, chaps. ii–iii.

37. *Ibid.*, pp. 24, 33–35. Nonspecialist writers, such as Gillie, and Alan Clark, *Barbarossa: The Russian-German Conflict, 1941–45* (New York: Morrow, 1965), p. 35, praise Christie's ideas much more lavishly than do those in closer contact with the technical aspects of tank development. See Constance McLaughlin Green, Harry C. Thomson, and Peter C. Roots, *The Ordnance Department: Planning Munitions for War (United States Army in World War II: The Technical Services*, Washington: Department of the Army, 1955), pp. 199–200.

38. Andrew Boyle, *Trenchard* (London: Collins, 1962); Giulio Douhet, *Command of the Air*, tr. Dino Ferrari (New York: Coward-McCann, 1943); Edward Mead Earle, ed., *Makers of Modern Strategy: Military Thought from Machiavelli to Hitler* (Princeton: Princeton University Press, 1943), pp. 485–501; Alfred F. Hurley, *Billy Mitchell: Crusader for Air Power* (New York: Watts, 1964); Louis A. Sigaud, *Douhet and Aerial Warfare* (New York: Putnam, 1941).

39. Army Air Forces Historical Studies, *Organization of Military Aeronautics, 1907–1935;* Army Air Forces Historical Studies, No. 39, *Legislation Relating to Air Corps Personnel and Training Programs, 1907–1939* (Washington: Government Printing Office, 1945); Hurley, *op. cit.*, pp. 84–86.

40. On Mitchell, Hurley's biography is superior to the early partisan ones. These are cited in Hurley's bibliography, along with the most important of Mitchell's own numerous writings.

41. The Morrow Board report was published: *Hearings Before the President's Aircraft Board* (Washington: Government Printing Office,

1925). See also R. Earl McClendon, *The Question of Autonomy for the United States Air Arm* (Montgomery: Air University, 1954). On the Army and the air mail, Schlesinger, *op. cit.*, pp. 448–53. On the heavy bomber, Air Force Historical Studies, No. 6, *The Development of the Heavy Bomber, 1918–1944* (Montgomery: Air University, 1951); Thomas H. Greer, *The Development of Doctrine in the Army Air Arm, 1917–1941* (Montgomery: Air University, 1955).

42. MacArthur is quoted in Bernardo and Bacon, *op. cit.*, p. 388. For weapons development in the 1920's and 1930's, Green *et al.*, *op. cit.*, chap. ii.

43. Green *et al.*, *op cit.*, pp. 21 n, 31, 35, 57–59, 65, 475–77.

44. Watson, *op. cit.*, *passim*, esp. pp. 29–31.

45. Report of chief of staff, 1939, quoted in Kriedberg and Henry, *op. cit.*, p. 438.

46. *Ibid.*

47. Watson, *op. cit.*, pp. 42–44.

48. Kreidberg and Henry, *op. cit.*, pp. 451–52.

49. Franklin D. Roosevelt, *The Public Papers and Addresses of Franklin D. Roosevelt* (13 vols., New York: Macmillan, 1941–50), VII, 66–71.

50. Watson, *op. cit.*, pp. 134–43.

51. Kreidberg and Henry, *op. cit.*, p. 547.

52. Watson, *op. cit.*, pp. 142–43, 154–55.

53. Kreidberg and Henry, *op. cit.*, pp. 548–52.

54. Green *et al.*, *op. cit.*, pp. 53–64; Watson, *op. cit.*, pp. 148–52.

55. Jim Dan Hill, *The Minute Man in Peace and War: A History of the National Guard* (Harrisburg: Stackpole, 1963), chap. xv.

56. Watson, *op. cit.*, pp. 152–55.

Chapter Eighteen

1. Address at Charlottesville, Virginia, June 10, 1940, quoted in Henry Steele Commager, ed., *Documents of American History* (6th ed., 2 vols. in 1, New York: Appleton-Century-Crofts, 1958), II, 612.

2. Forrest C. Pogue, *George C. Marshall: Education of a General, 1880–1939* (New York: Viking, 1963), *passim*, esp. p. 138.

3. *Ibid.*, p. 131.

4. Franklin D. Roosevelt, *The Public Papers and Addresses of Franklin D. Roosevelt* (13 vols., New York: Macmillan, 1941–50), VIII, 488–489.

5. Mark S. Watson, *Chief of Staff: Prewar Plans and Preparations* (*United States Army in World War II: The War Department*, Washington: Department of the Army, 1950), pp. 158–59.

6. *Ibid.*, pp. 164–65.

7. Marvin A. Kreidberg and Merton G. Henry, *History of Military Mobilization in the United States Army, 1775–1945* (Washington: Department of the Army, 1955), pp. 570–71; William L. Langer and S. Everett Gleason, *The Challenge to Isolation, 1937–1940* (New York: Harper, 1951), pp. 469–76; Watson, *op. cit.*, pp. 164–71.

8. Langer and Gleason, *op. cit.*, pp. 476–80; Watson, *op. cit.*, pp. 172–177.

9. Langer and Gleason, *op. cit.*, pp. 507–8, 680–83; Watson, *op. cit.*, pp. 188–97.

10. Elting E. Morison, *Turmoil and Tradition: A Study of the Life and Times of Henry L. Stimson* (Boston: Houghton Mifflin, 1960), pp. 475–76, 479–83; Henry L. Stimson and McGeorge Bundy, *On Active Service in Peace and War* (New York: Harper, 1947), pp. 345–48.

11. Jim Dan Hill, *The Minute Man in Peace and War: A History of the National Guard* (Harrisburg: Stackpole, 1963), pp. 370–72; Watson, *op. cit.*, pp. 197–209, 212–14.

12. *Statutes at Large*, LIV, 858, 885; Langer and Gleason, *op. cit.*, p. 683.

13. Quoted in Richard M. Leighton and Robert W. Coakley, *Global Logistics and Strategy, 1940–1943* (*United States Army in World War II: The War Department*, Washington: Department of the Army, 1955), p. 42. See Kent Roberts Greenfield, Robert R. Palmer, and Bell I. Wiley, *The Organization of Ground Combat Troops* (*United States Army in World War II: The Army Ground Forces*, Washington: Government Printing Office, 1947), pp. 32–43.

14. Omar N. Bradley discusses his experiences in training the 28th Division in *A Soldier's Story* (New York: Holt, 1951), pp. 12–15. See also Greenfield *et al.*, *op. cit.*, pp. 34–38; Hill, *op. cit.*, chap. xvi.

15. Quoted in Watson, *op. cit.*, p. 270. See *ibid.*, pp. 241–77; Kreidberg and Henry, *op. cit.*, p. 613.

16. William R. Keast, "Service Schools of the Army Ground Forces" and "The Training of Officer Candidates," in Robert R. Palmer, Bell I. Wiley, and William R. Keast, *The Procurement and Training of Ground Combat Troops* (*United States Army in World War II: The Army Ground Forces*, Washington: Government Printing Office, 1948), pp. 245–364; Kreidberg and Henry, *op. cit.*, pp. 511–14.

17. Greenfield *et al.*, *op. cit.*, pp. 1–55; Watson, *op. cit.*, pp. 2, 206–7, 212.

18. William R. Keast, "The Training of Enlisted Replacements," in Palmer *et al.*, *op. cit.*, pp. 369–428.

19. Greenfield *et al.*, *op. cit.*, pp. 15–31; Watson, *op. cit.*, pp. 149, 295–296.

20. Watson, *op. cit.*, pp. 204, 213–14.

21. For industrial mobilization in World War II, see Donald M. Nelson, *Arsenal of Democracy: The Story of American War Production* (New York: Harcourt, Brace, 1946); David Novik, Melvin Anshen, and W. C. Truppner, *Wartime Production Controls* (New York: Columbia University Press, 1949); R. Elberton Smith, *The Army and Economic Mobilization; The United States at War: Development and Administration of the War Program by the Federal Government* (Washington: Government Printing Office, 1946).

22. William L. Langer and S. Everett Gleason, *The Undeclared War, 1940–1941* (New York: Harper, 1953), chaps. vii–viii; Watson, *op. cit.*, *passim*, esp. pp. 312–16, 318–21, 331–38.

23. Leighton and Coakley, *op. cit.*, chaps. iii–v; Watson, *op. cit.*, chap. x.

24. Leighton and Coakley, *op. cit.*, pp. 103–6.

25. Kreidberg and Henry, *op. cit.*, pp. 678–79; Leighton and Coakley, *op. cit.*, pp. 304–9.

26. Watson, *op. cit.*, pp. 222–31.

27. *Ibid.*, pp. 360–66.
28. *Ibid.*, chap. xi.
29. *Ibid.*, chap. xv; Kreidberg and Henry, *op. cit.*, pp. 596–97.
30. Greenfield *et al.*, *op. cit.*, pp. 198–206; Palmer *et al.*, *op. cit.*, pp. 433–39.
31. Robert R. Palmer, "Mobilization of the Ground Army," in Greenfield *et al.*, *op. cit.*, pp. 189–259.
32. *Ibid.*, pp. 189–94.
33. *Ibid.*, pp. 190–95.
34. Quoted *ibid.*, pp. 214, 236. See *ibid.*, pp. 191–94, 252–59.
35. Leighton and Coakley, *op. cit.*, p. vii.
36. Roy S. Cline, *Washington Command Post: The Operations Division* (*United States Army in World War II: The War Department*, Washington: Department of the Army, 1951), pp. 70–74, 90–93; John D. Millett, *The Organization and Role of the Army Service Forces* (*United States Army in World War II: The Army Service Forces*, Washington: Department of the Army, 1954), chaps. i–ii.
37. Cline, *op. cit.*, pp. 67–70; Wesley Frank Craven and James Lea Cate, *The Army Air Forces in World War II* (6 vols., Chicago: University of Chicago Press, 1948–53), I, *Plans and Early Operations*, chaps. ii–iii; Watson, *op. cit.*, chap. ix.
38. Cline, *op. cit.*, pp. 90–98; Craven and Cate, *op. cit.*, I, 258–65; Greenfield *et al.*, *op. cit.*, pp. 143–55; Millett, *op. cit.*, pp. 36–42.
39. Cline, *op. cit.*, p. 95.
40. *Ibid.*, p. 28.
41. *Ibid.*, pp. 257–62; Leighton and Coakley, *op. cit.*, pp. 221–27; Millett, *op. cit.*, pp. 28–42.
42. Cline, *op. cit.*, pp. 128–30, 168, 175–77, 206, 278–86; Millett, *op. cit.*, pp. 111–23.
43. Leighton and Coakley, *op. cit.*, pp. 223–46; Millett, *op. cit.* For the services incorporated into the Army Service Forces, see the various volumes of *United States Army in World War II: The Technical Services*.
44. Leighton and Coakley, *op. cit.*, chap. xiii. On the Transportation Corps, see Chester Wardlow *et al.*, *The Transportation Corps* (3 vols., *United States Army in World War II: The Technical Services*, Washington: Department of the Army, 1951–57).
45. Leighton and Coakley, *op. cit.*, chap. xi.
46. *Ibid.*, pp. 282–85.
47. *Ibid.*, esp. chap. xiii; Millett, *op. cit.*, chaps. iv–v.
48. Leighton and Coakley, *op. cit.*, p. 348.
49. *Ibid.*, pp. 348–49; Greenfield *et al.*, *op. cit.*, p. 175.
50. Leighton and Coakley, *op. cit.*, pp. 244–46; Millett, *op. cit.*, chap. viii.

Chapter Nineteen

1. Walter Millis, ed., *The Forrestal Diaries* (New York: Viking, 1951), pp. 79–81.
2. Quoted in Elting E. Morison, *Turmoil and Tradition: A Study of the Life and Times of Henry L. Stimson* (Boston: Houghton Mifflin, 1960), p. 543.

3. *Ibid.*, p. 499.
4. John D. Millett, *The Organization and Role of the Army Service Forces* (*United States Army in World War II: The Army Service Forces*, Washington: Department of the Army, 1954), esp. p. 26 n; Morison, *op. cit.*, pp. 491–92. Patterson's relationships with General Somervell and ASF paralleled Stimson's with Marshall and the General Staff. Patterson and Somervell felt a high degree of mutual confidence and respect, the door between their offices was an open one through which both passed frequently, and meanwhile Patterson retained the right to deal directly with any office of ASF. Patterson was especially close to the Legal Branch of ASF, which drafted procurement regulations.
5. Morison, *op. cit.*, pp. 493–94.
6. Stetson Conn, "The Decision To Evacuate the Japanese from the Pacific Coast," in Kent Roberts Greenfield, ed., *Command Decisions* (Washington: Department of the Army, 1960), pp. 125–49; Stetson Conn, Rose C. Engelman, and Byron Fairchild, *Guarding the United States and Its Outposts* (*United States Army in World War II: The Western Hemisphere*, Washington: Department of the Army, 1964), chap. v.
7. Roy S. Cline, *Washington Command Post: The Operations Division* (*United States Army in World War II: The War Department*, Washington: Department of the Army, 1950), chap. xvi.
8. Quoted *ibid.*, p. 105. On Roosevelt as Commander in Chief, see William Emerson, "Franklin Roosevelt as Commander in Chief in World War II," *Military Affairs*, XXII (1958–59), 181–207, and in Ernest R. May, ed., *The Ultimate Decision: The President as Commander in Chief* (New York: Braziller, 1960), pp. 135–77; Henry L. Stimson and McGeorge Bundy, *On Active Service in Peace and War* (New York: Harper, 1947); and among biographies of Roosevelt, especially Robert W. Sherwood, *Roosevelt and Hopkins: An Intimate History* (New York: Harper, 1948).
9. For Churchill, there is of course his own eloquent history, Winston S. Churchill, *The Second World War* (6 vols., Boston: Houghton Mifflin, 1948–53). The capriciousness of his military judgment is often evident therein. For criticisms that are also sometimes capricious but sometimes well founded, see J. F. C. Fuller's various writings on World War II, including *The Conduct of War, 1789–1961: A Study of the Impact of the French, Industrial, and Russian Revolutions on War and Its Conduct* (New Brunswick: Rutgers University Press, 1961), pp. 252–55, 260–61, 279–87, and Arthur Bryant, *The Turn of the Tide: A History of the War Years Based on the Diaries of Field-Marshal Lord Alanbrooke, Chief of the Imperial General Staff* (Garden City: Doubleday, 1957), and *Triumph in the West* (Garden City: Doubleday, 1959). Fuller and Alanbrooke do not have a high opinion of Roosevelt or most of the other American strategists either.
10. Cline, *op. cit.*, chaps. viii, ix, x, xii. For Anglo-American strategic planning, see Herbert Feis, *Churchill-Roosevelt-Stalin: The War They Waged and the Peace They Sought* (Princeton: Princeton University Press, 1957); Kent Roberts Greenfield, *American Strategy in World War II: A Reconsideration* (Baltimore: Johns Hopkins

Press, 1963); Trumbull Higgins, *Winston Churchill and the Second Front, 1940–1943* (New York: Oxford University Press, 1957); Maurice Matloff, "The American Approach to War, 1919–1945," pp. 213–43, in Michael Howard, ed., *The Theory and Practice of War: Essays Presented to Captain B. H. Liddell Hart* (London: Cassel, 1965); Maurice Matloff and Edwin M. Snell, *Strategic Planning for Coalition Warfare, 1943–1944* (*United States Army in World War II: The War Department*, Washington: Department of the Army, 1959); Samuel Eliot Morison, *Strategy and Compromise* (Boston: Little, Brown, 1958).

11. For the British command system, see J. R. M. Butler *et al.*, *Grand Strategy* (7 vols., *United Kingdom Military Series*, London: H. M. Stationery Office, 1956–57), II, 4–9.
12. Cline, *op. cit.*, *passim*, esp. pp. 100–101.
13. *Ibid.*, pp. 101–2.
14. *Ibid.*, p. 218.
15. *Ibid.*, chap. xiii. For the views of the chairman of JCS, see his recollections, William D. Leahy, *I Was There* (New York: McGraw-Hill, 1950).
16. Cline, *op. cit.*, pp. 249–57; R. Earl McClendon, *The Question of Autonomy for the United States Air Arm* (Montgomery: Air University, 1954).
17. Cline, *op. cit.*, pp. 242–47 and chap. xv. For an overseas theater command, see especially Forrest C. Pogue, *The Supreme Command* (*United States Army in World War II: The European Theater*, Washington: Department of the Army, 1954).
18. Quoted in Cline, *op. cit.*, p. 95.
19. *Ibid.*
20. *Ibid.*, esp. chap. viii.
21. *Ibid.*, p. 124.
22. *Ibid.*, pp. 120–21, 162–63; Dwight D. Eisenhower, *Crusade in Europe* (Garden City: Doubleday, 1948), pp. 31–50.
23. Kent Roberts Greenfield, Robert R. Palmer, and Bell I. Wiley, *The Organization of Ground Combat Troops* (*United States Army in World War II: The Army Ground Forces*, Washington: Government Printing Office, 1947), p. 283; see also pp. 271–73, 277.
24. *Ibid.*, p. 308; see pp. 305–18.
25. *Ibid.*, p. 318.
26. *Ibid.*, pp. 300–318.
27. The Tables of Organization and Equipment of the redeployment division of 1945 reflected such experience; see *ibid.*, pp. 454–83.
28. *Ibid.*, pp. 351–56, 359–71, 381–82.
29. *Ibid.*, pp. 356–59, 374–80.
30. Robert R. Palmer, "Organization and Training of New Ground Combat Elements," *ibid.*, pp. 387–434.
31. *Ibid.*, p. 322.
32. *Ibid.*, pp. 327–28; see pp. 322–35. For an early denial of the omnipotence of tanks and armored forces, see S. L. A. Marshall, *Armies on Wheels* (New York: Morrow, 1941), pp. 131–84.
33. Greenfield *et al.*, *op. cit.*, p. 334. For the shortage of infantry divisions in Europe in the winter crisis of 1944–45, see H. M. Cole, *The Lorraine Campaign* (*United States Army in World War II: The Euro-*

pean Theater of Operations, Washington: Department of the Army, 1950).

34. Histories of the campaigns of World War II are numerous, but there is as yet no outstanding interpretative work on the tactical developments of the war; the rapid pace of tactical and technological change after 1945 has surely tended to forestall such a work. For a brief survey of the American campaigns, with an extensive bibliography, see A. Russell Buchanan, *The United States and World War II* (2 vols., New York: Harper and Row, 1964).

35. George Raynor Thompson *et al.*, *The Signal Corps* (2 vols., *United States Army in World War II: The Technical Services*, Washington: Department of the Army, 1956–57).

36. Greenfield *et al.*, *op. cit.*, pp. 336–50. On the airborne divisions, see James M. Gavin, *Airborne Warfare* (Washington: Infantry Journal, 1947). On the Army's usual indifference to unit traditions, see Edmund G. Love, "The Case of the 'Fighting Irish': An Illustration of American Indifference to Regimental Traditions," *Military Affairs*, XI (1947), 46–48.

37. Constance McLaughlin Green, Harry C. Thomson, and Peter C. Roots, *The Ordnance Department: Planning Munitions for War* (*United States Army in World War II: The Technical Services*, Washington: Department of the Army, 1955), pp. 13, 189–203, 211–212, 236–39, 250–57, 448–50, 481–85, 494, 513–14. On German and Russian tanks, there is useful information in Alan Clark, *Barbarossa: The Russian-German Conflict, 1941–1945* (New York: Morrow, 1965); Raymond L. Garthoff, *Soviet Military Doctrine* (Glencoe, Ill.: Free Press, 1953); Heinz Guderian, *Panzer Leader* (New York: Dutton, 1952); Augustin Guillaume, *Soviet Arms and Soviet Power* (Washington: Infantry Journal, 1949); B. H. Liddell Hart, ed., *The Red Army* (New York: Harcourt, Brace, 1956); F. W. von Mellinthin, *Panzer Battles* (Norman: University of Oklahoma Press, 1956). There is a good discussion of infantry assault tactics in Jac Weller, *Weapons and Tactics: Hastings to Berlin* (New York: St. Martin's Press, 1966), pp. 118–22. See also John Kirk and Robert Young, Jr., *Great Weapons of World War II* (New York: Walker, 1961).

38. Green *et al.*, *op. cit.*, pp. 178–88, 196–97, 236–39, 315–27, 341, 370–371, 432–46. Among the volumes on combat operations in the Army's official history, there is especially interesting and detailed material on artillery support in Charles B. MacDonald and Sidney T. Matthews, *Arnaville, Altuzzo, and Schmidt* (*United States Army in World War II: Three Battles*, Washington: Department of the Army, 1952).

39. Quoted in R. Ernest Dupuy, *The Compact History of the United States Army* (New York: Hawthorn, 1956), p. 642.

40. Quoted in Fairfax Downey, *Sound of the Guns: The Story of American Artillery from the Ancient and Honorable Company to the Atom Cannon and Guided Missile* (New York: McKay, 1956), p. 253.

41. Wesley Frank Craven and James Lea Cate, *The Army Air Forces in World War II* (6 vols., Chicago: University of Chicago Press, 1948–53), III, *Europe: Argument to V-E Day, January 1944 to May 1945*, esp. pp. 43–48 and chap. xxii; United States Strategic

Bombing Survey, *Over-all Report (European War)* (Washington: Government Printing Office, 1946).

42. Quoted in Dupuy, *op. cit.*, p. 265.

43. Cline, *op. cit.*, p. 295.

44. Chester Wilmot, *The Struggle for Europe* (New York: Harper, 1952), p. 512. See Wilmot's own praise of the military qualities of American troops, pp. 425–28, especially interesting in the light of this Australian writer's general critical-mindedness and British orientation.

45. See Omar N. Bradley, *A Soldier's Story* (New York: Holt, 1951), pp. 18–21; Morris Janowitz, *The Professional Soldier: A Social and Political Portrait* (Free Press paperback ed., New York: Free Press of Glencoe, 1964), pp. 150–65; Forrest C. Pogue, *George C. Marshall: Education of a General, 1880–1939* (New York: Viking, 1963).

46. For the background of modern scientific efforts in weapons development, and the confused beginnings in World War I, see again Irving B. Holley, *Ideas and Weapons: Exploitation of the Aerial Weapon by the United States During World War I* (New Haven: Yale University Press, 1953). See also A. Hunter Dupree, *Science in the Federal Government: A History of Policies and Activities to 1940* (Cambridge: Harvard University Press, 1957). For World War II see James Phinney Baxter III, *Scientists Against Time* (Boston: Little, Brown, 1946); Vannevar Bush, *Modern Arms and Free Men: A Discussion of the Role of Science in Preserving Democracy* (New York: Simon and Schuster, 1949).

47. See Wilmot, *op. cit.*, pp. 425–28.

48. E.g., Allan Nevins, "Should American History Be Rewritten?" *Saturday Review*, XXXVII (Feb. 6, 1954), 7–9.

49. In addition to the works cited in note 6 above, see Morton Grodzins, *Americans Betrayed: Politics and the Japanese Evacuation* (Chicago: University of Chicago Press, 1949); Jacobus ten Broek, Edward N. Barnhart, and Floyd W. Matson, *Prejudice, War and the Constitution: Japanese American Evacuation and Resettlement* (Berkeley: University of California Press, 1954); D. S. Thomas and R. S. Nishimoto, *The Spoilage: Japanese American Evacuation and Resettlement* (Berkeley: University of California Press, 1946).

50. J. W. Campbell, *The Atomic Story* (New York: Holt, 1947); Leslie R. Groves, *Now It Can Be Told: The Story of the Manhattan Project* (New York: Harper, 1962); W. L. Laurence, *Dawn over Zero: The Story of the Atomic Bomb* (New York: Knopf, 1960); Henry De-Wolf Smyth, *Atomic Energy for Military Purposes: The Official Report on the Development of the Atomic Bomb Under the Auspices of the United States Government, 1940–1945* (Washington: Government Printing Office, 1945).

PART FOUR

1. The Thomas Hobbes translation, Thucydides, *The Peloponnesian War*, David Grene, ed. (2 vols., Ann Arbor: University of Michigan Press, 1959), I, 68–69.

CHAPTER TWENTY

1. The Truman Doctrine, in Henry Steele Commager, ed., *Documents of American History* (6th ed., 2 vols. in 1, New York: Appleton-Century-Crofts, 1958), II, 705.

2. Henry M. Adams, "Allied Military Government in Sicily, 1943," *Military Affairs*, XV (1951), 157–65, and "Operations of an American Military Government Detachment in the Saar, 1944–45," *ibid.*, XIX (1955), 121–36; Harry L. Coles and Albert K. Weinberg, *Civil Affairs: Soldiers Become Governors* (*United States Army in World War II: Special Studies*, Washington: Department of the Army, 1964); Carl J. Friedrich and associates, *American Experiences in Military Government in World War II* (New York: Rinehart, 1948); Kazuo Kawai, *Japan's American Interlude* (Chicago: University of Chicago Press, 1960); Douglas MacArthur, *Reminiscences* (New York: McGraw-Hill, 1964), Part VIII; Grant E. Meade, *American Military Government* (New York: Columbia University Press, 1951); *Military Government of Germany, U. S. Zone, Monthly Reports* (50 issues, Office of Military Government for Germany (U.S.), 1945–1949); John D. Montgomery, *Forced To Be Free: The Artificial Revolution in Germany and Japan* (Chicago: University of Chicago Press, 1957).

3. C. Joseph Bernardo and Eugene R. Bacon, *American Military Policy: Its Development Since 1775* (Harrisburg: Stackpole, 1955), pp. 444–45, 448; Harry S Truman, *Memoirs by Harry S Truman* (2 vols., Garden City: Doubleday, 1955–56), I, 506–9.

4. Martha Derthick, *The National Guard in Politics* (Cambridge: Harvard University Press, 1965), pp. 72–74; Eilene Galloway, *History of the United States Military Policy on the Reserve Forces, 1775–1957* (Washington: Government Printing Office, 1957), a review of legislation with emphasis on the recent past; Jim Dan Hill, *The Minute Man in Peace and War: A History of the National Guard* (Harrisburg: Stackpole, 1963), pp. 498–502.

5. Roy S. Cline, *Washington Command Post: The Operations Division* (*United States Army in World War II: The War Department*, Washington: Department of the Army, 1950), chap. xviii.

6. *Ibid.*, pp. 352–61.

7. *Ibid.*, p. 358.

8. *Ibid.*, pp. 359–60.

9. Roy S. Cline and Maurice Matloff, "Development of War Department Views on Unification," *Military Affairs*, XIII (1949), 65–74; Paul Y. Hammond, *Organizing for Defense: The American Military Establishment in the Twentieth Century* (Princeton: Princeton University Press, 1961), pp. 87–90; John McAuley Palmer, *Statesmanship or War* (Garden City: Doubleday, 1927), pp. 68–69. A general history is Lawrence J. Legare, "Unification of the Armed Forces," Ph.D. thesis, Harvard University, 1951. See also John C. Ries, *The Management of Defense: Organization and Control of the U.S. Armed Services* (Baltimore: Johns Hopkins Press, 1964).

10. Among the works in which command problems in the Pacific can be followed, see especially Louis Morton, *Strategy and Command: The First Two Years* (*United States Army in World War II: The War in the Pacific*, Washington: Department of the Army, 1962), and

Samuel Eliot Morison's *History of United States Naval Operations in World War II* (15 vols., Boston: Little, Brown, 1947–60).

11. R. Earl McClendon, *The Question of Autonomy for the United States Air Arm* (Montgomery: Air University, 1954); for the creation of the Twentieth Air Force, see Cline, *op. cit.*, p. 256.

12. 78th Congress, 2nd Session, House Report 1645, Hearings before the Select Committee on Postwar Military Policy; Hammond, *op. cit.*, pp. 186–92.

13. Hammond, *op. cit.*, pp. 196–203; Walter Millis, ed., *The Forrestal Diaries* (New York: Viking, 1951), pp. 14, 59–64.

14. Ferdinand Eberstadt, *Unification of War and Navy Departments and Postwar Organization for National Security. A Report to Hon. James Forrestal* (Washington: Government Printing Office, 1945); Hammond, *op. cit.*, pp. 203–13.

15. J. Lawton Collins, "National Security—The Military Viewpoint," *Vital Speeches of the Day*, XIII (June 1, 1947), 488–92; Hammond, *op. cit.*, pp. 213–15.

16. Hammond, *op. cit.*, pp. 220–26; Millis, *op. cit.*, pp. 162–63, 167–68, 200–206, 246–47, 269–71, 274, 291–95; Truman, *op. cit.*, II, 46–52.

17. *Statutes at Large*, LXI, 495–510; William R. Kintner, *Forging a Sword: A Study of the Department of Defense* (New York: Harper, 1958).

18. *Statutes at Large*, LXI, 496–99.

19. On the National Security Council, see Henry M. Jackson, ed., *The National Security Council: Jackson Subcommittee Papers on Policy-Making at the Presidential Level* (New York: Praeger, 1965), including testimony before the subcommittee, documents such as excerpts from the Eberstadt report and the National Defense Act of 1947, and conclusions; also Hammond, *op. cit.*, esp. chap. xii.

20. Henry A. Kissinger, *Nuclear Weapons and Foreign Policy* (New York: Harper, 1957), pp. 26–28, 407–9; Millis, *op. cit.*, pp. 389, 392–96, 462, 468, 476–79.

21. Hammond, *op. cit.*, p. 239.

22. *Statutes at Large*, LXIII, 578–92.

23. *Ibid.*, LXIV, 263–75; Hammond, *op. cit.*, esp. p. 272. On the Military Police, see Jacob B. Lishchiner, "Origin of the Military Police," *Military Affairs*, XI (1947), 67–79.

24. *The Army Almanac: A Book of Facts Concerning the United States Army* (Harrisburg: Stackpole, 1959), pp. 19–22.

25. War Department Circular 347 is printed in The President's Advisory Commission on Universal Training, *A Program for National Security* (Washington: Government Printing Office, 1947), pp. 397–99, and Frederick Martin Stern, *The Citizen Army: Key to Defense in the Atomic Age* (New York: St. Martin's Press, 1957, pp. 353–356.

26. *The War Reports of General of the Army George C. Marshall, General of the Army H. H. Arnold, and Fleet Admiral Ernest J. King* (Philadelphia: Lippincott, 1947), p. 296. See Marshall's extended argument for universal military training, *ibid.*, pp. 289–300.

27. President's Advisory Commission, *op. cit.*, pp. 393–97; Russell F. Weigley, *Towards an American Army: Military Thought from Washington to Marshall* (New York: Columbia University Press, 1962), pp. 246–47.

28. President's Advisory Commission, *op. cit.*, pp. 401–4.
29. Bernardo and Bacon, *op. cit.*, pp. 448–49; Truman, *op. cit.*, II, 53–55.
30. Truman, *op. cit.*, I, 511.
31. *The New York Times*, Oct. 24, 1945, cited in Bernardo and Bacon, *op. cit.*, p. 447.
32. *Statutes at Large*, LXV, 75–89.
33. *Army Almanac*, pp. 142–43; Millis, *op. cit.*, pp. 374–76, 400–402.
34. Department of Defense Semiannual Report, Report of the Secretary of the Army, January 1–June 30, 1950, p. 68; Bernardo and Bacon, *op. cit.*, pp. 476–77.
35. Roy E. Appleman, *South to the Naktong, North to the Yalu* (*United States Army in the Korean War*, Washington: Department of the Army, 1960), pp. 49–50, 69–73, 113–14, 180, and *passim; Department of Defense Semiannual Report, Report of the Secretary of the Army, January 1–June 30, 1950;* R. Ernest Dupuy, *The Compact History of the United States Army* (New York: Hawthorn, 1956), p. 282; T. R. Fehrenbach, *This Kind of War: A Study in Unpreparedness* (New York: Macmillan, 1963), pp. 91, 101–3, 109, 128–129, 220. For a summary of the Uniform Code of Military Justice and a brief historical sketch, see *Army Almanac*, pp. 288–94. See also Richard A. McMahon, "Military Discipline of the U.S. and U.S.S.R.," *Army*, XII (Jan., 1962), 45–55. For a professional officer's highly critical assessment of the Doolittle report, see Fehrenbach, *op. cit.*, pp. 39, 431–34.

CHAPTER TWENTY-ONE

1. 82nd Congress, 1st Session, Hearings Before the Committee on Armed Services and the Committee on Foreign Relations, *Military Situation in the Far East* (Washington: Government Printing Office, 1951), p. 366.
2. Roy E. Appleman, *South to the Naktong, North to the Yalu* (*United States Army in the Korean War*, Washington: Department of the Army, 1960), pp. 46–47. Appleman's is the first volume to be published in a new series. For brief and early official accounts, see Orlando Wood, *Korea, 1950* (Washington: Department of the Army, 1952), and John Miller, Jr., Owen J. Carroll, and Margaret E. Tackley, *Korea, 1951–1953* (Washington: Department of the Army, 1956).
3. Appleman, *op. cit.*, pp. 69–73, 113–14, 180, and *passim;* T. R. Fehrenbach, *This Kind of War: A Study in Unpreparedness* (New York: Macmillan, 1963), pp. 101–3, 109, 220.
4. Appleman, *op. cit.*, pp. 176–77; Fehrenbach, *op. cit.*, pp. 142–46. For Dean, see also William F. Dean, *General Dean's Story* (New York: Viking, 1954).
5. *Statutes at Large*, LXIV, 254–55.
6. Jim Dan Hill, *The Minute Man in Peace and War: A History of the National Guard* (Harrisburg: Stackpole, 1963), pp. 506–14.
7. *Statutes at Large*, LXV, 75–89.

8. Fehrenbach, *op. cit.*, pp. 503–4, 514; Hill, *op. cit.*, pp. 503–14. See also a sociological study of replacement systems, David J. Chester, Niel J. Van Steenberg, and Joyce E. Bruechel, "Effect on Morale of Infantry Team Replacement and Individual Replacement Systems," *Sociometry*, XVIII (Dec., 1955), 587–97.

9. C. N. Barclay, *The First Commonwealth Division: The Story of British Commonwealth Land Forces in Korea, 1950–53* (Aldershot: Gale and Polden, 1954), p. 196; David Rees, *Korea: The Limited War* (New York: St. Martin's Press, 1964), p. 190; James G. Westover, *Combat Support in Korea* (Washington: Combat Forces Press, 1955).

10. For MacArthur's interpretation of his role in Korea see his *Reminiscences* (New York: McGraw-Hill, 1964), and Vorin E. Whan, Jr., ed., *A Soldier Speaks: Public Papers and Addresses of General of the Army Douglas MacArthur* (New York: Praeger, 1965), Parts VI–IX; also two works by friends and confidents, Courtney Whitney, *MacArthur: His Rendezvous with History* (New York: Knopf, 1956), and Charles Willoughby and John Chamberlain, *MacArthur, 1941–1951* (New York: McGraw-Hill, 1955). For the attitudes of the Joint Chiefs toward MacArthur, see John W. Spanier, *The Truman-MacArthur Controversy and the Korean War* (Norton Library ed., New York: Norton, 1965), esp. chap. v.

11. Harry S Truman, *Memoirs by Harry S Truman* (2 vols., Garden City: Doubleday, 1955–56), II, 256, 429, deals with the President's admiration for Marshall and the latter's appointment as Secretary of Defense.

12. Paul Y. Hammond, *Organizing for Defense: The American Military Establishment in the Twentieth Century* (Princeton: Princeton University Press, 1961), esp. pp. 248–49.

13. *Ibid.*, p. 249; Rees, *op. cit.*, pp. 127–28.

14. Appleman, *op. cit.*, pp. 109–13; Fehrenbach, *op. cit.*, pp. 217, 242, 263, 313, 316, 506; Rees, *op. cit.*, pp. 38–39.

15. Appleman, *op. cit.*, pp. 489–92, 609–12, 618–21, 684–88, 729–48; Rees, *op. cit.*, p. 79 and *passim*.

16. Rees, *op. cit.*, chaps. vi–viii; Spanier, *op. cit.*, chaps. v–vii.

17. Appleman, *op. cit.*, chaps. xxxiii–xxxv; S. L. A. Marshall, *The River and the Gauntlet: Defeat of the Eighth Army by the Chinese Communist Forces, November, 1950, in the Battle of the Chongchon River, Korea* (New York: Morrow, 1953).

18. MacArthur's address to Congress on April 19, 1951, reprinted in his *Reminiscences*, pp. 400–405.

19. For MacArthur's long-standing special pretensions, see Rees, *op. cit.*, pp. 66–72. John Gunther, *The Riddle of MacArthur* (New York: Harper, 1951) offers a perceptive portrait of MacArthur, mainly as proconsul in Japan.

20. Rees, *op. cit.*, chaps. ix–xi; Spanier, *op. cit.*, chaps. viii–ix.

21. Truman, *op. cit.*, II, 444.

22. Rees, *op. cit.*, pp. 176–83.

23. *Ibid.*, pp. 214–18; Truman, *op. cit.*, II, 436–50. Spanier, *op. cit.*, and Trumbull Higgins, *Korea and the Fall of MacArthur: A Précis in Limited War* (New York: Oxford University Press, 1960) are the fullest and best balanced accounts. Arthur M. Schlesinger, Jr.,

and Richard Rovere, *The General and the President* (New York: Farrar, Straus and Young, 1951) evidences its hasty preparation. For a larger view of civil-military relations in the modern United States, see Denis W. Brogan, "United States Civil and Military Power," in Michael Howard, ed., *Soldiers and Government* (London: Eyre and Spottiswoode, 1957), pp. 169–85; Harry L. Coles, ed., *Total War and Cold War: Problems in Civilian Control of the Military* (Columbus: Ohio State University Press, 1962); Walter Millis, ed., *Arms and the State: Civil-Military Elements in National Policy* (New York: Twentieth-Century Fund, 1958); Harold Stein, ed., *American Civil-Military Relations* (Tuscaloosa: University of Alabama Press, 1963). See also Burton Sapin and Richard C. Snyder, *The Role of the Military in American Foreign Policy* (Garden City: Doubleday, 1954).

24. On Van Fleet's successes and plans just before the opening of truce negotiations, see Rees, *op. cit.*, pp. 251–63. Ridgway dissented from MacArthur and Van Fleet and accepted the rationale of limited war; see his *Soldier: The Memoirs of Matthew B. Ridgway* (New York: Harper, 1956). In 1953, however, Ridgway became chief of staff of the Army and was succeeded in the Far East by another general impatient with limited war, Mark Clark; see the latter's *From the Danube to the Yalu* (New York: Harper, 1954), and "You Can't Win a War If Diplomats Interfere," *U.S. News and World Report*, XXXVII (Aug. 20, 1954), 75–81. On the American attitude toward limited war, the indispensable study is Robert E. Osgood, *Limited War: The Challenge to American Strategy* (Chicago: University of Chicago Press, 1957).

25. On this theme, see especially Fehrenbach, *op. cit.*, which argues for a professional army strong enough to carry the major burden of limited wars.

26. The literature relating to United Nations soldiers in Communist prisons includes: Albert D. Biderman, *The March to Calumny* (New York: Macmillan, 1962); Kenneth K. Hansen, *Heroes Behind Barbed Wires* (Princeton: Van Nostrand, 1957); Edward Hunter, *Brainwashing in Red China* (New York: Vanguard Press, 1951); *Journal of Social Issues*, XIII, no. 3 (1957), a special issue on brainwashing; Eugene Kinkeid, *In Every War but One* (New York: Norton, 1960); Robert J. Lifton, *Thought Reform and the Psychology of Totalism: A Study of "Brainwashing" in China* (New York: Norton, 1961); *POW, the Fight Continues After the Battle* (Washington: Department of Defense, 1955); *Treatment of British Prisoners of War in Korea* (London: H.M. Stationery Office, 1955); William L. White, *The Captives of Korea* (New York: Scribner, 1956). For the "President's Code of Conduct" of 1955, see *The Army Almanac, A Book of Facts Concerning the United States Army* (Harrisburg: Stackpole, 1959), pp. 381–82.

27. The Chinese phase of the Korean War is surveyed in both Fehrenbach, *op. cit.*, and Rees, *op. cit.* S. L. A. Marshall dissects one of the late battles in *Pork Chop Hill: The American Fighting Man in Action in Korea, Spring, 1953* (New York: Morrow, 1956).

28. Robert Frank Futrell, *The United States Air Force in Korea 1950–1953* (New York: Duell, Sloan and Pierce, 1961).

29. For a glossary of weapons used in Korea, see Fehrenbach, *op. cit.*, pp. 665–71.
30. *Ibid.*, pp. 444–87; Rees, *op. cit.*, chap. xiv.
31. C. Turner Joy, *How Communists Negotiate* (New York: Macmillan, 1955); William H. Vatcher, Jr., *Panmunjom* (New York: Praeger, 1958).
32. Fehrenbach, *op. cit.*, p. 611.
33. George M. Lewis and John Mewha, *History of Prisoner of War Utilization by the United States Army, 1776–1945* (Washington: Department of the Army Pamphlet 20–213, 1955).
34. Fehrenbach, *op. cit.*, pp. 539–82; Rees, *op. cit.*, pp. 315–27; Hal Vetter, *Mutiny on Koje Island* (Rutland, Vt.: Tuttle, 1964). Stanley Weintraub, *The War in the Wards: Korea's Unknown Battle in a Prisoner-of-War Hospital Camp* (Garden City: Doubleday, 1964) is a wry eyewitness account by a hospital administrative officer.
35. For Dulles's speech announcing the policy of "massive retaliation," see *Department of State Bulletin*, XXX, No. 761, Jan. 25, 1954; reprinted in Raymond G. O'Connor, ed., *American Defense Policy in Perspective: From Colonial Times to the Present* (New York: Wiley, 1965), pp. 326–30. See also Dwight D. Eisenhower, *The White House Years: Mandate for Change, 1953–1956* (Garden City: Doubleday, 1963), chap. vii, and Rees, *op. cit.*, chaps. xxii–xxiii, for the ending of the Korean War. For an early criticism of the "massive retaliation" doctrine, see William W. Kaufmann, "The Requirements of Deterrence," in William W. Kaufmann, ed., *Military Policy and National Security* (Princeton: Princeton University Press, 1956), pp. 12–38.
36. For Ridgway, Taylor, and Gavin, see their books: Ridgway, *op. cit.;* Maxwell D. Taylor, *The Uncertain Trumpet* (New York: Harper, 1959); James M. Gavin, *War and Peace in the Space Age* (New York: Harper, 1958).
37. Discussions of the Kennedy-McNamara defense policy, especially as it applied to the Army, include: C. V. Clifton, "Hail to the Chief!" *Army*, XIV (Jan., 1964), 28–33; George Fielding Eliot, *Reserve Forces and the Kennedy Strategy* (Harrisburg: Stackpole, 1962); Paul R. Ignatius and Finn J. Larsen, "Industry and Army Organization," *Army*, XII (May, 1962), 47–54, 88–92; William W. Kaufmann, *The McNamara Strategy* (New York: Harper and Row, 1964); Forrest K. Kleinman, "The Changing Army," *Army*, XII (Feb., 1962), 16–20; Jack Raymond, *Power at the Pentagon* (New York: Harper and Row, 1964), esp. pp. 277–311; Arthur M. Schlesinger, Jr., *A Thousand Days: John F. Kennedy in the White House* (Boston: Houghton Mifflin, 1965), pp. 152–54, 312–19; Theodore Sorensen, *Kennedy* (New York: Harper and Row, 1965), pp. 602–633; Maxwell D. Taylor, "Our Changing Military Policy," *Army*, XII (Mar., 1962), 54–56; "The Why and How of the Reorganization of the Army: The Case for Change," *ibid.*, (Feb., 1962), pp. 26–31.

CHAPTER TWENTY-TWO

1. *Public Papers of the Presidents of the United States. John F. Kennedy . . . , 1963* (Washington: Government Printing Office, 1964), p. 232.
2. Robert S. McNamara, "Remarks Before the Economic Club of New York," Nov. 18, 1963, Department of Defense News Release 1486-63; reprinted in part in Walter Millis, ed., *American Military Thought* (Indianapolis: Bobbs-Merrill, 1966), pp. 522–35.
3. Army organization through the late 1950's is described in *The Army Almanac: A Book of Facts Concerning the United States Army* (Harrisburg: Stackpole, 1959), esp. pp. 74–93. Convenient sources of more current information are the periodicals *Army, Army Information Digest, Armor, Infantry,* and *Military Engineer.* A useful popular work is Forrest K. Kleinman and Robert S. Horowitz, *The Modern United States Army* (Princeton: Van Nostrand, 1964).
4. *Statutes at Large,* LXV, 75–89; LXVI, 481–509.
5. *Army Almanac,* pp. 127–29; C. Joseph Bernardo and Eugene R. Bacon, *American Military Policy: Its Development Since 1775* (Harrisburg: Stackpole, 1955), pp. 480–83; *Statutes at Large,* LXIX, 598–605; Hobart N. Young, "Fragment from the Recent History of the Organized Reserve," *Military Affairs,* XIX (1955), 137–44.

   Another post-Korean development of importance to the history of the National Guard is the use of federalized Guard units in civil disturbances, as in Arkansas in 1957, Mississippi in 1962, and Alabama in 1963 and 1965. Not since the Whiskey and Fries Rebellions of the 1790's and the era of Jefferson's embargo had the federal government employed militia in such circumstances. In the interval the Regular Army grew so much more reliable and efficient than the militia that the federal government relied on it alone for civil emergencies requiring military force, including the labor disturbances of the late nineteenth and early twentieth centuries; only the states employed the militia for police duty. But after World War II federal control of the Guard was sufficient to have made it an efficient and reliable instrument, and during the civil rights crises in the South there were political advantages in removing the state militias from the governors' control and using Guardsmen rather than Regulars to enforce the national will on the local population. It is striking testimony to the extent to which the policies of Governors Orval Faubus, Ross Barnett, and George C. Wallace were already anachronistic that the National Guards of their states became faithful and obedient federal instruments in thwarting them, responding without question to federal calls.
6. Jack Raymond, *Power at the Pentagon* (New York: Harper & Row, 1964), p. 300.
7. George Fielding Eliot, *Reserve Forces and the Kennedy Strategy* (Harrisburg: Stackpole, 1962); William W. Kaufmann, *The McNamara Strategy* (New York: Harper and Row, 1964), pp. 63–64, 68.
8. Jim Dan Hill, *The Minute Man in Peace and War: A History of the National Guard* (Harrisburg: Stackpole, 1963), pp. 547–49. A popular discussion of the Guard that takes up the Berlin crisis is James

C. Elliott, *The Modern Army and Air National Guard* (Princeton: Van Nostrand, 1965).

9. Kaufmann, *op. cit.*, pp. 80–82; William V. Kennedy, "New Goals, New Muscle for the Army National Guard," *Army*, XIV (July, 1964), 31–36; Raymond, *op. cit.*, pp. 300–301; W. H. S. Wright, "The Reserves in Transition," *Army*, XIV (Dec., 1963), 42–44, 81–84.

10. The outlines of the controversy over consolidation can be traced in *The New York Times*: Dec. 13, 1964, pp. 1, 83–84; Dec. 14, p. 34; Dec. 16, p. 1; Dec. 17, p. 40; Dec. 20, Sec. 4, p. 5; Mar. 2, 1965, p. 10; Mar. 11, p. 16; Mar. 26, p. 17; Mar. 28, p. 24; May 16, p. 1.

11. Quoted in Kaufmann, *op. cit.*, p. 81.

12. On this issue, see "Again the Question—Why Not Reserves?" *The New York Times*, Aug. 21, 1966, Sec. 4, p. 4; Hanson W. Baldwin, "The Case for Mobilization," *The Reporter*, May 19, 1966, pp. 20–23.

13. Norman S. Paul, quoted in Raymond, *op. cit.*, p. 314. For a representative discussion, see "The Draft Is 'Universal' but Is It Fair?" *The New York Times*, Aug. 14, 1966, Sec. 4, p. 5.

14. Henry A. Kissinger, *Nuclear Weapons and Foreign Policy* (New York: Harper, 1957). On Project Vista, see Raymond, *op. cit.*, p. 391.

15. Raymond, *op. cit.*, pp. 143–48. Eventually there was an acrimonious rupture of the Army's relationship with Johns Hopkins, which seems to have been caused by personality as well as policy differences. Thereupon the Army established the Research Analysis Corporation, more literally following the Rand model. For a study of Rand with implications for all the organizations of this type, see Bruce L. R. Smith, *The Rand Corporation: Case Study of a Nonprofit Advisory Corporation* (Cambridge: Harvard University Press, 1966).

16. *Army Almanac*, pp. 5, 9, 13, 68–69, 301; Marvin L. Worley, Jr., *A Digest of New Developments in Army Weapons, Tactics, Organization, and Equipment* (Harrisburg: Military Service Publishing Co., 1958).

17. John F. Kennedy, *The Strategy of Peace*, Allan Nevins, ed. (New York: Harper, 1960), p. 185.

18. Kaufmann, *op. cit.*, pp. 82–87, 98–99; James H. McBride and John I. H. Eales, *Military Posture: Fourteen Strategic Issues Before Congress, 1964* (New York: Praeger, 1965), pp. 105–22 on "Air and Sea Lift."

19. Among representative discussions of the ROAD division are: Edwin W. Chamberlain, "The Hidden Versatility of Our New Divisions," *Army*, XIV (April, 1964), 61–63; Charles H. Hollis, "This Is a ROAD Brigade," *ibid.*, XIII (April, 1963), 31–35; Forrest K. Kleinman, "ROAD Sign for Big Sixes" and "On the Road to ROAD," *ibid.*, XII (July, 1962), 12, 62–66; Anthony L. Wermuth, "High on the ROAD: Some Observations on the Role of the Brigade," *ibid.*, XIV (Nov., 1963), 39–43; Robert T. Winfree, "ROAD Can Be Geared to the Needs of the Nuclear Battlefield," *ibid.*, XII (Dec., 1961), 62–63. With the eclipse of the regiment as a tactical unit, a "Combat Arms Regimental System" was planned whereby battalions and other active formations would be assigned to historic regiments to preserve their traditions and identities.

20. For a survey of the Communist approach to unconventional war, see

Peter Paret and John W. Shy, *Guerrillas in the 1960's* (New York: Praeger, 1962).

21. Quoted in Kaufmann, *op. cit.*, p. 62. For discussions of President Kennedy's attitudes toward unconventional war, see Schlesinger, *op. cit.*, pp. 340–42, and Sorensen, *op. cit.*, pp. 632–33.

22. Department of the Army, *Guerrilla Warfare and Special Forces Operations* (Washington: Government Printing Office, 1958), and Barksdale Hamlett, "Special Forces: Training for Peace and War," *Army Information Digest* (June, 1961), pp. 2–9, cover the origins and early development of the Special Forces. An issue of *The Annals of the American Academy of Political and Social Science* devoted to "Unconventional Warfare," CCCXLI (May, 1962) includes information on the history of the Special Forces as part of a variety of useful discussions of its subject. Robin Moore's fictional *The Green Berets* (New York: Crown, 1965) should not be ignored.

23. See esp. *The New York Times*, Aug. 7, 1966, pp. 2, 6.

24. J. K. Zawodny, "Guerrilla and Sabotage: Organization, Operations, Motivations, Escalation," *Annals*, CCCXLI (May, 1962), 12.

25. On disappointment with the M-14 in Vietnam, see *The New York Times*, June 26, 1966, p. 38. On contemporary small arms, Frank F. Rathbun, "The Rifle in Transition," *Army*, XIV (Aug., 1963), 19–25; W. H. B. Smith, *Small Arms of the World* (Harrisburg: Stackpole, 1964); Jac Weller, *Weapons and Tactics: Hastings to Berlin* (New York: St. Martin's Press, 1966). On recent developments in artillery see Jack F. Coles, "Cannon Have a Future," *Army*, XII (June, 1962), 40–44; on tanks, Jerry Greene, "Panzer Wedding," *ibid.*, (Feb., 1964), 32–36.

26. Bernardo and Bacon, *op. cit.*, pp. 506–11; Paul Y. Hammond, *Organizing for Defense: The American Military Establishment in the Twentieth Century* (Princeton: Princeton University Press, 1961), pp. 247–66; Samuel P. Huntington, *The Common Defense: Strategic Problems in National Politics* (New York: Columbia University Press, 1961); Warner B. Schilling, Paul Y. Hammond, and Glenn H. Snyder, *Strategy, Politics, and Defense Budgets* (New York: Columbia University Press, 1962).

27. Bernardo and Bacon, *op. cit.*, pp. 511–21; Hammond, *op. cit.*, chap. xi.

28. Hammond, *op. cit.*, pp. 381–84; Raymond, *op. cit.* See also Andrew F. Henry, John W. Masland, and Laurence I. Radway, "Armed Forces Unification and the Pentagon Officer," *Public Administration Review*, XV (Summer, 1955), 173–80.

29. Hammond, *op. cit.*, chap. xiii.

30. A good outline is in Kleinman and Horowitz, *op. cit.*, pp. 82–88.

31. John W. Masland and Laurence I. Radway, *Soldiers and Scholars: Military Education and National Policy* (Princeton: Princeton University Press, 1959), pp. 131–34, 140–44, 156–65, and Part V; Frank F. Rathbun, "The Armed Forces Staff College: Where They Teach Joint Togetherness," *Army*, XIV (Oct., 1963), 33–37.

32. Masland and Radway, *op. cit.*, pp. 134–39, 144–56, 323–29.

33. Stephen E. Ambrose, *Duty, Honor, Country: A History of West Point* (Baltimore: Johns Hopkins Press, 1966), pp. 322–33; Warren W. Hanson, "ROTC: A National Asset That Transcends Military Needs," *Army*, XIV (Aug., 1963), 31–35; Masland and Radway,

op. cit., Part III; "Some Ideas for Stimulating Interest in ROTC," *Army*, XIV (Aug., 1963), 36–39. On a related development, the growing interest in national security studies in civilian institutions, see Gene M. Lyons and Louis Morton, *Schools for Strategy: Education and Research in National Security Affairs* (New York: Praeger, 1965). The Army of the 1960's also maintained a huge general education system; see Harold F. Clark and Harold S. Sloan, *Classrooms in the Military: An Account of Education in the Armed Forces of the United States* (New York: Teachers College, Columbia University, 1964); *Report to the Secretary of Defense of the Advisory Committee on Nonmilitary Instruction, Karl R. Bendetson, Chairman* (Washington: Government Printing Office, 1962); Jane C. Shelburne and Kenneth J. Groves, *Education in the Armed Forces* (New York: Center for Applied Research in Education, 1965).

34. Morris Janowitz, *The Professional Soldier: A Social and Political Portrait* (New York: Free Press of Glencoe, 1964), esp. chap. vii.

35. See *ibid.*, Part III.

36. Gene Grove, "The Army and the Negro," *The New York Times Magazine*, July 24, 1966, pp. 4–5, 48–52; David G. Mandelbaum, *Soldier Groups and Negro Soldiers* (Berkeley: University of California Press, 1952); *Report of President's Committee on Equal Opportunity in the Armed Forces* (Washington: Government Printing Office, 1963).

37. Janowitz, *op. cit.*, chap. v. Janowitz's study suggests the necessity to read with caution C. Wright Mills's contentions regarding the officer corps in *The Power Elite* (New York: Oxford University Press, 1956), but Mills's provocative arguments should not be ignored. For related material on military sociology, see: *American Journal of Sociology*, LI (March, 1946), special issue on "Human Behavior in Military Society"; Morris Janowitz, "Changing Patterns of Organizational Authority: The Military Establishment," *Administrative Science Quarterly*, III (March, 1959), 473–93, and ed., *The New Military: Changing Patterns of Organization* (New York: Russell Sage Foundation, 1964), and in collaboration with Roger Little, *Sociology and the Military Establishment. Revised Edition. A Revision of the Bulletin Prepared in 1959 for the American Sociological Association* (New York: Russell Sage Foundation, 1965); A. J. Mayer and T. F. Hoult, "Social Stratification and Combat Survival," *Social Forces*, XXXIV (Dec., 1955), 155–59; Robert K. Merton and Paul F. Lazarsfeld, eds., *Studies in the Scope and Method of "The American Soldier"* (Glencoe, Ill.: Free Press, 1950); F. J. Ryan, *Relation of Performance to Social Background Factors of Army Inductees* (Washington: Catholic University Press, 1958); G. Dearborn Spindler, "The Military: A Systematic Analysis," *Social Forces*, XXVII (Oct., 1948), 83–88; Samuel A. Stouffer *et al.*, *The American Soldier* (2 vols., Princeton: Princeton University Press, 1949), the classic study of American military morale; J. T. Ungerleider, "The Army, the Soldier, and the Psychiatrist," *American Journal of Psychiatry*, CXIX (Mar., 1963), 875–77. For an interesting Army viewpoint on the growing political involvement of the officer corps, see George A. Kelly, "Officers, Politics, Ideology," *Army*, XII (Jan., 1962), 30–33.

☆ INDEX ☆